THE WILEY-BLACKWELL COMPANION
TO MAJOR SOCIAL THEORISTS

WILEY-BLACKWELL COMPANIONS TO SOCIOLOGY

The Wiley-Blackwell Companions to Sociology provide introductions to emerging topics and theoretical orientations in sociology as well as presenting the scope and quality of the discipline as it is currently configured. Essays in the Companions tackle broad themes or central puzzles within the field and are authored by key scholars who have spent considerable time in research and reflection on the questions and controversies that have activated interest in their area. This authoritative series will interest those studying sociology at advanced undergraduate or graduate level as well as scholars in the social sciences and informed readers in applied disciplines.

The Blackwell Companion to Major Classical Social Theorists
Edited by George Ritzer

The Blackwell Companion to Major Contemporary Social Theorists
Edited by George Ritzer

The Blackwell Companion to Political Sociology
Edited by Kate Nash and Alan Scott

The Blackwell Companion to Sociology
Edited by Judith R. Blau

The Blackwell Companion to Criminology
Edited by Colin Sumner

The Blackwell Companion to Social Movements
Edited by David A. Snow, Sarah A. Soule, and Hanspeter Kriesi

The Blackwell Companion to the Sociology of Families
Edited by Jacqueline Scott, Judith Treas, and Martin Richards

The Blackwell Companion to Law and Society
Edited by Austin Sarat

The Blackwell Companion to the Sociology of Culture
Edited by Mark Jacobs and Nancy Hanrahan

The Blackwell Companion to Social Inequalities
Edited by Mary Romero and Eric Margolis

The New Blackwell Companion to Social Theory
Edited by Bryan S. Turner

The New Blackwell Companion to Medical Sociology
Edited by William C. Cockerham

The New Blackwell Companion to the Sociology of Religion
Edited by Bryan S. Turner

The Wiley-Blackwell Companion to Major Social Theorists
Edited by George Ritzer and Jeffrey Stepnisky

Also available:

The Blackwell Companion to Globalization
Edited by George Ritzer

The New Blackwell Companion to the City
Edited by Gary Bridge and Sophie Watson

THE WILEY-BLACKWELL COMPANION TO

Major Social Theorists

Volume II
Contemporary Social Theorists

EDITED BY

GEORGE RITZER AND JEFFREY STEPNISKY

A John Wiley & Sons, Ltd., Publication

This edition first published 2011
© 2011 Blackwell Publishing Ltd

Blackwell Publishing was acquired by John Wiley & Sons in February 2007. Blackwell's publishing program has been merged with Wiley's global Scientific, Technical, and Medical business to form Wiley-Blackwell.

Registered Office
John Wiley & Sons Ltd, The Atrium, Southern Gate, Chichester, West Sussex, PO19 8SQ, United Kingdom

Editorial Offices
350 Main Street, Malden, MA 02148-5020, USA
9600 Garsington Road, Oxford, OX4 2DQ, UK
The Atrium, Southern Gate, Chichester, West Sussex, PO19 8SQ, UK

For details of our global editorial offices, for customer services, and for information about how to apply for permission to reuse the copyright material in this book please see our website at www.wiley.com/wiley-blackwell.

The right of George Ritzer and Jeffrey Stepnisky to be identified as the authors of the editorial material in this work has been asserted in accordance with the UK Copyright, Designs and Patents Act 1988.

Wiley also publishes its books in a variety of electronic formats. Some content that appears in print may not be available in electronic books.

Designations used by companies to distinguish their products are often claimed as trademarks. All brand names and product names used in this book are trade names, service marks, trademarks or registered trademarks of their respective owners. The publisher is not associated with any product or vendor mentioned in this book. This publication is designed to provide accurate and authoritative information in regard to the subject matter covered. It is sold on the understanding that the publisher is not engaged in rendering professional services. If professional advice or other expert assistance is required, the services of a competent professional should be sought.

Library of Congress Cataloging-in-Publication Data

The Wiley-Blackwell companion to major social theorists / edited by George Ritzer, Jeffrey Stepnisky.
　　p.　cm. – (Blackwell companions to sociology; 27)
　Published in 2000 under title: The Blackwell companion to major social theorists.
　Includes bibliographical references and index.
　ISBN 978-1-4443-3078-6 (hardback)
1. Sociologists–Biography.　2. Social sciences–Philosophy.　I. Ritzer, George.　II. Stepnisky, Jeffrey.
III. Blackwell companion to major social theorists.　IV. Title: Major social theorists.
　HM478.B583 2011
　301.092′2–dc22
　[B]
　　　　　　　　　　　　　　　　　　　　　2011003987

A catalogue record for this book is available from the British Library.

Set in 10/12.5pt Sabon by SPi Publisher Services, Pondicherry, India

Printed and bound in Singapore by Markono Print Media Pte Ltd

1　2011

Contents

List of Contributors   vii

Preface   xv

Introduction   1
Jeffrey Stepnisky

1   Norbert Elias   13
Richard Kilminster and Stephen Mennell

2   Henri Lefebvre   44
Kanishka Goonewardena

3   Robert K. Merton   65
Charles Crothers

4   Harold Garfinkel   89
Anne Warfield Rawls

5   Erving Goffman   125
Greg Smith

6   Zygmunt Bauman   155
Peter Beilharz

7   Gilles Deleuze   175
Ian Buchanan

8   Richard M. Emerson   193
Karen S. Cook and Joseph M. Whitmeyer

9   James S. Coleman   219
    Guillermina Jasso

10 Michel Foucault   240
    Couze Venn

11 Dorothy E. Smith   268
    Marie L. Campbell and Marjorie L. DeVault

12 Niklas Luhmann   287
    Rudolf Stichweh

13 Jean Baudrillard   310
    Douglas Kellner

14 Jürgen Habermas   339
    William Outhwaite

15 Pierre Bourdieu   361
    Craig Calhoun

16 Immanuel Wallerstein   395
    Christopher Chase-Dunn and Hiroko Inoue

17 Edward W. Said   412
    Patrick Williams

18 Anthony Giddens   432
    Christopher G. A. Bryant and David Jary

19 Giorgio Agamben   464
    Catherine Mills

20 Ulrich Beck   480
    Iain Wilkinson

21 Donna Haraway   500
    Janet Wirth-Cauchon

22 Bruno Latour   520
    Sal Restivo

23 Judith Butler   541
    Moya Lloyd

Index   561

Contributors

Peter Beilharz is Professor of Sociology and Director of the Thesis Eleven Centre for Cultural Sociology at La Trobe University, Australia. He is past Professor of Australian Studies and William Dean Howells Fellow at Harvard and is a Fellow in Cultural Sociology at Yale. He is author or editor of 23 books, most recently *Socialism and Modernity* (2009). He has published six books on the work of Zygmunt Bauman, and is collecting his essays for a seventh volume. Work in progress includes the intellectual biography of the founding mother of Australian sociology, Jean Martin; a study of Australian modernity in the twentieth century; and a collaborative project on the history of rock music in Australia.

Christopher G. A. Bryant is Emeritus Professor of Sociology in the Faculty of Arts, Media and Social Sciences at the University of Salford, UK, and an Academician of the Social Sciences. He is the author of *Sociology in Action* (1976), *Positivism in Social Theory and Research* (1985), *Practical Sociology: Post-empiricism and the Reconstruction of Theory and Application* (1995), and *The Nations of Britain* (2006), and the co-editor of six other books. Three of these, *Giddens' Theory of Structuration* (1991), *Anthony Giddens: Critical Assessme*nts (4 vols, 1997) and *The Contemporary Giddens* (2001) are with David Jary. In addition to social theory, he has research interests in political sociology. His latest research is on the reconfiguration of Britain.

Ian Buchanan is Professor of Critical and Cultural Theory at Cardiff University. He is the author of *The Dictionary of Critical Theory* (OUP, 2010) and the founding editor of the journal *Deleuze Studies*.

Craig Calhoun is President of the Social Science Research Council and University Professor of Social Sciences at NYU. He received his doctorate from Oxford University and he has also been a professor at the University of North Carolina and Columbia University as well as a visiting professor in Asmara, Beijing, Khartoum, Oslo, and Paris. Calhoun's most recent book is *Nations Matter: Culture, History, and the*

Cosmopolitan Dream (2007). He has also edited *Lessons of Empire: Historical Contexts for Understanding America's Global Power* (with F. Cooper and K. Moore, 2006), *Sociology in America* (Chicago, 2007), *Knowledge Matters: The Public Mission of the Research University* (with Diana Rhoten, forthcoming) and anthologies of both classical and contemporary social theory (new editions, Blackwell, 2011). Among his best-known earlier books are *Critical Social Theory: Culture, History and the Problem of Specificity* (Blackwell, 1995) and *Neither Gods Nor Emperors: Students and the Struggle for Democracy in China* (California, 1994). His new book, *Cosmopolitanism and Belonging,* will appear from Routledge this fall.

Marie L. Campbell is Professor Emerita from the University of Victoria, Canada, where she was a member of the Faculty of Human and Social Development. Institutional ethnography has inspired all her teaching, research, and publications. Her most recent book is *Managing to Nurse: Inside Canada's Health Care Reform,* co-authored with Janet Rankin, and published in 2006 by University of Toronto Press. Since retirement, she has taught at the American University-Central Asia in Bishkek, Kyrgyzstan, and with Elena Kim from AUCA, conducted an institutional ethnography on the discursive organization of international development in Kyrgyzstan. The first publication from this research, co-authored with Katherine Teghtsoonian, is published in *Signs: A Journal of Women in Culture and Society,* in the Summer 2010 issue.

Christopher Chase-Dunn is a Distinguished Professor of Sociology and Director of the Institute for Research on World-Systems at the University of California, Riverside. He is the author of *Rise and Demise: Comparing World-Systems* (with Thomas D. Hall), *The Wintu and Their Neighbors* (with Kelly Mann) and *The Spiral of Capitalism and Socialism* (with Terry Boswell). He is the founder and former editor of the *Journal of World-Systems Research*. Chase-Dunn is currently doing research on global party formation and antisystemic social movements. He also studies the rise and fall of settlements and polities since the Stone Age and global state formation.

Charles Crothers is Professor of Sociology in the Department of Social Sciences at AUT University, Auckland after previously serving as a Professor of Sociology at the University of Natal, Durban, South Africa. Prior to this, Charles had lectured in the Departments of Sociology at the University of Auckland, and Victoria University and had been President of the New Zealand Sociological Association and Secretary and currently Vice-Chair of the History of Sociology Research Committee of the International Sociological Association. His research interests cover Sociological/Social Theory (especially the analytical theories in the work of Robert K. Merton, and to develop a robust conceptualization of social structure), Social Research Methodology/methods, Sociology of Science and Social Science (especially the Columbia Tradition of Sociology, national sociologies, and most broadly comparative patterns in world sociology and organization of social research) and Studies of New Zealand (and other settler societies) and Auckland.

Karen S. Cook is the Ray Lyman Wilbur Professor and Chair of Sociology at Stanford University. She is also the Director of the Institute for Research in the Social Sciences

(IRiSS) at Stanford. Professor Cook has a long-standing interest in social exchange, social networks, bargaining, and social justice and is currently involved in a large interdisciplinary project focusing on trust in social relations. She has edited a number of books in the Russell Sage Foundation Trust Series including *Trust in Society* (2001), *Trust and Distrust in Organizations* (with R. Kramer, 2004), *Whom can you Trust?* (2009), and *eTrust: Forming Relations in the Online World* (with C. Snijders, V. Buskens, and C. Cheshire, 2009). She is co-author of *Cooperation without Trust?* (with R. Hardin and M. Levi, 2005). She was elected to the National Academy of Sciences in 2007 and in 2004 she received the ASA Cooley Mead Award for Career Contributions to Social Psychology.

Marjorie L. DeVault is Professor of Sociology in the Maxwell School of Citizenship and Public Affairs at Syracuse University. Her research focuses on gender and work, including unpaid household and family work, and she has written extensively on qualitative and feminist research methodologies, especially institutional ethnography. She is the author of *Feeding the Family: The Social Organization of Caring as Gendered Work* and *Liberating Method: Feminism and Social Research*, and editor of *People at Work: Life, Power, and Social Inclusion in the New Economy*.

Kanishka Goonewardena was trained as an architect in Sri Lanka and is Director, Program in Planning, Department of Geography, University of Toronto, where he teaches urban design and critical theory. He is co-editor of *Space, Difference, Everyday Life: Reading Henri Lefebvre* (Routledge, 2008) and has written in both popular venues and academic journals such as *Radical History Review*, *Review of Radical Political Economics*, *Antipode: A Radical Journal of Geography*, *International Journal of Urban and Regional Research*, *Planning Theory*, *New Formations*, *Theory and Event* and the publications of INURA (International Network of Urban Research and Action). The Social Science and Humanities Research Council (Canada) funded his book manuscript in progress, *National Ideology in Sri Lanka: A Question Concerning Technology, Modernity, and the West?* He is also working on a study of the appropriations of critical theory in urban studies entitled *The Future of Planning at the End of History*.

Hiroko Inoue is a PhD candidate in the Sociology Department at University of California-Riverside. Her research interests are sociological theory, world-systems analysis, formal modeling, ecological analysis, sociocultural evolution, and social network analysis. She is also a research associate at the Institute for Research on World-Systems at UCR helping to conduct several research projects. The research topics that she has been involved in are: the growth/decline phases of cities, states, and empires, globalization, global state formation, and the world-systems analysis on the Internet. Her publications include: "Global State Formation and Global Democracy" with Chase-Dunn, Alvarez, and Niemeyer in Yildiz Atasoy (ed.) *Hegemonic Transitions, the State, and Crisis in Neoliberal Capitalism* and "Scale Transitions and the Evolution of Global Governance since the Bronze Age" with Chase-Dunn, Niemeyer, and Alvarez in William R. Thompson (ed.) *Systemic Transitions: Past, Present and Future.*

David Jary is Visiting Research Professor at the Centre for Higher Education Research and Information (CHERI) at the Open University, and he holds an Emeritus Professorship at Staffordshire University, where he was previously Dean of the Graduate School. Between 2001 and 2005 he was a Visiting Professor at the Higher Education Academy Subject Centre for Sociology, Anthropology and Politics based at the University of Birmingham. He has published widely on social theory and his writing on contemporary social theory includes a number of volumes on the work of Anthony Giddens (with Chris Bryant), including *The Contemporary Giddens – Social Theory in a Globalizing Age* (2001). His recent volume on higher education is *Improving What Is Learned at University* (2010). He is editor of the *Collins Dictionary of Sociology* and also an editor of the journal *Widening Participation and Lifelong Learning*.

Guillermina Jasso (PhD, Johns Hopkins University) is Silver Professor and Professor of Sociology at New York University. Her main research interests are basic theory and international migration, together with inequality, probability distributions, and factorial survey methods, topics on which she has published widely, including such articles as "How Much Injustice Is There in the World?" "A New Unified Theory of Sociobehavioral Forces," "Two Types of Inequality," "Two New Distributions," "Estimating the Previous Illegal Experience of New Legal Immigrants," and "How Many Highly Skilled Persons Are Waiting in Line for U.S. Legal Permanent Residence?" She is currently Co-Principal Investigator of The New Immigrant Survey. She was a Fellow at the Center for Advanced Study in the Behavioral Sciences and is an elected member/fellow of the Johns Hopkins Society of Scholars, the Sociological Research Association, and the American Association for the Advancement of Science.

Douglas Kellner is George Kneller Chair in the Philosophy of Education at UCLA and is author of many books on social theory, politics, history, and culture, including *Critical Theory, Marxism, and Modernity* and *Jean Baudrillard: From Marxism to Postmodernism and Beyond*; works in cultural studies such as *Media Culture* and *Media Spectacle*; a trilogy of books on postmodern theory with Steve Best; and a trilogy of books on the media and the Bush administration, encompassing *Grand Theft 2000, From 9/11 to Terror War*, and *Media Spectacle and the Crisis of Democracy*. Kellner's *Guys and Guns Amok: Domestic Terrorism and School Shootings from the Oklahoma City Bombings to the Virginia Tech Massacre* won the 2008 AESA award as the best book on education. In 2010, Kellner published with Blackwell *Cinema Wars: Hollywood Film and Politics in the Bush-Cheney Era*. His website is at www.gseis.ucla.edu/faculty/kellner/kellner.html

Richard Kilminster is Senior Lecturer in Sociology at the University of Leeds, where he also gained his PhD under Zygmunt Bauman in 1976, having previously studied sociology at the Universities of Essex and Leicester. He has written many articles on the sociology of knowledge and the work of Norbert Elias in particular. In the 1980s he worked with Elias at the University of Bielefeld and in Amsterdam and edited his last major work, *The Symbol Theory*, in 1991. He is author of *Praxis and Method: A Sociological Dialogue with Lukács, Gramsci and the Early Frankfurt School*

(1979), *The Sociological Revolution: From the Enlightenment to the Global Age* (1998) and *Norbert Elias: Post-philosophical Sociology* (2007). He is Chair of the Editorial Advisory Board for the *Collected Works of Norbert Elias*, has edited volume I, *The Early Writings* (2006) and co-edited (with Stephen Mennell) three further volumes of *Essays* (2008–2009). He is currently working on a new edition of *The Symbol Theory* for that series (2010) and on the role of psychoanalytic schools in the formation of sociology.

Moya Lloyd is Professor of Political Theory at Loughborough University. She has published widely in the areas of contemporary political theory and gender theory. Her most recent books include *Beyond Identity Politics: Feminism, Power, Politics* (2005), *Judith Butler: From Norms to Politics* (2007), and with Adrian Little (eds) *The Politics of Radical Democracy* (2009). She is currently at work on two projects: a book on *Sex, Gender and Sexuality* for Acumen Press, and a project examining the relation between social orders, norms, and "who counts."

Stephen Mennell is Professor Emeritus of Sociology at University College Dublin, from which he retired in 2009. He read economics at Cambridge (1963–1966), and then spent the year 1966–1967 in the old Department of Social Relations at Harvard, before teaching at the University of Exeter (1967–1990) and at Monash University, Australia (1990–1993). His books include *All Manners of Food: Eating and Taste in England and France from the Middle Ages to the Present* (1985), *Norbert Elias: Civilization and the Human Self-Image* (1989, paperback *Norbert Elias: An Introduction*, 1992, 1998), and *The American Civilizing Process* (2007). He holds the degrees of Doctor in de Sociale Wetenschappen (Amsterdam) and Doctor of Letters (Cambridge). He is a member of the board of the Norbert Elias Foundation, Amsterdam, of the Royal Netherlands Academy of Arts and Sciences, and of the Royal Irish Academy.

Catherine Mills is Sesqui Lecturer in Bioethics at University of Sydney, Australia. Her main research interests lie in the areas of biopolitics and bioethics, especially in relation to technologies of reproduction. She is particularly interested in ideas of subjectivity, normalcy, and responsibility. She has previously published *The Philosophy of Agamben* (2008) and is currently completing a manuscript on reproductive ethics. She has also published numerous articles in feminist theory, bioethics, and political theory.

William Outhwaite is Professor of Sociology at Newcastle University. His recent publications include *The Future of Society* (Blackwell, 2006), *European Society* (2008) and (with Larry Ray) *Social Theory and Postcommunism* (Blackwell, 2005). His 1994 book on *Habermas* has just appeared in a new expanded edition (2009). He is currently working on social and political change in Europe since 1989, supported by a Leverhulme Major Research Fellowship.

Anne Warfield Rawls is a member of the Sociology Department at Bentley University, and Associate Researcher at Centre d'Etude des Mouvements Sociaux, EHESS, Paris. She writes about Garfinkel, Goffman, Durkheim, and the importance of the idea of constitutive orders in the development of sociological theory, studies of practice and ethics. Her research explores aspects of constitutive orders, including the social constitution of information, the interface between communication, technology and work, and the relationship between Interaction Orders and inequality. Her publications include *Epistemology and Practice: Durkheim's Elementary Forms of the Religious Life* (2004); "Harold Garfinkel: Ethnomethodology and Workplace Studies," *Organization Studies* (2008); "An Essay on Two Conceptions of Social Order," *Journal of Classical Sociology* (2009); "Garfinkel's Conception of Time," *Time and Society* (2005); "Social Order as Moral Order," *Handbook of the Sociology of Morality* (2010); "'Race' as an Interaction Order Phenomenon: W. E. B. Du Bois' 'Double Consciousness' Thesis Revisited," *Sociological Theory* (2000); "Dialectics of Belief and Practice" (with Bonnie Wright), *Critical Sociology* (2006); "Accountably Other: Trust, Reciprocity and Exclusion in a Context of Situated Practice," *Human Studies* (2005).

Sal Restivo is Professor of Sociology, Science Studies, and Information Technology at Rensselaer Polytechnic Institute in Troy, NY, and Special Lecture Professor at Northeastern University in Shenyang, China. He is a founding member and former president of the Society for Social Studies of Science and specializes in the sociology of science, knowledge, mathematics, and mind and brain. He is the author of *The Social Relations of Physics, Mysticism, and Mathematics* (1983), *Mathematics in Society and History* (1992), *Science, Technology, and Society: A Sociological Perspective* (2005; with W. Bauchspies and J. Croissant), and other books and articles in science studies, editor-in-chief of *Science, Technology, and Society: An Encyclopedia* (2007), and co-editor with Peter Denton of *Battleground: Science and Technology, An Encyclopedia* (2008). His current work focuses on science and anarchism, and the social brain.

George Ritzer is Distinguished University Professor at the University of Maryland. Among his awards: Honorary Doctorate from La Trobe University, Melbourne, Australia; Honorary Patron, University Philosophical Society, Trinity College, Dublin; the American Sociological Association's Distinguished Contribution to Teaching Award. He has chaired the American Sociological Association's Section on Theoretical Sociology, as well as the Section on Organizations and Occupations, and is currently the first Chair of the section-in-formation on Global and Transnational Sociology. Among his books are *The McDonaldization of Society* (5th edn, 2008), *Enchanting a Disenchanted World* (3rd edn, 2010), and *The Globalization of Nothing* (2nd edn, 2007). His most recent book is *Globalization: A Basic Text* (Blackwell, 2010) and he edited *The Blackwell Companion to Globalization* (2008). He is currently working on *The Outsourcing of Everything* (with Craig Lair, forthcoming). He was founding editor of the *Journal of Consumer Culture*. He also edited the eleven-volume *Encyclopedia of Sociology* (2007) and the two-volume *Encyclopedia of Social Theory* (2005) and is currently editing the *Encyclopedia of Globalization* (forthcoming). Current essays deal with the "prosumer" (one who simultaneously produces and consumes), especially on Web 2.0 sites such as Wikipedia and Facebook, and he is editing a special double-issue of the *American Behavioral Scientist* on that topic. His books have been translated into over twenty languages, with over a dozen translations of *The McDonaldization of Society* alone.

Greg Smith is Professor of Sociology at the University of Salford, UK. His publications include *Analysing Visual Data* (1992), *Goffman and Social Organization: Studies in a Sociological Legacy* (1999), *Erving Goffman* (4 vols, 2000), *Erving Goffman* (2006), and *Introducing Cultural Studies* (2nd edn, 2008). He is presently working on further books about the interactionist tradition, including an intellectual biography of Goffman.

Jeffrey Stepnisky is Assistant Professor of Sociology at Grant MacEwan University in Edmonton, Alberta, Canada. He teaches courses in social theory, social psychology and the sociology of mental illness. His research interests are in the area of self and subjectivity with particular attention to the impact of contemporary biotechnologies, such as antidepressants, on self-understanding. He has published papers on this topic in *Social Theory & Health* and *The Bulletin of Science, Technology & Society*. He also has an ongoing interest in the work and writing of Canadian philosopher and social theorist Charles Taylor.

Rudolf Stichweh studied sociology and philosophy in Berlin and Bielefeld. He received his Doctorate from the University of Bielefeld in 1983 and he has worked at the Max-Planck-Institut für Gesellschaftsforschung, Köln (1985–1989), the Maison des Sciences de l'Homme, Paris (1987), and the Max-Planck-Institut für europäische Rechtsgeschichte, Frankfurt a.M. (1989–1994). He was Professor for Sociological Theory from 1994 to 2003 at the University of Bielefeld and a guest professor at EHESS, Paris in 2000. Since 2003 he has been Professor for Sociological Theory, University of Lucerne, Switzerland and in 2005/6 was a fellow at Wissenschaftskolleg zu Berlin. From 2006 to 2010 he was rector of the University of Lucerne. In the Spring of 2011 Stichweh will be visiting professor at Princeton University. His areas of research include: theory of world society, sociocultural evolution, history and sociology of science and universities, sociology of the stranger, sociological theory and systems theory and historical macrosociology. He has published the following books: *Zur Entstehung des modernen Systems wissenschaftlicher Disziplinen: Physik in Deutschland* 1740–1890 (1984), *Der frühmoderne Staat und die europäische Universität* (1991), *Wissenschaft, Universität, Professionen* (1994), *Die Weltgesellschaft* (2000), *Inklusion und Exklusion* (2005) and *Der Fremde: Studien zu Soziologie und Sozialgeschichte* (2010).

Couze Venn is Emeritus Professor of Cultural Theory at the Theory, Culture & Society Centre, Nottingham Trent University, and Research Fellow, University of Johannesburg. He is the author of *Occidentalism. Modernity and Subjectivity* (2000), *The Postcolonial Challenge: Towards Alternative Worlds* (2006), and co-author of *Changing the Subject: Psychology, Social Regulation and Subjectivity* (1984). He was a founding editor of *Ideology & Consciousness* which promoted Foucauldian research from the 1970s, and is the Review Editor and sits on the editorial board of *Theory, Culture & Society* and *Body & Society*.

Joseph M. Whitmeyer is the Professor of Sociology at UNC, Charlotte. Among his research interests are social interaction in small groups and the construction of mathematical models of social processes. He has published a number of articles on social power and on social networks. He is co-author (with S. Brenner, 2009) of *Strategy on the United States Supreme Court*.

Iain Wilkinson is a Senior Lecturer in Sociology at the University of Kent, UK. His publications include *Anxiety in a Risk Society* (2001), *Suffering: A Sociological Introduction* (2005), and *Risk Vulnerability and Everyday Life* (2009). He is currently collaborating with Arthur Kleinman to write a new book on "social suffering."

Patrick Williams is Professor of Literary and Cultural Studies at Nottingham Trent University, where he teaches courses on postcolonial theory and culture, film, diaspora, and race and nation in twentieth century Britain. His publications include *Colonial Discourse and Post-Colonial Theory* (1993); *Introduction to Post-Colonial Theory* with Peter Childs (1996), *Ngugi wa Thiong'o* (1999); *Edward Said* (2000); and *Postcolonial African Cinema* with David Murphy (2007). Forthcoming books include *The Routledge Companion to Diaspora Studies*, (edited with Alison Donnell and John Noyes), and a collection on Orientalism in Routledge's "Major Works" series. He is on the editorial boards of *Theory, Culture & Society*, and *Journal of Postcolonial Writing*.

Janet Wirth-Cauchon is Associate Professor of Sociology at Drake University. She is the author of *Women and Borderline Personality Disorder: Symptoms and Stories* (2001), a study of the gendered history and application of the borderline diagnosis in psychoanalysis and psychiatry. Her research interests are in the areas of feminist cultural theory, science studies, and gender and psychiatry. She is currently researching feminist conceptualizations of materiality, and the political and ethical implications of changing relations between embodiment, technology, and nonhuman nature.

Preface

This volume of *The Wiley-Blackwell Companion to Major Social Theorists* is a significant expansion and revision of *The Blackwell Companion to Major Contemporary Social Theorists* originally published in 2000 and in slightly modified form in 2003. While the first edition featured chapters on thirteen contemporary social theorists, this version includes twenty-three essays. Sixteen of the twenty-three chapters are written by authors new to this edition. The authors of essays that appeared in the previous edition have thoroughly revised their pieces by rewriting parts of the original, adding new sections and ideas, commenting on the relevance of theory in the present moment, and updating the list of primary and secondary sources. In addition, all essays include a feature new to this volume – a reader's guide. Located at the end of each chapter, this short guide gives readers a quick summary of the most important entry points into a theorist's work. Ultimately this companion comes together as a fresh piece of scholarship that enlarges our understanding of the major contemporary social theorists.

In addition to the original essays, this companion includes chapters on eleven theorists not included in the original edition. Some of these theorists were added because of their general importance for contemporary social theory. Smith gives us the hugely influential standpoint theory, Luhmann's systems theory is now recognized as one of the most original and interdisciplinary developments in contemporary theory, Lefebvre has long been recognized as a unique interpreter of Marx and the pre-eminent social theorist of space, and Agamben has come into prominence for his work on political power and the "bare life." The choice of theorists new to this edition is also influenced by developments in social theory over the last ten years. Beyond the metatheoretical debates of the 1980s and 1990s, we now see a social theory increasingly concerned with substantive social and political problems. This is due, in part, to the increasing significance of globalization and globalization theory, the growing importance of science studies, and the continuing importance of consumerism and the spread of consumer society. Essays on Bauman, Beck, Said, and Wallerstein were added for their contributions to globalization theory. However, as the essays show, their contributions are also wider ranging than this – for example,

Bauman helps us to think about consumerism, and through his risk society thesis Beck contributes to science and technology studies. Latour and Haraway are included because of their contributions to science studies, although they are also helpful in demonstrating new ways of doing social theory. Deleuze has also been influential in science studies, although his work can also be read for its contribution to theories of culture and consumer culture. This companion also includes a new introduction that discusses major social theoretical topics found across the essays. This includes perennial themes such as identity, politics, power, and social structure as well as the aforementioned themes of globalization, science, and consumer culture.

All the chapters in this volume are written by contemporary theorists who are experts on the theorist discussed in their chapter. However, even for experts there is a great deal of work that goes into researching and writing one of these essays. One of the strengths of this volume is that the essays are quite deep and extensive, including not simply a rehearsal of the major features of each theorist's ideas, but also the biographical and historical contexts that frame each theorist's work. The editors are grateful then not only for expertise of the contributors but also for the time commitment involved in writing such essays. The dedication of each contributor shows in the quality of the essays produced.

The editors would also like to thank the team at Wiley-Blackwell for their efforts in bringing these volumes together. In particular, we thank Justin Vaughan who first approached us to expand and revise the volumes. Throughout the writing, editing, and production process Ben Thatcher has been an invaluable resource and helpful guide. At various points, Barbara Duke, Sally Cooper, and Joanna Pyke provided helpful feedback. We are also grateful for Alta Bridges's work as copy-editor. These volumes also owe something to Douglas Goodman and Todd Stillman, both of whom helped George Ritzer to edit and develop the first edition of this companion. Finally, Jeff Stepnisky would like to thank Michelle Meagher for her support and feedback throughout the editorial process.

George Ritzer and Jeff Stepnisky

Introduction

JEFFREY STEPNISKY

The purpose of this volume of *The Wiley-Blackwell Companion to Major Social Theorists* is to provide a comprehensive engagement with the work of 23 major contemporary social theorists. This means not simply describing the central components of a theorist's work, but also putting these ideas into personal, social, intellectual, and historical context. Indeed, each author approached to write an essay for this volume was asked to place the theorist's work in these multiple contexts.

Here "contemporary" is more-or-less defined as the period stretching from the end of the Second World War until the present. This heralds not only a major geopolitical and economic re-organization in which the United States emerges at the core of the world system (as discussed in Chase-Dunn and Inoue's essay on Wallerstein) but also the origins of international organizations (United Nations, World Bank, International Monetary Fund) that facilitated the process of what is now called globalization. It is a historical period that witnesses decolonization, the growth of the democratic welfare state, the emergence of civil rights movements, the establishment of consumer society, the Cold War and nuclear threat, the intensification of scientific inquiry, the rise of neoliberalism, the development and spread of high speed travel and telecommunication technology, and the growth of the environmental movement. Reading the essays in this volume, we also come across specific events that have either shaped the work of contemporary theorists or have been the focus of social theoretical investigation: the Great Depression, the Second World War, the Holocaust, the Nasserite Revolution, the Vietnam War, the 1967 Israeli-Palestinian War, the student protests of May 1968, the collapse of the Berlin Wall, the oil crisis of the 1970s, the Chernobyl disaster in Ukraine and the Union Carbide disaster in India, the Clinton sex scandals and the O.J. Simpson trial, the AIDS crisis, foot and mouth disease, avian flu, 9/11, the wars in Afghanistan and Iraq, prisoner

The Wiley-Blackwell Companion to Major Social Theorists, First Edition.
Edited by George Ritzer and Jeffrey Stepnisky.
© 2011 Blackwell Publishing Ltd. Published 2011 by Blackwell Publishing Ltd.

detention at Abu Ghraib and Guantanamo Bay, and Hurricane Katrina. This indicates only a few of the events mentioned in these essays, but as a preliminary collection they tell a story of massive social transformations, conflicts, violence, the breakdown of old identities and structures, the emergence of new identities and structures, and a growing list of globally dispersed dangers and threats.

Like the period in which they write, the work of the theorists described in these volumes is rich and complex. Indeed, the value of a collection such as this one is that it shows how a particular theorist's ideas change not only in relation to the dynamics of his/her own thought, but in response to inputs from the intellectual, political, and social climates in which they live. Most theorists included in this volume are popularly identified with a single important contribution (e.g. Lefebvre on space, Smith on institutional ethnography, Merton on mid-range theory, Beck on risk society, Butler on queer theory), but the character of a theorist's work can change over a lifetime and the interpretations of that theorist's work are equally varied. Michel Foucault shifts from analyses of modern disciplinary institutions to analyses of the more intimate forms of Greek and Roman self-care, Judith Butler shifts from her famous work on sex and gender identity to problems in warfare, violence, and human rights, and Anthony Giddens shifts from his metatheoretical studies of structure-agency relations to his current interest in the politics of climate change. One further element of complexity: while many of the theorists covered in this volume are sociologists, the work of social theory is largely interdisciplinary. This means that in addition to the theories of sociologists, this volume also contains coverage of work by philosophers and literary theorists (Agamben, Deleuze, Said, Butler). Moreover, nearly all of the thinkers covered in this volume draw on a wide variety of disciplinary sources including sociology, political theory, cultural theory, literary theory, philosophy, anthropology, biological science, cybernetic theory, and so on.

The multifaceted character of theories poses a problem for an introduction such as this one. Namely, it is impossible to describe in a few pages everything that is contained in this volume, or even to describe adequately the contribution of each theorist. With this in mind, the remainder of this introduction is arranged to draw attention to a few persistent theoretical themes (social structure, selfhood and identity, politics and power) as well as a few of the more important emerging themes in contemporary theory (consumerism, globalization, science and technology). These brief discussions introduce the theorists covered in this volume by describing the way that they have contributed to the definition and growth of these topical areas. At the same time this introduction can be treated as a reader's guide, or map, for those who wish to follow how these themes have been handled by different theorists over the last 60 years. This gives a sense of theory as a dynamic and moving entity.

STRUCTURES, NETWORKS, AND SYSTEMS

Social structure is a founding concept in sociology, and for this reason it also plays a role in the development of social theory. Broadly, structure deals with the problem of social patterning, a characterization that links it to the concepts of network and system. Indeed, increasingly social theorists use the language of networks and systems rather than structures – this is meant to capture the presumed dynamism of current societies.

In this volume, Crothers's chapter on Merton provides the most explicit discussion of structure. He introduces Merton's work on cultural and social structure, discusses this in relationship to Merton's famous analysis of mid-range institutions, and even his less known work on microsociology. Uniquely, Crothers integrates the otherwise dispersed components of Merton's social theory into a picture of the whole. James Coleman, a former student of Merton, gets at the whole another way. While Coleman is generally known as the founder of rational choice theory, in her chapter Jasso puts such familiar characterizations aside to show how mathematical sociology informs Coleman's work. In a challenging essay, Jasso demonstrates how social status, power, and power structures cannot only be mathematically mapped as social structure, but also linked to smaller scale micro-phenomenon such as self-esteem and adolescent behavior.

Both Crothers and Jasso draw out the multileveled character of their theorists' respective work – indeed, Jasso dedicates an entire section of her chapter to "Coleman and the micro-macro" link. This draws attention to the structure-agency, or micro-macro debates that were so important to social theory in the 1980s and 1990s. The problem was that classical social theories were either seen to focus too much on small-scale interactive processes or larger scale social processes with little effort to show how the two are related. The importance of this debate is evidenced in the fact that it's now difficult to find a work in social theory that doesn't at least mention the importance of bridging this gap. Anthony Giddens and Pierre Bourdieu are the two social theorists most central to resolving the issue. In their essay on Giddens, Bryant and Jary show how Giddens bridged the gap by treating structure and agency as co-constituting recursive practices. Challenging the notion that structuration theory is too abstract, too disconnected from actual practice, Bryant and Jary also describe the numerous contexts in which the theory has been applied – accounting, management, gender relations, surveillance, and bureaucratic power. Bourdieu also sought to overcome the structure-agency distinction as well as the conceptual split between objective and subjective phenomena. His theory includes an idea of structure conceptualized through the language of field and capital that is ultimately, as Calhoun notes, drawn together through the tremendously fruitful concept of *habitus* – a term that evokes the way that objective structures are lived and reproduced in everyday commonplace practices. When read through these lenses we see that the structure-agency debate is not just a metatheoretical endeavor but rather has given rise to a well-grounded set of theoretical tools increasingly described under the title *practice theory*.

Harold Garfinkel represents another kind of intervention into the discussion of structure. In particular, as Rawls reminds us, he challenges the very idea of structure. There are no structures, only the interpersonal generation of the idea of structure – a legitimation and justification of the discipline of sociology. To describe this oftentimes-challenging position, Rawls outlines the history of Garfinkel's work including not only his famous *Studies in Ethnomethodology*, but also recently available editions of early work on communication and information theory. Garfinkel's critique of structure also anticipates the more recent work of Bruno Latour. Together with John Law and Michel Callon, Latour is one of the founders of actor-network theory. Rather than thinking of society as a set of structures, or pre-existing patterned realities into which actors are then inserted (with varying degrees of agency), Latour traces the ways that agents make connections with other agents. These connections constitute networks. The shift from structure to network has a leveling effect. Society no longer consists of several levels – micro-social, meso-social, macro-social – each of which is handled with a different kind of analysis. Instead, using one of Gilles Deleuze's terms, society is a series of "assemblages." The problem is not to understand how different levels in a society function, but rather to understand how assemblages are produced and held together. Indeed, this is one of the places where Deleuze, the philosopher, becomes relevant for social theory. He recasts social thought in terms of what Ian Buchanan calls a "practical ontology" – a way of describing the ever-shifting connections that compose social life.

The network concept is also found in the work of American sociologist Richard Emerson. Like Latour, for Emerson a network is relational and therefore focuses not on the isolated social actor but on the relationship that constitutes the actor. However, Emerson is different from Latour because, borrowing from microeconomic theory, networks are built out of cost-benefit analysis – they are *exchange* networks. Again unlike Latour, Emerson treats network as a kind of structure – a lasting pattern that organizes behavior. Differences aside, two things should be clear. First, the appeal of network as a description of contemporary societies resonates with the more popular sense that we are living in a networked society where one's ability to make connections is of equal importance to one's predetermined place in a social hierarchy. Second, though Latour and others oppose overarching concepts such as structure it is not clear that network is by definition anathema to structure.

A few words, then, about "systems." Even though the concept of system has been around since the classical period (in the work of Spencer and Parsons), it has a contemporary resonance with network theories, especially the focus on fluidity and transformation. This becomes clear in Stichweh's chapter on Niklas Luhmann. Stichweh notes that Luhmann was one of the most prolific sociologists of the twentieth century and one of the few contemporary social theorists to develop a universal social theory. Immensely interdisciplinary, Luhmann reformulated systems theory as a non-hierarchical account of system self-formation – in particular the formation of social systems. Though Luhmann's theory seems to resonate with the aspiration of an earlier grand sociology it is worth noting that his work has been adopted by scholars in both the humanities and social sciences who are seeking a theoretical approach that could take them beyond the postmodernisms and poststructuralisms of the 1980s and 1990s (Rasch, 2000). This is perhaps because of his emphasis on communication as the basic element of social systems – here we also find an interesting overlap with Garfinkel's ideas, especially the aforementioned work in communication and information theory.

What should become clear from this brief review is that even though the concept of structure (social patterning) is maintained into the contemporary moment, gone are the days when structure is conceived as a stable overarching entity. Instead, we have a variety of approaches that describe the mechanisms through which connections among elements, and thereby patterns, are generated, sustained (for varying periods of time), and then transformed.

Self and Identity

The concepts of self and identity have been intrinsic to social theory since the classical period. Products of early capitalism, the urban space, and cross-cultural interaction, processes of self and identity formation are sped-up within the context of an information-saturated consumer culture. In the theorists covered in this volume there is a drift from the more general discovery that selves are made up in social interaction to work that studies cultural, political, and historical contexts under which these selves and identities are forged.

Erving Goffman is the contemporary theorist who has had the most profound effect on social theories of the self. His dramaturgical approach treats selves as social productions that, as Smith emphasizes, function within "interaction orders." Indeed, for Smith, Goffman's overarching contribution was to map out the interaction order, thus detailing the fundamentally relational character of selves. Relationality is an important concept for social theories of self and subjectivity. It also comes up in the work of Norbert Elias, though under the title of "figurational sociology." Elias was not a micro-sociologist like Goffman. However, as Kilminster and Mennell show, he was concerned with the processes of subject formation. How are the bodily habits, manners, and practices of Western people shaped over time? Moreover, Elias's analysis of subject formation emphasizes the role that state formation and the control of violence play in the construction of modern persons. From this view, figurational sociology treats people not as isolated individuals, self-contained atoms, but always as part of larger configurations – related through structures of power.

This focus on the body, politics, and power is also central to Dorothy Smith's and Judith Butler's work, though they introduce the central dimensions of sex and gender. For Smith and Butler identities are political constructions that impact not merely a person's sense of self but also their corporeal identity. Though coming from different scholarly traditions, they both argue that traditional social theory overlooks the centrality of the physical body to the production of identity. Butler, as Lloyd shows, uses the techniques of poststructuralist analysis and psychoanalytic theory to describe how gender and sex are socially produced. Smith studies the body, but comes out against poststructuralist analyses. Indeed, in their chapter, Campbell and DeVault provide a very helpful comparison of the work of Smith and poststructuralist Michel Foucault. Smith places the lived experience of body (a concept deconstructed by poststructuralists) at the center of analysis and from this theoretical vantage point develops standpoint theory as a critique of capitalism, patriarchy, and social science.

In the most recent developments, social theory has been interested in the ethics of self-other relations. Effectively, this work revolves around the problem of *recognition*. For example, Patrick Williams's discussion of Edward Said shows how Western colonial powers have failed to recognize non-Western identities and cultures. Introducing the concept of Orientalism, Said describes the cultural practices through which unfamiliar people are made into cultural others. Said deconstructs the concept of the "Orient" showing it to be a product of Western scholars and politicians – a place and identity that only exists for the West. Orientalist imaginaries, Williams is quick to point out, are not just a description of nineteenth-century colonial practices – they remain alive and well mediating East–West relations in the globalizing world and in particular the recent wars in Iraq and Afghanistan. Butler, Agamben, and Bauman also consider the problem of recognition, though they take one step back and consider the conditions under which certain persons and groups are rendered *un*recognizable. Agamben and Bauman use the Holocaust as their example. Butler refers to 9/11 and the subsequent wars as her examples. In all these cases, the question arises as to what is the "liveable life" and who will be recognized as human. Here social theories of self and identity begin to overlap with theories of political power.

POWER AND POLITICS

Another central problem for social theory, power, and the political is addressed repeatedly in this volume. Emerson, who was discussed earlier for his work on exchange networks, is also recognized for his theory of power. Emerson provides a formal definition of power, construed in the language of network theory. He renders power measurable and subject to experimental testing. As Cook and Whitmeyer put it in their chapter: "the power of actor A over B is equated to the dependence of Actor B on Actor A," where these dependencies are mediated by network structures. While its formality seems to place this theory of power worlds apart from those developed by European thinkers like Lefebvre and Foucault (discussed below), there is one important commonality: power is relational; it is not, contrary to common sense, a product of the singular abilities of an actor or institution.

Indeed, Lefebvre develops a theory that sees power emanating not from persons but from the spaces of everyday life. Goonewardena introduces Lefebvre by calling him the most important and creative interpreter of Marx. As Goonewardena argues, while we need to be careful not to pigeonhole Lefebvre, he has come to be known for his theories of space and everyday life. Contrary to the Cartesian view, space is not simply a backdrop to everyday life (a series of mathematical co-ordinates into which people are inserted), but it is constructed within and out of everyday activity. The power of capital then is exerted in and through the spaces of everyday life, hence the challenge that comes in transforming social relations and in seeking new forms of social and economic arrangement.

Lefebvre's importance has only recently been recognized, perhaps because of the way that space becomes important in the age of globalization. Foucault, however, has long been recognized as one of the most important theorists of power in the late twentieth century. He is best known for his "capillary" approach to power and for his discussion of the shift from sovereign to disciplinary power, a shift, by the way, which is also treated by Norbert Elias in his analysis of the formation of the modern subject. Both theorists show that in the modern era power is not exercised through a single political sovereign. Power, instead, is produced and reproduced in everyday practice. Power produces subjects. Subjects internalize power and in this learn to exercise power over themselves and in their relations with others. In his chapter on Foucault, Venn covers these familiar aspects of Foucault's work but most interestingly he spends time discussing Foucault's only recently translated lectures on political economy. This opens up yet another dimension of Foucault's work. Consistent with the earlier concepts of episteme and discourse, the analysis of political economy offers a vision of power in capitalism, under the influence of the neoliberal ideal. In short, as Venn explains, for Foucault, neoliberalism is not a product of magical, hands-off market forces, but as Karl Polanyi (2001 [1944]) once showed, it depends upon the way that the state sets up the conditions for the operation of the economy.

Foucault also draws attention to the importance of "biopolitics," and this is where we can bring in the work of Giorgio Agamben. As Mills shows, Agamben develops Foucault's ideas through the work of scholars such as Karl Schmitt and Walter Benjamin. In this we get a more visceral theory of power. Foucault, of course, talked about the body and the discipline of the body, but there the body was always studied through discursive regimes. There is something more primordial at work in Agamben. As noted, he takes the Holocaust and the concentration camps as his model of state power and thereby provides a vision of power as something that operates on "the bare life." Life and death decisions are made in a pre-discursive space before they can be socially recognized. They are both within the social, yet hidden from the social. The growing popularity of Agamben's work is likely owing to this darker view of power – in a globalizing world populated by war, refugee claims, industrial disaster, and ecological collapse – decisions are increasingly made about who is worthy and who is unworthy of state care. In short, this allows for a discussion of the ways that access to "life itself" is mediated by the state. Here Butler's recent work should also be mentioned. Indeed, she is an excellent example of a theorist who has taken her earlier, quite focused, work on sexuality and turned it into a larger theory of ethics and power, especially in the context of war and violence. In particular, as Lloyd points out, Butler suggests that we can combat violence if we are able to identify with the suffering of the Other. Butler draws on Emmanuel Levinas and psychoanalysis to develop a theory of grief and mourning. It is by learning to grieve the loss of the Other that we will be drawn to a more general understanding of human fragility and thereby better equipped to overcome the desire for vengeance.

Though space doesn't permit further discussion, it is worth adding to this list Giddens's definition of power as the combination of rules and resources. Bourdieu also offers an important analysis of power, and Calhoun draws particular attention to his concept of symbolic violence. Smith, as Campbell and DeVault show, provides a fully developed theory of patriarchy, capitalism, social science, and power. Indeed, to some extent, every theory in this volume discusses the nature and deployment of power in social, political, and economic systems.

CULTURE AND CONSUMPTION

There can be little question that the emergence of consumer culture following the Second World War has significantly shaped contemporary social life, especially in the West, and thereby social theory. Capitalism is now consumer capitalism, and where identity was once shaped by religious, political, and ethnic cultures, consumer culture seems positioned to replace or at least pose a formidable challenge to these historical forms. Processes of globalization frequently meet with resistance because they carry with them the economy, identity, and ethics of consumer culture (most often associated with American consumer culture). Numerous theorists described in this volume either describe or critique consumer culture. Henri Lefebvre's work, as Goonewardena documents, is developed in concert with Guy Debord and the Situationists who offer a critique of the society of spectacle. Lefebvre later develops this critique through analysis of what he calls "the bureaucratic society of controlled consumption." At times, Agamben's work critiques "spectacular capitalism" and in particular the way that it colonizes social relations. Deleuze and Guattari describe the "desiring subjects" generated in late capitalism and Deleuze theorizes cinema, a medium central to the operation of consumer capitalism. Foucault, in his archeology of neoliberalism shows the relationship between enterprise society and the consumer society. Each of these participates in a shared economy of desire.

In this volume, the theorists who provide the most developed tools for thinking about the consumer culture are Jean Baudrillard, Pierre Bourdieu, and Zygmunt Bauman. Baudrillard gets us started with his early books, in particular *The Consumer Society*. This work was written, Kellner points out, when Baudrillard was still under the influence of Marxian theory and hence serves as a critique of consumerism. To the Marxist concepts of exchange and use value, Baudrillard adds sign value. Consumer objects are given their value within sign systems. Eventually consumer signs come to define all of society, threatening in turn to absorb and define all of reality. This is only the beginning of Baudrillard's trajectory and he offers increasingly provocative and, according to some, obscure engagements with modern and then postmodern society. The point to make for the present discussion is Baudrillard's critical approach to the consumer society: a self-replicating sign system in which consumers are mere connective nodes.

Bourdieu is the theorist in this volume who offers the most developed theory of culture, and as a consequence, tools for helping to think about consumerism. Where for Baudrillard the consumer is a mere appendage to the consumer culture, Bourdieu's attack on the distinction between structure and agency recognizes the consumer as a strategic actor that positions itself within cultural fields. The actor is not free to position herself in any way that she chooses – she is constrained by the habitus built into her by her social location – but nevertheless she moves with an agency unthinkable to Baudrillard. Furthermore, unlike Baudrillard, Bourdieu retains the connection to Marxism or at least sociological theories of inequality. Taste, conspicuous consumption, and other consumer practices are used by agents not simply to satisfy desire but to distinguish themselves in relationship to others.

Finally, for Bauman, also a critic, consumerism is associated with individualization and privatization (topics also addressed by Giddens and Beck). In his discussion of Bauman, Beilharz cites Parisian graffiti "1968: Changing the World; 1989: Renovating the Kitchen." This gets to the core of the issue. Bauman who started his career writing about labor movements now observes a capitalist consumer culture that operates at a furious pace, exacerbates the inequalities between rich and poor, individualizes identity, and in this threatens the possibility for collective change. Indeed all aspects of social life are transformed through the "liquid" logic of consumer capitalism. Selves acquire identity through consumer commodities, love relationships are unstable, momentary accomplishments that reflect the ever-shifting desires generated in consumer culture, children become objects of "emotional consumption." Indeed in this system the poor are coded, Beilharz argues, as "flawed consumers" who act as "scarecrows" for the well-to-do bourgeoisie consumer class.

All this said, we should not go too far. Yes, consumerism is a defining feature of the contemporary moment, but other theorists have described the continuing importance of traditional cultures. Habermas, as explained by Outhwaite, has recently struggled with ethical issues around science and religion. He describes a *post-secular society* in which religious cultures continue to exist alongside secular cultures. Secular, consumer culture doesn't win the day, but rather must find ways to co-exist with the religious culture. Habermas has also detailed the importance of national and regional identities in defining contemporary politics and identities. Patrick Williams also makes this point in his chapter on Edward Said, where he argues that Said's life and work is a testament to the continuing relevance of national and ethnic cultures and identities, even as these are taken up and transformed in late modernity. Or perhaps, as some such as Beck and Giddens suggest, consumer culture is not all that bad – insofar as it brings with it the requirement for reflexive self-construction it impels new forms of social co-ordination that are well-suited to handling emerging social and environmental problems.

SCIENCE AND TECHNOLOGY

Science studies is a growing interdisciplinary field of research. Although in this volume several sociologists theorize science, technology and, society (Merton, Beck), the two major theorists of science are a philosopher (Latour) and, at least originally, a biologist (Haraway). Though it has mid-century origins, the study of science really responds to rapid development in the natural sciences over the last twenty years. This includes accomplishments such as the decoding of the human genome, the saturation of society with teletechnology, and the increasing everyday use of biotechnologies. Science studies also points to the inextricable relationship between science, capitalism, and politics. Indeed, science studies make a significant contribution to social theory because it re-theorizes the social through science.

Merton, as Crothers points out, is one of the early figures in the sociology of science. His approach was to treat science as a social institution that could be understood using the tools of sociology. Science is socially and culturally structured, its discoveries mediated by social processes, in particular the norms that regulate scientific practice. From this point forward the story of science studies is elaborate and by no means can it be fully told using the chapters in this volume. Fortunately the two chapters on more recent contributors to science studies, Bruno Latour and Donna Haraway, provide some of the story.

In his chapter on Latour, Restivo (himself one of the founding members of the Society for the Social Studies of Science), contextualizes Latour's work by drawing out the general contours of science studies. Early work included field studies and ethnographies of scientific laboratories. This was more or less acceptable to practicing scientists. More troubling was when social scientists started studying the content of science; this lead to the idea that scientific knowledge could be treated as a social construction. Latour was front and center in the subsequent science wars. He claimed, for example, that science was inseparable from politics and other social institutions. It could not be studied as one isolated component of the social but rather as an entity networked through a variety of other "non-scientific" practices.

Donna Haraway also treats technoscience as constitutive of the contemporary social order, but in particular, as Wirth-Cauchon shows, her work is grounded in feminist science studies. Thus she initially works to deconstruct the masculinist, but also racist and ablest, assumptions built into scientific practice. Famous for her introduction of the cyborg concept, Haraway wants to transcend historical dichotomies, in particular the distinction between human and machine or more recently human and companion species. Here, Haraway and Latour share another point of view – historically social theory has only treated the relationship between human beings. It has assumed that societies are built out of persons in relationship with one another. This, however, excludes all the non-human agents (animals, bacteria, machines) that have helped to constitute those orders. Here, as with Baudrillard, some critics argue that social theory borders on science fiction. Others suggest that these kinds of radically distinctive social theories are the only kind that can speak to the present moment.

Though Ulrich Beck's work is tremendously broad, he is also drawn into these debates about science, in particular through his theory of the risk society. Wilkinson shows us that for Beck risk can only be understood in the context of his larger theory. This includes ideas about reflexivity (which are also found in Giddens and Bourdieu), individualization, and second modernity. In brief, industrial and scientific developments of first modernity have created the conditions for a second modernity. This includes the proliferation of risks (environmental, economic, political) that can no longer be handled by any single nation. This also draws the theory of risk society into the terrain of globalization theory. Risk consciousness, especially around technoscience (as both a danger and a savior), defines the current moment.

GLOBALIZATION

Is globalization the master process of the current moment? It seems to have replaced postmodernism as the theoretical buzzword. Most major living theorists address globalization, presumably because it is the process that has the largest impact on the organization of contemporary social life. Its influence has been noted in discussion of the previous themes: globalization creates new kinds of networks and social systems, it generates new challenges for self and identity formation, it spreads the logic of consumer capitalism, and it is part and parcel of the definition of risk society. The definitions vary. Bauman defines it against the solidity of an earlier capitalism: globalization is liquid and ever shifting. This is similar to anthropologist Arjun Appadurai who has used the metaphor of flows to describe globalization. Cultures, commodities, and people flow across the global landscape. The problem is to understand the way that flow is both facilitated and controlled (see Ritzer 2010). These processes, as Bauman points out, work in favor of the wealthy – those who can move in global circles. Further, insofar as globalization empties out the welfare protections of the nation-state, the poor are left behind in increasingly desperate conditions.

Venn's chapter on Foucault addresses globalization when he describes the development and spread of the neoliberal model of the economy. Globalization is also addressed in Campbell and DeVault's chapter on Dorothy Smith where they describe how Smith's institutional ethnography has been deployed to understand the effects of neoliberal globalization in human services or other public sector professions. Baudrillard addresses globalization in a number of ways. First, consistent with the Baudrillard described above, he treats it as a process through which every corner of the globe is absorbed into a virtual reality. Second, in seeming contrast to the first point, globalization pushes the system to brink, opening up the possibility of a return to reality. Indeed, Kellner notes that, for Baudrillard, 9/11 was the first "real" event to occur in decades. Said's discussion of Orientalism and imperialism helps to work out some of the identity politics that have been central to globalization. Agamben and Butler, as described earlier, develop their work on politics and ethics within the context of global human rights and warfare. Habermas and many of his European colleagues have been writing about processes of regionalization, an important component of global social formation. In particular and within the context of his more familiar writings on democracy, the public sphere and rational communication, Habermas advocates European integration. Here Europe is not conceived as a new kind of super-nation but rather as a post-national entity readied to participate in global dialogue and process.

Beck's contributions should also be noted. Indeed, as Wilkinson points out, for years now Beck has been hard at work to develop a cosmopolitan sociology. He argues that traditional sociology and social theory are organized around the model of the nation-state. This model no longer works and social theorists need to reconceive the social as a global phenomenon. In particular, by placing globalization front and center, cosmopolitanism encourages what Beck calls "responsible globalization" against the unchecked globalization fueled by capitalism. In a similar vein, Bryant and Jary suggest that Giddens advocates a third way politics as a means of addressing the threats of unhindered globalization.

Among those covered in this volume, Immanuel Wallerstein is the one whose name is most closely associated with globalization theory. Ironically, Wallerstein does not believe that there is anything new about globalization. It is an example of a capitalist world system that has been in development since the sixteenth century. Chase-Dunn and Inoue's chapter is helpful in emphasizing the basic elements of Wallerstein's theory, especially its prioritization of core-periphery economic relations. However, it is also useful because it provides a number of prominent critiques of Wallerstein's work. This not only helps to refine Wallerstein's position, but introduces a range of other works in globalization theory, both from within the world systems perspective and elsewhere. In this sense, Chase-Dunn and Inoue's chapter can also be read as a quick primer to recent debates on globalization theory.

What is most striking about the theorists described in this volume is their continual engagement with the surrounding social world. Even in the more abstract descriptions of the social world there is always a sense that the theorist is trying to "get it right" – to describe the world as it demands. This is what makes each theory so compelling: they offer visions of what the world looks like, and in some cases could look like. The idea that social theory could get it right, of course, flies in the face of postmodern arguments that were so popular 10 or 20 years ago. In that context the very claim that there could be authentic or truthful knowledge was contested. Social theory has certainly taken lessons from that moment, and now almost all practicing social theorists recognize the social, historical, and political conditions under which knowledge is produced. But that is only to say that social theory has to work harder to get the contexts right and to recognize that these contexts are always changing. No single theory, of course, gets it right, but a collection of 23 essays, such as we have put together in this volume should allow for a "triangulation" of perspectives that will at least clarify the important dynamics and draw attention to the most important issues. We have sought to capture some of these through the above discussion of six thematic areas. Of course, these should not be viewed as a final characterization of a settled field, but as an effort to hold the social world still for a moment so that it can be brought into view. The individual chapters will provide support for this discussion, but they also offer challenges and suggest new and different themes. Indeed, we hope that readers will engage these chapters not only to learn about the theorists under discussion but to help think through the issues of the current moment and the role that social theory can play in advancing our collective understanding of these.

References

Polanyi, Karl (2001[1944]) *The Great Transformation: The Political and Economic Origins of Our Time*. Boston: Beacon Press.

Rasch, W. (2000) *Niklas Luhmann's Modernity: The Paradoxes of Differentiation*. Stanford, CA: Stanford University Press.

Ritzer, G. (2010) *Globalization: A Basic Text*. Oxford: Wiley-Blackwell.

1

Norbert Elias

RICHARD KILMINSTER AND STEPHEN MENNELL

But my whole conviction is that our image of and orientation in our social world will become very much easier once we realize that human beings are not economic in one of their pockets, political in another and psychological in another, in other words that no real divisions correspond to the traditional divisions.

(Norbert Elias, 1970: 148)

INTRODUCTION

Norbert Elias (1897–1990) is most celebrated for his classic work *Über den Prozess der Zivilisation*, first published obscurely in German in 1939, but little known in the anglophone world until the publication of a translation (*The Civilizing Process*) in 1978–1982.[1] In this book, Elias traces long-term connections between changes in power balances in society at large and changes in the embodied habitus – or cultural personality makeup – of individual people, among the secular upper classes in Western Europe from the late Middle Ages to the nineteenth century. His work constitutes an endeavor – rare in the history of sociology – to bridge the gap between "micro" and "macro" sociology in a *theoretical–empirical*, rather than merely conceptual way. Although it was originally grounded in a study of European history, the theory of civilizing processes points to linked changes in power, behavior, and habitus which can be demonstrated to have been at work elsewhere and in many other periods. In later books and articles, Elias greatly extended the scope of the original theory.[2]

Elias's work constitutes a radical rejection of many of the common assumptions of sociology in the second half of the twentieth century. He conceived of the discipline

The Wiley-Blackwell Companion to Major Social Theorists, First Edition.
Edited by George Ritzer and Jeffrey Stepnisky.
© 2011 Blackwell Publishing Ltd. Published 2011 by Blackwell Publishing Ltd.

in the broadest terms, not as just "hodiecentric" (or "present-centered"), nor as the study solely of "modern" societies, but as including the study of long-term processes over the whole course of the development of human society. He was hostile to the hegemony of philosophy and what he sometimes called "philosophoidal" modes of thought in sociology, and he told his fellow sociologists to stop making obeisance to the philosophers. His own sociological work is grounded in a *sociological* theory of knowledge and the sciences, rather than in the traditional assumptions of mainstream philosophical epistemology and philosophy of science. This is one of the main ways in which he differs from contemporary "social theorists" who are generally more deferential to philosophy, such as Anthony Giddens, Jeffrey Alexander, and Jürgen Habermas. In general, his work has closer affinities with that of his friend Pierre Bourdieu. Elias referred to his way of doing sociology as "process sociology" – it is also commonly referred to as "figurational" sociology – and it involves the rejection of many of the static polarities and false dualities that pervade sociological thinking.

LIFE AND TIMES

Perhaps the most striking fact about Norbert Elias's career is how extremely late in life he gained recognition. He published fifteen books, but all of them, except the little-noticed first edition of *Über den Prozess der Zivilisation*, appeared after he reached normal retirement age – indeed most of them when he was in his 80s and 90s. Someone who in 1928 appeared on the same panel of discussants as Ferdinand Tönnies, Werner Sombart, and Alfred Weber (Elias, 2006a[1929]) – figures whose work we associate with the nineteenth and early twentieth centuries – thus finally came to seem a very contemporary presence to sociologists at the end of the twentieth century.

Elias was one of the generation of Jewish scholars who fled Germany in 1933 when Hitler came to power. Some of them were immediately able to establish themselves in universities in English-speaking countries; we can only guess how many more of them, having escaped with their lives, failed to re-establish themselves as academics. Elias was almost one of the latter group.

He was born on June 22, 1897 in Breslau, the only son of Hermann and Sophie Elias. His father was a businessman in the textile trade. Although, since the frontier changes at the end of the Second World War, Breslau is now the Polish city of Wrocław, the city was then fully German. At the distinguished *Johannes-Gymnasium* there, Elias received a first-class, all-round education in the humanities and sciences; he was immersed from an early age in the classics of German literature, Latin, Greek (a reading knowledge of both which served as a useful research skill into his old age), and French, as well as being given a good grounding in mathematics, physics, and chemistry. Asked in old age whether, as a child, he felt more a member of the Jewish community or of the wider German society, Elias (1994: 10) said that the very question reflected events that have unfolded since then. He knew as a child he was both a German and a Jew, but at the time the two identities did not conflict. There were isolated incidents of anti-Semitic remarks, but anti-Semites were people to look down upon. While this may indeed be true of his perceptions as a child, research since his death has revealed that his suggestion that he had never been involved in politics was not entirely true: this may have been the case in relation to normal German politics, but from his teenage years he was a leading light in the Zionist youth movement Blau-Weiß (Hackeschmidt, 2004). One of his earliest articles was on anti-Semitism in Germany (Elias, 2006b[1929]).

In 1915, reaching the age when he became eligible for conscription, Elias enlisted in a signals regiment of the German army and saw action on both the Eastern and Western Fronts in the First World War. He remembered the carnage, especially seeing a comrade killed nearby, and he probably suffered shellshock but could not remember the circumstances. How he came to leave the front and return to Breslau remained a blur, but he served out the war back in his hometown as an army medical orderly and recalled watching a famous surgeon amputating limbs. After the Armistice he enrolled at Breslau University, for some time managing to pursue courses in both medicine and philosophy. He completed the pre-clinical part of the medical training and always considered that his experience in the dissecting room had left a lasting mark on his understanding of how human beings work as social animals. For nothing he observed – especially dissecting the brain and the musculature of the face – corresponded to the distinction taken for granted in philosophy between the "external" world and the "internal" world of "the mind." But then, to his father's disappointment, he recognized that he could not pursue both disciplines and dropped medicine in favor of completing his doctoral degree in philosophy.

Elias's student years were a time of enormous political and social instability in Germany after its defeat in the war, the abdication of the Kaiser, and the establishment of the Weimar Republic. Armed left-wing and right-wing militias fought each other in the streets. One of Elias's school friends, a mild and scholarly youth but apparently suspected of left-wing leanings, was among those killed by the right-wing *Freikorps*. A little later, Germany experienced the great runaway hyperinflation of 1922–1923, which destabilized many aspects of society and in Elias's own case meant that he had for a time to take a job in industry (as export manager for a local manufacturer of iron goods) in order to help support his temporarily financially embarrassed parents.

So, even before the rise of Hitler, Elias had seen a great deal at first hand of war, civil unrest, violent death, and social instability. It is important to bear this in mind as an antidote to a once-common misapprehension about *The Civilizing Process*: Elias did not set out in that *magnum opus* to write a celebration of Western civilization in the popular sense, still less to depict it as the outcome of inevitable "progress." On the contrary, Elias was very conscious of how hard won was the outward show of "civilization," yet how brittle a veneer it remained. That is made abundantly clear at the very end of his life in *The Germans*, in which he describes himself thus: "Standing half-hidden in the background of the studies published here is an eyewitness who has lived for nearly ninety years through the events concerned as they unfolded" (1996: 1).

Elias wrote his doctoral thesis at Breslau under the neo-Kantian philosopher Richard Hönigswald, from whom he acknowledged that he learned a great deal, even though the relationship ended in their estrangement. The thesis was entitled

"Idea and Individual" (2006d[1922]), and was eventually accepted in January 1924, after a delay of more than a year occasioned by a dispute between student and supervisor. Their dispute concerned a fundamental issue: whether there are any grounds for postulating a notion of truth that is transcendental, *a priori* to and independent of human experience and human history. Although he could not then formulate his viewpoint with the precision and clarity that came later, Elias recalled that he had begun at this time to come to the conclusion

> that all that Kant regarded as timeless and given prior to all experience, whether it be the idea of causal connections or of time or of natural and moral laws, together with the words that went with them, had to be learned from other people in order to be present in the consciousness of the individual human being. (1994: 91)

Ever afterwards, Elias argued that the whole central tradition of modern Western epistemology, from Descartes through Kant to twentieth-century phenomenology, was misconceived. It was based on asking how a single, *adult*, human mind can know what it knows. Elias called this the model of *homo clausus*, the "closed person," and found it lurking in much of modern sociology (2000[1939]: 470–9; 1978: 119ff.; Mennell, 1998: 188–93; Kilminster, 1998: 57–92). He argued that we must instead think in terms of *homines aperti*, "open people," and in particular of "long lines of generations of people" building up the stock of human knowledge. The crucial point, however, which he developed in *The Civilizing Process* and other later works, was that the image of *homo clausus* corresponded to a *mode of self-experience* that was *not* a human universal but was a social product, particularly of European society from the Renaissance onwards.

The dispute with Hönigswald appears to have influenced Elias's decision, after he had received his doctorate and when his parents' finances had recovered, to resume his studies in Heidelberg not as a philosopher but as a sociologist. Max Weber had died four years earlier, but his circle, centered on his younger brother Alfred and his widow Marianne, was still a dominant presence in Heidelberg. Elias presented his first paper as a sociologist, a sociological interpretation of the differences between Gothic cathedrals in France and Germany, at a meeting of Marianne's salon, on the balcony of the Webers' house.[3] Elias had earlier interpolated a semester at Heidelberg (when he also attended a student Zionist conference) during his studies at Breslau, and there had met Karl Jaspers, who introduced him to the work of Max Weber and also encouraged him to write an essay on the notions of *Zivilisation* and *Kultur* in German thought, with special reference to Thomas Mann's essay "Civilization's Literary Man" (1983[1918]). Now Elias enrolled as a *Habilitation* student with Alfred Weber and set out to write a thesis on the transition from pre-scientific to scientific thinking common both to the arts and sciences in Renaissance Florence.[4] Alfred Weber was very interested in questions of "civilization" and "culture." He argued that culture could not be reduced to economic relationships or explained in terms of economic interests. It always had to be understood in terms of social behavior, but its pattern of development differed from that of economics, science, and technology; in these there was progress, but in art, religion, and culture in general there were no progressions or regressions – culture was rather to be seen as the self-realization of the soul of a people (Weber, 1998[1921]). Elias's later theory of civilizing processes may be understood as in part an attempt to demonstrate that, *pace* Weber, structured long-term processes can be discovered in "culture movements" too.

Around this time, Elias became friendly with a young *Privatdozent*, Karl Mannheim, four years his senior, who introduced him into the Weber circle. In 1929, when Mannheim became Professor of Sociology at the then relatively new University of Frankfurt, Elias went with him as his academic assistant. There were mixed motives for the move: friction had developed between Mannheim and Alfred Weber, making it uncomfortable for Elias as the friend of one and *Habilitation* candidate of the other; and Mannheim promised Elias earlier *Habilitation* than Weber was able to do.

At Frankfurt, Elias embarked on a new topic for his *Habilitationsschrift*: a sociological study of life at the court of France in the seventeenth and eighteenth centuries. All the stages of Elias's *Habilitation* – which would give him the rank of *Privatdozent* – were rushed through, except for the inaugural lecture, early in 1933, just as Hitler came to power and shortly before Elias fled into exile. But the thesis remained unpublished until 1969, when Elias revised and enlarged it considerably; it appeared as *Die höfische Gesellschaft* (in English, *The Court Society*, 2006g[1983]).

Mannheim headed the Department of Sociology and, as one of his assistants, Elias was particularly involved in supervising doctoral dissertations. The Department was housed in rented space in a building owned and occupied by the *Institut für Sozialforschung* – later celebrated as "the Frankfurt School" – of which Max Horkheimer was director. Relations between the two groups seem to have been polite but distant, although Elias seems to have been on good personal terms with Theodor Adorno despite disagreeing with the direction of his thought (Elias, 2009b[1977]). There is a degree of thematic similarity between the problems addressed in *The Civilizing Process* and by Horkheimer and Adorno in their *The Dialectic of Enlightenment* (1979[1944]) – the relations between control of nature, control of society, and self-control – but also a strikingly symptomatic difference. Horkheimer and Adorno write from within a very traditional philosophical discourse, whereas Elias sets out to turn questions traditionally posed in philosophical terms into empirically researchable socio-historical questions (Bogner, 1987).

Elias stayed long enough in Frankfurt after the Nazis came to power to be able to observe later that the process through which they came to power contained both highly rational *and* very violent elements – the two are not opposites. But, having lost his post and salary in the Nazi takeover of the university, later in 1933 he went into exile in Paris. He then spoke excellent French but little English. But he failed to secure academic employment. He invested what remained of the money his father had given him in a business making wooden toys. It was not a success; Elias lost all his money and was effectively destitute. At the urging of his old friend Alfred Glucksmann, who had already emigrated to Cambridge, Elias moved to England in 1935 where he secured a meager stipend from a Dutch Jewish charity.

Although in later years he claimed that *The Civilizing Process* was written in the Reading Room of the British Museum, it is possible that the first volume at least was begun in Paris, where he may have first encountered Lucien Febvre's essay on the origins of the concept of "civilization" (1930), which is cited in *The Civilizing Process*. In the early 1930s he also read Freud's *Civilization and its Discontents* ([1962]1930), which he acknowledged as the greatest single intellectual influence on *The Civilizing Process*. Freud's book serves as a reminder that in the 1930s a concern with "culture" and "civilization" was by no means associated with a naïve faith in "progress" and its benefits.

The two volumes of *The Civilizing Process* were completed in a white heat of inspiration in London, by 1938 at the latest. The problem was how they were to be published. Elias's parents visited him in London that year and he tried to persuade them to join him in exile. They refused. All their friends were in Breslau and, said his father, "They can't touch me – I've never broken a law in my life." His father died in Breslau in 1940 and his mother in Auschwitz in 1941. But before that, his father had arranged for *Über den Prozess der Zivilisation* to be printed in Breslau. Before it could actually be published, however, the printer too fled the country. Hermann Elias then surreptitiously arranged for the unbound sheets to be exported to Switzerland where they were bound and eventually published by Haus zum Falken in 1939. That year, as Bryan Wilson was later wryly to observe, was not the most propitious moment for the publication of a two-volume work, in German, by a Jew, on, of all things, civilization. Few people read it. Among those who did, appreciatively, were Thomas Mann and two prominent reviewers in The Netherlands (Goudsblom, 1977b: 61).

On the publication of *The Civilizing Process*, Elias was awarded a Senior Research Assistantship at the London School of Economics, which was evacuated to Cambridge during the war. He was briefly interned with other "enemy aliens" during 1940, but returned to Cambridge and worked for British Intelligence at the end of the war. Afterwards, he lived in near poverty, scraping a living by teaching extramural lectures. In the early 1950s, with his old friend S. H. Foulkes, he was one of the founders of the Group Analytic school of psychotherapy (Elias, 2009c[1969]; Pines, 1997; Mennell, 1997). These were years when Elias published almost nothing, however, the trauma of his mother dying in Auschwitz may be at least part of the explanation for that. Only in 1954, when he was already 57, did he get his first secure academic post, at the respectable but obscure University College Leicester, soon to be the University of Leicester. There, with Ilya Neustadt, he helped to build up one of the most distinguished departments of sociology in Britain; both Anthony Giddens and John Goldthorpe – among many other notable figures – gained their first teaching posts in the Leicester department. On his retirement in 1962 he served for two years as Professor of Sociology at the University of Ghana, and on his return continued to teach part-time at Leicester. These were the years when he published *The Established and the Outsiders* with John Scotson (2008[1965]) and began to develop the whole area of the sociology of sport with Eric Dunning (Elias and Dunning, 2008[1986]). In 1969, however, *Über den Prozess der Zivilisation* was republished and consequently he rapidly became an intellectual celebrity in Germany and The Netherlands (see Elias, 1970). In the 1970s, he was in demand in both countries as a Visiting Professor and gradually abandoned residence in Britain for residence in Amsterdam and – for a time – in Bielefeld. The 1970s and 1980s were years of unparalleled productivity in which books and articles that had been gestating for decades finally flowed from his pen. This productivity was considerably aided by the devoted editorial assistance of Michael Schröter. Elias died, still writing at the age of 93, on August 1, 1990.

INTELLECTUAL CONTEXT AND INFLUENCES

One of the problems which anyone introducing Elias immediately faces is that of situating his highly original work within the theoretical schools, paradigms, and sociological language familiar to mainstream sociologists. As Johan Goudsblom has pointed out (1977a: 60, 77ff.), the difficulty of "placing" him in the European sociological tradition has always been a problem for commentators. It is difficult to find a place for Elias's "figurational" sociology within the paradigms of recent sociology such as phenomenology, action theory, functionalism, structuration theory, Marxism, Weberianism, post-structuralism, critical realism, rational choice theory, or neo-positivism. Elias seems to fall between all stools. Echoes of, and parallels and similarities with, the work of others abound in Elias's sociology, as do concepts and problems common to other traditions of social science, but in a strange way Elias's contribution remains stubbornly unique. How? To answer that question we need to take a brief detour.

Elias did not assign much importance to delineating carefully his intellectual debts and situating himself in relation to other writers in the detail that we have come to expect and find in the writings of, say, Parsons, Habermas, or Bourdieu. All this interpretative work of debt assignment and influences in relation to Elias has had to be done by others much later, following up clues in his writings and interviews and drawing on broader knowledge of the state of sociology in Germany in the first quarter of the twentieth century. For many years Elias would avow only one significant intellectual debt. In a footnote to the first volume of *The Civilizing Process* (2000[1939]: 526–7), he acknowledged how much the study owes to the discoveries of Freud which, he says, is obvious to the reader anyway, so did not need to be pointed out in all instances. Even then, he explicitly stressed the "not inconsiderable *differences* between the whole approach of Freud and that adopted in this study" (our emphasis). Rather than "digressing into disputes at every turn," he continues, it seemed more important "to build a particular intellectual perspective as clearly as possible."

Later, Elias further complicated the issue by challenging the conventional assumption that an "influence" always had to come from a book: "I am extremely conscious of the fact that others have influenced me, that I have learned from others – though not only from books, but also from the events of my age" (quoted by Goudsblom, 1977b: 78). He also claimed that, at the time he was writing *The Civilizing Process*, his knowledge of those writers whom we think of today as our sociological ancestors was "extremely deficient" (quoted by Goudsblom, 1977b: 78). But this admission has to be taken with a pinch of salt. Even if he did not know these writers in quite the depth that we take for granted today, he nevertheless still participated in the particularly rich sociological culture of Weimar Germany, in which many of these ancestors had already been discussed, absorbed and processed, and areas of enquiry established (see Mannheim, 1953[1934]: 209–28; Aron, 1957; Schad, 1972; Kettler, Loader, and Meja, 2008).

The problem-agenda of the generation of Weimar sociologists, which included Elias, was a remarkably fertile one set by gifted people such as Max Weber, Georg Simmel, Veblen, Freud, Alfred Weber, Sombart, prominent Marxists such as Lukács, and the more sociologically sympathetic phenomenologists and existentialists such as Hannah Arendt and Karl Jaspers, in the aftermath of one European war and in the build-up to another. The origins of Elias's sociology lie in the complex political conflicts and alignments of the Weimar period, although the applicability of his insights goes well beyond that. In the decades after the Second World War, the central conflicts in sociology between American functionalist systems theory and varieties of Marxism (in effect reflecting the Cold War) for long obscured the rich inheritance from Weimar Germany. If Elias's work can be placed anywhere it is as a development out of the German *Wissenssoziologie*, to which it bears a family resemblance (Kilminster, 2007: 40–71).

Having said all that, the question remains: in what does the uniqueness of Elias's sociology consist? Following Goudsblom again (1977b: 79), our view is that the key to answering this question lies in grasping how Elias managed to integrate *through empirical research* many seemingly incompatible perspectives into a "workable synthesis," a single testable model of human interdependence. This enabled him to solve in a preliminary way problems shrewdly posed, but left in the air, by (among others) the gifted writers just mentioned. These problems had already been made available, so to speak, in the sociological culture in which Elias participated. To name just a few significant sociological themes he found, ready-to-hand: discussions of and research into the conspicuous consumption of elites; "two-front" strata; the monopoly of the means of violence; rationalization; social equalization; competition; social differentiation and integration; the internalization of what is external; and the development of civilized self-restraint. All these, and many more, Elias integrated into his sociological synthesis, as concepts or problems requiring solution. In doing so, he did not undertake a great deal of conceptual work to demonstrate how his concepts differed from those developed by other writers in different traditions. For him, the integrity of the synthesis and its empirical extension were everything.

By and large, Elias seems to have assumed that people reading *The Civilizing Process* would see the explanatory power of the "workable synthesis" and would seek to test it further in their own research. Working directly from the sociological model to empirical areas and back again in this high-minded, but unorthodox, way was not without its dangers. It exposed Elias to the risk that readers would find in his books apparent similarities with the ideas of other sociologists and philosophers but, failing to appreciate the *synthetic* character of his work, accuse him of unacknowledged derivation or lack of originality. Some of the controversy surrounding the belated recognition of his work has arisen from this feature of his approach and his failure not always to make this aspect of his way of working clear to his readers.

There is a parallel here with the holistic approach to society found in the work of Elias's colleague and friend of many years, Karl Mannheim, which may illuminate this issue. Perhaps Elias's being out of step with the expectations of the sociological profession regarding the elaborate acknowledgement and documentation of sources of inspiration is also *organically* related to the character of his integrating research strategy. As Kettler and Meja (1995) point out, in his restless attempts to uncover the *Zeitgeist*, Mannheim was open to ideas and inspiration from many sources in his pursuit of a political synthesis. Although Elias's work was not moving in that particular political direction, he did share with Mannheim the idea that the significance of a social event, social grouping or cultural item lies in its relationship with other aspects of the developing social structure as a whole. Subject to the further caveat that Elias would have no truck whatsoever with any talk in a sociological context of spirit (*Geist*), the succinct description given by Kettler and Meja of Mannheim's way of working with concepts and research materials resonates with that of Elias:

> [Mannheim] would subject key concepts to a "change of function." It was unnecessary to criticize others; it was enough to correct and balance what they said by drawing on something said by someone else. All participants were seen as sharing the same condition or expressing the same spirit. (1995: 318)

READING ELIAS

Certain unusual features of Elias's writings set his work apart from the dominant forms of professional sociology to which we are accustomed. It is worth briefly outlining them as an aid to understanding Elias.

1 For most of his long career, for reasons often beyond his control, Elias was on the periphery of the sociology establishment and thus distanced from it. He therefore felt few of the pressures of the institutionalized world of the academic social sciences. One consequence of this is that his works have an unfamiliar structure and character. The reader will not find the customary beginning with a review of the literature or contemporary debates about the problem or topic addressed. Elias did not work that way. Rather, he always went for the problem or object of inquiry (for example, symbols, scientific establishments, Mozart, art, utopias, time, violence, sport, ageing and dying, work, or gender – to name just a few of the subjects he investigated in his later years) which he would explore in his own way, in his own language of figurational or process sociology.

2 In the later writings in particular, Elias typically lists very few references; indeed, in some books and articles there may only be one, perhaps to an obscure book published many years ago. If one complained to Elias that he had failed to address the contemporary literature, or suggested that he was out of date, he would reply that you had a fetish for the new, that just because a book is old it does not mean that it may not still be the best treatment of a problem. And conversely, new books did not necessarily represent an advance simply because they were new. It was the intrinsic cognitive worth of the book that counted, not whether it was currently *à la mode* (see Elias, 2007a[1987]: 121–2n). He worked within a very long scientific time scale detached from current orthodoxies.

3 It is worth mentioning the style of Elias's writings. Wolf Lepenies (1978: 63) aptly described their qualities: "a jargon-free concern with clarity, a careful training in sociological observation, and a thoroughgoing combination of theoretical discussions with often surprising references to details." Elias was very alert to the subtleties and associations of the language and concepts we employ

in sociology. He writes about social processes in a controlled language carefully cleansed of all traces of reification and static metaphysics and highly sensitive to evaluative nuances. Elias will talk of "party establishments" when others refer to "the political"; or economic specialists rather than "the economic sphere"; or social specialists for violence control instead of "repressive state apparatuses"; or means of orientation rather than "ideological practice."

4   The more one reads Elias the more aware one becomes of how he convinces readers not so much by conventional "logical" arguments for this or that position, as by expressing issues (particularly in his articles) in such a way as to provoke people into reflecting upon the categories or assumptions that they routinely employ in dealing with them. As well as containing a theoretical model and empirical materials, *The Civilizing Process* embodies a mode of experiential persuasion that cannot be described as entirely rational. As we read through the picturesque extracts from contemporary documents about farting, bedroom behavior, spitting, torture, the burning of cats, or whatever, we gain insight *through this experience itself* into our own feelings of shame, repugnance, and delicacy derived from the standards of our own society, representing a later stage of development. Our reactions themselves exemplify the rising of the thresholds of shame, embarrassment, and repugnance which Elias is demonstrating. This effect partly explains why the book is so memorable.

THE SOCIOLOGICAL IMPERATIVE

For an adequate understanding of Elias, it is essential to appreciate how his sociology developed out of the desire to transcribe philosophical discussions of knowledge, society, culture, and the human condition into a form amenable to empirical sociological investigation. This leaves the status of philosophy ambiguous and disputable. These questions included those traditionally grouped under epistemology, ontology, and ethics (that is, "evaluative" or "normative" questions) which reappear in Elias's works transformed into a sociological idiom. We cannot stress too much the robustly sociological character of Elias's world view. The failure of various commentators to understand this dimension of Elias's work has led to a number of misunderstandings. Readers of Elias need to be prepared for his controversial and uncompromising views about philosophy and his rather sweeping denunciations of its practitioners, which have not won him many friends. He considered that his work presupposed the supersession of philosophy and consistently questioned the authority of philosophers (see Elias, 2009a; Kilminster, 1998: 3–26; Kilminster, 2007).

On the subject of *epistemology*, from as early in his career as when he was a doctoral student under Hönigswald, there were indications in Elias's work that he was moving in the direction of developing a sociological epistemology to replace the traditional philosophical one (Kilminster and Wouters, 1995). This transformed epistemology would relate ways of knowing to the patterned ways in which human beings live together and remodel the traditional issue of validity (*Geltung*). This realization gathers momentum in his work to a point where he makes a complete break with philosophy, decisively turning his back on the tradition. The failure to grasp this feature of his thinking has sometimes led some commentators to try to pull Elias back into the philosophy from which his life's work was a sustained attempt at emancipation (see for instance Maso, 1995); or to criticize him from philosophical positions that he regarded himself as already having moved beyond (Sathaye, 1973).

The neo-Kantian philosophy in which Elias was initially schooled did, however, alert him to key areas of enquiry, including the problems of the historical validity of knowledge, the origins and status of universal categories of thought, and the prevalence of the model of the individual knowing subject in epistemology. The classical German philosophical tradition generally, and neo-Kantianism in particular, thus constituted a point of departure for Elias's transfer of his intellectual energies into a dynamic and historical sociology, which he believed could provide a more inclusive and adequate framework for the solution of those problems. Once Elias had begun to make this break, we would argue, then his sociological enquiries became *structurally different* from philosophy, despite odd similarities of terminology. For example, philosophical speculations about the "objects" of the different sciences and the so-called "modes of being" postulated by fundamental ontologists in the line of Heidegger and philosophical realists such as Hartmann and Whitehead, provided the stimulus for Elias to develop a *testable* theory of the levels of integration (physical, chemical, biological, social, etc.) of the social and natural worlds investigated by the different sciences (Elias, 2007a[1987], 2009a). Similarly, discussions of values, value-relevance, and value-freedom in Rickert and Weber are recast by Elias as the theory of involvement and detachment in which the conceptions of "autonomous" and "heteronomous" evaluations play a central role (Elias, 2007a[1987] – more on this below). Generally, therefore, one finds in Elias a principled avoidance of philosophical concepts and the consistent substitution of sociological alternatives which are more amenable to empirical reference. More examples include: "truth" is recast as "reality congruence"; "part/whole" becomes "unit and part-unit"; and "abstractions" are transformed into "symbols at a high level of synthesis."

On the subject of "*evaluative*" or "*normative*" matters, Elias commented very early in his career that "ethical questions are always, and quite wrongly, separated from other scientific questions" (Elias, 2006c[1921]: 15). Furthermore, Elias's total commitment to sociology as a "mission," which comes out clearly in his autobiographical *Reflections on a Life* (1994), tells us something. He saw sociology as potentially able to assist human beings to orientate themselves in the figurations they form together and to help them to control the unintended social entanglements which threaten to escalate into destructive sequences such as wars and mass killings. The figurational view of society, and Elias's theories of civilizing processes and established–outsiders relations, are implicitly underpinned by the perceived imperative of generating knowledge to help groups in achieving greater "mutual identification" and thus to live in controlled antagonism with each other (De Swaan, 1995, 2001; Mennell, 1994). Writers who have failed to grasp this aspect of his work have tended, in their criticisms of Elias, to confuse the technical and normative dimensions of some of Elias's concepts, for example, "civilization" and "civilizing processes" (e.g. Leach, 1986; Bauman, 1988), when Elias was aware of the normative issue right from the start and had already, to his own satisfaction anyway, transformed the question and the relevant concepts into a sociological form amenable to empirical investigation (Fletcher, 1997: chapter 8).

The intensive commitment of Elias and his followers to empirical research can all too easily lead to a misunderstanding of the "moral" dimension of his work, and to its being wrongly assimilated into the mode of "value-free" sociological empiricism. The matter can be clarified through examining the links between Elias's thinking and Karl Mannheim's sociological program from the 1920s and 1930s, in the development of which Elias participated (Kettler, Loader, and Meja, 2008). He shared the spirit, if not the last letter, of this intellectual venture. In addition to advocating a "relational" or "perspectival" view of society (echoes of which we find in Elias – see Kilminster, 1998: 47–51), Mannheim's programme was at the same time intended to deal with questions normally gathered together under the umbrella of "ethics," "politics," or "evaluative" and "existential" questions. These pertained to the ways in which humankind might achieve greater happiness and fulfillment individually and socially within what Mannheim called "the forms of living together of man" (Mannheim, 1957[1935]: 43).

In Mannheim's scheme of things, when considering evaluative matters the investigator makes a theoretical move sideways, the intention of this method being to redefine the scope and limits of assertions by politicians, philosophers, and others about the possibilities of human freedom, democracy, and happiness, by showing them to be coming inevitably from differing ideological perspectives. It was only through these one-sided perspectives that access was even possible to knowledge of society, all knowledge being existentially bounded and perspectival. Objectivity is sought by "the translation of perspectives into the terms of another" (1936[1929]: 270–1). Having made these moves, the investigator is then potentially able to evaluate the feasibility or validity of "ethical" or "political" issues in the form in which they were originally raised by the particular politician, party, or ideology. Mannheim refers to this theoretical journey as attaining a new form of "'objectivity' … in a roundabout fashion" (1936[1929]: 270). These analytic steps then reach a point where the process "becomes a critique" (1936[1929]: 256).

Elias's version of the journey specifies that it is only by a "detour via detachment" that sociologists can hope to gain more adequate knowledge of the structure of social events in which they themselves are also emotionally caught up (Elias, 2007a[1987]: 169–70). He integrated a psychoanalytic dimension into the basic perspectivistic insight. He shared the Mannheimian ambition to transcribe so-called ethical and evaluative matters into sociologically manageable terms and thus to put the questions raised philosophically or ideologically on to another level. This position constitutes the pith and marrow of Elias's whole sociological programme and is observable sometimes even in the interstices of his more empirical work. Consider, for example, the following statement in *The Court Society* on the historians' fear that sociological research threatens to extinguish human freedom and individuality:

If one is prepared to approach such problems through two-pronged investigations on the theoretical and empirical planes in closest touch with one another, rather than on the basis of preconceived dogmatic positions, the question one is aiming at with words such as "freedom" and "determinacy" *poses itself in a different way*. (Elias, 2006g[1969]: 33, our emphasis)

This "evaluative" intention also pervades the empirical–theoretical presentations that are laid out in *The Civilizing Process*. Elias opens the first volume with a sociogenetic inquiry, typical of the sociology of knowledge, into the origins of the concepts of *Kultur* and *Zivilisation*, which, as we have seen, were both redolent of the covert ideological dimension of Alfred Weber's sociology and other highly charged ideological conflicts at the time over whether civilized behavior was the acme or the nadir of the human social achievement. Amongst other things, the tacit task of *The Civilizing Process* is to reframe the range, applicability, and realistic usefulness of these two key terms via the sociological enquiry into their genesis in the European civilizing process in general. Significantly, Elias returns to the concepts in the final part of his book (2000[1939]: 363–447) at a new level and *re-poses* the questions about human satisfaction, fulfillment, and constraint embodied more ideologically in the antithesis which partly provided the starting point.

THE PRINCIPAL WORKS

Elias wrote substantial parts of his first book, which we now know as *The Court Society*, in the Frankfurt years, but it was not published in any form until 1969. It is a sociological study of aristocratic society in France in the century and a half before the Revolution. The reign of Louis XIV (1643–1715) was particularly crucial in completing the process of the "taming of warriors" and transforming some of them into courtiers devoid of independent military power and increasingly the creatures of the king.[5] The courtly nobility were a "two-front stratum" (Georg Simmel's phrase), squeezed between the king and the rich bourgeoisie. Elias shows how much of what seems to us the bizarre detail of court ritual can be understood as mechanisms through which the king could manipulate courtiers through tiny expressions of favor and disfavor. The "ethos of rank" became all-pervasive. He shows, for example, how rank determined the courtiers' expenditure, quite regardless of their *income*, and as a result many became impoverished. In an important corrective to the common assumption that bourgeois economic rationality (Max Weber's *Zweckrationalität* or the Frankfurt School's "instrumental rationality") is the characteristic and even unique form of Western rationality, Elias contends that although the extravagance of courtiers appears "irrational" from a bourgeois point of view, it was a manifestation of a "court-rationality" which itself involved a high degree of restraint of short-term affects for longer-term objectives; it was a form of rationality in which prestige and rank, rather than capital and income, were made calculable as instruments of power.

Within the hotbed of faction and intrigue that was the court, courtiers had to develop an extraordinary sensitivity to the status and importance that could be attributed to a person on the basis of fine nuances of bearing, speech, manners, and appearance. Observing, dealing with, relating to, or avoiding people became an art in itself. And self-observation was inextricably bound up in that: greater *self-control* was required. To later sociologists reared on Erving Goffman,[6] that may seem a universal characteristic of human society; in some degree it is – there is no zero-point, as Elias was fond of remarking in this and many other contexts – but Elias argued that this sensitivity was developed in court society to an exceptional *extent* through the competitive struggle for prestige with vital interests at stake.

The courtly ethos of self-control, Elias argues, is reflected in the literature, drama, and even in the French formal gardens of the period. But, above all, it is seen in the philosophy of Descartes and his successors. The image of the person as *homo clausus* so evident in "*cogito, ergo sum*" is not just a philosophical idea but also the characteristic mode of upper class self-experience that had been developing in Europe since the Renaissance and the Reformation (Elias, 2010[1991]). Elias saw his demonstration of the part played by court society in the development of this mode of self-experience as a supplement to, and not necessarily contradictory in all respects to, Max Weber's parallel account in *The Protestant Ethic and the Spirit of Capitalism*. What was needed was a more comprehensive theory of the development of the modern self-image and mode of self-experience, and that is what Elias set out to provide in *The Civilizing Process* and his later writings.

In this complex *magnum opus*, Elias speaks of civilizing processes on two levels.[7] The first is the individual level, and is rather uncontroversial. Infants and children have to acquire through learning the adult standards of behavior and feeling prevalent in their society; to speak of this as a civilizing process is more or less to use another term for "socialization," and ever since Freud and Piaget there has been little dispute that this process possesses structure and sequence. But the second level is more controversial. Where did these standards come from? They have not always existed, nor always been the same. Elias argues it is possible to identify long-term civilizing processes in the shaping of standards of behavior and feeling over many generations within particular cultures. Again, the idea that these standards *change* is not controversial; the controversy is about whether the changes take the form of structured processes of change with a discernible – though unplanned and by no means irreversible – *direction* over time.

The Civilizing Process often strikes new readers as being about quite different subjects: on the one hand the history of manners in Western Europe from the late Middle Ages to the Victorian period, and on the other hand a detailed model of the process of state formation, again in Europe, since the Dark Ages. The basic idea, and the basic link between the two halves, is that there is a connection between the long-term structural development of societies and long-term changes in people's social character or habitus. (*Habitus* was a word in common use among German academics in the early twentieth century; Marcel Mauss also used *habitus* in French. Elias used the word when writing in German, but in the earlier English editions of his work it was translated as "personality makeup." The word was later popularized by Pierre Bourdieu.) In other words, as the structure of societies becomes more complex, manners, culture and personality also change in a particular and discernible direction, first among élite groups, then gradually more widely. This is worked out with great subtlety for Western Europe since the Middle Ages.

Elias began the first volume of *The Civilizing Process* by reviewing the accretion of evaluative meanings around the notion of "civilization." The word was derived from *civilité* – the term used by courtiers to denote their own ways of behaving – but by the nineteenth century it had come to have a single general function, as a badge of the West's sense of superiority:

> this concept expresses the self-consciousness of the West. ... It sums up everything in which Western society of the last two or three centuries believes itself superior to earlier societies or "more primitive" contemporary ones. By this term, Western society seeks to describe what constitutes its special character and what it is proud of: the level of *its* technology, the nature of *its* manners, the development of *its* scientific knowledge or view of the world, and much more. (2000[1939]: 3)

By the nineteenth century, the ways people in the West used the *word* civilization showed that they had largely forgotten the *process* of civilization. Confident of the superiority of their own, now seemingly inherent and eternal, standards they wished only to "civilize" the natives of the lands they were now colonizing (or the lower orders of their own societies). They lost awareness that their own ancestors had undergone a learning process, a civilizing process, through which they *acquired* the characteristics now perceived as marks of an imagined *innate* superiority.

In order to retrieve an awareness of this forgotten process from the European past, Elias studied the development of social standards governing eating, nose blowing, spitting, urinating and defecating, undressing, and sleeping. The reason for investigating these most "natural" or "animalic" facets of behavior was that these are things that by their biological constitution all human beings have to do in any society, culture, or age. Moreover, human infants are born in more or less the same emotional and physical condition at all times and places, and in every society they have to learn how to handle these matters. Therefore if the way they are handled changes over time, it stands out rather clearly.

Elias's principal sources were French, German, Italian, and English manners books from the Middle Ages to the mid-nineteenth century. In earlier centuries these basic matters of behavior – discussion of which would later cause embarrassment, or at least the humorous sensation of a taboo having been broken – were spoken of openly and frankly, without shame. Then gradually, from the Renaissance, a long-term trend towards greater demands on emotional management in adults becomes apparent: the child has further to travel, so to speak, to attain the adult standard. Codes of behavior become more differentiated, and thresholds of shame and embarrassment advance. Many things become hidden behind the scenes of social life – and also repressed behind the scenes of conscious mental life.

Elias produces evidence to show that this long-term civilizing process cannot be explained away simply by reference to rising levels of material prosperity or to advances in scientific knowledge of health and hygiene, although these were still involved. Moreover, a similar civilizing curve can also be discerned in the development of social standards of self-restraint over resort to the use of *violence*. The explanation is found in the dynamic of social interdependencies. Over a period of many centuries in Europe, chains of social interdependence have grown longer and people have become more subject to more multipolar social constraints. In other words, "more people are forced more often to pay more attention to more other people" (Goudsblom, 1989: 722). In the course of this process, the *balance* of the controls by which individual people steer their conduct shifts from the preponderance of external constraints (*Fremdzwänge* – constraints *by other people*) towards more internalized self-constraints (*Selbstzwänge*). Here the influence of Freud on Elias is evident. But it is not just a matter of *more* self-restraint, rather the balance tilts towards self-constraint being more *automatic*, more *even* (volatility of mood becomes less than in medieval times), and more *all-embracing* (standards apply more equally in public and private, and to all other people irrespective of rank, and so on). Elias pointed to the extreme self-restraint of which Native American warriors or medieval ascetics were capable. In complex modern societies, self-constraint is not *greater*, but it operates in a different fashion.

In the second volume, Elias puts forward a detailed theory of state formation in Europe, implicitly beginning from Max Weber's definition of the state as an organization which successfully upholds a claim to binding rule-making over a territory, by virtue of commanding a monopoly of the legitimate use of violence. Elias, however, is more interested in the process through which a monopoly of the means of violence – and taxation – is established and extended. That innocent addition – *taxation* – is significant. Elias insisted that Marxist attempts to accord causal primacy to economic "factors" or "forces" or "modes of production" were misleading. The means of production, the means of protection (including attack), and the means of orientation could not be reduced to each other; moreover, in the period of which Elias was talking, the means of violence and the means of production were simply inextricable.

Elias does not regard state formation as the sole cause; indeed, he rejects the use of that concept entirely in this context. State formation, he argues, is only one process interweaving with others to enmesh individuals in increasingly complex webs of interdependence. It interweaves with the division of labor, the expansion of trade, the growth of towns, the use of money and administrative apparatuses, and increasing population in a spiral process. The internal pacification of territory facilitates trade, which facilitates the growth of towns and division of labor and generates taxes which support larger administrative and military organizations, which in turn facilitate the internal pacification of larger territories, and so on – a cumulative process experienced as a compelling force by people caught up in it. Furthermore, this has long-term effects on people's habitus:

> if in a particular region, the power of central authority grows, if over a larger or smaller area people are *forced* to live at peace with one another, the moulding of the affects and the standards of the demands made upon emotional management are very gradually changed as well. (2000[1939]: 169, our emphasis; translation modified to reflect Elias's later terminology)

According to Elias, the gradually higher standards of habitual self-restraint engendered in people contribute in turn to the upward spiral – being necessary for example, to the formation of gradually more effective and calculable administration.

The Civilizing Process is based entirely on European evidence. It is not so much that it is Euro*centric* as that it is *about* Europe. Elias recognized that one of the most important gaps in his work, and one of the most interesting lines for further research, was the study of equivalent – but no doubt different in detail – civilizing processes in other historic cultures. Examples of investigations of civilizing processes outside the context of Western Europe include Ikegami (1995), Mennell (2007), Stauth (1997), Volkov (2000), and Young (1997).

LATER EXTENSIONS

The theory of civilizing processes has provoked much scholarly debate.[8] Meanwhile, Elias extended his original thesis in many directions. What follows is a brief account of a selection of what we judge to be the most important, major extensions and developments of his ideas which he himself undertook, in chronological order. (A number of other works, monographs, and lectures have been omitted.)

1. In *The Established and the Outsiders: A Sociological Inquiry into Community Problems*, written with John L. Scotson (2008[1965]), Elias develops, through a detailed piece of empirical research of three neighborhoods in a Leicestershire village, the theory of established–outsider relations, which has a wider application. This theory (which is foreshadowed in *The Civilizing Process* and in early writings such as Elias's essay on the Huguenots (2006f[1935]) is designed to provide simpler but more inclusive concepts than class, status, and party, which have dominated Marxian and Weberian approaches to inequality.[9] For Elias, class relations are only one form of social oppression and we should not generalize from their features to all types. The theory of established and outsider relations is conceived as part of the theory of civilizing processes, being particularly useful for understanding the complex dynamics of *varieties* of group oppression and group ascent, and the effects of such social ascendance on social and behavioral codes. In Eliasian language, it enables us to grasp with one concept the changing patterns in the uneven balances of power between many different kinds of interdependent groups in a figuration. These power balances include – in addition to those between economic classes – the relations between men and women, homosexuals and heterosexuals, blacks and whites, parents and children (or, more generally, between older and younger generations), governors and governed, and colonizers and colonized.

According to the theory (which has been applied in a considerable range of empirical research: see works cited in Kranendonk, 1990: 158–69 and Mennell, 1998: 125–39) when the power gradient between groups is very steep, outsiders are often stigmatized as unworthy, filthy, shifty, or perhaps as childlike, as in the case of whites stigmatizing blacks. At this stage, images of outsiders are highly fantasy-laden and the attitudes of established towards outsiders are extremely rigid. The differences between the behavior and attitudes of established and outsiders are frequently (wrongly) explained biologically. The "group charisma" of the established is such that power superiority is equated with human merit or the grace of nature or God. In cases of great power imbalance, outsiders take into their conscience the view of themselves that the established have formed, and so come to accept that they are unworthy, even inhuman. They come to internalize their own "group disgrace." There is an echo of Anna Freud's (1968[1936]: ch. 9) "identification with the aggressor" here, the difference being that rather than regarding the phenomenon *individualistically* as a constant in relations between parent and child, or leader and follower,

Elias refashions it as symptomatic of a particular *stage* of the shifting power relations between specific interdependent *groups*.

Where the balance of power is becoming more equal, tilting more in favor of the outsiders, then one finds symptoms of rebellion and emancipation as in the case of the relations between older and younger generations, men and women, homosexuals and heterosexuals, and blacks and whites in recent times. At this stage of the process, images of outsiders become less fantasy-laden and the attitudes of the established groups towards the outsiders more flexible and accommodating. Outsiders begin to develop their own "we-image" and to deny the one imposed by the established. In the early stages of an emancipatory phase there are often calls for separatism (both blacks and women have been through this) and self-help groups form to build new self-images for the rising group (the slogan "black is beautiful" epitomizes this part of the process). As the balance of power becomes *relatively more* equal (not entirely equal) compared with the earlier phase, and outsiders begin to merge with the established to form a new establishment, then more realistic mutual perceptions become possible between groups as the tensions between them diminish.

2. The three books *Involvement and Detachment* (2007a[1987]), *An Essay on Time* (2007c[1992]), and *The Symbol Theory* (2011[1991]) represent major extensions of the theory of civilizing processes to the history of humanity as a whole in the context of biological evolution. These three later works, together with the essays now collected in volume 14 of the Collected Works (2009a), constitute Elias's theory of knowledge and the sciences to which he himself, in various interviews, assigned considerable importance. In all of them Elias's very long-term orientation is much to the fore. He also argues in these works, amongst many other things, that an adequate understanding of social development needs to be integrated into the overall evolutionary process. As he puts it in *The Symbol Theory:*

> The natural constitution of human beings prepares them for learning from others, for living with others, for being cared for by others and for caring for others. It is difficult to imagine how social scientists can gain a clear understanding of the fact that nature prepares human beings for life in society without including aspects of the evolutionary process and of the social development of humankind in their field of vision. (Elias, 2011[1991]: 145)

In the perspective of the development of human knowledge over the whole history of the species, the "double-bind" relationship between the dangers people faced and the fears they experienced posed formidable initial obstacles to an escape from emotionally charged, fantasy-laden, and "involved" knowledge. Escape can never be complete, but control over social dangers and fears has lagged behind control over natural forces and the fears arising from the human experience of them; and by extension the social sciences remain *relatively* less autonomous and "detached" than the natural sciences. Elias argues that the predominant form of explanation gradually changes across the spectrum from the physical through the biological to the social sciences, with law-like theories becoming less important. The aim of the social scientist should be to construct "process theories" in *five* dimensions – the three dimensions of space, plus time and *experience*. For exemplars of the pursuit of process theories resting on an image of humankind as "open people," one need look no further than Elias's own sociological research.

In *An Essay on Time* (2007c[1992]) Elias argues that "time" refers not to any universal substance or capacity of the human mind, as philosophers have variously claimed, but to the human social *activity* of *timing*. This activity rests on the human biologically endowed capacity for memory and synthesis, for making connections through the use of symbols. More than any other creatures, humans are orientated by the experience not of each individual but also of long chains of generations, gradually improving and extending the human means of orientation. It is simply a means of using symbols to connect two or more sequences of changes – physical, biological, or social – using one as a frame of reference for the others. Hence, "time" is not just "subjective," but has evolved through experience in a long intergenerational learning process.

The social need for timing was much less acute and pervasive in earlier societies than in the more highly organized modern industrial states. Increased differentiation and integration of social functions mean that in modern societies many long chains of interdependence intersect within the individual, requiring constant awareness of time in the co-ordination of numerous activities. People have to adjust themselves to each other as part of an increasingly intricate mesh of contacts and social necessities, which requires a socially standardized, high-level symbol of timing to enable this to be done with accuracy and predictability. A particularly complex system of self-regulation and an acute individual sensibility with regard to time has developed. The individualization of social time-control thus bears all the hallmarks of a civilizing process.

The Symbol Theory (2011[1991]), which turned out to be the last extended work to be completed for publication by Elias prior to his death in August 1990, is an inquiry into the survival value in the evolutionary process of reality-congruent knowledge made possible by the human capacity for symbol making. Part of the task of this book is to look at the human social and biological condition in a detached, non-reductionist, and non-religious way, so as to enable us to develop a more realistic model of humankind as being caught up in the evolutionary process on another level. For Elias, evolutionary theory is not to be identified solely with Darwin's version, which he regards as incomplete and representing an early stage of elaboration. Anticipating the accusations of evolutionary determinism or teleology, he draws the crucial distinction here, as in several other places in this group of writings, between largely irreversible biological *evolution* and potentially reversible social *development*. Unlike processes of biological evolution, it is possible for social processes to go into reverse and return to an earlier stage of their development. (It is in this sense that he acknowledged the possibility of civilizing processes going into reverse as processes of "*de*civilization": see below.)

Within this broad framework of socio-natural development, which he calls the Great Evolution (2007b [1987]: 179–233), Elias sees the technical human capacity for communication via symbols to be a unique consequence of the blind inventiveness of nature. Symbols, he insists, are also *tangible* sound patterns of human communication, made possible by the evolutionary biological precondition of the unique and complex vocal apparatus of humans. The capacity of humans to steer their conduct by means of learned knowledge gave them a great evolutionary advantage over other species which were unable to accomplish this at all or only to a very limited extent.

3. *The Germans: Power Struggles and the Development of Habitus in the Nineteenth and Twentieth Centuries* (1996) is a late collection of essays and lectures on German social development and national character and the rise of the Nazis, originally published in German in 1989, exactly 50 years after *The Civilizing Process*. The later volume expands and develops the triangular comparison between Britain, France, and Germany which runs through the earlier work, through a detailed analysis of the German case. Elias focuses on the successive historical diminution, through the wars of 1866 and 1914–1918, of German territory in the west and east, resulting in the hegemony of Prussia in the German Confederation. This meant that a centralized German nation-state did not emerge with the ease and speed of other European states, such as England and France. The character of the German habitus, personality, and social structure which combined to produce the rise of Hitler and the Nazi genocides is best understood in relation to this feature of Germany's past.

The comparatively late unification of Germany occurred under the leadership of the militaristic ruling strata of Prussia. This was a process in the course of which large sections of the middle classes abandoned the humanistic values which had hitherto predominated in their social circles, and adopted instead the militaristic and authoritarian values of the hegemonic Prussian elite. German society became orientated around a code of honor in which dueling and the demanding and giving of "satisfaction" occupied pride of place. Elias argues that Germany's unification involved the "brutalization" of much of the middle classes. The code of behavior which they adopted was essentially a warrior code which emphasized the cult of hardness and obedience and unyielding attitudes of contempt for weakness and compromise. Along with these features of the emerging German habitus was a need to submit to a strong state authority and a decided decline in people's ability to empathize with others. Or, in Elias's words, there occurred a contraction in the scope of "mutual identification." Combined with the weakening of the state's monopoly of violence in the Weimar Republic and the consequent escalation of violence and social fears, these preconditions gave rise to a compelling sequential development (a likely, but *not inevitable*, process) which produced a society-wide process of "decivilization," accelerating during the Weimar Republic and culminating in the Second World War and the Holocaust (see Fletcher, 1997).

PRINCIPLES OF PROCESS SOCIOLOGY

The central recommendations of Elias's sociology, as a theoretical–empirical research strategy, are set out most systematically and succinctly in *What is Sociology?* (1978). (The highly stimulating theoretical reflections contained in *The Society of Individuals* (Elias, 2010[1991]) are a good supplement.) These recommendations grew out of the vast amount of research and reflection some of which we have tried to summarize. Elias states that sociology is about studying real people in the plural in webs of social interdependencies. People are bonded to each other not only economically or politically, but also *emotionally*. (The latter dimension had been a central theme of his work since the beginning. He anticipated the contemporary specialisms of the sociology of emotions and of the body a very long time ago.) Figurational sociology is committed to studying people "in the round," simultaneously in *all* the ways in which people are tied to each other in their social existence. It is best summarized as a dynamic sociology of human bonding and the formation of individuals, which centrally stresses the role of power in human relationships. Primacy is given to the developing structure of the social interdependencies (including local, national, regional, and global dimensions) in which people are actually integrated, not to "the social system" in the abstract, nor to analytically distinguished "spheres" or conditions of social action. As Elias declared, in a polemic against Talcott Parsons:

> Why put "actions" in the centre of a theory of society and not the people who act? If anything, societies are networks of human beings in the round, not a medley of disembodied actions. (Elias, 2008[1970]: 109)

Since sociologists are part of the figurations which they are seeking to understand and to explain, one of the problems they face is controlling for their wishes, fears, and prejudices ("involvements" in Elias's terminology) which stem from their own enmeshment in the tensions generated by social interdependencies which comprise their society. This problem presents itself simply because there is no place outside the antagonisms and conflicts of the figuration from which to observe it. So, for Elias, the problem of achieving a greater degree of sociological detachment is integral to his theory of knowledge and thus to his sociology (Elias, 2007a[1987]). It also means that at this stage of the development of the discipline, the cognitive status of sociological texts cannot but be bound up to some degree with the social perspective, location, or position of their authors, and so must be to some degree "involved." So, if standards of detachment and fact orientation ("autonomous evaluations" in Elias's terminology) are only relatively weakly institutionalized in sociology, it is likely that a great deal of sociological output will be more informed by extra-sociological involvements ("heteronomous evaluations"). In other words, under present conditions the inquiries of many sociological practitioners will tell us more about them than about the objects of their investigations. Or to put it another way, their involvement/detachment balance will be tilted towards the former pole.

In summary, Goudsblom (1977a: 6) has distilled from Elias four principles of process sociology. The fact that readers may initially be suspicious of the simplicity and obviousness of these points may be indicative of the expectations of sophistication and difficulty which sociologists commonly associate with the language of the discipline, particularly its theoretical side.

1   Human beings are interdependent in a variety of ways; they are inextricably bonded to each other in the social figurations they form with one another, including with people they do not know.
2   These figurations are continually in flux, undergoing changes, some rapid and ephemeral, others slower and more lasting.

3 The long-term developments taking place in human figurations have been and continue to be largely unplanned and unforeseen but are nonetheless structured.

4 The development of human knowledge (including sociology itself) takes place within human figurations and forms one important aspect of their overall development.

SUMMARY AND EVALUATION

The reception of Elias's work and his reputation have varied from country to country. In The Netherlands, France, and in Germany his intellectual standing and reputation are considerable, whilst in Britain, France and in the USA, he is appreciated only patchily (Mennell, 1998[1989]: 278–84).[10] The obstacles to the appreciation of Elias in the USA are many. In their history, Americans have little experience of courtly elites or monopolistic model-setting upper classes who feature prominently in Elias's studies of European history, although Mennell (2007) has shown in great detail the insights that can be derived by applying Elias's ideas to the USA. Americans may also feel more uncomfortable than Europeans about Elias's depiction of the social patterning of basic bodily functions in *The Civilizing Process*. But, besides such broader questions, there are peculiarities of the sociological profession in the USA (which increasingly serves as a model for the rest of the world). One of the prerequisites for making a successful career in sociology today is the choice of a specialism; say medical, political, or urban sociology, or perhaps methods. Specialization has gone a very long way in sociology generally, but particularly far in the USA, perhaps to the point where even some of the specialists themselves have lost sight of the core of the discipline (Di Maggio, 1997: 193). With one or two exceptions, there has been a decline (on both sides of the Atlantic) of the sociological generalist who can cross specialisms and draw things together. This, however, is precisely the (unfashionable) strength of Elias's perspective – that is, its explanatory potential as a synthesis. We take the view that this potential extends not only to drawing together data from specialisms within sociology, but also between sociology and other social sciences.

In the face of the forces of specialization the synoptic thrust of sociology has been diverted into the artificial field of "social theory" which tries to accomplish this aim on a purely conceptual terrain. As a result, "theory" itself has ironically become yet another specialism. Here, however, the holistic, generalizing, connecting impetus is not carried out in the substantive, theoretical–*empirical* fashion so typical of Elias. Furthermore, the expansion of social theory has tended to pull sociology back into philosophy, something upon which Elias had firmly turned his back (see Kilminster, 1998: Part II; 2007: ch. 2). Karl Mannheim expressed the problem of balancing specialization and synthesis in a way with which Elias would probably have agreed. In a letter dated April 24, 1942 to Alexander M. Carr-Saunders, the then Director of the London School of Economics, Mannheim wrote:

As there is recently a growing movement proclaiming that the Social Sciences cannot remain in a state of *disjecta membra* for good and that there must be a concept of

science which admits both specialization and integration, there are less obstacles today
to the acceptance of the synthetic concept than have been before. Synthetic, or structural sociology gradually developed a technique of careful handling of the data gained
by the specialist and specific methods for their combination. Whereas the specialist is
competent as long as the accuracy of his data is concerned, as to the technique of synthesis those are the experts who have greater practice in the study of getting into relations and of the comprehensive patterns of society. (Cited in Gábor, 2003: 276)

It is clearly hard to find a fertile soil in which Elias's unique brand of sociology
can grow and flourish. In the case of Britain, the pattern had already been established. Although Elias lived and worked there for about 40 years, scarcely anyone
seemed to have noticed; at any rate, very few took up his work. Unlike Mannheim,
he did not have an academic post of professorial rank at the LSE, had until late in
his British sojourn published little in English, and was unknown in the public sphere.
Like many other continental social-scientific émigrés, Elias encountered the inertia
of the British traditions of social administration, Fabianism, and empiricism in the
service of social reform (Kilminster and Varcoe, 1996: 5–10). Again unlike Mannheim,
Elias was not prepared to adapt his sociology to the political and cultural context in
which he found himself. In contrast, the Dutch were from early on receptive to
Elias's work. *Über den Prozess der Zivilisation* was well reviewed in The Netherlands
in the months before the German invasion in 1940, and a major research school
inspired by Elias developed there from 1969 onwards under the intellectual leadership of Johan Goudsblom. The question of why precisely The Netherlands should
have been so much more receptive than Britain or the USA has not yet been fully
answered.

In the ten years since the first edition of this book was published, however, it is
fair to say that Elias's status as a sociologist of the first rank has become firmly
established. The more seriously misleading criticisms of his work that may have
impeded his reception at an earlier time have been refuted and he is now better
understood. The reception of Elias has moved from a combative stage to one of
consolidation. There are signs that his intellectual standing will continue to rise in
the next few decades as this consolidation spreads further in world sociology.
Harbingers of this process include the fact that translations of Elias's works are
appearing in many languages, including Chinese, Japanese, Korean, and Portuguese
and that active research groups are emerging in Japan, Italy, Brazil, Argentina,
and Mexico.

The next generation is taking for granted the nuanced understanding of Elias's
work established by the one which preceded them and is bringing it to bear, along
with other perspectives, on the burning issues of their generation. In the last edition [of this companion] we identified the emerging fields of research in anglophone sociology where Elias's ideas were then finding expression as (a) gender,
sexuality, and identity and (b) the reorientation of sociological theory. This double
trend is continuing, notably with the publication of two major works by Wouters
(2004, 2007) on the management of social relations, including sexual relations,
between men and women and people of different rank in a long-term perspective,
using evidence from manners books from four countries. (These scant remarks do
not do justice to the empirical richness and theoretical depth of Wouters's studies

which are highly significant works.) In the second broad area of theoretical reflection and reorientation, two advanced readers have recently appeared examining the tradition established by Elias (Loyal and Quilley, 2004; Salumets, 2001); a comparison of Freud, Weber, Adorno, and Elias on the relation between psychology and sociology (Cavalletto, 2007); a study contrasting Elias with Hannah Arendt, Zygmunt Bauman, Talcott Parsons, and Michel Foucault (Smith, 2001); and a study of the origins, reception, and significance of Elias, focusing on the "post-philosophical" theme in his writings and its implications for the enterprise of sociology (Kilminster, 2007).

Looking back over the last ten years through the regular reports of recent articles and books that apply, test, or develop Elias's theories reported in *Figurations*, the biannual newsletter of the Norbert Elias Foundation, an intriguing proclivity emerges. It is probably the synoptic, connecting character of Elias's theories that make them appeal to researchers working on the margins of sociology and other disciplines, for example, in the liminal areas of criminology (Garland, 1990; Rodger 2008; Wood 2004, 2007; Pratt 2002), International Relations (Linklater, 2003, 2004, 2005a, 2005b, 2007), and the study of organizations (Van Iterson *et al.*, 2003; Newton, 1999, 2003; Van Vree, 1999; Mastenbroek, 1999; Dopson, 1997). Increasingly, too, empirical studies have been applying Elias's ideas in non-European contexts, including for example, the socio-political development of the United States of America (Mennell, 2007); the water supply as an important power resource in Mexico (Castro 2006); civilizing processes in rural China (Brandstädter, 2003); the history of Singapore (Stauth, 1997); South-East Asia (Young, 1997); Russia and Stalinism (Volkov, 2000); West Africa (Ouédraogo, 1997); and aboriginal children in Australia (Van Krieken, 1999a, 1999b, 2002). In addition, figurational sociologists have followed Elias in developing a research interest in world history and extremely long-term processes. The most spectacular instance of this is Goudsblom's study of the role of fire in human development – both the biological evolution and the social development of human beings – in his book *Fire and Civilization* (1992), which reaches far back beyond the emergence of the species *Homo sapiens* in its present form.

In addition to those trends, a proliferation of recent empirical studies reveals the diverse subjects that have been illuminated through Elias's work, including tobacco use (Hughes, 2003); alcohol and opiates (Gerritsen, 2000); sport (Dunning, Malcolm, and Waddington, 2004; Maguire 1999); pain and injury in sport (Loland, Skirstad, and Waddington, 2006); drugs in sport (Waddington and Smith, 2009); sociology of the natural environment (Sutton, 2004); narcissism (Kilminster, 2008); a comparison of national character in Austria and Britain (Kuzmics and Axtmann, 2007); perspectives in the sociology of knowledge and science (Power, 2000); and decivilization, violence, war and genocide (Zwaan, 2001; Haring and Kuzmics, 2008; Watson, 2007).

Elias often said that his work was unfinished, simply an early elaboration of problems to be taken further by others. He offered his synthesis as an invitation to others to work empirically and theoretically to confirm or to refute and thus to amend the basic propositions. Our view is that his work is a rich and enduring source of inspiration for the sociological imagination.

Reader's Guide to Norbert Elias

Elias's Collected Works are being published in 18 volumes by University College Dublin Press, Dublin, Ireland. These volumes contain many texts that have not previously been published in English, and earlier English versions have been carefully corrected and annotated. Especially important are the three volumes (14, 15, 16) that contain all of Elias's essays, including some published only after his death. The project will be completed in 2013.

The most recent book in English on Elias's work is that of Richard Kilminster (2007), *Norbert Elias: Post-Philosophical Sociology*, an advanced study which probes the ways in which Elias's approach differs fundamentally from mainstream sociology. Earlier introductions to Elias are also useful: Stephen Mennell's (1998[1989]) comprehensive *Norbert Elias: An Introduction*; the shorter introduction by Robert Krieken (1998), *Norbert Elias*. Jonathan Fletcher's (1997) *Violence and Civilization: An Introduction to the Work of Norbert Elias* is an incisive assessment of Elias's work focusing on the important concept of "decivilizing processes." Of the many books by Elias himself, two introduce his way of thinking as a whole in an engaging and accessible way: *What Is Sociology?* (1978) and *The Society of Individuals* (2010[1991]).

Another route into Elias works is through readers of various kinds. Two volumes edited by Johan Goudsblom and Stephen Mennell, *The Norbert Elias Reader: A Biographical Selection* (Goudsblom and Mennell, 1998) and *Norbert Elias: On Civilization, Power, and Knowledge: Selected Writings* (Mennell and Goudsblom, 1998) contain different combinations of extracts from Elias's writings, respectively organized biographically and thematically. Two substantial readers which have pulled together expert commentaries on aspects of Elias's work are Thomas Salumets (2001) *Norbert Elias and Human Interdependencies* and Steven Loyal and Stephen Quilley (2004) *The Sociology of Norbert Elias*.

Notes

1 The German text was republished in 1969, and Elias's reputation in Germany and The Netherlands grew rapidly from then onwards. A French translation was published in the early 1970s, but the English version was not only long delayed but has a troubled history. The first volume was published under the misleading title *The History of Manners* in 1978. There was then a four-year gap before the appearance of the second, which appeared under two different titles, *State-Formation and Violence* in Britain and the unauthorized and misleading *Power and Civility* in the United States. As a consequence, many readers and some reviewers failed to appreciate that the two volumes were inseparable halves of a single work. In 1994, Blackwell published a one-volume edition under the title *The Civilizing Process*, which reproduced all the textual faults of the earlier English edition and introduced many more. A revised version, corrected by Eric Dunning, Johan Goudsblom, and Stephen Mennell, was published by Blackwell in 2000, and (pending the publication of a definitive edition as volume 3 of the Collected Works of Norbert Elias in English) that is the best text available. The Collected Works edition will appear under the more accurate title *On the Process of Civilization* – because the emphasis should be on the word *process*, not *civilization*.

2   The Collected Works of Norbert Elias in English are being published in 18 volumes by
    UCD Press, Dublin. These volumes contain heavily corrected texts, and will become the
    standard editions of Elias's writings. The project will be completed in 2013.
3   This paper has been lost.
4   Elias's outline of his intended thesis was found among Alfred Weber's papers in Heidelberg,
    and is included as an appendix, "On the emergence of the modern natural sciences"
    (2006e [c.1925–1926], in Elias's *Early Writings*.
5   Elias argued that the taming of warriors was a process of significance not just in European
    history but in the development of human societies generally, and that it had been rela-
    tively neglected by sociologists. See Ikegami (1995) for a study of this process in Japanese
    history.
6   Goffman cited the original edition of *Über den Prozess der Zivilisation* in *Asylums*
    (1961) and *Behaviour in Public Places* (1963); that is quite remarkable, considering
    the obscurity of Elias's work in the early 1960s. (He was apparently introduced to the
    book by Edward Shils in Chicago, where he was a graduate student in the late
    1940s.)
7   In fact, especially in his later works such as *An Essay on Time* (2007c[1992]) and *Humana
    Conditio* (2010), Elias also spoke of civilizing processes on a third level, that of humanity
    as a whole. See Mennell (1998: 200–24).
8   For a fuller discussion of the controversies, see Mennell (1998), especially Chapter 10.
9   These general considerations are set out most clearly in "A Theoretical Essay on
    Established and Outsider Relations," written by Elias in 1976 and included (along with
    further reflections on established–outsiders relations in an essay, "The Maycomb Model,"
    written only weeks before his death in 1990) in the new edition of *The Established and
    the Outsiders* which constitutes volume 4 of the Collected Works (Elias and Scotson,
    2008[1965]).
10 One sign that American sociologists are coming to regard Elias as a sociologist of the first
    rank is the inclusion of a selection of his writings in the famous Heritage of Sociology
    series (Mennell and Goudsblom, 1998).

Bibliography

Writings of Norbert Elias

1970. Interview met Norbert Elias. *Sociologische Gids*, 17(2): 133–40. (Reprinted as An
    Interview in Amsterdam in Johan Goudsblom and Stephen Mennell (eds) *The Norbert
    Elias Reader: A Biographical Selection*. Oxford: Blackwell, 1998, pp. 141–51.)
1978. *What is Sociology?* London: Hutchinson (Collected Works, vol. 5, forthcoming).
1994. *Reflections on a Life*. Cambridge: Polity Press (to be included in *Interviews and
    Autobiographical Reflections*, Collected Works, vol. 17, forthcoming).
1996. *The Germans: Power Struggles and the Development of Habitus in the Nineteenth and
    Twentieth Centuries*. Cambridge: Polity Press (*Studies on the Germans*, Collected Works,
    vol. 11, forthcoming).
2000[1939]. *The Civilizing Process*, rev. edn. Oxford: Blackwell (*On the Process of Civilization*,
    Collected Works, vol. 3, forthcoming).
2006a[1929]. Contributions to the debate on Karl Mannheim, the importance of competition
    in the intellectual field, in *Early Writings*. Dublin: UCD Press (Collected Works, vol. 1,
    2006), pp. 67–70.

2006b[1929]. The sociology of German anti-Semitism, in *Early Writings*. Dublin: UCD Press (Collected Works, vol. 1), pp. 77–83.

2006c[1921]. On seeing in nature, in *Early Writings*. Dublin: UCD Press (Collected Works, vol.1), pp. 5–21.

2006d[1922]. Idea and Individual: a critical investigation into the concept of history, in *Early Writings*. Dublin: UCD Press (Collected Works, vol. 1), pp. 23–53.

2006e[c. 1925–1926]. On the emergence of the modern natural sciences, in *Early Writings*. Dublin: UCD Press (Collected Works, vol. 1), pp. 111–23.

2006f[1935]. The expulsion of the Huguenots from France, in *Early Writings*. Dublin: UCD Press (Collected Works, vol. 1), pp. 97–104.

2006g[1983]. *The Court Society*. Dublin: UCD Press (Collected Works, vol. 2).

2007a[1987]. *Involvement and Detachment*. Dublin: UCD Press (Collected Works, vol. 8).

2007b[1987]. Reflection on the great evolution: two fragments, in *Involvement and Detachment*. Dublin: UCD Press (Collected Works, vol. 8), pp. 179–233.

2007c[1992]. *An Essay on Time*. Dublin: UCD Press (Collected Works, vol. 9).

2008[1970]. Processes of state formation and nation-building in *Essays II: On Civilising Processes, State Formation and National Identity*. Dublin: UCD Press (Collected Works, vol. 15), pp. 105–18.

2008[1986]. (with Eric Dunning) *Quest for Excitement: Sport and Leisure in the Civilizing Process*, rev. edn. Dublin: UCD Press (Collected Works, vol. 7).

2008[1965]. (with John L. Scotson) *The Established and the Outsiders*, enlarged edn. Dublin: UCD Press (Collected Works, vol. 4).

2009a *Essays I: On the Sociology of Knowledge and the Sciences*. Dublin: UCD Press (Collected Works, vol. 14).

2009b[1977]. Address on Adorno: respect and critique, in *Essays III: On Sociology and the Humanities*. Dublin: UCD Press (Collected Works, vol. 16), pp. 82–92.

2009c[1969]. On sociology and psychiatry, in *Essays III: On Sociology and the Humanities*. Dublin: UCD Press (Collected Works, vol. 16), pp. 159–79.

2010. *Humana conditio*: observations on the development of humanity on the fortieth anniversary of the end of a war (8 May 1985), in *The Loneliness of the Dying and* Humana Conditio. Dublin: UCD Press (Collected Works, vol. 6).

2010[1991]. *The Society of Individuals*. Dublin: UCD Press (Collected Works, vol. 10).

2011[1991]. *The Symbol Theory*. Dublin: UCD Press (Collected Works, vol. 13).

Further Reading

Aron, Raymond (1957) *German Sociology*. London: Heinemann.

Bauman, Zygmunt (1988) *Modernity and the Holocaust*. Cambridge: Polity Press.

Bogner, Artur (1987) Elias and the Frankfurt School. *Theory, Culture and Society*, 4(2–3): 249–85.

Brandtstädter, Susanne (2003) With Elias in China: Civilising process, local restorations and power in contemporary rural China. *Anthropological Theory*, 3(1): 87–105.

Castro, José Esteban (2006) *Water, Power, and Citizenship: Social Struggle in the Basin of Mexico*. Basingstoke: Palgrave Macmillan.

Cavalletto, George (2007) *Crossing the Psycho-Social Divide: Freud, Weber, Adorno and Elias*. Aldershot: Ashgate.

Di Maggio, Paul (1997) Epilogue: Sociology as a Discipline. In Kai Erikson (ed.) *Sociological Visions*. Lanham, MD and Oxford: Rowman & Littlefield Publishers, Inc.

Dopson, Sue (1997) *Managing Ambiguity and Change: the Case of the NHS*. London: Macmillan.

Dunning, Eric, Malcolm, Dominic, and Waddington, Ivan (2004), *Sport Histories, Figurational Studies of the Development of Modern Sports*. London: Routledge.

Febvre, Lucien (1930) Civilisation: Evolution of a Word and a Group of Ideas. In John Rundell and Stephen Mennell (eds) (1998) *Classical Readings in Culture and Civilisation*. London: Routledge, pp. 160–90.

Fletcher, Jonathan (1997) *Violence and Civilisation: An Introduction to the Work of Norbert Elias*. Cambridge: Polity Press.

Freud, Anna (1968 [1936]) *The Ego and the Mechanisms of Defence*, rev. edn. London: Hogarth Press, pp. 109–121.

Freud, Sigmund (1962 [1930]) *Civilisation and its Discontents*. New York: W. W. Norton.

Gábor, Éva (ed.) with the assistance of Dézsö Banki and R. T. Allen (2003) *Selected Correspondence (1911–1946) of Karl Mannheim, Scientist, Philosopher, and Sociologist*. Lampeter: Edwin Mellen Press.

Garland, David (1990) *Punishment and Modern Society: A Study in Social Theory*. Oxford: Clarendon Press.

Gerritsen, Jan-Willem (2000) *The Control of Fuddle and Flash: A Sociological History of the Regulation of Alcohol and Opiates*. Leiden: Brill.

Goffman, Erving (1961) *Asylums*. Garden City, NY: Doubleday.

Goffman, Erving (1963) *Behavior in Public Places*. New York: Free Press.

Goudsblom, Johan (1977a) *Sociology in the Balance*. Oxford: Blackwell.

Goudsblom, Johan (1977b) Responses to Norbert Elias's work in England, Germany, The Netherlands and France. In Peter Gleichmann, Johan Goudsblom, and Hermann Korte (eds), *Human Figurations: Essays for Norbert Elias*. Amsterdam: Stichting Amsterdams Sociologisch Tijdschrift, pp. 37–97.

Goudsblom, Johan (1989) Stijlen en beschaving [Styles and Civilization]. *De Gids*, 152: 720–722.

Goudsblom, Johan (1992) *Fire and Civilisation*. London: Allen Lane.

Gouldsblom, J. and Mennell, Stephen (eds) (1998) *The Norbert Elias Reader: A Biographical Selection*. Oxford: Blackwell.

Hackeschmidt, Jörg (2004) The Torch Bearer: Norbert Elias as a Young Zionist, *Leo Baeck Institute Year Book* 49. Oxford: Berghahn Books, pp. 59–74.

Haring, Sabine A. and Kuzmics, Helmut (eds) (2008) *Das Gesicht des Krieges: Militär aus emotionssoziologischer Perspektive* [The Face of War: The Military Seen from a Sociology-of-Emotions-Perspective]. Vienna: Sicht.

Horkheimer, Max and Adorno, Theodor W. (1979 [1944]) *Dialectic of Enlightenment*. London: New Left Books.

Hughes, Jason (2003) *Learning to Smoke: Tobacco Use in the West*. Chicago: University of Chicago Press.

Ikegami, Eiko (1995) *The Taming of the Samurai: Honorific Individualism and the Making of Modern Japan*. Cambridge, MA: Harvard University Press.

Iterson, Ad van, Mastenbroek, Willem, Newton, Tim, and Smith, Dennis (eds) (2003), *The Civilised Organisation: Norbert Elias and the Future of Organisation Studies*. Amsterdam: John Benjamins.

Kettler, David and Meja, Volker (1995) *Karl Mannheim and the Crisis of Liberalism: The Secret of These New Times*. New Brunswick, NJ: Transaction Publishers.

Kettler, David, Loader, Colin, and Meja, Volker (2008) *Karl Mannheim and the Legacy of Max Weber: Retrieving a Research Programme*. Aldershot: Ashgate.

Kilminster, Richard (1998) *The Sociological Revolution: From the Enlightenment to the Global Age*. London: Routledge.

Kilminster, Richard (2007) *Norbert Elias: Post-philosophical Sociology*. Abingdon: Routledge.

Kilminster, Richard (2008) Narcissism or Informalisation?: Christopher Lasch, Norbert Elias and Social Diagnosis. *Theory Culture and Society*, 23(3): 131–151.

Kilminster, Richard and Varcoe, Ian (1996) Introduction: Intellectual Migration and Sociological Insight in Richard Kilminster and Ian Varcoe (eds) *Culture, Modernity and Revolution: Essays in Honour of Zygmunt Bauman*. London: Routledge.

Kilminster, Richard and Wouters, Cas (1995) From philosophy to sociology: Elias and the neo-Kantians: A response to Benjo Maso. *Theory, Culture and Society*, 12(3): 81–120.

Kranendonk, Willem H. (1990) *Society as Process: A Bibliography of Figurational Sociology in The Netherlands* [up to 1989]. Amsterdam: Sociologisch Instituut, Universiteit van Amsterdam.

Krieken, Robert van (1998) *Norbert Elias*. London: Routledge.

Krieken, Robert van (1999a) The Barbarism of Civilisation: Cultural genocide and the "stolen generations." *British Journal of Sociology*, 50(2): 295–313.

Krieken, Robert van (1999b) The "stolen generations": on the removal of Australian indigenous children from their families and its implications for the sociology of childhood, *Childhood* 6(3).

Krieken, Robert van (2002) Reshaping civilisation: Liberalism between assimilation and cultural genocide. *Amsterdams Sociologisch Tijdschrift*, 29(2): 215–247

Kuzmics, Helmut and Axtmann, Roland (2007) *Authority, State and National Character: the Civilizing Process in Austria and England, 1700–1900*. Aldershot: Ashgate.

Leach, Edmund (1986) Violence, *London Review of Books*, October 23.

Lepenies, Wolf (1978) Norbert Elias: an outsider full of unprejudiced insight. *New German Critique*, 15: 57–64.

Linklater, Andrew (2003) Norbert Elias and international relations. *Figurations: Newsletter of the Norbert Elias Foundation*, no. 19: 4–5.

Linklater, Andrew (2004) The "Civilising Process" and the sociology of international relations. *International Politics*, 41: 3–35.

Linklater, Andrew (2005a) Dialogic politics and the civilising process. *Review of International Studies*, 31: 141–154.

Linklater, Andrew (2005b) A European Civilising Process, in Christopher Hill and Michael Smith (eds) *International Relations and the European Union*. Oxford: Oxford University Press, pp. 368–387.

Linklater, Andrew (2007) *Critical Theory and World Politics: Citizenship, Sovereignty and Humanity*. London: Routledge.

Loland, Sigmund, Skirstad, Berit, and Waddington, Ivan (eds) (2006), *Pain and Injury in Sport*. London: Routledge.

Loyal, Steven and Quilley, Stephen (eds) (2004) *The Sociology of Norbert Elias: Introduction and New Directions*. Cambridge: Cambridge University Press.

Maguire, Joseph (1999) *Global Sport: Identities, Societies, Civilizations*. Cambridge: Polity Press.

Mann, Thomas (1983 [1918]) *Reflections of a Non-political Man*. New York: Frederick Ungar.

Mannheim, Karl (1936 [1929]) *Ideology and Utopia*. London: Routledge & Kegan Paul.

Mannheim, Karl (1953 [1934]) German Sociology (1918–1933). In Karl Mannheim (ed.) *Essays on the Sociology and Social Psychology*. London: Routledge & Kegan Paul.

Mannheim, Karl (1957 [1935]) *Systematic Sociology: An Introduction to the Study of Society*. London: Routledge & Kegan Paul.

Maso, Benjo (1995) Elias and the Neo-Kantians: Intellectual backgrounds of *The Civilizing Process*. *Theory, Culture and Society*, 12 (3): 43–79.

Mastenbroek Willem (1999) Negotiating as emotion management. *Theory, Culture and Society*, 16(4): 49–73.

Mennell, Stephen (1994) the formation of we-images: A process theory. In Craig Calhoun (ed.) *Social Theory and the Politics of Identity*. Oxford: Blackwell, pp. 175–197.

Mennell, Stephen (1997) A sociologist at the outset of group analysis: Norbert Elias and his sociology. *Group Analysis*, 30(4): 489–514.

Mennell, Stephen (1998[1989]) *Norbert Elias: An Introduction*. Dublin: University College Dublin Press.

Mennell, Stephen (2007) *The American Civilizing Process*. Cambridge: Polity Press.

Mennell, Stephen and Goudsblom, Johan (eds) (1998) *Norbert Elias on Civilisation, Power and Knowledge: Selected Writings*. Chicago: University of Chicago Press.

Newton, Tim (1999) Power, subjectivity and British industrial and organisational sociology: the relevance of the work of Norbert Elias. *Sociology*, 33(2): 411–440.

Newton, Tim (2003) Credit networks and civilisation. *British Journal of Sociology*, 54(3): 347–372.

Ouédraogo, Jean-Bernard (1997) *Violences et communautés en Afrique noire*. Paris: L'Harmattan.

Pines, Malcolm (ed.) (1997) Special section: Centennial celebration to commemorate the birth and work of Norbert Elias. *Group Analysis*, 30(4): 475–529.

Power, Richenda (2000) *A Question of Knowledge*. Harlow: Pearson Education.

Pratt, John (2002) *Punishment and Civilization: Penal Tolerance and Intolerance in Modern Society*. London: Sage.

Salumets, Thomas (ed.) (2001) *Norbert Elias and Human Interdependencies*. Montreal: McGill–Queen's University Press.

Sathaye, S. G. (1973) On Norbert Elias's developmental paradigm. *Sociology*, 7(1): 117–123.

Schad, Susanne Petra (1972) *Empirical Social Research in Weimar Germany*. The Hague: Mouton.

Smith, Dennis (2001) *Norbert Elias and Modern Social Theory*. London: Sage.

Stauth, Georg (1997) Elias in Singapore: Civilising processes in a tropical city. *Thesis Eleven*, 50: 51–70.

Sutton, Philip W. (2004) *Nature, Environment and Society*. Basingstoke: Palgrave Press.

Swaan, Abram de (1995) Widening circles of identification: Emotional concerns in socio-genetic perspective. *Theory, Culture and Society*, 12(2): 25–39.

Swaan, Abram de (2001) Dyscivilisation, mass extermination and the state. *Theory, Culture and Society*, 18(2–3): 265–76.

Volkov, Vadim (2000) The concept of *kul'turnost'*: Notes on the Stalinist civilizing process. In Sheila Fitzpatrick (ed.) *Stalinism: New Directions*. London: Routledge.

Vree, Wilbert van (1999) *Meetings, Manners and Civilisation*. London: University of Leicester Press.

Waddington, Ivan and Smith, Andy (2009) *An Introduction to Drugs in Sport: Addicted to Winning?*. Abingdon: Routledge.

Watson, Katherine D. (ed.) (2007), *Assaulting the Past: Violence and Civilization in Historical Context*. Newcastle upon Tyne: Cambridge Scholars Publishing.

Weber, Alfred (1998 [1921]) Fundamentals of Culture Sociology: Social process, civilisational process and culture-movement. In John Rundell and Stephen Mennell (eds) *Classical Readings in Culture and Civilisation*. London: Routledge, pp. 191–215.

Wood, J. Carter (2004) *Violence and Crime in Nineteenth-Century England: The Shadow of Our Refinement*. London: Routledge.

Wood, J. Carter (2007) Recent work on Elias and violence: history, evolutionary psychology and literature. *Figurations: Newsletter of the Norbert Elias Foundation*, no. 28: 6–8.

Wouters, Cas (2004) *Sex and Manners: Female Emancipation in the West, 1890–2000*. London: Sage.

Wouters, Cas (2007) *Informalization: Manners and Emotions since 1890*. London: Sage.

Young, Ken (1997) State formation in Southeast Asia. *Thesis Eleven, 50*: 71–97.

Zwaan, Ton (2001) *Civilisering en decivilisering: Studies over staatsvorming en geweld, nationalisme en vervolging* [*Civilising and Decivilising: Studies on State-formation and Violence, Nationalism and Persecution*]. Amsterdam: Boom.

2

Henri Lefebvre

KANISHKA GOONEWARDENA

The last great classical philosopher.

Fredric Jameson

I am a Marxist today, so that we can be anarchists tomorrow.

Henri Lefebvre

WHO IS LEFEBVRE?

The most prolific writer in the tradition of Western Marxism, Henri Lefebvre (1901–1990), still remains something of a curiosity in contemporary critical theory. For he is without doubt the least studied socialist thinker among the great twentieth-century political-intellectual icons, not least among Marxists. Compared to the sprawling secondary literatures devoted to Antonio Gramsci or Theodor Adorno, Lefebvre occupies a strikingly small space in the landscape of radical thought. Much more has been written about the much less that Louis Althusser – his antipode in post-war French theory – or Guy Debord – his fellow traveler for some years – wrote. Less is more, sometimes, but here is something of a puzzle. How could the man who really introduced Marx to French intellectual life – and remained a most energetic artisan and partisan of Marxism to the end of his life, from within and without the French Communist Party – not detain Perry Anderson for more than a few passing references in his classic study, *Considerations on Western Marxism* (1976), or escape altogether the attention of Alain Badiou in his little red book of eulogies to a motley crew of celebrated French philosophers, *The Pocket Pantheon* (2008)?

The Wiley-Blackwell Companion to Major Social Theorists, First Edition.
Edited by George Ritzer and Jeffrey Stepnisky.
© 2011 Blackwell Publishing Ltd. Published 2011 by Blackwell Publishing Ltd.

Space, Time, Revolution

A few postmodern geographers have suggested that his unjust marginalization in critical theory issued from an occupational hazard of its exponents: the privileging of time at the expense of space. There is an element of truth in what they say against the backdrop of various academic specializations still unconcerned with space. Yet, this exaggerated claim also represents the besieged mentality of some professors worried about their disciplinary identity, and less the actuality of Lefebvre, whose significance for the so-called "spatial turn" in contemporary theory has been registered with almost exclusive reference to his *The Production of Space* (published in 1974, translated into English in 1991). True, writings on the "production of space" and "cities" rank among the most original aspects of Lefebvre's stunningly wide-ranging work, as we will see, but he was no less concerned with understanding history, as evidenced by the breadth and depth of his engagement with the classic themes of Hegel, Marx, and Lenin in his earliest exegeses: *Morceaux choisis de Karl Marx* (1934), *La conscience mystifiée* (1936[1999]), *G. W. F. Hegel: Morceaux choisis* (1938), *Cahiers de Lénine sur la dialectique Hegel* (1938), *Dialectical Materialism* (1939[2009]). The attention devoted to time and history in these texts marks an enduring feature of Lefebvre's thought, persisting through more famous explorations of space, to reemerge most suggestively in the last published work, co-authored with his communist lover Catherine Régulier: *Elements of Rhythmanalysis* (1992). Even *The Production of Space*, more often than noted, betrays a profound historical consciousness, especially in its account of the *history* of space – centered on abstract and contradictory space produced by state and capital, but beckoning beyond.

Open Marxism

Adopting a famous phrase from Jean-Paul Sartre, it is safe to say that Lefebvre was no doubt an iconoclastic twentieth-century Marxist philosopher, but not every iconoclastic twentieth-century Marxist philosopher was Lefebvre. Indeed, differences and similarities between Lefebvre and other leading exponents of Marxism in contemporaneous Europe help to situate him in the specificity of his French political-intellectual milieu, while also indicating how he stretched the boundaries of French Marxism, spicing up on occasion its Hegelian heritage with bits and pieces of Schelling, Nietzsche, and Heidegger. What, then, distinguishes Lefebvre's reading of Marx – which forms the unyielding core of his entire oeuvre? In the 1961 foreword to the fifth French edition of *Dialectical Materialism*, Lefebvre identified the key concepts of Marx that first commanded his attention in the 1920s and the 1930s, which were beginning to be suppressed at the time in the official Marxisms of the USSR and the PCF (French Communist Party): "alienation, praxis, the total man and social totality." An unwavering commitment to these politically loaded theoretical categories nourished not only his heterodox identity in relation to the party lines of Comintern Marxism during the last century, but also his palpable distaste to the dominant intellectual fashions of the post-war French Left, especially structuralism and post-structuralism. Lefebvre's spirited opposition to the theoretical anti-humanism of the latter – championed by Althusser, Michel Foucault, and Jacques Derrida, with whom he shared several interests including ideology, power, and language – renders the impressionable Anglo-American sketch of him as a "postmodern" student of space philologically unsustainable. It also calls into question the coherence of his own selective appropriations of Heidegger and Nietzsche, whose more rigorous readers place these thinkers firmly within an anti-humanist problematic, to which he was resolutely opposed. Lefebvre for one – unlike Derrida or Foucault – seems not to have received Heidegger's famous "Letter on Humanism" (1946).

Uses of Alienation

If Lefebvre was a peculiar kind of Marxist, that peculiarity had to do on the one hand with a certain intellectual eclecticism, marked by a predilection to raid the philosophical ice boxes of Nietzsche, Heidegger, and other assorted philosophers to gather food for his own romantic-revolutionary thoughts; and on the other hand an uncanny originality in the study of urban modernity as a global phenomenon subtended by state and capital, wherein we see a series of novel contributions to Marxism in particular and critical theory more broadly. The resultant conceptual innovations focused above all on everyday life, urbanization, space, time, difference, state, and modernity, turning several phenomena hitherto sidelined within the mainstreams of Marxism into suggestive theoretical concepts for radical politics. This prodigious intellectual endeavor was of course underwritten by Lefebvre's fidelity to those foundational concepts he found in Marx and Hegel: alienation, praxis, total man, and social totality. It is worth recalling in this regard Anderson's 1984 note on him in *In the Tracks of Historical Materialism* (1984), reflecting on the mutation of a largely Marxisant French intelligentsia into variations of *Nouvelle Philosophie* following May 1968: "The oldest living survivor of the ... tradition I discussed, Henri Lefebvre, neither bent nor turned in his eighth decade, continuing to produce imperturbable and original work on subjects typically ignored by much of the Left." The "price of such constancy," however, "was relative isolation," especially in the heartland of existentialism, structuralism, and post-structuralism. But just as "no intellectual change is ever universal," so no conjuncture is eternal (1984: 30). Four decades after May 1968, Lefebvre has been reincarnated in the Anglo-American academia, with barely a thought on his quixotic communism or septuagenarian return into the PCF orbit, just as his once untimely meditations began to appear innocuously in English bookstores.

Aesthetics and Politics

Any reckoning of Lefebvre's rebirth requires a return to the conjuncture of his birth: the moment of modernism bounded by the two European World Wars, which was pregnant with an explosive combination of revolutionary politics, radical art, and new technology. He was born near the Pyrenees at Hegetmau to middle-class parents and was a sixteen-year old philosophy student at the time of the Bolshevik Revolution. Lefebvre completed his degree in philosophy at the Sorbonne guided by Léon

Brunschvicg and Maurice Blondel, focusing on Jansen and Pascal, before teaming up in the early 1920s with a small but influential group of intellectuals with radical artistic and philosophical inclinations, including Paul Nizan, Georges Politzer, Norbert Guterman, Georges Friedmann, and Pierre Morhange. They produced a key journal of radical ideas named *Philosophies*, committed to a critique of both Bergsonian mysticism and forms of rationalist-positivist thought then dominating French intellectual life. In the challenge to reigning ideology mounted by this group known also as *philosophies*, art played a central role, drawing on the movements of Dada and especially the Surrealists, led respectively by Tristan Tzara and André Breton. In tandem with their excursions into Rabelais, Pascal, Schelling, Nietzsche, and Freud, Surrealism served them as a weapon against the rationalist rigidities of both mind and world, with which the official Marxisms of the day were also complicit, as these tended to be conceived as expressions rather than *critiques* of political economy. Yet Lefebvre saw here a limitation in Surrealism as well, notwithstanding its critical-utopian force derived in large part from a radical rendition of Freud's concept of the unconscious, for remaining at the level of *critique* and falling short of revolutionary *praxis*. It is for the sake of the latter that he joined the PCF in 1928 with his *philosophies* friends, following a stint behind bars for protesting the French attack on Moroccan Rif in 1925. He was to carry the Party Card for the next thirty years, and, for the rest of his life as an intellectual and an activist, a dialectical-humanist approach to revolution nourished more by avant-garde art and radical philosophy than economistic or otherwise "orthodox" Marxism.

FOR AND AGAINST THE PCF

Lefebvre's relationship to the Party was predictably fraught. For the kind of Marxism to which he subscribed ran against the grain of the PCF's increasingly Stalinist tendencies beginning in the Comintern era after Lenin. Yet the *philosophies* group retained in their new location and vocation an influential voice in the French Left, both inside and outside the PCF. Lefebvre maintained among them the highest quality and quantity of publications during this heyday of Stalinism leading up to the Second World War, becoming in Anderson's words "the most distinguished and prolific philosopher in the Party." To this end, his collaboration with Guterman proved to be particularly fruitful. This yielded a path-breaking work on ideology, *La conscience mystifiée* (1936[1999]), augmenting George Lukács's founding text of Western Marxism *History and Class Consciousness* while also broaching key questions explored in greater depth in Lefebvre's subsequent writings on "everyday life." They also made fresh contributions to the study of the dialectical method and Marxist philosophy, especially with a critical edition of Lenin's 1914/15 "philosophical notebooks" on Hegel's *Logic*, published in 1938 as *Cahiers de Lénine sur la dialectique Hegel*. The title of Lefebvre's most significant contribution to Marxism in the interwar years bore a striking similarity to the "scientific philosophy" of Marxism expounded by Stalin himself in *Dialectical and Historical Materialism* (1938). To be sure, Lefebvre's *Dialectical Materialism* was in fact written in almost direct opposition to Stalin's conception of Marxism, as explained in Stefan Kipfer's excellent "Preface" to the latest edition of this book in 2009. Whereas "Stalin

declared dialectical materialism 'the world outlook of the Marxist-Leninist Party' "
with reference to a "nominally dialectical philosophy of nature" and a "mechanical
conception of materialism" based on a "narrow and schematic reading of Engels's
Dialectics of Nature and *Anti-Dühring*," Lefebvre argued that "Marxism was above
all a dynamic movement of theory and practice, not a fixed doctrine and instrument
of Party strategy" (2009: xiv–xv). It should be noted that Lefebvre's record under
such circumstances is, however, not so clear-cut: on occasion he followed the Party
line on demand, not least in his virulent attacks on Sartre and existentialism, which
represented around the Second World War the most influential left alternative to
Marxism in French intellectual life: *L'existentialisme* (1946[2001]) and "Autocritique"
in *La nouvelle critique* (1949).

HUMANISM

The decisive theoretical event for Lefebvre in the pre-War period was the belated
discovery of Marx's early philosophical work, the Paris manuscripts of 1844. David
Ryazanov, who was the director of the Marx–Engels Institute in Moscow when he
discovered them in its archives, was fired from his job and sent to a labor camp two
years before its publication in 1932. He died in 1938, on an order of Stalin, but
Marx's *Economic and Philosophic Manuscripts of 1844* that saw the light of day
thanks to his exemplary efforts – with editorial assistance from Lukács then exiled in
Moscow – had a more mercurial fortune. This was due essentially to three pioneers
of Western Marxism, who were profoundly and independently influenced by the
young Marx. Lukács vividly recalled in his 1967 preface to *History and Class
Consciousness* the "overwhelming effect" Marx's Paris manuscripts had on his
thought, which led him to revise radically the overweening "reification" thesis of this
book derived more out of Hegel than Marx, by drawing a line between the concepts
of objectification and alienation, to register against Hegel and following Marx that
while the former category refers to a necessity of human praxis as such, the latter
denotes a particular form of it stemming from oppressive social relations. In 1932,
Herbert Marcuse's reaction to the Paris manuscripts in Berlin was no less striking,
when he wrote in *Die Gesellschaft* that these philosophical writings put "the entire
theory of 'scientific socialism' on a new footing" (cited in Anderson, 1976: 51). And
"in Paris," Anderson notes, "Lefebvre was responsible for the first translations from
the Manuscripts into a foreign language – his edition of them, prepared in collaboration with Guterman, appeared in 1933; while the first major theoretical work to
advance a new reconstruction of Marx's work as a whole in the light of 1844
Manuscripts was Lefebvre's *Dialectical Materialism*, written in 1934–5" (1976: 51).

READING HEGEL

Anderson is correct: *Dialectical Materialism* (1939[2009]; most recent English
edition cited here, 2009) was not merely an influential exegesis of Marx, but also a
novel interpretation that foreshadowed many of Lefebvre's original contributions to
Marxism. Having already highlighted the vitality of Hegel for Marxism, not least for

Marx and Lenin, Lefebvre offers here a consideration of the German philosopher's works on "logic," by first noting the inadequacies of formal logic for either understanding or changing the world, and then pointing out how Hegel's dialectical logic enables us to not simply abolish but sublate the formalisms of rationalist philosophy in a movement of thought anchored to the not so formal dynamics of society and history. Marked here is the distance traveled by Hegel in his "recreation of the movement of the real, through a movement of thought" beyond Kant, whose insurmountable antinomies Lefebvre views as a symptomatic expression of the systemic contradictions of bourgeois society:

> When Hegel set out on his philosophical career he found Reason, which is thought in its most highly developed form, profoundly rent by these internal conflicts. Kantian dualism had aggravated them to the point where they became intolerable, by deliberately dissociating form from content, thought from the "thing-in-itself," and the faculty of knowing from the object of knowledge. Hegel's purpose was to resolve these conflicts. (13)

There exists certainly shared ground between Lefebvre's appreciation of Hegel here and the middle sections of Lukács's seminal essay "History and Class Consciousness" (1923) with its arresting narration of the history of bourgeois philosophy as the actualization of capitalist alienation in the realm of thought. Hence the reference to Lefebvre by some commentators as the "French Lukács," a label rejected by him with good reason. For in spite of some overlaps between Lefebvre and Lukács, differences between them are also significant, and they hinge on the question of how a Marxist must out-Hegel Hegel. The need to do so arises in spite of as well as because of Hegel's methodological achievement. For although Hegel aimed at a dynamic unity of thought and reality, he remained in the end a philosopher rather than a revolutionary to the extent that his theodicy could not fully escape the alienated realm of the mind; whereas the real task of the dialectic, for Lefebvre as much as for Marx, was not to interpret but to change the world. Hegel's attempt to deal with this problem in *Philosophy of Right* with an apologia for the Prussian state was deemed by Lefebvre, much like Marcuse in *Reason and Revolution* (1941), to be the most disappointing moment of his work. Nor was he much impressed by Lukács's solution to the same problem in *History and Class Consciousness*, which posited the Communist Party as the decisive mediation between an objectively commodified working class and its subjective consciousness of the commodity form – the mediation that guaranteed the political capacity of the proletariat to transform capitalism. For Lefebvre, the failure of such "final solutions" to the fundamental problems of alienation is not only political, but also methodological, because they betray a tendency for the dialectical method severed from revolutionary politics to become a formalism in spite of its best intentions, making reality (content) conform to theory (form) in a fatal disavowal of their mutual constitution in praxis. Then "it is no longer a matter of raising the content freely to the notion, but of finding in the content a certain form of the notion, posited *a priori* in relation to the content: circular, enclosed and total...as a closed totality" (40–41). As a keen student of the Hegelian–Marxist concept of totality, Lefebvre has been consistently critical of teleological, deterministic and, essentialist versions of it, admonishing Lukács among others on this issue, from a standpoint sharing Sartre's emphasis in *The Critique of Dialectical Reason* (1960) on *totalization* vis-à-vis totality. The kind of "thought" tending towards closed totality "grasps only itself" (41) and "abolishes both contradiction and the Becoming," without which the dialectic is as good as dead. "But," Lefebvre notes, "contradiction does not allow itself to be destroyed by Hegel any more than by the pure logicians; it takes an ironic revenge on him" (45). "Dialectical materialism," which recognizes this, is "more Hegelian than Hegelianism" (92).

PRAXIS

Lefebvre argued that "the dialectic, far from being an inner movement of the mind, is real." As such, "the contradictions in thought do not come simply from thought itself," but also "from the content" and "together they tend towards the expression of the total movement of the content and raise it to the level of consciousness and reflection" (97). Against formalist temptations, Lefebvre also warned:

> Our quest for knowledge cannot be thought of as having been terminated by dialectical logic; quite the reverse, it must acquire a fresh impetus from it. The dialectic, a movement of thought, is true only in a mind that is in motion. In the form of a general theory of Becoming and its laws, or of a theory of knowledge, or of concrete logic, dialectical materialism can only be an instrument of research and action, never a dogma. (97–98)

"Nor," says Lefebvre, "can dialectical materialism be enclosed within an exhaustive definition." Anticipating Adorno's *Negative Dialectics* (1966), he adds that "it is defined negatively, by being exposed to those doctrines which limit human experience, either from without or within, by subordinating it to some external existence or else by reducing it to a one-sided element or partial experience seen as being privileged and definitive" (98). The unity of thought and being at which dialectical thinking aims therefore "cannot be reduced to an idea, but must be achieved concretely." Such emphases on contradiction, becoming, and praxis enabled Lefebvre to formulate a conception of dialectical materialism resisting the lure of "closed totality," while embracing the praxis of "open totality":

> Dialectical thinking has never ceased to evolve.... Every truth is relative to a certain stage of the analysis and of thought, to a certain social content. It preserves its truth only by being transcended. We must go on constantly deepening our awareness of the content and extending the content itself.... No expression of dialectical materialism can be definitive, but, instead of being incompatible and conflicting with each other, it may perhaps be possible for these expressions to be integrated into an open totality, perpetually in the process of being transcended, precisely in so far as they will be expressing the solutions to the problems facing concrete man. (98–99)

TOTAL MAN

"Praxis" for Lefebvre is the essence of the dialectic. Accordingly, much of the second half of *Dialectical Materialism* offers an elaboration of the concept of praxis. Lefebvre draws here from not only the Paris manuscripts (1844) but also *Capital*

(1867), arguing against both the structuralist and the humanist camps within Marxism that there exists no "epistemological break" between "early" and "late" work in Marx. On the contrary, he finds in Marx a remarkable consistency, seeing especially the sections on the commodity in *Capital* as a rewarding application of the concept of alienation to the capitalist mode of production – which yields not a "political economy," but a "*critique* of political economy." State and capital figure in this view as forms of human alienation and actualizations of *in*human labor. Lefebvre reads here the dialectical sign that "man has not yet been born"; that "he is still in throes of childbirth." For "man" exists yet "only in and through his opposite: the inhuman" (140). In the "production of man by man" that Lefebvre takes as the basis of humanism, these inhuman forms in which humanity realizes itself are "themselves grounded in a certain praxis" that has its "own economic and social structure" – which "must be overcome so that we can create a new praxis…" (149). Praxis in this sense involves what Hegel termed *Aufhebung* (sublation) because "total humanism does not aim to destroy" actually existing social relations, "but, on the contrary, to free them from their restrictions." In this struggle for the "total man" Lefebvre places the decisive emphasis not so much on science as *art*, which he viewed not simply as an embodiment of "the highest values of the past," but also as a "productive form of labour freed from the characteristic of alienation" (153). Yet he was well aware that "what ought (in ethical terms) to be an 'end in itself' is still only a means: man's creative activity, his essence, his individuality" (143). Hence the emphasis placed in "the dialectical notion of alienation" on a "description of man in his Becoming," that is, the "historical drama of the human" and the "significance of praxis" in the making of the "total man" (149):

> The total man is both the subject and the object of the Becoming. He is the living subject who is opposed to the object and surmounts this opposition. He is the subject who is broken up unto partial activities and scattered determinations and who surmounts this dispersion. He is the object of action, as well as its final object…. The total man in "de-alienated" man…. Human alienation will end with the "return of man to himself"…. This will not put an end to history, but rather to man's "pre-history," his "natural history"…. It will inaugurate the era of an authentic humanity, in which man will control his own destiny and try at last to resolve the specifically human problems: those of happiness, knowledge, love and death. (149–151)

WHAT IS REVOLUTION?

The most enduring concern among Lefebvre's original contributions to Marxism and critical theory was the concept of everyday life. As the subject of his three-volume work *Critique of Everyday Life* (1947[1958], 1961, 1981), as well as *Everyday Life in the Modern World* (1968) and *Rhythmanalysis* (1992/2004), it also plays a crucial role in his post-war works on modernity, space, city and state. And Lefebvre made no secret of its centrality to his own oeuvre when he defined "Marxism as Critical Knowledge of Everyday Life" in the first volume of *Critique of Everyday Life* (*CEL* I, 138) in unison with Debord and the Situationists, with whom he collaborated closely on this and related questions of urbanism in the early 1960s. That

Lefebvre's longstanding fascination with everyday life grows naturally out of his creative engagement with the concepts alienation and praxis is already evident from *Dialectical Materialism*:

> Praxis is where dialectical materialism both starts and finishes. The word itself denotes, in philosophical terms, what common sense refers to as "real life," that life which is at once most prosaic and more dramatic than that of the speculative intellect. Dialectical materialism's aim is nothing less than the rational expression of the Praxis, of the actual content of life – and, correlatively, the transformation of present praxis into a social practice that is conscious, coherent and free. (1939[2009]: 100)

This formulation anticipates how a few revealing moments of praxis in the revolutionary socialist tradition shaped Lefebvre's thinking: the Paris Commune, the Bolshevik Revolution, and May 1968. Both Lefebvre and the Situationists urge us to think of the Commune not in terms of conventional categories as merely a political event, but rather as a revolution *of* urban space *and* everyday life. Their close collaboration on it led to the radical conclusion that the ultimate test for the revolution lies in everyday life. Hence Lefebvre's poignant question in *Critique of Everyday Life, Volume II*: "What did Marx want"? And his response: "Marx wanted to change everyday life," because, "to change the world is above all to change the way everyday, real life is lived." Indeed, Lefebvre goes "so far as to argue that critique of everyday life – radical critique aimed at achieving the metamorphosis of everyday life – is alone in taking up the authentic Marxist project again and continuing it: to supersede philosophy and to fulfill it" (*CEL* II: 35, 23).

MOMENTS AND SITUATIONS

Lefebvre was centrally implicated in the events of May 1968 as a charismatic professor at the University of Nanterre, pulling crowds to courses such as "music and society" and counting among his students such radicals as Daniel Cohn-Bendit. Kristin Ross's superb account *May '68 and Its Afterlives* (2002) displays a subtle Lefebvrean awareness of this late-capitalist watershed, the interpretation of which proved to be a battleground for post-1968 French theory arguing for and mostly against revolution. *May '68* therefore offers a fine vantage point from which to observe not only Lefebvre's intervention in it, but also some innovative features of his radical thought. As Ross notes:

> The functionalist campus at Nanterre, inaugurated in 1964 and built on the site of the worst immigrant slums outside Paris, provided students with a direct "lived" lesson in uneven development – a daily experience that Henri Lefebvre, for one, never tired of remarking was the foremost "cause" of May '68. Nanterre students … acted as a catalyst for distinctly new forms of expression, representation, and mobilization of immigrant workers; by 1970, rent strikes, hunger strikes, squatting, and other collective struggles unseen before May '68 began to bring immigrants into direct confrontation with the state apparatus. (Ross, 2002: 95–96)

Ross shows here how urban space and everyday life constituted May 1968, which Lefebvre was among the first to examine critically in 1968 from a revolutionary perspective in *The Explosion: Marxism and the French Upheaval*. This "irruption" was also the moment at which he himself got a taste of his own theorizations of everyday life and urban space, which were fashioned out of Marx's concept of alien-ation in order to critique dialectically the exemplary forms of French post-war lived experience as both instances of domination and resources for liberation. While pointing to the necessity of engaging these new realities of urban and everyday life for revolutionary praxis – the research of which include some noteworthy anti-colonial (immigrants' experiences) and proto-feminist insights (engendering of work and leisure) in his critiques of everyday life and writings on the state – *The Explosion* also offers a theorization of the *moment*. This too is informed by Lefebvre's own involvement in May 1968, as he vividly recalls in an interview with Ross (Lefebvre and Ross, 1997):

> On Friday evening, May 13, ... there were maybe seventy or eighty thousand students discussing what to do next. The Maoists wanted to go out to the suburbs ... the anarchos and the situationists wanted to go make noise in the bourgeois quarters. The Trotskyists were in favour of heading for the proletarian districts ... while the students from Nanterre wanted to go to the Latin Quarter. Then some people cried out, "We've got friends in the Prison de la Santé – let's go see them" and then the whole crowd started off ... towards the Prison de la Santé. We saw hands at the windows, we yelled things, and then we headed off towards the Latin Quarter. It was chance. Or maybe it wasn't chance at all. There must have been a desire to go back to the Latin Quarter, to not get too far away from the centre of student life .... It was curious; after that hour of floating around, not knowing which way to go. And then, in the Latin Quarter, the television was there, until midnight, that is. Then there was just the radio, Europe No.1. And at about three in the morning – in complete bedlam, there was noise from all directions – a radio guy handed the microphone to Daniel Cohn-Bendit who had the brilliant idea of simply saying: "General strike, general strike, general strike." And that was the decisive moment; it was then that there was action. That was what took the police by surprise. That students were making trouble, that there was a little violence, some wounded, tear gas, paving stones, barricades, and bombs: that was all just the children of the bourgeoisie having a good time. But a general strike, well, that was no laughing matter. (82–83)

Everyday Life

Seeing that "everyday life is the native soil in which the moment germinates and takes root," Lefebvre defined the latter as "the attempt to achieve the total realiza-tion of a possibility" (*CEL* II: 348, 357). These concepts – moment and everyday life – are for him not only philosophical but also sociological, and he approached them innovatively after the War as a research director at CNRS (Centre national de la recherche scientifique) and as a professor at the universities of Strasbourg and Nanterre. And it was during the course of such sociological research that Lefebvre also developed his novel understanding of the spatiality of social relations – arguing for the revolutionary transformation of both space *and* society. As such, his celebrated theorization of space and subsequent writings on the state exist in an inextricable relationship with everyday life, which he defined in a famous passage:

> Everyday life, in a sense residual, defined by "what is left over" after all distinct, superior, specialized, structured activities have been singled out for analysis, must be defined as a totality. Considered in their specialization and their technicality, superior activities leave a "technical vacuum" between one another which is filled by everyday life. Everyday life is profoundly related to all activities, and encompass them with all their differences and their conflicts; it is their meeting place, their bond, their common ground. And it is in everyday life that the sum total of relations which make the human – and every human being – a whole takes its shape and its form. In it are expressed and fulfilled those relations which bring into play the totality of the real, albeit in a certain manner which is always partial and incomplete: friendship, comradeship, love, the need to communicate, play, etc. (*CEL* I: 97)

This view clearly owes something to the classic avant-garde critique of the separation between (specialized) art and (everyday) life, which regards the revolution as the deconstruction of this distinction in order to dissolve art into life and life into art, transforming both. But just as the avant-garde identified a relationship between art and life to be revolutionized, so Lefebvre must clarify the location of everyday life relative to those "specialized" phenomena handled by experts: the state (the object of political science), the economy (the domain of political economy), or culture (the province of anthropology). He does this with a striking image, arguing that all non-everyday (higher) activities derive from everyday (residual) activities, as the former become alienated expressions of the latter:

> There is a cliché which with a certain degree of justification compares creative moments to the mountain tops and everyday time to the plain, or to the marshes. The image the reader will find in this book differs from this generally accepted metaphor. Here everyday life is compared to fertile soil. A landscape without flowers or magnificent woods may be depressing to the passer-by; but flowers and trees should not make us forget the earth beneath. (*CEL* I: 87)

THE BUREAUCRATIC SOCIETY OF CONTROLLED CONSUMPTION

Lefebvre diagnoses the colonization of everyday life by capital and state with a concept announced in *Everyday Life in the Modern World* (1968) that rivals Adorno and Horkheimer's more famous notion of the "Culture Industry": "The Bureaucratic Society of Controlled Consumption." In its dialectical perspective, the everyday appears as a terrain of struggle, not as a lost cause à la Heidegger. For although "residual" with respect to "specialized activities," everyday life cannot be fully characterized *only* as such, because a vital, indeed growing part of it also lives under the shade of those "higher" activities. Hence the need to define everyday life further as "doubly determined" – both as the "residual deposit" and as the "*product*" of all "elevated" activities. According to philosopher Peter Osborne's penetrating reading in *The Politics of Time* (1995), in Lefebvre's concept of everyday life "there is the 'good,' but unrealized universality of an historically produced species-being and the 'bad,' abstract but realized universality of its alienated forms (money, the commodity, the state, etc.)" (191). Lefebvre's own account of "everyday life" (*la vie quotidienne*) in his essay "The Everyday and Everydayness" (1987) aligns "the everyday" (*le quotidian*) with the former, the incomplete, embattled yet actually existing "species-being" à la Marx, and "everydayness" (*la quotidienneté*) with the latter, "the homogeneous, the repetitive [and] the fragmentary" forms of being-in-the-everyday of late-capitalist modernity. This renders everyday life contradictory to the core: Lefebvre sees it as a struggle between its "human" aspect and its "bourgeois" aspect. By the same token, no specialized activity – fetishized economy, bureaucratic state, rarefied culture, *l'art pour l'art* – can sever its umbilical link to everyday life. "Innumerable human beings have been tortured by innumerable conflicts," Lefebvre writes, "since abstract (rational) social processes became detached from" the "realm" of "immediate and direct relations between individual people," a "realm" that is "situated within the everyday" (*CEL* II: 210). To the extent that the non-everyday cannot quite let go of the everyday, however, the struggle of the "human" against the "inhuman" launched from everyday life remains alive; and it is in the nature of alienation, for Marx's as much as for Lefebvre's humanism, that in the inhuman lives the human:

> The human…was and remains at the mercy of forces which in fact come from the human and are nothing but human – but torn apart and dehumanized. This alienation was *economic* (the division of labour; "private" property; the formation of economic fetishes: money, commodities, capital); *social* (the formation of classes); *political* (the formation of the state); *ideological* (religions, metaphysics, moral doctrines). It was also *philosophical*: primitive man, simple, living on the same level as nature, became divided up into subject and object, form and content, nature and power, reality and possibility, truth and illusion, community and individuality, body and consciousness…. With its speculative (metaphysical) vocabulary, philosophy is itself a part of human alienation. But the human has only developed through alienation. (*CEL* I: 249)

THE URBAN REVOLUTION

Lefebvre's interest in space evolved in tandem with his inquiries into modernity and everyday life, especially as he became aware of how urbanization constitutes a decisive mediation of late-capitalist society. He advances with this knowledge an audacious thesis: urbanization has *superseded* industrialization as the leading force shaping late capitalism. It is better therefore to call the world we live in *urban* rather than industrial, noting how space is no mere "container" nor simply an "expression" of social relations, but a productive and constitutive element of them. Space is a social product; society is spatially constituted. This radical geographical insight on socio-spatial *mediation* holds enormous import for Marxism, as Debord also underlined in *The Society of the Spectacle* (§171): "While all the technical forces of capitalism contribute toward various forms of separation, urbanism provides the material foundation for those forces and prepares the ground for their deployment. It is the very *technology of separation*." What Lefebvre called "the urban phenomenon," in other words, provides now an essential condition of possibility for the reproduction of late capitalism – which cannot be transcended without revolutionizing space, by claiming the "right to the city." It is the rationale for this struggle for a *new* city, which for Lefebvre is also the struggle for a *different* society characterized by maximal *difference*, that we find elaborated in *The Urban Revolution*. Here Lefebvre underlines the supreme formal feature of "the urban" as *centrality*.

> What does the city create? Nothing. It centralizes creation. And yet it creates everything. Nothing exists without exchange, without union, without proximity, that is, without relationships. The city creates a situation, the urban situation, where different things occur one after another and do not exist separately but according to their differences. The urban, which is indifferent to each difference it contains, often seems to be as indifferent as nature, but with a cruelty of its own. However, the urban is not indifferent to all differences, precisely because it unites them. In this sense, the city constructs, identifies, and delivers the essence of social relationships: the reciprocal existence and manifestation of differences arising from or resulting in conflicts. Isn't this the rational delirium known as the city, the urban? (1970: 117–118)

As the essence of social relations, the city centralizes power and wealth, forming the locus of social struggle. With respect to the socio-spatial *process* of urbanization that forms the ground for such struggle, *The Urban Revolution* explicates the dialectic of urban *form* as an "implosion-explosion" of the city, wherein *various* manifestations of centrality are both created and destroyed. In this sense, Lefebvre speaks here of *two* urban revolutions. The first is the creative-destructive "implosion" of the traditional pre-industrial city and its classical form of centrality bounded by walls and experienced in squares, coupled with its scalar "explosion" in the fragmented, polycentric suburban megalopolis dotted with malls and crisscrossed by highways. In a nutshell: "The merchant bourgeoisie, the intellectuals, and politicians modeled the city. The industrialists demolished it" (127–128). The second urban revolution then refers to the *possible* city, yet to be achieved in a revolutionary transformation of late capitalist social space. Clearly, this does not involve going back from highways and malls to squares and walls, notwithstanding "new urbanist" attempts to appropriate Lefebvre, who was romantic, but not nostalgic. Just as communism meant for Marx the dialectical sublation of the primitive commune on a higher plane by going all the way through class struggle, so the revolutionary city for Lefebvre represents the re-realization of the centrality of the classical city in a superior form, by going all the way through its late-capitalist creative-destruction towards a radically new "space of encounter."

SPACE AND DIALECTICS

The Production of Space is Lefebvre's most cited work, but not the best understood. The Swiss Lefebvre scholar and author of *Stadt, Raum, Gesellschaft: Henri Lefebvre und die Theorie der Produktion des Raumes* (2005) Christian Schmid is right to note in his paper "Henri Lefebvre's Theory of the production of space" (2008) that the "postmodern reformulation and monopolization" of Lefebvre in the 1980s and

1990s in the USA "has contributed to a great deal of confusion" (28). At least part of the difficulty in grasping head or tail of this inimitable book lies in its immense accumulation of different theoretical reference points drawn from virtually the full sweep of Lefebvre's formidable erudition. Its *form* recalls that of the urban itself, given the veritable "implosion-explosion" of theory that one witnesses in it: Hegel, Marx, Nietzsche, phenomenology, linguistics, semiotics, psychoanalysis, art history, political economy, sociology, anthropology, and much else recast in Lefebvre's own meta-philosophical mold of "three dimensional" dialectics. *The Production of Space* is therefore not an easy introduction to Lefebvre; rather, an awareness of the totality of Lefebvre's work becomes a prerequisite to make sense of it. Schmid offers much help here, by clarifying the "three sources and component parts" of this book stretching across spatial, social, and symbolic terrains: first, an original conception of a triadic dialectic, erroneously termed a "spatial dialectic"; second, a theory of language drawn heavily from Nietzsche, Roman Jacobson, and others emphasizing the relationships between its syntagmatic, paradigmatic, and symbolic dimensions, as spelled out in Lefebvre's *Le langage et la société* (1966); and, third, a substantive appropriation of French phenomenology from Sartre, Maurice Merleau-Ponty, and Gaston Bachelard, in addition to Heidegger. Such are the resources from which emerge Lefebvre's celebrated three moments in the production of space: "spatial practice," "representations of space" and "space of representation" in the phenomenological register; or "perceived," "conceived," and "lived" space seen through the linguistic-semiotic lens. The greatest source of confusion in all of this concerns of course the dialectic, and what Lefebvre is alleged to have done with or to it. In the best account on this issue, Schmid explains how Lefebvre attempted to take the dialectic beyond Hegel (philosophy) and Marx (praxis) by mixing it up with Nietzsche (poesy), a story Lefebvre himself tells in greater detail in *Logique formelle, logique dialectique* (1947[1969]), *Métaphilosophie* (1965[2001]), and *Le retour de la dialectique* (1986). Lefebvre's claim to originality here lies in abandoning the teleological cast of the Hegelian "thesis-antithesis-synthesis" and the Marxist "affirmation-negation-negation of the negation" formulas in favor of a dialectic premised on *three* simultaneously and variously correlated *moments* – such as the perceived-conceived-lived in space; melody-harmony-rhythm in music; syntactic-paradigmatic-symbolic in language; and so on – that do not lend themselves towards a reconciliation. Contrary to postmodern misconception, there is *nothing* especially spatial about *this* dialectic, which can be just as musical, linguistic, or indeed philosophical (Hegel–Marx–Nietzsche). Intriguing as it is, however, this "three dimensional" dialectic still raises a question, not about Schmid's unrivaled exegesis of it, but about Lefebvre's own judgment. For the whole triadic operation makes sense only to the extent the dialectical methods of Hegel or Marx can be captured in such simple formulas, rather than as more open-ended attempts to theorize socio-historical *totality* and its diverse forms of *mediation*. The "thesis-antithesis-synthesis" formula, foreign to Hegel himself, belongs to one widespread but limited interpretation that is most attractive to detractors of dialectics ranging from Karl Popper to Gilles Deleuze; the same may be said about "affirmation-negation-negation of the negation," which in any case is more Sartrean than Marxist. As Lefebvre of all people should know better than most of us, the dialectic ought to follow formulas only as much as does the reality it engages; and its best practitioners proceed not formulaically but negatively, towards open totality by way of manifold mediations, rather like Adorno and Fredric Jameson, or indeed, *The Production of Space*. A way out of such dialectical confusions may indeed demand taking Lefebvre at not so much his word as his work.

STATE AND REVOLUTION

A basic insight in Lefebvre's spatial thought revolves around the role of the state in reproducing the relations of late-capitalist production at an expanded, worldwide scale. In tackling this question of the "survival of capitalism" as a socio-spatial process, Lefebvre offers yet another striking contribution to radical thought by proposing a new conception of the state, especially in his four-volume essay *De l'État* (1976–1978), which remains the least studied major area of his scholarship. Following a review of state theories "from Hegel to Mao via Stalin," this work demonstrates the value of studying the state as the dominant political force producing social space that is itself shaped by such space. In doing so, he adds a nuanced spatial dimension to the Marxist theory of uneven development beyond the classics of Lenin, Trotsky, and Luxemburg; and urbanizes especially the Gramscian concepts of hegemony and "integral state" (state + civil society) to reveal the presence of the state in urban as well as everyday life. "State mode of production" (*le Mode de production Étatique*), "state-space" (*l'espace étatique*) and *mondialisation* ("becoming worldwide") rank among the leading concepts that Lefebvre mobilizes to theorize the state as a relatively autonomous condensation of power and form of rationality combining with capital in a relentless will to *produce* and *grow*, while anticipating key geo-political-economic developments of late capitalism. Among the latter is a distinctly oppressive socio-spatial relation, as noted by Lefebvre in *The Survival of Capitalism* (1973[2002]):

> Having become political, social space is on the one hand centralised and fixed in a political centrality, and on the other hand specialized and parcelled out. The state determines and congeals the decision-making centres. At the same time, space is distributed into peripheries which are hierarchised in relation to the centres; it is atomised. Colonisation, which like industrial production and consumption was formerly localised, is made general. Around the centres there are nothing but subjected, exploited and dependent spaces: neo-colonial spaces. (84–85)

Centrality for Lefebvre is the essential form of both the state and the urban. Understood dialectically, it leads to the question of center-periphery relations; and this in turn yields a new perspective on colonialism as the *modus operandi* of socio-spatial power in our era of postcolonial imperialism, especially at the scale of the city, which now serves as the main instrument for globalizing uneven development. Lefebvre's view of socialism also emerges from this prognosis of centrality, with reference to the Marxist and Leninist concept of the "withering away of the state," as articulated in his advocacy for *autogestion*: self-management. This term reignites for the struggle against late capitalism Marx's classical conception of radical socialist democracy worked out in his political writings – from the "Critique of Hegel's

Philosophy of Right" (1843) to *Critique of the Gotha Program* (1875) – but since abandoned by state socialism, for which Lefebvre credits Ferdinand Lassalle, calling him a "Hegelian who thought he was a Marxist." Warning against co-optation, and resisting formulaic definitions, Lefebvre saw *autogestion* as not a condition, but the name for a struggle. In his essay "Theoretical Problems of *Autogestion*" (1966), Lefebvre had already pointed out the stakes of this struggle "to constitute itself as a power which is not that of the State" (147).

> We must never forget that society constitutes a whole and does not consist of a sum of elementary units. Even radicalized, an *autogestion* that only organized itself into partial unities, without achieving globality (*le global*), would be destined to failure…. The State of *autogestion*, which is to say that State at whose core *autogestion* is raised to power, can only be a State that is withering away. Consequently, the party of *autogestion* can only be a party that leads politics towards its termination and the end of politics, beyond political democracy…. Only through *autogestion* can the members of a free association take control over their own life, in such a way that it becomes their work (*oeuvre*). This is also called appropriation, de-alienation. (150)

TOTALITY

The revolution will be total, or not at all. This conviction on Lefebvre's part explains his unique commitment to the concept of *totality*. And the frequency with which he invokes it signals arguably his most profound *and* undervalued gift to Marxism: a new theory of totality. Lefebvre's concept of totality emerges from the totality of his work, as we consider the *unity* of his three major thematic innovations: the everyday, the urban, and the state. Each of these refers to the other two in their mediated relations, such that together they form three *levels* of a triadic socio-spatial totality. To wit: the traditional concepts of mediation in Marxist theories of totality involve a view of society as a systemic whole comprised of analytically distinct levels, as does Lefebvre's, but the former understand these with reference to some variation of Marx's "base-superstructure" dialectic. Lefebvre proposes – most succinctly in the "Levels and Dimensions" chapter of *The Urban Revolution* – a promising alternative. His totality has three levels of socio-spatial reality: at the "top" reigns the *global level* of the state (neo-dirigisme) and capital (neo-liberalism), consisting of the most abstract and universal forces of the social order; in the "middle" sits the *urban level*, serving as the "mixed" and "mediating" level between the top and the bottom levels; and at the "bottom" lies the *level of everyday life* (sometimes called the level of "habiting" or "the private," when Lefebvre speaks in Heideggerian). Whenever the alienating rationality of the "bureaucratic society of controlled consumption" rules the world, the global level of this social totality projects its logic onto the urban level, which introjects it and then injects itself into the level of everyday life. But for Lefebvre here operates also a dis-alienating counter-rationality springing up from everyday life, capable of projecting itself upwards, through the urban level, onto the global level. The mediating urban level – where opposed rationalities from the global and the everyday clash – assumes therefore decisive political import. Indeed, the revolution for Lefebvre is premised precisely on the prospect of the everyday acting upon the urban, and the urban upon the global. A revolution is possible, that is, only if "the level of the everyday and the level of the historical can interact" (*CEL* II: 119–120). Hence the essence of Lefebvre's fundamental contribution to radical thought: there can be no socialist revolution without an urban revolution, no urban revolution without a socialist revolution, and neither without a revolution in everyday life.

WHITHER LEFEBVRE?

Quoting Hegel from memory in German, Lefebvre once claimed that the "familiar is not necessarily the known … ('Was ist bekannt ist nicht erkannt' [sic])" (*CEL* I: 15). (What Lefebvre was recalling from Hegel's "Preface" to his *Phenomenology* reads: "Das Bekannte überhaupt ist darum, weil es *bekannt* ist, nicht *erkannt*"; just because it is familiar, the familiar is not known.) The point is well taken, although Lefebvre could not have realized how presciently he was describing in these words his own fate in the Anglo-American academy. But how could he be both popular and unknown? Several explanations offer themselves, some of which have something to do with the idiosyncratic style and the sheer variety of his writings. Anglo-American academic habits of reading, typically organized by sampling bits and pieces of different authors rather than sustained engagement with their oeuvres, militate against wholistic understanding, especially for such a wide-ranging writer as Lefebvre. In the English speaking world, where Lefebvre is mostly understood as a student of space, initial readings of his work were skewed by the two theoretical orientations dominant in post-May 1968 urban studies: political economy in the 1970s and postmodernism in the 1990s. Neither was well disposed to appreciate the scope and nature of Lefebvre's radical intervention. In critical theory more generally, his critique of everyday life was respectfully noted, but overshadowed by the deconstructed Frankfurt School, the decommunized Gramsci, and the mystified Benjamin of postmodern cultural studies. The early works on Hegel, Marx, and dialectics were also effectively eclipsed by the towering presence of Lukács and Sartre in the Western Marxist view of the world, before being overtaken in the 1960s by Althusser. Lefebvre's reckless philosophical eclecticism also contributed to his unjust marginalization within the political tradition he was committed to rejuvenating: Marxism. His status within Nietzsche or Heidegger scholarship by comparison is virtually and justifiably non-existent. As Geoffrey Waite aptly notes in his polemic "Lefebvre without Heidegger" (2008), "Lefebvre was a sometimes avid and always mediocre and careless reader of Heidegger," who "did not need to be a careful reader for his productive appropriations" (95). Nietzsche and Heidegger featured provocatively in Lefebvre's work, yes, but largely to furnish a dimension of poesy in his critique of statist and capitalist rationality, as an occasional addition rather than an alternative to his Hegelian–Marxist humanism. What, then, are the present prospects for his critique of alienation, and his call for the right to the city and self-management? Lefebvre will not protest if we leave the last word on this question to those engaged in radical *praxis* – the struggle to wrest a properly human world from the inhuman Planet of Slums in the Age of Empire, which may yet stretch his work to new frontiers, just as he did Marx's.

Reader's Guide to Henri Lefebvre

Among book-length studies in English, Andy Merrifield's *Henri Lefebvre: A Critical Introduction* (2006) brings the reader closest to Lefebvre the political animal while making him relevant to radical politics today; whereas Stuart Elden's *Understanding Henri Lefebvre: Theory and the Possible* (2004) offers the most comprehensive intellectual-historical survey. *Space, Difference, Everyday Life: Reading Henri Lefebvre* edited by K. Goonewardena, S. Kipfer, R. Milgrom and C. Schmid (2008) includes essays by more than a dozen writers on most of his major concepts, informed by French and German literature in addition to earlier English scholarship. Merrifield's (2009) review essay "The Whole and the Rest: Remi Hess and *les lefebvriens français*" offers a useful survey of recent French writings on Lefebvre. Lefebvre is sometimes, not always, the best guide to his work; and on certain topics there is no better alternative to reading his own words. On everyday life, the reader may begin with the three volumes of *Critique of Everyday Life*; on space and the city, *Writings on Cities* and *The Urban Revolution* are the best starting points, before tackling *The Production of Space*; on the state, the collection superbly edited by Neil Brenner and Stuart Elden, *State, Space, World* is the place to begin. Lefebvre's *Dialectical Materialism* and *The Sociology of Marx* also offer excellent points of entry into his oeuvre. An exemplary reader of Lefebvre, Kristin Ross provides a fine lesson in extending his thought into new areas of research such as colonialism, gender, and popular culture in *Fast Cars, Clean Bodies* (1995).

Acknowledgments

I thank Stefan Kipfer and Andrew Shmuely for their help with this chapter.

Bibliography

Writings of Henri Lefebvre

An adequate list of Lefebvre's publications in forms other than books exceeds the space limitations here; but readers can find bibliographies of them in R. Shields, *Lefebvre, Love and Struggle: Spatial Dialectics* (London: Routledge, 1999) and S. Elden, *Understanding Henri Lefebvre: Theory and the Possible* (New York: Continuum, 2004).

1934 (with N. Guterman). *Morceaux choisis de Karl Marx*. Paris: Gallimard.

1936[1999] (with N. Guterman). *La conscience mystifée*, 2nd edn. Paris: Éditions Syllepse.

1937[1988]. *Le nationalisme contre les nations*, 2nd edn. Paris: Méridiens Klincksieck.

1938 (with N. Guterman). *G. W. F. Hegel, Morceaux choisis*. Paris: Gallimard.

1938 (with N. Guterman). *Cahiers de Lénine sur la dialectique de Hegel*. Paris: Gallimard.

1938. *Hitler au pouvoir, les enseigements de cinq années de fascisme en Allemagne*. Paris: Bureau d'Éditions.

1939. *Nietzsche*. Paris: Éditions Sociales Internationales.

1939[2009]. *Le matérialisme dialectique*. Paris: Alcan. Trans. by J. Sturrock, *Dialectical Materialism*, Preface by S. Kipfer. Minneapolis: University of Minnesota Press.

1946[2001]. *L'existentialisme*, 2nd edn. Paris: Anthropos.

1947[1969]. *Logique formelle, logique dialectique*, 2nd edn. Paris: Anthropos.

1947. *Descartes*. Paris: Éditions Hier et Aujourd'hui.

1947. *Marx 1818–1883*. Genève-Paris: Trois Collines.

1947. *Pour connaître la pensée de Karl Marx*. Paris: Bordas.

1947[1958]. *Critique de la vie quotidienne I: Introduction*, 2nd edn (with new foreword). Paris: L'Arche (1991, trans. by J. Moore, *Critique of Everyday Life Volume I: Introduction*. London: Verso).

1948. *Le marxisme*. Paris: Presses Universitaires de France.

1949[1983]. *Diderot ou les affirmations fondamentales du materialisme*, 2nd edn. Paris: L'Arche.

1949. *Pascal: Tome Premier*. Paris: Nagel.

1949. Autocritique: contribution à l'effort d'éclaircissement idéologique. *La nouvelle critique*, 4: 41–57.

1953[2001]. *Contribution à l'esthétique*, 2nd edn. Paris: Anthropos.

1954. *Pascal*: Tome Deux. Paris: Nagel.

1955[1970]. *Musset*, 2nd edn. Paris: L'Arche.

1955[2001]. *Rabelais*, 2nd edn. Paris: Anthropos.

1956. *Pignon*. Paris: Édition Falaise.

1957. *Pour connaître la pensée de Lénin*. Paris: Bordas.

1958[1960]. *Problèmes actuels du marxisme*, 2nd edn. Paris: PUF.

1959[1989]. *La somme et le reste*, 3rd edn. Paris: Méridiens Klincksieck.

1961. *Critique de la vie quotidienne II: Fondements d'une sociologie de la quotidienneté*. Paris: L'Arche (2002, trans. by J. Moore, *Critique of Everyday Life Volume II: Foundations for a Sociology of the Everyday*. London: Verso).

1962. *Introduction à la modernité: Préludes*. Paris: Les Éditions de Minuit (1995, trans. by J. Moore, *Introduction to Modernity: Twelve Preludes*. London: Verso).

1963. *La vallée de Campan: Étude de sociologie rurale*. Paris: PUF.

1963 (with N. Guterman). *Karl Marx: Oeuvres choisis*, tome I. Paris: Gallimard.

1964. *Marx*. Paris: Gallimard.

1964. *Allemagne*. Paris: Braun & Cie.

1965. *La proclamation de la commune*. Paris: Gallimard.

1965[2001]. *Métaphilosophie*, 2nd edn. Paris: Éditions Syllepse.

1965[2000]. *Pyrénées*, 2nd edn. Pau: Cairn.

1966. *Le langage at la société*. Paris: Gallimard.

1966. *Sociologie de Marx*. Paris: PUF (1982, trans. by N. Guterman, *The Sociology of Marx*, with a new preface. New York: Columbia University Press).

1966[2009]. Theorectical problems of *Autogestion*. In H. Lefebvre, *State, Space, World* (eds) N. Brenner and S. Elden. Minneapolis: University of Minnesota Press, pp. 138–152.

1966 (with N. Guterman). *Karl Marx: Oeuvres choisis*, tome II. Paris: Gallimard.

1967. *Position: Contre les technocrates en finir avec l'humanité-fiction*. Paris: Gonthier.

1968. *La droit à la ville*. Paris: Anthropos. (1996, trans. by E. Kofman and E. Lebas, The right to the city. In Henri Lefebvre, *Writings on Cities* edited by E. Kofman and E. Lebas. Oxford: Blackwell, pp. 63–181).

1968. *La vie quotidienne dans le monde moderne*. Paris: Gallimard (1971, trans. by S. Rabonovitch, *Everyday Life in the Modern World*. Harmondsworth: Allen Lane).

1968[1998]. *L'irruption de Nanterre au sommet*, 2nd edn. Paris: Éditions Syllepse (1969, trans. by A. Ehrenfeld, *The Explosion: Marxism and the French Upheaval*. New York: Monthly Review Press).

1970. *Du rural à l'urbaine*. Paris: Anthropos.

1970. *La fin de l'histoire*. Paris: Les Éditions de Minuit.

1970. *La manifeste différentialiste*. Paris: Gallimard.

1970[2003]. *La révolution urbaine*. Paris: Gallimard. Trans. by R. Bononno, *The Urban Revolution*, Foreword by N. Smith. Minneapolis: University of Minnesota Press.

1971. *Au-delà du structuralisme*. Paris: Anthropos.

1971. *Vers le cybernanthrope*. Paris: Denoël/Gonthier.

1972[2000]. *Espace et politique: La droit à la ville II*, 2nd edn. Paris: Anthropos.

1972. *La pensée marxiste et la ville*. Paris: Casterman.

1972. *Trois texte pour le théâtre*. Paris: Anthropos.

1973[2002]. *La survie du capitalisme: La re-production des rapports de production*, 3rd edn. Paris: Anthropos. Trans. and abridged by F. Bryant, *The Survival of Capitalism*. London: Allison & Busby, 1976.

1973 (with P. Fougeyrollas). *Le jeu de Kostas Axelos*. Paris: Fata Morgana.

1974. *La production de l'espace*. Paris: Anthropos (1991, trans. by D. Nicholson-Smith, *The Production of Space*. Oxford: Blackwell).

1975. *Actualité de Fourier: Colloque d'Arcs-et-Senans sous la direction de Henri Lefebvre*. Paris: Anthropos.

1975. *Hegel, Marx, Nietzsche ou le royaume des ombres*. Paris: Anthropos.

1975. *Le temps de méprises*. Paris: Stock.

1975. *L'idéologie structuraliste*. Paris: Anthropos.

1976–1978. *De l'État*, 4 vols. Paris: UGE.

1978 (with C. Régulier). *La révolution n'est plus ce qu'elle était*. Hallier: Éditions Libres.

1980. *La présence et l'absence: Contribution à la théorie des représentations*. Paris: Casterman.

1980. *Une pensée devenue monde: Faut-il abandonner Marx?* Paris: Fayard.

1981. *Critique de la vie quotidienne III: De la modernité au modernisme (Pour une métaphilosophie du quotidienne)*. Paris: L'Arche (2005, trans. by G. Elliott, *Critique of Everyday Life Volume 3: From Modernity to Modernism (Towards a Metaphilosophy of Daily Life)*, Preface by M. Tebitsch. London: Verso).

1985. *Qu'est-ce que penser?* Paris: Publisad.

1986. *Le retour de la dialectique: 12 mots clefs*. Paris: Messidor/Éditions Sociales.

1986 (with P. Tort). *Lukács 1955* and *Être marxiste aujourd'hui*. Paris: Aubier.

1987. The everyday and everydayness. *Yale French Studies*, 73: 7–11.

1990 (with Navarrenx de Le Group). *Du contrat de citiyenneté*. Paris: Éditions Sociales.

1991 (with F. Combes and P. Latour). *Conversation avec Henri Lefebvre*. Paris: Messidor.

1992. *Éléments de rythmanalyse: Introduction à la connaissance de rythmes*. Paris: Éditions Syllepse 2004 (trans. by S. Elden and G. Moore, Elements of rhythmanalysis: Introduction to the understanding of rhythms. In H. Lefebvre, *Rhythmanalysis: Space, Time and Everyday Life*, edited by S. Elden. London: Continuum, pp. 1–69).

1996. *Writings on Cities* (eds) E. Kofman and E. Lebas. Oxford: Blackwell.

1997 (with K. Ross). Lefebvre on the Situationists: An interview. *October*, 79: 69–83.

2002. *Méthodologie des sciences: Un inédit*. Paris: Anthropos.

2003. *Key Writings* (eds) S. Elden, E. Kofman and E. Lebas. London: Continuum.

2007. *Le cœur ouvert*. Navarrenx: Cercle Historique de l'Arribère.

2009. *State, Space, World: Selected Essays* (eds) N. Brenner and S. Elden. Minneapolis: University of Minnesota Press.

Further Reading

Anderson, P. (1976) *Considerations on Western Marxism*. London: Verso.

Anderson, P. (1984) *In the Tracks of Historical Materialism*. Chicago: University of Chicago Press.

Debord, G. (1961) *Perspectives for Conscious Changes in Everyday Life*. Trans. K. Knabb (2006). Bureau of Public Secrets. Available online at www.bopsecrets.org/SI/6.everyday. htm (accessed November 18, 2010).

Debord, G. (1967) *The Society of the Spectacle*. Trans. K. Knabb (2002). Bureau of Public Secrets. Available online at www.bopsecrets.org/SI/debord/index.htm (accessed November 18, 2010).

Elden, S. (2004) *Understanding Henri Lefebvre: Theory and the Possible*. London: Continuum.

Goonewardena, K., Kipfer, S., Milgrom, R., and Schmid, C. (eds) (2008). *Space, Difference, Everyday Life: Reading Henri Lefebvre*. New York: Routledge.

Merrifield, A. (2006) *Henri Lefebvre: A Critical Introduction*. London: Routledge.

Merrifield, A. (2009) The whole and the rest: Remi Hess and *les lefebvriens français. Society and Space*, 27: 936–949.

Osborne, P. (1995) *The Politics of Time: Modernity and Avant-Garde*. London: Verso.

Ross, K. (1995) *Fast Cars, Clean Bodies*. Cambridge, MA: The MIT Press.

Ross, K. (2002) *May '68 and its Afterlives*. Chicago: University of Chicago Press.

Schmid, C. (2008) Henry Lefebvre's theory of the production of space. In K. Goonewardena, S. Kipfer, R. Milgrom and C. Schmid (eds) *Space, Difference, Everyday Life: Reading Henri Lefebvre*. New York: Routledge, pp. 27–45.

Waite, G. (2008) Lefebvre without Heidegger: Left Heideggerianism *qua Contradictio in Adiecto*. In K. Goonewardena, S. Kipfer, R. Milgrom and C. Schmid (eds) *Space, Difference, Everyday Life: Reading Henri Lefebvre*. New York: Routledge, pp. 94–114.

3

Robert K. Merton

CHARLES CROTHERS

THE PERSON

Robert Merton was born on July 4, 1910 to working class Jewish immigrant parents in Philadelphia. His family included an older sister, and while close to her and his mother, Merton's relationship with his father was distant. He was educated at the South Philadelphia High School for Boys, and became a frequent visitor of the nearby Andrew Carnegie Library, The Academy of Music, Central Library, Museum of Arts, and other cultural and educational centers. His father scraped out a living as a shop-keeper, carpenter, and then truck driver. From a young age he was reading in all fields, particularly biography, and by twelve he became a magician who performed for money at neighborhood social functions. Indeed, during his teenage years he changed his name from Meyer R. Schkolnick to Robert King Merton which was considered a more appropriate "stage name."

In 1927 he won a scholarship to Temple University in Philadelphia where he first studied philosophy, then taking a major in sociology under the influence of George Simpson who excited interests in empirical investigation. In 1931 he won a fellow-ship to Harvard University for graduate work in sociology (the first Temple student ever to go to Harvard). He went to study under Pitirim Sorokin, and in 1932 he gained a Harvard MA. He began his doctoral dissertation completing in 1935, and in 1936 became an instructor and tutor at Harvard spending several years working on a range of topics which provided a platform for much of his later work and completed his "professional socialization."

In 1939 he was appointed as associate professor and then professor at Tulane University, New Orleans serving as chairman of the department. In 1941 he became assistant professor at Columbia University in New York at the invitation of prominent social theorist Robert McIver. Merton's "joint" appointment to the Columbia

The Wiley-Blackwell Companion to Major Social Theorists, First Edition.
Edited by George Ritzer and Jeffrey Stepnisky.
© 2011 Blackwell Publishing Ltd. Published 2011 by Blackwell Publishing Ltd.

faculty with Paul Lazarsfeld was a fortunate accident. When a full professorship fell vacant in 1940 the department was split between Robert Lynd and Robert McIver and could not agree on a nomination. A compromise was effected by the University President (Nicholas Murray Butler) who split the position into two assistant professorships – one emphasizing social theory and the other empirical research. Merton was appointed to the former and Lazarsfeld to the latter. For a while the two had little contact, but then followed an intellectual seduction. Lazarsfeld invited Merton and his wife to dinner but diverted him that evening to assist with his research enterprise on audience-testing a government pre-war morale-building radio program and thus began a very long and close collaboration.

Merton was subsequently promoted to associate professor (1944) and full professor (1947), succeeding Lazarsfeld as Chairman of the department in 1961 (and on and off for a number of years) and often deputizing for him as Associate Director of the Bureau of Applied Social Research (BASR: which was strongly associated with the department) from 1942 through to 1971 when the BASR was closed (eventually to be replaced by successive research centers). In 1963 he was appointed Franklin Henry Giddings Professor of Sociology, in 1974 acquired the rank of "University Professor," and from 1979 was "Special Service Professor" and "University Professor Emeritus." A key advisor from 1966 to 1989, Merton was Russell Sage Foundation's first "Foundation Scholar."

He died in 2004 of a multiple attack from several cancers. He was survived by his (second) wife (sociologist Harriet Zuckerman), three children (one of whom is Economics Nobel Prize winner Robert C. Merton), nine grandchildren and nine great-grandchildren.

Intellectual Career

Merton's scholarly output was considerable and much of his work had a complex publishing history. (A useful synopsis of Merton's approach to writing is provided by Coser, 1975: 91). Particular characteristics of his work included close and active editing of other scholars' writings, active book reviewing and a love of words and language which led to the creation (or redeployment) of many widely used evocative neologisms. The fame of his teaching was widespread and has been written of in many accounts (e.g. Caplovitz, 1977: 142; see also Marsh, 2010). He disliked organizational involvements but nevertheless played a prominent part in professional activities.

Merton's research and writing program can be broadly divided into five phases, which approximate to the various decades of his academic working life and to the decades of his own age-periods. However, as with any such schema it is used only to provide a general framework for understanding the progression of his interests, and the relationships amongst its various phases.

In his undergraduate days Merton became well schooled in then-contemporary American sociology. At Harvard this was extended by intensive reading of European sociology, including a systematic review of French sociology which he wrote up in his first publications (Merton, 1934a, 1934b).

On the empirical side he was involved in a series of research studies that included work on Simpson's research study on references to "Negroes" over some decades of

Philadelphia newspapers, and then at Harvard fieldwork amongst the homeless of Boston, and several laborious library projects developing long-term quantitative indicators of changes in science, technology, and medicine. His own doctoral work involved quantitative analyses of shifts in the foci of scientific interests, shifts in the occupational interests of the English elite which involved hand-tabulating six thousand biographies from the *Dictionary of National Biography*, and the experiments recorded in the *Transactions of the Royal Society*.

His theoretical work, especially in the sociology of deviance and also race relations, largely flowed out of teaching tasks and the developing theoretical concerns of the small sociological community at Harvard (see Nichols, 2010). This work was published as the "Unanticipated Consequences of Purposive Social Action" (1936) and the essay on "Social Structure and Anomie" (1938b). These essays were important for sketching out Merton's more general sociological stance, and had a far-reaching impact within sociology. Later in the 1930s his theoretical attention focused on a more formal "functional approach" and he never adequately reconnected with his earlier work. The core of the anomie theory is the subversive view that capitalism breeds systematic failure; that in societies which highly stress achievement goals and yet where there is class-differentiated limitations in means for obtaining success, there can be structural pressure on those with more limited resources to indulge in "innovative" (and often illegal) means to achievement.

The "second" phase of work in the 1940s included several empirically based studies arising from research projects carried out in the Bureau of Applied Social Research at Columbia University, especially in the areas of morale and propaganda studies, media sociology, and the sociology of housing. Merton also participated in an extensive post-war review of various empirical studies sponsored by the American army during the Second World War, teasing out and developing Herbert Hyman's concept of "reference groups." His methodological interests during this period included fieldwork in community settings and the methodology of "the focused interview" (1956) that was the platform on which the very widely used "focus group" methodology was later built by the market and social research industries. His theoretical interests included reference-group behavior and the social processes of friendship formation.

In addition to this work on research projects, Merton assembled the various writings that constituted his composite theoretical and methodological stance within sociology and which formed the themes of *Social Theory and Social Structure* ([1949]1968). This included work on the methodology of functional analysis and the interplay of theory and research, and the selection and arrangement of much of the array of theoretical writing, commentary, and empirical studies he had produced to that point.

The "third phase" in the 1950s included a broad program which had a higher theoretical emphasis and less explicit methodological concerns than his previous set of work. A key piece in this empirical program was a comparative study of medical education at Cornell University and several other medical schools. During this period Merton also continued his work on updating and extending several of the theoretical essays laid down previously in a series of "continuities" which were included in a much-expanded version of *Social Theory and Social Structure* published in 1957. Merton developed his "role-set" theory. Work on the properties of groups was facilitated by examination of this area by a seminar of graduate students with a reading program on Simmel's writings.

Merton also played an important role (flowing from his presidency of the American Sociological Association) in developing two major texts that brought together much of then-contemporary American sociology. These were *Sociology Today* (1959) which comprised a set of some two dozen chapters each of which attempted to lay out the significant sociological analytical problems and the state of the art in addressing these concerns for each of a range of specialist areas, and *Contemporary Social Problems* ([1961]1976) which reviewed the relationship between social issues and sociological knowledge.

Merton's "fourth" phase of work, beginning in the late 1950s and extending through the 1960s, is marked by a noticeable restriction in the span of his writing interests and a concentrated return to his "first love" – the sociology of science. This return was staged on the highly visible occasion of his presidential address to ASA (1957). Whereas his earlier (1930s) work in the sociology of science had focused on the interrelationship between the social institution of science and other areas of society, Merton's later sociology of science centered on the key internal features of science as an autonomous institution. Central to his image of science was the idea that scientific discoveries were, in principle at least, *multiples* (likely to be uncovered by any of many competitors) and that the reward systems of science impel scientists to seek recognition for their discoveries by others in forms such as citations or eponymous labels or awards which acknowledge intellectual debts. As a result of the fateful conjunction of these two principles, scientists expend energy in attempting to secure their property rights of public recognition of their discoveries – if necessary, through occasionally clamorous "priority disputes." If the pressure for discovery is too great, social pathologies (e.g. fraud, plagiarism) may result.

Much of his work from the late 1950s was in the Columbia Program in the Sociology of Science supported by the National Science Foundation with his colleagues including Harriet Zuckerman, Stephen Cole, Jonathan Cole, and later Thomas Gieryn. This program included empirical studies of the evaluation systems across several scientific disciplines of age-structures and the differential effects of codification in science.

Merton also published an empirical study (couched in a delightful Shandean mode) – *On the Shoulders of Giants* (1965) – of the historical trajectory of the uses of this metaphor over time. This has some links to his more formal analysis of science as an institution as the "Shoulders of Giants" aphorism is a key metaphor through which the scientific norm of humility is expressed; but the main message of the book emphasizes the non-linear development of scientific concepts. At much the same time he drafted with Elinor Barber a book on the travels and adventures of *Serendipity* – but not published for another 40 years (2004).

During this period Merton also attempted to come to terms with broadening streams in the development of sociology – both through his sociological accounts of social theory and through theoretical restatements in which he signaled the importance of recognizing the "sociological ambivalences" that are generated by social structures (1976: essay first published in 1963). Alongside these two major foci of interest there continued a stream of tasks associated with being a prominent figure in American sociology, especially providing commentaries, forewords, and updating previously published material. A third, and final, edition of *Social Theory and Social Structure* was produced in 1968.

The "fifth" phase of the 1970s, and through to his death, covered much in a "reminiscent" vein – often in the form of obituary material for colleagues he had outlived – together with some rearguard action defending parts of his earlier writings against recent criticism, and some writing tasks which accompanied his "elder statesman" position. During this period there was a further flowering of Merton's contributions to "*belles lettres*" as a humanist. Theoretical interests continued, with Merton signaling a change in emphasis from a preferred "functional analysis" mode to a "structural analysis" approach (1976), and developing his work on "socially expected durations" (1984). This period saw the piecemeal development of "Sociological Semantics" as a research program (cf. Zuckerman in Calhoun, 2010) that "takes words, phrases, aphorisms, slogans and other linguistic forms as subjects of inquiry."

Did Merton notably change his theoretical approach in tune with any phases in his research trajectory? For the most part, there was relatively little change, since his basic sociological orientation was clearly laid down during the first decade of his writing and its basic features can be discovered within his early set of essays and investigations. However, there have been changing emphases: an earlier interest in "action" followed by the self-conscious concern with functional analysis which dominated his "1940s" period, while by the "1970s" he worked in a "structuralist" mode. Another change seems to have been the social psychological approaches more often involved with Bureau of Applied Social Research studies in the "1940s" and were complemented in several essays from the "1950s" onwards with a more conscious emphasis on "social structure." Although much of his more humanist writings was crafted in the late 1950s, this style of his writing only fully emerged much later in his intellectual career alongside his writings on sociological semantics.

SOCIAL AND INTELLECTUAL CONTEXTS

Any attempts to reduce Merton's writings as directly being "read off" his social context would not get very far, despite the conceit of various "strong programs" in sociology that even the content of ideas is shaped by society (Merton always resiled from these). Indeed, his very settled career at Columbia insulated him from too much direct outside influence. Yet, the imprint of several successive societal periods on his intellectual life is visible including the Depression, the Second World War and totalitarianism, the post-war economic boom with the period of university expansion and Cold War, the student rebellions of the 1960s and 1970s, and the collapse of communism. Although Merton always kept a clear eye on the long-term future of sociology, some of his work directly linked to ongoing events and others were discussions of how societal events influenced sociology. Clearly the Depression affected him and led to short-term research as well as reinforcing a long-term concern with social justice. Merton threw himself into war-related social research work and into assessing possibilities in post-war social reconstitutions and especially civil rights. However, later in his life he was more removed, keeping a distance from the campus troubles of the late 1960s and engaging little with intellectual and social movements emanating from younger generations and imported from Europe.

Merton has established his own official intellectual lineage in the acknowledg-
ments to his *Social Theory and Social Structure* where he thanks:

- Charles Hopkins (his brother-in-law, friend, and teacher of life-skills);
- George Simpson (his undergraduate teacher for introducing him to sociology);
- Pitirim Sorokin (his graduate teacher for bringing the range of European social
  thinking to his attention);
- George Sarton (historian of science and early sponsor for close assistance with
  his historical studies of science);
- Talcott Parsons (graduate advisor and colleague for his enthusiastic pursuit of
  theoretical concerns);
- Paul Lazarsfeld (Columbia colleague for his long-term close engagement with
  Merton over the analytical issues of formulating a sociology that interfaced
  theory and research).

But these are only his "masters-at-close-range." Much of Merton's concern was,
as Coser puts it a "self-conscious effort to ransack the whole house of European
erudition" (1975: 89). Whereas Parsons focused clearly and deeply on a very limited
range of European theorists, Merton drew very widely but less systematically on a
very wide array of European social theorists, many minor, but including several
neglected by Parsons. Merton chose Durkheim as a role model, especially in respect
to the strategy of following an open-ended train of inquiry across a scatter of topics.
Durkheim was a major source in the development of the anomie theory of deviance,
the functional mode of analysis, the emphasis on the facticity of structures and the
importance of wider cultural categories, and more generally Merton's methodological approach. He chose Weber in developing the "Merton hypothesis" of the religious impetus to the development of seventeenth-century science, in analysis of
bureaucracy, and more generally the interpenetration and autonomy of different
social spheres and the importance of interpretive aspects; Mannheim in sociology of
knowledge; Simmel for work on group properties; and Marx for a concern about the
operation of class. The ideas of Pareto were exposed through the Henderson seminar
at Harvard, which Merton attended along with Parsons, but these did not attract.
Each was not just written about but actively used and reformulated in developing an
approach to a particular theoretical problem.

Merton's use of earlier American theorists is less marked. Further sources were
Anglo-American social anthropology (Linton, Malinowski and Radcliffe-Brown,
Murdock), contemporary sociology which he closely monitored, and a range of
historians and social critics. Sorokin's notions of culture and immanent cultural
change are used and extended. Chicago influences such as Thomas's "definition of
the situation" were drawn on and Homans's insistence on "bringing men back in"
affirmed. Much extends Parsons's work: there is a similar foundation in terms of
"action theory" and similar analyses of broader structures. Although the "Frankfurt
School in Exile" inhabited the Columbia campus during the early 1940s, and
despite Merton's involvement with Lazarsfeld in advising on the "Authoritarian
Personality" research, there seems to be little direct theoretical influence from them.
Moreover, the rise of European social theorizing in the last decades of the century
was of little interest.

Although Merton's own image of himself was of a lone scholar at work in his study, there were two immediate intellectual contexts which strongly influenced his work. One was the effervescence around sociological thinking in the Harvard situation of the 1930s (see Nichols, 2010) and the other the longer-term dynamics of the Columbia Sociology department (Crothers, 1996).

THEORY

Discipline-building and sociological theory

When Merton began his professional career, sociology in North America was at best empiricist. On the other hand, there was a legacy of broad theory from Continental writers which was far too general to guide more detailed sociological research and too confused with the history of social theory. Merton had a life-long concern to chart out a course that sociology might follow to allow the complexities of social life to be handled rigorously within both qualitative and quantitative frameworks. He had a life-long involvement in empirical projects.

An early methodological contribution was a pairing of short essays that dealt with each side of the interplay between theory and research ("The bearing of sociological theory on empirical research" and "The bearing of empirical research on sociological theory"). The first essay differentiates several conceptions of theory, especially contrasting theory proper with general sociological orientations on the one hand and empirical generalizations and *ad hoc* explanations on the other. In the paired essay, research is seen as initiating, reformulating, deflecting, and clarifying theory. In particular, Merton urges alertness to the possibility of "serendipity" – the unanticipated discovery of theoretically strategic facts. In a later (1968) essay on the "History and Systematics of Social Theory" he indicates the potential for theoretical insights to be gained from (re)reading classical writers and the "humanistic" aspects of sociology. And more generally, in several essays on conflicting and competing approaches in sociology, he pointed out a conception of sociology as a multi-paradigm or theoretically pluralist science in which theories derived from different theoretical approaches can shed *complementary*, rather than *incommensurate*, insights into social phenomena.

The (pre-Kuhn) conceptual device of "paradigms" is advanced to encourage the systematic consolidation of areas of study. Examples are his paradigms for functional analysis in sociology and the sociology of knowledge, and as worked examples ("delimited paradigms") those relating to anomie, intermarriage, and prejudice-discrimination. Paradigms are seen as not just notational devices, but as "logical designs for analysis" which "bring out into the open the array of assumptions, concepts and basic propositions employed in a sociological investigation" (1976: 211) and also as "preliminary efforts to assemble propositional inventions of sociological knowledge" (1976: 211). In particular, a paradigm provides the agenda of problematics in an area.

Within the framework provided by a paradigm Merton was able to show how different theories can *complement* each other. In a comparison of four alternative theories of deviance he ([1961]1976: 31–37) shows how each highlights a particular area of phenomena while leaving other aspects in darkness. While some theories can be combined, others clash or give rise to competing hypotheses and others "talk past each other." For example, the differential deviance generated by anomie-and-opportunity structures explains the original development of deviance whereas labeling theory explains the perpetuation of subsequent deviant careers.

The central methodological precept for which Merton is undoubtedly most famous is his advocacy of "theories of the middle-range." Middle-range theories are distinguished from general sociological orientations. "Such orientations involve broad postulates which indicate *types* of variables which are somehow to be taken into account" (1968: 41–42), and empirical generalizations "an isolated proposition summarizing observed uniformities of relationships between two or more variables" (1968: 149). The key passage was indicated in an address in 1947 and published in 1949 (1968: 39):

> Middle-range theory is principally used in sociology to guide empirical inquiry. ... Middle-range theory involves abstractions, of course, but they are close enough to observed data to be incorporated in propositions that permit empirical testing. Middle-range theories deal with delimited aspects of social phenomena, as is indicated by their labels. One speaks of a theory of reference groups, of social mobility, or role-conflict and of the formation of social norms just as one speaks of a theory of prices, a germ theory of disease, or a kinetic theory of gases.

One outcome of his work was the development of a "theory-construction school" within sociology which stressed the importance of the more formal stating of theories. Foundational to this enterprise was Merton's startling formalized casting of Durkheim's theory of Suicide (1968: 151).

Moreover, Merton was not a great exponent of the "covering law" model and rather, in his own work, preferred to isolate social mechanisms which he saw at work in various areas of social life, for example, conflict between the demands of several statuses might be (partially) handled through consideration of the issues amongst other family members. This has been seen as a forerunner to current methodological interests in the analysis of mechanisms amongst "analytical sociologists" (e.g. Hedstrom and Swedberg, 1998).

Theory

As well as helping to shape the "form" of post-war sociology, Merton had a considerable influence on its "content," and it is to an elucidation of this that this study now turns.

Merton made no claim to providing a "general theory," and some commentators have criticized this (e.g. Bierstedt, 1981). Yet other sociological theorists have made that claim on his behalf and have taken steps to advance this view (e.g. see Clark, 1990; Crothers, 1987; Erikson, 1997; Stinchcombe, 1975; Sztompka, 1986). Needless to say, the following sketch still falls short of reaching any goal for a general theory of sociology, although the possibilities are promising. However, it is one thing to suggest that such a latent theoretical framework exists, and quite a different matter to make this explicit. Help is at hand: Stinchcombe has provided a highly

successful general model of the core social psychological processes or micro-
foundations which brought together key elements common to a range of Merton's
more substantive works (which Merton has endorsed). However, this model needs to
be extended to incorporate more of the cultural and social structural properties
central to Merton's approach.

One immediate difficulty lies in Merton's clear identification with "functional
analysis." Functionalism was originally an approach fashioned by anthropologists
to analyze regularities behind the cultural complexities of non-literate societies,
rather than the earlier theoretical practice of tracing the *evolution* of cultural forms.
Merton was able to take this approach, and to convert it to one suited to the analysis of modern societies. He therefore rejects three postulates usually held to be
"essential" to classical functional analysis (1968: 79–91). This rejection requires
that functional analysis of the consequences of social units for other areas of social
life need to be recognized as:

- multiple,
- specified as either functional or *dys*functional, and
- not inherently tied to a particular form (but rather, units may have alternatives).

It is important to realize that a considerable commitment to structural analysis
was built into his schema and that it differed in major ways from that advanced by
Talcott Parsons.

Over subsequent decades a consensus in sociology steadily grew that functional
explanation in its more simple form was fatally flawed by the fallacious teleological
pseudo-causal mechanism at its heart and the theoretical position was evacuated.
However, it is also widely agreed that the debate helped enormously in clarifying
some of the opportunities and limitations of social theorizing, and that despite its
severe limits, the functional mode of analysis has considerable heuristic advantages.

The Stinchcombe version of the core process of Merton's model centers on variation
between people in their rates of choice amongst alternatives which are structurally
produced and in which the rates of choice loop back to affect the institutional patterns
which had shaped the rates of choice "in the first place." People differ in their rates of
choice amongst structurally given alternatives depending on their location in the social
order. On the one hand, choices are causally structured, and on the other hand, choices
causally influence the development of institutional patterns which structure that choice:
the causal chain goes backwards, and also forwards from the core process. The
key-phrase "choices with institutional consequence" nicely sums this up.

For example, as Merton has shown, scientists are particularly concerned with the
publication of research reports of original investigations, and the institutional pattern of science supports and motivates this. In turn, the importance of open publication rather than secrecy, and the continued availability of journals to publish in, is
enhanced when scientists choose to publish their research work in journals.

Stinchcombe then thickens out this account by identifying three particular ways
through which institutional patterns shape individual choice behavior (through
structurally induced motives, control of information, and sanctions), and also a
causal loop in which the development of "social character" is influenced by choices,
and then in turn affects the ways choices are made.

The first part of Stinchcombe's extension of the core model provides more detail about how Merton's theoretical work explains the linkage between institutional pattern and individual rates of choice. People in different social positions will have different goals or motivations, stemming from some mix of a range of structural sources – the cultural beliefs they have acquired through socialization, reward systems (including the striving after status), seeking to affirm social identities valued by reference groups, and the need to maintain everyday life. Another key mechanism linking institutional pattern and individual choice behavior is the structural governance of information. The availability of information influences the knowledge of the range of choice (as well as, presumably, the person's weighing up of the costs and benefits of each alternative they are aware of). The flow of information may itself be a resource that affects the success in carrying out an activity (and in turn, success reinforces the choice of continuing in that activity). And the application of sanctions (rewards and punishments) is dependent on knowing when and whom to reward or punish. Further, a person's choice behavior may be influenced by the social pressure which others bring to bear on them through their ability to reward or punish the person.

The last component which Stinchcombe adds into the model is a feedback loop involving socially patterned character or personality development. As a result of being placed in a particular social situation (for example, as a bureaucrat – see Merton, 1968), and making repeated similar choices, a particular social character is formed. This is further reinforced as it influences the style in which choice behavior is carried out, which limits a person's exposure to alternative sources of information or social pressure. Thus a style of operating becomes cemented in.

But, Stinchcombe's account stresses processes rather than structures. He is rather too ready to show how Merton sees "social structures" as working, and not careful enough to show how Merton sees the components and organization of the "social structure" in the first place. Alongside this is an overemphasis on micro-sociological or social psychological components rather than structural levels of analysis. Rather, Merton is a theorist particularly concerned with the essential properties and types of social structure, as well as the detailed ways in which they work. Where the biggest departure from Stinchcombe's model is required is in building forward from choices into Merton's views of the social environment shaping those choices. The social environment needs to be subdivided into "cultural structure" and "social structure." Merton used these terms to represent quite different aspects of social reality. Broadly, cultural structure consists in the shared ideas which shape people's images of social reality and provide motivations and ideological justifications for institutional patterns and cultural products. On the other hand, social structures are patterned social relationships amongst people. Social structures mediate between cultural patterns and the behavior patterns resulting from choices. Whereas the cultural structure sets goals (albeit selectively reinforced by social arrangements), social structure provides the means for making and implementing choices. As Merton points out, there may be marked disjunctions between aspects of cultural and social structures, and congruence should not be assumed. A related aspect of many of Merton's analyses which Stinchcombe under-emphasizes is the three-layer model in which macro-structures, especially social class, are seen as "working behind," and through, intermediate social structures to influence social practices.

In his earlier writing, Merton did not give much attention to the micro-contexts of interaction in which people's behavior is set. However, this is explicitly addressed in his later work, and so will be treated as a separate element in the extended model. His more recent theoretical writings featured analysis of "socially expected durations," and this will also receive separate attention.

One set of mechanisms involves the consequences of behavior for the maintenance and change of the institutional structures (which induce and shape the behavior in the first place). Choices and their resultant behavior will have consequences not only for the institutional structures in which they are directly embedded, but also for other institutional structures. An obvious example of this is the "Merton thesis" that in the early development of science, the puritan ethos legitimated a concern with nature and technology. So, "feedback" effects need to be separated from "leakage" effects. Both are likely to be usually unintended and unanticipated although not necessarily.

Components of the model

CULTURAL STRUCTURE   Merton's model of cultural structure is not particularly sophisticated, and is conducted with a very considerable eye to the social consequences of beliefs, or knowledge, or values. This contrasts with more analytical concerns with the internal interrelationships within cultural structures themselves and their impacts which so dominate the attention of French "structuralists," and a variety of other more recent approaches in social theory. Later in life though, Merton worked on the study of sociological semantics, a topic at the core of cultural sociology.

There are several crucial distinctions which Merton deploys in constructing descriptions of cultural structures: especially in terms of different levels of abstractness. Much emphasis is placed on the built-in complexity of normative structures. This can be portrayed as patterns of norms and counter-norms, in which each norm is "balanced" by its opposite, although the two seldom receive equal weighting. Culture is considered to have several levels, with values being more abstract than attitudes. Another distinction is made between the more technical and the more social components of cultural structure, which are likely to have different social effects. The former covers beliefs, knowledge, and values concerning material production and the latter concerns, beliefs, knowledge, and values in relation to social structure.

In several passages, Merton makes interesting suggestions about the interplay between cultural norms and social structures, and in fact most of his analyses feature centrally the implications of cultural values for people's behavior. His early work concerns the puritan impetus towards science, and his later analysis of science the shaping force of the underlying scientific "ethos." An early contribution was suggestions for empirically developing the sociology of knowledge. One particular life-long theme was the implications of falsely held beliefs or self-fulfilling prophecies (and their opposites – suicidal prophecies).

SOCIAL STRUCTURE   Merton has a strongly developed analytical approach to social structure. This is organized around the key concepts of status-set and role-set, but also includes attention to characteristics of membership groups, reference groups, status-sequences, and role-sequences. The partial and multiplex interlocking of statuses and roles and how individuals and collectivities are involved with these can form a complex social architecture, usually fraught with a diversity of tensions as well as synergies. Merton was concerned to show the mechanisms which linked parts of the social structure and especially how conflict and difficulties might be resolved. Embedded within his discussion of reference-group theory Merton attempts to sketch out a sociological analysis of membership groups. This is accomplished through an examination of the characteristics of group membership and through the listing of 26 properties groups are considered to possess.

Merton distinguishes between three different types of social formation – groups, collectivities, and social categories. Social categories are aggregates of people with the same social statuses, the occupants of which are not in social interaction. They have like social characteristics – of sex, age, marital condition, income, and so on – but are not necessarily orientated toward a distinctive and common body of norms. Having like statuses and, consequently, similar interests and values, social categories can be mobilized into collectivities or into groups (1968: 353, 354). Merton also addressed some of the analytical properties associated with organizations, communities and societies, although did not develop well-honed theories relating to these higher levels of social and institutional organization.

In his work on science, Merton also drew attention to the way in which particular clusters of cultural and social life can be bundled into large-scale "institutions" (or institutional areas) which can develop a considerable autonomy in their own right, as well as comprising particular constellations of social arrangements (these points were particularly expounded in Storer's commentary on his work: see Storer's editorial material in Merton, 1973).

INTERACTION CONTEXTS OR MILIEU   Although Merton has never accorded it systematic and explicit attention, an interest in the micro-sociology of interaction is a continual thread throughout his work. For example, in further formulations of his anomie theory (1968: 233–235) Merton makes it very clear that he considers that the interaction context plays a significant role either in amplifying or damping-down the vulnerability of individuals to anomic strain and their likelihood of converting this into deviant behavior. In later commentary, there is often reference to "micro-environments" in which, for example, scientific creativity occurs.

SOCIAL CHARACTER   Personality or character structure is occasionally deployed as an intervening "variable" between cultural and social structures on the one hand and social choices and social practices on the other. There are several examples of Merton including a personality "level of analysis": the bureaucratic personality (1968: 259), leadership capacity (1968: 402, 404), eminent scientists (1973: 458, 459), or even in the propensity to adopt a ritualistic mode of adaptation (1968: 205). But, as a sociologist, Merton rightly shuns close attention to character structure.

SOCIAL CHOICES AND SOCIAL ACTION   At the center of the Mertonian analytical system is the action of individual people (and perhaps sometimes collectivities) in making choices amongst structurally given alternatives. The actor is only partly socially determined in the Mertonian schema, and is conceptualized as having room to maneuver within structurally imposed constraints and opportunities. The flesh-and-blood individual is also recognized as actively "manning" the positions in the social structure and not just determined by these positions. By standing at the center of often-diverse status-sets, the individual "pulls together" the diverse strands and complexities of the social structure. In turn, the impulses and strains affecting an individual are structurally channeled along the lines of the social structure.

The central place of the actor was developed in two discussions – the early treatment in the essay on "The Unanticipated Consequences of Purposive Social Action" (1936) and the more recent recapitulation by Stinchcombe (1975). Merton's essay is concerned to show how objective consequences can arise unbidden from purposive action. One of the major ways in which unanticipated consequences may arise is through limitations to the "existing state of knowledge" on which social action is based. These limitations are barriers to the correct anticipating of consequences, and include ignorance, error, imperious immediacy of interest, basic values, and self-defeating predictions. This model of the actor differs from several alternative options (e.g. Stinchcombe, 1975: 12, 14).

Some social change arises through sub-conscious "drift" as incremental micro-changes eventually give rise to qualitative shifts. But other mechanisms of change can be more directive, such as "social learning" in which accumulated experience of social actors is brought to bear in helping the social structure to operate and to adapt to changing circumstances.

SOCIAL PRACTICES   Choices tend to be embedded within broader strategies. In his essay on Anomie, Merton famously develops a typology of five individual "modes of adaptation" which cover acceptance or rejection of present cultural goals on the one hand, and acceptance or rejection of present institutionalized means for achieving these goals on the other. In addition, he provides a stance of rejection-and-substitution (1968: 41). Cross-tabulating orientation to cultural goals against orientation to institutional means generates a typology in which each cell is then "labeled" as a different "mode of adaptation." Such orientations to various levels of social grouping are very broad types of social choice.

FEEDBACK AND LEAKAGE LOOPS: CONSEQUENCES   Some of Merton's essays have examined mechanisms of social dynamics and change – in general unanticipated (and/or unintended) consequences and specifically the self-fulfilling prophecy, the self-defeating or suicidal prophecy, and at a more institutional level, latent and manifest functions. This part of the Mertonian schema is concerned with how the social practices resulting from social choices fold back to affect structures. In particular, it is one of the more innovative aspects of the ways in which Merton provides a "take" on the agency/structure issue (as it later came to be called). He defines a self-fulfilling prophecy as "a false definition of the situation evoking a new behavior which makes the originally false conception come true" (1968: 477). The examples he offers include the collapse of banks under "runs" and the way in which people in minority groups have often not been allowed access to institutions and then been damned because, instead, they pursued alternatives. The suicidal prophecy involves changing the course of behavior such that the prophecy fails to be brought about. Merton is careful to point out that there are social mechanisms that can intervene in such vicious cycles and that institutional controls are often able to quell rumors and panics that feed at the informal interactional level of operation.

In addition to the feedback effects specified by Merton and others there are what I designate "leakage effects." This is where social practices affect the development of structures other than those which generated the behavior patterns in the first place. The obvious example of this is Merton's hypothesis that the puritan impulse may have led to the increased pursuit of scientific knowledge. Leakage effects are not randomly sprayed around from their source, but are contained by the status-sets that people are simultaneously placed within. Often, however, this leakage effect will be unanticipated and unintended by the actors involved. It is a consequence of the way social structures are complexly organized.

The most obvious way in which consequences affect institutions is through building or collapsing the social support for a particular institution over against its rivals – the structural alternatives. However, the relationship may be more varied than this. For example, as a result of scientists' productivity, scientific work may accumulate into massive flows of articles. The resultant growth may in turn have effects on individual behavior (e.g. the types of literature-citing practices needed by scientists to cope with the volume available).

SOCIAL MECHANISMS   Having provided a conceptual framework for describing the various elements of social structure, Merton then deploys a variety of conceptual frameworks which provide analytical purchase on how the social structure works, and especially, how it connects up with patterns of behavior. These might be broadly referred to as "social mechanisms" which provide various ways in which things are made to happen or social needs and difficulties are overcome (albeit with further follow-on consequences which set in motion further needs or further difficulties; see Hedstrom and Swedberg (1999) for a partially overlapping discussion of social mechanisms).

The best known of these is "reference-group theory." Merton's reference-group theory is an attempt to show the mechanisms through which groups shape the behavior of members. Perhaps the more interesting aspect, which Merton points out, is the way people are influenced by groups they are not members of, and even by non-groups (i.e. by fictional or virtual groups). What is sociologically problematic is not so much that individuals are affected by social frames of reference, but *which* particular frames of reference are relevant in influencing them.

Another feature of Merton's conception of social structure is that it is a framework around which there is built social distributions of resources. He specifically notes authority, power, influence, and prestige (1976: 124) and more generally means for achieving legitimate or illegitimate goals. The concept of "opportunity-structure" is a general term which points to these social distributions of resources, and the choices they make available or close down. Because it can be pushed and pulled by various social actors "opportunity structures" themselves can change over time, often then altering the possibilities different people have for accessing resources. Another key concept is that of "accumulated (dis)advantage" – sometimes referred to as the "Matthew Effect." There is a tendency for those with initial advantage to cumulatively build on (and extend) that advantage, and vice versa.

An important property of social structures is the extent to which they shape information flows. As Stinchcombe points out, "many of Merton's central concepts have to do with information" (1975: 20), and he summarizes these as involving three major mechanisms (cf. Merton, 1968: 373–376). First, sanctions depend on information: one person cannot sanction another for something he or she does not know the other has done. Second, information affects people's ideas about what choices they are confronted with. People do not choose alternatives they do not know about. Third, people use information in the concrete construction of successful activities, and success in an activity makes the activity more likely to continue. The collective competence of a science to solve scientific problems would be impossible if scientists could not find out the answers of other scientists to their questions (Stinchcombe, 1975: 20, 21).

The way in which social structures motivate people through their reward-structures is important in Mertonian analyses. Indeed, one of the central questions Merton poses in any context is to examine what kinds of signals for effort are given, and also what pointers of displeasure are conveyed so that the likely consequences for different categories of actors can be assessed. This is always a complex situation as people's behavior is not totally determined by reward-structures but is mediated by their position in the social structure. Alongside this concern with the way in which motivation for behavior is shaped by reward-structures, Merton places ideas about the way in which behavior is constrained by mechanisms of social control. He has nicely summed up the variability in the extent to which social norms are socially enforced in his alliterative formula of the "4Ps": prescription, preference, permission, and proscription (1968: 187).

POWER   Merton has developed a theory of power, or more precisely, a theory of the maintenance and operation of power – once structural power has been established. This stresses that authority, in general, is accorded by those who are prepared to obey as the exercise of power must meet with compliance. This in turn means that leaders must be sensitive to the norms of the group and have considerable information about the norms and group operation so that the compliance can be maintained. Thus leaders are ironically perhaps more trapped in the ongoing structure than their followers. However, leaders have a further responsibility to ensure adaptation to changes to secure long-term survival of the group, and this requires them to initiate or at least support change.

SOCIAL EXPECTED DURATIONS   People and collectivities must deal with time and space. Merton's contribution in this area of analysis has been his concept of "socially expected durations" (SEDs) which are:

> socially prescribed or collectively patterned expectations about temporal durations imbedded in social structures of various kinds: for example, the length of time that individuals are institutionally permitted to occupy particular statuses (such as an office in an organization or a membership in a group); assumed probable durations of diverse kinds of social relationships (such as friendship or a professional client relation); and the patterned and therefore anticipated longevity of individual occupants of statuses, of groups and of organizations. (1984: 265, 266)

STRUCTURES IN PROCESS   It is clear that in this model there is a strong image of social groups requiring a cultural structure and institutional structure that operate to damp down the inherent conflicts and divergences to at least an operable level. The model

assumes widespread consensus, within which there is considerable, but not unlimited, room for dissensus. Social disorganization arises only when the normal coping
mechanisms are overwhelmed. However, there is some room for innovation and
long-term change, as his central image of social structure indicates:

> The key concept bridging the gap between statics and dynamics in functional theory is
> that of strain, tension, contradiction or discrepancy between the component elements of
> social and cultural structure. Such strains may be dysfunctional for the social system in
> its then existing form; they may also be instrumental in leading to changes in that sys-
> tem. In any case, they exert pressures for change. When social mechanisms for control
> are operating effectively, these strains are kept within such bounds to limit change of the
> social structure. (1968: 1761)

Having sketched out Merton's multi-layered analytical account, it is important to
show how this is then "set in motion" or "made to work."

At the center of the schema is some pattern of choices faced by actors, and this is
seen as constrained and often routinized in continually repeated patterns, but still
with a considerable role for "free will." However, the act of choice is framed by a
variety of sources – both psychological and sociological. Merton's sociological analytical apparatus focuses on the structuring of choices and motivation so that the
actor plays a subordinate role in the system, at least in the sociological analysis of it.

Instead, Merton's analytical schema tends to locate the seat of what might be seen
as "energy" in the cultural structure, but as mediated, reinforced, or dampened by
the social structure. Or sometimes it seems social energy is generated by the rough-
textured friction and interaction between the cultural and social. It is their joint
effect that shapes the range of choice for individuals. While the cultural structure
provides the knowledge and values which circumscribe and motivate social action,
these are variously effected by social structure, not least through differential exposure to the cultural structure. At the center of all Merton's analyses are social structural features, which more specifically shape social practices, and which in turn
differentially affect the development of culture and also feedback to gradually
reshape the social structure itself.

> Social structures generate both changes within the structure and changes of the structure
> and…these changes come about through cumulatively patterned choices in behavior
> and the amplification of dysfunctional consequences resulting from certain kinds of
> strains, conflicts and contradictions in the differentiated social structure. (1976: 125)

This architecture and imagery has several attractive features. The scale at which
the analysis is cast "brings men in," but also shows how their behavior is socially
shaped. There is a focus on regularity in human affairs but also attention to ambivalence, deviance, and reaction, and the vulnerability of the accepted social order to
change and conflict. Social structure is portrayed as being *real* in its effects, but it
is seen as permeable rather than *reified*. Private troubles and joys are linked to
structure but structure is shown to grow out of individual behavior in a complex
interplay of the objective and subjective. The mix of handling the ordinary and the
exotic, the obvious and the mysterious is nicely grasped: Merton urges attention to

the unobvious hidden side of the social which only sociologists can reveal, but he also attempts to confront the commonplace by showing the limitations of common-sense assumptions. Nevertheless the mundane is built into his sociology as much as the newly revealed. Other useful summaries of Merton's approach are provided by Rose Coser (1975: 239) and Kai Erikson (1997: 223–224).

Beneath the intricate Mertonian facade there lurks an understanding of Realpolitik that is seemingly invisible elsewhere! But it is precisely through such mechanisms that the Mertonian analytical system is able to explain how the structure is itself able to induce structural changes, whereas in some contrast, the Parsonian system seems only to react to external changes.

While the Mertonian system is clearly able to handle variety in human behavior, its ability to explain change and its handling of power need closer examination. In Stinchcombe's exegesis the feedback-looping is given a prominent place. But, in Merton's own work, examples of changing structures are not prominent, despite the central point in functional analysis that structural equivalents might be expected to "come in" once a particular structure is seen to be failing, and despite his concern that long-term viability of any social structure is dependent on mechanisms that induce change in order for the structure to adapt to changes in its environment.

Merton's "Theory of Society"

Merton did not develop an explicit "theory of society" which draws attention to key differentiating characteristics of the modern social world, although there are glimpses of one. He encouraged a rounded understanding of an emerging post-war society which encompassed such key structures as urban communities, the mass media, knowledge and attitudes, bureaucracies, professions, knowledge and science.

Merton's normative stance

Merton experienced a variety of political contexts (see above) which influenced his work and provided opportunities for him to stake out ideological positions he felt important to enunciate. However, his reactions tended to be circumscribed and an overall framework was not elicited. Nevertheless, several interesting and more recent accounts of Merton's writings have placed them within a broader intellectual frame.

Merton's first foray into staking an ideological claim came in reflections on the nature of the relationship between science and other institutions in a society. Merton opined that other institutions should both be hospitable to and respect the autonomy of science if it was to develop effectively, whereas he critiqued Nazi science of that time for incorrectly using the race and the creed of the scientist in validating knowledge. His 1942 formalization of the four key beliefs underlying science as an institution – namely universalism, disinterestedness, organized skepticism, and communism – further reinforced the necessary cultural autonomy of science if it is to operate successfully.

Merton's media work had a critical and historical edge not always found in other media studies of the time although more recently popular. In his study of actress Kate Smith's radio appeals marketing war bonds Merton explicitly drew attention to the possibilities of psuedo-*Gemeinschaft*, "the feigning of personal concern with the other fellow in order to manipulate him the better" ([1946] 1971: 142).

His work on a planned housing estate explored possibilities for racial and other forms of community social integration and this segued into backroom support for Kenneth Clark's social science-backed case which led to the historic US court decision on racial segregation of schooling and its effects. The interaction between democracy and bureaucracy was another problematic of the 1950s decade which Merton addressed.

The overall image of Merton's stance has been defined by Hollinger (1996; see also Katznelson, 2003) as recognizing complexities and unintended consequences of planned social change but nevertheless retaining a faith that gradual social improvement is possible and to be pursued. Finally, more generally the complexities of Merton's status-and-role theory both configure a more complexly inter-locked social structure but also the freedoms that such complex structures provide to individuals to maneuver their way within them, as their opportunities to exercise choice are maximized given the more limited pressure social structure can exert.

Merton's normative stance was always muted and analytical and was a relatively minor component in his overall corpus of work. Moreover, there is a definite long-term trajectory (perhaps congruent with his rising status as a senior professor), from some engagement towards an increasingly distanced stance.

IMPACT

Impact begins with professional recognition. Merton's professional activities included the Presidencies of the American Sociological Association (1956–1957), the Eastern Sociological Society (1968–1969), the Sociological Research Association (1968), and the Society for Social Studies of Science (1975–1976). Honorary degrees were awarded by nearly 30 universities including Temple, Emory, Leyden, Western Reserve, Colgate, Yale, Wales, Chicago, Pennsylvania, Harvard, Jerusalem, Maryland, Brandeis, State University of New York, Columbia, and Oxford. Merton has been a Fellow of the Guggenheim Foundation (1962–1963), the Center for Advanced Studies in Behavioral Science and has been Resident Scholar at both the Russell Sage Foundation and Adjunct Professor at the Rockefeller University since 1979. Prizes have been awarded him by the American Council of Learned Societies, the National Institute of Medicine, the American Academy of Arts and Sciences (Talcott Parsons Prize for Social Science), the Memorial Sloan–Kettering Cancer Center, Society for Social Studies of Science (Bernal Award), American Sociological Association (Common Wealth award and Career Distinguished Scholarship award), he has been a MacArthur Prize Fellow (1983–1988), and, perhaps most prestigious of all, he was awarded the National Medal of Science in 1994 by President Bill Clinton – the first and only time it has been awarded to a sociologist.

Merton's influence on contemporary sociology has been broad and pervasive. Moreover, as is perhaps appropriate for a scholar with an interest in scientific influences there have been some studies of his own influence, and to some degree such studies have a "self-exemplifying aspect" since he wrote more generally on this topic. An array of studies of Merton's impact have enumerated many of its features (see Crothers, 2005). Several features of Merton's writings strain the normal procedures of bibliometric studies.

His reception remains centered in several substantive areas of sociology, and there is declining attention from the mainstream core. Because his general approach was not clearly "branded," different expositions emphasize one or other of its "faces": so in various introductory textbooks (for example) we find Merton referred to as Parsons's junior partner in the functional approach, as a sociologist of anomie and deviance, as the inventor of focus groups, or of the concept self-fulfilling prophecy, and so on. The effect is coruscating.

Over time, the concerns of sociology and its theoretical language and style of discourse change and as a result the influence of some theorists waxes and wanes. His first "functional analysis" phase became superseded by, or rather over-layered by, a quantitative mode of carrying out sociology and this (with other subtle barriers) has tended to limit Merton's direct impact. Although the language remains fresh, there is insufficient theoretical "baggage" to attract attention in the contemporary theory-saturated age of sociology.

To use his own term, much of Merton's work has been subject to "obliteration of source of ideas or findings by their incorporation in currently accepted knowledge" (1968: 28 ff.; this is abbreviated as *OBI*). Many of his contributions are so central that they are built into the unconsciously accepted foundations of sociology and thus have a particularly powerful but often unrecognized intellectual influence.

Although Merton has worked with a range of collaborators (especially his close Columbia University colleagues and students) on a sequence of projects, and his work has inspired a series of research programs and indeed fully fledged "fields of study," he has not otherwise attracted a general school of followers, or even a small sect of committed devotees. On the other hand there clearly has been a diffuse "Columbia Tradition" (Crothers, 1996). Merton's influence has broadly affected much of what Mullins (1973) has termed "Standard American Sociology," and Calhoun (2007) "Mainstream Sociology." The Columbia School is seen as a *joint* product of both Merton and Lazarsfeld. Throughout the 1940s, 1950s, and 1960s Merton played a major role as both a graduate teacher in training a large cohort of sociologists and as an editor in helping shape through editing a wide range of the sociological writing from this group and more generally other sociologists. Columbia was a central seat from which to influence much of the mid-century development of sociology. Besides his impact within his own university, Merton was also able to exert a wider, if more diffuse, influence throughout American and world sociology.

Since Merton established several programs that for a time each shaped research in a particular area of sociology he has become labeled as the "father" of that area and attracts some influence as a result. Moreover, there are signs of renewed attention to Merton's work, especially as their 50th (and later) anniversaries have been reached.

Moreover, there are national differences in the reception of his work. Alongside other American sociologists – usually Talcott Parsons and Paul Lazarsfeld – Merton had a major influence across a wide swathe of countries as European sociology re-emerged from the ashes of the Second World War and as sociology sprang up across a wide range of developing countries and these influences have been described in various case studies.

ASSESSMENT

In sum, Merton drew on an array of classical sociology thinking and helped forge a theoretically informed but empirically grounded sociology from reformulations of its ideas. His style of conducting sociology remained connected with the ways classical sociology had been presented but reached out to newer, more scientific modes of carrying out sociology.

He took the "culture, society, personality" schema, differentiated more finely within it, connected it up and set it to work on explaining behavior, and on showing how structural changes arose out of behavior and in turn how these shaped behavior. For most of his work Merton worked through the various explanatory requirements for a sociological analytical methodology and theoretical framework. As with most other creative activities Merton was able to find the various conceptual and empirical materials needed for the extension of his work. But each additional piece needed to be activated, and then located within the continually evolving structure. Keeping track of it all was difficult, if not impossible. But showing some of the possibilities of a more coherent presentation of Merton's range of ideas gives an indication of how subtle and powerful his approach can be.

The micro-foundations of Merton's approach in action theory were laid down very early in his writing emphasizing not just the limitations of purposive action but also the very considerable impacts of the unanticipated and/or unintended consequences of actions on social structures: indeed, much of social life carries on "behind the backs" of its participants. However, these micro-foundations were not always adequately linked to more structural analyses.

Merton was an avowed functional analyst (but not a functionalist) for most of his academic life (during the late 1940s through to the early 1970s), and before this operated with a simplified and truncated version of this approach. In the mid-1970s he partially recanted, but did not clearly enunciate what was involved in the non-Parsonian structural "variant" he now was prepared to accept, and he did not clarify his attitude to his earlier work. I argue that under the cover of this functional framework, Merton in fact largely deployed a structuralist approach, in which behavioral outcomes are tied to structural sources, and which is sensitive to conflicts and ambiguities. The top-layer of Merton's *functional analysis* has distracted attention from the rather more important underlying *structural analysis*, although Merton's position on each was only generally indicated and not fully spelled out.

It is not clear if Merton's career and impact suffered at all from his "failure" to adopt a more clear-cut branding of an individualized theoretical project. He was favorably received in American sociology and recognized worldwide as a leader of a broad functional analysis "theoretical movement." Within that "broad church" he was able to emphasize particular themes which gave him his own signature tune. His work was more empirically linked, less pitched at a societal level, and more structurally orientated than that of most other functionalists. When the broad theoretical movement began to founder, Merton's sociology was sufficiently sound in its own right that little damage ensued from the demise of the wider branding. But Merton's apparent inability to project a clear theoretical pathway ahead has limited the extent to which his work has been appreciated in terms of its overall structure, and its role in general theoretical debates. By discarding his contributions as rather too eclectic, some of his finely honed theoretical contributions have not been sufficiently incorporated into general sociology, and this has been a considerable loss.

Reader's Guide to Robert K. Merton

Almost all the significant writings by Merton have been assembled in four volumes (with a very slight overlap in content). *Social Theory and Social Structure* was first published in 1949 with subsequent further-expanded editions in 1957 and in 1968. In 1973 most of Merton's work in the *Sociology of Science* was assembled by Norman Storer into a volume with the same title. Another 13 essays are gathered from symposia and journal articles into the 1976 collection *Sociological Ambivalence*. A further selection is reproduced in *Social Research and the Practicing Professions* edited by Aaron Rosenblatt and Thomas F. Gieryn, who also provide a useful introduction. Finally, Piotr Sztompka was responsible for assembling an array of Merton's writings into a 1996 volume for the University of Chicago series on the Heritage of Sociology.

Writings on Merton comprise book-length treatments of his intellectual biography (in some need of updating) by Sztompka (1986) and Crothers (1987). Festschriften or collections of commentary include those edited by Coser (1975) which is useful for the authoritative commentary provided by the assembled array of colleagues, Gieryn (1980) which casts a wider span of contributors in terms of disciplinary area, Mongardini and Tabboni ([1989]1997) which assembles a more international cast, Clark (1990) in which a large number of commentaries are organized in a pro vs con argumentative framework, Cohen (1990) concerned solely with Merton's historical sociology of science, and Calhoun (2010) which concentrates more on Merton's more recent sociology of science and also his theoretical approaches. Many other articles and some special issues of journals are readily available.

Bibliography

Writings of Robert K. Merton

1934a. Recent French sociology, *Social Forces*, 12: 537–545.

1934b. Durkheim's division of labor in society, *American Journal of Sociology*, 40: 319–328.

1936. The unanticipated consequences of purposive social action, *American Sociological Review*, 1: 894–904.

1937 (with Pitirim A. Sorokin). Social time: A methodological and functional analysis. *American Journal of Sociology*, 42: 615–629.

1938a. Science, technology and society in seventeenth century England. In George Sarton (ed.) OSIRIS: *Studies on the History and Philosophy of Science and on the History of Learning and Culture*. Bruges, Belgium: The St. Catherine Press, pp. 362–632. (1970, New York: Howard Fertig, Inc.; Harper Torchbooks, Harper & Row.)

1938b. Social structure and anomie, *American Sociological Review*, 3: 672–682.

1940. Fact and factitiousness in ethnic opinionnaires, *American Sociological Review*, 5(1): 13–28.

[1946]1971 (with the assistance of Marjorie Fiske and Alberta Curtis). *Mass Persuasion*. New York: Harper & Brothers. (1971, Stamford, CN: Greenwood Press and 2003, New York: Howard Fertig Publishers.)

[1949]1968. *Social Theory and Social Structure*. New York: The Free Press. (1957, Revised and enlarged edition. New York: Free Press. 1968, Enlarged edition. New York: Free Press.)

1950 (with Paul F. Lazarsfeld (eds)). *Continuities in Social Research: Studies in the Scope and Method of "The American Soldier"*. New York: The Free Press.

1952 (with Alisa P. Gray, Barbara Hockey and Hanan C. Selvin (eds)). *Reader in Bureaucracy*. New York: The Free Press.

1956 (with Marjorie Fiske and Patricia L. Kendall). *The Focused Interview*. New York: The Free Press.

1957 (with George G. Reader and Patricia L. Kendall (eds)). *The Student-Physician: Introductory Studies in the Sociology of Medical Education*. Cambridge, MA: Harvard University Press.

1959 (with Leonard Broom and Leonard S. Cottrell, Jr. (eds)). *Sociology Today: Problems and Prospects*. New York: Basic Books. (1967, New York: Harper & Row)

[1961]1976. *Contemporary Social Problems* (edited with Robert A. Nisbet). New York: Harcourt Brace Jovanovich. (1976 Fourth edition.)

1961. Social conflict in styles of sociological work, *Transactions, Fourth World Congress of Sociology*, 3: 21–46.

1965. *On the Shoulders of Giants: A Shandean Postscript*. New York: The Free Press. (1993, *The Post-Italianate edition* (Foreword by Umberto Eco). Chicago: University of Chicago Press.)

1971a (with Harriet A. Zuckerman). Patterns of evaluation in science: Institutionalization, structure and functions of the referee system. *Minerva*, 9(1), January, 66–100.

1971b. The precarious foundations of detachment in sociology. In Edward A. Tiryakian (ed.) *The Phenomenon of Sociology*. New York: Appleton-Century-Crofts, pp. 188–199.

1973. *The Sociology of Science: Theoretical and Empirical Investigations*. Edited by Norman Storer. Chicago: University of Chicago Press.

1976. *Sociological Ambivalence*. New York: The Free Press.

1977 (with Jerry Gaston and Adam Podgorecki (eds)). *The Sociology of Science in Europe*. Carbondale: University of Southern Illinois Press.

1978 (with Yehuda Elkana, Joshua Lederberg, Arnold Thackray and Harriet Zuckerman (eds)). *Toward a Metric of Science: Thoughts Occasioned by the Advent of Science Indicators*. New York: John Wiley.

1979a (with James S. Coleman and Peter H. Rossi (eds)). *Qualitative and Quantitative Social Research: Papers in Honor of Paul F. Lazarsfeld*. New York: The Free Press.

1979b. *The Sociology of Science: An Episodic Memoir*. Carbondale: University of Southern Illinois Press.

1981 (with Peter M. Blau (eds)). *Continuities in Structural Inquiry*. London: Sage Publications.

1982. *Social Research and the Practicing Professions*. Cambridge: Abt Books.

1984. Socially expected durations: A case study of concept formation in sociology. In W.W. Powell and Richard Robbins (eds) *Conflict and Consensus: In Honor of Lewis A. Coser*, New York: Free Press, pp. 262–283.

1987. Three fragments from a sociologist's notebooks: Establishing the phenomenon, specified ignorance and strategic research materials. *Annual Review of Sociology*, 13: 1–28.

1988. The Matthew effect in science, II: Cumulative advantage and the symbolism of intellectual property, *Isis*, 79: 606–623

1990 (with David L. Sills) *Social Science Quotations: Who Said What, When, and Where. International Encyclopedia of the Social Sciences*, vol. 19. New York: MacMillan Publishing Company.

1994a. Durkheim's division of labor in society: A sexagenarian postscript, *Sociological Forum*, 19(1): 27–36.

1994b. A life of learning: Charles Homer Haskins Lecture, *American Council of Learned Societies*. An Occasional Paper, no. 25.

1995a (with Alan Wolfe). The cultural and social incorporation of sociological knowledge. *The American Sociologist*, 26(3), fall: 15–38.

1995b. Opportunity structure: The emergence, diffusion, and differentiation of a sociological concept, 1930s–1950s. In Freda Adler and William S. Laufer (eds) *Advances in Criminological Theory: The Legacy of Anomie Theory*, vol. 6. New Brunswick, NJ: Transaction Publishers, pp. 3–78.

1995c. The Thomas Theorem and the Matthew Effect, *Social Forces*, 74(2), December: 379–424.

2004 (with Elinor Barber). *The Travels and Adventures of Serendipity: A Study in Sociological Semantics and the Sociology of Science*. (Bologna: II Mulino (Italian), with an introduction by James L. Shulman). Princeton: Princeton University Press.

Further Reading

Barbano, Filipo (1968) Social structures and social functions: The emancipation of structural analysis in sociology, *Inquiry*, 11: 40–84.

Bennett, James (1990) Merton's "social structure and anomie": Suggestions for rhetorical analysis. In Albert Hunter (ed.) *The Rhetoric of Social Research: Understood and Believed*. New Brunswick and London: Rutgers University Press.

Besnard, Philippe (1987) *L'Anomie*. Paris: PUF.

Bierstedt, Robert (1981) Robert K. Merton. In *American Sociological Theory – A Critical History*. New York: Academic Press, pp. 443–489.

Calhoun, Craig (ed.) (2010) *Robert K. Merton: Sociological Theory and the Sociology of Science*. New York: Columbia University Press.

Calhoun, Craig and Van Anwerpen, Jonathan (2007) Orthodoxy, heterodoxy, and hierarchy: "Mainstream" sociology and its challengers. In Craig Calhon (ed.) *Sociology in America: A History*. Chicago: University of Chicago Press, pp. 367–410.

Caplovitz, David (1977) Robert K. Merton as an editor: Review essay, *Contemporary Sociology*, 6: 142–150

Clark, Jon (ed.) (1990) *Robert K. Merton: Consensus and Controversy*. London and Philadelphia: The Falmer Press, Taylor and Francis.

Cohen, I. Bernard (ed.) (1990) *Puritanism and the Rise of Modern Science: The Merton Thesis*. New Brunswick: Rutgers University Press.

Collins, Randall ([1977]1981) Merton's functionalism. In R. Collins (ed.) *Sociology Since Midcentury*, New York: Academic Press, pp. 197–203.

Coser, Lewis A. (ed.) (1975) *The Idea of Social Structure: Papers in Honor of Robert K. Merton*. New York: Harcourt Brace Jovanovich.

Crothers, Charles (1987) *Robert K. Merton: A Key Sociologist*. London and New York: Tavistock Publications.

Crothers, Charles (1996) The postwar "Columbia tradition" in sociology: Its cognitive commonalities and social mechanisms, *Work-Organization-Economy Working Paper, Series 38*, Department of Sociology, Stockholm University.

Crothers, Charles (2004) Merton as a general theorist: Structures, choices, mechanisms and consequences, *The American Sociologist*, 35(3): 23–36.

Crothers Charles (2005) Merton's legacy: Influences from Merton. *American Sociological Association Conference*, Philadelphia, August (Centenary Session).

Erikson, Kai (1997) *Sociological Visions*. Lanham, Maryland: Rowman and Littlefield.

Gieryn, Thomas F. (ed.) (1980) *Science and Social Structure: A Festschrift for Robert K. Merton*. New York: The New York Academy of Sciences.

Gouldner, Alvin Ward (1973) *For Sociology: Renewal and Critique in Sociology Today*. London: Allen Lane.

Hedstrom, Peter and Swedberg, Richard (eds) (1998) *Social Mechanisms*. Cambridge: Cambridge University Press.

Hollinger, D. A. (1996) *Science, Jews, and Secular Culture: Studies in Mid-twentieth-century American Intellectual History*. Princeton, NJ: Princeton University Press.

Hunt, Morton M. (1961) How does it come to be so? Profile of Robert K. Merton. *New Yorker*, 28(36), January: 39–63.

Jaworski, Gary D. (1997) *George Simmel and the American Prospect*. Albany, NY: State University of New York Press.

Katznelson, Ira (2003) *Desolation and Enlightenment: Political Knowledge after Total War, Totalitarianism and the Holocaust*. New York: Columbia University Press.

Marsh, Robert (2010) Merton's sociology 215–216 course, *The American Sociologist*, 41(2): 99–114.

Mongardini, Carlo and Tabboni, Simonetta (eds) ([1989]1997) *L'Opera di Robert K. Merton e la sociologia contemporanea*. Genoa: ECIG. (English translation: *Merton and Contemporary Sociology*. New Brunswick: Transaction Publishers.)

Mullins, Nicholas (1973) *Theories and Theory Groups in Contemporary American Sociology*. New York: Harper and Row.

Nichols, Lawrence (2010) Merton as Harvard sociologist: Engagement, thematic continuities, and institutional linkages, *Journal of the History of the Behavioral Sciences*, 46(1): 72–95.

Rigney, Daniel (2010) *The Matthew Effect: How Advantage Begets Further Advantage*. New York: Columbia University Press.

Schultz, Ruth (1995) The improbable adventures of an American Scholar: Robert K Merton, *American Sociologist*, 26(3): 68–77.

Stimonson, Peter (2010) *Refiguring Mass Communication: A History*. University of Illinois Press, History of Communication series.

Stinchcombe, Arthur (1975) Merton's theory of social structure. In L. Coser (ed.) *The Idea of Social Structure*. New York: Harcourt Brace Jovanovich, pp. 11–34.

Sztompka, Piotr (1986) *Robert K. Merton: An Intellectual Profile*. London: MacMillan/New York: St. Martin's Press.

Sztompka, Piotr (ed.) (1996) *Robert K. Merton on Social Structure and Science*. The Heritage of Sociology. A series edited by Donald N. Levine. Chicago: The University of Chicago Press.

Zuckerman, Harriet (1989) The other Merton thesis, *Science in Context*, 3: 239–67.

4

Harold Garfinkel

ANNE WARFIELD RAWLS

THE THEORY

Since the publication of *Studies in Ethnomethodology* in 1967, Harold Garfinkel has come to be known as the "father" of "ethnomethodology." His theory and corresponding research program have had a widespread and growing influence in the United States, Canada, the UK, EU, Russia, Australia, and Japan. In spite of the controversy into which it emerged and the rise and fall of a number of "new" sociologies since, its influence has been felt continuously across sociology from social theory to specialty areas like medical sociology, science and technology, sociology of work, race and gender, and criminology. Influence on the fields of communication, linguistics, studies of work and technology, and human machine interaction is also substantial. Wherever researchers must explain how people make sense together, and why, ethnomethodology is likely to have become a resource. There are affinities to Durkheim on scientific practices, Wittgenstein on meaning as "use" and Burke and Mills on "accounts." There are also points of resemblance to pragmatism, phenomenology, and gestalt psychology and the theory was first put to paper while Garfinkel was at Harvard with Parsons. But, it is not a phenomenological argument, or a pragmatist or Wittgensteinian argument. Nor does it simply "reject" Parsons. What Garfinkel asks is that we think differently about social processes. He borrows insights from many traditions and then respecifies them with an empirical focus on the local and witnessable character of constitutive social action. The result is a unique focus on how participants accomplish mutual intelligibility by cooperating to make the social processes they are engaged in exhibit a mutually recognizable order. Rather than assuming an allegedly "human" capacity to communicate as a starting point, Garfinkel insists that mutual intelligibility be explained. The position is inherently sociological, addressing fundamental epistemological questions at the heart of the

The Wiley-Blackwell Companion to Major Social Theorists, First Edition.
Edited by George Ritzer and Jeffrey Stepnisky.
© 2011 Blackwell Publishing Ltd. Published 2011 by Blackwell Publishing Ltd.

sociological enterprise. In specifying empirically the constitutive use practices involved in cooperative sensemaking, and elaborating the "Trust" requirement that sustains them, Garfinkel makes a unique contribution to social theory and research.

The publication of three additional volumes of Garfinkel's work since 2002 makes essential foundational arguments and additional research available: *Ethnomethodology's Program: Working out Durkheim's Aphorism* (2002, collection of essays), *Seeing Sociologically: The Routine Grounds of Social Action* (2006, manuscript from 1948), and *Toward a Sociological Theory of Information* (2008, manuscript from 1952).

Despite its acknowledged influence, there remains considerable debate and misunderstanding about what Garfinkel actually meant by ethnomethodology. For instance, ethnomethodology has often mistakenly been associated with a focus on the individual and Garfinkel is said to be concerned with the values and beliefs of individual participants. Another widespread misunderstanding is that Garfinkel's research consists primarily of "breaching experiments" in which persons violate social expectations to demonstrate the existence of underlying rules governing social behavior. Others have associated ethnomethodology with a social indeterminacy similar to Baudrillard's postmodernism. Garfinkel's idea of practice has also been associated with "practice" and "routine" in Bourdieu and Giddens. But, there are essential differences. One problem with these interpretations is that ethnomethodology is not a single research program, nor does it focus on a single social phenomenon, whether individual or collective. Ethnomethodology, as elaborated by Garfinkel, while borrowing from various classic traditions, involves a complete theoretical reconceptualization of social order and a corresponding multifaceted research program.

The word "ethnomethodology" itself represents a very simple idea. If one assumes, as Garfinkel does, that the meaningful, patterned, and orderly character of everyday life is something people must continually work cooperatively to achieve, then one must also assume they have some methods for doing so. One way of understanding this is by analogy with the idea that to make sense by speaking in a language, persons have to speak the same language, using the same meanings for words and the same grammatical forms. Another analogy is with the idea that in order to play a game persons have to play with the same rules. It is not possible to play baseball by running downfield with a football. The essential rules of baseball are in important respects constitutive of the game of baseball. Constitutive means that the rules define recognizable boundaries of the objects and practices of the game.

There are problems with these analogies because Garfinkel does not think of members' methods in terms of rules or grammars, which are themselves oversimplified conceptualizations of the constitutive features of social practices. In fact, according to Garfinkel the idea that social order is a result of following rules is responsible for many classic problems in social theory. But the idea is important nevertheless. Garfinkel gave lectures on "rules" for many years developing his notions of "instructed action" and "praxeological validity" to avoid the classic problems with rules. These difficulties noted, the analogies help illustrate what it means to say that the methods used by persons to create the orderliness of ordinary social occasions are constitutive of those occasions.

Ethnomethodology, then, is the study of the methods people use for producing recognizable social orders. "Ethno" refers to members of a social situation or cultural group and "method" refers to the things members continually do using those methods to create and recreate various recognizable social actions or social practices. "Ology," as in the word "sociology," implies the study of, or the logic of, these methods and their use. Thus, ethnomethodology means the study of members' methods for producing recognizable social orders.

Ethnomethodology is not itself a method. It is a study of members' methods based on the theory that a careful analysis of the details of social phenomena can reveal social order. The word ethnomethodology itself does not name a set of research methods any more than the word sociology designates a specific set of research methods. Ethnomethodologists have done their research in many and varied ways. The object of all these research methods, however, is to discover the things that persons in particular situations do, the methods they use, to create the patterned orderliness of social life. Not all research methods are capable of revealing this level of social order. But there are many that can.

Ethnomethodologists generally favor methods that require total immersion in the situation being studied. They hold the ideal that they learn to be competent practitioners of whatever social phenomena they are studying. This ideal is referred to by Garfinkel as "unique adequacy." When the subject of research is something that most persons participate in regularly, such as ordinary talk, the game of tic-tac-toe, driving, walking, etc., then unique adequacy can usually be assumed. However, with regard to practices with specialized populations, unique adequacy can be very hard to achieve. An ethnomethodologist pursuing unique adequacy within a specialized population may spend years in a research site becoming a competent participant in its practices, in addition to collecting various sorts of observational, documentary, and audiovisual materials. Ethnomethodologists have taken degrees in law and mathematics, worked for years in science labs, become professional musicians, and worked as truck drivers and in police departments, in an effort to satisfy the unique adequacy requirement.

Ethnomethodology involves a multifaceted focus on the local social orders that are enacted in various situations. The individual persons who inhabit these situations are, as individuals, uninteresting, except in so far as personal characteristics, such as blindness, reveal something about the competencies required to achieve the recognizable production of the local order that is the object of study.

The mistaken identification of ethnomethodology with a specific methodology, and in particular with "breaching experiments," may be due to the fact that in teaching ethnomethodology Garfinkel found it helpful to develop what he refers to as "tutorial exercises," so that students could have first-hand experience of the "phenomenal field properties" of socially constituted phenomena. These tutorial exercises generally involved disrupting the orderly achievement of intelligibility in some way. Students were assigned tutorial tasks which revealed the work involved in the individual and bodily mastery of the various practices constitutive of local orders. For instance, they might be asked to perform ordinary tasks wearing headgear that distorted their vision. The idea is that tasks and situations that problematize everyday life actions can make students aware of the need for the constant achievement of the social orderliness of local settings.

Garfinkel's attention to moments of "breach" and "incongruity" are sometimes interpreted as having to do with opportunities for change and innovation which such incongruities are thought to make possible. But, this involves a misconception.

In Garfinkel's view local orders of practice do not constrain creativity, they make the mutual intelligibility of creative acts possible. By contrast with habits and routines which are reproductions of prior actions and do constrain creativity, local orders of practice provide a means, more like the order of grammar or chess, for producing an unlimited variety of inventive moves while nevertheless constituting a shared medium of action within which participants can recognize one another's moves. The breach is important for Garfinkel not as an opportunity for innovation, but rather, because it demonstrates that without cooperating to produce an order of practice there is no mutual intelligibility.

Studies in ethnomethodology

Garfinkel's research was available primarily in *Studies in Ethnomethodology* for 35 years. "Studies," as the 1967 volume came to be called, is a collection of papers, each demonstrating a different theoretical and/or methodological facet of ethnomethodology: indexicality, accountability, mutual commitment to shared practices, social construction of identity, rationality as a property of social action, and the documentary method of interpretation, among them. Garfinkel recommended the policy "that any social setting be viewed as self-organizing with respect to the intelligible character of its own appearances as either representative of or as evidences-of-a-social-order" (1967: 33).

The book opens with the question "What is Ethnomethodology?" which involves a discussion of indexicality, an idea that is important to ethnomethodology. Treating the indexicality of talk and social action as a problem, Garfinkel points out, has motivated endless studies directed to its remedy. However, since people do manage to make sense and almost every situation in which they do so exhibits indexicality, it cannot in practice be the problem it appears to be in theory. Garfinkel recommends treating indexicality as it occurs in social interactions as a research topic rather than as a problem. Indexicality here does not mean ambiguity or contingency. It means that the "things" (words, turns, gestures) people use to make meaning have many possible meanings and take on a particular meaning only as participants build an order of practice together using them.

There are important implications for moral obligations involved. The second chapter opens with a reference to the idea that for Kant the mystery was the moral order "within." For sociology, Garfinkel goes on to say, the mystery is the moral order without. The reference sets up an important contrast between philosophical and sociological approaches to morality. Social and moral order are technical and not logical mysteries for Garfinkel. Participants encounter this moral order as the "natural facts of life" as if they did not need to be constituted and did not require their constant attention and effort. Yet, they only exist if we cooperate to make them together. Mutual intelligibility depends on these processes and thus they are moral. This he says is sociology's central topic. But, in spite of its importance, the question of how these moral facts are constituted and how they can be so stable as to be routinely taken for granted is rarely taken seriously. Their constitution should be a topic in its own right. But, for mainstream sociology concepts like "socialization" and "language" that treat these essential processes as givens, predominate. "Language" for instance, is often treated as explaining communication. Garfinkel insists that it is essential to know just how mutually recognizable social facts are constituted. This is a process that must be done again "each next first time," which produces a very different picture of things like "socialization," language, and "social order" from that of mainstream sociology.

The obligation to engage in a coordinated mutual reflexivity with those with whom we interact extends to all meaningful interactions. For instance, if persons find themselves at a movie theater where people line up in a particular way, then they must figure out what methods for lining up are being used and line up that way too. Otherwise, they may find after much waiting that they have not in fact been in line. That is, they have not been "recognizably" waiting in line, and the others in the theater will not accept their claim that they have been waiting in line. There will be a moral censure of their activities, "Hey you, don't cut in line" with the anger and moral outrage that accompanies moral censure.

Garfinkel treats these members' methods as unspecified and unspecifiable in ways that distinguish them from the more problematic idea of rules. Rules and grammars are conceptual simplifications of constitutive features of actual social practices. Because members must use the same methods in order to produced recognizable social orders, a level of commitment to shared methods is necessary in order for mutual intelligibility to be achieved. Garfinkel called this the "Trust" requirement. There is a resemblance to Habermas's argument that persons make a set of foundational assumptions before they can sit down and reason publicly with one another. But, for Habermas the commitments remain hypothetical. For Garfinkel, "Trust" is not motivated by anything more than the mutual interest in producing recognizable orders. Thus it introduces a stringent requirement of interactional reciprocity; replacing traditional morality with something stronger that does not depend on shared beliefs. When social institutions encroach on this domain of Trust, minimum requirements of mutual intelligibility and self must be satisfied, or those institutions will fail.

Garfinkel's discussion of the "Documentary Method of Interpretation" (chapter 3) has inspired studies of institutional and everyday life accounting practices. He argues that persons in everyday life construct carefully documented accounts (in ordinary and institutional contexts) to warrant claims they make about the orderliness of social events. In all cases, however, such documented accounts gloss over and thus lose the details of social processes. This common everyday life practice, Garfinkel argues, parallels the practices of formal analytic theorizing. In the very same ways that the everyday life practice of documentary reasoning glosses over the details of practices in producing a documented account, formal analytic reasoning glosses those practices as well.

While there are similarities to Mannheim and the argument has been interpreted as a sociology of knowledge, Garfinkel's point is that the documentary method is not in fact a way of knowing anything, but rather, a way of explaining things after the fact that gives the appearance of being knowledge while actually obscuring what is being explained. Using documented accounts, persons are always able to retrospectively reconstruct a plausible explanation of why something happened which appears to have predictive power. But, Garfinkel argues, such retrospective documented accounts bear little or no relationship to how and why events actually unfolded prospectively in the way that they did. Therefore, when such accounts are used to explain or predict social behavior the results are notoriously inaccurate.

Because, in Garfinkel's view, social life is organized by the production of recognizable practices, the details of those practices are critical to the understanding of society. Yet the documented accounts of both common-sense reasoning and formal analytic theorizing treat conceptual schemes as more important than the contingent details of practices. Therefore, formal analytic theorizing, based as it is on documented accounts, inevitably misses the essential orderliness of society. Where scientific sociology places the clarity of concepts at the heart of its science, Garfinkel blames this same reliance on clear concepts for the "loss of the phenomenon."

Although Garfinkel's interest in accounts and accountability was primarily influenced by his reading of Kenneth Burke between 1936 and 1940, it bears important similarities to C. Wright Mills's (1940) argument that institutions are not organized prospectively according to rules, but retrospectively according to shared vocabularies of motive. Garfinkel goes farther than Mills, however, in insisting that social order is not only constituted retrospectively through the enactment of a shared vocabulary of motives (or accounts), but also prospectively through the enactment of detailed sets of shared practices. One of the primary distinctions Garfinkel makes is between the order properties of retrospective (documented, accountable, and institutional) versus prospective (sequentially and embodiedly ordered over its course) social objects.

The "Jury Study" discussed in chapter 4 explores how conflicting rules for making sense and conflicting contexts of accountability are managed by jurors. It was during this project in 1953–1954 that Garfinkel came up with the term ethnomethodology. He distinguishes between the "rules of decision making in everyday life" and the "official line" that decision makers must take within a formal institution or organization such as the court/jury. Jurors respect and must preserve aspects of both. Garfinkel examines the ways in which jurors modify the rules of everyday life decision making just slightly to accommodate the particular work they are charged with doing. The need to manage the ambiguity that results from juggling the two sets of rules is what he finds to be characteristic of the work of a juror. The conflicts between organizational accountability, which works after the fact, and ordinary practices which work prospectively, is one of the big issues.

The "Agnes" study (chapter 5, and its corresponding appendix), which explored the practices involved in achieving a recognizable gendered image, has been the subject of much debate and has had a great deal of influence, particularly on gender studies. The research began in 1959 and continued through 1967. Garfinkel presents a detailed account of discussions with a young person who was seeking (and eventually received) a sex change operation. The critics have sometimes argued over whether or not Garfinkel and the doctors were "taken in" by Agnes, who claimed to be a young woman mistakenly labeled a young man. The question of whether Garfinkel was able to observe Agnes from an "objective" research standpoint, or whether his own beliefs and values influenced what he observed, seems to dominate that discussion.

This debate misses the point. What interested Garfinkel was the idea that gender must be socially managed. If Agnes, in being a man who was really a woman, or a man who was pretending to really be a woman, or a woman who had the biology of a man, etc., had to recognizably reproduce actions, expressions of emotion, posture, etc., that were recognizably female, then by watching and talking to Agnes it might be possible to discover the essential features of recognizable actions involved in the social construction of gender. If Agnes was "fooling" anyone, then the performance would, from Garfinkel's standpoint, be *more* valuable as a subject of research, not *less* valuable.

Critics often assume that gender is something biological and that Agnes either "really" had the biology or did not. Garfinkel was assuming something much more radical; that gender is a social production, such that persons who are said to be biologically male can produce recognizably female actions and thereby make the claim that they are female and be believed. The question Garfinkel raises is not the indeterminate biological one of whether Agnes is "really" male or female. The question is how, and in exactly what way, Agnes used members' methods to reproduce herself or himself recognizably socially as a female in each and every particular situation.

"Good Reasons for Bad Clinic Records" (chapter 6) reported on a field study of a psychiatric outpatient clinic. The chapter following (chapter 7) outlines problems with conventional research on clinic intake processes based on an understanding of how clinic workers actually do their work. The researchers had originally been interested in coding clinic files. But they found the files were for their purposes "hopelessly incomplete." What interested Garfinkel about this was that the incompleteness of the files was not random. It reflected a combination of internal clinic practices and concerns for the accountability of those practices to outside agencies. He argued that, because of the need for institutional accountability, clinic workers had to manage the information contained in the files carefully. Therefore, it could not be assumed that clinic files and the statistics they generated reflected what "outsiders" would consider an accurate record of patient histories. They were not designed to do so. Rather, they were designed to meet the needs of the institution and its workers.

Garfinkel's point is not only negative. Together with the discussion of documentary methods of interpretation it has inspired studies of institutional recordkeeping and institutional accountability. Any institutional database constitutes data objects that are meaningful only in relation to the work done by that particular institution. While the statistical records produced are therefore problematic when compared with records produced by other institutions (i.e. they cannot be treated as an "accurate" account of cases), they can be used to show how clinic workers keep their records and why. To a traditionally trained social scientist the clinic files are "bad" files. But they are not bad files from the clinic workers' point of view. They provide just those materials clinic workers need in order to produce the orderly routines of the clinic day and then account for those routines to those to whom they are accountable. For the clinic workers there are "good" reasons for these "bad" records. For the ethnomethodologist, the records provide important information about the way the social order of the clinic is achieved. The caution is that institutional databases define information uniquely such that objects in one database are not equivalent to the "same" objects in other databases.

Garfinkel maintained from the beginning that the rationality of daily life is different from rationality as assumed by scientific theorizing and the last chapter on "The Rational Properties of Scientific and Commonsense Activities" takes up this point. Because participants in social life must assume something about the other person's knowledge of the world, sociologists cannot avoid the question of rationality, but, they usually define it by selecting features from the properties of scientific action as ideally described. This is inappropriate according to Garfinkel because "scientific rationalities occur as stable properties of action and as sanctionable ideals only in the case of actions governed by the attitude of scientific theorizing" (270). Meaningfully adequate action occurs often in contexts that fail utterly to meet the scientific criteria of rationality. In fact, he says, "actions governed by the attitude of daily life are marked by the specific absence of these [scientific] rationalities" and attempts to impose those rationalities in daily life will only multiply the anomic features of interaction. He proposes "rationalities" plural as a subject of empirical investigation, rather than "rationality" as defined theoretically and in advance. The argument leans heavily on Schutz in elaborating 14 rationalities (1–10 occur in daily life without anomie, 11–14 represent the scientific rationalities).

Garfinkel's theory of communication

Seeing Sociologically: The Routine Grounds of Social Action written in 1948 and published for the first time in 2006 (hereafter *Seeing*), outlines a theory of how interaction and communication work. The notions of reflexivity, constitutive rules, and a performative self are introduced in this early work and the manuscript represents an early elaboration by Garfinkel of the relationship between his developing framework of ideas and mainstream sociology at the time. The manuscript was written as a preliminary proposal for a dissertation too ambitious to be completed, his actual dissertation elaborating parts of the first section of this manuscript on the problem of the scientific description of action and the actor's point of view. Whereas, Garfinkel in his later work increasingly refused to articulate theoretical questions, this document attempted a thorough theoretical elaboration of problems and conflicts on the one hand in the work of those he had worked closely with: Gurwitsch, Schutz, and Parsons, and those he appreciated but distinguished himself from: James, Peirce, Mead, and Dewey, and on the other hand mainstream scientific sociology, and did so as a way of staging the initial theoretical space for his own argument.

Originally titled "Prospectus for an Exploratory Study of Communicative Effort and the Modes of Understanding in Selected Types of Dyadic Relationship," the document has an interesting history. Distributed in mimeograph to a group of graduate students at Harvard in 1948, it fell into the hands of several key thinkers early on: Erving Goffman, Anselm Strauss, and Harvey Sacks among them. While its intersection with, and influence on, the work of these and other prominent scholars, would alone make the manuscript important, it elaborates essential issues that Garfinkel does not address theoretically anywhere else. It also highlights the degree to which Garfinkel was, from the first, focused on communicative interaction and situated reason broadly conceived. As such, the manuscript makes evident a deep continuity between Garfinkel's early theoretical writing and his later empirical research on both conversation/communication and members' methods more generally.

By "communication," in the original title, Garfinkel meant "interaction" a term which he says he preferred, but avoided because it had direct connections to stimulus response theory at the time. However, interaction has become an important focus of theory and research in the 60 years since Garfinkel wrote the manuscript, and the word no longer bears the connotations of stimulus response. The term interaction, as we now use it, more accurately connotes what Garfinkel intended.

"Effort" invoked the idea that interaction involved cooperative "work" between actors to construct a mutually intelligible world and that this work was a public, visible, and orderly passing back and forth of recognizable sounds and movements, according to orders of expectation and could therefore be profitably studied in details. It was not the study of behavior. It was the study of how actions were given public and mutual meaning by actors working together within shared fields of practice to create witnessable orders. While it involved meaning, this interactional work was not carried by, or accomplished through, concepts, beliefs, ideas, or typifications. Nor was it embodied in projects as Schutz had proposed. Rather, the recognizability of projects and concepts was made possible in and through this mutual and reflexive work of ordering interaction in its material details.

The new subtitle, "The Routine Grounds of Social Action," reflects Garfinkel's argument that social action has "routine grounds," or expectations, that are both a condition for, and an outcome of, this interactive effort, as he also argued in a later paper (1964) "The Routine Grounds of Everyday Activities." Communicative work is accomplished in an interactional time frame that Garfinkel referred to as "sequential," which is situated entirely and completely within a context of action, and made on the spot, but on the basis of expectations that are established before the action in question is undertaken. This conception of sequential time is essential to Garfinkel's position, as all mutually intelligible actions are situated actions in a sequence of actions, passed back and forth between actors, in a developing horizon of intelligible meaning, in a developing sequential time series, against which the recognizable boundaries of objects ("social things") can become visible. Sequential time is embodied and consists of a series of interpretive acts within recognizable mutually engaged fields of practice.

Since, as Garfinkel says, "anything can mean anything," nothing has any particular meaning except in so far as its position in some ordered sequence of interaction, in accordance with some mutual expectations, establishes an understanding between the participants. Situated actors place their interpretations into this developing order of sequences for the others to see and comment on. The actors have methods for doing this and, among other things, these methods allow them to correct and elaborate on the interpretations made of the mutually developing line of action at any point.

The relationship between the problem of scientific description and various phenomenological and gestalt issues with regard to intelligible communication, and the actor themselves as a situated accomplishment, are given more detailed theoretical articulation here than in later writing. The relationship between Garfinkel's argument and pragmatism is also taken up at some length. Thus, the manuscript has the potential to connect later, more empirical, demonstrations with the original theoretical questions as Garfinkel saw them. This manuscript represents Garfinkel's earliest attempt to bridge a gap between social practice and scientific description that was emerging in American Sociology in the post-war 1940s.

Seeing, in Garfinkel's view, requires a focus on the routine details that comprise the coherence of activities, not on the beliefs and motives of actors: Seeing in new ways, seeing society anew, and in details. This is not a trivial point, as

Garfinkel's argument becomes heavily involved with the way in which "gestalts," seen, heard, felt and embodied, "educated eyes" and "educated ears" are both enacted by, and comprise social action. Learning to *see differently* sociologically means learning to see social orders *in* their details *as* they are achieved in real time *by* persons *through* the enactment *of* those details instead of through conceptual glosses on those details after the fact.

Garfinkel's theory of information

Toward a Sociological Theory of Information (2008), completed in 1952 (hereafter *Information*), builds a sociological approach to information on the earlier theory of communication. Written by Garfinkel as Memo no. 3 for a seminar he was teaching at Princeton University on information and formal social organizations, the manuscript outlines an inherently *social* theory of information. Garfinkel maintains that information is not only put to social uses, but becomes information in the first place through situated social processes, in details. Thus, he argues, it is impossible to understand information, either intrinsically, or in application, without addressing its social and constitutively organized character. Included as appendices in the 2008 volume are two manuscripts (prepared for the seminar as Memos no. 1 and no. 2) in which Garfinkel outlined his theories of communication, self and social order. Two draft research proposals and a study of Bastrop, Texas completed in 1942 are also included.

Far from being outdated, in the 60 years since it was written, the argument has become increasingly relevant as technical worksites and computer-mediated interaction have become more prevalent, traditional approaches more problematic, and ethnomethodologically informed studies of those issues make an increasingly significant contribution.

In the manuscript, Garfinkel assesses classic information theory and the semantic and linguistic theories of communication it assumed. As Garfinkel points out, information theory has, from the first, been informed by theories of language. Therefore, changing the theory of language changes information theory. Garfinkel grounds his theory of information on a theory of communication, selves and objects, which treats them as constituted by the order properties of the situations in which they occur, and as having no other "objectivity" (mutually intelligible coherence). This alternative theory remains innovative and is the heart and soul of the manuscript.

By the time Garfinkel did this work at Princeton, the information age had ushered in a new focus on information, the design and management of information systems, and the need for easy information retrieval. Because signals must be paired with codes, and "noise" distinguished from information, in order for any of this to work, theories of information necessarily raise the problem of the relationship between ideas and symbols. In other words, information raises the classic problem of language and meaning in a new and very pragmatic form. Representations in information systems must match the content assigned to them in ways that are easily accessible by many different people. Theories about how people are believed to ordinarily manage a process of transferring ideas from one "mind" to another, through ordinary language and communication, have typically been invoked. In this way, assumptions (many of them problematic) about language, epistemology, ontology, and the nature of mind, cognition, categorization, and classification have found their way into technical specifications of work and information.

Information theorists have wanted language to work in logically driven and referential ways that can be easily engineered, but which do not match up well with the way language and meaning actually work. Because of this, information theory continues to struggle with theories of meaning and classification, and with epistemological and ontological assumptions. Social processes have become increasingly relevant.

The contemporary turn toward language in philosophy and social science intersects with the pragmatic organization, management, and retrieval of information in a profound way. Frustrated researchers in information sciences sometimes appeal to philosophers and social theorists to take seriously the problems of meaning, categorization, and epistemology they face. Ironically, problematic assumptions made by such researchers about definitions, categories, semantics, and grammars that get caught up not only in definitions of information, but in the organization, access and retrieval of information, have been seriously contested for centuries. What is new is that such "theoretical" questions have in the last two decades been recognized as practical problems for workers and systems designers in the world of information. More contact between disciplines is required to recognize the amazing conjunction between esoteric questions of theory and practical relevance that inhabit information and its domain.

Garfinkel's insistence that sociology stops taking communication and language as givens and address the epistemological issues that are foundational to any mutual intelligibility sets him squarely in the midst of these questions. His manuscript on information is an important piece of the historical debate that helps to situate and clarify the current state of both research and theory and to put information theory in touch with the philosophical and socio-theoretical issues. Those inspired by Garfinkel, along with followers of James, Durkheim, Lévi-Strauss, Wittgenstein, Foucault, and others, have for years engaged in a sustained critique of conventional information theory as based on a cognitivist and individualist model of communication that does not take the Wittgensteinian critique of referential (linguistic/semantic) meaning into account, does not reflect Whitehead's pragmatist critique of positivism (the fallacy of misplaced concreteness), does not consider social aspects of information, or the social character of categorization and classification (Durkheim, Lévi-Strauss, Foucault, Bourdieu).

Garfinkel's main point is that objects, selves, things, of *any sort* must be "thingified" in the context of some shared practice in order to be rendered in mutually intelligible ways; made recognizably and mutually coherent for more than one person at the same time. It is only in that way that they become objects. In Garfinkel's view, it is not possible to apprehend information, objects, or information exchange adequately without situating objects, meanings, and actions in the ordered social processes that constitute them. Other currently popular approaches that seem to take the constitutive and situated character of action and perception into account, escape into abstraction at some point. The currently popular idea of "boundary objects" for instance, objects that are allegedly the "same" across many contexts, solves the problem of "same object" by positing types of objects (such as birds) that are "durable" enough to escape the constraints of constitutive practice. The view consistent with Garfinkel's position is that if there are objects that cross situated boundaries it is not because some objects are common to more situations than others, but rather, because the practices which constitute them as mutually intelligible objects are themselves common across many situations and memberships. It is not the objects that have "durability," as ontological presences, but the practices which constitute them.

Articles published since studies

Between the publication of *Studies in Ethnomethodology* in 1967 and the three books published after 2002, Garfinkel published five principle articles: "On Formal Structures of Practical Action" with Harvey Sacks in 1970, "The Work of a Discovering Science Construed with Materials from the Optically Discovered Pulsar" with Michael Lynch and Eric Livingston in 1981, "Evidence for Locally Produced, Naturally Accountable Phenomena of Order, Logic, Reason, Meaning, Method, etc., in and as of the Essential Haecceity of Immortal Ordinary Society" (hereafter referred to as "Parsons's Plenum") in 1988, "Two Incommensurable Asymmetrically Alternate Technologies of Social Analysis" with Larry Weider in 1992, and "Ethnomethodology's Program" in 1996.

The paper "On Formal Structures of Practical Action," co-authored with Harvey Sacks, stands as a statement of the joint theoretical interest of ethnomethodology and conversation analysis. Garfinkel and Sacks spent several years working closely with one another in the early 1960s when Sacks was developing what would become known as conversational analysis. "Formal Structures" presents the argument that even the most mundane of practical actions have observable structures. While the idea is necessarily pursued differently in studies of conversation per se, and studies of practical activities that involve other sorts of practice along with conversation, the principle is the same. In order for practices to be mutually intelligible they must be recognizably produced and mutually confirming. This idea that all mutually intelligible actions have an observable structure is a distinctive characteristic of ethnomethodology and conversational analysis.

Ethnomethodology's program

This book consists of a collection of papers, lectures and research notes compiled by Garfinkel between 1967 and 2002. The paper on Galileo's Inclined Plane Experiment was compiled specifically for this book. There are chapters on Phenomenal Fields and Occasioned Maps that reflect Garfinkel's influence on various lines of research over the years.

The earlier "Parsons's Plenum" paper appears again in this book and outlines the relationship between Garfinkel's work and mainstream sociology as represented by Parsons. It stands as a summary statement of concerns that preoccupied Garfinkel's later work. Until at least 1964 he was hopeful of convincing Parsons to modify his position. He also gave a set of lectures called "Parsons's Primer" at UCLA that read Parsons through a set of modifications. The lectures remain unpublished. Garfinkel argues that there are two very different assumptions made about the nature of the social world by Parsons and himself and that those assumptions define their respective research programs in essential respects.

According to Garfinkel, the "Plenum" assumes a world in which individual persons, while possessed of a degree of freedom to act according to personal drives and motives, nevertheless come to realize that there are culturally accepted ways for doing most things. Thus individuals, in pursuing their individual interests, will usually attempt to choose courses of action that are socially acceptable. Furthermore, the very ways in which they interpret their feelings and even their physical needs will be socially constrained. For instance, individuals may have a drive to dominate others. In modern Western society, however, they will, if properly socialized, learn to interpret this drive as an impulse to achieve power or prestige in any of a number of socially acceptable ways.

Of course at some level this is right. Certainly individuals are constrained by social values. However, if one accepts the proposal that social order is composed *entirely* of the relationship between individuals and social constraint, then social order will appear to be merely the net result of general tendencies to comply with norms: order is then merely a summary or aggregate of individual actions. This is what Garfinkel says mainstream sociology does. Evidence of an "underlying social structure" that maintains norms and values and constrains persons to follow them in such a model comes to depend on the statistical manipulation of large aggregate data sets, as individuals are expected to vary in their degree of compliance. The result, according to Garfinkel, is "Parsons's Plenum": a theoretically constructed world in which order can only be discovered after and as a result of the application of a social scientific method.

Garfinkel contrasts this with a constitutive order of social action in which order is an inherent property of the mutual intelligibility of social activity. His concern is that the widespread focus of what he calls "formal analytic theory" and methods on aggregating data across large populations is preventing the discovery of the production of social order itself. The irony is that the dominant approach in the discipline of sociology to the problem of social order obscures the very processes of social orderliness that are being sought: the "what more" there is to social order than formal analytic theorizing can ever find. Garfinkel, for his part, argues that all socially recognizable actions must be produced in orderly and expected ways, and that they display their orderliness in their concrete details. Therefore, studying concrete practices in the situations in which they are produced can give the researcher direct access to the process of constituting local orders without aggregation.

It is the view of "structure" as a plenum that leads to the characterization of non-statistical approaches to sociology, and ethnomethodology in particular, as individualistic "micro" sociologies that are indifferent to the problem of social order. From Garfinkel's perspective, it is the mainstream view that fails to examine the most fundamental aspects of social order. How are persons able to recognize valued courses of action? How similar do actions need to be to be recognizably the same? When persons do not choose valued courses of action are they sanctioned? In Parsons's system a great deal of behavior that does not fit the norms is possible and goes unsanctioned. Post-structuralism and pragmatism are no different in this respect. For Garfinkel this explains neither the high degree of order experienced in everyday life, nor the routine achievement of intelligibility.

Garfinkel is not examining society at an "individual" or "micro" level. He is looking at the essential collectivities of modern life: examining the great classic questions of social order. He interprets Durkheim's immortal society to refer to the local production of order which Garfinkel calls "Immortal Ordinary Society." Society, in this view, does not depend on the tendencies of individuals to more or less comply with social norms. Society is immortal in that the patterned orderliness of situations outlives the particular persons who staff them. Persons know, according to Garfinkel, "of just these organizational things that they are in the midst of, that it preceded them and will be there after they leave; the great recurrences of ordinary society, staffed, provided for, produced, observed and observable locally and accountably, in and as of an 'assemblage of Haecceities'."[1]

The classic way of looking at social order places the emphasis on the populations who staff the scenes and thereby appear to create those scenes and on their demographic characteristics: gender, race, income, religion, education, etc. Garfinkel's focus places the emphasis on the patterned order of the scene. Any population coming on a particular scene could only recognizably reproduce it by recognizably producing the practices that identify it as a scene of a particular sort. Reconstructing the actor's point of view thus involves taking into account the various contingencies faced by any actor in attempting to produce recognizable practices. It does not involve the perspective of any particular actor.

According to Garfinkel, practitioners of formal analysis know about local orders. But, they don't know what to do with them. They "know" about them only in a special sense: as problems, recurrent irritations, and errors in "measurement" that need to be "controlled" for. They do not know them as social orders. Ethnomethodology recognizes these recurrent irregularities as the achieved orderliness of the "Immortal Ordinary Society." They are Durkheim's "social facts" conceived of not as external and coercive social norms, shared values, collective concepts, or goals, but as the achieved and enacted concrete detail of particular recognizable social practices and their occasions.

Garfinkel rejects the widespread idea that chaos and contingency are primary attributes of ordinary social scenes as individual actors struggle against institutional constraint. Struggle against institutional constraint takes place against a background of the underlying constitutive order practices of sense making. Mutually intelligible actions must have recognizably recurrent features and are therefore necessarily orderly. His insistence on the ongoing production of social order at all mutually intelligible points has sometimes been interpreted as evidence that his sociology is conservative because it does not seem to allow the individual actor any room to rebel or create. But sharing a local practice together, like playing a game together, does not work by constraint, but rather by mutual commitment to a practice. Such practices afford endless opportunities for creativity. In fact, Garfinkel's position allows for a great deal more "rebellion" against institutional values than most theories – because it argues for a layer of order beneath such institutions from which they can be criticized and resisted.

Nor does Garfinkel's argument deny the reality of institutional constraint. Accountability and documentary methods are responses to institutional constraint. What Garfinkel does is replace the vague notion of a conceptual, or structural, constraint on goals and values with concrete descriptions of how mutual intelligibility is achieved. The message is not that social inequality is not of concern to the analyst. Far from believing that all is well with the status quo, Garfinkel spent his career warning that many of the most trusted methods, methods presumed to be objective, are themselves shaped in essential ways by constraints on the social practices that constitute the essence of those methods, resulting in "critical" studies biased in favor of the status quo.

THE PERSON

Harold Garfinkel was born in Newark, New Jersey, on October 29, 1917. His formative years were spent in Newark during the Depression, where his father, Abraham Garfinkel, owned a small business selling household merchandize to immigrant families on the installment plan. The neighborhood in which he was raised consisted of a large Jewish community, at a time when ethnicity was important, and the problem of how to overcome poverty and disadvantage to succeed in the "chosen" country a pressing one. Many extremely bright young men and women, second and third-generation immigrants, were struggling not only to find a place in American society, but to formulate that place in their own terms.

For the elder Garfinkel, raising a son during the Depression, employment was the most important concern, and he wanted to be sure that his son learned a trade. Harold, on the other hand, wanted a university education. There was in the family an in-law who was not Jewish and was therefore credited with knowledge about what sorts of professions were viable in the world outside of the Newark Jewish community.

This in-law agreed to give advice with regard to Harold's future. One night at the dinner table he asked Harold what profession he would pursue at a university. Harold, who didn't really want to pursue a profession, recalls that he had been reading an article on surgeons in the *New York Times* and it sounded interesting. He answered that he wanted to become a surgeon. His in-law then told his father, "surgeons and lawyers are driving taxicabs." It was the middle of the Depression (1935). Thereupon, it was decided that Harold would go into the installment business with his father. Courses in business and accounting were germane to the business, however, so it was agreed that Harold would attend the University of Newark, an unaccredited program at the time, majoring in business and accounting during the day, and working in his father's installment business at night.

This early thwarting of the young Garfinkel's plans for a university education had some unpredictably happy results. The courses in accounting, in combination with friends made at the university, had an important and positive influence on the later development of his sociological theory and research. Because the program was unaccredited, the teaching was done primarily by graduate students from nearby universities. In the case of business courses at the University of Newark, the lecturers were quite often graduate students in economics from Columbia. This meant not only that courses were often taught by the best and brightest young minds in the country, but also that in business courses Garfinkel was apt to be taught the theory of business in place of procedure.

According to Garfinkel, his later work on accounts owes as much, or more, to a business course at the University of Newark called the "theory of accounts" as it does to Kenneth Burke whose theory of accounts he also studied. The course dealt with double entry bookkeeping and cost accounting. From this course, Garfinkel came to understand that even in setting up an accounting sheet he was theorizing the various categories into which the numbers would be placed. Choosing, for instance, whether to place an item in the debit or assets column was already a decision. Furthermore, that decision was accountable to superiors and other agencies in a variety of complex ways. The course, although a course in accounting, didn't deal with mathematics. "How do you make the columns and figures accountable?" was the big question according to Garfinkel.

These accountants and economists weren't describing events, they were describing "indicators," and unlike the social theorists Garfinkel was to encounter later, they were very frank about it. They didn't pretend their indicators constituted an underlying order or an existence independent of their accounting practices. There are clear connections between this approach to accounting and Garfinkel's later work. The argument of "Good Reasons for Bad Clinic Records," focusing, as it does, on the ways in which clinic workers render the files accountable, is an obvious parallel. So is the argument that formal analytic theorizing creates an orderly social world from "indicators" aggregated across large data sets.

At the University of Newark Harold hung out with a group of Jewish students who were interested in sociology. The group included Melvin Tumin, Herbert McClosky, and Seymour Sarason. According to Garfinkel, Philip Selznick and Paul Lazarsfeld, who were at Columbia at the time, were also known to members of the group. In fact, he recollects that Lazarsfeld taught a course in social statistics at the University of Newark attended by Tumin, McClosky, and Sarason. Students at this unaccredited university were able to take courses, developed by ambitious graduate students, not yet available at more traditional universities.

Discussions with this group turned Garfinkel's interests toward sociology. All the members of the group, along with their friends from Columbia, were later to rise to prominence, a fact that had a very positive influence on Garfinkel's career. Tumin became prominent as an anthropologist at Princeton. McClosky went on to join the political science faculty at Berkeley and helped introduce survey research to political science. Seymour Sarason went on to join the psychiatry faculty at Yale. Philip Selznick joined the sociology department at UCLA and later went on to Berkeley (where he supported the graduate careers of Sacks, Schegloff, and Sudnow). Lazarsfeld, unknown at the time, went on to establish scientific sociology at Columbia.

By the time Garfinkel graduated from the University of Newark in the summer of 1939 he knew that he could not go into the installment business with his father. He had a professor of insurance, Lawrence Ackerman, in whom he confided. Ackerman told him not to worry; he would help Harold to "get away." A Quaker, Ackerman arranged for Harold to attend a Quaker work camp that summer, building an earth dam for a rural community in Cornelia, Georgia. In that work camp, Garfinkel met a number of idealistic young people from Columbia and Harvard. By the end of the summer he knew he wanted to be a sociologist. At the camp, Morris Mitchell, from the Columbia School of Education, advised him that the sociology department at the University of North Carolina, which placed an emphasis on sociology as an effective means of furthering public service projects, was the place to go. So, at the end of the summer of 1939 Harold packed his bags and hitchhiked directly from the summer camp in Georgia to the University of North Carolina at Chapel Hill.

At North Carolina Guy Johnson became Harold's mentor and introduced him to the work of W. I. Thomas. Johnson was a former student of Howard W. Odum, the Chair at North Carolina, and his particular expertise was in race relations. Very active in local community associations that dealt with issues of race, Johnson generously made his own early research on race and interracial homicide available to Garfinkel, suggesting that he pursue the subject for his master's thesis. Garfinkel now owned a car, purchased for him by his father, and his fellowship freed him from the need to work, so he was able to visit all the courthouses in a ten county area, observe courtroom procedures and dig the information he needed out of the courthouse records. The result was his thesis on interracial homicide.

At North Carolina Garfinkel was introduced to a broad range of theoretical perspectives that shaped the development of ethnomethodology in significant ways. In addition to W. I. Thomas, he studied Florian Znaniecki's *Social Actions*, which he refers to as a highly significant, though much neglected, theoretical work. He was also introduced to the theories of accounts and vocabularies of motive of Kenneth Burke. He studied a broad range of phenomenological philosophy with a fellow student, James Fleming, with whom he discussed courses in the philosophy department that dealt with Husserl, Schutz, and Gurwitsch. Seymour Koch in the psychology department introduced Garfinkel to Lewin and gestalt psychology. *The Structure of Social Action*, by Talcott Parsons, had been published in 1937 and Harold purchased a first edition from McGraw-Hill that first Christmas at North Carolina. He says that he can still remember sitting in the backyard fingering the book, smelling the newness of its pages. According to Garfinkel it was a "love affair" with sociology from the beginning.

While immersed in the study of sociology at North Carolina, Garfinkel was befriended by a group of five students at the university who challenged Odum's view of sociology. While it seemed to Harold that the great political and social questions of the day were being debated with great energy at North Carolina, these students felt that the "real" debate was going on elsewhere. While Odum was committed to a program of documenting southern folk society, which he believed was the key to generic stable society, the students from New York City and Chicago were dreaming of Parsons at Harvard and Lazarsfeld and Merton at Columbia. It was going to be a scientific sociology, with Parsons, providing for order in ordinary society with grand heroic theories, at its head.

According to Garfinkel, Lazarsfeld was seen as the emissary to the new scientific sociology from Germany. He promised that sociology would become scientific with the use of social statistics and within ten years would be entirely mathematical. The idea was that if economists could make economic affairs accountable with indicators that made up a time series, then a scientific sociology should be able to do the same thing for social behavior in general. This determination would dominate sociological thinking in the 1940s. Everyone was singing the same chorus of models and modeling, and quantitative methods were the *sine qua non* if you wanted to be taken seriously.

In the sociology department at North Carolina, however, there was one graduate student, James Fleming, who was not taken up with the pursuit of empirical "scientific" (quantitative) sociology. Fleming was engaged in reading "across the disciplines," looking for the actor's point of view. Znaniecki's book *Social Action*, not the study of the Polish peasant, was the canonical text with regard to the actor's point of view. According to Garfinkel, Znaniecki was the first to insist vociferously on the adequate description of social action, an issue which became a primary concern of Garfinkel's and remained so throughout his career. The problem facing Znaniecki's theory of social action, however, according to Garfinkel, was what an adequate description of action could consist of, given the insistence on the relevance of the actor's point of view.

Garfinkel's combination of the theory of accounts with the problem of the actor's point of view would provide a novel approach to this problem. His first publication, "Color Trouble," an early effort at an adequate description of accounting practices, exhibits the skeleton of his mature view. It was first published in 1939, Garfinkel's first winter at North Carolina. His master's thesis examined accounts produced in court in homicide cases. There was a deep racial bias evident in the accounts, which disappeared when outcomes were aggregated. This he found was because black defendants who had killed black victims were characterized as doing the community a favor as were white defendants who had killed black victims. The accounts made evident the importance of the race and social standing of the victim in determining the outcome.

Garfinkel's graduate career at North Carolina was interrupted by the entry of the United States into the Second World War. After completing his master's thesis in the spring of 1942, Garfinkel went to Bastrop, Texas to do fieldwork for Wilbert Moore. His final report was written to Moore on July 24, 1942 (published as an appendix to *Information*). He was drafted and assigned to the air force that fall. He says he took with him thoughts on Parsons and Znaniecki and his theorizing with regard to accounts. He was by that time also familiar with Husserl, Schutz, and Gurwitsch, and the idea of multiple realities in James and Schutz. In the air force, Garfinkel was assigned to designing and teaching strategies for small arms warfare against tanks and rose to the rank of corporal. It was also during the war that Garfinkel married his wife Arlene.

The task of training troops in small arms warfare against tanks was the most ironically appropriate assignment one can think of for the future "father" of ethnomethodology. Garfinkel was given the task of training troops in tank warfare on a golf course on Miami Beach in the complete absence of tanks. Garfinkel had only pictures of tanks from *Life* magazine. The real tanks were all in combat. The man who would insist on concrete empirical detail *in lieu* of theorized accounts was teaching real troops who were about to enter live combat to fight against only imagined tanks in situations where things like the proximity of the troops to the imagined tank could make the difference between life and death. The impact of this on the development of his views can only be imagined. He had to train troops to throw explosives into the tracks of imaginary tanks; to keep imaginary tanks from seeing them by directing fire at imaginary tank ports. This task posed in a new and very concrete way the problems of the adequate description of action and accountability that Garfinkel had taken up at North Carolina as theoretical issues.

During the war Garfinkel also did a study of pilot training and wrote up several sets of observations: a study of labeling sick soldiers at the Gulfport Army hospital (described in *Seeing*) and a study of leadership (published in the appendix to *Information*).

After the war, Garfinkel went on to Harvard to study for his PhD with Talcott Parsons.[2] The relationship between Garfinkel's work and Parsons's social theory, as it developed at Harvard, is an important one. Garfinkel insisted on the adequacy of description and a focus on contingent detail. Parsons relied on conceptual categories and generalization. The engagement between their positions would develop into one of the most important theoretical debates of the past several decades. In his doctoral thesis, Garfinkel took on Parsons more or less directly and continued to work with Parsons until at least 1964 in an attempt to modify his position. Parsons's "Response to Dubin" in 1960 (ASR) shows evidence of some success in this regard. However, sometime after 1964 Garfinkel withdrew from this debate, maintaining that his position could be demonstrated only empirically, not theoretically. What is only now coming to light is the deep regard that Garfinkel and Parsons had for one another.

While pursuing his degree at Harvard, Garfinkel worked again for Wilbert Moore on The Organizational Behavior Project, funded by the Ford Foundation, at Princeton University.[3] While at Princeton, he taught seminars in sociology and information theory for two years and organized a conference for the project in 1952, called "Problems in Model Construction in the Social Sciences." The idea was to develop interdisciplinary studies in organizational behavior. Garfinkel sought out innovative theorists for this conference, inviting Herbert Simon, Talcott Parsons, Kenneth Burke, Kurt Wolff, Alfred Schutz, Gregory Bateson, Philip Selznick, and Paul Lazarsfeld. Garfinkel kept up a correspondence with Simon and arranged to spend time with him after he left Princeton. However, instead when Garfinkel left Princeton in 1952, after receiving his degree from Harvard, he joined Kurt Wolff at Ohio State University at the "Personnel Research Board," a group of industrial psychologists with federal funding to support studies of leadership on submarines and airplanes.

The following year Fred Strodbeck, another classmate from Harvard who was at Wichita engaged in his jury study project, asked Garfinkel to join him and Saul Mendlovitz. While Garfinkel was at Wichita, the three reported on their work at the American Sociological Association meetings in the summer of 1954. In preparing for this talk, Garfinkel searched for what to call what they found so interesting in their discussions with the jurors. He examined the Yale cross-cultural survey and saw all the "ethnos" – ethnoscience, ethnobotany, etc. – and thought of the jury members' close reasonings with one another as "ethnomethods." The word "methods" was, according to Garfinkel, an extrapolation from Felix Kaufmann, a philosopher, who spoke of the term methodology as the theory of correct decisions in deciding the grounds for action and further inference. Together the two words seemed to apply to what the jurors were doing. Thus, the term "ethnomethodology" was born.

In the fall of 1954 Harold was asked to join the faculty at UCLA. Selznick's earlier move to UCLA turned out to be of particular importance to Garfinkel; it was Selznick along with Tumin who talked the then-chair at UCLA, Leonard Broom, into hiring Harold when Selznick moved from UCLA to Berkeley. UCLA was a joint sociology/anthropology department at the time, and the anthropologists appreciated Garfinkel's attention to interactional detail. This was an unexpectedly lucky move for Garfinkel, as UCLA, which was practically unknown at the time, quickly rose to become one of the top universities nationally. From the very beginning at UCLA Garfinkel used the term ethnomethodology, developed in Wichita, in his seminars.

At UCLA Garfinkel worked with a number of students and colleagues who became prominent proponents of ethnomethodology and conversational analysis. They very often worked together in teams and held meetings at which they presented their research. Many of these meetings were audio taped. Garfinkel could be an inspiring teacher and patient with his colleagues over long periods. But, he is also an exacting thinker and was often disappointed in the end. Garfinkel's relationship with Harvey Sacks, who did research with Garfinkel at UCLA and then joined the faculty at UC Irvine after completing his dissertation with Erving Goffman at Berkeley, was of particular importance. There were also meetings between Parsons, Garfinkel, Goffman, and Sacks at which they discussed research at the Suicide Prevention Center in Los Angeles being done by Garfinkel and Sacks. Sacks, along with Emmanuel Schegloff, also from Berkeley, and Gail Jefferson, outlined what has essentially become a new field of conversational studies, referred to as "conversational analysis," within the general parameters of ethnomethodology.

Garfinkel and his wife Arlene, married during the war, have lived in Pacific Palisades, California, continuously from 1961. They raised two children and supported one another's intellectual endeavors during 60 plus years of marriage. Arlene Garfinkel's work as a lipid chemist inspired many of Garfinkel's insights into scientists' work. Garfinkel formally retired from UCLA in 1987 but remained active as an emeritus professor.

THE SOCIAL CONTEXT

Garfinkel grew to maturity at a critical moment in American history. The Depression, the Second World War, and the immediate post-war period were times of sweeping social transition. This social context created a mood of both opportunity and criticism that turned Garfinkel toward an interest in social issues. The Depression was a particularly difficult time for the American working class, whose jobs were eliminated by the failure of industry. During the Depression a new spirit of democracy and anti-elite sentiment swept the nation, and the New Deal placed an emphasis on the problems of the American poor and working classes for the first time. These circumstances led to a heightened political awareness among the working class, and the young Garfinkel found himself caught up in debates over politics, economics, and the possibility of general social transformation going on in the community around him.

With the onset of the Second World War, however, the situation began to change. There were now jobs to be had in industries related to the war effort. In white working-class communities the perception that all was well with America quickly replaced the anxiety of the Depression years. The great majority of the white working class was eager to parlay its newfound job security into upward mobility into the middle class. Race-based government housing and lending programs, begun during the Depression, fueled this interest, enabling the white working class to distance themselves from African American and ethnic minority communities by building all-white suburbs.

This created a crisis within the working class. The gains made during the Depression were really very small. Political organs of the working class, like the UAW (United Auto Workers), which had been so strong during the Depression, began to wither in the mid-1940s. Even in so strong a union town as Detroit the union was unable to elect a mayor after this period. According to UAW leaders, their political position was weakened by large numbers of the white working class, who simply pretended they had achieved middle-class status, voting middle-class interests.

This wholesale adoption of middle-class values did not penetrate to Jewish and other ethnic minority communities. While they did benefit to some extent from the increase in jobs, the preferential treatment of the white working class during the war and post-war period raised the level of debate over social issues in minority communities to new levels. African American and Jewish leaders continued to talk about equality and social change throughout the war and post-war years.

Thus, at a time when the majority of white working-class Americans were becoming more politically conservative, those Jewish, African American, and other ethnic minorities who were excluded by housing and other forms of discrimination from participation in this exclusive all-white group, became further politicized. Socialism became increasingly popular and labor unions during this time increasingly identified with a socialist or Marxist framework. While it was not the only factor, race and ethnicity played a key role in the determination of political awareness during this period.

This early exposure to the importance of race and ethnicity is reflected in Garfinkel's early writings, in his master's thesis on interracial homicide, and in his first publication "Color Trouble." Both deal with the situated social production of African American inequality and demonstrate a clear concern for, and understanding of, the plight of African Americans, a group whose tenuous relationship to the mainstream Garfinkel well understood. A critical attitude toward the institutions of mainstream American society, political, social, and intellectual, continued to characterize Garfinkel's later studies in ethnomethodology.

In addition to the general social upheaval of the period and the debate it fostered over social issues, the Second World War was a particularly significant time in which to be Jewish in America. Because of the conflict with Hitler's fascist anti-Semitism, the widespread discrimination against Jews in the United States came to be seen generally for the first time as a social problem. After the war, when Americans realized the extent of German atrocities, an unprecedented effort was made to confront anti-Semitism.

Within the Jewish community this combination of events created a highly politicized atmosphere, much as a new awareness of post-war segregation and inequality did in the African American community. Young Jewish men and women, particularly in New York, earnestly discussed politics, the war, and the creation of a Jewish state. When Garfinkel attended the University of Newark, even as a business and accounting student, he found himself continually caught up in these discussions.

This atmosphere of discussion and debate, because of its emphasis on the transformation of the social and political system, resulted, for the first time, in a widespread interest in the discipline of sociology. The social theories of Karl Marx, John Dewey's argument connecting social relations to Democracy, and Talcott Parsons's vision of voluntaristic egalitarian social action were widely read during this period of wartime antifascism. Sociology, the efficacy of New Deal social programs, and the future of capitalism were all seriously debated in the 1930s and early 1940s at a time when most universities did not yet have sociology departments. This interest influenced the career choices of many young students, including Garfinkel.

The resulting increase in the demand for courses in sociology forced many universities to open sociology departments, a trend that continued through the 1950s and

1960s. Undergraduate and graduate students alike turned to sociology as a discipline relevant to the social issues of the day. New academic positions were created for those, like Garfinkel, who were attracted to academic life by the social upheaval of the times. Sociology promised to provide solutions to many pressing social problems, and there was room in the thriving new discipline for many innovative young thinkers.

The Intellectual Context

Critical to an understanding of Garfinkel's work is the fact that he began his graduate education at the University of North Carolina at Chapel Hill prior to the Second World War and saw active service during the war. He belongs to a generation, educated before the war, and seeing wartime service, that embraced sociology as a set of broad theoretical and methodological issues, deeply relevant to the morality of the times and not constrained by scientific sociology as it developed during and immediately after the war.

A tendency to focus on Garfinkel's graduate training at Harvard, overlooking the years he spent at North Carolina, has led to the view that the genesis of his position can be traced to a conflict with Parsons, and an admiration for Schutz. In fact, he took issue with both making use of each in highly selected ways. It is more accurate to set the development of Garfinkel's ideas against the intellectual backdrop of the sociology department at North Carolina. Garfinkel went to Harvard with a set of well-formulated ideas about the actor's point of view, the essential character of reflexivity, the importance of adequate description, and a reinterpretation of Burke and Mills on accounts, developed at North Carolina. During the war he engaged in significant research projects that sharpened his perspective. It was in the contrast between these already deeply held and well worked out ideas, and Parsons's teaching, that Garfinkel began to develop his mature views. But, the most important continuing factor was Garfinkel's attention to the empirical details of actual ongoing practices.

Sociology, as Garfinkel initially encountered it in the 1930s, was a multifaceted discipline, with many widely divergent theories and methods. The Chicago School, inspired by the work of Robert Park, W. I. Thomas, Charles Horton Cooley, George Herbert Mead, and Florian Znaniecki, was still a dominant force. The perspective of the actor and interaction were serious issues. The work of Karl Marx was actively debated, and Parsons and scientific sociology had not yet come to dominate the discipline.

When Garfinkel arrived at the University of North Carolina as a graduate student in the summer of 1939 he encountered a group of scholars committed to addressing issues of poverty, inequality, and race relations. Both theoretically and methodologically, the department reflected the eclectic nature of the discipline at that time. The graduate training that Garfinkel and others received during this period was broadly theoretical, with a social problems emphasis. Preserving the social fabric of society against the onslaught of modernity was a pressing issue. Ethnography was an important and widespread methodological tool.

By the time Garfinkel reached Harvard after the war, however, there was a recognized dominant type of sociology considered by most people to be more scientific and valid than the types of sociology that preceded it. Parsons was its acknowledged leader. Znaniecki, the Chicago School, C. Wright Mills, phenomenology, and

Marxist sociology all but disappeared for a number of years. Even Max Weber and Émile Durkheim were for years only interpreted and studied in terms set by Parsons. Durkheim's important arguments about the emergence of self-organizing practices in modern society (1893) and his epistemological arguments (1912) were neglected entirely.

How and why a combination of statistical methods and Parsonian structural functionalism came to define the notions of "scientific" and "objective" is an interesting issue. Marx, Weber, Toennies, Simmel, and Mead had not really made use of statistics. Even Durkheim, who introduced the idea that statistical trends might represent underlying social facts in his book *Suicide*, made only very limited use of them. However, by the 1950s the world had changed. The old social order had been, if not radically transformed, at least given that appearance. Miracle drugs, invented to fight infectious diseases, were widely available. The power of the atom had been unleashed on Hiroshima and Nagasaki. Scientific and mathematical challenges directly related to the war had spurred the development of computers.

A struggle to define the parameters of adequate scientific description came to dominate American Sociology in the 1940s as sociologists, concerned with their lack of influence on war related policy making, attempted to increase their influence by adopting what they considered more scientific standards of research. Scientists were the ones who had influence. Prominent sociologists advocated a unified theory and method. The solution, it was said, lay in numbers and the clarity of concepts. The problem was that they could not agree on either the theory or the method. When Paul Lazarsfeld moved to the United States from Germany, the social statistics he advocated were just what an eager population of sociologists committed to becoming more scientific wanted. But, these statistics made their way into many competing theories and theoretical differences ironically increased.

Post-war sociologists also became increasingly preoccupied with what they saw as a problem of eroding morality and character in post-war "modern" society. The idea of character as a social construction, and debates over the social organization of interaction were first emerging. David Reisman's *Lonely Crowd*, the first of many influential attempts to come to terms with the new situated quality of morality, personal character, and interaction in post-war society was published by Harvard Press in 1950 while Garfinkel was a graduate student there. The theme of the relationship between character and society was taken up also in studies of the family by Talcott Parsons among others. The contrast between traditional ideas about morality, and the moral demands of practices became a focus. Interaction tended to be seen as a dimension for the exercise of individualism, not a domain of inherently collective social action.

For Garfinkel, however, the need for participants to maintain a commitment to the background expectations of situations, which he referred to as the "Trust" requirement, makes successful interaction inherently collective, and constitutes a moral dimension in its own right. While this morality does threaten traditional belief-based moral systems, they in turn conflict with the requirements of public interaction in a pluralistic society. The background expectations of members' methods, on the other hand, support the practice of public civility. A public civil and secular morality may thus be seen as emerging from the collective need to be mutually engaged in practices.

Garfinkel was not entirely alone in his pursuit of these questions; forms of sociology committed to the adequate description of social action continued to be practiced. Studies focused on interaction continued at the University of Chicago where Erving Goffman and Everett Hughes argued that the details being lost were essential to meaning, order, coherence, and understanding. A number of studies consistent with Garfinkel's position on both trust and institutional accountability appeared in the 1950s demonstrating a connection between the development of particular forms of character and forms of interaction, in prisons (*Society of Captives*, Gresham Sykes), mental institutions (*Asylums*, Erving Goffman), mental health (*Manufacture of Madness*, Thomas Szasz). But in the new intellectual context anything other than the new scientific sociology had to be justified by contrast to the prevailing view. It was a difficult time to be different.

From the early fifties until the late sixties "statistical" sociology with a functional orientation reigned almost unchallenged. It began to be clear, however, that there were deep theoretical problems involved. For one thing, when notions of scientific and mathematical clarity are applied to the study of human society something essential is lost. Because human actions are meaningful and involve reflexivity, human intelligibility does not lend itself to "objective" mathematical study. Furthermore, models perfected in advance of research cannot take what is learned from observation into account. The discipline faced a crisis and sociologists began to search for alternatives. Earlier trends in theorizing, temporarily eclipsed by the new statistically driven scientific theorizing, regained some of their former status. Marxist and Weberian approaches to sociology enjoyed a newfound legitimacy in the 1960s and 1970s. Interactionism, labeling theory, social problems, and symbolic interactionism became popular. Pragmatism made a resurgence in philosophy. Sociological perspectives influenced by phenomenological philosophy, existentialism, and Wittgenstein also gained ground. French post-structuralist theories were embraced.

Into this social climate stepped Garfinkel, with his emphasis on interactional detail and adequate description. For many young sociologists, Garfinkel provided the first introduction to phenomenology, philosophy, pragmatist issues, questions of epistemology as they apply to sociology, and a new and different appreciation of classical social theory. He was one of the first to argue that phenomenological texts were central to the sociological enterprise. Confronted by a discipline in crisis Garfinkel and other Interactionists like Erving Goffman and Howard Becker seemed for many to have arrived "just in time" to save sociology. Very few students in the 1960s were interested in understanding how to maintain the status quo. They were interested instead in change and challenge; in social movements; in new ways of thinking that were not so Western, logical, and middle class in emphasis.

Garfinkel challenged the prevailing criteria for adequate research: that studies could be considered scientific only if they aggregated numerically across clear conceptual classifications theoretically defined. In so doing, he challenged the very notion of technical reason that was the driving force behind scientific sociology and the validity of the classifications it depended on. He authored a sociological theory of information which proposed that every object needed to be "thingified" through social practices. These efforts constitute an important American counterpoint to the development of Critical Theory in Germany that is rarely acknowledged as such. Garfinkel believed that the processes of theoretical and mathematical justification required for acceptance by scientific sociology were logically incompatible with the phenomena of social order. Furthermore they tended to validate the status quo. Scientific sociology, as it had emerged in the 1940s and 1950s at Harvard and Columbia, was, according to Garfinkel, obscuring, rather than clarifying, the understanding of social reality.

Ethnomethodology stands as a direct contradiction to the faith in formalism, technical reason, and mathematicized representations of social behavior that came to define post-war sociology. Garfinkel argued that formalism depends on the enactment of social practices which remain unexamined. Even engineers and mathematicians do not work in a pure mathematical vacuum. They must speak to one another and make mutual sense of the domain in which they work. Engineers must imagine the uses to which persons will put the products they are engaged in producing. These activities involve the use of practices which are in essential respects constitutive of what science, mathematics, and engineering will turn out to be. In fact no domain of human endeavor is free from this requirement. Ironically, in order to succeed at work based in technical reason, a detailed understanding of those ordinary practices through which persons regularly achieve recognizable and mutually intelligible sense is required.

IMPACT

Since the publication of *Studies in Ethnomethodology* in 1967, Harold Garfinkel's work has had an enormous influence on many disciplines in the social sciences and humanities worldwide. The more recent publication of his early work is underscoring its relevance to technical domains of work and sensemaking. Shortcomings with the "scientific" study of human society laid bare by critiques of structural functionalism and positivism in the 1960s and 1970s fueled a search in many disciplines for a new approach. Garfinkel's arguments introduced aspects of the problem of social order and intelligibility that promised to address these concerns. He took seriously the problem of interpretation proposed by hermeneutic philosophy as the alternative to positivism and sought to restore the perspective of the actor. However, he also and at the same time sought to restore the validity of adequate empirical description of the details of social action. In addition, Garfinkel's demonstrations of the taken-for-granted constitutive features of members' methods oriented the discipline toward the observation of social practice in a deeper and more detailed way.

The promise of simultaneously addressing all these issues had great appeal. There has been a subtle shift since the 1960s and 1970s in what counts as adequate description, and Garfinkel played an important part in creating it. The shift crossed disciplinary boundaries and many scholars who would not think of themselves as having been interested in ethnomethodology were nevertheless influenced by Garfinkel's emphasis on members' methods and adequate empirical description.

Researchers began to look for the underbelly of society. Informal orders were discovered everywhere: in formal institutions, in scientific practice, in classroom instruction. Wherever researchers looked there were previously unsuspected levels of order in detail to be uncovered. While Garfinkel was joined by Goffman and others in leading the discipline toward a more detailed look at interaction and the Interaction

Order, it was Garfinkel who moved beyond the problems of self and interpretation to take a serious look at the problem of mutual intelligibility and its relationship to constitutive practices at its most fundamental level.

His argument that even scientific practices and scientific objects are recognizably constituted social orders directly challenged the mainstream assumptions about what is scientific, and has inspired important studies in the sociology of science. His criticisms of technical reason and formalism in the scientific workplace gave rise to studies of practices in mathematics and engineering, and the application of computers and other technology in the workplace. Studies of conversation influenced by Garfinkel, Sacks, Schegloff, Jefferson, and Pomerantz impacted communication, semiotics, linguistics, and studies of communication in applied areas such as doctor–patient interaction, intercultural communication, legal reasoning, and various institutional and workplace settings.

Studies of institutional accounting practices, inspired by Garfinkel's theory of accounts, have focused on the generation of records during plea bargaining, on truck drivers' log-keeping practices, police recordkeeping practices, and coroners' decisions with regard to suicide. For many with an interest in social reform Garfinkel's argument pointed toward the organizational production of those statistics which are offered by scientific sociology as representations of the "real" world. If administrators, politicians, and institutional workers all have ongoing organizational reasons for manipulating the generation of statistics, then surely the generation of statistics should be an important topic for a critical social science.

Furthermore, the idea that a social institution that is believed to discriminate by class and race, such as the police, the courts, schools, or a workplace, should be allowed through its own worksite practices to generate statistical accounts that support its own claims not to be discriminating, and that those statistical accounts should be taken as undeniable scientific evidence of social structure, is, in Garfinkel's view, unthinkable. Yet even today the vast majority of the articles published in the *American Sociological Review* use secondary statistical data sets generated by institutional accounts.

From Garfinkel's position, a scientific sociology based on such data can never be politically disinterested. It can only confirm the prevailing views of those institutions that generated its data. That may explain its popularity. Ethnomethodology, on the other hand, generally represented as indifferent to issues of structure and politics, is indifferent only to institutionalized structures of accountability. Ethnomethodology cannot be indifferent to political, ethical, or theoretical critique because that is essentially what it is. Garfinkel seeks to reveal the methods persons use to create the appearance that various "facts" exist independently of those methods.

Ethnomethodologists have also undertaken studies of specific disciplinary methods, such as survey research and focus group interviews. In all these studies the emphasis has been on the practices used to achieve the results in question. Garfinkel's insistence that researchers achieve the "unique adequacy" requirement of methods before they attempt to answer these how and why questions has generated many studies that could be considered practical or applied research. Such "hybrid studies," done by outsiders who are also insiders, have as their aim that practitioners in the specialty area being studied will be as interested in the studies as professional sociologists. Many of the practices essential to the constitutive features of any social setting make use of conversation, and there are essential constitutive features of conversation to which practitioners at any worksite must attend. Thus, many who have developed a serious interest in ethnomethodology have also used conversational analysis as one of their research tools. The constitutive features of talk are inexorably intertwined with the achievement of ordinary practices.

From small beginnings with a handful of graduate students at UCLA, ethnomethodology spread quickly around the world. While several of Garfinkel's students and colleagues like Sacks, Sudnow, and Schegloff played an important role in promoting the popularity of ethnomethodology, its spread depended heavily on the interest of sociologists who never studied with Garfinkel and who initially knew little about ethnomethodology. Their interest had its origins in a deep dissatisfaction with the state of social theory and methods.

In the 1980s and 1990s a number of sociologists, dissatisfied with the discipline's lack of response to these concerns, turned to poststructural and postmodern alternatives. Ironically, poststructuralists and postmodernists tend to view structure in a Parsons's Plenum sort of way, accepting the individual versus structure dichotomy, while they reject the moral validity of structures. Thus, both sides in structure–poststructure debate share a conception of structure that Garfinkel challenged.

Poststructuralism owes a great deal to French anthropology and begins with the understanding that it is against structures that the shared meanings of everyday life are achieved. Meanings are defined in structural opposition either to one another – "up" can only be understood in contrast to "down" and "black" to "white" – or to institutional structures, as when a person's actions in waiting for a bus to get to work are seen to be defined by the institutions of work, or one's gender role is seen to be defined by the conceptual structure of gender terms in a given society. The essential idea is that "structures," in some fashion or other, impart meaning to everyday language and action. Then, in order to "break out," persons have to "deconstruct" the structures.

The problem is that the result of deconstruction should be a meaningless infinite regress if all shared meaning (and most private meaning) really were produced by relations between persons (or actions) and formal structure as poststructuralists argue. But, in fact, the operation is often quite meaningful and revealing. This is hard to explain from within either the poststructural or the postmodern position.

For Garfinkel, however, there are an unlimited number of ways of constructing the intelligibility of social action at the local level. When persons rebel against structure, the rebellion is made possible by these underlying endogenously produced intelligibilities. In fact, something like what Garfinkel is articulating seems to be the only explanation for how persons can rebel against structure yet have their language and activities remain mutually intelligible.

From Garfinkel's perspective, the popularity of deconstruction as a method is easy to explain. Poststructuralism is another version of theorized reality. While it is in some respects new, it is also very familiar. It promises novelty without requiring changes in the basic theorized assumptions of sociology as a discipline. In the rush to deconstruct, the social world is once again being theorized, and the interactional practices which are actually constitutive of intelligibility are being overlooked again in favor of an institutionalized view of meaning.

More recently the popularity of Bourdieu, Giddens, and the turn to pragmatism in social theory have caught ethnomethodology up in their wake. While these

perspectives present more serious alternatives to the mainstream than poststructuralism did, they still retain elements of the individual versus structure dichotomy and
the reification of social objects, selves and meanings that differentiate them from
Garfinkel's perspective. Social practices in empirical details are not beliefs, local
orders are not routines – they are always done for the "next first time" – and meaning and identity are not either properties of individuals or defined by social institutions: they must be continually achieved. Differences between his position and
pragmatism were taken up at length by Garfinkel in the 1948 manuscript (*Seeing*).

Critics often ask why Garfinkel did not himself engage in clarification with regard
to issues that have been so consequential for the reception of his work. The consideration of pragmatism in the 1948 manuscript shows that he once did. But, given his
commitment to an empirical demonstration of his claims, and his experience with
misunderstandings of his earlier attempts at theoretical clarification, I believe his
silence is due to a conviction that as an argument his position could only be demonstrated empirically. In Garfinkel's view, theoretical demonstrations depend hopelessly
on imagined orders of affairs and if an argument cannot be persuasive without being
theorized, it is because the empirical demonstrations still fall short of adequate description. Thus, Garfinkel has consistently met theoretical criticism by attempting to
deepen the level of empirical detail in his research. This has often confused critics.

Because he felt that the generic and theorized terminology of mainstream sociology rendered social orders invisible, Garfinkel has also been wary of using generic
terms and generalizations in his own work. His invention of new words and phrases
to express the empirical social relations discovered through his research is part of
what makes his work so hard to read. One must make a commitment to treating his
terminology as essential to his argument. In this regard, Garfinkel's writing resembles that of Marx, who, in his attempt to avoid treating mutually dependent social
processes as though they were independent entities (reification), constructed sentences in which the subject is also the object of the same sentence. In Garfinkel's case,
the attempt to avoid theorized generalities led to an emphasis on words and phrases
that specify the concreteness of things and at the same time specify the contingency
of the various positions in which things are constituted. Phrases like "as of which,"
that multiply the propositional relationships between "objects" and the occasions
upon which they are socially constituted as such, are common.

The continual emphasis in Garfinkel's work on "just-thisness," "haecceities,"
"details," "order," and "contingencies" is an attempt not to lose the phenomena
through generalization. Trying not to refer to local order phenomena in general
terms is linguistically strange. However, the importance of the contingencies of local
order phenomena to his argument justifies the attempt. The spotlight falls on the
constitutive practices that order these contingencies.

Garfinkel has opened the way for a new sort of theorizing. Theorizing more broadly
conceived does not have to be of the generic, categorizing, plenum sort. There is no
reason, in principle, why theorists cannot be faithful to the phenomena; no reason
why they have to proceed in generic terms. Garfinkel has shown us the possibility of
empirical theorizing and it is in these terms that I want to refer to Garfinkel as one of
the great social theorists of the twentieth century. However, he is quite right that contemporary theory has, for the most part, proceeded in terms of categories and generic
terms. If I call Garfinkel a theorist, there are sure to be sociologists who will want to

reduce his arguments to categories and generic terms. It is essential to note that this understanding of social theory is entirely incompatible with Garfinkel's view.

ASSESSMENT

Garfinkel's relationship to the discipline of sociology is both highly significant and extremely ironic. Ethnomethodology has from first to last been an exercise in sociology. Garfinkel dedicated his life work to documenting the empirical details of orderly social practices. This is an empirical work of scientific discovery focused on the details of constitutive collective social processes.[4] However, the sociological elite during the 1940s defined scientific empiricism as the study of abstract conceptual representations of individuals and their normative values, represented in numerical form. Because Garfinkel's approach did not fit this definition of empirical it has been characterized by the discipline as a "micro" sociology focused on individual, contingent, and subjective matters, and not on the collective empirical aspects of social order and mutual intelligibility it actually investigates.

Many sociologists who have been labeled micro do accept a version of sociology that treats conceptual representations as the foundation of social order and meaning. Because they think of "practices" in terms of concepts and ideas, they also reject Garfinkel's claim that in studying concrete witnessable practices he is engaged in empirical research. They argue that Garfinkel is theorizing the relationship between individual concepts and shared symbolic meanings, not engaging in empirical research, as he claims. Consequently, they criticize him for ignoring the infinite regress entailed by representational accounts of meaning.

Because Garfinkel rejects assumptions fundamental to both micro and macro sociology, sociologists from both camps make mirror versions of the same criticism of his work. It is incorrect to assess Garfinkel's work as a conceptual or interpretive exercise – although interpretation is involved in the enactment of constitutive practices themselves. Garfinkel does not set up a relationship between conceptual meanings and symbolic representations. Meaning is accomplished as the outcome of a reflexive and ordered social process. Ethnomethodology is a thoroughly empirical enterprise devoted to the discovery of social order and intelligibility as witnessable collective achievements. Ethnomethodology is not indifferent to issues of social structure; only to issues of institutional structure as defined by mainstream sociology.

The true irony is that Garfinkel focused on members' methods for achieving recognizable social phenomena because he *did* believe that empirically observable, collectively enacted, social structures existed and were being obscured by conventional methods of research, *not* because he wanted to study individuals. Because these orders are actual they can be empirically observed. Because these orders are inherently collective, a focus on individual subjectivity would obscure them. Mainstream sociology focused on statistical indicators of individual tendencies to orient toward normative goals because they *did not* believe that there were social structures that could be observed empirically. They thought they had to aggregate across general concepts to get rid of the details of particular settings and thereby reveal order as a general principle.

The misinterpretations of Garfinkel originate in the fact that his position conflicts with basic assumptions about the institutional character of social order, and the symbolic and representational nature of meaning; assumptions essential to the macro/micro distinction, and the emphasis on unified theory and conceptual clarity which have dominated the discipline since the mid-twentieth century. The basic disciplinary assumptions were formalized as sets of dichotomies in textbooks that taught the doctrine that sociology either took a formal institutionalized collective view (macro) or was individualistic and contingent (micro). This doctrine left no room for the idea that Interaction Order phenomena are collective, made for and with one another, according to shared criteria.

Before 1940 the bias in favor of conceptual reduction and aggregated indicators was not so strong. At the end of the nineteenth century close observations of situated events played a central role in social theory and research. Although there was a tendency to reduce observations to generalizations and ideal types, it was really only in the period after the Second World War, that generalizations defined the research subject from the beginning. Durkheim, usually credited with introducing statistics and a focus on formal institutions, actually argued (in *The Division of Labor*, 1893) for the importance in modern society of a level of self-organizing constitutive order (embodied in occupational groups and scientific practice) that resists more formal levels of order such as government and the law. This argument grounds his claim that justice will become a functional requirement in modernity.

Sociology went from a concern with documenting the details of social order and its moral implications to a concern with becoming more mathematical and generalizable, in order to justify itself as a science. The classical concerns with the meaning and epistemological foundation of social action and its moral implications were almost completely forgotten.

Garfinkel's position preserves those earlier concerns. The difference is that his approach to social order places the emphasis on constitutive local orders, rather than on either institutional or conceptual (representational) orders.

Insisting that Interaction Orders are fundamental, or indispensable, to sociology has been one of Garfinkel's greatest contributions. As the postmodern crisis made clear, without an explanation of underlying intelligibility, social orders cannot be given a valid explanation. Sociology cannot solve the problem by connecting concepts with symbolic representations. Representational approaches to meaning are as problematic as trying to explain social order in terms of formal structures.

In treating local orders as a collective accomplishment, Garfinkel did not give up the actor's point of view. But he transformed it substantially, locating the experiential and contingent features of action, originally treated as belonging to the actor, in the regularities of actual practices. The actor's point of view was transformed into a concern with what populations do in particular settings to achieve the mutual recognizability of particular practices. According to Garfinkel, a population is constituted not by a set of individuals with something in common, but by a set of practices common to particular situations or events: the crowd at the coffee machine, the line at the supermarket, the "gang" at the science lab, and so on.

Instead of talking about the phenomenal properties of experience, Garfinkel began talking about the phenomenal field properties of objects. Thus, in an important sense the actor's point of view and the achieved meaning of social action no longer had to be thought of as subjective. Because, in Garfinkel's view, intelligibility is achieved in and through the collective enactment of observable practices, not through interpretive processes in the minds of individual actors, empirical studies of observable practices could reveal the actor's point of view. It is in mainstream sociology that individual subjectivity, in the form of operationalized variables, theorized accounts, and individually produced institutional accounts, can be found, not in ethnomethodology.

Critics argue that the study of local social orders is not sociological because it consists only of a description of what people do and ignores the real social (i.e. institutional) constraints within which those actions took place. The constraint argument is fundamental to post-Second World War sociology; part of the assumption that social order comes from formal institutions. The discipline of sociology was, in an important sense, founded on Durkheim's argument that in traditional societies social facts exist as relations of external constraint, rather than as artifacts of the combined psychosocial or biological impulses of a large number of persons. Therefore, when Garfinkel is interpreted as having argued against the existence of external constraint, he is thought to have repudiated the idea of social facts and thus to have rejected sociology as a whole. However, Garfinkel has not rejected the idea of external constraint, he has argued that in its classic form as beliefs and values it does not explain the local orders that constitute mutual intelligibility. In taking this position Garfinkel is actually more in line with Durkheim's argument that the social order of modernity will be organized quite differently, developing a form of constitutive order that does not work by external constraint. Mainstream sociology has largely ignored this argument and its implications.

Other critics, from what is sometimes called the "left" of ethnomethodology, and from the postmodern position, argue that ethnomethodology is hopelessly conceptual and theorized, and thus falls victim to its own criticisms of mainstream sociology. Such critics, however, tend to set up a straw man argument. They attribute to ethnomethodology a representational theory of meaning, equating enacted practices with subjective interpretive procedures (often mistakenly equated with the documentary method), and render practices in terms of concepts and beliefs. As Garfinkel treats practices as consisting of their concrete witnessable details, the attribution is incorrect. There is nothing circular in the argument that to convey meaning visible concrete actions must be recognizable to others as actions of a sort: that the constitutive features of what counts and does not count as actions of a sort must be witnessable to participants and therefore available for empirical observation.

For Garfinkel, structure and order are primarily located in local practices, which constitute a set of foundational expectations and obligations. Formal institutions act as a constraint in limited and specific ways via institutional contexts of accountability. According to Garfinkel, "The instructably observable achieved coherent detail of the coherence of objects *is* the fulfillment of Durkheim's promise that the objective reality of social facts is sociology's fundamental principle."[5] Persons are accountable both at the local level for a commitment to a local order of practices, and, at what sociology has generally termed the institutional level, accountable to what Mills (1940) referred to as a shared "vocabulary of motives."

In Mills's view, institutional practices bear a peculiar relationship to institutional rules. The rules constitute a context of justification for action, rather than something followed to produce the action. Therefore, while the rules constrain the practices, in this peculiar way of constraining what will count after the fact as having been a case of following the rules, they are not constitutive of action in its course.

Garfinkel's treatment of accounts goes beyond Mills in proposing a level of constitutive orders of action in addition to a complex network of contexts of accountability at various levels of social organization. In Garfinkel's view persons can be accountable to formal institutions, such as government agencies or scientific disciplines, at the same time that they are accountable to the expectations of their colleagues with regard to normal workplace procedures. Persons are constantly accountable for their production of recognizable talk and movements, even while they are managing institutional levels of accountability.

But, it is constitutive orders not accounts that constitute the foundation of mutual intelligibility. The fact that local orders may be accountable does not explain their order. Constitutive orders orient sets of background expectancies and obligations in details. When members enact them recognizably in a situation with other cooperating members they will not be asked for accounts. It is only when mutual intelligibilities fail that accounts must be given for actions and if the accounts are successful justifications are not required.

Extending the theory of accounts Garfinkel is able to consider a wide range of theoretical issues. The theoretical line of argument which Garfinkel's inquiry into "rules" (i.e. instructed action) and accountability develops includes: the classic distinction between traditional and modern rational action (Durkheim, Weber, Toennies, Simmel); the seminal arguments of Burke and Mills regarding contexts of accountability; many of the Chicago School studies of organizations and bureaucracies, which revealed the paradox of rules and informal cultures within organizations; and contemporary work in philosophy on justifications as a form of moral reasoning.

Garfinkel's position also runs parallel to other arguments developed during the 1950s and 1960s regarding the relationship between rules and practice, including: Goffman's study of asylums (1961); similar studies in prisons and psychology by Sykes (1958) and Szasz (1961); labeling theory, which examines the relationship between institutional behavior, the institutional production of statistics, and the beliefs and practices of the populations which staff those organizations; the distinction in philosophy between constitutive and summary rules and between social objects and brute facts (Rawls, 1955; Warnock, 1958; Searle, 1964); and the extension of this argument into game theory. The recognition that social facts have a special status is important.

Garfinkel's focus on intelligibility also extends a second line of inquiry: attempts by classical social theorists to frame epistemology and intelligibility sociologically (Durkheim, 1915; Weber, 1921; Rawls, 1996). It is important to understand that classical social theorists were philosophers who challenged the limits of their discipline on the issues of epistemology and intelligibility. If, for instance, one begins with Durkheim's theory of the social origins of the categories of the understanding (in *The Elementary Forms*), then one finds Garfinkel continuing the inquiry into the question of intelligibility raised by Durkheim, and extended by Mead, Husserl, Heidegger, Wittgenstein, Mills, and Schutz, but all but forgotten by both mainstream scientific sociology. If one begins with Durkheim's argument for the increasing importance of constitutive orders (in the *Division of Labor*) one finds Garfinkel extending this inquiry as well.

In locating the conditions for intelligibility in the concrete social surroundings of daily life, and in taking the problem of intelligibility as the central problem sociology must address before constructing a theory of social order, Durkheim stands as a direct precursor of Garfinkel. Garfinkel continues to search for the foundations of human intelligibility, reason, and logic in the details of collaborative social practice.

Garfinkel has from the beginning been blessed with a vision of social order that allowed him to see order being produced around him in ordinary events which the rest of us experience as finished products, but which Garfinkel experienced as events produced from patterned details over their course. This is brilliantly evident in his first paper, "Color Trouble." In this paper, we get a picture of Garfinkel as a young student taking a bus home from college. When black passengers are ordered to the back of the bus and won't go, Garfinkel sees something the rest of us would have missed. As the driver engages in his dispute with the black passengers, he is formulating his actions in terms of the account he will have to give for being late at the end of the line. He is accountable not for his morals, but for being on time. The longer the dispute takes, the more important will be the acceptability of the account the driver can give, and it turns out that color is one of the troubles with busses which are accepted as an account for their lateness on certain southern runs.

Garfinkel's description of this incident is masterful, and the essay won an award as one of the best short stories of 1941. More importantly, however, it demonstrates the continuity of vision which has characterized Garfinkel's career as a social thinker. We can imagine Garfinkel sitting in social theory classes being confronted with generic categorizations. He recalls that in his first theory class at Harvard the students were told to make up a social theory. The thing was to be purely an invention, an exercise in logic and the generic use of categories. As a young man with a keen sense for the actual unfolding of social order in the everyday world around him, this sort of theorizing, which operated on the assumption that everyday social scenes were not inherently orderly, and that their details were irrelevant, rubbed the wrong way. He quickly realized that his vision of a stable constitutive order of practice stood in contradiction to the received and approved methods of formal analytic theorizing. Through the years Garfinkel has remained true to his vision.

Reader's Guide to Harold Garfinkel

Those interested in reading further about Garfinkel and Ethnomethodology should read *Studies in Ethnomethodology* and progress to Garfinkel's other works. Reading Garfinkel in the original is important because writing about his work has been very uneven. It is also important to read empirical studies by highly respected Ethnomethodologists. The theoretical arguments simply cannot be understood in the absence of empirical studies. Because of the unique relationship between theory and research that Garfinkel proposes, conventional interpretations tend to misconceive his argument and much of what has been written about Ethnomethodology is simply wrong. Even the best work can be problematic when authors emphasize a single aspect of Garfinkel's position (such as its relevance to phenomenology,

Parsons, breaching, indeterminacy, accounts) thus obscuring the overall perspective into which all of these aspects fit. Just as Garfinkel has insisted that understanding his texts requires doing some of the research problems they propose and not merely reading them – it is important for those interested in his work to do more than read "about" it.

Notes

1 Haecceities is one of many words that Garfinkel has adopted over the years to indicate the importance of the endless contingencies in both situations and practices. He has also used the words quiddities, contingencies, and details in this regard. The terminology changes frequently to maintain the open and provisional nature of the idea. As a conventional sense develops for a word he has used, he changes it.

2 His Harvard cohort included Gardner Lindsey, Henry Riecken, David Schneider, David Aberle, Brewster Smith, Duncan MacRae, Bernard Barber, Frank Sutton, James Olds, Fred Strodbeck, Marion Levy, Hans Lucas Taueber, and Renee Fox, many of whom became prominent sociologists and several of whom were instrumental in furthering Garfinkel's career.

3 The faculty at Princeton included Marion Levy and Duncan MacRae, who had been at Harvard with Garfinkel, and Wilbert Moore. Elliot Mishler was also at Princeton with Garfinkel. Edward Tiryakian, an undergraduate at Princeton for whom Garfinkel served as senior thesis advisor, would later publish Garfinkel's paper, co-authored with Harvey Sacks, "On Formal Structures of Practical Action."

4 Unfortunately, most of these studies remain unpublished.

5 Personal communication.

Bibliography

Writings of Harold Garfinkel

1941. Color trouble. In Edward O'Brian (ed.) *Best Short Stories of 1941*.

1949. Research note on inter- and intra-racial homicide. *Social Forces*, 27:370–381.

1963. A conception of, and experiments with, "trust" as a condition for stable concerted actions. In O. J. Harvey (ed.) *Motivation and Social Interaction*. New York: Ronald Press.

1964. Studies of the routine grounds of everyday activities. *Social Problems*, 11:225–250.

1967. *Studies in Ethnomethodology*. Englewood Cliffs, NJ: Prentice Hall.

1970 (with Harvey Sacks). On formal structures of practical action. In Edward Tiryakian and John McKinney (eds) *Theoretical Sociology*. New York: Appleton Century Crofts.

1981 (with Michael Lynch and Eric Livingston). The work of a discovering science construed with materials from the optically discovered pulsar. *Philosophy of the Social Sciences*, 11(2): 131–158.

1988. Evidence for locally produced, naturally accountable phenomena of order, logic, reason, meaning, method, etc., in and as of the essential haecceity of immortal ordinary society. *Sociological Theory*, 6(1): 103–109.

1992. (with Lawrence Weider) Two incommensurable asymmetrically alternate technologies of social analysis. In Graham Watson and Robert M. Seiler (eds) *Text in Context*. Newbury Park, CA: Sage, pp. 172–206.

1996. Ethnomethodology's program. *Social Psychology Quarterly*, 59(1): 5–21.

2002. *Ethnomethodology' Program: Working Out Durkheim's Aphorism*. Edited by A. Rawls. Lanham, MD: Rowman & Littlefield.

2006. *Seeing Sociologically: The Routine Grounds of Action*. Edited by A. Rawls. Boulder, CO: Paradigm Publishers.

2008. *Toward a Sociological Theory of Information*. Edited by A. Rawls. Boulder, CO: Paradigm Publishers.

Further Reading

Baudrillard, Jean (1975) *Mirror of Production*. St Louis: Telos Press.

Becker, Howard (1963) *Outsiders: Studies in the Sociology of Deviance*. New York: Free Press.

Blumer, Herbert (1969) *Symbolic Interaction: Perspective and Method*. Berkeley: University of California Press.

Bourdieu, Pierre (1990) *The Logic of Practice*. Stanford, CA: Stanford University Press.

Cooley, Charles Horton (1902) *Human Nature and the Social Order*. New York: Scribner's.

Durkheim, Emile (1893) *The Division of Labor in Society*. Trans. Simpson. New York: The Free Press.

Durkheim, Émile (1912) *The Elementary Forms of The Religious Life*. Chicago: Free Press.

Goffman, Erving (1961) *Asylums*. New York: Anchor Books.

Goffman, Erving (1963) *The Presentation of Self in Everyday Life*. New York: Anchor.

Goffman, Erving (1983) The interaction order. *American Sociological Review*, 48: 1–17.

Gurwitsch, Aron (1964) *The Field of Consciousness*. Duquesne, PA: Duquesne University Press.

Habermas, Jürgen (1981) *The Theory of Communicative Action*. Boston: Beacon Press.

Heidegger, Martin (1962) *Being and Time*. London: SCM Press.

Husserl, Edmund (1962) *Ideas*. New York: Collier Books.

Kaufmann, Felix (1944) *Methodology of the Social Sciences*. Oxford: Oxford University Press.

Lewin, Kurt (1938) *The Conceptual Representation and the Measurement of Psychological Forces*. Durham, NC: Duke University Press.

Mead, George Herbert (1934) *Mind, Self, and Society*. Chicago: University of Chicago Press.

Mead, George Herbert (1938) *Philosophy of the Act*. Chicago: University of Chicago Press.

Mills, C. Wright (1940) Situated action and the vocabulary of motives. *American Sociological Review*, 5: 904–993.

Parsons, Talcott (1937) *The Structure of Social Action*. Chicago: Free Press.

Rawls, Anne (1996) Durkheim's epistemology: The neglected argument. *American Journal of Sociology*, 102(2): 430–482.

Rawls, Anne (2008) Harold Garfinkel, ethnomethodology and workplace studies. *Organization Studies*, 29(5): 701–732.

Rawls, Anne (2009) Special issue: John Rawls' "Two concepts of rules" (ed.) *Journal of Classical Sociology*, 9(4).

Rawls, John (1955) Two concepts of rules. *The Philosophical Review*, 64(1): 3–32.

Sacks, Harvey, Schegloff, Emmanuel, and Jefferson, Gail (1977) The simplest systematics for turntaking in conversation. *Language*, 50: 696–735.

Schutz, Alfred (1967) *The Phenomenology of the Social World*. Evanston, IL: Northwestern University Press (originally published in German in 1932).

Searle, John (1964) How to derive ought from is. *The Philosophical Review*, 73(1): 43–58.

Sykes, Gresham (1958) *The Society of Captives*. Princeton, NJ: Princeton University Press.

Szasz, Thomas (1961) *The Myth of Mental Illness: Foundations of a Theory of the Social World*. New York: Harper & Row.

Thomas, W. I. (1927) *The Polish Peasant in Europe and America*. New York: Alfred A. Knopf.

Warnock, Geoffrey J. ([1958]1967) *The Philosophy of Perception*. London: Oxford University Press.

Weber, Max (1921) *Economy and Society*. New York: Bedminster Press.

Winch, Peter (1958) *The Idea of a Social Science*. Routledge and Kegan Paul: London.

Wittgenstein, Ludwig (1953) *Philosophical Investigations*, trans. G.E.M. Anscombe. Oxford: Basil Blackwell.

Znaniecki, Florian (1936) *Social Actions*. New York: Farrar and Rinehart.

5

Erving Goffman

GREG SMITH

Introduction

Erving Goffman was a unique presence in twentieth-century sociology. From the early 1950s to his premature death in 1982, Goffman produced a series of dazzling publications that aimed to found a discrete area of inquiry – the interaction order (Goffman, 1983a), the realm of social life brought into being whenever persons are in one another's presence. Goffman showed how what transpired during moments of co-presence – "the glances, gestures, positionings, and verbal statements that people continuously feed into the situation" (Goffman, 1967:1) – was more socially organized than was previously understood. Goffman's place in the canon of twentieth-century sociological thought was assured by his pioneering and inventive analyses of the interaction order written in an unmistakable signature style.

Goffman's primary achievement was to discover and classify those largely out-of-awareness social rules and presuppositions that underpin the forms of conduct of co-present persons. He populated this new domain with a host of concepts now sedimented into sociology's commonsense. Those concepts include presentation of self, impression management, performances, front and back regions, role distance, stigma, total institution, civil inattention, deference, demeanor, frame, and footing among others. Goffman's intellectual outlook and analytic commitments remained firmly rooted in sociology throughout his career, yet his ideas became widely known outside academic sociology. Surveys and citation counts testify to Goffman's ongoing influence. Goffman's first book, *The Presentation of Self in Everyday Life* (1959), ranked tenth in the International Sociological Association's (1998) "Books of the Century" poll. A 2007 analysis of frequently cited authors of books in the humanities and social sciences ranked Goffman its sixth most cited author – ahead of Weber, Freud, Heidegger, Kant, and Chomsky (Anon., 2009).

The Wiley-Blackwell Companion to Major Social Theorists, First Edition.
Edited by George Ritzer and Jeffrey Stepnisky.
© 2011 Blackwell Publishing Ltd. Published 2011 by Blackwell Publishing Ltd.

Exploring the dimensions of the social situatedness of co-present persons remained the abiding focus of Goffman's work. Yet he became even better known as the author of *Asylums* and *Stigma* (Goffman, 1961a, 1963b), books that reached beyond the academy and which significantly influenced the shape of public debate and policy in North America and Europe. In these widely read books Goffman applied his general ideas about the interaction order to the situation of mental patients and those, such as ethnic minorities or the disabled, who found themselves disqualified from full social acceptance. Goffman's popular appeal was powerfully added by a lucid and subtle writing style that conveyed an utterly distinctive analytic attitude. Goffman worked hard to produce the perceptive writing that expressed his starkly ironic stance towards the vagaries and vicissitudes of interpersonal conduct and social organization. While he always insisted that sociology was fundamentally an obser-vational, empirical discipline, his own sociology anticipated postmodernism-inspired debates about the role of rhetoric in sociological description and analysis (e.g. Clifford and Marcus, 1986).

For all the acclaim Goffman's work attracted, his sociology also proved to be enduringly controversial. He had not merely theories about social life but a trade-mark perspective towards it. There is an unmistakable look and feel to the pages of his books and papers. Goffman never felt it necessary to situate his work in relation to the established figures and debates of academic sociology. Unlike Harold Garfinkel, with whom he is often compared, Goffman's name was not attached to a specific methodology or school of thought. His sociology modestly promoted description and classification rather than fully predictive theory. Goffman's steadfast interest in the minutiae of everyday conduct was never theoretically ambitious, yet the subtle-ties of his analyses suggest a thinker who was fully conversant with sociology's theo-retical disputes – enough for one commentator to observe that Goffman's sociology met "the most important requirement of modern social theory – to be self-conscious about the meaning of what it is to know" (Williams, 1983: 102).

The Person

Max and Ann, Goffman's Ukrainian Jewish immigrant parents, married in Winnipeg in 1918. Their son, Erving, was born in Mannville, Alberta, in 1922. He spent most of his childhood and adolescence in the small town of Dauphin, Manitoba with an older sister, Frances Bay, who in later life enjoyed a successful acting career in film and television. The family moved to the city of Winnipeg when Erving was in his mid-teens. His father was a successful storekeeper whose business prospered through the 1930s. The Goffmans were neither orthodox nor secular Jews. They observed the major religious festivals and dietary traditions and spoke a little Yiddish at home but were not closely integrated into synagogue life. As Winkin (2010) suggested, compared to many Jewish households in Winnipeg at the time, Goffman's family probably enjoyed more economic capital but less cultural capital than their fellow co-religionists. At high school in Winnipeg Goffman already appeared distant and self-contained. He did not embrace the ideological convictions of fellow Jewish classmates. He was remembered as a good gymnast, a formidable chemistry student, and a practical joker (Winkin, 2010). Erving Goffman, then, was not in any simple sense the marginal Jew celebrated by Simmel's essay, "The stranger." He was doubly marginal, both to the mainstream and to the group identification that provided his initial marginality.

At 17 Goffman enrolled at the University of Manitoba in Winnipeg as a student of natural sciences. Over the following three years his interests gradually shifted towards the social sciences. He left in 1942 without completing his degree but used his credits to return to study sociology at the University of Toronto in 1943–1944, graduating in 1945. In between Manitoba and Toronto he worked for a time at the National Film Board of Canada in Ottawa where he met Dennis Wrong who encouraged him to resume his studies at Toronto. While at Toronto he became close to Elizabeth Bott, who would later become well known as author of the landmark study, *Family and Social Network* (1957). Goffman went with Bott to begin graduate work at the University of Chicago in 1945 (Winkin, 1988). The work and person of W. Lloyd Warner (1898–1970) impressed Goffman as a beginning graduate student. Warner was an anthropologist who held a joint appointment in anthropology and sociology at Chicago. The fieldwork methods Warner first learned researching the Murngin of Australia he later turned to good advantage in his investigations of urban communities, notably the Yankee City series. An academic entrepreneur, Warner was highly effective at getting funding and organizing and motivating research teams. Under Warner's supervision, Goffman wrote a master's thesis that reported a research project spun off from Warner and Henry's (1948) study of audience responses to a popular radio programme (Smith, 2003). Goffman would later claim that Everett C. Hughes was his most influential Chicago teacher (Verhoeven, 1993; Jaworski, 2000). Hughes also championed fieldwork methods and encouraged ethnographic approaches to the study of occupations. Goffman also took courses in theory with Louis Wirth.

However, it was Warner's patronage that enabled Goffman to take up an instructor's post in the Social Anthropology department at the University of Edinburgh at the beginning of the 1949–1950 academic year. In December 1949 he arrived at the Springfield Hotel, Baltasound, on the most northerly of the Shetland Islands. Over the next year and a half Goffman spent about 12 months in Baltasound gathering the data that would become his PhD dissertation, "Communication Conduct in an Island Community." At first he lived in the hotel, then in a small cottage at the back of the hotel. He became well known in the village, in particular through his casual work at the hotel kitchen and his participation in the socials held regularly at the village hall (Winkin, 2000).

In summer 1951 he departed for Paris to begin drafting his dissertation. He married a fellow University of Chicago student, Angelica Choate, in 1952. Back in Chicago, Goffman worked on several projects apart from his dissertation: for Edward Shils, for Edward C. Banfield and for Warner's market research company, Social Research, Inc. The dissertation was a controversial work. Goffman was grilled intensively in his oral defense (Winkin, 1988). It was difficult to categorize: not the community study that Warner might have expected, nor an ethnography in the tradition of Hughes. It drew upon Goffman's fieldwork data about conversational interaction in the remote community of Baltasound in order to shed light on islanders' "communication conduct." Yet the dissertation itself was ambitious. It was designed to contribute to "a systematic framework useful in studying interaction throughout our society." With its expressly generalizing ambitions and its orientation to conversational interaction as one species of social order (Goffman, 1953: 33–38), it seemed to be an affiliation with Talcott Parsons's theoretical project. Nevertheless, Goffman graduated at the end of 1953. He stayed in Chicago for most of the year following his dissertation defense. During this time he assembled the first draft of *The Presentation of Self in Everyday Life* (originally titled, *The Management of Impressions in Social Establishments*) and "On face-work." *Presentation* was not, as is sometimes thought, simply the book of the dissertation. It was a substantially new work. Goffman activated his Edinburgh connections to secure the book's publication in 1956. It is noteworthy that it was not published by Edinburgh University Press but rather by a small unit within the university, the Social Science Research Centre (Goffman, 1956a). In 1959, Anchor Books, a division of the large Doubleday publishing corporation of New York, published an expanded edition of *Presentation*. While it was this later publication that shot Goffman to fame, the earlier Edinburgh edition was influential in helping to consolidate his fast growing reputation as an original thinker in British and North American sociological circles.

At the end of 1954 Goffman took up an appointment as Visiting Scientist at the National Institute of Mental Health, Bethesda, Maryland. In this position he carried out the year's participant observation of patient life at Saint Elizabeths Hospital, Washington DC that led to *Asylums* (Goffman, 1961a). Saint Elizabeths (spelled without an apostrophe) was the oldest federal mental hospital in the USA. In the informal role of "assistant to the athletic director," Goffman was free to roam the wards and grounds observing both official and unofficial treatment of the patients and the "underlife" they created for themselves. Ironically, around this time a decline in the mental well-being of Goffman's wife was becoming evident. Early versions of *Asylums* were presented at the Josiah Macy Jr. Foundation conferences in the mid-1950s. The first presentations led to some robust exchanges among the specially selected conference participants. The anthropologist Margaret Mead was one persistently critical voice in these discussions (see Goffman, 1957).

At the start of 1958 Goffman was appointed assistant professor at the University of California, Berkeley. Herbert Blumer arrived at Berkeley from Chicago in 1952 and quickly built up a strong Department of Sociology. Goffman's colleagues included Reinhard Bendix, Kingsley Davis, Nathan Glazer, Seymour Martin Lipset, Leo Lowenthal, David Matza, Philip Selznick, and Neil Smelser. Goffman taught classes in social psychology and deviance, attracting large student audiences. His productivity (he published five books between 1959 and 1963) and his rising standing ensured that he became full professor by 1962. Awarded the prestigious MacIver Prize in 1961 for the best book in sociology (*Presentation of Self*), by the early 1960s Goffman's reputation as one of the outstanding sociologists of his generation had been established.

At Berkeley, Goffman regularly visited the casinos of Reno and Las Vegas, a leisure interest that eventually became a professional one. Goffman trained and secured employment as a blackjack dealer. The position allowed him to carry out fieldwork for a study of gambling behavior that was never fully written up (but see "Where the action is" (Goffman, 1967)). He influenced a number of graduate students at Berkeley, including John Lofland, Gary Marx, Harvey Sacks, Dorothy Smith, and David Sudnow. In 1964 Angelica Goffman's mental problems deteriorated to the point where she took her own life. Although never openly acknowledged, Goffman's

(1969) essay, "The insanity of place," seemed to be pointedly founded on Goffman's own experience of living with Angelica's difficulties. The essay examined the "havoc" a person with mental symptoms makes for others living in the same household.

In 1966–1967 Thomas Schelling facilitated a visiting fellowship at Harvard University, allowing Goffman to deepen his understanding of developments in game theory (see Goffman, 1969a). In 1968 Goffman accepted a Benjamin Franklin Chair in Anthropology and Sociology at the University of Pennsylvania. There he became involved in the work of the Center for Urban Ethnography, drawing him closer to the sociolinguistics of Dell Hymes and William Labov. The focus on conversational interaction was manifested in the papers collected as *Forms of Talk* (1981a), his last book, and was supported by his marriage to Gillian Sankoff, a linguistics professor. (Their daughter, Alice, has become an accomplished ethnographer (see Goffman, 2009).) Goffman's academic honors included a Guggenheim Fellowship (1977–1978), election as Fellow to the American Academy of Arts and Sciences, and election to the Presidency of the American Sociological Association 1981–1982. He died from stomach cancer on November 20, 1982.

Erving Goffman came a long way from small town Canada to an elevated position in the US academy and an impressive international reputation. If Goffman is to be regarded as "the chosen one" in post-war interactionist and ethnographic sociology, then he helped the process along. He early acquired an intimidating reputation – he would happily employ the strategies and break the face-to-face rules his sociology described and analyzed. He covered his tracks in his publications, where the references provided in footnotes were rarely a good guide to influences on the text. He stayed away from the blandishments of academic fame: refusing to give interviews, avoiding photographers, shunning radio and TV appearances, and discouraging interest in his work as an object of attention in its own right. In public Goffman refused the trappings of the celebrity intellectual, consistently directing his attention to writing that examined facets of the interaction order.

One explanation for this reticence lies in Goffman's lifelong respect for the fieldwork tradition: Goffman the ethnographer did not want his cover blown. Although his later work in particular depended heavily on documentary sources, the temper of his sociology is ethnographic to the core. Living the ethnographic life – a book title that Goffman suggested to his student, Dan Rose (1990) – was a key element of Goffman's mode of sociological being. Observation was the gold standard against which other data collection methods were to be adjudged. Goffman was a constitutional sociologist who saw the world the way he wrote about it. Goffman had absorbed early the Durkheimian precept that social facts were to be explained socially. His work was driven by a belief – inspired by a creative adaptation of the ideas of Émile Durkheim, George Herbert Mead and Georg Simmel – that the sociological analysis of interaction and experience had not yet been pursued far enough. This idea was memorably captured in Goffman's suggestion that the concept of role distance "helps to combat the touching tendency to keep a part of the world safe from sociology" (Goffman, 1961b: 134). From the prizing of observation it followed that you might "treat your own life as data" (Strong, 1983: 147) – and the lives of those you were with. Goffman the ethnographer seemed always to be switched on, never missing an opportunity to observe and analyze, which partly explains why there are so many reports of how difficult it could be to be in Erving's company.

Goffman quickly acquired a formidable reputation as a "difficult" personality. In graduate school his classmates nicknamed him the "little dagger" (Winkin, 1988). Gary Marx, a Berkeley graduate student in the early 1960s, remembers Goffman's self-presentation as "a detached, hard-boiled intellectual cynic, the sociologist as a 1940s private eye" (Marx, 1984: 53). His sharp wit and pithy observations could be penetrating, wounding, and hilarious all at once. Goffman's ready facility for insightful and incisive remarks contributed to the development of a mythology (what Lofland calls "tales of Goffman") unmatched in sociology (Lofland, 2000[1984]; Shalin, 2008). Perhaps Goffman's remarks were practical devices for cutting through the everyday and taken-for-granted, the merely conventional and acceptable? Maybe – although these remarks were not always received or treated as such. John Lofland, who knew Goffman well, suggests that the brilliance evident in his writing was also there in the person: "he had been constituted a restless insight machine, almost constantly quipping, snipping, teasing, reflecting, questioning" (Lofland, 2000[1984]: 173) even beyond the point where that became oppressive to his listeners. Later life may have blunted some of Goffman's barbs but in private gatherings at least he seems to have retained the capacity to make people edgy.

Goffman's career was devoted to the production of original sociology. He took very seriously the development of his scholarly work, often secluding himself to ensure that his academic writing was not neglected. He was never an enthusiastic committee man and saw scholarship as a thing apart from such organizational demands of university life. Research and scholarship was to be prized and nurtured. Goffman was single-minded about developing his sociological gifts. He did not collaborate with co-authors and did not produce edited collections featuring others' work. He did not encourage the growth of a large graduate student circle but was meticulous with those students he did supervise. His work attracted admirers and fans, not followers. Goffman was a sociologist whose efforts were strongly oriented toward publication, which was where, as he would tell would-be interviewers, the most considered statements of his ideas could be found.

THE SOCIAL CONTEXT

Goffman's career progression paralleled what now seems a golden age for American sociology in the 1950s and 1960s. From the end of the Second World War through to the early 1970s the number of academic positions available in universities grew and so did opportunities for research funding and publication. When Goffman was in graduate school, sociology was still small enough for everyone to keep abreast of almost all the papers appearing in the professional sociology journals. That soon changed. A discipline that was a modest cottage industry moved into an era of large-scale production. In particular, the rapid expansion of sociology generated increasing demand for textbooks and monographs. Goffman capitalized on this emergent market, writing serious but accessible books that were published simultaneously in hardback and paperback editions.

Goffman's rise to international fame coincided with a period of unprecedented economic prosperity combined with great political and cultural change in North America and Western Europe, a phenomenon now known simply as "the Sixties."

In the USA, the civil rights movement succeeded in removing the remaining formal barriers to full legal and civic participation faced by black people. Popular culture, and in particular television and pop music, came to the fore in a way it had never done before. Students demanded rights and representation in universities (the Berkeley campus was at the forefront of student protest in the mid-1960s). Students also supported workers' movements for political change, notably in "les événements" of May 1968 in Paris. The Vietnam War became the object of widespread political protest. Feminist ideas were rekindled at the end of the 1960s. Goffman seldom referred to these major shifts, though they were filtered through oblique comments in his writings. In particular the growth of uncertainty and insecurity in urban streets and other public places prompted on his part an intensified scrutiny of the sources of social order. This can be seen most clearly in "Normal appearances" (Goffman, 1971), a chapter that captured the erosion of traditional bases of trust between the unacquainted that was a conspicuous feature of the 1960s (Dawe, 1973). Some 1960s countercultural movements, Goffman acknowledged, had effectively turned the interaction order into a battleground. There was a "complex unsettling expressed variously in the current unsafety and incivility of our city streets, the new political device of intentionally breaking the ground rules for self-expression during meetings and contacts, the change in the rules of censorship, and the social molestation encouraged in the various forms of 'encounter group' and experimental theater" (Goffman, 1971: ix–x).

Goffman's own work in the early 1970s could be understood, for one influential commentator at least, as an anti-Utopian backlash (Jameson, 1976). Certainly Goffman retained a sociological distance from Utopian projects and radical sentiments in this period. He acknowledged that his analysis did not address issues of class disadvantage. Much work was required to "combat false consciousness and awaken people to their true interests…because the sleep is very deep" Goffman (1974: 14) wrote, adding, "I do not intend here to provide a lullaby but merely to sneak in and watch the way the people snore." Goffman never accepted theoretical or moral agendas other than his own. If convictions were to be found in Goffman's writings, they surfaced most clearly in *Asylums* and *Stigma* where Goffman was resolute in defending the individual against the encroachments of unreasonable social demands. Goffman came to maturity during the Second World War and its aftermath, which may explain the potency for Goffman of images of concentration camps, brainwashing programs, and the other assaults on the integrity of the individual that George Orwell's writings so eloquently exposed. It was a small step conceptually from Orwell's "unperson" to Goffman's "non-person" (Travers, 1999).

While Goffman consistently confined his analytic attention to unraveling the units and processes of the interaction order, commentators chose to make links, often speculative, between Goffman's theoretical ideas and features of contemporary society. Alvin Gouldner's dozen pages on Goffman in *The Coming Crisis of Western Sociology* (1970) led the way. Gouldner saw Goffman's dramaturgy as a symptom of the crisis. While Gouldner welcomed Goffman's challenge to the dominance of Parsonsian functionalist orthodoxy, he was plainly unhappy with many features of Goffman's approach including its neglect of history and its concentration on the face-to-face to the exclusion of wider structural factors. Above all, Gouldner disapproved of dramaturgy's emphasis on the manipulation of appearances, which he saw as a partial account that gave theoretical expression to the experiences of the new middle classes working in offices and service occupations. This class fraction understood that appearances really did matter and yet could be fabricated easily. Goffman's dramaturgy, for Gouldner (1970: 380), "declared a moratorium on the conventional distinction between make-believe and reality," with the attendant moral loosening that implied. Perhaps Goffman's sociology did "resonate" with the experiences of some class fractions more than others. Goffman's sociology itself seemed intent on more general ambitions however dated some of its illustrative material may now appear. Like Simmel before him, Goffman sought analyses that extended beyond specific class or occupational groupings to encompass the universal elements of the interaction order, wherever and whenever they occurred.

The Intellectual Context

Goffman's intellectual outlook was first shaped by his education and experiences growing up in Canada in the 1930s and 1940s (McGregor, 1986; Winkin, 2010). Undoubtedly it was his graduate apprenticeship at the University of Chicago in the immediate post-war period that was the most decisive source of intellectual influence. When Goffman arrived at Chicago in 1945 its sociology department could look back on nearly half a century as a world-leading presence in the discipline. However, the dominance of Chicago in American sociology was challenged first by the new theoreticism that Talcott Parsons championed at Harvard, then by the sophisticated forms of survey research pioneered by Lazarsfeld at Columbia. In 1945 the Chicago department was small and the graduate population bigger than it ever was, due mainly to the influx of students supported by the provisions of the GI Bill. Their wartime experiences gave them a worldliness possibly lacking in previous generations. Goffman was pitched into this intense environment. His classmates included many figures who would make important contributions to the symbolic interactionist tradition including Howard S. Becker, Fred Davis, Eliot Friedson, Joseph Gusfield, Lewis M. Killian, Gladys and Kurt Lang, Bernard Meltzer, Warren Peterson, Gregory P. Stone, and Ralph Turner. This group formed the core of what came to be known as the second Chicago School of sociology (Fine, 1995). However, it was far from a unified "school." Sometimes a caricature of the history is sketched: qualitative methods were extensively employed by Robert Park and his students in the 1920s and 1930s and these methods were refined and linked to G. H. Mead's social psychology to produce a post-war symbolic interactionist hegemony at Chicago. Close inspection of the history shows that this version of the history was a myth. There was always a wide range of different kinds of sociology taking place at Chicago; there was no methodological orthodoxy or dominance of a particular method; and even the two figures said to head up the interactionist/qualitative tradition at Chicago, Herbert Blumer and Everett Hughes, were at odds with one another, Blumer considering Hughes theoretically unsophisticated, Hughes implying that Blumer was afraid of empirical research (Becker, 1999). There was never an interactionist dominance of the Chicago department while Goffman was there in the 1940s and early 1950s (Abbott, 1999). Goffman for his part audited Blumer's course but did not complete the coursework needed for credits. He managed to get Hughes on to his dissertation committee only for Hughes to withdraw when he became departmental head. Warner, the anthropologist trained by Radcliffe-Brown, was the abiding presence throughout Goffman's graduate studies, giving Goffman his first research opening in 1946, then the opportunity to go to Edinburgh. Warner also served on both Goffman's master's and dissertation committees.

Notwithstanding these qualifications, it has proved possible to identify some common features of the sociological attitude of the Chicago group. Winkin (1999) suggested three key elements of the Chicago "scientific habitus." First, there was a bias toward observation of the empirical world. To believe it, Chicagoans have to see it. The features of the world took precedence over the concepts and theories used for its sociological apprehension. Priority was accorded data, preferably in observational form. Second, theoretical constructions tended to be sparse, stripped down, pitched at "the lower range" (Goffman, 1981c). Goffman's theoretical minimalism was eloquently stated: "better, perhaps, different coats to clothe the children well than a single splendid tent in which they all shiver" (Goffman, 1961a: xi). Goffman wanted to allow his data to shape his concepts rather than have them forced into premature theoretical straitjackets. Third, the Chicagoans favored an ironic, distanced stance towards the analysis of the world's workings. They attempted to remain apart from the various interests at play in the world, or at least were not seduced by those interests. Humor and irony played important roles in securing some critical distance from worldly stakes and claims (Fine and Martin, 1990). The Chicagoan attitude was "cool" but not cynical or disenchanted.

These features of the Chicago scientific habitus promoted by Goffman's teachers and developed by Goffman and his fellow students help to explain Goffman's own diffidence about being labeled a symbolic interactionist (Verhoeven, 1993). Part of Goffman's opposition grew out of his antipathy to the growing tendency in the 1960s and 1970s of placing a scholar's work within a specific perspective or paradigm and then using that identification as a basis for criticism. When the strategy was applied to Goffman's own work, he was withering in reply:

> One proclaims one's membership in some named perspective, gives pious mention of its central texts, and announces that the writer under review is all off by virtue of failing to qualify for membership. A case of guilt by pigeonholing. As if a writer's work is a unitary thing and can be all bad because he or she apparently does not apparently subscribe to a particular doctrine, which doctrine, if subscribed to, would somehow make writings good. (Goffman, 1981b: 61)

Labeling for Goffman was a crude method of critical assessment, which explains Goffman's reluctance to embrace the symbolic interactionist label. But, given how this label was used, Goffman fully appreciated that he had as much right as anyone to be described in these terms. The issue for Goffman was that symbolic interactionism was a category awaiting content. It provided a general orientation to the world and to theorizing that Goffman found "very congenial" (Verhoeven, 1993: 320) but it did not offer the substance needed to carry out sociological analysis.

For that substance Goffman turned in his dissertation to the classical figures of Durkheim, Simmel, and Mead. Durkheim furnished Goffman with a cogent statement of the significance of ritual that would prove a key resource for his interaction analyses. Durkheim's repeated emphasis that social facts are moral facts found expression in Goffman's abiding concern with the moral dimensions of interaction. Simmel offered an associational conception of society that sat comfortably with Goffman's notion of the interaction order. Simmel's formal sociology also presented a model for Goffman's own efforts to identify the forms and processes of the interaction order. Mead's emphasis on the role of symbols in communication and the centrality of the process of role-taking in accounting for the rise of mind and self was sufficiently well known in Chicago of the 1940s and 1950s as to justify little direct mention in Goffman's writings. Indeed, a case has been made that C. H. Cooley was even more influential on Goffman than Mead (Scheff, 2005). Goffman's broader argument was that classical figures in the sociological tradition were not to be treated as ornaments to be venerated but rather as sources to be adapted and developed to understand new fields of inquiry. That is exactly what Goffman did in his dissertation. The decision to treat the interaction order as a domain in its own right drew its inspiration in part from the functionalism of Durkheim and Radcliffe-Brown (Goffman, 1981b).

Two key teachers at Chicago with influences on Goffman's work were Warner and Hughes. As a Radcliffe-Brown protégé Warner was important in reaffirming the Durkheimian tradition for Goffman, a tradition to which he was first exposed by C. W. M. Hart at Toronto. Warner provided opportunities, encouragement, and may well have been a role model for Goffman of how to be a successful academic. Goffman's (1951) first paper on class status symbolism bears the hallmarks of Warner's interests in class and how it was represented in social life. Hughes's influence was also, in part, as a bearer of a tradition. Hughes was a doctoral student of Robert E. Park in the 1920s and Park obtained his principal schooling in sociology from attending Georg Simmel's lectures in Berlin at the start of the twentieth century. Hughes held a pluralist approach to research methods but was especially prominent in teaching fieldwork to Chicago students (see Junker, 1960). In addition Hughes championed a comparative approach that drew upon Kenneth Burke's (1965[1935]) "perspective by incongruity." Hughes suggested that plumbers, prostitutes, and psychiatrists all shared some common problems that comparison of the three occupations could reveal (Jaworski, 2000). The Hughesian influence could be seen most sharply in the first truly Goffmanesque paper, "On cooling the mark out" (Goffman, 1952) where Goffman races away with the comparative possibilities afforded by the confidence game model. Goffman came to Chicago as a student with a strong observational ability. The Chicago habitus provided the environment that gave shape and direction to this capacity, transforming it into what Hymes (1984) described as Erving's "gift."

THE WORK

Making sense of any single piece of Goffman's writings can be a deceptively easy undertaking. Goffman invariably starts from conceptual scratch, explaining his usages as he goes along. All that is needed is some patience and perhaps a good recall of the concepts and distinctions introduced earlier. However, making sense of Goffman's writings as a whole is a much more difficult task that begs fundamental questions about the broad nature of his intellectual output. The shapeliness of individual pieces contrasts with the shapelessness of his entire output – each of his books appears to be written as if none of the others had been (Sharrock, 1976). There is little cross-referencing to earlier works (Goffman did begin to remedy this absence in his later books). Indexes are absent or inadequate. New conceptual usages are introduced without clarifying how they supersede earlier cognate terms. Goffman gives little guidance about how to situate his sociology in relation to established perspectives and approaches. All this can appear an odd if not a perverse way to develop a new sociological domain, especially one that was devoted to conceptual articulation.

Goffman's publications can be broadly grouped under three major headings. First there were the interaction studies of the 1950s and 1960s that built upon the fundamental reasoning about the interaction order set out in his 1953 doctorate. They included *Presentation of Self* (1959), *Encounters* (1961b), *Behavior in Public Places* (1963a), *Interaction Ritual* (1967), *Strategic Interaction* (1969), and *Relations in Public* (1971). The 1974 publication of *Frame Analysis* marked a watershed, providing a phenomenological re-grounding of earlier concerns with co-present conduct, phrased and inflected in a distinctively Goffmanesque manner. Goffman's late works, notably *Forms of Talk*, showed the impact of these new analytic preoccupations. Finally, there are the "popular" works – *Asylums* (1961a), *Stigma* (1963b), and *Gender Advertisements* (1979) – that concentrate on issues of difference or disadvantage and that develop the conceptual terminology of the general works.

Interaction studies

Underpinning the multiplicity of Goffman's interactional analyses was a model of the "situated expressivity" (Manning, 2010: 100; Smith, 2006: 35–36) of co-present persons. Most generally the expressive aspect of behavior referred to how the character of the person spilled over into the character of their acts (Goffman, 1953: 50). How was this made manifest in face-to-face interaction? Goffman (1959: 2) famously proposed that expressions may be "given" or "given off," that is directly communicated through talk or exuded by the tone of the talk, the look of the eyes, the posture struck or the gesture made. Individuals monitored the expressive information that others convey – a process that could be quite complex since co-present persons were "transceivers" (Goffman, 1981a) of information, giving information about themselves and receiving information from others in the social situation. Through this account of situated expressivity Goffman began to unpick how the Meadian process of taking the role of the other was actually worked out by co-present persons.

Goffman (1963a) distinguished three important aspects of co-presence. A "social gathering" was when two or more persons come into one another's presence. A "social situation" referred to the spatial environment within which persons in the gathering monitored one another. A "social occasion" was the wider social entity that brought together a group of people to a specific time and place. For example, a birthday party could be seen as a social occasion providing a background in which gatherings and situations can occur. Situations and their gatherings were regulated by a moral code known as the "situational proprieties." This moral code includes the "common courtesies" and those matters concerning posture, gesture, tone of voice, and so forth deemed appropriate to the situation. How human conduct was responsive to the immediate situation remained an abiding concern of Goffman's. As he once wrote, the "neglected situation" (Goffman, 1964) was that situations were neglected as topics for sociological inquiry.

Goffman identified two steps in the "communicative traffic order" between co-present persons. The first, "unfocused interaction," typically occurred in places where people in a social situation are unacquainted with one another, as in a waiting line or a busy city street. The second step was "focused interaction" where the participants "openly cooperate to sustain a single focus of attention" (Goffman, 1963a: 24), for example by telling someone a story, playing a board game, or dancing a *pas de deux*.

Much of Goffman's substantive analysis of the interaction order was premised around the unfocused/focused steps. The "civil inattention" that typically occurred between passers by on city streets was perhaps his most famed example of the practice of unfocused interaction. In this situation persons sized up each other as they approached and then turned their gaze and attention elsewhere – a display Goffman likened to passing automobiles dipping their lights. Civil inattention served to display mutual regard and absence of threat between unacquainted persons. This situational propriety was regarded as the cardinal rule regulating conduct between the unacquainted in public places. Goffman's point was that public places were not some asocial void. Others were not simply ignored through our situated conduct in public places. Rather, we comport ourselves in a manner that indicates the absence of threat to others. The sociological apprehension of the features of unfocused interaction was developed in *Behavior in Public Places* (1963a) and *Relations in Public* (1971) through numerous concepts including "body gloss," "tie signs," "vehicular units," "singles," and "withs," all of which articulated aspects of situated social being in public places.

How was the transition from unfocused to focused interaction to be made? Although it is not difficult to speak to a person we do not know – an "unacquainted" person – nonetheless a fundamental shift occurs because "acquainted persons in a social situation require a reason not to enter" an encounter, "while unacquainted persons require a reason to do so" (Goffman, 1963a: 124). Of course, there are cultural differences in these practices but Goffman went on to identify different kinds of openness to overtures for focused interaction shaped by position in local interaction orders. Police officers and shop counter staff were in structurally more "exposed" or "open positions" than the general citizenry. Some, like the very young or very old, could be regarded as inhabitants of perpetually open positions, so that they become "open persons." There were also "opening persons" like priests or nuns who enjoyed the license to accost others at will, and "open regions" like parties and congregation where heightened openness was sustained among all those present.

Encounters or focused gatherings are made up of "interchanges" that take a broad statement–reply dialogic form. The basic unit of encounters was thus the "move," defined by Goffman (1967: 20) as "everything conveyed by an actor during a turn at taking action." Move was thus distinct from the "turn at talk" of conversation analysis and the "message" of communication theory. The centrality of "move" to the analysis of interaction structures was one of the distinctive features of Goffman's approach. The other was the priority he accorded involvement. Spontaneous involvement was regarded as the desired state for conversational interaction yet this "socialized trance" could easily dissipate into various forms of "alienation from interaction" (Goffman, 1967: 133). When alienation occurred, too little attention was shown for the situational proprieties. Here Goffman was no simple Durkheimian apologist. He recognized that challenging the situational proprieties was sometimes the right thing to do – a theme he returned to in his analyses of the mental patient's situation.

Goffman was surely modern sociology's most creative user of metaphor as an analytical device. So much of what transpires in face-to-face interaction is taken for granted or out of the conscious awareness of the participants. Goffman used metaphor to thematize those overlooked aspects of situated conduct. Three metaphors recurred in Goffman's work: drama, game, and ritual. Each caught a different aspect of conduct in the interaction order. The dramaturgical metaphor of *Presentation of Self* – an adaptation of the "life as theater" analogy – highlighted the enacted and displayed aspects of our everyday "performances." Self was something to be "presented" by the interactant's "performances" in order to "manage impressions" in everyday life. Goffman gave new life to this old metaphor by attending to the stage or setting ("front and back regions") and to the collaboration of the performers ("teamwork") in successfully providing a convincing performance for an audience. Goffman's fascination for the dramaturgical metaphor reappeared in subsequent writings, notably in the chapter on "The theatrical frame" (Goffman, 1974), in the concept of gender display (Goffman, 1979), and in his claim in his final book that "deeply incorporated into the nature of talk are the fundamental requirements of theatricality" (Goffman, 1981a: 4).

The game metaphor represented the calculative aspect of Goffman's analysis of the interaction order. The game metaphor is evident in Goffman's (1959) emphasis on the potential of individuals to control and manage information about themselves in encounters as well as in the notion of the "move" as the basic analytic unit for understanding how interaction unfolds. It was here that Goffman first attracted notoriety for his apparent portrayal of interaction and interactants in what critics saw as excessively rational, opportunistic, and manipulative terms. Ten years later, Goffman (1969) devoted a short book to what he called "strategic interaction," which worked through some of the implications of games theory for an understanding of interactional processes. Certainly Goffman was always quick to see the calculative possibilities in his analyses of interaction. He offered sociology a subtle understanding of the role of calculation and instrumentality. But the game metaphor served other functions in his analyses, notably to highlight the opportunities for fun, engrossment and the display of "character" in social situations (Smith, 2006: 45–50).

The moral dimensions of interaction were chiefly expressed through the ritual metaphor, which Goffman creatively adapted from Durkheim's *Elementary Forms*. For Durkheim, religious ritual directed people towards things symbolically significant to them. Consequently, it called for attitudes and acts of respect. Goffman took Durkheim's idea and secularized it. In Goffman's hands the ritual metaphor articulated the forms of regard and respect manifested interactionally:

In contemporary society ritual performed to stand-ins for supernatural entities are everywhere in decay, as are extensive ceremonial agendas involving long strings of obligatory rites. What remains are brief rituals one individual performs for and to another, attesting to civility and goodwill on the performer's part and to the recipient's possession of a small patrimony of sacredness. What remains … are interpersonal rituals. (Goffman, 1971: 63)

Of course what Goffman pointed to was a variable feature of interpersonal conduct, best understood as a continuum with concern and regard clustering at one end and contempt and insult occupying the other.

The ritual metaphor provided the basis of some of Goffman's most compelling concepts. His magnificent paper "On face-work" (1955; reprinted Goffman, 1967) analyzed the encounter in terms of the ways people sustained the "face" (the positive social value expressed through their interactional conduct) they claimed and how threats to face were handled. The concepts of "deference" and "demeanor" pointed to the ways interactants must guard the symbolic implications of their talk and conduct while in the presence of that all-important deity, the individual. Goffman's (1971) chapters on "supportive interchanges" and "remedial interchanges" underlined the significance of greetings and farewells, and apologies and explanations respectively.

In Goffman's analyses metaphor was used as analytic device to tease out overlooked or hidden from view features of interactional conduct. It was never a simple mechanical application of the metaphor to some data. Goffman was always ready to mix his metaphors in the interests of generating insight into the social organization of the interaction order. In developing the dramaturgical analysis in *Presentation*, Goffman insisted that there was a moral character to self-presentations; in "On face-work," the ritual and the game models intersected in the proposal that persons may be regarded as players of a "ritual game." While this mixing may have illuminated interactional analysis, it also invited the criticism that Goffman was less than systematic in his work. Certainly, Goffman's early publications orbited around some focal concerns but never seemed to move in the direction of general theory. That apparent lack of interest in consolidation of his theoretical ideas became, particularly for those of orthodox social science persuasions, a major source of unease as Goffman developed his project. Others saw Goffman's project as a "blurred genre" (Geertz, 1980) that was not bound by such concerns because it fell outside of conventional conceptions of the humanities and social sciences. Meanwhile Goffman himself largely ignored such debates, consistently avoiding being drawn into debate about the standing of his work (and succumbing only once: see Goffman, 1981b). Like his teacher W. Lloyd Warner, Goffman seems to have regarded this kind of intervention as a sidetrack that would divert his attention from his current work and next publication.

Frame analysis and later work

Through the 1960s ethnomethodology made increasing inroads into the intellectual space first colonized by Goffman. Garfinkel's project attracted increasing attention, not least from talented young graduate students like Harvey Sacks, Emanuel Schegloff, Dorothy Smith, and David Sudnow who all attended Goffman's Berkeley classes. Partly in response to the challenge represented by the rise of ethnomethodology and other phenomenological approaches, Goffman produced a major alternative formulation in the shape of *Frame Analysis* (1974), a long book centered on the question of how we make sense of ordinary events. His focus widened beyond the interaction order to accommodate (in the book's subtitle) the "organization of experience." His analytic attention shifted from the pragmatics of commingling represented in his earlier "moments and their men" (Goffman, 1967: 3) approach towards an analysis of the sense that persons made of moments. Any strip of activity could support several different interpretations. In Goffman's (1974: 10) own example: "a couple" kissing can also be a "man" greeting his "wife" or "John" being careful with "Mary's makeup."

Thus participants in any strip of activity have to find an answer to the question, "what is going on here"? Is this strip of activity a joke or a game or a play or a rehearsal or a test? How sense was made became Goffman's focus. His general solution was that sense making comes about because we are able to apply frames to events – frames that are sustained both in mind and in activity. For Goffman the central analytical question became: "How can frames be classified and analyzed?" He proposed that the first or elemental framing of an activity was achieved through the application of a "primary framework." The primary framework made sense of an otherwise unintelligible activity. However, any frame might be transformed into something else. A "fight" (primary framework) could be transformed into "playing at fighting" or "reporting a fight." These transformations involved a "keying" of an activity. Sometimes, however, asymmetrical understandings of what is going on could emerge: a "good deal" might actually turn out to be a "con." Such "fabrications," designed to mislead one party to an experience, were the second major way that primary frameworks could be transformed. Fabrications were termed "benign" when not engineered against the target's interests and "exploitative" when they were. Fabrications were plainly tied to Goffman's earlier preoccupations with the game metaphor.

Goffman inventively used the frame concept to articulate the recursive and reflexive dimensions of social life. Throughout, Goffman argued against any kind of easy social constructionism. Social situations were not created entirely anew every time people interact. Individuals were not free to define situations just how they please. Rather, the world is constructed so as to supply the frames that individuals will employ in the situation. Goffman's frame analysis provided social answers to cognitive questions about sense making. Experience was seen as very fully socially organized. While this represented an imaginative engagement with the ideas of Alfred Schutz and the phenomenological tradition more broadly, it was perhaps less successful at addressing phenomenologists' concerns with the particularity of the individual's specific experiences (Smith, 2005).

Frame analysis re-invigorated Goffman's perspective in his last works. This was most clearly evident in *Forms of Talk* (1981a), where the reflexive actions of the conversational interactant were repeatedly foregrounded. Goffman rejected what he saw as the deterministic picture of talk provided by conversation analysis, a picture in which the sequential organization of turn-taking seemed to trump all other analytical considerations. He proposed instead that conversation provided a fire that "can burn anything" and "the box that conversation stuffs us into is Pandora's" (Goffman, 1981a: 38, 74). He analyzed instances of "self-talk," words apparently designed for only the individual's own consumption, such as "Oops!" and "Shit!," to show how they were actually responsive to the interactant's dramaturgical need to display an orientation to the norm of "controlled alertness." He examined closely the asides of the lecturer and the slips of the radio announcer's tongue in order to establish how a lively human presence was conveyed through various small acts that breached the frame of the ceremonial lecture and radio talk.

At the center of this late work was the notion of "footing" (Goffman, 1981a), a concept aimed at sociologically grasping the moment-by-moment shifts in identity enacted in conversational interaction. Goffman began his analysis with a newspaper report of a 1973 bill-signing ceremony in the Oval Office. A woman journalist wearing slacks attracted President Nixon's attention. He requested that she pirouette to show off her outfit to the mainly male company. Both Nixon and the journalist experienced a shift in the alignment that they took to themselves and to the others present who witness the scene. Goffman suggested that the notions of speaker and hearer were too simple to offer an adequate basis for a satisfactory analysis. Goffman dis-aggregated the broad concept of the speaker into three components: "animator" (the speaker of words), author (the originator of the words), and principal (the believer of the words). The speaker's footing at any moment in talk depended upon the configuration of these roles. Similarly, hearership was seen to depend on participant status as ratified or unratified (e.g. an overhearer) and addressed or unaddressed (e.g. a bystander). The woman journalist finds that Nixon shifts the ground of her participation in the occasion by removing her from the unaddressed group of journalists and giving her a speaking and performing part: she does a twirl and explains that her husband is happy for her to wear slacks. The analytic terminology of footing looms large in Goffman's late studies of lecturing and radio talk, shedding fresh sociological light on the self-referential features of conversational interaction. Together with the frame schema, they demonstrate how, through to the end, Goffman was continuing to develop and refine his studies of the interaction order, taking them in new directions sensitive to issues of context, experience, and reflexivity.

Popular works

Under this heading we can consider those three books – *Asylums* (1961a), *Stigma* (1963b), and *Gender Advertisements* (1979) – where Goffman applied some of his general ideas about the interaction order to specific topics, mental illness, social disadvantage, and gender difference. Taking his cue from Durkheim and Freud, Goffman suggested that much could be learned about normal social conduct by examining its abnormal forms. Each of these books is a study in the nature of difference, otherness, and exclusion, seen from Goffman's distinctive interactional vantage point.

Asylums enjoyed classic status not only because of its extensive citation both in specialist research papers and introductory texts but also because of its use in legal proceedings and its broad public influence. Goffman drew extensively on his field-work experience at Saint Elizabeths Hospital. The mental hospital was positioned as an instance of a "total institution," a type of formal organization that broke down the customary separation of places for work, sleep, and play. Instead, the daily round was carried out in the company of like-situated others (batch living), activities were scheduled by rules and officials, and the activities themselves were devised as part of a plan to realize the institution's goals. Prisons, care homes, military barracks, POW camps, isolation hospitals, and convents are all examples of the total institution. The key groupings are "staff" and "inmates." Life in the total institution was contrasted with civil society and domestic family life. The contrast was used as "strategic lever-age" in the management of inmates.

The special relevance of total institutions for Goffman was that they were: "forc-ing houses for changing persons; each is a natural experiment on what can be done to the self" (Goffman, 1961a: 12). Induction into the total institution typically involved "a series of abasements, humiliations, and profanations of self" (Goffman, 1961a: 14). The inmate's biography was recorded, his/her picture taken, hair cut, body inspected or searched, personal belongings taken away, and civilian clothing changed for institutional issue. "Initiation rites" and "obedience tests" that function as "will-breaking contests" for inmates were undergone. The net consequence of such "mortification processes" was to remove the inmate's usual sources of self-identification: "total institutions disrupt or defile precisely those actions that in civil society have the role of attesting to the actor and those in his presence that he has some command over his world – that he is a person with 'adult' self-determination, autonomy and freedom of action" (Goffman, 1961a: 43). The total institution tended to successfully break down sources of inmate group solidarity and high morale. When resistance occurred, it took covert and defeasible forms: "playing it cool," "situational withdrawal," and "intransigence." These forms of resistance helped inmates restore some sense of self-worth. Despite the total instititution's power to re-define the inmate's self, the effects seldom endured long beyond release into civil society. The "proactive status" that graduation from the total institution conferred, however, depended on the nature of the institution. It was very different for those who could look back to a spell in an elite officer-training academy than a prison or a mental hospital.

In keeping with his Chicagoan ethnographic heritage it was organizational proc-esses rather than structures that became Goffman's primary focus. His chapter on the mental patient's "moral career" identified the changes in conception of self and framework for appraising self and others occasioned by the patient's path from civil society to the mental hospital. Goffman challenged psychiatric orthodoxy in seeing the "sick behavior" of the mental patient not as the result of illness but rather as a consequence of social distance from the patient's immediate situation. Goffman's point was that in this "prepatient phase" various kinds of improper behavior were typically overlooked or tolerated until a complaint was made. The patient would then find themselves the target of an "alienative coalition" of complainant, next-of-kin, psychiatrists, police, social workers, and the like, who seemed to the patient to collectively conspire to ensure the patient's incarceration. From the patient's point of view, those who were supposed to have the patient's welfare and interests at heart instead constituted a "betrayal funnel" leading to the patient's hospitalization. In the "inpatient phase," mortification processes eroded previous conceptions of the patient's self. Initial acts of resistance to hospital procedures often eventually gave way to a demoralized, albeit temporary condition in which the patient practiced "the amoral arts of shamelessness" (Goffman, 1961a: 169).

Asylums also analyzed patients' "ways of making out" at Saint Elizabeths. Goffman chronicled the arrangements through which patients construct a life for themselves outwith the demands of the hospital. Goffman described an "underlife" made up of patients' scavenging, "make-do's," exploitation of outside contacts, "stashes," and "free places," that went on largely beneath the radar (or at least the action) of staff. For all its ethnographic detail, Goffman's analysis remained driven by more general themes, in this case the nature of the social bond. The notion of "secondary adjustments" was coined to capture the ways such activities represented an alternative to the hospital's conceptions of the patient's self. Secondary adjustments were not mere pranks or silly games. Instead, Goffman saw them as "methods to keep some distance, some elbow room between himself and that which others assume he should be identified" (Goffman, 1961a: 319) in an oppressive environment. Goffman showed the intelligibility of these actions and restored rationality to the mental patient. Foucault may well have popularized "resistance" as an element of social and cultural theory but Goffman provided the ethnographic basis on which such analyses could be made compelling.

Goffman's general approach was not conventionally ethnographic. It did not, in the terminology made famous by Geertz, aim to generate thick descriptions of the native's point of view. In *Asylums* and elsewhere, Goffman's primary aim was to develop an "ethnography of concepts" (Manning, 2009). Ethnographic investigation was used as a springboard for conceptual innovation. This distinctive model of ethnographic research has not always been well understood by critics. Goffman's study attracted other complaints. For a book that does not contain any explicit recommendations for change ("Nor…do I mean to claim that I can suggest some better way of handling persons called mental patients" (Goffman, 1961a: 384)), *Asylums* proved both controversial and influential (Weinstein, 1994). Goffman's organizational analysis was criticized for presenting as "characteristics" of total institutions – for example, batch living – features that would be better treated as variables. Goffman's method played up the similarities between different kinds of total institution at the expense of differences between them, often in order to capitalize rhetorically on the negative associations attached to coercive institutions such as prisons or conscripts barracks. The degree to which admission to the total institution is voluntary has been suggested as a key variable for understanding inmates' experiences, differentiating the convict's lot from the monk's.

The popularity of *Stigma* (Goffman, 1963b) owed something to its underlying themes of difference, disadvantage, and otherness. Once again Goffman focused on how these matters manifested themselves in everyday encounters. The book soon became a key text in the sociology of deviance, medical sociology, and disability studies. Goffman's (1963b) interest in stigma may have been sparked by consideration of the ex-patient phase mentioned but not analyzed in the "Moral career" paper. The status of ex-mental patient was certainly stigmatizing to its holders, who, in Goffman's (1963b: Preface) first definition of stigma, were "disqualified from full social acceptance." The concept rounded up three sources of social disqualification: physical deformities, character faults, and the delicately described "tribal stigma of race, nation and religion" (Goffman, 1963b: 4). Of course, Goffman's interest was not so much in the discrediting attributes themselves as it was in the interactions and relationships set up around the presentation and management of the stigmatizing attribute. Goffman's analysis was driven by three identity concepts – social, personal, and ego or felt identity – each of which facilitated the examination of a different aspect of stigma. Social identity referred to the everyday ways of identifying and characterizing the person. The concept allowed Goffman the opportunity to explore some general features of stigmatization as a social process. Those who were already "discredited" on account of their visible disability or tribal stigma often shared a common "moral career" and required the support of "sympathetic others." Included among the latter the "own," others sharing the stigma, and the "wise," persons familiar with their plight even though they did not share the stigma.

Personal identity concerned those features that marked the person out as distinct from all others. Goffman linked the notion of the "discreditable" to personal identity. A discreditable stigma was not self-evident in social situations (a character fault or a damaging fact from the person's biography, for example) and therefore it could be managed through careful information control. Goffman emphasized the thoroughly contextual reasoning informing control of information about personal identity: "To display or not to display; to tell or not to tell; to let on or not to let on; to lie or not to lie; and in each case, to whom, how, and where" (Goffman, 1963b: 42). A large part of Stigma was devoted to documenting the interactional strategies that discreditable persons employed to control the vagaries of the situations they encountered.

Ego or felt identity enabled Goffman to address how the person felt about their stigma and the sources of advice they received about their stigmatized identity. Goffman emphasized that many standards for grading people were widely shared: persons stigmatized in some situations readily acted as normals in another. Goffman's tough-minded analysis emphasized the competing loyalties the stigmatized often faced as they attempted to find a way through the wider society's standards of worthiness and the contrasting standards espoused by activists for their own group. In the end a "politics of identity" (possibly the earliest use of the identity politics concept (Lemert, 1997)) emerged as the stigmatized worked through the arguments about what their ego identity ought really to be (Goffman, 1963b: 123–125). Just as Asylums took the psychological normality of the mental patient as its point of departure, so too Stigma made no presumption of psychological difference between the normal and the stigmatized. "A stigmatized person" wrote Goffman (1963b: 134) "is first of all like anyone else, trained first of all in others views of persons like himself." Thus normal and stigmatized "are not persons but rather perspectives," interactional roles rather than persons defined essentially by the attributes of supposed "shameful difference" that they display. If Stigma can be considered Goffman's most morally compelling work, it is because he succeeded in making persuasive arguments, grounded in the close analysis of the situations of the stigmatized, about the futility of claims about essential human difference.

Essentialist claims were also a target for Goffman's writings on gender. There he offered strong social constructionist arguments that gender difference was best understood as an enactment encoded in situated practices such as the gender displays conspicuous in advertising imagery. The ideas Goffman developed in the 1970s seem to have been rediscovered by the performative turn linked to Judith Butler's work in the 1990s. The eye-catching volume Gender Advertisements also made an important contribution to the emergent fields of visual sociology and visual studies (Emmison and Smith, 2000). This 1979 book, containing over 500 images drawn mainly from pictorial advertisements was originally published as a special issue of a visual communication journal in 1976. Apparently Goffman toured a number of

US universities equipped with several carousels of slides of advertising images that he had collected. The book was developed from his interpretations and commentaries on the sets of slides he showed. While the rise of feminism in the early 1970s and the interests of feminist-oriented graduate students in his classes at the University of Pennsylvania may have acted as a catalyst for this work, it is fair to say that an awareness of the significance of gender and of the special interactional predicaments women sometimes face on grounds of their gender went back to Goffman's writings of the early 1950s.

Gender Advertisements was an empirically grounded application of a more general framework for understanding gender relations proposed in Goffman's 1977 article in *Theory and Society*. There he argued for an "institutional reflexivity" theory of gender. In its basics, this proposed that the arrangements institutionalized in a society to mark and honor the presumed biological differences between the sexes turn out to be the real sources of gender difference. Gendered first names, segregated toilet facilities in public places, household divisions of labor, and the like did not, as is commonly supposed, merely honor the more fundamental, biological differences in the natures of men and women. Rather, these institutionalized arrangements actually generated those differences in the human natures of men and women. This implied that if institutionalized practices were changed, then so too would the gendered conceptions based upon them.

The institutional reflexivity theory was particularized and extended in *Gender Advertisements*. The key analytic unit in the book, "gender display," isolated the situated, non-verbal "conventionalized portrayals" correlated by the culture with sex. More simply, gender displays concerned how femininity and masculinity could be seen and shown. The book described and showed some leading forms of gender display, including "function ranking," where men were typically shown taking the executive role; the "ritualization of subordination," where women lowered their bodies in canting gestures symbolizing their lesser status; and "licensed withdrawal," where women assumed rights to disengage from full involvement in the matter at hand. The book itself used a novel format. Sets of images were presented to illustrate a theme first briefly outlined by Goffman's written text. The reader of *Gender Advertisements* was thus cast into an active role. The reader (or reader-scanner) was effectively asked to engage in a search procedure. First Goffman's prose statement needed to be read then the arrays of images scanned in order to find the specific sense in the images indicated by the prose. The book continues to be a major reference point for studies of advertising images. It also offers a plea for visual sociological thinking (Smith, 2010) that has largely gone unheard in subsequent replications of the study.

IMPACT AND ASSESSMENT

Goffman initiated his singular sociological project over half a century ago, yet many puzzles remain about its character and contribution. While unquestionably readable, Goffman's work remains a true "enigma": texts that seem designed "to afford an exercise for the ingenuity of the reader ... in guessing what is meant" (Lemert, 2003: xii). It is not surprising that so many ways of categorizing Goffman (Jacobsen and

Kristiansen, 2010) have developed as understandable responses to this enigmatic status and that each categorization succeeds in capturing only part of the complexity of Goffman's sociology. The most general question concerns the nature of Goffman's legacy. An adequate review would be a substantial undertaking. It would examine the many substantive areas of sociology in which Goffman's ideas have made a significant impact. A far from comprehensive list of these areas would include: mental illness and deinstitutionalization policies (Gronfein, 1992); disability studies and the cultural politics of recognition (Jacobsen, 2010b); gender and performativity (Gardner, 1989; West, 1996); sociological approaches to emotion (Hochschild, 1983; Scheff, 2006); public places (Cahill, 1994); and face-work and politeness theory (Ting-Toomey, 1994). There is also the speculative but intriguing question about the areas and topics he might have ventured into had he lived longer (Collins, 1986).

A broader assessment of Goffman's contribution to social theory might focus on the controversies his work stimulated. Three Goffman controversies can be identified: Goffman provoked debate about the self, about method, and about textuality. In each case Goffman's view generated a debate that helped to refine sociological sensitivities about these important areas.

One major node of controversy about Goffman's sociology concerned its emphasis on the human agent and its portrayal of the individual. Many critics complained that Goffman's sociology was, in a word, cynical. They suggested that it gave undue prominence to a view of human nature that was predatory and manipulative. It seemed to depict people as overly self-conscious in the ruthless pursuit of self-interest through strategies of impression management and the opportunistic control of personal information. While Goffman gave a good deal of attention to the capacity of humans to design and control interactional activity, this calculative side of his thinking about interaction was only one part of the fuller theory he offered. In particular, Goffman's appropriation and creative development of Durkheim's ritual model yielded a very different view of human nature, one that emphasized consideration rather than calculation and moral considerations directed towards not just the pursuit of personal ends.

To many observers, Goffman seemed to play up the role of agency and play down the role of structure in accounting for social action. The characterization of Goffman as an agency theorist, however, does little justice to his own emphasis on the importance of the notion of the local determination of action – the idea that many aspects of action can be accounted for by the demands of the interaction order (Rawls, 1987). Taking Goffman as an agency theorist buys into the distinction between agency and structure that is increasingly questioned in contemporary social theory (Martin and Dennis, 2010). Goffman can easily be assimilated into what is coming to be known as "the practice turn" (Schatzki *et al.*, 2001) – indeed, Goffman's ideas influenced two of its key exponents, Pierre Bourdieu and Anthony Giddens. The individual agent mattered in Goffman's scheme but it was the locally occurring "moments" rather than "their men" (Goffman, 1967: 3) that consistently occupied analytical center stage.

Goffman's arguments about the relative analytical autonomy of the interaction order are the key to understanding his view of the individual. Goffman (1961b; 1983a) rejected the idea that macro social structures were simply built up from what transpired interactionally. Social structure was not just an aggregate of interactions.

Equally, what actually took place in interaction cannot be simply read off from the interactant's social structural position. It is as if there is a "membrane" around the interaction that sifts and sorts the structural attributes (race, gender, class, etc.) that will be brought into play in the encounter. In general Goffman proposed a loosely coupled relation between interactions and social structures, not a straightforward determinism in either direction. It was from this vantage that Goffman's sociologization of the self proceeded.

One of the unsettling features of Goffman's project was its identification of hitherto unthought-of sociological determinants of the individual as an interactant. Actions commonly held to be random or idiosyncratic to the person became transformed, in Goffman's sociological gaze, into instances of patterned co-present conduct. The consequence was that Goffman succeeded in making "the self a visible, sociological phenomenon" (Anderson *et al.*, 1985). Goffman took very seriously Mead's "social behaviorist" approach. This advocated studying the self through the implications of the person's conduct for their self. At its simplest, Goffman's behaviorist approach to the self concentrated upon the ways co-present conduct could be read as an indicator of the self's mood, orientation, competence, etc. But it was also used to show how evidence of the individual's "unique self" was produced interactionally and how the "perduring self" depended for confirmation of its existence upon frames and situationally appropriate actions (Goffman, 1967: 85, 1974: 298).

At the same time that Goffman was extending the scope of sociological determinations of the self, he also sought to understand the ways persons attempt to escape social bondedness. Most fundamentally, Goffman suggested that local interaction orders provided the resources for resistance to social role expectations and obligations. In striking examples such as the skittish behavior of surgeons during surgery and the secondary adjustments of mental patients Goffman demonstrated how interactional resources allowed them to be something other than merely exponents of their roles as surgeons or mental patients. Thus for Goffman resistance to social bonds could also be understood sociologically – no part of the world was safe from his sociology. This theme was pursued through to his later writings where the concept of footing captured the live performance elements of ordinary interaction – what lends a spark to our everyday dealings. While people could escape the obligations of roles and institutionalized demands, apparently they could not escape their obligations as interactants. Persons may possess a "simultaneous multiplicity of selves" that made them unique but the "dance of identification" (Goffman, 1961b: 144) through which the multiplicity depended for expression required the resources furnished by the interaction order. In sum, Goffman's sociology presented a novel understanding of the social bases of "person production" (Cahill, 1998) that encashed the leads set down by Marcel Mauss and Michel Foucault as well as George Herbert Mead and Charles Horton Cooley.

A second source of productive controversy centered on Goffman's method or, rather, his apparent lack of one. Very many readers of Goffman like what they read, even though they may confess some bafflement about exactly *what* it was that his sociology was doing, and precisely *how* that sociology was done. There has been a proliferation of attempts to locate Goffman in established sociological perspectives – symbolic interactionist, functionalist, structuralist, existentialist, phenomenologist, critical theorist, and postmodernist among them – none of which have been finally adequate or satisfying (Jacobsen and Kristiansen, 2010). However, there is wide agreement that doing sociology Goffman's way is not easy to copy or to teach students. Commentators have remarked that Goffman seemed too empirical in his preoccupations to be considered a theorist, yet too theoretical to be regarded as simply an ethnographer. Adjudged next to conventional social scientific methodological criteria, it was easy to find Goffman wanting. Bernard Meltzer *et al.* (1975) noted this when listing some of the conventional objections to Goffman's procedure:

> We find in his work no explicit theory, but a plausible and loosely organized frame of reference; little interest in explanatory schemes, but masterful descriptive analysis; virtually no accumulated evidence, but illuminating allusions, impressions, anecdotes, and illustrations; few formulations of empirically testable propositions, but innumerable provocative insights. In addition, we find an insufficiency of qualifications and reservations, so that the limits of generalization are not indicated. (Meltzer *et al.*, 1975: 70–71)

Goffman himself acknowledged some of the conventional social scientific criticisms, although he never seemed to accept them as telling censures. However philosophers (Louch, 1966; Cioffi, 2000) added another layer of complaint, arguing that as members of society we already possess sound explanations of the matters Goffman described so that genuine discoveries are absent in his writings. All Goffman offered, according to the philosophers, was a reassuringly well-packaged rearrangement of what we already know. Such critiques beg the question of the role of conceptual innovation in Goffman's sociology.

Goffman took a methodologically minimalist approach to his work in following Georg Simmel's attempts to identify conceptually the basic forms or structuring principles of social life. It was minimalist in that the most his work attempted was the classification of the concepts he felt that sociology would need in order to explore the new territory of the interaction order. Goffman possessed a remarkable talent for "nomination" (Jameson, 1976: 127), giving names to new social objects (teams, discrepant roles, unfocused interaction, and many more – around one thousand concepts have been identified in Goffman's writings). The year before his death he expressed doubt about the value of grand and middle range theory, recommending something more basic, "a modest but persistent analyticity: frameworks of the lower range":

> I believe that the provision of a single conceptual distinction, if it orders, and illuminates, and reflects delight in the contours of our data, can warrant our claim to be students of society. And surely, if we can't uncover processes, mechanisms, structures and variables that cause others to see what they hadn't seen or connect what they hadn't put together, then we have failed critically. (Goffman, 1981c: 4)

A leading issue about Goffman's method was why he chose to proliferate conceptual frameworks without ever consolidating them. A plausible case was made by Robin Williams (1988) and Philip Manning (1992) that Goffman's own conceptual and classificatory work was driven by an interior logic that sought to test and refine the adequacy of his concepts and metaphors. However, the recovery of that testing and the reconstruction of what survived have proved difficult to identify, although fragments are discernible (e.g. the way the footing terminology replaces the earlier role distance concept). The primarily conceptual character of Goffman's legacy has meant that a wide range of methodologies have been used to test the applicability of his concepts. As Goffman (1959, 1981a) recognized, it was in such further empirical testing by other researchers that the real worth of his concepts was to be located.

On the other hand, the initial plausibility of the concepts Goffman presents is a matter thoroughly indigenous to the texts themselves. Goffman's textuality is a third area of critical commentary that points to wider implications of his work. Even though Goffman considered sociology a fundamentally empirical discipline, there is plenty of evidence that he worked hard to craft the prose that made his books so compelling. His "socio-literary method" (Manning, 1976) centered on his imaginative and inventive use of metaphor and his application of literary critic Kenneth Burke's notion of "perspective by incongruity." Goffman was a strong writer who understood the role of textual persuasion in promoting his distinctive perspective towards the world. Sociological substance and literary style were clearly intertwined in his writings. A number of studies have sought to understand how textual persuasion works in his writings. They have focused upon topics such as Goffman's metaphorical practices (Brown, 1977; Smith and Jacobsen, 2010), his use of irony, sarcasm and satire (Fine and Martin, 1990), the sequencing of words and phrases in Goffman's texts (Atkinson, 1989), and shifts in narrative voice (Cohen and Rogers, 1994; Manning, 1989). Academic interest in the "crisis of representation" largely post-dated Goffman's own work, yet he has now been reclaimed as a writer in the vanguard of the rhetorical turn.

Everett Hughes once wrote of Goffman as "our Simmel" (Winkin, 1999: 28). Certainly, the parallels with the great German philosopher and sociologist are striking at many levels (Smith, 1994; Davis, 1997; Gerhardt, 2003). One of the best summations of Goffman's contribution can be found by borrowing Max Weber's (1972) assessment of his contemporary, Georg Simmel. Weber's comments about Simmel seem to apply with equal facility to Goffman:

> certain crucial aspects of his methodology are unacceptable ... his mode of exposition strikes one at times as strange ... On the other hand one finds oneself compelled to affirm that his mode of exposition is simply brilliant and ... attains results that are intrinsic to it and not to be attained by any imitator ... nearly every one of his works abounds in important new theoretical ideas and the most subtle observations ... Altogether then, even when he is on the wrong path, he fully deserves his reputation as one of the foremost thinkers, a first-rate stimulator of academic youth and academic colleagues. (Weber, 1972: 158)

Close readers of the critical literature on Goffman will have come across this comparison before. Stanford Lyman (1973) first noted the appositeness of the Weber passage to Goffman. Robin Williams (1988) saw to it that Lyman's comparison reached a wider audience.

Goffman's writings helped shift the analytic reach of sociological analysis. Yet, in comparison with Howard S. Becker or Anselm Strauss, Goffman made no substantial contributions to methods of naturalistic observation. Nevertheless, in and through the impact of his writings on his readership, Goffman effectively raised the bar for sociological observation. Part of the "revolutionary character" of Goffman's work compared to his precursors (Parsons, Bales, the symbolic interactionists), according to Dorothy Smith (quoted in West, 1996: 366, n.13), was that they "did not know how to 'look' as Goffman taught us." In Goffman's sociological gaze, of course, perception and conception were united. Goffman's delicate conceptual distinctions permitted matters to be noticed that were previously held to be in the province of creative writers. Goffman's concepts have found their way into thousands of studies, showing how the conceptual substance of his writings has proved (as Lévi-Strauss might have put it) "good to think with." But Goffman did more than merely provide a rich array of concepts that facilitated further research studies. His mode of procedure, as the controversies around method and textuality indicated, continually gave readers pause for thought, demanding that they themselves consider what they deemed to be adequate standards for conducting sociological research and providing an acceptable sociological account. In this respect Goffman was indeed "a first-rate stimulator of academic youth and academic colleagues" who will continue to be read for a long time to come.

Reader's Guide to Erving Goffman

Goffman's publications are easy for readers to enter at any point. Nearly all of his books are still in print in paperback. The last work that Goffman knew would be published, "The interaction order" (1983a), gives his final assessment of some general questions posed by his sociology. *Interaction Ritual*, Goffman's (1967) collection of essays mainly written in the 1950s, still offers a good introduction to many of his central analytic concerns. Of this earlier work, "On face-work" (Goffman, 1967, orig. 1955) is an important statement while the somewhat overlooked essay "Fun in games" (in *Encounters*) offers much to ponder about the games metaphor and the micro–macro relationship. Of the later work, "Footing" (Goffman, 1981a) articulates some very general issues about alignment. The extensively illustrated *Gender Advertisements* (1979) brings together some key themes in a novel and provocative textual format that vividly exposes key elements of his method. Charles Lemert and Ann Branaman's (1997) *The Goffman Reader* supplies a good selection from across the range of the published work and is prefaced by a thoughtful essay apiece from each editor.

Substantial commentary in English begins with Jason Ditton's (1980) still useful edited collection, *The View from Goffman*. A major international conference on Goffman held at the University of York (UK) in 1986 resulted in two edited collections, by Paul Drew and Anthony Wootton (1988) and by Frances C. Waksler (1989). Two monographs assessing Goffman's work appeared in 1992. Tom Burns's *Erving Goffman* benefited from a friendship begun in Edinburgh in 1949. Philip Manning's *Erving Goffman and Modern Sociology* provides a good guide to just why Goffman was so provocative a thinker. Two more monographs appeared in 2006. In *Goffman Unbound!* Thomas Scheff, a former Berkeley student of Goffman's, argues that Goffman's vision centers upon his discovery of the "emotional/relational world." Greg Smith's 2006 volume in the Routledge Key Sociologists series gives a focused overview of the central features of Goffman's life and work. The critical literature collected Gary Alan Fine and Smith's (2000) four-volume collection on Goffman traces the major responses to Goffman's ideas in and around sociology.

The continuing relevance of Goffman's ideas and analytic attitude to a wide range of sociological concerns comes across in contributions to four edited collections of original papers, by Stephen Riggins (1990), Greg Smith (1999), Javier Treviño (2003) and Michael Hviid Jacobsen (2010a), respectively. The contributions to Jacobsen's volume, aptly entitled *The Contemporary Goffman*, in turn "dissect," "reframe," and "extend" Goffman's sociology. The studies extending Goffman show the relevance of his ideas for understanding new media technologies and communicative forms and contemporary tourist and urban mobilities. Goffman never wanted his work to be turned into museum artifacts. The critical literature not only assesses aspects of the substance and approach of Goffman; it contains many examples where Goffman's ideas have stimulated further sociological work. For Goffman's intellectual biography, see the writings of Yves Winkin (1988, 1999, 2000, 2010). A collection of biographical materials assembled by Dmitri Shalin is available online at www.unlv.edu/centers/cdclv/ega/index.html

Bibliography

Writings of Erving Goffman

1949. Some characteristics of response to depicted experience. MA thesis, Department of Sociology, University of Chicago.

1951. Symbols of class status. *British Journal of Sociology*, 2(4): 294–304.

1952. On cooling the mark out: Some aspects of adaptation to failure. *Psychiatry*, 15(4): 451–463.

1953. Communication conduct in an island community. PhD dissertation, Department of Sociology, University of Chicago.

1955. On face-work: An analysis of ritual elements in social interaction. *Psychiatry*, 18(3): 213–231.

1956a. *The Presentation of Self in Everyday Life*. Edinburgh: University of Edinburgh, Social Sciences Research Centre.

1956b. Embarrassment and social organization. *The American Journal of Sociology*, 62(3): 264–271.

1956c. The nature of deference and demeanor. *The American Anthropologist*, 58(3): 473–502.

1957. Interpersonal persuasion. In B. Schaffner (ed.) *Group Processes: Transactions of the Third Conference* (October 7–10, 1956). New York: Josiah Macy Jr. Foundation, pp.117–193.

1959. *The Presentation of Self in Everyday Life*. New York: Doubleday, Anchor Books.

1961a. *Asylums: Essays on the Social Situation of Mental Patients and Other Inmates*. New York: Doubleday, Anchor Books.

1961b. *Encounters: Two Studies in the Sociology of Interaction*. Indianapolis: Bobbs-Merrill.

1963a. *Behavior in Public Places: Notes on the Social Organization of Gatherings*. New York: The Free Press.

1963b. *Stigma: Notes on the Management of Spoiled Identity*. Englewood Cliffs, NJ: Prentice-Hall.

1964. The neglected situation. *The American Anthropologist*, 66(6), Part 2: 133–136.

1967. *Interaction Ritual: Essays on Face-to-face Behavior*. New York: Doubleday, Anchor Books.

1969. The insanity of place. *Psychiatry: Journal of Interpersonal Relations*, 32(4): 357–387.

1969. *Strategic Interaction*. Philadelphia, PA: University of Pennsylvania Press.

1971. *Relations in Public: Microstudies of the Public Order*. New York: Basic Books.
1974. *Frame Analysis: An Essay on the Organization of Experience*. Cambridge, MA: Harvard University Press.
1977. The arrangement between the sexes. *Theory and Society*, 4: 301–332.
1979. *Gender Advertisements*. London: Macmillan.
1981a. *Forms of Talk*. Oxford: Basil Blackwell.
1981b. A reply to Denzin and Keller. *Contemporary Sociology*, 10(1): 60–68.
1981c. Program committee encourages papers on range of methodologies. *ASA Footnotes*, 9(6): 4.
1983a. The interaction order. *American Sociological Review*, 48(1): 1–17.
1983b. Felicity's condition. *The American Journal of Sociology*, 89(1): 1–53.
1989. On fieldwork. *Journal of Contemporary Ethnography*, 18(2): 123–132.

Further Reading

Abbott, A. (1999) *Department and Discipline: Chicago Sociology at One Hundred*. Chicago: University of Chicago Press.
Anderson, R., Hughes, J. A., and Sharrock, W. W. (1985) *The Sociology Game: An Introduction to Sociological Reasoning*. London: Longman.
Anon. (2009) Most cited authors of books in the humanities, 2007. *Times Higher Education*, March 26. Available online at www.timeshighereducation.co.uk/story.asp?storyCode=405956&sectioncode=26#leftnavend (accessed June 18, 2010).
Atkinson, P. A. (1989) Goffman's poetics. *Human Studies*, 12: 59–76.
Becker, H. S. (1999) The Chicago School, so-called. *Qualitative Sociology*, 22(1): 3–12.
Bott, Elizabeth (1957) *Family and Social Network*. London: Tavistock Publications Limited.
Brown, R. H. (1977) *A Poetic for Sociology: Toward a Logic of Discovery for the Human Sciences*. Cambridge: Cambridge University Press.
Burke, K. (1965[1935]) *Permanence and Change*. Indianapolis: Bobbs-Merrill.
Burns, T. (1992) *Erving Goffman*. London: Routledge.
Cahill, S. E. (1994) Following Goffman, following Durkheim into the public realm. *Research in Community Sociology*, Supplement 1: 3–17.
Cahill, S. E. (1998) Toward a sociology of the person. *Sociological Theory*, 16: 131–148.
Cioffi, F. (2000) The propaedeutic delusion: What can "ethogenic science" add to our pre-theoretic understanding of "loss of dignity, humiliation and expressive failure"? *History of the Human Sciences*, 13: 108–123.
Clifford, J. and Marcus, G. E. (1986) *Writing Culture: The Poetics and Politics of Ethnography*. Berkeley, CA: University of Berkeley Press.
Cohen, I. J. and Rogers, M. F. (1994) Autonomy and credibility: Voice as method. *Sociological Theory*, 12(3): 304–318.
Collins, R. (1986) The passing of intellectual generations: Reflections on the death of Erving Goffman. *Sociological Theory*, 4(1): 106–113.
Davis, M. S. (1997) Georg Simmel and Erving Goffman: Legitimators of the sociological investigation of human experience. *Qualitative Sociology*, 20(3): 369–388.
Dawe, A. (1973) The underworld view of Erving Goffman. *British Journal of Sociology*, 24(2): 246–253.
Ditton, J. (ed.) (1980) *The View from Goffman*. London and Basingstoke: Macmillan.
Drew, P. and Wootton, A. (eds) (1988) *Erving Goffman: Exploring the Interaction Order*. Cambridge: Polity.
Emmison, M. and Smith, P. (2000) *Researching the Visual*. London: Sage.

Fine, G. A. (1995) *The Development of a Postwar American Sociology*. Chicago: University of Chicago Press.

Fine, G. A. and Smith, G. (eds) (2000) *Erving Goffman*, Four vols. London: Sage.

Fine, G. A and Martin, D. D. (1990) Sarcasm, satire and irony as voices in Erving Goffman's *Asylums*. *Journal of Contemporary Ethnography*, 19(1): 89–115.

Gardner, C. B. (1989) Analyzing gender in public places: Rethinking Goffman's vision of everyday life. *The American Sociologist*, 20(1): 42–56.

Geertz, Clifford (1980) Blurred genres: The refiguration of social thought. *The American Scholar*, 29: 165–179.

Gerhardt, U. (2003) Of kindred spirit: Erving Goffman's oeuvre and its relationship to Georg Simmel. In J. Treviño (ed.) *Goffman's Legacy*. Lanham, MD: Rowman and Littlefield, pp.143–165.

Goffman, A. (2009) On the run: Wanted men in a Philadelphia ghetto. *American Sociological Review*, 74(3): 339–357.

Gouldner, A. (1970) *The Coming Crisis of Western Sociology*. New York: Basic Books.

Gronfein, W. (1992) Goffman's *Asylums* and the social control of the mentally ill. *Perspectives on Social Problems*, 4: 129–153.

Hochschild, A. R. (1983) *The Managed Heart: Commercialization of Human Feeling*. Berkeley: University of California Press.

Hymes, D. (1984) On Erving Goffman. *Theory and Society*, 13: 621–631.

International Sociological Association (1998) *Books of the century*. Available online at www.isa-sociology.org/books/vt/bkv_000.htm (accessed February 1, 2008).

Jacobsen, M. H. (ed.) (2010a) *The Contemporary Goffman*. New York and London: Routledge.

Jacobsen, M. H. (2010b) Recognition as ritualized reciprocation: The interaction order as a realm of recognition. In M. H. Jacobsen (ed.) *The Contemporary Goffman*. London: Routledge, pp.199–231.

Jacobsen, M. H. and Kristiansen, S. (2010) Labelling Goffman: The presentation and appropriation of Erving Goffman in academic life. In M. H. Jacobsen (ed.) *The Contemporary Goffman*. London: Routledge, pp. 64–97.

Jameson, F. (1976) On Goffman's *Frame Analysis*. *Theory and Society*, 3(1): 119–133.

Jaworski, G. D. (2000) Erving Goffman: The reluctant apprentice. *Symbolic Interaction*, 23(3): 299–308.

Junker, B. (1960) *Fieldwork: An Introduction to the Social Sciences*. Chicago: University of Chicago Press.

Lemert, C. (1997) "Goffman." In C. Lemert and A. Branaman (eds) *The Goffman Reader*. Malden, MA: Blackwell.

Lemert, C. (2003) Goffman's enigma: Series Editor's foreword. In J. Treviño (ed.) *Goffman's Legacy*. Lanham, MD: Rowman and Littlefield, pp. xi–xvii.

Lemert, C. and Branaman, A. (eds.) (1997) *The Goffman Reader*. Malden, MA: Blackwell.

Lofland, J. (2000[1984] Erving Goffman's sociological legacies. In G. A. Fine and G. Smith (eds) *Erving Goffman*. London: Sage.

Louch, A. R. (1966) *Explanation and Human Action*. Oxford: Clarendon.

Lyman, S. M. (1973) Civilization: Contents, discontents, malcontents. *Contemporary Sociology*, 2(4): 360–366.

Manning, P. D. (1989) Resemblances. *History of the Human Sciences*, 2: 207–233.

Manning, P. D. (1992) *Erving Goffman and Modern Sociology*. Cambridge: Polity Press.

Manning, P. D. (2009) Three models of ethnographic research: Wacquant as risk-taker. *Theory and Psychology*, 19(6): 756–777.

Manning, P. K. (1976) The decline of civility: A comment on Erving Goffman's sociology. *Canadian Review of Sociology and Anthropology*, 13 (1): 13–25.

Manning, P. K. (2010) Continuities in Goffman: The interaction order. In M. H. Jacobsen (ed.) *The Contemporary Goffman*. New York and London: Routledge, pp. 98–118.

Martin, P. J. and Dennis, A. (eds) (2010) *Human Agents and Social Structures*. Manchester: Manchester University Press.

Marx, G. T. (1984) Role models and role distance: A remembrance of Erving Goffman. *Theory and Society*, 13: 649–662.

McGregor, G. (1986) A view from the fort: Erving Goffman as Canadian. *Canadian Review of Anthropology and Sociology*, 23(4): 531–543.

Meltzer, B. N., Petras, J. W., and Reynolds, L. T. (1975) *Symbolic Interactionism: Genesis, Varieties and Criticism*. London: Routledge and Kegan Paul.

Rawls, A. W. (1987) The interaction order sui generis: Goffman's contribution to social theory. *Sociological Theory*, 5: 136–149.

Riggins, S. H. (ed.) (1990) *Beyond Goffman: Studies on Communication, Institution and Social Interaction*. Berlin and New York: Mouton de Gruyter.

Rose, D. (1990) *Living the Ethnographic Life*. Newbury Park, CA: Sage.

Schatzki, T. R., Knorr-Cetina, K., and von Savigny, E. (eds) (2001) *The Practice Turn in Contemporary Theory*. London: Routledge.

Scheff, T. J. (2005) Looking-glass self: Goffman as symbolic interactionist. *Symbolic Interaction*, 28(2): 147–166.

Scheff, T. J. (2006) *Goffman Unbound! A New Paradigm for Social Science*. Boulder, CO: Paradigm.

Shalin, D. N. (2008) Goffman's biography and the interaction order: A study in biocritical hermeneutics. Available online at www.unlv.edu/centers/cdclv/ega/bios.html (accessed July 15, 2010).

Sharrock, W. W. (1976) Review of *Frame Analysis*. *Sociology*, 10(2): 332–334.

Simmel, G. (1950) *The Sociology of Georg Simmel*. K. H. Wolff, ed. New York: The Free Press.

Smith, G. (1994) Snapshots *sub specie aeternitatis*: Simmel, Goffman and formal sociology. In D. Frisby (ed.) *Georg Simmel: Critical Assessments*, vol. III. London: Routledge, pp. 354–383.

Smith, G. (ed.) (1999) *Goffman and Social Organization: Studies in a Sociological Legacy*. London: Routledge.

Smith, G. (2003) Chrysalid Goffman: A note on *Some Characteristics of Response to Depicted Experience*. *Symbolic Interaction*, 26(4): 645–658.

Smith, G. (2005) Enacted others: Specifying Goffman's phenomenological omissions and sociological accomplishments. *Human Studies*, 28(4): 397–415.

Smith, G. (2006) *Erving Goffman*. London: Routledge.

Smith, G. (2010) Reconsidering *Gender Advertisements*: Performativity, framing and display. In M. H. Jacobsen (ed.) *The Contemporary Goffman*. London: Routledge, pp. 165–184.

Smith, G. and Jacobsen, M. H. (2010) Goffman's textuality: Literary sensibilities and sociological rhetorics. In M. H. Jacobsen (ed.) *The Contemporary Goffman*. London: Routledge, pp. 119–146.

Social Research Incorporated (1953) The service station dealer: The man and his work. Mimeographed report prepared for the American Petroleum Institute. Chicago, IL: Social Research Inc.

Strong, P. M. (1983) On the importance of being Erving: Erving Goffman, 1922–1982. *Sociology of Health and Illness*, 5: 345–355.

Ting-Toomey, S. (ed.) (1994) *The Challenge of Facework: Cross-Cultural and Interpersonal Issues*. Albany: State University of New York Press.

Travers, A. (1999) Non-person and Goffman: Sociology under the influence of literature. In G. Smith (ed.) *Goffman and Social Organization: Studies in a Sociological Legacy*. London: Routledge, pp. 156–176.

Treviño, J. (ed.) (2003) *Goffman's Legacy*. New York: Rowman and Littlefield.

Verhoeven, J. C. (1993) An interview with Erving Goffman, 1980. *Research on Language and Social Interaction*, 26(3): 317–348.

Warner, W. L. and Henry, W. E. (1948) The radio daytime serial: A symbolic analysis, *Genetic Psychology Monographs*, 37: 3–71.

Waksler, F. C. (1989) Erving Goffman's sociology: An introductory essay. *Human Studies*, 12: 1–18.

Weber, M. (1972) Georg Simmel as sociologist. *Social Research*, 39: 155–163.

West, C. (1996) Goffman in feminist perspective. *Sociological Perspectives*, 39: 353–369.

Weinstein, R. M. (1994) Goffman's *Asylums* and the total institution model of mental hospitals. *Psychiatry*, 57(4): 348–367.

Williams, R. (1983) Sociological tropes: A tribute to Erving Goffman. *Theory, Culture and Society*, 2: 99–102.

Williams, R. (1988) Understanding Goffman's methods. In P. Drew and A. Wootton (eds) *Erving Goffman: Exploring the Interaction Order*. Cambridge: Polity, pp. 64–88.

Winkin, Y. (1988) Erving Goffman: Portrait du sociologue en jeune homme. In Y. Winkin (ed.) (1988) *Erving Goffman : Les Moments et Leurs Hommes*. Paris: Seuil/Minuit, pp. 11–92.

Winkin, Y. (1999) Erving Goffman: What is a Life? The uneasy making of an intellectual biography. In G. Smith (ed.) *Goffman and Social Organization: Studies in a Sociological Legacy*. London: Routledge, pp. 19–41.

Winkin, Y. (2000) Baltasound as the symbolic capital of social interaction. In G. A. Fine and G. Smith (eds) *Erving Goffman*, vol. 1. London: Sage, pp. 193–212.

Winkin, Y. (2010) Goffman's greenings. In M. H. Jacobsen (ed.) *The Contemporary Goffman*. Routledge, New York, pp. 51–63.

6

Zygmunt Bauman

PETER BEILHARZ

THE PERSON

Over the past twenty years Zygmunt Bauman has become one of the most influential sociologists in the world. Partly this is because, from a solid earlier research base, he chose to go public, to write for an imaginary audience that commutes through the everyday life of our cities, rather than hiding in its libraries. Partly it is because of his capacity to identify central problems of concern and anxiety, and to mediate them with some of the central wisdoms of classical and modern sociology. The result might be called a postmodern sociology, though that was a category he resisted, preferring the idea of a sociology of the present, a sociology of the postmodern. This is what, more recently, might be called a sociology of liquid modernity. It moves, it slips and slides, it surprises us daily – and so do we.

Bauman is a solitary actor, founding no center, no journal, no school. Though he is open to all, he is a private person; his most intimate companion over sixty-one years was Janina Bauman, whose work had a significant effect on his. He does not seek influence, he is not a TV celebrity, he eschews opportunities to court or to influence power, not least because it bites you, or threatens to swallow you up. Bauman is a private person, and we do not know a great deal about his life. The model for his work is conversational, and his conversation shifts rapidly across whatever associations appear. Ask him a question and chances are he will answer with a question back. For this is how he sees our vocation. Our job is to ask questions, more importantly than to offer answers. Intellectuals are important, in this way of thinking, but no more important than anyone else. And if social problems have putatively practical solutions, best we work on these together rather than expect the eggheads or scientists to come up with the perfect solution. Humanity muddles through, and sometimes the mess of its achievements is stacked high, and counted in lives, in bodies, hearts, and souls.

The Wiley-Blackwell Companion to Major Social Theorists, First Edition.
Edited by George Ritzer and Jeffrey Stepnisky.
© 2011 Blackwell Publishing Ltd. Published 2011 by Blackwell Publishing Ltd.

When pressed, Bauman sometimes says that he is (we should be) interested in birds, not in ornithologists. We should be concerned with the problems of the world, not with the attributes or frailties of its interpreters. We do, nevertheless, know something of this ornithologist.

The Context

Bauman was born in Poznan in 1925. His family fled into the Soviet Union with the invasion of Poland by the Nazis in 1939. Bauman studied in the Soviet Union, but joined the Polish Army in the Soviet Union in order to fight the Nazis and defend his homeland. Elevated to the rank of major, he was sacked in the anti-Semitic purge of 1953, and instead became a sociologist, working in the continental tradition with thinkers like Stanisław Ossowski and Julian Hochfeld, for whom there was a significant connection between sociology, philosophy, and social criticism.

This story fits the pattern of a kind of East European Critical Theory, sometimes called a dissident or Renaissance Marxism, which came out of Hungary, Czechoslovakia, Yugoslavia, and Poland into the 1960s. It has strong sympathies with the humanist Marxist sympathies of those times. From the 1950s Bauman identifies strongly not only with socialism and Marx, but also with sociology. He has disdain for mainstream American sociology which he calls "Durksonian" (i.e. Durkheim plus Parsons) but he loves Simmel, "who started it all."

Along with others like Leszek Kołakowski, Bauman was sacked again in the 1968 anti-Semitic purge, now charged with the most noble crime of all – "corrupting the youth." He and his family were "allowed to leave" on a one-way exit visa, via Tel Aviv and Canberra, to Leeds, which became his other home. Earlier, he had studied in Manchester and at the London School of Economics. England he knew was a place that tolerated foreigners, even if it did not embrace them; and in this he followed in Marx's footsteps and shared Marx's connection to the home of industrialism and the strange combination of class struggle and communitarianism which it called out.

His is a sociology which solidarizes with C. Wright Mills's vocation, the sociological imagination, and it is no accident that Mills was a visitor to Poland in the 1950s, a connection Bauman later followed up with mutual friend Ralph Miliband, who also came to Leeds. Bauman at no stage of his career hesitates to call himself a sociologist; only he also knows that sociologists, and intellectuals in general, are all too human, too tribal, too particularistic, too defensive, too much prone to repetition and self-reproduction, and too open to the charms of influence and power where they imagine they can set the world to rights.

Bauman's work is both reactive and programmatic. Across the path of his life, there are sixteen books in Polish and more than thirty in English. His production schedule increases with age, especially after his retirement from Leeds, and it accelerates together with his embrace of the popular format "little books" which have become a staple for him in recent years. These are books you might find in the high street bookshop, and read on the bus or train. What this reflects is a highly variegated body of work, less a clear project or trajectory than might be discerned in the work of a more single-minded thinker. His work is reactive, but also innovative, and its diversity makes it difficult to categorize (a fact that he would delight in). Consider some of his topics: sex, death, love, consumption, production, labor, socialism, culture, modernity, ambivalence, hermeneutics, fragmentation, classes and elites, structuralism, the postmodern, freedom and dependence, the Holocaust, Poland and other Soviet-type societies, Stalin, ethics, globalization, community, Europe, identity, flux, uncertainty, and so on. Some larger, world historic themes coordinate this life and work. Bauman was compelled to experience and to deal intellectually with fascism and communism. He then had to make sense of capitalism in its British heartland, in the wake of Marx, and with its transformation into a culture of consumption. Bauman's work is special because it connects the small detail of daily life to these world historic themes and shifts which made us, and the last century, the age of extremes, and what follows.

How to put order into this chaos which so dutifully reflects the mess of the world which we inhabit? Bauman's work can be organized around many themes or optics. The four used here are socialism and culture; the postmodern turn; modernity and the Holocaust; and the most recent, liquid turn.

Bauman's English language work can be said to have two pivotal intellectual shifts or moments: one in 1987, when he takes on the postmodern; the second in 1989, when he takes on the Holocaust. These involve a significant shift of emphasis away from the ideas of capitalism and socialism, towards modernity. Accompanying these shifts, belatedly, there is the shift of addressee, from the well-documented academic monograph to the popular work, the "little books" of the recent period. With the decline or closure of politics in the public sphere, Bauman turns his own energy towards expanding the sphere of public criticism upon which the prospect of a democratic politics depends.

THE WORK

Socialism and culture

In the beginning, for Bauman, there was socialism, its British narrative, told by Marx, and its Polish hopes. Socialism, in this story, was many things. It was the manifestation of the real struggles of ordinary men and women, engaged both in hope and in fear, looking forward to the prospect of better worlds and longing for memories, nostalgic or real, of the lost worlds of lives calmer and steadier before the factory system arrived.

These issues are opened in what might be Bauman's most conventionally scholarly work in sociology, his first book in English, *Between Class and Elite* (1972). Like the later text *Thinking Sociologically* (1990) this book connects vitally to earlier Polish-language anticipations. Here it is labour, and the British labour movement which is to be the bearer of socialism. But in bearing socialism, it carries it, belatedly, into the state after the Second World War, with the result that labour and the Labour Party become completely institutionalized, transformed into creatures of the state and in this sense the best lieutenants of capital. In the beginning, of course, there was more. The labour movement was the exemplary social movement. And its nineteenth-century intellectuals were also exemplary of problems to come later, into the twentieth century.

Messianic intellectuals could not help but project their own dreams onto others, typically more modest folk who dreamed of more bread and a safe roof later than the utopias hatched for them by others.

Labour, then, has a culture, or cultures, both those of aspirations modest or immodest, and those of activity, of the *habitus* and experience of everyday life and its accumulated traditions. Labour had its own intelligence and *raison d'être*, as well as carrying its own dreams and those of others. Labour would always be looking back, as well as forward. Labour also had its own elite, and its medieval memories of guild and artisanal life. The mass worker and the image of mass society changed all this.

As it becomes legitimized and trade unions and labour parties become hesitantly accepted, the labour movement also becomes a career escalator. It generates new elites. These elites, in turn, have their own cultures.

Socialism, in all this, would remain beyond definition. Bauman quotes Hubert Bland: "It seems that we are to work for socialism, fight for socialism, even die for it, but not, for God's sake, to define it!" Or at least this was the story once the Labour Party became a significant institutional actor. Bauman, for his part, had a clearer sense of what socialism was; and it was less a state of affairs actual or to be realized (as in Poland) than a utopia. This sense resulted in one of his most powerful early works, *Socialism: The Active Utopia* (1976). Here Bauman argued three of his most powerful pertinent claims: first, that we are all utopians, like it or not; second, that the definition of socialism as utopia indicates that it is not a state of affairs but a horizon never to be reached; and third, that socialism becomes the counter current or counter movement of modernity.

Utopia, indeed, could be the singular image under which almost all of Bauman's work could be organized. For it contains our hopes and dreams, as moderns or post-moderns, and our fears and disillusion. It changes, for us as moderns, for we believe ourselves to be capable of realizing it, socially, for others, publically, or privately, at home, in our private lives. For utopia becomes dystopia, after the Russian Revolution and Nazism; and then what is left of utopia becomes privatized, channeled into the pursuit of love or intimacy or the consumer paradise.

Utopia matters for Bauman because it is ubiquitous; everyone has a utopia, larger or smaller, more or less systematic or implicit. The utopian impulse is real; it makes us want more; it makes us want to do better, it refuses to accept (for socialists) that the poor must always be among us. Utopias relativize the present; they serve to remind us of our own historicity and contingency. Utopias are driven by hope, they are future-oriented but they also connect to the present. Yesterday's dreams (full employment, healthcare insurance, whatever) sometimes come true, across the path of the twentieth century. Utopias pluralize, or open possibilities regarding social alternatives, for there are always alternatives, even when we cannot see them. Utopias actually work, not globally but incrementally; little bits of them finally come to pass.

Yet the cold stream of socialism, that which leads to Bolshevism, becomes fundamentally implicated in the practice of social engineering. The proletariat (or whoever) needs to be led by those who know, and these wise men have a habit of sticking around after the revolution. This practical utopianism, where utopia is a design to be actually realized, is necessarily connected to order building. Engineering and technology become the solutions to all problems, in this way of thinking. Technocracy threatens to rule. The pursuit of certainty threatens to kill us all, or at least to imprison us with cages of iron and steel, bound together by piles of paperwork that lead to the heavens. Yet in its critical sense, associated with the warm stream of socialism, the utopia of socialism is as Romanticism is to the Enlightenment; its partner and necessary corrective. In one sense socialism is bound to be and to remain a utopia; for as Weber is rumored to have said to Lukács, this experiment (the Russian Revolution) will set the cause of socialism back one hundred years. Read negatively, perhaps socialism will never recover from the experience of communism; read positively perhaps it is rather the case that socialism remains, simply, as one of the warring gods, always ahead of us of, inspiring in its very impossibility.

The argument of *Socialism: The Active Utopia* points in many directions, one towards the problem of sociology of intellectuals, those who claim to represent others and may well later represent a class or elite project of their own. That is not a new idea nor is it by any means only an idea with a right wing lineage. Libertarians have always been suspicious of intellectuals and perhaps especially of the state and not only of capital; and there is clearly a libertarian impulse in Bauman's thinking, one that aligns his sympathies with those of Luxemburg rather than Lenin. For Bauman also insists on connecting the problems of socialism and intellectuals to culture, and by no means wants to limit culture to its high cultural or aesthetic dimension.

Why is culture so important for Bauman? Because it is to us humans what water is to fish. Everything that we do, including economic life, is mediated by culture; the idea that they can be separated is an example of the kind of analytical logic which Bauman views as so pernicious. Alongside these other early works of Bauman, another foundation work is *Culture as Praxis* (1973). Bauman begins from the recognition that culture is a hierarchical practice; it is based on discrimination, on claims regarding "real" or high and other, or popular culture. Some have it, and others do not; even its semantics make it clear that culture needs cultivation, as in agri-culture. But there is also a second, widely shared use of the idea of culture, which presumes in a less hierarchical manner that all peoples and all loci or situations have cultures. The labour movement, for example, has not only a culture but many cultures, or at least it used to. Culture indicates ways of being, which Bauman wants to address less as structures, in the manner of the then widely influential school of structuralism, than of practices, as in processes. Intuitively this aligns his thinking with that of Antonio Gramsci, and later Pierre Bourdieu. Structure, here, is less an outcome than an aspiration. Cultures seek to make chaos into order. Sometimes its ordering project can be lethal; for Nazis, and communists also had cultures, indeed the German and Soviet experiences depended entirely on their cultural ambitions. For it is not enough to carry the people with you passively; they have to believe in Big Brother.

Cultures also generate insiders and outsiders; they are exclusive as well as inclusive. Bauman turns in this early work to the figure of the stranger, or the outsider. So here he already anticipates later work like *Modernity and the Holocaust*, where the figure of the stranger is the Jew, and his work on the postmodern, where the outsider is the flawed consumer. But Bauman also wants to insist that there is a culture of critique, and this line of argument is developed further in *Towards a Critical Sociology* (1976). For sociology too readily becomes comfortable, aligned with the status quo and the insiders, even at the same time as sociology burns the fingers of those who claim too easily to represent the people, the poor or the outsiders.

A central category in *Towards a Critical Sociology* is the idea of second nature. Second nature, indeed, is a kind of synonym for culture, for the idea that we learn very easily to naturalize the worlds into which we are born, to universalize our own cultures, ways of thinking, being, doing, living, hoping. The tragedy of culture is that it ossifies; our greatest triumphs entrap us. And here another theme is posited which returns later: the problem of conformism, of playing along, of following the rules even when we are not subject to instruction or the threat of sanction. But more, playing along might be just that, understanding full well that obedience does not imply inner acceptance or conversion. Sociology, on this way of thinking, should be aligned with the dream of freedom, even as freedom itself should be aligned with the counter factual of dependence rather than imagined independently.

Arriving at the postmodern

For Bauman's generation of East European Marxists, the most powerful conceptual dyad was capitalism/socialism. But if capitalism and socialism were conceived as cultures, even if (as in Castoriadis) actually existing socialism was viewed as a variation of capitalism, all these phenomena were nevertheless understood as cultural in their constitution. This was not a matter of comparing or contrasting two different economies or economic models. What was interesting and disturbing about these phenomena was their cultures, their ways of life and being, the personality types that they made available, encouraged, or prohibited.

It was only later, however, that this discourse became known as a discourse about modernity. The temptation for Marxists was to identify capitalism and modernity. These days, however, it is common for people to talk about modernity whether in the seminar room or in the daily news (e.g. does modernity have a future when it comes to ecology or sustainability). In retrospect, when it comes to critical or academic discourse, it seems reasonably clear that one of the reasons we speak more or less comfortably about modernity today is because twenty years ago there was a massive fuss about the idea of the postmodern. The controversy over the postmodern was multifaceted and multiform. It elided or combined at least two different concerns or anxieties. One concerned the idea that modernism as an aesthetic category was over; that abstract international style was no longer hegemonic, that pastiche now ruled whether in art or music or whatever else. The other concern involved the possibility that modernity as a social form was over; that we (whoever this we was) no longer wanted to live in the modular, American post-war model of growth, suburbia, cars, malls, and marriage. The meeting point, or vital seam which connected modernism and modernity, or postmodernism and postmodernity, was arguably most evident in the theory and practice of architecture. For here aesthetics and technology or economy combined. It was not just modernist aesthetics that rankled, here it was the chicken-coop idea of mass standardized housing and mass standardized human subjects, men, women, and children.

All this seems reasonably apparent in retrospect. It was less obvious what was at risk at the time, for many reasons. Postmodern enthusiasm appealed to many, back then, as it carried on the earlier modernist love of the new. Away with the post-war world! Away with cardboard people and one-dimensional lives! If Bauman was right, that culture ossified, then it would be reasonable to expect that the post-war world, which itself looked like utopia to those who had suffered wars and depression, would soon enough itself look like a concrete cage. Nothing stands still, not least culture and its horizons of expectations.

Several of these issues, then, called out to Zygmunt Bauman. And he was to share, however momentarily, in this enthusiasm for the sense that the postmodern might offer us a new hope out from under the incubus of modernism, that new creative forces might be released that would remind us that other ways of living were possible. Perhaps, as he later put it, the postmodern would offer us nothing more than modernity without illusions, or at least without the most disabling illusions of the twentieth century, fascism, communism, and the "there is no alternative" (TINA) philosophy of economic liberalism. When Bauman responded to the idea of the postmodern, however, the particular theme to which he chose to connect was that of intellectuals and the sociology of intellectuals. The point of identification was powerful. The postmodern critique of modernity itself often took the form of the critique of Enlightenment. The Enlightenment was a project, a set of ideas and so on; but it was also necessarily identified with its carriers: the intellectuals, the saviors, the savants, Those Who Knew, the scientists, eventually the social scientists – us. This of course meant that we were invisible, the Elephant in the Room of Modernity. For social scientists learned very quickly how to represent those who could not readily represent themselves. Social science became a kind of social ventriloquism.

The key work in Bauman's project here was *Legislators and Interpreters* (1987). The postmodern only appeared as a subtitle, and so provisionally that it remained hyphenated: *On Modernity, Post-Modernity and Intellectuals*. Still, at this earlier moment of postmodern debate optimistic as to its productive potential, Bauman's interest was to contrast the intellectual styles or personality types of moderns and postmoderns. Modern and postmodern were less historic phases of development or actual social states of affairs; rather they represented intellectual cultures and choices. Modern and postmodern represented different cultures, or worldviews, modern instrumental, rational and calculative, postmodern pragmatic, skeptical, suspicious. Modern was built on the pursuit of the idea of the rational mastery of the world; postmodern, on the sense of the impossibility and dangers of this stratagem. Modern played into the strategy of social engineering. Postmodern was gentler than this, more contemplative, but also more open to the risk of complacency.

Thus the two strong types of his title. Moderns fancy themselves as legislators, those who know how to put the world to rights, and view the negative consequences of social engineering merely as the next set of challenges. Interpreters want to move more slowly and cautiously, to act as mediators or messengers rather than as the Heroes of Modern Times. Interpreters are given less to absolutes and universalism. Yet as Bauman is wont to insist, these are not clear cut or simple distinctions. All of us appeal to universals at some point, as in claims regarding universal rights. And interpreters retain a significant kind of power.

Viewed from the perspective of *Modernity and the Holocaust* and its critique of fascism as social engineering, *Legislators and Interpreters* begins to look like a critique of Bolshevism, or of Marxism in power. Its critical message is also self-critical. For it is addressed to the engineering ambitions of the likes of Lenin, who believed in *What is to be Done?* that ten wise men (=us) were worth a hundred fools. Read further back, Bauman's work viewed as a critique of *les philosophes* is actually a critique of Jacobinism. Conceptually, the argument connects to that in *Culture as Praxis*, for Bauman's critical metaphor of choice is not, as in Foucault, the pastoral, but the idea of modernity as a gardening culture. Moderns, on this account, do not know to leave well alone. They cannot give countenance to gamekeeping, which is Bauman's own preferred ethic. Humanism too easily becomes twentieth-century paranoia evidenced in the anxious imperative that nothing can be left alone. The object of Bauman's critique is the Faustian impulse of modernity, to build and rebuild the world, to destroy and build it again, to fuse and weld creation and destruction as the central dynamic of modern times. Modern culture, for Bauman, may not always self-destroy, but it cannot leave behind the imaginary horizon within which all that is solid deserves constantly to be melted by us, as actors who cannot help ourselves. We are bound, after Marx, to be sorcerers' apprentices. We can no longer fool ourselves that we control this process, humanly created or unleashed, which now seems only and completely to control us.

Modernity and the Holocaust

Modernity turns back on itself; moderns turn into barbarians. This was also the theme of Max Horkheimer and Theodor Adorno, in *Dialectic of Enlightenment*. And it, in turn, becomes the leitmotif for Bauman's most widely influential work, *Modernity and the Holocaust* (1989). But for Bauman, the point was not that the loftiest of Europeans – the Germans – had turned into barbarians. It was more general. Any one of us could do this; any one of us could, or would, comply, serve, follow orders, stack up the corpses, pull the trigger, sign the forms authorizing extermination. In itself this was shocking enough. For Bauman refused, in this, to follow the conventional morality which divides humanity into good souls and evil monsters. The point was not that there were no such monsters, but that modernity (which here meant the twentieth century's greatest achievement) made such behavior so much more possible. The development of the means of destruction developed apace with the development of the means of production. It became easier for modern humans to kill or to maim because they did not have to look into the face of other, simply flick a switch.

Bauman's intellectual formation was influenced by those continental sociologists, like Hochfeld and Ossowski, for whom there was no firm distinction between sociology and philosophy, or between social sciences, liberal arts, and humanities. Across the path of his life he was deeply influenced by thinkers like Marx, Simmel, and Gramsci. The path of his work is littered with references to those thinkers whose ideas spark for him, which associate or condense or enable him to mediate past classics and present predicaments. Alongside these many influences, one most profound on the thinking of Zygmunt Bauman was that of his wife and companion, Janina.

The Holocaust arrives as something of a surprise in his work. It is also something of a surprise for sociology, which hitherto left its study to disciplines like politics or history. The Holocaust serves as a modern light bulb or tragic Eureka for Bauman; and this is one source of the controversy and originally negative response to his work, which could easily be seen as disrespectful to its victims, given to using the Holocaust as a symptom rather than as the great modern tragedy itself.

Bauman tells us that his book, *Modernity and the Holocaust*, was prompted by Janina's *Winter in the Morning* (1986). Janina's book contains the memoirs of her childhood in the Warsaw Ghetto, and her subsequent escape and survival. It is a remarkable book, written entirely without self-pity, looking into the abyss of Jewish daily life in Nazi Warsaw without succumbing to it innerly. As Zygmunt Bauman puts it, the power of the experience of her own distance, writing daily, monthly, yearly, and its result, combining presence and humanity with all these horrors, all this made him think that he had misplaced the Holocaust intellectually. He had viewed it as though it were a painting on the wall. Now, after Janina's self-interpretation, he viewed the Holocaust as a window on the wall. Its optic was that of modernity itself. The Holocaust told a story about all of us, not only a tragedy of Germans and Jews.

For Bauman, the Holocaust was a rational and rationalized project of state-sponsored, ideologically motivated mass murder delivered by the best available German technology. It was a kind of murderous Fordism, the logic of mass production in the manner of Detroit here applied to mass destruction factory style. This is not, however, a technological determinism at work in Bauman's thinking. Nazism is or was a culture, a murderous variation on the idea of creative destruction, where the creation of the Third Reich as a geopolitical project rested on the destruction of the Jews and others. Nazism was not only a politics or an ideology or a technology combining freeways with cinema propaganda and gas ovens; it was a population strategy whose purpose was to rebuild a greater Aryan land for the world, or at least for its Aryan citizens. For Bauman, then, the Holocaust involved a kind of modern chemistry where all the existing ingredients – bureaucracy, anti-Semitism, and technologies – were combined into a newly explosive result. This does not make modernity and the Holocaust identical, or even co-extensive. But it does give us the optic of the eye in the modern storm.

Nazism represented the apogee of the gardening state. It sought to eliminate the Jews, the "weeds," and to cultivate the superior stock. More, the Jews had to be destroyed because they represented disorder. This involved the most systematic destruction of the state-identified *Other* in living memory. The result was a particular kind of reactionary modernism. For modernity would, and would ever be imagined as exclusively modern. All modernities were mixed, combining traditionalistic throwbacks and inventions with technological advance. The Germany of the Black Forest was an invented tradition. Racism, as we know it, is a modern phenomenon. Racism is a modern weapon used often to seek out traditionalistic ends. Nazism exemplifies the social engineering project, now applied to genetic business itself.

Bauman wants us to look into the mirror of Auschwitz, to contemplate the possibility that we could have done this. This opens the possibility that his is a sociology of conformism, a critique of conformism. Perhaps this is underwritten by the critique of technology, for there is a residual sense in which any critique of Enlightenment rationality still draws on the legacy of Romanticism. As Bauman says, the problem with technology is that we have no way of saying no to it. We are too weak to say no individually to what is presented to us as the onward march of progress, and we have no collective or social means by which to discuss or to limit the growth of science and technology politically. Thus Bauman's analysis of modernity and the Holocaust shifts into discussion of the Milgram and Zimbardo experiments, not German, not Nazi, but American, Ivy League, democratic, liberal, and civilized. The point, again, is that all of us potentially will follow orders, will inflict pain on instruction, just as the university students in those experiments did. Obedience becomes the substitute for conscience. The image of the rational, self-legislating personality so central, say, to Kant's view in "What is Enlightenment?" is lost, absent. Moderns find it very difficult to escape from the horizons of heteronomy. Society, as Bauman puts it, becomes a factory for morality. And let there be no mistake, Nazi culture, too, had its morality, its own strong and clear conceptions of wrong and right, who were the real citizens and who were the parasites, who was visible and who was invisible, who had the right to the space to live and who had to go.

Bauman's "German" book thus ends up in the United States, or stretching across the globe itself. The German question is pursued, meantime, in one of Bauman's most conceptually powerful books, *Modernity and Ambivalence*. Here Bauman shifts from the critique of modern action to the critique of modern thinking, or classificatory logic. Bauman seeks to value ambivalence, or at least to respect it. For it makes us human, this kind of uncertainty that makes us feel radical on Thursday, conservative on Friday; and its serves to remind us that our judgments are perspectival, or institutional. We need, then, to classify, to separate, or discriminate, but we also seem to need too readily to fix these sensibilities, so that A is not B when it may be both. Once classified, too much fixity or certainty ensues. We set out to distinguish, but end up essentializing. One can only be German or Jewish, bourgeois or proletarian, friend or foe, insider or outsider. Yet we all know what it means to cross over, even as we kid ourselves that we know the world because we have it classified and categorized.

The theme points back to Horkheimer and Adorno, to *Dialectic of Enlightenment*, to the critique of that European civilization which strides (and stumbles) forward, turning the dream of progress into the mixed modernity of barbarism. And it also points back to Germany, and to the other Jews, the non-German Jews or *Ostjüden*. The East European Jews were even more liminal than the Jews of Germany, for they were cast as failed German Jews. After the worst of modernity's excess in the Holocaust, what is left is the thin gruel of assimilation, or inclusion on borrowed time, at the grace of the host culture and at their discretion. Assimilation is better than exclusion, but it always remains provisional, and it threatens the strangers with being accepted only at the cost of being denied, or swallowed up.

As Bauman puts it later, modernity seems to combine or to alternate between two differing strategies which Claude Lévi-Strauss claims characterize some other, earlier tribes. These are called *anthropoemia* and *anthropophagia*. The first involves assimilation in the literal sense, to include the other by swallowing him or her up, digesting them. The second indicates expulsion, vomiting out, rejecting the other in a visceral way. Bauman suggests that modern states constitute their populations through a combination of these strategies.

Turning liquid?

Bauman retired from Leeds in 1990. His last seriously academic monograph, duly referenced and thoroughly argued, was *Modernity and Ambivalence*. His next step was to turn, or to return, to the essay form, though Bauman has always been an essayist even when writing at length. He follows Montaigne: the essay is an attempt at understanding, never final, and it invites response, further questioning and discussion. So the interval between the larger books and the little books is filled with collections of essays, including *Life in Fragments* (1995), *Postmodernity and its Discontents* (1997) and *Postmodern Ethics* (1993).

Then come the little books, themselves signaling a postmodern or liquid turn in terms of style, culture, or audience. If this is a publishing choice then it was a choice Bauman made consciously at the time, and not only a trend or pattern that is evident only in retrospect. The idea of a liquid turn, in contrast, only seems to make sense after the fact, when there is now a series of titles constituted with reference to this new icon: *Liquid Love* (2003), *Liquid Life* (2005), *Liquid Times: Living in an Age of Uncertainty* (2006). Whence this sense of liquidity? In some ways, the idea of liquid modernity represents a semantic or symbolic solution to the problem of the postmodern. In its earlier configurations, into the 1980s, the postmodern seemed to hold some prospect of emancipation from the stodgier constraints of modernism. Twenty years later the postmodern had well passed its "use-by." The controversy over the postmodern was exhausted, and a more nuanced sense of valuing modernity both positively and negatively was one result. Increasingly the postmodern was viewed as another modernist or *avant-garde* moment in the reaction against institutionalized or actually existing modernism.

At the same time, it remained the case that there was something going on, something changing in the West at an alarming rate. In the 1980s, the word often used to try to capture this sense of accelerating change was the postmodern. Then another, bigger word came along to claim the job: globalization. Bauman also wrote a book about globalization. But his new position was marked by the idea of liquidity.

The intellectual reference, characteristically, was to Marx, to the famous winged phrase mistranslated in the English version of *The Communist Manifesto* as "all that is solid melts into air."

Bauman's reference was contemporary rather than poetic or lyrical. He was not referring to the apparent solidity of the capitalism of the 1840s or the traditional regime of the same time. The solid capitalism or modernity Bauman referred to was of his own time: it stood for the long post-war boom and the period of affluence, consumerism and the welfare state, full employment, nuclear family, Fordism, the American Dream and its British and other European sub-versions, antipodean, Latin American, and so on. This new post-war world achieved a kind of apparent solidity which made the postmodern turn itself look revolutionary, as the new uncertainty and anxiety of neoliberalism and globalization took its place. Liquid modernity meant that the set repertoire of the post-war boom was gone: fixed, relatively clear gender roles, full male employment, a fixed working week and weekend for leisure, cold war clarities setting political parties well apart over a Keynesian consensus underneath, jobs for life – all gone. Liquidity replaced it with the manifold meanings of the German word *Unsicherheit* – uncertainty, unsafety, insecurity, a kind of existential loneliness in the face of endless change and the end of loyalty, whether personal, intimate, or institutional. Everybody and everything was now replaceable. An intimate relationship could be cast aside like a dead biro; for to embrace the liquid modern restlessness it was necessary always to be ready to move on, embrace change, and endlessly reshape the self, externally, physically, and physiognomically, and internally, viewing the subject or self as the material of endless transformation. The spirit of Faust had truly come home to haunt us.

Before the "liquid turn" there is a political turn. This is signaled already in *In Search of Politics* (1999). Glossy globalization, the good news for the well heeled and cashed up, works brilliantly for those Bauman calls tourists, but to the detriment of the landlocked outsiders he calls vagabonds. Globalization is an attack on the nation state; by this virtue it is an attack on social democracy and the welfare state, for their practical parameters for reform have typically been national. Capitalism becomes even more globally footloose, while workers, peasants and vagabonds, especially the illiterate, unskilled, or non-English speakers are stuck. In this context, the singular presenting problem atop this global woe is the absence of political spheres, institutions, and mentalities that might begin to provide spheres in which we could address these problems. This is not only a problem at the global level, where we lack globally effective institutions or arrangements. Now it is also the case that local or state-based organizations have been politically emptied out. Not only is there no alternative, there is no one responsible. Nation states take advantage of globalization by washing their hands of local responsibilities; everything now can be blamed on the whims or machinations of the world system. As a Brazilian acquaintance put it, "the economy took my job away. Globalization took my job." Poetically profound, this is nevertheless exactly the view that globalization encourages.

Locally, or nationally, the problem is that there is no properly political sphere anymore. If we discuss the good life at all it is likely in our backyards, and in terms of the fleeting pleasures of hedonism. There are no open institutions in which we discuss how we should live. Actually existing institutional politics, in any case, has become the playground of media and celebrity. Perhaps the problem ultimately lies outside the political. For the underlying problem is the way we live, the culture we inhabit. This is a culture of speed, repetition, and gratification undergirded by a solid layer of anxiety that at any stage we might fall off, and end up with the vagabonds. Ours is a culture of restlessness, where the most dangerous and therefore impossible thing would be exactly to ask, how should we live? The prospect of a serious politics would depend on some sufficient space for contemplation, conversation, and debate. What we encounter instead is the televisualized circus of electoral politics, where the only significant issue is how many degrees of neoliberalism or regulation we are prepared to tolerate.

Contemplation of these issues took Bauman back to the realms he had visited earlier in *Between Class and Elite* and in *Memories of Class*. The result was a book called *Work, Consumerism and the New Poor* (1998). The poor, historically, are always with us; only now they become essential. Where they used to be surplus population, the queue outside in the cold looking in, they now have a function, in order for the rest of us to keep our noses to the grindstone. Now the poor are a scarecrow; their fate drives us on, and away from them, but they can never hope fully to be absolved or assimilated into society. To be a scarecrow, today, is to be what Bauman calls a "flawed consumer," a latent rather than actual consumer; for while we are still judged by our status in work, our capacity to consume becomes vitally significant too. The Protestant Ethic is alive and well, at least in postmodern form; but this is a Brave New World we are entering, where uncertainty rules and loyalty is a liability. Bauman is backing into the idea of liquid modernity, itself to be formally announced in the book of that title two years later. At this point, he still refers to the present as "modernity mark two," consumers' modernity.

Producers' modernity, modernity mark one, might on this account look back to the nineteenth century, when the "people" look like the "proletariat." The stronger contrast, later made by Bauman into "solid modernity," is with the post-war regime of the long boom, growth, security, and the Keynesian welfare state. Now the shopping mall replaces the factory as the symbolic center of everyday life. Under the influence of Claus Offe, Bauman now revisits the claim that the highpoint of the Keynesian welfare state offered a missed opportunity, one which still exists: the in-principle possibility of uncoupling work and income. But all that is scrambled by the arrival, in Britain, of Thatcherism, which begins to liquefy the solid achievements of the post-war bipartisan consensus.

Thatcher famously announced that there was no such thing as society, only individuals and their families. Her regime did not introduce but reinforced and legitimated the contemporary trend towards individualization. And so Bauman's next book takes on *The Individualized Society* (2001). If *Work, Consumerism and the New Poor* connects to Offe, this book connects later to Ulrich Beck and, behind him, to the figure of C. Wright Mills, who observed much earlier that one of the standard pathologies of modern times was the imperative that we should somehow seek personal solutions to what are actually social problems. Only things now are more extreme; as the Paris graffiti was to put it, "1968: Changing the World; 1989: Renovating the Kitchen."

The pendant to *The Individualized Society*, and to this political turn, is the collection of essays called *Society Under Siege* (2002). As politics has been sublimated into media, entertainment, or management by the suits, Bauman's interest now turns into culture, Big Brother, liquid modern pizza, and TV in lieu of the earlier bread and circuses. Prurience replaces politics. Privatization replaces the idea of the public. We are consumed by our own consumption, like the snake eating its own tail.

Newism or nowism

Now comes the liquid turn. It is formally announced in *Liquid Modernity* (2000). Liquids morph and move. This is Bauman's starting point – the metaphor of liquidity and its capacity to suggest contingency, transformation, chaos, movement, uncertainty. Fluids travel easily; they flow, spill, run out, pour over, leak, flood, spray, drip, seep, ooze; they are indeterminate, unlike solids, and unpredictable. These Bauman tells us, are reasons why notions like "fluidity" or "liquidity" speak to our times, or to our sense of these times. At the same time, the idea of liquidity suggests lightness of being. Liquid modernity not only corrodes solidity, it attacks time.

What has changed since Marx is that this new fluid world anticipated in *The Communist Manifesto* of 1848 itself solidified into the twentieth century and especially after the Second World War. The spirit of modernism melts, and then hardens into those new institutions of Fordism and the welfare state that we then take for granted, at least for a few decades. Modernity promised the prospect of a new solidity, of a kind even firmer than that offered by feudalism earlier. But it then began to disintegrate itself, at least in these post-war forms. The economy came to free itself even more than before from traditions, cultural, and political forms. More, power itself has become extraterritorial; we no longer know where it is, so that even if "we" had the revolutionary will, we would not know where to find power in order to overthrow it, and we certainly would be in the dark as to what to do after that.

Solid modernity gave us the Fordist factory, bureaucracy, the Panopticon, Big Brother, and the concentration camp. Its class text was *1984*. It coincided with the logic of the Gardening State and it gave us the Iron Cage. But the process of creative destruction did not stop with that dystopia; and nothing, finally, stands still. Today, our lives are characterized by endless frenzy, and by heightened individualism. No one, and nothing, can be allowed to stand still. We end up shopping for life, to the point that we are no longer able to tell the difference. We cannot escape from newism, or nowism.

From *Liquid Modernity* there follows *Liquid Love* (2003). Its subject matter is the frailty of human bonds. All that is solid melts into air, not least when it comes to human relationships. This occurs not only in the workplace or in the public sphere, but also in the private and in the intimate sphere. We disperse of our relationships with the same ease as we throw out our old shoes. Connections become "virtual relations." We keep running, not least from commitment or from working at relationships that falter.

Love concerns care for the other, and this is a big ask in the age of super individualism. Love is brittle, until-further-notice, "top pocket," so you take it out only when you need it, not as the other needs you. And children? They become objects of emotional consumption. We no longer know how to do intimacy, except when it comes to sexual contact and the exchange or exercising of bodily fluids. The only love left to us, in the common culture of our times, is literally liquid love.

And what happens locally also happens globally. Trust evaporates; cities become more divided and hostile; xenophobia multiplies. Modernity produces waste, and as Bauman proclaims in *Wasted Lives* (2004). Here the liquidity image is pushed to another logical extreme: the outcasts of modernity are as its excreta. Modernity expels its outcasts. Our planet is now imagined as full. Surplus populations represent waste, the redundant, the excess. The worries of Generation X, according to Bauman, are redundancy worries, anxieties about being classified as surplus to requirement, and missing out. There are too many people, too much waste, too much civilization, too much information, too many wasted lives. Refugees and prisoners become the most pathetic examples of this stigma.

Liquid Fear (2006) takes further Bauman's interest in uncertainty. The power of the imagery of liquidity peaks after the experience of Hurricane Katrina in New Orleans. Here, modernity literally (again) liquefies: it disappears, disintegrates, the city in effect disappears. The last piece in this string is entitled *Liquid Times – Living in an Age of Uncertainty* (2006). On Bauman's thinking, we (no longer?) cope because we now have abandoned the idea of dealing with consequences, or of planning. National governments license the abandon which they easily claim globalization has forced upon them. Cities become dumping grounds for globally conceived and gestated problems. Urban politics become hopelessly overloaded.

These themes intersect with many others in Bauman's "little books." Several of the volumes are actually formatted as little books. These include *Globalization: The Human Consequences* (1998); *Community – Seeking Safety in an Insecure World* (2001); *Identity* (2004); and *Europe – An Unfinished Adventure* (2004). The first two of these titles, on globalization and community, are works of provocation, Cassandra or Jeremiah warnings of dire straits ahead in the absence of decisive human action to divert further social disaster. Bauman's views on globalization here are almost unremittingly negative. Almost, because Bauman is also skeptical of the G word. It is a phenomenon in its own right, like the postmodern. Even if it were completely fantastic, an utter fabrication, it would be of interest for what it says about us. For "globalization" has already become a vogue word; there is as much fuss about "globalization" as there is about globalization. The more the word is stretched, the more experiences it seeks to make transparent, the more it rather actually renders the social world opaque. To the contrary, Bauman wants to argue, globalization is a far less unified process than is often presumed. Yet it divides as much as it unites, and in this sense it is merely the contemporary extension of much older imperial processes of the world system. At the same time, its effects are diverse, too: what appears as globalization for some means localization for others. And localization and globalization are mutually constitutive, like master and slave, or freedom and domination, or tourist and vagabond. The much-acclaimed trend to "liquidity" goes together with new and pernicious forms of tribalism. Meantime, new forms of "absentee landlordship" develop, as the global rulers and elites are less and less tied to any significant sense of place or political responsibility. The globalized society is increasingly mobile, but asymmetrically so. Being "on the move" means quite different things for generals and foot soldiers. The extension of criminalization goes together with the expansion of the ranks of the vagabonds, those *sans papiers*.

Bauman makes it clear, however, that if he is here to tell us the bad news, it is because silence leads ultimately to complicity. He agrees with Cornelius Castoriadis that the trouble with contemporary civilization is that it has lost the capacity to question itself. Bauman's adventures in globalization then take us through the city, urban design and utopia, the desperate attempt of moderns to expunge the chaos which always returns immediately via the back door, and to the sterile landscapes of planned cities such as Brasilia. The result is uniformity, which breeds conformity, and conformity's other face is intolerance. Ours is a world in which no one seems now to be in control.

The problem with the idea of community, in contrast, is that it has been emptied of all content. Everybody likes the idea of community, which is proof enough that there must be something fundamentally wrong with it. It "feels" good. Community is unavailable to us, which makes us lust after it all the more. It is a modern paradise lost. At least since Tönnies's *Gemeinschaft und Gesellschaft* (1887) – at least since Rousseau – modernity has generated premodern nostalgia for pasts real, or mostly, imagined. But the acid of the capitalist revolution melted these traditional solids. The prospect of community is destroyed by capitalism, not in recent times, as the prize for success is secession. The rich and powerful exit their relations and commitments; the rest of us, and those below us, are stuck, and stay put. "Cosmopolitanism," in this context, belongs to the tourists, not to the vagabonds. Like Rorty, Bauman worries here that what is left of the "cultural left" too often misses the point: it thinks more about stigma than about money, whereas two thirds of the global population do not know the difference or at least the finer distinctions involved. Struggles over recognition replace those over redistribution, arguments for multiculturalism elide those to equality. In all this, we miss community because we miss security.

Communitarianism, then, is as much a response to globalization as it is to neoliberalism. We rediscover the need for community at the very moment that its feasibility is least likely. Traditionalism of identity is a predictable reaction to modernization; nationalism or parochialism is a predictable response to globalization. And so it is that "identity" becomes the new mantra.

There is too much fuss about identity, not least from comfortable middle-class intellectuals with overwhelming public neuroses. Bauman begins his book on identity by acknowledging the pertinence of his own identity – Polish, more than British, yet he had been denied his Polish identity by the regime that expelled him, or allowed him to leave; Jewish, as he discovered, even though his primary chosen identity was as a Polish communist and socialist. The implication, for Bauman, is clear. In these modern times identity is often itself equated with nationality; but nationality can be given and taken away. Being out of place is just as routine an experience as belonging, for many of us. And locality matters for many as much or more than nation or nationalism does. Identity is a relatively new obsession, coinciding with the wave of change that begins with decolonization through to the contemporary process we call globalization. For the need of identity is also bound up with the widespread sense of insecurity.

But if identity can be confused with, and by nationalism, or as much by consumption as it used to be by production, then there are also other repertoires of identity available. One that Bauman identifies for himself, non-Jewish Jew, post-Pole, incomplete Briton, is larger. It is that of Europe itself. This is the subject of Bauman's little book *Europe – An Unfinished Adventure*. Ambivalence holds this together. For Bauman is also the ruthless critic of Europe and its remarkable capacity to achieve civilization through and upon its own barbarism. Yet, Europe also remains an idea, or a project, and not only a place or an experience. Europe has been a great adventure, an aspirant world system, as well as a misadventure. Europe offered the nastiest state experiments, but also pioneered welfare or social state. The dream of universalism persists. Socialism, after all, was also a European project.

INTERPRETATIONS OF BAUMAN

This much on Bauman. But what is the Bauman Effect? What is striking about the secondary materials on Bauman, given the extent of his influence, is that they are relatively sparse and recent. In comparison, say, to the literature on Foucault or Habermas, work on Bauman is recent and thin. The first hallmark study was a *festschrift* edited by Richard Kilminster and Ian Varcoe, *Culture, Modernity and Revolution. Essays in Honour of Zygmunt Bauman* (1996). As its title and form suggests, these five essays center around interests of Bauman's rather than analyzing his work in detail, with the exception of the editorial contributions. The following year two special issues of journals appeared – one with *Theory, Culture and Society*, the other in *Thesis Eleven*. The first two monographs on Bauman were published in 2000. Dennis Smith's *Zygmunt Bauman. Prophet of Postmodernity* combines significant theoretical sophistication with a detective-like suspicion of Bauman's intellectual path and an enthusiasm to proclaim him a prophet of the postmodern, probably a role and certainly a phenomenon Bauman was later to reject. Peter Beilharz's *Zygmunt Bauman: Dialectic of Modernity* focuses on themes of socialism and culture, modernity, utopia and intellectuals. In 2000 Beilharz published the edited *Bauman Reader*, which is mainly retrospective and historical in orientation. In 2002 Beilharz published the four-volume collection *Zygmunt Bauman: Critical Assessments*, drawing together all hitherto existing essays on Bauman's work, mainly in the English language.

Two more significant books were published in 2001. These were Keith Tester's in-depth *Conversations with Zygmunt Bauman*, and Junge and Kron's edited volume *Zygmunt Bauman – Sociology between Postmodernity and Ethics* (2007). In 2004 Keith Tester published the third monographic study of Bauman's work, entitled *The Social Thought of Zygmunt Bauman*. Tester, Bauman's student, shows with especial sensitivity the literary, filmic, and ethical dimensions of Bauman's project, fully cognizant of the centrality of Bauman's life path, communism, and fascism to his work. Tester and his colleagues also generated two extremely helpful edited collections, *Bauman before Postmodernity: Invitation, Conversations and Annotated Bibliography 1953–1989* with Michael Hviid Jacobsen; and *Bauman beyond Postmodernity: Critical Appraisals, Conversations and Annotated Bibliography 1989–2005* with Jacobsen and Sophia Marshman. These are extremely valuable in their attention to scholarly detail. As their titles imply, both volumes seek to save, or distance Bauman from the postmodern or at least to minimize the identification of his life's work with the postmodern. They seriously deepen the levels of analysis in Bauman scholarship.

A second wave of Bauman literature builds on this work. It begins with Tony Blackshaw's *Zygmunt Bauman* (2005). This is a work which tries to make Bauman easy, by adding an independent line of contemporary social criticism of the present. Does Bauman's work sufficiently cut into bite-size pieces? Readers can decide. The question begged is whether students are so immersed in liquid modernity as to necessarily need a quick fix.

A second major work of new analysis is to be found in Michael Hviid Jacobsen and Paul Poder's *Sociology of Zygmunt Bauman: Challenges and Critique* (2008). The purpose of this collection is to develop a reading of Bauman's work as a general sociology. Here the parallel is made between Bauman's project as a sociological hermeneutics and C. Wright Mills's sociological imagination, and themes such as metaphor, globalization, genocide, consumerism, and freedom are privileged over the texts themselves. The work is conceptually clustered and connected out rather than in to Bauman's work. Whether this volume differs with the work of the first wave, or rather builds upon it, is less immediately apparent. What is beyond dispute, however, is the intellectual sophistication and depth of these essays.

A parallel text is Mark Davis's *Freedom and Consumerism – A Critique of Zygmunt Bauman's Sociology* (2008). Davis foregrounds the theme of freedom as the central coordinate of Bauman's work. Davis begins from the conviction that the first wave of Bauman interpretation is insufficiently critical. The first imperative is trying to work out what Bauman came to say. It is precisely because Bauman's work is hermeneutic and open ended, necessarily unfinished that the idea of external critique and connection may be difficult. On the other hand, to foreground an issue like conservatism may throw light on Bauman's thinking but may also rather suggest that, quite reasonably, there is a point at which we should stop reading Bauman and simply turn to other currents again. No one thinker can do everything, not even one as catholic and as stimulating as Bauman.

Anthony Elliott's edited collection *The Contemporary Bauman* (2007) takes a different approach, combining the exegetical approach, extracting Bauman's own work with a more strikingly immediate emphasis on the contemporary – contemporary social life, and contemporary Bauman. Implicit here is one central debate: is the image of liquid modernity a metaphor, or a theory? Arguably it can be rendered as either, though viewed as a theory liquidity may overstretch its suggestive capacity. The idea of the postmodern, in contrast, was not primarily metaphorical, so much as putatively historical (modernity then, postmodern now) and negative (postmodern equals not modern). Liquidity is at the same time both a much larger and yet smaller category, image or device. The achievement of Elliott's collection, like this other second wave literature, is to build on the establishment phase indicated by the first wave. Contrary to the assertion that literature on Bauman is now abundant, the field is really just opening. The challenge remains to think with Bauman as well as through his work; to take in his interlocutors as well as his own views; and, finally to move on.

Finally, a bridge between the two waves of work on Bauman has been published by Davis and Tester together in their edited volume "*Bauman's Challenge: Sociological Issues for the Twentieth Century*" (2010). This collection connects interpretation and extension out. Bauman's ideas again are opened out to broader horizons from Abu Ghraib to the future of Europe.

Alongside this literature, and Bauman's own work, there nevertheless remains one especially privileged line of access to his project. This is to be found in the work of Janina Bauman, especially in *Winter in the Morning* (1986), republished in 2006 in a second edition as *Beyond These Walls*. Zygmunt Bauman's own work continues, meantime, and each new installment contains surprises as well as elements of continuity. For his project, like our lives, is characterized by both. Now read on.

Reader's Guide to Zygmunt Bauman

Is there a simple way into Bauman's work? Given its spread and diversity, the short answer is no. The early work is more demanding. *Socialism: The Active Utopia* (1976) might be the clearest early short work, followed by *Freedom* (1988). *Thinking Sociologically* (1990) is a wonderful introduction to Bauman's style of continental sociology. *Modernity and the Holocaust* (1989) remains a key work, followed by *Modernity and Ambivalence* (1991). Of the later, little books, *Work, Consumerism and the New Poor* (1998) and *Wasted Lives* (2004) remain among the most powerful. Any of the books on liquidity provide a fine point of entrance; as Bauman says, his is a house with many doors. But be patient, the little books are less easy than they might seem at first; every Bauman book is an invitation to a conversation, so there will always be demands placed on the reader, however brief the encounter.

Traditionally minded readers may find it useful to start with the first wave of Bauman interpretation, after his own texts, before attending to the newest work. But if there remains one privileged way in, it is via the work of Janina Bauman. Her autobiographical work, read in sequence, is a wonderful place to start for those who are not in too much of a hurry.

Bibliography

Writings of Zygmunt Bauman

1972. *Between Class and Elite: The Evolution of the British Labour Movement. A Sociological Study*. Manchester: Manchester University Press (Polish original 1960).

1973. *Culture as Praxis*. London: Routledge & Kegan Paul.

1976. *Socialism: The Active Utopia*. New York: Holmes and Meier Publishers.

1976. *Towards a Critical Sociology: An Essay on Commonsense and Emancipation*. London: Routledge & Kegan Paul.

1978. *Hermeneutics and Social Science: Approaches to Understanding.* London: Hutchinson.

1982. *Memories of Class: The Pre-history and After-life of Class.* London and Boston: Routledge & Kegan Paul.

1985. *Stalin and the Peasant Revolution: A Case Study in the Dialectics of Master and Slave.* Leeds: University of Leeds Department of Sociology.

1987. *Legislators and interpreters – On Modernity, Post-Modernity, Intellectuals.* Ithaca, NY: Cornell University Press.

1988. *Freedom.* Philadelphia: Open University Press.

1989. *Modernity and The Holocaust.* Ithaca, NY: Cornell University Press.

1990. *Paradoxes of Assimilation.* New Brunswick: Transaction Publishers.

1990. *Thinking Sociologically: An introduction for Everyone.* Cambridge, MA: Basil Blackwell.

1991. *Modernity and Ambivalence.* Ithaca, NY: Cornell University Press.

1992. *Intimations of Postmodernity.* London and New York: Routledge.

1992. *Mortality, Immortality and Other Life Strategies.* Cambridge: Polity.

1993. *Postmodern Ethics.* Cambridge, MA: Basil Blackwell.

1995. *Life in Fragments: Essays in Postmodern Morality.* Cambridge, MA: Basil Blackwell.

1996. *Alone Again – Ethics after Certainty.* London: Demos.

1997. *Postmodernity and its Discontents.* New York: New York University Press.

1998. *Globalization: The Human Consequences.* New York: Columbia University Press.

1998. *Work, Consumerism and the New Poor.* Philadelphia: Open University Press.

1999. *In Search of Politics.* Cambridge: Polity.

2000. *Liquid Modernity.* Cambridge: Polity.

2001. *Community: Seeking Safety in an Insecure World.* Cambridge: Polity.

2001 (with Keith Tester). *Conversations with Zygmunt Bauman.* Cambridge: Polity.

2001. *The Individualized Society.* Cambridge: Polity.

2001 (with Tim May). *Thinking Sociologically*, 2nd edn. Oxford: Blackwell Publishers.

2002. *Society under Siege.* Cambridge: Polity.

2003. *City of Fears, City of Hopes.* London: Goldsmith's College.

2003. *Liquid Love: On the Frailty of Human Bonds.* Cambridge: Polity.

2004. *Europe: An Unfinished Adventure.* Cambridge: Polity.

2004. *Identity: Conversations with Benedetto Vecchi.* Cambridge: Polity.

2004. *Wasted Lives. Modernity and its Outcasts.* Cambridge: Polity.

2005. *Liquid Life.* Cambridge: Polity.

2006. *Liquid Fear.* Cambridge: Polity.

2006. *Liquid Times: Living in an Age of Uncertainty.* Cambridge: Polity.

2007. *Consuming Life.* Cambridge: Polity.

2008. *Does Ethics Have a Chance in a World of Consumers?* Cambridge, MA: Harvard University Press.

2008. *The Art of Life.* Cambridge: Polity.

2009. *Living on Borrowed Time: Conversations with Citlali Rovirosa-Madrazo.* Cambridge: Polity.

Further Reading

Bauman, Janina (1986) *Winter in the Morning: A Young Girl's Life in the Warsaw Ghetto, 1939–1945.* London: Virago.

Bauman, Janina (1988) *A Dream of Belonging: My Years in Postwar Poland.* London: Virago.

Bauman, Janina (2006) *Beyond These Walls: Escaping the Warsaw Ghetto – A Young Girl's Story.* London: Virago.

Beilharz, Peter (2000) *Zygmunt Bauman: Dialectic of Modernity*. London: Sage.

Beilharz, Peter (2001) *The Bauman Reader*. Oxford: Blackwell Publishers.

Beilharz, Peter (ed.) (2002) *Zygmunt Bauman – Masters of Social Thought*, 4 vols. London, California and New Delhi: Sage Publications.

Blackshaw, Tony (2005) *Zygmunt Bauman (Key Sociologists)*. London and New York: Routledge.

Davis, Mark (2008) *Freedom and Consumerism: A Critique of Zygmunt Bauman's Sociology*. Aldershot: Ashgate.

Davis, Mark and Tester, Keith (eds) (2010) *Bauman's Challenge: Sociological Issues for the 21st Century*. Basingstoke: Palgrave MacMillan.

Elliott, Anthony (ed.) (2007) *The Contemporary Bauman*. London: Routledge.

Jacobsen, Michael Hviid and Poder, Poul (eds) (2008) *The Sociology of Zygmunt Bauman: Challenges and Critique*. London: Ashgate.

Junge, Matthias and Kron, Thomas (eds) (2007) *Zygmunt Bauman – Sociology Between Postmodernity and Ethics*. Wiesbaden, Germany: Verlag für Sozialwissenschaften.

Kilminster, Richard and Varcoe, Ian (eds) (1996) *Culture, Modernity and Revolution: Essays in Honour of Zygmunt Bauman*. London: Routledge.

Smith, Dennis (2000) *Zygmunt Bauman: Prophet of Postmodernity (Key Contemporary Thinkers)*. Cambridge: Polity.

Tester, Keith (2004) *The Social Thought of Zygmunt Bauman*. Basingstoke: Palgrave MacMillan.

Tester, Keith and Jacobsen, Michael Hviid (2006) *Bauman Before Postmodernity: Invitation, Conversations and Annotated Bibliography 1953–1989*. Aalborg: Aalborg University Press.

Tester, Keith, Jacobsen, Michael Hviid, and Marshman, Sophia (2007) *Bauman Beyond Postmodernity: Conversations, Critiques and Annotated Bibliography 1989–2005*. Aalborg: Aalborg University Press.

7

Gilles Deleuze

IAN BUCHANAN

Undoubtedly one of the most influential philosophers of the twentieth century (the century his friend Michel Foucault mischievously suggested would one day be named after him), Deleuze's (1925–1995) work was propelled to the height of intellectual fashion in the early part of the twenty-first century, in both the humanities and social sciences, spawning literally hundreds of books and articles about his work. Although notoriously difficult to read and often frustratingly elusive, Deleuze's writing has broad appeal because it invites creative application rather than strict adherence. His political outlook is highly optimistic about the possibility of change, but still relentlessly critical of the current state of affairs, and for that reason his work has been well received internationally by a wide variety of social movements.

The Person and the Context

The details of Deleuze's younger days are now reasonably well known thanks to François Dosse's comprehensive (though not flawless) biography, *Gilles Deleuze et Félix Guattari: Biographie Croisée* (2007). Born in Paris in 1925, Deleuze's father was an aeronautical engineer and the family's sole breadwinner. His family was well enough off so that his mother could stay at home and care for Gilles and his brother Georges. When war broke out in 1939 Deleuze's parents sent the two teenage boys to a boarding school in Deauville on the Normandy coast. There Gilles met Pierre Halbwachs, whom Deleuze later described as his first true teacher, crediting him with inspiring his interest in French literature and philosophy in the course of their long walks in the sand dunes. The son of the great philosopher Maurice Halbwachs, Pierre joined the resistance with his father. They were captured by the Gestapo and both perished in concentration camps.

The Wiley-Blackwell Companion to Major Social Theorists, First Edition.
Edited by George Ritzer and Jeffrey Stepnisky.
© 2011 Blackwell Publishing Ltd. Published 2011 by Blackwell Publishing Ltd.

After the armistice, Deleuze was able to return to Paris to continue his studies. He completed his *baccalauréat* at the Lycée Carnot and then his *khâgne* at the Lycée Henri-IV. His brother Georges joined the resistance and was captured by the Germans and died en route to a concentration camp. The loss of both his mentor and brother in short succession dealt a grievous blow to Deleuze – it also resulted in a deep gulf opening up between him and his family, who tended to regard the "lost" brother as the hero Gilles could never measure up to. According to Dosse, this is the source of Deleuze's so-called anti-familialism, but the explanation itself is the product of exactly the kind of familialism Deleuze criticizes in psychoanalysis, namely the assumption that the subject is wholly formed in the crucible of the family. In his later work, Deleuze does not reject the family per se, as Dosse implies; what he rejects is the idea that the family is the only aspect of a child's life that is formative. As Deleuze and Guattari put it in *Anti-Oedipus*: "what a grotesque error to think that the unconscious-as-child is acquainted only with daddy–mommy, and that it doesn't know 'in its own way' that the father has a boss who is not a father's father, or moreover that its father himself is a boss who is not a father" (2004:106).

From the Lycée Carnot Deleuze went to the Sorbonne to study philosophy, graduating in 1948. His classmates included François Châtelet, Jean-François Lyotard, Michel Butor, Pierre Klossowski, Claude Lanzmann, maker of the epic film *Shoah* (1985), and the novelist Michel Tournier, who remembers Deleuze in his memoir, *Le Vent Paraclet* (1977), translated as *The Wind Spirit* (1988). According to Tournier, as an undergraduate Deleuze was already a powerful innovator:

> We soon came to fear his talent for seizing upon a single one of our words and using it to expose our banality, stupidity, or failure of intelligence. He possessed extraordinary powers of translation and rearrangement: all the tired philosophy of the curriculum passed through him and emerged unrecognizable but rejuvenated, with a fresh, undigested, bitter taste of newness that we weaker, lazier minds found disconcerting and repulsive. (Tournier, 1988: 128)

Another fellow pupil, Maurice de Gandillac, said that he and the other students thought of Deleuze as a new Sartre (Dosse, 2007: 116). As surprising as it might sound, Deleuze would probably have regarded this accolade as a compliment – although his work shows few traces of Sartre's influence, Deleuze clearly admired him, describing him as "breath of fresh air from the backyard...which gave us the strength to tolerate the new restoration of order" (Deleuze, 1987: 12).

Deleuze found the atmosphere at the Sorbonne claustrophobic. He respected and admired his teachers, such as Maurice Merleau-Ponty and Jean Hyppolite, but he nonetheless rejected their teaching very firmly. "I could not stand Descartes, the dualisms and the Cogito, or Hegel, the triad and the operation of the negation" (Deleuze, 1987: 14). The exception was Sartre, but even then Deleuze did not feel drawn to existentialism or phenomenology. Deleuze said he belonged to a generation, "that was more or less bludgeoned to death with the history of philosophy" (Deleuze, 1995: 5). Although Deleuze singles out the dialectic as one of the things he wanted to escape from, ultimately it was not the specific concepts that bothered him (indeed, in his later works he would say he was trying to develop a "superior" form of the dialectic), but the repressive way the history of philosophy was used to

constrict thought and effectively put it in the straightjacket of the imperative injunc-
tion "you can't do this until you've read that" with which all students are familiar.
Similarly, as his collaborations with Guattari demonstrate vividly, Deleuze also
rejected the rather traditionalist position that philosophers should only read philosophy and that only philosophers do philosophy.

Characteristically, Deleuze's own career followed an alternative path to the one
prescribed by the institution. He quite consciously created his own philosophical
cannon, one that privileged the work of such out of favor authors as Hume, Bergson,
Nietzsche, and Spinoza. That these authors, with the exception of Hume, have
enjoyed a remarkable renaissance in the last forty years is due in no small part to the
efforts of Deleuze. Yet it can hardly be said that these authors are all alike – there are
vast gulfs between them, a fact that has perplexed many Deleuze scholars, particularly in philosophy where such yawning chasms are treated with suspicion. One
solution has been to treat Deleuze's work on these authors as so many unrelated
experiments, as though he sampled Hume, then moved on to Bergson, and so on.
But this does not hold because it is evident in his later work that he draws on all of
these authors, yet does so without reducing them to the same. Deleuze's own solution is to see each of these authors as trying (but not always succeeding) to create a
philosophy of immanence, which is a mode of philosophy that does not assume that
external or transcendent coordinates are necessary preconditions. Insofar as he is
concerned, then, they are like so many master craftsmen from whom one learns certain techniques, so as to be able to create one's own works, which may or may not
resemble that of the master's. His work then combines the various "solutions" to the
problem of constructing a philosophy of immanence in order to create something
new. As Deleuze frequently insists in his work, the means by which an object or idea
is constructed can tell us nothing about its actual use.

Deleuze's academic career progressed quite slowly, and indeed he never rose to the
lofty heights that Foucault did. Partly this was due to poor health – Deleuze had a
chronic lung condition that frequently prevented him from working (the fact that he
was also an inveterate smoker doubtless did not help things in this respect) – but it
was also due to the fact that he never played the academic game in the way his friend
did. As is customary in the French academic system, after completing his first doctorate Deleuze did his time in the Lycée system, first in Amiens, then Orleans, and
finally back in Paris, for nearly a decade before obtaining a post as a junior lecturer
at the Sorbonne in 1957, where he remained until 1964. After a very brief stint at the
Centre National de la Recherche Scientifique, Deleuze obtained a teaching post in
philosophy at the University of Lyon, during which time he prepared the requisite
two theses for his Doctorat d'État, both of which appeared in the watershed year of
1968. *Différence et répétition*, translated as *Difference and Repetition* (1994), and
Spinoza et le problème de l'expression, translated as *Expressionism in Philosophy:
Spinoza* (1992). By his own account, *Difference and Repetition* was the first book in
which he did *his own* philosophy, the first book in which he broke away from writing the history of philosophy and began to create new philosophy. Written in the
same period, though not published until a year later, *Logique du Sens* (1969), translated as *The Logic of Sense* (1990), ostensibly a study of Lewis Carroll's work, but
really a profound meditation on the philosophy of language, completes this phase of
Deleuze's career.

The year 1968 was of course a watershed year in French and indeed world history for reasons other than the publication of Deleuze's doctorate. In May of that year, a student protest that began in the outer suburban university of Nanterre but rapidly spread to include students in even the most conservative Latin Quarter institutions grew into a national disruption when blue-collar workers joined in and went on strike. At one point during the so-called "events of May" some 10 million people were on strike, effectively bringing the country to a standstill. History is undecided as to the overall effectiveness of the dissident actions taken during this period, which included violent street protests, because at the end of it all there was no change in the political regime. Yet, as theorists like Deleuze himself insisted, everything had changed because the government lost its credibility and with it its authority. While Deleuze did not participate in the events of May 1968, he nonetheless took a keen interest in its results. On the one hand, he was impressed by the fact that such a large number of people felt strongly enough to show their dissent in such a strident manner; but on the other hand, he detected fascist elements in the operations of some of the groups. He was particularly opposed to the Maoists' demand for self-renunciation, which he saw as helping no one and doing nothing to change the political situation. Unlike many colleagues of his own generation, Deleuze did not accept the revisionist line that "nothing happened" that May because it did not result in a genuine change in the French political system, but he was nevertheless at a loss as to how he should respond since it could not easily be shown what exactly had happened.

The beginnings of an answer to the problem of how to account for the intangible but nonetheless significant changes wrought by the events of May would present themselves a year later when a young psychoanalyst, Félix Guattari, sought him out in the summer of 1969. Several years younger than Deleuze, Guattari had neither a degree nor a book to his name when he visited Deleuze's summer residence at the suggestion of friends. Guattari had a gift for intellectual invention and organizing people, for conceiving new ideas and bringing people together. He was the living embodiment of "transversality," the concept he invented to describe relations between subjects and objects, or subjects and subjects, which is neither unifying nor totalizing. Before he met Deleuze, Guattari had already gained notoriety in France as a political activist. He was known in the French press as "Mr Anti-" for his public campaigning on a range of causes from the decolonization of Algeria, the improved treatment of prisoners in French prisons (he was a member of Michel Foucault's Groupe d'Information sur les Prisons), the improved treatment of the mentally ill in French insane asylums, the establishment of free radio, to Gay rights and Green politics. Guattari received formal training in psychoanalysis from Jacques Lacan, but his relationship to Lacan and Lacanian psychoanalysis was at best ambivalent. Guattari wanted to meet Deleuze not only because he admired his work (particularly the concept of "the body without organs," which appears for the first time in *The Logic of Sense*), but also because he thought Deleuze could help him resolve a number of theoretical impasses he found in the work of Jacques Lacan. It proved to be a meeting of true minds, and was not the encounter between a disciple and a master as it is sometimes portrayed.

Following the success of *Anti-Oedipus* and *A Thousand Plateaus*, written with Guattari, Deleuze returned to more singular and specialized topics, producing first a book on Francis Bacon, then a two-volume "natural history" of cinema. These were followed by books on Foucault and Leibniz and one final book with Guattari, *What is*

Philosophy?, which functions as a kind of master key to everything Deleuze had worked on previously. Deleuze eschewed the trappings of fame that the success of his collaborations with Guattari had brought him. He did not accept lucrative visiting appointments in the US, as did several of his illustrious peers (Derrida, Foucault, and Lyotard in particular), nor did he accept many of the frequent invitations to present at conferences around the world. He traveled to the US once, with Guattari, to give a series of talks at several different universities, but it was not an agreeable experience for him and he never repeated the journey. In interviews he made a virtue of not traveling very much, saying that too much movement interrupted one's becoming. Deleuze is often accused of being withdrawn from worldly affairs in the last years of his life, but this charge is as unjust as it is untrue. His writing was always politically charged and he actively supported several high profile causes, including the plight of the Palestinian people.

THE WORK

It is customary to divide Deleuze's work into two basic periods, before and after he met Guattari, and though there is an element of truth in this division it is ultimately too simplistic to be of much use. Leaving aside the fact that the usual reason for doing this is the abusive one of wanting to single out Guattari's "bad influence" on Deleuze (Alain Badiou, Manuel DeLanda, and Slavoj Žižek take this line), it fails to capture the manifold nature of Deleuze's career. I want to propose that Deleuze's career can be divided into five different stages. The lines dividing these stages are fuzzy or inexact (as Deleuze himself might say) because there is a great deal of overlapping between the stages, but by the same token the lines are sharp enough to indicate the tectonic movement of Deleuze's thought.

1 The apprenticeship (to adopt Michael Hardt's useful designation), the period between the publication of his first book on Hume and the appearance of his book on Sacher-Masoch;
2 The doctorate (*Difference and Repetition*, *Expressionism in Philosophy* and *The Logic of Sense*), which undoubtedly overlaps with the previous period, but also represents a maturing of Deleuze's philosophical thinking;
3 The schizoanalytic period of collaboration with Guattari – *Anti-Oedipus*, *Kafka*, *A Thousand Plateaus*, but not *What is Philosophy?*, which belongs to a later period;
4 The "return to self," which culminated in the two books on cinema, but also saw the publication of monographs on Foucault and Bacon – although published slightly later, the book on Leibniz seems to belong to this period;
5 Late Deleuze (in Edward Said's sense of the term "late"), which include *What is Philosophy?*, *Essays Critical and Clinical* (although many were written much earlier), and *L'abécédaire de Gilles Deleuze*.

Apprenticeship

In a book that was effectively his own apprenticeship in philosophy, *Gilles Deleuze: An Apprenticeship in Philosophy* (1993), Michael Hardt argues that Deleuze's early career was very much in the spirit of the times – like his colleagues and peers, the group of scholars that would collectively create post-structuralism, Deleuze defined his philosophical goal in terms of an escape from Hegel and the all pervasive Hegelianism of the generation that came before him (Hyppolite, Kojève, Sartre, etc.). But as Hardt is careful to point out, Deleuze is not merely anti-Hegelian; he is much more creative than that in his approach. To adapt a locution Hardt uses in his later work, we might say that Deleuze is alter-Hegelian because his work constitutes a radical alternative to Hegel that is constructed by confronting and resolving by different means the same basic philosophical problem that motivated Hegel, namely the question of the genesis of being. In this regard, as Hardt rightly points out, Deleuze cannot be grouped among the "antifoundationalist" poststructuralists (such as Richard Rorty) because his project is not concerned with getting rid of foundation per se; rather, his purpose is to reorient philosophy from a transcendental foundation towards an immanent foundation. Ultimately, Deleuze's goal is "to think transcendence within the immanent" (Deleuze and Guattari, 1994: 47), and thus create a form of philosophical thinking Deleuze calls "transcendental empiricism." In other words, it is a mistake to think that Deleuze gets rid of the transcendental altogether; rather, he resituates as it as a secondary form of philosophy conditioned by immanence.

Hardt maps out Deleuze's apprenticeship as a progression from Bergson to Nietzsche to Spinoza, thus omitting Hume from consideration. Hardt seems to think Deleuze's first book on Hume was something of a misstep that took several years of reading other philosophers to correct. By the same token, Hardt also sets aside the books on Sacher-Masoch (1967) and Proust (1964) as though these were not somehow philosophical experiments too. None of these omissions is consistent with Deleuze's own account of his apprenticeship years – his own telling of the story always begins with Hume and it is not difficult to see why, and always includes mention of his apparently literary works too. Deleuze was attracted to Hume at this point in his career because Hume offers a way of conceiving the mind as an immanent system that contains the means within itself not only to bring itself into being, but to function in an ongoing manner. Immanence for Deleuze is the power of the indefinite, the indeterminate, and the indivisible that simultaneously shapes and disrupts the transcendental – if the latter is the power of determination, the ability to synthesize and differentiate one object from another, then it is a power that finds its meaning in and against the indeterminacy of immanence. Devising the means to take philosophy in this direction was the principal goal of the first stage of Deleuze's career, which (it is worth remembering) refers to a period of work lasting nearly two decades and includes an eight year gap in which he published nothing, and his work on Hume was crucial to that goal.

Empiricism and Subjectivity: An Essay on Hume's Theory of Human Nature (1991), was first published in 1953 while Deleuze was still a student. His first full-length book, it was not his first publication, but it is the first work that Deleuze recognizes as "his." In later life Deleuze repudiated everything he wrote prior to this point – several essays on Christo-philosophical and related theological subjects. In his own eyes then, his work on Hume marks the true starting point of his philosophical career. Deleuze's book focuses on Hume's theory of the externality of relations to ideas. As becomes clear during Deleuze's schizoanalytic period, this notion is crucial to Deleuze's subsequent development as a philosopher of immanence.

In contrast to Kant, and the whole critical tradition of philosophy that developed in Kant's wake, Hume does not suppose that there is anything "within thought that surpasses the imagination"; consequently, there is nothing transcendental in Hume's account of the imagination because the principles of association he proposes "are simply principles of *our* nature" which "render possible an experience without at the same time rendering necessary the objects of this experience" (Deleuze, 1991: 111–112). As Deleuze explains, the basic problem Hume addresses is how is it possible for a subject that transcends the given to be constituted in the given? In other words, how does the subject form out of the multiple sensations and impressions that bombard the mind? Hume's answer is the notion of associationism. Yet it is clear from the fact that it took him eight years to write another book that Hume did not provide all the answers Deleuze was looking for and one may suppose that the delay was because he got stuck on how to solve the problem that Hume's work exposes without satisfactorily resolving, namely the problem of a dualistic ontology.

As Jeffrey Bell explains in *Deleuze's Hume* (2009), this turn toward a dualistic ontology is the source of the considerable difficulty many of Deleuze's peers, particularly Alain Badiou, have with his work. But this difficulty arises from an inability to grasp that for Deleuze the virtual and actual do not comprise a dual system as such; rather, they are two states of being, which should not be confused with the apparently cognate binary non-being and being. As Deleuze puts it in his short book on Bergson, the virtual exists in such a way that "it is actualised by being differentiated and is forced to differentiate itself, to create its lines of differentiation in order to be actualised" (Deleuze, 1988: 97). In other words, the virtual and the actual do not resemble one another; the former is not the mirror image of the latter, nor is it its condition, or pre-formation. The concept of the crowd does not give rise to the crowd, but it is nevertheless actualized by the crowd when a large group of people gathers. In *A Thousand Plateaus*, Deleuze and Guattari explain the difference between virtual and actual in terms of limits and use the example of the drunk to articulate what they mean. The drunk, they argue, is concerned to determine his or her second last drink, that is, the last drink they can have before things begin to change (i.e. the last drink before they pass out, fall over, feel sick, or whatever); the actual limit is what must be avoided at all costs. The actual limit, until it is reached, exists on a virtual plane, but what is both curious about this, and absolutely central to Deleuze's thought, is that it is no less real for being virtual because its effects are real. The virtual is not imagined or fantasized, it is completely real without being actual, and without it, according to Deleuze, we are unable to explain fully how the subject interacts with the world without resorting to phenomenology.

Deleuze's second book, *Nietzsche et la philosophie* (1962), translated as *Nietzsche and Philosophy* (1983), is credited with sparking a profound "return to Nietzsche" after more than half a century of neglect. Deleuze overturned the gloomy image of Nietzsche as the ultimate nihilist and dismissed the suspicions of those who accepted the distorted picture of him as a Nazi philosopher created by his sister Elisabeth. He presented Nietzsche as a philosopher of joy, and natural successor Spinoza, who calls on us to overcome our *ressentiment* and live life in an active rather than reactive manner. Under different guises, this theme would remain constant throughout Deleuze's writings. The terms "active" and "passive" disappear from Deleuze's work by the end of the 1960s, to be replaced by affirmative and negative, but the problematic underpinning them remains constant and simply evolves into what many see as a variant on vitalist philosophy. Whilst Deleuze uses the term "vitalism" to describe his work, he also qualifies it as a "machinic vitalism," thus making it difficult to place his thought in the vitalist tradition in any straightforward way. Machinic, and indeed machinic vitalism, refers to a mode of connectivity which is independent of the terms it relates (he takes this idea from Hume, who insisted that relations are independent of terms). Perhaps the best example of what Deleuze has in mind is the notion of the constellation (a notion that also intrigued both Walter Benjamin and Theodor Adorno, and although Deleuze uses this notion himself in *A Thousand Plateaus*, he does not refer to either of these authors): the constellation is the name we give to a group of stars that are not in fact physically connected in any way; so the connection is imposed. But the crucial point is that it is the connections that create the object – the constellations we see in the night sky exist only because of the connections that have been mapped onto them. Deleuze and Guattari would later call this mode of connectivity "rhizomatic."

Deleuze's next books explore this problematic of what constitutes "vitalism" for our time, somewhat obliquely it has to be said, through an examination of literature. Inspired by Nietzsche's idea that the philosopher is a kind of physician Deleuze looked to the work of Proust and Sacher-Masoch to see whether this idea applied to literature as well. *Proust et les Signes* (1964), translated as *Proust and Signs* (1972), and *Presentation de Sacher-Masoch* (1967), translated as *Masochism: Coldness and Cruelty* (1989), inaugurate a trajectory in Deleuze's work he named the "clinical" that culminated in the publication of *Critique et Clinique* (1993), translated as *Essays Critical and Clinical* (1997). Although Deleuze himself regarded this aspect of his work as important, there is a case to be made that he in fact abandoned the project and never really completed it because he never resolves the basic problem it confronts, that of the symptom, which is in many ways an anathema to his entire mode of thought. As he argues in his work with Guattari, the problem with the symptom as it is conceived by both psychoanalysis and psychiatry is that it projects a surface layer of signification (manifest content) over a hidden depth of meaning (latent content). For this hermeneutic arrangement to work, psychoanalysis has to presuppose that all symptoms, however they manifest themselves, have as their basic etiology some kind of an impasse or blockage in the libidinal relation between the patient and their family. This relationship has come to be known simply as the Oedipal complex following Freud's observation in *The Interpretation of Dreams* that the child's situation recalls that of Oedipus who is fated to kill his father and marry his mother. The other problem Deleuze and Guattari have with this is that it privileges the therapist as the one who is uniquely able to decode the hidden meaning and thereby tell the patient what they are really thinking. These disagreements with psychoanalysis would be worked out more fully by Deleuze in his collaboration with Guattari.

In between the books on Proust and Sacher-Masoch, Deleuze wrote on commission textbooks on Bergson and Kant. The former is generally taken as evidence that Deleuze was indeed a vitalist, while the latter is read as a sign that Deleuze's philosophical project consisted in completing Kant's critique – this is made explicit in Deleuze's later collaborative works. Awarded the Nobel Prize for literature in 1927, Bergson had fallen into relative obscurity by the time Deleuze came to write about him in 1966. As with Nietzsche, Deleuze's book on Bergson did a lot to restore the latter's reputation, but the process was much slower. Doubtless this is because his reputation had suffered many more blows – Bergson's work was attacked along two interrelated lines: on the one hand, he was accused of bad science (particularly in his ill-judged "debate" with Albert Einstein), while on the other hand, he was accused of spiritualism for his attempt to posit an intangible or metaphysical life force (*élan vital*) as an explanation for evolution. For the most part, Deleuze steers clear of these issues in his book on Bergson and instead focuses on the one area in which Bergson's work remains as relevant and as robust as ever, namely his theory of time. At the most rudimentary level, Bergson's theory of time is simply this: both the past and the future are dimensions of the present, but their existence is virtual rather than actual. In this sense, then, the past is a present that is no longer actual, while the future is a present that is not yet actual. Both past and future are real, but they are not actual. This distinction is fundamental to the whole of Deleuze's work, but especially to his collaborations with Guattari as will be seen in a moment.

In contrast to Bergson, Kant's stock as a philosopher has never been less than bullish. As one of the heralds of the so-called Enlightenment, Kant is the effective starting point for the entire transcendental tradition in modern or what is also known as continental philosophy. For this reason, Kant is the polar of opposite of Deleuze, and though Deleuze depicts him as the old enemy and caricatures him as the Chinaman of the North, his respect for Kant is obvious. Both *Anti-Oedipus* and *A Thousand Plateaus* position Kant's work on *a priori* synthesis as a necessary precursor to schizoanalysis. Deleuze's argument with Kant is never that Kant was wrong as such, but always that he did not go far enough in the development of the categories, and in the end remained within the limited and limiting confines of moral judgment.

Doctorate

In his doctoral phase, Deleuze concluded that there has only ever been one satisfactory theory of ontology and that is the notion of univocal being first enunciated in Duns Scotus and then given its most powerful expression in Spinoza. It takes time for him to arrive at this viewpoint and to get there he needs to sort out a number of problems that this position presents both philosophically and ethically. It seems he turned to Bergson for the sake of the philosophical problems it presents, principally those that concern memory and the passage of time, and to Nietzsche for the sake of the ethical problems, which for Deleuze is never a matter of deciding how one should act in a prescriptive sense, but always turns on how one should deal with what has happened. The principal philosophical problem posed by univocal being is this: if everything already is, if everything is part of one thing, then how can there be change? More precisely, if everything already is, if everything is part of one thing, then how can something that used to exist cease to exist? To put it another way, if everything already is, if everything is part of one thing, then how can something that did not exist start to exist? As Deleuze points out, the category of the "possible" is useless in resolving this problematic because if something is possible then in a sense it already exists. The same applies to the category of "potential." Bergson's solution, which Deleuze adopts and integrates into the very heart of his own thinking (in spite of Bergson's frequently stated antipathy for Hume), is to distinguish between the "virtual" and the "actual," both are categories of the real inasmuch that they both exist, but only the latter has tangible, concrete form.

This solution is articulated in three different ways in the three books constituting this phase of Deleuze's career: *Difference and Repetition, Expressionism in Philosophy* and *The Logic of Sense*. In *Difference and Repetition* the actual and virtual are mobilized to explain the twin processes of difference, which Deleuze distinguishes as differen*c*iation (with a "c") and differen*t*iation (with a "t"). "We call the determination of the virtual content of an Idea differen*t*iation; we call the actualisation of that virtuality into species and distinguished parts differen*c*iation" (1994: 207). This is Deleuze's way out of what he sees as the blind path of dialectics and its explanation of genesis and transformation as a labor of the negative, that is, that something is what it is only by power of its ability to separate itself from what it is not. But perhaps Deleuze's most provocative argument in this book is his thesis that only the different can be repeated. In effect, Deleuze is saying no such separation is necessary because only that which is different can in fact be actualized and thereby result in difference. In *Expressionism in Philosophy* the virtual and actual are implicit in the distinction between Spinoza's attribute (expression) and substance to which Deleuze draws our attention. As Deleuze shows, this distinction parallels the one he himself draws between differen*c*iation (with a "c") and differen*t*iation (with a "t"): attributes are the virtual univocal forms of being which do not change regardless of the type of being they are attributed to, while substance is the actual form of being which attributes modify (Deleuze, 1992: 47–49). In *The Logic of Sense* the virtual and actual are once again deployed to account for the multiplicity of meanings texts are capable of generating – Deleuze's originality in this respect is to show that this multiplicity is not a "hidden" potential, but an active constituent part of the "surface" of the text.

The schizoanalytic period

Deleuze and Guattari describe their first book together, *Anti-Oedipus*, as a May 1968 book, by which they mean its central problematic is one that the events of May made apparent. Theory as it stood then was not equipped to properly comprehend, much less articulate what happened that summer, which so far as Deleuze and Guattari were concerned boiled down to the irruption of two apparently contradictory trajectories among those involved in the events, either towards progressive collective political action or regressive neo-fascistic political factionalism. I say apparently contradictory trajectories because in reality the two tendencies are often found side by side: many progressive political groups are also highly factionalist, policing their membership with the pernicious vigilance of fascists. As Deleuze complained, the Maoists put forward radical ideas for the transformation of society, but in order to participate in their activities one had to first of all renounce one's bourgeoisie past and perform excoriating acts of self-criticism. Deleuze could see no point in such demands, which in his view simply played to the masochistic tendencies of intellectuals. It was this coincidence of tendencies – the progressive and regressive, for the want of better words – that intrigued and concerned Deleuze and Guattari. To explain it they felt that they had to short-circuit the connection between Freud and Marx established by the Frankfurt School (as well as the connection between

Lacan and Marx established by Althusser and the Althusserians). The reason for this is twofold: on the one hand, they dispute the theory that capitalism persists in spite of its exploitativeness because people are unaware of its true nature (a situation Marxism terms "false consciousness"); on the other hand, they dispute the theory that people adhere to fascist models of government because it appeals to their instincts, or their irrational side.

Deleuze and Guattari start from the assumption, rather, that the persistence of capitalism and/or the adherence to fascism (which for Deleuze and Guattari really just means any official or institutionally supported exercise of power) is at once fully conscious and fully rational. According to Deleuze and Guattari the fundamental problem of political philosophy, is "one that Spinoza saw so clearly, and that Wilhelm Reich rediscovered: 'Why do men fight *for* their servitude as stubbornly as though it were their salvation?'" (Deleuze and Guattari, 2004: 31). This question resonates throughout the three schizoanalytic books, *Anti-Oedipus*, *Kafka*, and *A Thousand Plateaus*. "Reich is at his profoundest as a thinker," they say,

> when he refuses to accept ignorance or illusion on the part of the masses as an explanation of fascism, and demands an explanation that will take their desires into account, an explanation formulated in terms of desire: no, the masses were not innocent dupes; at a certain point, under a certain set of conditions, they *wanted* fascism, and it is this perversion of the desire of the masses that needs to be accounted for. (Deleuze and Guattari, 2004: 31)

Reich, however, fails to provide an adequate answer to his own question because he frames it in terms of rational and irrational acts. In *A Thousand Plateaus*, Deleuze and Guattari revisit this problematic and frame it as follows:

> Why does desire desire its own repression, how can it desire its own repression? The masses certainly do not passively submit to power; nor do they "want" to be repressed, in a kind of masochistic hysteria; nor are they tricked by an ideological lure. Desire is never separable from complex assemblages that necessarily tie into molecular levels. (1987: 215)

Deleuze and Guattari are sometimes referred to as "philosophers of desire," and as the previous quote makes apparent there is some justice in this description, but this label only makes sense insofar as it is understood that their approach to desire is materialist. Desire is assembling, according to Deleuze and Guattari; it makes connections and it makes things happen.

Short-circuiting the connection between Marx and Freud is only the first step in establishing schizoanalysis and its purpose is not to then jettison either or both Marxism and psychoanalysis as many of their readers seem to assume. Deleuze and Guattari's rhetoric does at times give the impression that this is in fact their purpose, so one does have to read them very carefully. Having said that, they are quite explicit that their twin aim in short-circuiting the connection between Marx and Freud is to create a position from which they can retool both. Schizoanalysis is, they suggest, at once a reengineering of psychoanalysis and a reorienting of Marxism. In the case of the former this amounts to shifting the focus of attention from neurosis to psychosis, or more particularly from pleasure to desire; while in the case of the latter it means shifting the focus of attention from consumption to production, or more particularly from commodity capitalism to finance capitalism. The latter shift is effectively the precursor to the former because what intrigues Deleuze and Guattari about finance capital is the way, according to Marx's formulations, it is able to bypass the commodity phase and simply reproduce itself, so that money gives rise to more money, without needing to be mediated via the manufacture and sale of actual products (the so-called "Credit Crunch" or "Global Financial Crisis" of 2007–2009 made apparent both the absurdity and riskiness of this situation). This pure form of production that is constantly producing without ever producing anything actual describes perfectly what, in a different discourse might be thought of as the "natural" or "pre-egoic" state of the unconscious which Deleuze and Guattari correlate with psychosis. This, they argue, is what the experience of schizophrenia is like for its sufferers, a constant form of production – largely in the form of connections between things, thoughts, ideas that do not otherwise have anything in common – that they are helpless to stop. Psychoanalysis misunderstands psychosis because it emphasizes the content of the psychotic's delusions, when it should instead have concentrated on the processes underpinning it.

The three schizoanalytic books are for most readers as confusing as they are exciting. One senses immediately that these books are saying something radical and important, it is just very difficult to see how all the different bits and pieces – the numerous flashes of brilliance, not to mention the bewildering array of new concepts – of the three books fit together in a systematic fashion. Compounding this problem is the lack of consistency in the use of certain concepts and terms between books, or indeed within the books as is notoriously the case with *A Thousand Plateaus*. *Anti-Oedipus* opens with a discussion of the notion of desiring-machines and makes it seem that schizoanalysis hinges on understanding of this term. Yet one labors in vain to find any mention of the term in the sequel *A Thousand Plateaus*. In interviews, Deleuze and Guattari explain that the concept of the desiring machine was not sufficiently complex in its construction to enable them to articulate fully their answer to the question of why desire desires its oppression so they developed new terms. What they fail to mention is which term should be seen as its replacement. Read alongside each other, the three books seem to work like this: *Anti-Oedipus* is a vast labor of the negative, a cleansing of theory's Augean stables if you will, in which the errors and misprisions made by both Marxism and psychoanalysis in the eyes of Deleuze and Guattari are laid bare in preparation for the establishment of what might be termed schizoanalysis proper found in *A Thousand Plateaus*. The next installment in the schizoanalytic trilogy, the book on Kafka, has been described by Fredric Jameson (2009:193) as a missing plateau, or lost chapter of *A Thousand Plateaus* that ought to be restored, because it steps towards *A Thousand Plateaus* but cannot easily be understood in isolation from it. For most readers, it is the concept of minor literature that is the most significant aspect of this work and for this reason it has gained a readership outside of Deleuze studies circles, particularly in comparative literature and postcolonial studies. *A Thousand Plateaus* is the capstone of the whole endeavor.

As a capstone to a decade-long project *A Thousand Plateaus* is fittingly compendious, seemingly offering a "theory of everything." Hubris aside, this is effectively what *A Thousand Plateaus* sets out to be: it is primarily an attempt to construct what might be termed a practical ontology, that is, an ontology that can encompass the constantly changing conditions of everyday life from its most minute and hidden forms (affects, feelings, desires) to its largest and most visible forms (economy, government, war). The ontology they construct consists of three interrelated elements – the assemblage, the machine, and the body without organs – which are bound together in a constant state of change Deleuze and Guattari refer to as becoming. The assemblage is the set of material conditions necessary for a certain "thing" to exist – these conditions may be both virtual and actual, ideas as much as objects. Deleuze and Guattari do not separate the "thing" from its assemblage; indeed, it would be better to say that the thing in its thinghood (to use a Heideggerian locution) is in fact an assemblage. Assemblages give rise to machines, which is Deleuze and Guattari's word for operative ideas such as symptoms, phobias, neuroses, but also passions, desires, and other forms of attachment (it is a cognate of both Melanie Klein's notion of object and Jacques Lacan's *objet petit "a,"* but differs in that it works only in connection with other machines). Machines are produced spontaneously according to the nature of the assemblage, which is constantly changing (i.e. becoming) – not all machines have an impact on the assemblage itself, but those that do are known as abstract machines. For example, Little Hans's horse phobia (in Freud's case histories) is an abstract machine because it is a machine that arose within the "street assemblage" and now dominates it, dictating future developments in the assemblage. Behind all this there is the body without organs which is effectively the desire to be free of the various machines (i.e. organs) that assemblage gives to; it is, in effect, a steady state of desire like Freud's "nirvana principle." What Deleuze and Guattari emphasize in their brief discussion of this example is Freud's failure to take into account anything except the "Oedipal" relation between Hans and his parents and his consequent neglect of the complex reality of Hans's everyday life. The assemblage is, in this sense, an attempt to formalize and make practical the Marxist concept of the "actual situation."

The "return to self"

After *A Thousand Plateaus* Deleuze said he needed to find himself again and his next works were in some ways quite personal. First he wrote a short and admiring book on the art of Francis Bacon, *Francis Bacon, Logique de la Sensation* (1981), translated as *Francis Bacon: The Logic of Sensation* (2003). This book makes use of some of the concepts developed in *A Thousand Plateaus*, but places more emphasis on terms like affect and sensation, which are relatively undeveloped in *A Thousand Plateaus* but would be important to his fourth collaborative work with Guattari, *Qu'est-ce que la philosohie?* (1991), translated as *What is Philosophy?* (1994). He showed the manuscript of the book to the artist himself who was, understandably, very flattered, and they agreed to meet. But, as Bacon's biographer puts it, "although there was a perceptible sympathy and admiration between the two men, no friendship evolved" (Peppiatt, 2008: 378). He followed the book on Bacon with two volumes on film, *Cinéma 1: L'Image-Mouvement* (1983), translated as *Cinema 1: The Movement-Image* (1986), and *Cinéma 2: L'Image-temps* (1985), translated as *Cinema 2: The Time-Image* (1989). Deleuze did not regard these books as exercises in film philosophy; he saw them as attempts to articulate the specifically philosophical dimension of film. Anglo-American film studies was so slow to appreciate these books, but has in the last couple of years become deeply fascinated by the way they reorient the discussion of film.

Deleuze's interest in cinema is twofold. As anyone who has counted up all the films he refers to in these two volumes can tell you, and bearing in mind that he wrote them before home video technology, he obviously had a great passion for cinema. But there was also a precise philosophical interest underpinning these books as well. As Deleuze argues in the introduction to the first volume, the cinematic image is a unique kind of ontological object that "exists" only insofar as it is in motion, hence his designation of it as a "movement-image." It also has its own unique way of conveying meaning which, Deleuze argues, is poorly understood by standard Saussurean semiotic models (including Lacan psychoanalytic permutation). Deleuze turns to C. S. Peirce instead and develops his own critical vocabulary for analyzing how cinema works. What follows is an extensive cataloguing and categorizing of image types – Deleuze unlocks not so much the grammar of cinema as, in his own words, its "natural history." This "history" divides cinema into two moments – the first, which begins in the silent era and ends with Hitchcock, is described by Deleuze as being dominated by what he calls the "sensory motor scheme"; the second, which commences with the Italian neo-realists (principally De Sica, Rossellini, and Fellini) and continues up until the present, is dominated by the appearance of "any-space-whatevers." The difference between these two moments is this: in the sensory motor scheme, the logic of action is always determined by what can be seen on the screen, whereas in the second mode, which Deleuze calls the "time-image" it is no longer possible to discern the logic of action solely by what can be seen.

His next two books were monographs on authors that were close to him personally and intellectually. The most personal of all these books in this period was the one he wrote about his friend Foucault, published two years after the latter's death: *Foucault* (1986), translated as *Foucault* (1988). His next book was on Leibniz, an author not mentioned often in the rest of his work yet clearly important to him, *Le Pli: Leibniz et le baroque* (1988), translated as *The Fold: Leibniz and the Baroque* (1993). This book has been well received by creative artists and geographers who see its core concept of the fold as a radically new way of thinking about space and spatial relations. By the end of the 1980s, Deleuze's health had deteriorated dramatically and he found it difficult to work, yet he continued to produce new works, such as the already mentioned collaboration with Guattari *What is Philosophy?* as well as the essays on the clinical approach to literature. But perhaps his most important work in these years was the magnificent eight hour video of him in conversation with Claire Parnet, *L'abécédaire de Gilles Deleuze*. In the decade since his death, the video archive has greatly enhanced by the various web-based archives making available many recordings of Deleuze's seminars.

Late Deleuze

The melancholic opening of Deleuze and Guattari's final collaborative work, *Qu'est-ce que la philosophie?* (1991), translated as *What is Philosophy?* (1994), is a perfect example of what Edward Said (2006) described as "late style." The authors begin by saying it is the kind of book that could only be written with the "arrival of old age and the time for speaking concretely" (1994: 1). Old age, the authors continue, "produces not eternal youth but a sovereign freedom, a pure necessity in which one enjoys a moment of grace between life and death" (1994: 1). This moment of grace, Deleuze would later describe in his final published work "Immanence: A life" as the moment of pure immanence itself, the moment his whole philosophical career had been spent trying to conceptualize and describe (Deleuze, 2001).

What is Philosophy? divides thought into three principal domains: art, science, and philosophy. It then seeks to describe the specific operation of each domain – so, art produces percepts, science produces functives, and philosophy produces concepts. Each domain is also shown to have its own material – art works with affects, science works with prospects, and philosophy works with singularities. Each of these domains constructs its own kind of plane of immanence, which is Deleuze and Guattari's term for the limit of what is thinkable given a certain set of ontological presuppositions (it is in this respect comparable to Foucault's notion of the episteme, but it is specific to an individual philosopher rather than an historical period). The planes of immanence of the three domains are, Deleuze and Guattari insist, irreducible to one another. Science's way of conceiving of the world is radically distinct from either art's or philosophy's way of apprehending things, which means one cannot simply combine functives, percepts, and concepts willy-nilly to produce theory. This appears to fly in the face of Deleuze and Guattari's own previous work – what is the rhizome if not a functive turned into a concept? So, in this, it must be read as a corrective, not of the previous works, themselves, however, but of popular misconceptions concerning previous works. It is a demand for what the authors call "sobriety," by which they mean clarity, precision, and patience – the willingness to take one's time to grasp a difficult concept whose "meaning" is not immediately apparent.

The status of Deleuze's last work is the subject of considerable critical interest. Italian philosopher Giorgio Agamben (1999) wants us to believe that "Immanence: A Life," which is Deleuze's last known piece of work, can be treated as the philosophical equivalent of a last will and testament. He corroborates this claim with the coincidental fact that Deleuze's friend Michel Foucault also happened to present as his last published work a short disquisition on "Life." Both produced these pieces when they were dying: Foucault presumably corrected the proofs of his piece (actually a modification of something written, as Agamben himself notes, several years earlier in 1978 as an homage to his mentor Georges Canguilhem) from his hospital bed at La Pitié-Salpêtrière, while Deleuze must have composed his, if indeed this is when he wrote it (we don't actually know for sure), at a time when already mortally ill, and thoughts of suicide were perhaps weighing on his mind. But two coincidences do not create a truth. There is nothing in the texts themselves to suggest that it is anything but a coincidence that these essays happened to be the last thing either Deleuze or Foucault worked on; and it is certainly *nothing but a coincidence* that these essays happened to be the last both Deleuze *and* Foucault happened to work on. In this way, Agamben attempts to position Deleuze's work on "Life" as his true legacy, as his last great unfinished work that defines his philosophical project as a whole.

While Agamben's "evidence" is highly questionable, it is nonetheless the case that as far as we know this was Deleuze's last piece of work so it does open the question as to whether he intended "Life" to be the term that summarized his philosophical oeuvre. There is of course no way of knowing what his intentions were, but we can try to determine whether such a move is consistent with his work. The trouble is that the term "Life" is suspiciously humanist in its scope and Deleuze was clearly not that – his work does not privilege human life. Assuming Deleuze did not recant his previous nonhumanist position on his deathbed, then we are compelled to see that any move to treat his last essay as a note on humanism, as many commentators have done (consciously or not), then we are being inconsistent with Deleuze's work overall. It is perhaps better thought of more simply as the name Deleuze gives to the achievement of a philosophy of pure immanence. In other words, we must set aside all humanist "traces" (as Derrida might call the various false trails one might follow), suggested by the term "Life" if we want to be consistent with his work overall. Thus, "Life" is not as Agamben suggests, just another word for biopower, nor is it an unfinished project. On the contrary, Deleuze's essay is the full stop one puts at the end of an essay that has achieved what it set out to do, namely create a philosophy of pure immanence. It is the suicide note of a thinker who felt he had nothing left to say, having already said all that he wanted to say.

IMPACT AND ASSESSMENT

What has been the impact of Deleuze's work? If it were simply a matter of measuring the enthusiasm for his work expressed in the countless books and articles that have been written about his work then there would be no question that Deleuze's impact on contemporary thought has been substantial. But if one were to ask which ideas of his have been taken up and how have they contributed to the development of thought in the latter part of the twentieth century and the beginning of the twenty-first century then it becomes more complicated. There are undoubtedly as many scholars thinking of themselves as Deleuzians now as there once were Lacanians, Foucauldians, and perhaps even Athusserians, but their allegiance to Deleuze's work is as often as not expressed by a conscious attempt not to adhere to his ideas, but rather to use them as stepping off points for highly individual experiments. Concepts like the assemblage, the body without organs and the rhizome, among others, have passed into standard academic usage, but there is very little consistency in the way they are used and definitions vary quite dramatically depending on context. While this situation presents its own problems, it is in many ways the key to Deleuze's success – his work is read by political activists, architects, artists, cultural studies scholars, literary theorists, as well as philosophers.

In the end, it is difficult to classify Deleuze's achievement. He saw himself as overturning Plato and creating a form of transcendental empiricist philosophy that took philosophy past the various impasses it had gotten itself into. How successful he was in this venture is still being decided. It is widely agreed, however, that he was one of the most important thinkers of the twentieth century.

Reader's Guide to Gilles Deleuze

Gilles Deleuze's work is not easy to dip into. He was not an essayist like Jacques Derrida or a master of the interview like Michel Foucault. His métier was the book and he usually wrote in such a way that one really has to read the whole book to get the full sense of his argument. Yet, having said that, it is useful to start with Deleuze's interviews and short interventions in *Dialogues* and *Negotiations*, provided it is understood that they will need to be supplemented later on. Deleuze's readers tend to be divided on which of his books should be regarded as entry points – my feeling is that if you are from a philosophy background, then it is best to start at the beginning with his book on Hume; but if your background is cultural studies, gender studies, or politics, then you will probably find it more stimulating to leap right into *A Thousand Plateaus*; while film and visual culture people will probably want to go straight to the books on Bacon and film. The secondary literature on Deleuze is vast, over three hundred titles and counting, so picking a starting point is difficult, but some names do stand out: Claire Colebrook's introductory book on Deleuze is an excellent place to look for a good general overview of Deleuze's thought; James Williams's volume by volume introductions to *Difference and Repetition* and *The Logic of Sense* offer the kind of detailed explanations philosophy students need to get into the heart of his thought; Ron Bogue's encyclopedic work on Deleuze is undoubtedly the best entry point into Deleuze's thought for literature students; David Rodowick is unsurpassed in his ability to decipher Deleuze's work on cinema; meanwhile those with a more political bent will find useful the work of Eugene Holland and Paul Patton. For creative applications and extensions of Deleuze's work into the realms of cultural studies, then one should turn to the work of Gregg Lambert and Brian Massumi. Architects have found Andrew Ballantyne's work helpful in thinking through the practical implications of Deleuze's thought. Gender theorists are well supplied with introductions and more particularly interventions by Elizabeth Grosz.

Bibliography

Writings of Gilles Deleuze

1972. *Proust and Signs*, Trans. R. Howard. London: Allen Lane.

1983. *Nietzsche and Philosophy*. New York: Columbia University Press.

1984. *Kant's Critical Philosophy: The Doctrine of the Faculties*. Trans. H. Tomlinson and B. Habberjam. Minneapolis: University of Minnesota Press.

1986. *Cinema 1: The Movement-Image*. Trans. H. Tomlinson and B. Habberjam. Minneapolis: University of Minnesota Press.

1986 (with F. Guattari). *Kafka: Toward a Minor Literature*. Trans. D. Polan. Minneapolis: University of Minnesota Press.

1987 (with F. Guattari). *A Thousand Plateaus: Capitalism and Schizophrenia*. Trans. B. Massumi. Minneapolis: University of Minnesota Press.

1987 (with C. Parnet). *Dialogues*. Trans. H. Tomlinson and B. Habberjam. London: Athlone.

1988. *Bergsonism*. Trans. H. Tomlinson and B. Habberjam. New York: Zone Books.

1988. *Foucault*. Trans. S. Hand. Minneapolis: University of Minnesota Press.

1989. *Masochism: Coldness and Cruelty*. Trans. J. McNeil. New York: Zone Books.

1989. *Cinema 2: The Time-Image*. Trans. H. Tomlinson and B. Habberjam. Minneapolis: University of Minnesota Press.

1990. *The Logic of Sense*. Trans. M. Lester. London: Athlone.

1991. *Empiricism and Subjectivity: An Essay on Hume's Theory of Human Nature*. Trans. C. Boundas. New York: Columbia University Press.

1992. *Expressionism in Philosophy: Spinoza*. Trans. M. Joughin. New York: Zone Books.

1993. *The Fold: Leibniz and the Baroque*. Trans. T. Conley. London: Athlone.

1994. *Difference and Repetition*. Trans. P. Patton. London: Athlone.

1994 (with F. Guattari). *What is Philosophy?* Trans. H. Tomlinson and G. Burchell. London: Verso.

1995. *Negotiations*. Trans. M. Joughin. New York: Columbia University Press.

1997. *Essays Critical and Clinical*. Trans. D. Smith and M. Greco. Minneapolis: University of Minnesota Press.

2001. *Pure Immanence: Essays on A Life*. Trans. A. Boyman. New York: Zone Books.

2003. *Francis Bacon: The Logic of Sensation*. Trans. D. Smith. London: Continuum.

2004 (with F. Guattari). *Anti-Oedipus*. Trans. M. Seem *et al*. London: Continuum.

Further Reading

Agamben, G. (1999) *Potentialities: Collected Essays in Philosophy*. Trans. D Heller-Roazen. Stanford: Stanford University Press.

Ballantyne, A. (2007) *Deleuze and Guattari for Architects*. London: Routledge.

Bell, J. A. (2009) *Deleuze's Hume: Philosophy, Culture and the Scottish Enlightenment*. Edinburgh: Edinburgh University Press.

Bogue, R. (2003) *Deleuze on Literature*. London: Routledge.

Colebrook, C. (2002) *Gilles Deleuze*. London: Routledge.

Dosse, F. (2007) *Gilles Deleuze et Félix Guattari: Biographie Croisée*. Paris: La Découverte.

Grosz, E. (2008) *Chaos, Territory, Art: Deleuze and the Framing of the Earth*. New York: Columbia University Press.

Hardt, M. (1993) *Gilles Deleuze: An Apprenticeship in Philosophy*. Minneapolis: University of Minnesota Press.

Holland, E. (1999) *Deleuze and Guattari's Anti-Oedipus: Introduction to Schizoanalysis*. London: Routledge.

Jameson, F. (2009) *Valences of the Dialectic*. London: Verso.

Lambert, G. (2002) *The Non-Philosophy of Gilles Deleuze*. London: Continuum.

Massumi, B. (2002) *Parables for the Virtual: Movement, Affect, Sensation*. Durham: Duke University Press.

Patton, P. (2000) *Deleuze and the Political*. London: Routledge.

Peppiatt, M. (2008) *Francis Bacon: Anatomy of an Enigma*. London: Constable.

Rodowick, D. (1997) *Gilles Deleuze's Time Machine*. Durham: Duke University Press.

Said, E. (2006) *On Late Style: Music and Literature Against the Grain*. London: Bloomsbury.

Tournier, M. (1988) *The Wind Spirit*. Boston: Beacon Press.

Williams, J. (2003) *Gilles Deleuze's Difference and Repetition: A Critical Introduction and Guide*. Edinburgh: Edinburgh University Press.

Williams, J. (2008) *Gilles Deleuze's Logic of Sense: A Critical Introduction and Guide*. Edinburgh: Edinburgh University Press.

8

Richard M. Emerson

KAREN S. COOK AND JOSEPH M. WHITMEYER

THE PERSON

Growing up in Utah within the confines of Mormon culture and community at the base of snowcapped mountains exerted a profound, but little acknowledged, influence on the life and work of Richard Marc Emerson (1925–1982). The mountains he seemed to have always loved were his escape from the closed and somewhat stifling nature of the town in which he was raised. Two themes that emerged subsequently in his work as a sociologist can be traced to these roots: (a) the idea that dependence upon another (or a group) grants them power over you; (b) the notion that the very uncertainty of success brings its own form of motivation. In many ways he was also drawn eventually to sociology by his deep personal understanding of the role of norms, community pressure, hierarchical power relations, and what being an outsider means in a close-knit town. The lure of the mountains that took hold at a very early age also fed his sociological imagination, and he became an astute first-hand observer of group performance under stressful situations as he joined many mountaineering expeditions during his career, including the first successful American attempt to climb Mount Everest in 1963.

During the last few years of his life he and his wife, Pat, who had studied anthropology and Southeast Asia, made many trips to Pakistan to live with and study the remote mountain villages to which their treks and mountain expeditions had taken them over the years. Having lost a son, Marc, at the age of 17 in a tragic mountain climbing accident, Dick and Pat had returned on a sabbatical to the mountains of Pakistan to come to terms with their loss and to gain the support of the mountain people they had come to love. In their joint work and in some of his final papers Emerson examined more deeply the nature of these communities, their historical roots

The Wiley-Blackwell Companion to Major Social Theorists, First Edition.
Edited by George Ritzer and Jeffrey Stepnisky.
© 2011 Blackwell Publishing Ltd. Published 2011 by Blackwell Publishing Ltd.

as outposts of the vast British empire, and the authority and power relations that had defined these communities in relation to the emergent nation state over time.

A web of intricate social and organizational arrangements made each expedition into the remote mountain villages of Pakistan a job of enormous proportions, especially for lengthy sojourns. Such challenges engaged the full range of talents and skills of Richard Emerson, from the academic and intellectual to the intensely physical. As a member of the elite mountaineering company of the Army during the Second World War, he was able to advance the considerable technical skills he had begun to develop in the mountains of Utah and Wyoming during his youth. He completed his undergraduate degree in sociology with a minor in philosophy at the University of Utah. Later he did graduate work at the University of Minnesota, where he received his MA in 1952 and his PhD in 1955. He was admitted for graduate training at both Harvard and Berkeley, but neither offered the financial assistance that Minnesota did. His master's thesis was entitled "Deviation and Rejection: An Experimental Replication," and was co-directed by Don Martindale, his advisor in sociology, and Stanley Schachter, then a faculty member in psychology at the University of Minnesota.

He was trained in both sociology and psychology, and his PhD thesis was an extensive field and experimental study of the determinants of social influence in face-to-face groups. The field study included an investigation of Boy Scout troops in what was to be one of his few empirical examinations of social influence outside of the laboratory. Perhaps it was precisely because of the difficulties of collecting data on these Boy Scouts that he returned to the more controlled environment of the experimental laboratory in much of his subsequent empirical work.

Another significant empirical adventure came when he stepped out of the lab into the "real world" to study social influence, though this time it was to conduct a unique study of group performance among mountain climbers on the 1963 Everest expedition. This research was supported by a National Science Foundation grant entitled "Communication Feedback in Groups under Stress." During this historic expedition, Dick Emerson, one of the strongest team members physically, also served as a field researcher, conducting both experimental and observational research on his colleagues during what amounted to highly complex maneuvers, often at very high altitudes. His mountain climbing friends still complain about the journals they had to keep and even more about the negative feedback they received (in one condition), often during a difficult traverse or climbing exercise. For this unusual and path breaking work Richard Emerson received the Hubbard Medal on behalf of the National Geographic Society. The medal was awarded to him at the White House by President Kennedy in 1963 upon his return to the United States from the expedition.

While many academics of his generation moved around during their careers, Emerson served only two institutions during his lifetime. His first job was at the University of Cincinnati, where he joined the faculty in 1955 and was awarded tenure in 1957. He left Cincinnati in 1965 to become a member of the Sociology Department at the University of Washington. His Seattle home looked out on the Cascade Mountains, where he often climbed with friends and colleagues, the same mountain that later claimed the life of his teenage son. It was at the University of Washington that he completed his first major theoretical papers on social exchange theory, written in 1967 and later published (1972) in a volume on sociological theories in progress. While this work came to fruition at the University of Washington, the earliest seeds of the theory were evident in his PhD thesis and in two of his most influential pieces, on power-dependence relations, published in 1962 and 1964, just before he left the University of Cincinnati. The 1962 paper, entitled "Power-Dependence Relations," became a citation classic in 1981 due to its enormous influence. We trace some of the influence of this work on the social sciences in the section on the intellectual impact of his work.

The tragedy of his life, which began with the death of his son, followed him throughout his life. He and Pat endured the loss of friends and loved ones, most associated with the tight-knit community of mountain climbers in the Pacific Northwest or with their friends in the remote villages of Pakistan, where the deaths of Sherpas were common, but never easy to accept. Willie Unsoeld, close friend, fellow mountaineer, and colleague at the Evergreen State University in Washington, was killed in an avalanche on Mount Rainier. The Unsoelds lost a daughter, Devi, to the mountains and had endured the long recovery of a son who received serious head injuries from a fall while mountain climbing. Despite the certainty of tragedy in the lives of mountain climbers, Emerson continued to climb until his untimely death in 1982. In fact, during the last year of his life he was deeply engaged in planning for a return trip to Pakistan for a long sojourn in remote mountain villages with his wife. In many ways he was just reaching the peak of his career when he died suddenly on the evening before his daughter, Leslie, was to be married in their living room, with the Cascades looming in the background. Cancer surgery a year earlier had taken its toll, but his death was unexpected.

For a career cut short by premature death, the impact of his work can be judged as even more impressive. His collaborative work with Karen Cook at the University of Washington was just beginning to show fruit, and the graduate students they jointly trained, including Mary Gillmore and Toshio Yamagishi, among others, were just beginning their research careers. It is clear that the impact of his work in the social sciences would have been even greater if he had not died in his late fifties.

One gets a clear image of the heart and soul of Richard Emerson in a passage he wrote in the early stages of his career for a book entitled *The New Professors*, by Bowen (1960). In this chapter he writes about his love of mountains:

> Some of the things I appreciate most for sheer beauty are high alpine mountains, their winding valley glaciers, and foreboding corniced ridges. I love to feel them beneath my feet, when climbing, as well as view them as a painter might…As I ascend the mountain, I can…read from its contours its past and its future, and my climb is placed in grand context. In fact, through the whole experience I am placed in context! And, mind you, people ask me why I climb mountains.

If he had not become a sociologist, he would have become a sculptor, he once admitted. But, whatever his chosen vocation, he would have never given up the mountains he loved and that had been the primary source of his self-worth even as a child.

In this chapter we focus on his academic work and its impact. For the record, he was also a formidable photographer, whose stark photos of sheer mountain ridges, snowcapped peaks at the top of the world, and close-up shots of the mountain people he loved and their villages are mainly unpublished, except for some that appear in various Sierra Club publications. This black and white legacy of unique pictures that chronicle various expeditions and social reality in remote locations may one day also prove to be a significant contribution to social science. Several of these photos hung for years in the Commons Room in the Department of Sociology at the University of Washington. Before discussing more fully the impact of his scholarly work, we will comment briefly on the social and intellectual context that influenced both the style and content of his research.

THE SOCIAL AND INTELLECTUAL CONTEXT

Richard Emerson was one of the large number of men who entered academia after the Second World War, supported by the GI Bill. Many in this cohort of scholars have now retired or passed away. As with most of his contemporaries, his graduate training was influenced by the Second World War and the research that had been funded during and following the war. As Cartwright (1979) noted in his review of the development of the field of social psychology, the Second World War had an enormous impact on the social sciences as researchers attempted to come to terms with the rise of Hitler and the events that precipitated the war. Common topics of research were authoritarianism, styles of leadership, group solidarity, loyalty, conformity and obedience, nationalism, and power. Emerson was influenced by these trends in his own graduate training, which spanned the disciplines of sociology and psychology. In his early career he studied leadership and social influence.

While at the University of Cincinnati he was jointly an assistant professor of sociology and a senior research associate in psychiatry, where he collaborated on a variety of projects on family relations. In this role he developed the Cincinnati Family Relations Inventory. He also participated with many other influential social psychologists in the leadership training that was offered at the National Training Laboratory at Bethel, Maine. Here he was trained not only in the science of leadership, but also in the practice of developing leadership skills. This laboratory was established with funding after the war to determine the factors that promoted the development in society of good leadership. In part, all these efforts nationwide were derivative of the deep political concerns that had emerged during the war over the rise of Hitler, a man who was able to lead a nation to tolerate genocide in the name of nationalism.

For over two decades after the Second World War, the field of social psychology can be said to have been in its heyday. Funding poured into universities and research and training centers in order to produce a science of human behavior and social dynamics. Much of the funding came from military-related sources like ARPA (Advanced Research Projects Agency) and the Navy (ONR – Office of Naval Research). NIMH (National Institute of Mental Health) and NSF (National Science Foundation) were also strong funding sources for social science. This stream of research carried the academics trained right after the war through the early stages of their careers, which coincided with the expansion of university education in the United States. During the 1950s and 1960s most universities and colleges were in expansionist mode and departments hired many of the PhDs that had been produced as a result of the GI Bill and other efforts to induce students to obtain graduate degrees and become college teachers. This growth was also fueled by the need to educate the "baby-boom" children, the largest cohorts of children the United States had known. The earliest boomers, born just after the war in 1946 and later, began entering higher education in the early 1960s. Emerson's career spanned these events.

Another significant component of the social and intellectual context in which Emerson's work was carried out was the strong emphasis placed on sociology as a science and social psychology, in particular, as a scientific subdiscipline. Logical positivism was making inroads into the social sciences in the late 1950s and the early 1960s, with the rising popularity in some sociological circles of the work of Popper (1961), Kuhn (1963), Hempel (1965), and others. This work emphasized the general theoretical strategy of deductive theorizing, the formulation of abstract theoretical principles that could be used along with clearly defined concepts to derive predictions that could be tested empirically. Emerson's training in sociological theory and experimental work in psychology made this form of theory development natural for him. It is most evident in his major theoretical pieces, "Exchange Theory, Parts I and II," written in 1967 and published subsequently in 1972. This formulation is described in greater detail in the section below. Here we will comment only on the general intellectual climate in the social sciences that influenced his work at the time this work was produced. Of course, not all sociologists trained during this same time frame were drawn to deductive theorizing.

Other more specialized influences on his substantive work can be traced to his mentors and the work of his colleagues at Cincinnati and Washington. At Minnesota, Don Martindale introduced Richard Emerson to general sociological theory and the significant philosophy of social science debates of the time. Stanley Schachter, one of his MA thesis advisors, trained him in experimental methods and the empirical investigation of hypotheses derived from theoretical propositions. As mentioned above, he also worked at Cincinnati on the development of various tools for empirically investigating family relations (i.e. the inventory and computer-based scoring system he helped to develop), and here he was exposed to small groups and leadership training. His contacts with social scientists outside of sociology at the University of Cincinnati were also influential in the development of his theoretical work on power. Alfred Kuhn, an economist at the University of Cincinnati, once informed Karen Cook that he and Richard Emerson had had many productive conversations about theoretical work in the social sciences, the philosophy of science, and general theories of power and exchange as colleagues. Kuhn's major work, *The Study of Society: A Unified Approach*, published in 1963, gives evidence of this cross-fertilization.

At the University of Washington, Emerson was influenced by his colleagues in the sociology department, especially those who were involved with him in the social psychology program, one of the most nationally visible programs in this subfield. The faculty involved with this program included Frank Miyamoto, Otto Larsen, Phillip Blumstein, Robert Leik, David Schmitt, and Robert Burgess. Long conversations over coffee about behaviorism with Bob Burgess and Dave Schmitt drew Emerson's attention to the developments in the empirical investigation of human behavior from a behaviorist perspective. During the 1960s behaviorism was growing as a result of the influence of B. F. Skinner (see, especially, *About Behaviorism*, 1974) and others who were charismatic and very optimistic about the development of a science of behavior. This theoretical development coincided with the growth of interest in the philosophy of social science and with the debate over the importation of natural science models and modes of theorizing into the social sciences. Together, these developments generated widespread optimism in the potential for producing a science of human behavior. It was against this backdrop that Emerson formulated his own theory of social behavior while at the University of Washington.

George Homans was the first social exchange theorist to explore the implications of behaviorism for the study of social interaction, but Emerson is noted for his more extensive treatment of behaviorism as the natural foundation for a theory of social exchange. These principles were spelled out in his chapter entitled, "Exchange Theory, Part I: A Psychological Basis for Social Exchange." This piece reflects both the formal deductive theorizing he had come to value and his attempt to provide a more developed micro-level theory of behavior based on the scientific principles being produced at that time by behaviorists like his colleague Robert Burgess. This informal influence, noted in a footnote in Emerson's chapter, was more formally acknowledged in a paper published by Emerson in a collection of readings on human social behavior edited by Burgess and Bushell (1969). Burgess and Emerson also co-taught for a while the undergraduate lecture class on social psychology at the University of Washington, which stimulated further cross-fertilization of ideas.

In 1972, Karen Cook joined the Department of Sociology at the University of Washington, attracted to the department by the strength of the social psychology program and the opportunity to work with Richard Emerson, to whose work she had been exposed in her own graduate training at Stanford University, where she was influenced by mentors Joseph Berger, Bernard P. Cohen and Morris Zelditch, who also emphasized training in formal theory, deductive models, and experimental methods. In 1973, Cook and Emerson collaborated in the development of a long-term program of research funded by the National Science Foundation to test empirically propositions derived from Emerson's theory of social exchange, focusing special attention on the development of a theory of the distribution of power in exchange networks. In addition, Cook and Emerson developed the first computer-based laboratory in sociology for the study of social exchange. This work is described more fully in the theory section. This fruitful collaboration continued until Emerson's death in 1982. Karen S. Cook continued this program of research with the help of several former students and collaborators, including Mary R. Gillmore (University of Washington), Toshio Yamagishi (Hokkaido University), Karen A. Hegtvedt (Emory), Jodi O'Brien (Seattle University), Peter Kollock (UCLA), and Joseph Whitmeyer (UNC, Charlotte).

The collaboration with Karen Cook led to the introduction of more cognitive concepts to the theory of social exchange that Emerson had developed, and a gradual move away from the behavioristic model that had been the hallmark of his original theoretical work. In addition, her work on equity and distributive justice influenced the research by introducing into their joint theoretical work concerns over fairness and equity, returning to some of the normative aspects of social exchange addressed only briefly by Homans and more extensively by Blau. The behavioral formulation was subsequently developed and advanced significantly by the work of Linda Molm, trained at the University of North Carolina, primarily by Jim Wiggins, a behaviorist. She developed a systematic theory of exchange originally based explicitly on the behavioral principles developed by Emerson in his early work, and in a very intensive program of experimental research she first explored the use of power in what she terms reciprocal, as opposed to negotiated, exchanges (Molm, 1997). In the development of social exchange theory it is clear that social networks linking the investigators and their collaborators and students have had significant influence. A more complete analysis of the ties among the various actors who subsequently developed Emerson's work is beyond the scope of this chapter. However, it is important to acknowledge that a large part of the social and intellectual context in which a theorist works is social relations including those with colleagues and students who influence his or her work.

Jonathan Turner (1986) clearly articulated the specific nature of Emerson's sociological contributions and the intellectual significance of his landmark pieces on power-dependence relations (1962, 1964) and social exchange theory (1972, parts I and II). In his evaluation of exchange theory in the late 1980s Turner argued that Emerson had resolved one of the key difficulties in developing exchange theory to apply across levels of analysis, with the introduction of the idea of connected exchange relations forming networks of exchange. For Turner, this obviated the need to develop ever more complex conceptions of exchange as the nature of the social unit shifted from an individual to a group, organization, or large social system, a hallmark of Blau's formulation. In Emerson's theory the "actors" could be individuals or corporate actors involved in networks of exchange (see Cook and Whitmeyer, 1992).

THE THEORY

Scientists know that, no matter how brilliant their theories, no matter how accurate their explanations, eventually their work will be improved upon and even superseded, no longer consulted directly. The most important scientists have impact not so much through the particular content of their theories, but through changing other scientists' perspectives. They introduce new concepts or reconceptualize old ones in new ways. They fashion new perspectives or ways of looking at familiar phenomena, raising a host of new questions that lead to the rapid development of new theoretical formulations. Their legacy is an approach, concepts, questions.

Richard Emerson is such a scientist, and he contributed much in the way of theory and explanations, but, even more importantly, presented a new way of conceiving and studying an old concept, social power. His approach to social power and subsequently social exchange has led to a large program of research and theory development within sociology and at the same time has informed and enhanced analysis in a variety of substantive areas of social science. Of his specific theoretical formulations, some are still used, some have been modified, and some have been superseded. His approach, however, will always be an essential part of social theory.

Emerson's legacy to social theory can be divided into three areas: theoretical approach, theoretical substance, and methodological approach. As with most scientists, during his life he and his collaborators and colleagues were occupied primarily with the second of these, theoretical substance. He worked to develop theories that offered explanations for particular social phenomena, to test these theoretical formulations, and to improve them, based on empirical research. In retrospect, however, his legacy in the other two areas has been equally important. Naturally, these three areas – approach, substance, and methodology – are intertwined in his work, and so they are in our description of it.

Emerson's most important contribution is his approach to social power. This approach is distinctive for several reasons. First, he believed that power could be quantified and measured and thus analyzed rigorously, even mathematically. As a result, his analytic theory of power could be tested through experiments. Second, he argued that a theory of power must be based on a conception of the nature of the social relations in which power is embedded. Third, the theory of power should include a behavioral model of the actor. These features of his perspective can be applied more generally than just to social power, but are key to Emerson's approach to the analysis of power relations.

Social power is a useful concept. It has been employed by major social thinkers for centuries: Machiavelli, Marx, and Weber, to name just three. Lay people commonly use the term to explain certain social outcomes, whether on the scale of countries or within small informal groups. Nevertheless its scientific use has been hampered by its lack of formalization and quantification. George Homans, co-pioneer along with Peter Blau and Richard Emerson of the exchange perspective in sociology, also discussed power and influence in a deductive framework. Emerson, however, took the crucial step of defining power as a quantifiable, measurable concept. This had two beneficial consequences. Theory could become formal and mathematical, with a gain in precision over purely verbal reasoning and deduction. In addition, empirical measures of power could be devised so that theoretical results could be tested.

The step of formalizing social power was taken in Emerson's 1962 article, "Power-Dependence Relations." The power of actor A over actor B is equated to the dependence of actor B on actor A:

$$Pab = Dba \tag{1}$$

The dependence of B on A in turn is a positive function of the "motivational investment" of B in "goals mediated by" A and a negative function of the "availability of those goals" to B outside the A–B relation (Emerson, 1962: 32). In this early work, it appears that Emerson takes equation (1) to be a theoretical postulate, with power and dependence considered at least conceptually distinct, rather than a definition of power. The fact that Emerson (1964) experimentally tests this equation suggests this as well. However, by 1972 apparently Emerson considers equation (1) to be a *definition* of power ("*Power* is redundant and unnecessary in this scheme, given our conception of dependence"; Emerson, 1972: 64). Some subsequent researchers, such as Pfeffer and Salancik (1978) and Molm (1997), likewise have taken equation (1) to be a definition and a measure of power.

Two crucial aspects of equation (1) are that power is a property of a *relation*; and that power is a *potential*. A more precise way of stating the first aspect is that an actor's power is not simply a property of that actor, but rather it has a referent, namely the other actor. The second aspect means that power exists prior to behavior and behavioral outcomes. It, therefore, can affect those outcomes. Moreover, power itself can be affected by factors such as aspects of social structure and characteristics of the actors (status, gender, etc.). The analysis of what causes and affects power is separate from and analytically prior to analysis of how power and other factors affects behavior.

An important and influential part of Emerson's power-dependence theory is his identification of *balancing operations*. He calls an exchange relation in which power (and dependence) is unequal *unbalanced*. Then, in view of the two variables that affect dependence, Emerson suggests four possible balancing operations, that is, processes that will make power more equal in unbalanced relations. Suppose A is more powerful than B; that is, $Pab > Pba$ and $Dba > Dab$. To balance this relation: (a) B can reduce the level of motivational investment in goals mediated by A ("withdrawal"); (b) B can come up with alternative sources (e.g. actor C) for those goals mediated by A ("network extension"); (c) B can increase A's motivational investment in goals B mediates (e.g. through "status-giving"); or (d) B can work to eliminate A's alternative sources for the goals B mediates (e.g. by engaging in coalition formation with other actors, in particular, other suppliers).

Emerson's approach to social power as developed in his 1972 theoretical formulation entails the conception of social interaction as exchange. Thus, this theory falls into two traditions in social science, the study of social power and what is sometimes called exchange theory. In fact, Emerson terms his general approach *social exchange theory*. As Emerson (1972: 39) notes, "My initial reason for beginning the work set forth in these two chapters was to formulate a more encompassing (and hopefully enriching) framework around previous work on power-dependence relations." This marriage of a relational conception of power and the study of social exchange relations was the key move that made Emerson's formulation so influential subsequently, along with the extension of his dyadic framework to incorporate networks of exchange.

Emerson then took the methodological step, largely unprecedented in sociology for research on social power, of testing his theoretical propositions with laboratory experiments using human subjects. Such experiments test theory by investigating hypotheses derived from the theory for the particular conditions of the laboratory experiment. Laboratory experiments may not be suitable for testing explanations of natural phenomena (for development of this argument see Zelditch, 1969, 2007). Just as in the physical sciences, however, they are ideal for *theory*-testing because factors exogenous to the theory can be controlled. Support for hypotheses derived from theoretical principles for specific experimental conditions usually provides unambiguous support for those principles. This is difficult to achieve outside the laboratory, because social processes are rarely isolated in any social context and, therefore, findings obtained using other methodologies often have alternative interpretations or somewhat ambiguous meaning. (Of course, this can also happen in poorly designed experimental studies.)

Experimental tests of power-dependence theory were possible for two reasons. First, the mathematical definition of dependence allowed it to be created and measured in the laboratory. Second, by conceiving of social interaction as exchange, it was possible to test the theoretical propositions by creating a setting for exchange through experimental design. The theory explicitly applies to exchange with reference to any goals or resources. Thus, experimentally convenient exchange could be used (see also Molm, 1997, on this point). Emerson published his first experimental tests supporting power-dependence theory in 1964.

In a two-part work dating from 1967, but published only in 1972, Emerson builds his social exchange theory by extending his analysis of power and dependence in exchange relations in two directions. Part I presents a basis in behavioral psychology for power-dependence theory. In his earlier work, Emerson did little more than assert the relationship between dependence and motivational investment in mediated goals and availability of alternatives, respectively. Here he derives those relationships from the principles of behaviorism.

"Exchange Theory, Part II: Exchange Relations and Network Structures" contains the crucial extension from exchange relations to exchange networks that is the basis for most of the remaining work of his career. A few definitions are important. An exchange relation is conceived in part I as a "temporal series" containing opportunities for exchange, which, he argues, evoke initiations of exchange that in turn produce or result in transactions. An *exchange network* is a set of actors linked together directly or indirectly through exchange relations. An actor is then conceived as "a point where many exchange relations connect" (Emerson, 1972: 57). More specifically, two exchange relations between actors A and B (represented as A–B) and between actors B and C (B–C) are *connected* at actor B if they share actor B and if transactions in one relation are somehow related to transactions in the other relation. Note that this is a specialized definition: a connection exists not between actors but between exchange relations. A connection between two exchange relations is either *positive* or *negative*. Suppose two exchange relations are connected. If exchange in one relation is positively related, in frequency or magnitude, to exchange in the other relation, the connection is *positive*. In this case, if A–B and B–C are positively connected exchange relations, for example, an increase in the frequency of A–B exchange could result in an increase in the frequency of B–C exchange. If exchange in one relation is negatively related, in frequency or magnitude, to exchange in the other relation, the connection is *negative*. In the case in which the A–B and B–C relations are negatively connected, an increase in the frequency of A–B exchange could result in a decrease in the frequency of B–C exchange. An example is the situation in which A and C are alternative dating partners for B. Finally, a negatively connected exchange network is *intra-category* if the resources any network member provides could substitute for the resources any other network member provides (such as friendship in a friendship network). A negatively connected network that is not intra-category is *cross-category* (such as a network of heterosexually dating people).

Ironically, given more recent developments, Emerson considered a move toward economic theory as the basis for his version of exchange theory, which was the strategy Blau had adopted, but he dismissed this idea by arguing that operant psychology provided a more "social" micro-level basis for the theory. The primary reason was that he viewed the social relation as the major focus of the theory (and the social structures created through the formation of exchange relations). That is, the focus was the relatively enduring interactions between particular actors rather than what he viewed as the dominant focus in economics at that time, the transaction in which actors were perfectly interchangeable. This fit with the primary task of developing an approach in which social structure was the major dependent variable. In part I, Emerson (1972: 41) states clearly that his purpose is to "address social structure and structural change within the framework of exchange theory." It was clear from this statement that Emerson was interested in both the causes as well as the consequences of the social structures created by relations of social exchange.

Before presenting descriptions of what he termed prototypical exchange network structures, Emerson developed several key concepts that define the factors that are significant in understanding exchange relations. These include reciprocity, balance, cohesion, power, and power-balancing operations. *Reciprocity*, for Emerson, was little more than a description of the contingencies intrinsic to all human social exchange, not an explanation. Norms of obligation emerge to reinforce this feature of social exchange, but they are not necessary as an explanation of continued exchange. The reinforcement principles and their link to initiation of exchange provide sufficient explanation for the continuity or extinction of exchange relations in this framework. In this sense Emerson's work had much in common with Homans's (1961) original emphasis on the "sub-institutional" or elementary social behavior, focusing on the explanation of the behavior that preceded that which was "enshrined" in norms.

Balance in an exchange relation is reflected in any difference in initiation probabilities. An exchange relation is balanced if $Dab = Dba$. That is, the relation is balanced if both parties are equally dependent on the other for exchange (i.e. for resources or services of value). The concept of balance is critical in the original formulation of power-dependence relations, because it set the stage for understanding the "balancing operations" Emerson developed to explain changes in exchange relations and the structure of networks.

Cohesion represents the "strength" of the exchange relation or its propensity to survive conflict and the costs associated with the impact of what Emerson called "external events." Relational cohesion was represented in the 1972 chapters as the *average dependence* of the two actors in the relation. It could range from a low level of mutual dependence to a much higher level, typically indicating a strong bond. Subsequently, Molm (1985) and others (e.g. Lawler *et al.*, 1988) have come to refer to this concept as average total power (or simply total power). The concept represents how much is at stake in the relation (not the relative power of each actor within the exchange relation, which is treated separately in further developments in the theory). Power is defined straightforwardly in this work as based on dependence, as indicated above, and this definition becomes the basis for specifying the various possible "balancing operations" available to actors in imbalanced exchange relations.

To conclude the 1972 work, Emerson used these definitions together with the theoretical apparatus he had built involving power, dependence, and balancing processes to predict changes in exchange networks. Examples are as follows. Actors who are weak because they are rivals or competitors in a negatively connected network tend either to specialize or to form a coalition. If they specialize they develop what is effectively a new division of labor, each providing a distinct resource. If they form a coalition they have merged to form a "collective actor" in the network, which then must operate as one. The coalition can drive a harder bargain since former competitors are now in collaboration with one another.

Intra-category exchange networks (or networks in which only one dominant kind of resource is exchanged, such as approval) tend to change until they are closed, meaning that social circles get formed and the boundaries are maintained. Such closed social circles, like socially exclusive clubs, are often difficult for new members to penetrate. Under certain circumstances, intra-category networks tend to become stratified, with closed classes of distinct actors. Here Emerson's theory becomes quite speculative in an effort to examine how networks become stratified, forming classes differentiated by resource magnitude. Both intraclass exchange and interclass exchange are investigated as elements in the emergence of stratified exchange networks. Tentative theoretical principles were developed to explain, for example, the tendency for initiations of exchange to "flow upward" in interclass exchange and for transactions within such relations to be consummated from above. Many of these theoretical insights embedded in the text of part II of Emerson's formulation have never been fully developed theoretically or investigated empirically, nor have the rudimentary notions of norm formation and groups as exchange systems been elaborated (an exception is the work of Stolte, 1987).

In 1978 and 1983, Emerson and his colleague Karen Cook, together with former students Mary Gillmore and Toshio Yamagishi in the case of the 1983 paper, published two papers that extend the theory to the analysis of exchange networks and present experimental tests of those extensions (Cook and Emerson, 1978; Cook et al., 1983). From power-dependence theory it follows that, all else being equal, actors who have more alternatives for obtaining their goals will be less dependent on individual partners and thus have more power. Thus, in a negatively connected network, actors who have more partners with whom they can engage in full exchange will have more power. Theoretically, in such cases access to alternatives increases the availability of the resources of value (or goals to be obtained through exchange).

Assuming that to have power is to use it (Emerson, 1972), this proposition can be tested by measuring power use. Use of power in an exchange relation entails obtaining terms of exchange more favorable to oneself. The more powerful actor in an exchange relation, therefore, should obtain more favorable terms of exchange. Exchange as operationalized in the 1978 and 1983 experiments consists of negotiating the terms of trade between two parties (or more) for resources of value that are converted into monetary payoffs at the end of the experiment. Assuming actors use their power, the more powerful actor in an exchange relation should obtain a larger share of the valuable resources to be exchanged; that is, receive more points than the partner.

The two experiments in the 1978 papers involve four-actor, fully linked networks. That is, each actor has exchange opportunities with the other three. In the experiment on the balanced network, all linked pairs were equivalent: all could obtain resources of similar value in exchanges with their trading partners (i.e. no actor had resources of greater value than the others). In the experiment on the unbalanced network one of the four actors offered a more valuable resource and thus was the more desirable exchange partner (the transaction was worth a total of 24 units of profit); exchanges between the other actors involved resources of similar, but lower, value (these transactions were worth a total of eight units of profit). In the unbalanced network, the actor with the more valuable resource was the best alternative for his or her partners, thus giving that actor the most power according to the theory. This prediction was supported. Not only did the powerful actor gain significantly more points than its partners, but he or she also gained significantly more points than any of the positionally equivalent actors in the power-balanced network.

The 1983 article is a natural extension of the theory to larger networks, but at the same time enters a new domain. In the 1978 article, the four-actor exchange network was simply the context for tests of predictions from power-dependence theory. In the 1983 article, network structure became an interesting factor in its own right, reflecting the growing interest in network analysis in the discipline at large. The network studied consisted of five actors, no longer fully linked, but linked in a ring, so that

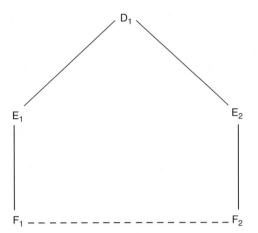

Figure 8.1

each actor had only two potential trading partners (see Figure 8.1). One of the five exchange relations was not very profitable (the transaction total was worth only eight points, as opposed to 24 units of profit in each of the other four potential trading relations). If we ignore that low-profitability relation (which concerns F_1 and F_2), we have a line (sometimes called "Line5") of five actors and four exchange relations, F_1–E_1–D_1–E_2–F_2. Previous theory on social networks at that time had supposed that *centrality* confers the most power and, thus, that D_1 would be most powerful in the network operationalized in this experiment. The 1983 study, however, used power-dependence theory to predict that if such a network were negatively connected, actors E_1 and E_2 would emerge as the most powerful actors.

The power-dependence reasoning was as follows. In each exchange relation, a partner with no alternatives will be more dependent and therefore less powerful than a partner with more alternatives (or technically greater availability of the resources of value). The *F*s, therefore, will be less powerful than the *E*s. D_1 has two alternatives, but because they have weak alternatives from whom they can obtain favorable outcomes, D_1 is more dependent on them than they are on D_1. As a result, D_1 is forced to reduce offers or demands down to the level of the *F*s to compete. Experimental results supported these general hypotheses, as has subsequent research in a number of research traditions including the work of Willer (see Willer, 1999) and his colleagues.

As is common in scientific investigation testing theoretical principles, the experiments reported in the 1978 and 1983 articles were designed to provide clear tests of theory, not to be instances of substantively important exchange phenomena. As a result, many of the substantive features of these experiments are not theoretically crucial. They are operationalizations of theoretical concepts, for which theory therefore makes precise predictions, which in turn can be evaluated as tests of theory. Thus, exchange is operationalized as coming to negotiated agreement over an exchange of resources (or profit points); "motivational investment" is operationalized as the conversion of points to money (at a constant rate); and negativity is operationalized by allowing each actor only one exchange per round. Many of these aspects of experimental design are not common in natural situations (e.g. one exchange per round), but they instantiate the theoretical concepts in ways easy to control and measure, and therefore permit clear tests of the theory. Thus tested and supported, the theory can then be applied to more complicated natural situations of exchange and exchange networks.

The 1983 paper also inaugurated two general trends in subsequent research on exchange networks. First, it presented computer simulation results for four networks: the Line5 and networks with seven, ten, and thirteen actors. Note again that in order to test the theory of exchange networks, exchange network experiments are designed to focus actors on a single goal: profit maximization. It is easy to embody this goal in simulations by incorporating simple procedures by which simulated actors pursue it. Simulations can thus show whether many actors simultaneously following these procedures produce the results that the theory of exchange networks predicts. Simulation results thus will be valid to the extent that the incorporated procedures match those followed by natural actors.

Second, the paper also presented an algorithm for determining the distribution of power in a negatively connected exchange network directly from the network structure. This algorithm was grounded loosely in power-dependence reasoning. However, application of the algorithm involved only analysis of the network structure and did not use power-dependence theory or models of actor behavior explicitly. This particular algorithm quickly came to be perceived as inadequate. However, many researchers later followed the lead of this paper in seeing it desirable to have such a structural-level algorithm, and have devised others that were more adequate, especially for more complex exchange networks (see the section on impact for citations to this work).

Emerson's last paper, which he did not complete before his death in 1982, was published in 1987 in an incomplete state. It is entitled, "Toward a Theory of Value in Social Exchange." As he notes in this paper, however, "A theory of value must be a theory of actors" (Emerson, 1987: 14). He attempts in this formulation to present a more complete model of the (human) actor than that used in his earlier theoretical work of 1962 and 1972. Here he is filling in important remaining lacunae in those theories, just as in his 1972 publications he went back and filled in a deductive basis for his 1962 work on power-dependence theory.

Value – that is, the relative importance actors place (behaviorally) on obtaining certain goals or resources – is crucial to both power-dependence theory and to its extension into a theory of exchange networks. For example, the first and third of the four balancing operations in a relationship of unequal dependence involve changes of value. Suppose B is more dependent on A than the reverse. B can decrease the value to itself of the goals A mediates or attempt to increase the value to A of the goals B mediates. The values of the resources to be obtained by network members also are integral to the categorization of different types of networks. A *negative* exchange connection exists when two members value the resources provided by a common partner, or when they provide resources that are substitutable for those valued by the common partner (a characteristic of the partner's values) and on which the partner satiates (i.e. "needs" no more). An intra-category network is one in which all network members place equal value on the resources available from other network members.

In these theories, however, two important simplifications are made concerning human actors – or, to put it differently, the scope of those theories is limited in two ways. First, the theories of power-dependence and exchange networks concern actors interested in but one or perhaps a few goals (or resources of value). Yet human actors are complex, having a variety of different things (goals) they value to different extents, with those values interrelated in complicated ways. A theory of social exchange and social power will become more useful to the extent that it can relax those restrictions and thus apply to situations in which a fuller panoply of goals is relevant.

Second, in those theories the values of different actors simply are given, without being explained. In 1972 Emerson wrote, and italicized, "In this chapter we will not presume to know the needs and motives of men," followed by, "We will see how far we can go on this skimpy basis" (Emerson, 1972: 44). Clearly, filling out some of this skimpiness would add to the scope and power of the theory. Understanding how value is created and changed clearly would inform our understanding of how and when the first (withdrawal) and third (e.g. status-giving) balancing operations are likely to occur. It also would provide for a theory of formation and change in the various types of exchange networks as values change (Whitmeyer, 1999) to complement the more structural theories of network change.

The Impact of Emerson's Work

Emerson's influence on contemporary social science falls into two main areas: work stemming from his original formulation of power-dependence theory and research based on his work on social exchange and exchange networks. Emerson's work on power and dependence itself has been carried forward in two directions: the theoretical investigation of power and more substantive studies of a wide variety of social phenomena. First, his approach has been incorporated into the development of general theory concerning social power. Many power theorists take a more general view, either conceiving of power more broadly or considering social processes in addition to exchange. Thus, Emerson's exchange perspective, in which power exists through dependence in an exchange relation, is included alongside other processes such as persuasion and legitimate authority (see, e.g. Wrong, 1988; Coleman, 1990; Friedkin, 1993b).

Second, Emerson's approach has found application in studies of a wide variety of social phenomena. Interactional dynamics in all types of settings frequently involve exchange and power. To the extent that power and power use is responsible for outcomes, Emerson's approach proves useful in analysis and explanation. Substantive areas of study in which it has been applied successfully include marriage and family dynamics, marketing, legal studies, deviance, geopolitics, and especially organizations.

Power-dependence theory is a cornerstone of one of the dominant perspectives in organizational studies, known as the *resource dependence* perspective (e.g. Pfeffer and Salancik, 1978). According to this perspective, organizations need a variety of resources from both outside and within the organization. Those entities – individuals, subunits, or other organizations – that exclusively provide the most needed resources will have the most power over or in the organization. This key postulate comes directly from the principle embodied in equation (1), although resource dependence theorists point out that for power actually to be exerted other elements are also necessary.

Because organizations are not self-sufficient, they must engage in exchanges with other organizations and entities in their environments to assure survival. Organizations, therefore, spend much of their time and energy involved in efforts to manage these strategic dependencies. As Scott (1992: 115) argues, "One of the major contributions of the resource dependency perspective is to discern and describe the strategies – ranging from buffering to diversification and merger – employed by organizations to change and adapt to the environment." An early treatment of these strategic options was presented in the work of James D. Thompson (1967) in his influential book, *Organizations in Action*. The application of power-dependence theory to the analysis of organizational exchange and interorganizational relations was pursued by Cook (1977) and subsequently by Cook and Emerson (1984). This work is also reflected in subsequent developments in the field of organizations. Many of the strategies available to organizations to manage their critical dependencies can be understood in terms of the balancing operations spelled out in power-dependence theory, because the goal is to acquire necessary resources without increasing dependence. Such strategies include, under different circumstances, joint venture, long-term contracting, specialization, consolidation, reduction in production arenas, and vertical integration of various types, among others. As Scott (1992: 193) puts it, "Unequal exchange relations can generate power and dependency differences among organizations, causing them to enter into exchange relations cautiously and to pursue strategies that will enhance their own bargaining position."

The work of Emerson and his colleagues has continued to inform research and theory development following the resource dependence perspective on organizations. Seabright, Levinthal, and Fichman (1992), for example, studied auditor–client relationships and found that as the fit between auditor and client declined, the likelihood of this relationship dissolving increased, as the resource dependence perspective predicts. The tendency to dissolve was attenuated, however, by the development of attachment (or commitment) between individuals – a development first predicted by Emerson and his collaborator Karen Cook (see Cook and Emerson, 1978).

Power-dependence theory as well as its descendent, the theory of exchange networks, has contributed also to the network perspective on organizations. Using power-dependence theory (Emerson, 1962; Cook and Emerson, 1978), Mizruchi (1989) expected and found that economic dependence and interdependence among businesses leads to similarity in their political behavior. Chok (2009) examined the situation and behavior of firms regulated by the Food and Drug Administration (FDA). Regulated firms often seek access to the regulator (the FDA) through the scientific advisors, taken from research institutions, the FDA uses. To the extent that a firm is ultimately dependent on the regulator, a tie through an advisor makes a firm dependent on that person and gives the person power over the firm, as power-dependence theory predicts. Also as the theory predicts, balancing operations are likely: Chok finds that the more dependent a firm is on the regulator, the more likely it is to employ a Scientific Advisory Board (SAB), which provides the firm with multiple ties to the regulator and, thus, lessens the power any particular individual has over the firm.

A number of studies have combined Burt's (1992) theory of structural holes with Emerson's (1962) power-dependence theory. A structural hole is a disconnection between two subnetworks, for example, two mutually exclusive, internally connected sets of employees in an organization. The theory of structural holes posits that an actor who fills that structural hole gains power in the network by so doing. This fits the power-dependence principle: to the extent that one subnetwork values resources, such as information, from the other subnetwork, it will be dependent on the actor filling the hole, thereby giving the actor power in much the same way as brokers gain power when linking actors with resources of mutual value (Marsden, 1982). More recently, Gargiulo *et al.* (2009), for example, studied informal exchanges between investment bankers in the equities division of a large financial services firm in 2001. They found that increased network density, that is, the absence of structural holes, hurts individuals who provide information and benefits individuals who seek information. The former have less power as redundant ties mean that others have less dependence on them, while the latter, correspondingly, have less of a power disadvantage.

Various organizational theorists also have extended the analysis of networks to the study of organizations and the role of networks more broadly in the economy (see especially Lincoln *et al.*, 1992; Powell, 1990; Sabel, 1991; Gerlach, 1992). Networks are examined as they affect labor practices, informal influence, ethnic enterprises, the organization of business groups, and the networking of companies across national boundaries (see Powell and Smith-Doerr, 1994, for a review). More recently, Emerson's power-dependence and exchange network theories have been applied to cross-sector collaborations between corporations and social enterprises (Di Domenico *et al.*, 2009) and to links between websites on the Internet (Gonzalez-Bailon, 2009). Central to these efforts is the attempt to analyze the relative power of the economic actors in the network and the strategies used to enhance network-wide power or to alter the distribution of power within the network. The focus of attention is on the structural location of the actors in the network and how that influences strategy. Exchange theory and the resource dependence perspective (e.g. Pfeffer and Salancik, 1978) based on power-dependence arguments are commonly used as the framework for analysis in these investigations of economic impact. Other topics of investigation include strategic alliances, collaborative manufacturing enterprises, vertical integration of firms, interlocking directorates, network diffusion of innovative practices, and mergers.

In the field of marketing too, theory has been developed from applying the theoretical ideas of Emerson, Cook, and colleagues to organizations. Cook and Emerson (1978) themselves pointed out the relevance of exchange networks to marketing, noting, for example, that vertically integrated markets and channels of distribution in fact are positively connected networks. In a recent article, Luo *et al.* (2009), studying buyer–supplier partnerships in China, found that relationship-specific investment, which strengthens the attachment, reduced the use of power in the relationship and increased the amount of commitment and cooperation. Anderson *et al.* (1994) discuss *business networks*, defined as two or more connected relations between businesses, each business conceived as a collective actor. One of their key propositions is that each firm in a network will develop a *network identity*. This identity has three dimensions: an orientation toward other actors, competence, and power. The last of these, power, is a function of an actor's resources and its network context, following Emerson, Cook, and colleagues. In examination of two case studies, Anderson *et al.*

note contrasting effects of positive and negative exchange connections. Further exploration of these cases led Anderson *et al.* to suggest mechanisms, typically involving network identity, that lead to changes over time in relations and connections in business networks.

In the area of family studies, power-dependence theory has contributed fruitfully to an understanding of the dynamics of relationships both within families and between family members and outsiders. In the study of dating couples, partners, and married people, various authors have applied exchange concepts to the analysis of the longevity and quality of such relationships despite the argument that an exchange "logic" does not work in close, personal relations. Michaels *et al.* (1984), for example, find that exchange outcomes are a more important predictor of relationship satisfaction than are equity concerns. Sprecher's (1988) research indicates that relationship commitment is affected more by the level of rewards available to partners in alternative relations than by fairness or equity considerations, although there is also evidence in various studies that fairness does matter (see review by Hegtvedt and Cook, 2001). Van de Rijt and Macy (2006) focus specifically on sexual activity in intimate relationships and find support for two power-dependence predictions. People whose partners provide them with more sexual favors and people whose partners are less emotionally attached will be more dependent on their partners. Van de Rijt and Macy found support for the predictions that, having less power, such people should provide their partners with more sexual favors. A recent study (Zuo, 2009) uses power-dependence theory to explain how a woman's position in the patriarchal family system in China has tended to improve over her life course as the dependence on her of the family into which she marries increases.

Cook and Donnelly (1996) applied the concepts of longitudinal exchange and generalized exchange relations to intergenerational relations both within the family and within the society at large. Relations between generations can be examined as implicit exchange relations in which each generation must determine how to allocate its resources to the next generation, and on what basis. Reciprocity, trust, dependence, power, fairness, and asymmetry in exchange benefits all play a significant role in these determinations. These dynamics are important within families and relate to social issues like long-term care, child care, elder abuse, health care, and the transfer of wealth. Many of these issues also arise at the aggregate level for the society at large in terms of the nature of the relations between the generations, with implications for property law, taxation, welfare policy, social and health services, and education. Such issues retain their valence during periods of economic recession, as being currently experienced worldwide.

Applications in fields like health care are less common, but interesting. Grembowski *et al.* (1998), for example, examined physician referrals under managed care using an exchange-based model of the nature of the decisions to refer and the network of providers involved in the delivery of health services under different degrees of "managedness." Issues of power and dependence are addressed in this literature at various levels, including the physician–patient relation, the relations between various categories of providers (e.g. physician to physician, primary care provider to specialist, physician to alternative health care provider, and physicians to hospital administrators or other managers within the health care system), and relations between organizational units with involvement in delivery of services (insurance carriers, suppliers of goods and services, other health and community agencies, etc.). Research based on models of exchange and power-dependence principles in the arena of health care continue to hold the promise of providing a more general theory of the processes involved than is currently available. The major shifts that have occurred in the delivery of health care have involved significant changes in the distribution of power among the key players in that organizational system (i.e. the shift in power from relatively autonomous physicians to the hospitals in which they practice and, more directly, to the insurers that pay them). Health care reform and the efforts to block it (e.g. as reflected in the "tea parties" of 2010) are often held hostage to the interests of those in power who stand to lose if reforms increase their dependence on government regulation of the market for health services or other forms of control over the enormous amount of resources at stake in this sector of the economy.

Finally, power-dependence theory also has been applied in the geopolitical realm, to relations between states. Jonathan Turner (1995), for example, proposed that ongoing exchange relations between states lead to balancing operations, as suggested by Emerson (1962, 1972). When dependence is unequal – that is, trade is imbalanced – the more dependent partner will take steps to reduce the imbalance, perhaps even resorting to coercion. A more recent study (Goodliffe and Hawkins, 2009) explains the surprising agreement between countries to strengthen the International Criminal Court as a result of the power some countries gained through other countries' trade dependence on them.

Emerson's fruitful extension of theory and research into exchange networks led to the experimental investigation of exchange networks, which has spawned a very large body of subsequent research that led in a number of different directions. Some research looks much more closely at exchange processes in addition to those Emerson investigated in his relatively brief career as a sociologist. Linda Molm, for example, has developed a highly influential research program into exchange networks in which network members not only can reward (i.e. confer resource gains on) each other, but also can punish (i.e. impose losses on) each other. In her extensive treatment of *coercive* power in social exchange, Molm (1997) presents the results of a ten-year program of experimental research that explores the nature of the effects of coercive power in exchange relations, a form of power that both Emerson and Blau defined as outside the scope of social exchange theory. The surprising finding she addresses in this work is the result that coercion is rarely used even by those in positions of power advantage. The primary reason is that the use of punishment power imposes losses on the exchange partner and raises the cost of the use of power, in terms of both opportunity costs (time better spent in active pursuit of other rewards) and the potential for retaliation. This work has initiated a more complete examination of the dynamics of exchange processes and the role of strategy in determining the outcomes that were viewed primarily in Emerson's work as structurally induced. In addition, in this work Molm was able to extend the underlying model of the actor to incorporate the loss avoidance that is characteristic of actors in many settings in which valued resources or activities are at stake (building on the award-winning work of Kahneman and Tversky, 1979).

Molm (e.g. Molm *et al.*, 2009) also has varied the exchange process by looking at reciprocal exchange, in which partners take turns rewarding or punishing (or not) each other, rather than negotiating the terms of an exchange, in which partners must come to an agreement about who gets what before the transaction is completed. Emerson's experimental research and much of the work that followed the lead of Cook and Emerson (1978) was restricted to negotiated exchange, although the theoretical formulation Emerson developed was not restricted in this manner, and it formed the basis of much of Molm's extensive research on reciprocal exchange (cf. Molm, 2010).

Edward Lawler and his collaborators (e.g. Lawler and Yoon, 1993, 1996; Lawler, Thye and Yoon, 2008) along with other investigators (e.g. Schaefer, 2009) have pursued research that explores in greater depth the notion of an exchange *relation*, that is, a situation of ongoing rather than one-time-only exchange. Lawler builds on the notion, from Emerson's (1962, 1972; Cook and Emerson, 1978) work on power-dependence theory, of *cohesion*, defined as the total dependence (of both partners) in an exchange relation. To this he adds emotional processes, and develops a theory of *commitment* in exchange relations. Not only does this research build on Emerson's work, but it is consistent with the spirit of that work, in its emphasis on an exchange relation as more enduring, and more meaningful for its members, than a simple one-shot economic opportunity for a trade or transaction. A key feature of Lawler's theory of relational exchange is the idea that instrumental exchange relations become transformed over time (based on the nature of the exchange dynamics) in such a way that the relation itself becomes a valued object worthy of commitment and affective orientation. In his studies of gift-giving, for example, he examines this transformation and measures it in terms of the emergence of commitment between exchange partners. A second feature that makes this work interesting is that it explicitly incorporates emotions into the theory (see Lawler, 2001), an aspect that is distinctly missing in Emerson's early work on exchange, but much less so in the work of the anthropologists, such as Mauss and Malinowski, who studied more primitive forms of exchange.

Another variant on exchange processes in exchange networks is *generalized exchange*. Under rules of generalized exchange, actors reward others who are different from the actors who reward them. Generalized exchange is a classic form of "indirect" exchange. The prominent existence of such exchange systems in some societies has been described by anthropologists, such as Malinowski's (1920) treatment of the Kula Ring in the Trobriand Islands. Inspired by these descriptions, Emerson (1981) himself suggested investigation into generalized exchange, but never had the opportunity to pursue it. It was left to his colleagues and former students (e.g. Gillmore, 1987; Yamagishi and Cook, 1993) to conduct the first experimental investigations of this type of exchange network (see also Takahashi, 2001). Frank's (2009) work includes a recent application of the exchange perspective on generalized exchange to teachers giving help to their colleagues.

One interesting feature of many systems of generalized exchange is that they produce *social dilemmas* through the incentive structures they create for network members. Namely, members do better than individuals by not giving to their partners, but if all refuse to give, they all do worse than if they all gave. Thus, we see investigation of exchange networks extending into the domain of social dilemmas, which is a vast area of research in its own right (see Yamagishi, 1995).

Considerable research has been conducted continuing the experimental study of the effect of network structures on power distributions in exchange networks.

Since the late 1980s much of this effort has gone into the development of models to predict accurately the distribution of payoffs among network members given a network structure. Most notably, David Willer and his colleagues have developed a series of algorithms for making such predictions for a wide variety of experimental exchange networks under a variety of experimental rules. Nevertheless, this work claims a theoretical basis in "elementary theory," which is defined as different from and much broader than power-dependence theory. Thus, we will not discuss it in further detail in this piece on Emerson's legacy. This tradition of research is described most completely in Willer's (1999) edited volume entitled, *Network Exchange Theory*. Noah Friedkin's interesting (1992, 1993a) *expected value model* incorporates the notion of actors behaving according to their dependence, and thus has more ties to Emerson's approach to the determination of the distribution of power in exchange networks.

Other approaches use techniques of microeconomic theory, in particular, game theory (e.g. Bienenstock and Bonacich, 1992) and general equilibrium analysis (e.g. Whitmeyer, 1994; Yamaguchi, 1996). Cook and Emerson (1978) note the relevance of microeconomic theory for exchange processes, but suggest that equity theory and power-dependence theory provide a more precise analysis of the social interactions in an exchange *relation*. In essence, the microeconomic models underlying the theory replace the behavioristic models Emerson used to describe basic underlying processes. Bienenstock and Bonacich (1997) point out the strong similarity of a game theoretic solution concept, the *kernel*, to the concept of *equidependence*, developed from Emerson's theory as a tool for predicting exchange network outcomes by Cook and Yamagishi (1992).

Presumably the rationale behind such model-building efforts is the idea that a model that accurately predicts outcomes somehow must capture the essential processes involved. Nevertheless, this research probably has not moved in the direction Emerson might have anticipated. Recall that Emerson came up with an experimental operationalization of exchange networks as a way of testing analytically derived theory. The concentration on predictive models entails a shift from considering experimental exchange networks simply as an operationally convenient way of testing theoretical propositions, to considering them as objects of interest in their own right. This shift also means, however, that less attention has been paid by these investigators to continuing the analytic development of theory concerning power, exchange, and network structure that would be more generally applicable.

Finally, we note numerous topics rooted in Emerson's work that are currently being investigated. These include applications of balancing processes, the role of emotions in exchange, the relationship between fairness assessments and strategy in negotiated and non-negotiated exchange, the nature of commitment and solidarity processes, and the emergence of trust in exchange processes (e.g. Cook, 2005; Molm *et al.*, 2009).

Assessment of Emerson's Legacy

Most social theorists die before the full impact of their work is revealed. Emerson was no exception to this rule. While he was alive in 1981 to learn that his 1962 paper on power-dependence relations had become a citation classic, he did not live long enough to accept the invitation to write about this contribution in his own words. This chapter completes this unfinished business. Nearly thirty years after his untimely death it is easier to assess the nature of the impact of the work Emerson began in the early 1960s. In a few words his 1962 and 1964 pieces fundamentally altered the social science view of power. Power viewed as a relational construct based on dependence is now the common view. It is the way we talk about power in most contexts (short of pure violence) at the individual, organizational, and societal levels. This is reflected in work on power in friendships, marital partnerships, families, organizational subunits or departments, organizations and interorganizational relations, governments in relation to citizens or other entities, and international relations. Examples of applications in some of these arenas have been provided in the section on the influence of Emerson's work.

Related to the impact of his work on power is the extent to which theories about social exchange within the field of sociology now draw on his conception of exchange networks. He was the first exchange theorist in sociology to extend the theory to apply to networks of connected exchange relations. Homans's theoretical work remained primarily at the dyadic and group level. Blau developed an exchange framework that extended into the macro-realm of social life and more complex forms of association, but he did not propose networks as the basis for the extension of exchange concepts beyond the micro-level, as Emerson subsequently did. The significance of this theoretical move, reflected in Turner's prophetic assessment discussed earlier in this chapter, is that it connects exchange theory directly to important developments in the analysis of social networks (a field that has expanded greatly in the past three decades) and to the continuing analysis of new forms of social and formal organization (e.g. Powell and Doerr-Smith, 1994) and global connections. As the "science of networks" now enters center stage encompassing a broad set of accomplishments across the social and natural sciences Emerson's legacy seems even more significant in hindsight.

Reader's Guide to Richard Emerson

Richard Emerson wrote clearly, so the best guide to his work is the work itself. His chapter "Social Exchange Theory" (1981) is a good and non-technical overview of his work up to that point, including power-dependence and early studies of exchange networks. The experimental studies (1964, 1978, 1983) are quite accessible. For those wishing to build on his theoretical foundations, "Exchange Theory, Parts I and II," although somewhat technical, are essential. Turner (1986) provides an excellent summary of his work and assessment of its importance and Molm and Cook (1995) have produced a useful overview of Emersons's formulation and subsequent developments

Bibliography

Writings of Richard M. Emerson

1962. Power-dependence relations. *American Sociological Review*, 27: 31–41.
1964. Power-dependence relations: Two experiments. *Sociometry*, 27: 282–298.

1969. Operant psychology and exchange theory. In R. Burgess and D. Bushell (eds) *Behavioral Sociology*. New York: Columbia University Press.

1972. Exchange theory, Part I. A psychological basis for social exchange. Exchange theory, Part II. Exchange relations and network structures. In J. Berger, M. Zelditch and B. Anderson (eds) *Sociological Theories in Progress*, vol. 2. Boston: Houghton Mifflin, pp. 38–87.

1977 (with John F. Stolte). Structural inequality: Position and power in network structures. In R. Hamblin and J. Kunkel (eds) *Behavioral Theory in Sociology*. New Brunswick, NJ: Transaction, pp. 117–138.

1978 (with Karen S. Cook). Power, equity and commitment in exchange networks. *American Sociological Review*, 43: 721–739.

1981. Social exchange theory. In Morris Rosenberg and Ralph Turner (eds) *Social Psychology: Sociological Perspectives*. New York: Basic Books, pp. 30–65.

1983 (with K. S. Cook, M. R. Gillmore, and T. Yamagishi). The distribution of power in exchange networks: Theory and experimental results. *American Journal of Sociology*, 89: 275–305.

1984 (with Karen S. Cook). Exchange networks and the analysis of complex organizations. In Samuel B. Bacharach and E. J. Lawler (eds) *Perspectives on Organizational Sociology: Theory and Research*, vol. 3. Greenwich, CT: Jai Press, pp. 1–30.

1987. Toward a theory of value in social exchange. In Karen S. Cook (ed.) *Social Exchange Theory*. Newbury Park, CA: Sage, pp. 11–46.

Further Reading

Anderson, James C., Håkan Håkansson, and Johanson, Jan (1994) Dyadic business relationships within a business network context. *Journal of Marketing*, 58: 1–15.

Bienenstock, Elisa Jayne and Bonacich, Phillip (1992) The core as a solution to negatively connected exchange networks. *Social Networks*, 14: 231–243.

Bienenstock, Elisa Jayne and Bonacich, Phillip (1997) Network exchange as a cooperative game. *Rationality and Society*, 9: 37–65.

Blau, Peter (1964) *Exchange and Power*. New York: John Wiley & Sons.

Bowen, R. O. (1960) *The New Professors*. New York: Holt, Rinehart & Winston.

Burgess, Robert G. and Bushell Jr., Don (eds) (1969) *Behavioral Sociology: The Experimental Analysis of Social Process*. New York: Columbia University Press.

Burt, Ronald S. (1992) *Structural Holes: The Social Structure of Competition*. Cambridge, MA: Harvard University Press.

Cartwright, Dorwin (1979) Contemporary social psychology in historical perspective. *Sociometry*, 42: 250–258.

Chok, Jay Inghwee (2009) Regulatory dependence and scientific advisory boards. *Journal of Research Policy*, 38: 710–725.

Coleman, James S. (1990) *Foundations of Social Theory*. Cambridge, MA: Harvard University Press.

Cook, Karen S. (1977) Exchange and power in networks of interorganizational relations. *Sociological Quarterly*, 18: 62–82.

Cook, Karen S. (1987) *Social Exchange Theory*. Newbury Park, CA: Sage.

Cook, Karen S. (2005) Networks, norms, and trust: The social psychology of social capital. *Social Psychology Quarterly*, 68: 4–14.

Cook, Karen S. and Donnelly, Shawn (1996) Intergenerational exchange relations and social justice. In Leo Montada and Melvin J. Lerner (eds) *Current Societal Concerns About Justice*. New York: Plenum Press, pp. 67–83.

Cook, Karen S. and Gillmore, Mary R. (1984) Power, dependence and coalitions. In Edward J. Lawler (ed.) *Advances in Group Processes*, vol. 1. Greenwich, CT: JAI Press, pp. 27–58.

Cook, Karen S. and Whitmeyer, Joseph M. (1992) Two approaches to social structure: Exchange theory and network analysis. In Judith Blake and John Hagan (eds) *Annual Review of Sociology*, vol. 18. Palo Alto, CA: Annual Reviews, pp. 109–127.

Cook, Karen S. and Yamagishi, Toshio (1992) Power in exchange networks: A power-dependence formulation. *Social Networks*, 14: 245–266.

Cook, Karen S., Cheshire, Coye, and Gerbasi, Alexandra (2006) Power-dependence and exchange theory. In Peter Burke (ed.) *Contemporary Social Psychological Theories*. Stanford, CA: Stanford University Press, pp. 194–216

Di Domenico, MariaLaura, Tracey, Paul, and Haugh, Helen (2009) The dialectic of social exchange: Theorizing corporate–social enterprise collaboration. *Organization Studies*, 30: 887–907.

Frank, Kenneth A. (2009) Quasi-ties directing resources to members of a collective. *American Behavioral Scientist*, 52: 1613–1645.

Friedkin, Noah E. (1992) An expected value model of social power: predictions for selected exchange networks. *Social Networks*, 14: 213–229.

Friedkin, Noah E. (1993a) An expected value model of social exchange outcomes. In Edward J. Lawler, Barry Markovsky, Karen Heimer, and Jodi O'Brien (eds) *Advances in Group Processes*. Greenwich, CT: JAI Press, pp. 163–193.

Friedkin, Noah E. (1993b) Structural bases of interpersonal influence in groups: A longitudinal case study. *American Sociological Review*, 58: 861–872.

Gargiulo, Martin, Ertug, Gokhan, and Galunic, Charles (2009) The two faces of control: Network closure and individual performance among knowledge workers. *Administrative Science Quarterly*, 54: 299–333.

Gerlach, Michael L. (1992) *Alliance Capitalism: the Social Organization of Japanese Business*. Berkeley: University of California Press.

Gillmore, Mary R. (1987) Implications of generalized versus restricted exchange. In Karen S. Cook (ed.) *Social Exchange Theory*. Newbury Park, CA: Sage, pp. 170–189.

Gonzalez-Bailon, Sandra (2009) Opening the black box of link formation: Social factors underlying the structure of the web. *Social Networks*, 31: 271–280.

Goodliffe, Jay and Hawkins, Darren (2009) A funny thing happened on the way to Rome: Explaining International Criminal Court negotiations. *Journal of Politics*, 71: 977–997.

Grembowski, David, Cook, Karen S., Patrick, Donald, and Roussell, Amy (1998) Managed care and physician referral: A social exchange perspective. *Medical Care Research and Review*, 55: 3–31.

Hegtvedt, Karen A. and Cook, Karen S. (2001) Distributive justice: Current research and theoretical developments. In Joseph Sanders and Lee Hamilton (eds) *Handbook on Social Justice*. New York: Plenum Press, pp. 93–128.

Hempel, Carl (1965) *Aspects of Scientific Explanation*. New York: Free Press.

Homans, George C. (1961) *Social Behavior: Its Elementary Forms*. New York: Harcourt, Brace and World.

Kahneman, Daniel and Tversky, Amos (1979) Prospect theory: An analysis of decision under risk. *Econometrica*, 47: 263–291.

Kuhn, Alfred (1963) *The Study of Society: a Unified Approach*. Homewood, IL: Irwin-Dorsey.

Kuhn, Thomas (1964) *The Structure of Scientific Revolutions*. Chicago: University of Chicago Press (2nd edn 1970).

Lawler, Edward J. (2001) An affect theory of social exchange. *American Journal of Sociology*, 107: 321–352.

Lawler, Edward J. and Yoon, Jeongkoo (1993) Power and the emergence of commitment behavior in negotiated exchange. *American Sociological Review*, 58: 465–481.

Lawler, Edward J. and Yoon, Jeongkoo (1996) Commitment in exchange relations. *American Sociological Review*, 61: 89–108.

Lawler, Edward J., Ford, Rebecca, and Blegen, Mary A. (1988) Coercive capability in conflict: A test of bilateral deterrence versus conflict spiral theory. *Social Psychology Quarterly*, 51: 93–107.

Lawler, Edward J., Thye, Shane R., and Yoon, Jeongkoo (2008) Social exchange and micro social order. *American Sociological Review*, 73: 519–542.

Lincoln, James R., Gerlach, Michael, and Takashi, Peggy (1992) Keiretsu networks in the Japanese economy: A dyad analysis of intercorporate ties. *American Sociological Review*, 57: 561–585.

Luo, Yadong, Liu, Yi, and Xue, Jiaqi (2009) Relationship investment and channel performance: An analysis of mediating forces. *Journal of Management Studies*, 46: 1113–1137.

Malinowski, B. (1920) Kula: The circulating exchange of valuables in the archipelagoes of Eastern New Guinea. *Man*, 20: 97–105.

Marsden, Peter V. (1982) Brokerage behavior in restricted exchange networks. In Peter V. Marsden and Nan Lin (eds) *Social Structure and Network Analysis*. Beverly Hills, CA: Sage, pp. 201–218.

Michaels, James, Edwards, John N., and Acock, Alan C. (1984) Satisfaction in intimate relationships as a function of inequality, inequity and outcomes. *Social Psychology Quarterly*, 47: 347–357.

Mizruchi, Mark S. (1989) Similarity of political behavior among large American corporations. *American Journal of Sociology*, 95: 401–424.

Molm, Linda D. (1985) Relative effects of individual dependencies: Further tests of the relation between power imbalance and power use. *Social Forces*, 63: 810–837.

Molm, Linda D. (1997) *Coercive Power in Social Exchange*. Cambridge, UK: Cambridge University Press.

Molm, Linda D. (2010) The structure of reciprocity. *Social Psychology Quarterly*, 73.

Molm, Linda D. and Cook, Karen S. (1995) Social exchange theory. In Karen S. Cook, Gary A. Fine, and James S. House (eds) *Sociological Perspectives in Social Psychology*. Needham, MA: Allyn and Bacon, pp. 209–235.

Molm, Linda D., Schaefer, David R., and Collett, Jessica L. (2009) Fragile and resilient trust: Risk and uncertainty in negotiated and reciprocal exchange. *Sociological Theory*, 27: 1–32.

Pfeffer, Jeffrey and Salancik, Gerald R. (1978) *The External Control of Organizations: A Resource Dependence Perspective*. New York: Harper and Row.

Popper, Karl (1961) *The Poverty of Historicism*. London, UK: Routledge & Kegan Paul.

Powell, Walter W. (1990) Neither market nor hierarchy: Network forms of organization. In L. L. Cummings and Staw (eds) *Research in Organizational Behaviour*, vol. 12. Greenwich, CT: JAI Press, pp. 295–336.

Powell, Walter W. and Smith-Doerr, Laurel (1994) Networks and economic life. In Neil Smelser and Richard Swedberg (eds) *The Handbook of Economic Sociology*. Princeton, NJ: Princeton University Press/New York: Russell Sage Foundation, pp. 368–402.

Sabel, Charles F. (1991) Moebius-strip organizations and open labor markets. In P. Bourdieu and J. S. Coleman (eds) *Social Theory for a Changing Society*. Boulder, CO: Westview Press, pp. 23–54.

Schaefer, David R. (2009) Resource variation and the development of cohesion in exchange networks. *American Sociological Review*, 74: 551–572.

Scott, W. Richard (1992) *Organizations: Rational, Natural, and Open Systems*, 3rd edn. Englewood Cliffs, NJ: Prentice-Hall.

Seabright, Mark A., Levinthal, Daniel A., and Fichman, Mark (1992) Role of individual attachments in the dissolution of interorganizational relationships. *Academy of Management Journal*, 35: 122–160.

Skinner, B. F. (1974) *About Behaviorism*. New York: Vintage Books.

Sprecher, Susan (1988) Investment model, equity, and social support determinants of relationship commitment. *Social Psychology Quarterly*, 51: 57–69.

Stolte, John F. (1987) Legitimacy, justice and productive exchange. In Karen S. Cook (ed.) *Social Exchange Theory*. Newbury Park, CA: Sage, pp. 190–208.

Takahashi, Nobuyuki (2001) The Emergence of generalized exchange. *American Journal of Sociology*, 105: 1105–1134.

Thompson, James D. (1967) *Organizations in Action*. New York: McGraw-Hill.

Turner, Jonathan H. (1986) *The Structure of Sociological Theory*. Homewood, IL: Dorsey Press.

Turner, Jonathan H. (1995) *Macrodynamics: Toward a Theory on the Organization of Human Populations*. New Brunswick, NJ: Rutgers University Press.

Van de Rijt, Arnout and Macy, Michael W. (2006) Power and dependence in intimate exchange. *Social Forces*, 84: 1455–1470.

Whitmeyer, Joseph M. (1994) Social structure and the actor: The case of power in exchange networks. *Social Psychology Quarterly*, 57: 177–189.

Whitmeyer, Joseph M. (1999) Power and interest-network structures in exchange networks. *Sociological Perspectives*, 42: 23–47.

Willer, David (ed.) (1999) *Network Exchange Theory*. Westport, CT: Praeger.

Willer, David, Thye, Shane, Simpson, Brent *et al.* (2002) Network exchange. In Joseph Berger and Morris Zelditch Jr. (eds) *New Directions in Sociological Theory: The Growth of Contemporary Theories*. New York, NY: Rowman and Littlefield, pp. 109–144.

Wrong, Dennis H. (1988) *Power, Its Forms, Bases, and Uses*. Chicago: University of Chicago Press.

Yamagishi, Toshio (1995) Social dilemmas. In Karen S. Cook, Gary A. Fine, and James S. House (eds) *Sociological Perspectives on Social Psychology*. Needham Heights, NY: Allyn and Bacon, pp. 311–354.

Yamagishi, Toshio and Cook, Karen S. (1993) Generalized exchange and social dilemmas. *Social Psychology Quarterly*, 56: 235–248.

Yamagishi, Toshio, Gillmore, Mary R., and Cook, Karen S. (1988) Network connections and the distribution of power in exchange networks. *American Journal of Sociology*, 93: 833–851.

Yamaguchi, Kazuo (1996) Power in networks of substitutable and complementary exchange relations: A rational-choice model and an analysis of power centralization. *American Sociological Review*, 61: 308–322.

Zelditch, Morris (1969) Can you really study the army in the laboratory. In A. Etzioni (ed.) *A Sociological Reader in Complex Organizations*. New York: Holt, Rinehart and Winston, pp. 428–539.

Zelditch, Morris (2007) The external validity of experiments that test theories. In Murray Webster, Jr. and Jane Sell (eds) *Laboratory Experiments in the Social Sciences*. San Diego, CA: Academic Press, pp. 87–112.

Zuo, Jiping (2009) Rethinking family patriarchy and women's positions in presocialist China. *Journal of Marriage and the Family*, 71: 542–557.

9

James S. Coleman

GUILLERMINA JASSO

COLEMAN AND SOCIOLOGY

James S. Coleman was born in the American Midwest, in Bedford, Indiana, on May 12, 1926. His family moved to Louisville, Kentucky, and there he graduated from DuPont Manual High School in 1944. After serving with the US military in the Second World War, Coleman graduated from Purdue University with a Bachelor of Science degree in 1949. After working briefly as a chemist, he enrolled in the graduate program in sociology at Columbia University. There he studied with Robert K. Merton, Paul F. Lazarsfeld, and Seymour Martin Lipset, and made enduring intellectual friendships with fellow students, obtaining the PhD in sociology in 1955. He then taught briefly at the University of Chicago, leaving for Johns Hopkins in 1959 to start the Department of Social Relations, to which he recruited Arthur L. Stinchcombe and Peter H. Rossi (who had preceded him at both Columbia and Chicago), with whom he would lead Hopkins in a golden moment far ahead of its time in rigorous interdisciplinary social science training. Together, Coleman and Rossi founded the journal *Social Science Research* in 1972. As the Hopkins experiment frayed, and with no signs yet of a second life, the crown jewels left – first Stinchcombe in 1967, then Coleman in 1973, and Rossi in 1974. Coleman taught for the rest of his life at the University of Chicago. There he died, tragically early, on March 25, 1995.

Coleman made many distinguished contributions to sociology – both theoretical and empirical – and received many honors, including membership in the US National Academy of Sciences and the Royal Swedish Academy of Sciences and ten honorary doctorates, including doctorates awarded by the Vrije Universiteit Brussels, the University of Erlangen-Nuremberg, the University of Haifa, and the Hebrew University of Jerusalem, as well as his alma mater Purdue University and the University of Notre Dame.

The Wiley-Blackwell Companion to Major Social Theorists, First Edition.
Edited by George Ritzer and Jeffrey Stepnisky.
© 2011 Blackwell Publishing Ltd. Published 2011 by Blackwell Publishing Ltd.

Important retrospectives of his work have appeared. These include the Festschrift edited by Sørensen and Spilerman (1993), the memorial volume edited by Clark (1996), the reflection by Lindenberg (2000), the comprehensive essay by Marsden (2005), and the analysis by Smith (2006). In this chapter, I will not tread again the ground covered by those major retrospectives. Rather I will hold to a few themes and insights of lasting importance for sociology and social science in whose development Coleman played an important part. Though these themes range widely – from mathematical functions and probability distributions to schooling and status – they coalesce in Coleman's passionate commitment to the rational action paradigm for understanding human behavior.

But I begin with a reminiscence of Coleman at Hopkins.

COLEMAN AT HOPKINS

During the years at Hopkins, Coleman published *The Adolescent Society* (1961), *Introduction to Mathematical Sociology* (1964), *Equality of Educational Opportunity* (1966), *Medical Innovation* (1966), *Resources for Social Change: Race in the United States* (1971), and *The Mathematics of Collective Action* (1973). Though *Equality of Educational Opportunity* had made him a towering public figure – invited to the White House to chat with President Nixon, invited to Cape Canaveral to watch spacecraft launches – at Hopkins, or at least among the students at Hopkins, it was *Introduction to Mathematical Sociology* (henceforth *Intro*) that really mattered. On the first day of graduate school, one of my fellow cohort mates told the story of ordering the book while he was serving in the Peace Corps in Africa and being so transfixed that he decided immediately to study with Coleman. That same student told the rest of the cohort that mathematical sociology is to theory what quantitative sociology is to empirical work. A beautiful analogy.

In the Department quarters on the fourth floor of Gilman Hall, there was a Student Room for the graduate students. And there the older students would tell the newcomers about science, about discovering laws, about the heroes they had known. They spoke with awe about previous Coleman students Spilerman and Sørensen; and Spilerman's (1970, 1971) articles on racial disturbances triggered widespread gratitude for the beauty of mathematics and for Coleman.

Re-reading *Introduction to Mathematical Sociology* now, it is striking what a watershed moment it was. *Intro* had set forth a few mathematical functions and a few differential equations, and now here were Spilerman and Sørensen fluidly using mathematical functions and differential equations to analyze a city's proneness to racial disturbances and a student's educational potential. More impressively, Spilerman and Sørensen were using probability distributions to model cities and students. In Spilerman (1970) alone, we find not only the Poisson and the binomial distributions used by Coleman but also the next step to new distributions, including continuous distributions – the gamma and its special cases, the exponential and the chi-squared. Clearly, Coleman had ushered in a new era, and the new era was at Hopkins.

Coleman would live 22 more years, his great work *Foundations of Social Theory* (henceforth *Foundations*) would be written at Chicago, he would found the journal

Rationality and Society, he would be President of the American Sociological Association, and many honors would come his way. But the intellectual excitement of the years at Hopkins – when discoveries lay around every corner and laws of nature sat on trees waiting to be plucked – would remain unequaled.

COLEMAN AND DEDUCTIVE THEORIES

There are two types of deductive theories. Outwardly they both look the same. They both have two parts, the first a tiny part containing the assumptions, the second a large and growing part containing the predictions.

But their souls differ. In the first type, the assumptions are known to be true, they may even be self-evident; or the assumptions may describe a set of arrangements under human control. Thus, the implications must be true. In the second type, the assumptions are what Popper (1963: 245) called "guesses" about the way a piece of the world works. The implications are testable predictions. If the predictions survive rigorous empirical test, such tests constitute evidence that the real world may resemble the world postulated in the guesses. This second type of theory, invented by Newton, is often called hypothetico-deductive theory (Toulmin, 1978: 378–379).

Coleman used and discussed both types of theories. Early, in *Intro* (1964: 10), he described, under the rubric of "synthetic" theory, the first type: "Sets of postulates are put down...From these postulates, which are known to be true, deductions are then generated." In *Intro* Coleman did not explicitly discuss hypothetico-deductive theory, although he did note that sometimes there are observations about the deductions in the "synthetic" theory (1964: 37) and although in the other form he described, not quite the hypothetico-deductive form, the predictions are tested against reality (1964: 36).

By *Foundations*, however, Coleman explicitly brings in the hypothetico-deductive approach, though still without naming it. Assumptions can now be more, or less, "realistic" (1990: 143) and more, or less, "tenable" (1990: 208); they can even be "untrue" (1990: 531) or "not correct" (1990: 646). Then comes this extraordinary passage (1990: 773):

> There may, of course, be utility functions that do assume cardinal utility, thus implying behavior that allows that assumption to be tested. The Cobb-Douglas utility function... used in this book, is an example. It implies something more specific...This specific function allows one, on the basis of observing the fraction of actor i's resources devoted to each resource in which he has some interest, to assign a number representing x^{ji}, actor i's interest in resource j...If one finds that the fraction is independent of the total amount of resources that i holds and independent of the price of resource j, then i's behavior is described by the Cobb-Douglas utility function.

In this remarkable passage, Coleman shows how sharp characterization of an assumption (in this case, assigning a particular functional form, called the Cobb-Douglas function, to the utility function of economics) yields predictions which if consistent with data reveal that the special utility function is indeed a faithful approximation to the real world. Thus, Coleman is staking out sociological territory for the Newtonian hypothetico-deductive method.

The stage is now set for the sociological theory of the future, whose assumptions are "genuine guesses about the structure of the world" (Popper, 1963: 245), whose predictions display the "marvellous deductive unfolding" of the theory (Popper, 1963: 221), and whose fruitfulness is evident in the "derivations far afield from its original domain," which "permit an increasingly broad and diversified basis for testing the theory" (Danto, 1967: 299–300).

COLEMAN AND MATHEMATICAL FUNCTIONS

The basic relations in a theory, both the relations that appear as postulates and the relations embodied in the deduced predictions, are usefully expressed mathematically. Across Coleman's work, there is strong rationale for using mathematics, especially in *Intro* (1964: 8–10, 48–49). Three reasons stand out: First is the parsimony of the mathematics language. Second is its precision. Third, mathematics is a power tool for deducing the implications of a set of assumptions, enabling the "marvellous deductive unfolding" of the theory (Popper, 1963: 221) and thus not only increasing the theory's fruitfulness but also making it easier to test (Danto, 1967: 299–300).

Coleman begins *Intro* (1964: 4–8) with the first step in constructing a mathematical relation, that is, find the variables which belong on the right-hand side of an equation expressing determination of a dependent variable y:

$$y = f(x_1, x_2, x_3, \ldots, x_k). \tag{1}$$

Choosing – or discovering – the independent variables that affect a dependent variable is only the first step. It remains to specify the nature of the relations between each independent variable and the dependent variable.

Accordingly, the second step is to specify, based either on theory or previous empirical research, the direction of the effects of each of the independent variables. For example, the researcher may believe that y is an increasing function of one independent variable, a decreasing function of another, and a nonmonotonic function of still another. This "signing" of the effects is often represented by the first partial derivatives; a positive first partial derivative indicates that, holding constant the other independent variables, as an independent variable increases, so does the dependent variable, a negative first partial derivative indicates a negative relation, and so on. For example, Coleman does this in discussing price (*Intro*, 1964: 95):

$$\frac{\partial y}{\partial x_1} > 0, \frac{\partial y}{\partial x_2} < 0. \tag{2}$$

But the task of describing the relations between the independent and dependent variables is not yet complete. The first derivatives indicate the direction of the effects but not the rate of change.

The stage is now set for the third step, which could be a specific function and/or a set of second derivatives. The second derivative indicates whether the rate of change is increasing, decreasing, or constant. For example, the combination of a positive first derivative and a positive second derivative indicates that as the independent variable increases, the dependent variable increases at an increasing rate; in contrast, the combination of a positive first derivative and a negative second derivative indicates that as the independent variable increases, the dependent variable increases at a decreasing rate. The second derivative is of the greatest importance in sociology because many outcomes vary with the same independent variables, and thus the challenge is to specify what is distinctive about each relation. To illustrate, power, status, and self-esteem all vary with wealth, and the task is to discover what is distinctive about each of these relations. Or are power, status, and self-esteem merely synonyms?

Coleman, keenly aware of the importance of fully describing the nature of social relationships, presents, in *Foundations* (1990: 674), the entire three-step procedure for the case of the utility function. He starts by writing the utility of the individual as a function of the amounts of goods held by the individual,

$$U = U(c_1, \ldots, c_m), \tag{3}$$

where U denotes utility and c denotes a good. Next he writes the first partial derivatives,

$$\frac{\partial U}{\partial c_j} > 0, \quad j = 1, \ldots, m. \tag{4}$$

Finally, he presents the second partial derivatives,

$$\frac{\partial^2 U}{\partial c_j^2} < 0, \quad j = 1, \ldots, m. \tag{5}$$

Together these expressions represent a vision of utility in which utility increases at a decreasing rate with each good.

Two features are noteworthy. First, it is not clear what the resource environment was for Coleman at the time of *Intro*. The great Bronshtein and Semendyayev (1985) had not yet been translated into English.[1] Neither had Gradshteyn and Ryzhik (1965). The classic Abramowitz and Stegun (1964), prepared at the US National Bureau of Standards (since 1988 the National Institute of Standards and Technology) as Publication 55 in the Applied Mathematics Series, was published the same year as *Intro*. Of course, there were numerous textbooks, and the classic two-volume work by Courant ([1934]1937) had appeared in English in 1934, followed quickly in 1937 by a second English edition. As well, Allen (1938) provided an introduction to mathematical methods useful in economics. Still, one does not get the impression of a rich resource environment. Thus, Coleman's achievement is all the more impressive.

Second, and relatedly, Coleman cites very little work of pure mathematics. There is no mention of, say, l'Hôpital's Rule or Euler's homogeneous function theorem, no joy that a difficult integral is already known or tabulated. Nor are there tips for the reader or the novice – "Start with Silvanus Thompson," or the like. Perhaps it was common knowledge that everyone studied A or read B. Below I return to questions it would be marvelous to ask Coleman.

It is interesting to speculate whether an environment richer in mathematical functions would have accelerated analytic advances in some of the topics of central concern to Coleman, such as prestige and status, social cohesion, and inequality. For example, had the resource environment been a bit richer, Coleman's (1964: 14, 28–30) discussion in *Intro* of Stephan and Mishler's (1952) work on the relation between rank and frequency of initiating/receiving participations in small groups might have led quickly to discovery of the status function, a discovery that would have to await Sørensen (1979).

How might such a discovery have been accelerated? Following Coleman (1964: 4–8), the first step would have been to express status as a function of relative rank, and the second step to sign the effect of relative rank, noting that status is an increasing function of relative rank. As described above, the third step would have been to propose a specific function and/or the sign of the second derivative. Could scrutiny of Stephan and Mishler's (1952) data, or of other data, have enabled a leap to either a specific function or a second derivative?

Both would happen 14–15 years later. The mathematical foundation for studying status was laid by Berger, Cohen, and Zelditch (1966), Berger *et al.* (1977), Goode (1978), and Sørensen (1979). Goode (1978) proposed that status increases at an increasing rate with relative rank, and Sørensen (1979) proposed the specific function which embeds Goode's (1978) convexity condition:

$$S = \ln\left(\frac{1}{1-r}\right), \qquad (6)$$

where S denotes status and r denotes relative rank on a valued quantitative characteristic. Quantitative characteristics of which more is preferred to less are called goods, and quantitative characteristics of which less is preferred to more are called bads (For fuller detail on the status function, see Jasso, 2001).

In groups of finite size, relative rank r is itself approximated by a function of the individual's raw rank i and the group size N:

$$r = \frac{i}{N+1}, \qquad (7)$$

where the raw ranks are represented by the sequence of integers from 1 to the group size N, with 1 assigned to the lowest-ranking person. The relative ranks lie on the unit interval, and have two important symmetry properties: the mth values from the bottom and top of the range are equidistant from zero and one, respectively, and also from the midpoint (for elaboration to mth ranges, see Stuart and Ord, 1987: 463).

Figure 9.1 provides the graph of the status function. As shown, status increases at an increasing rate with relative rank.

COLEMAN AND PROBABILITY DISTRIBUTIONS

Probability distributions represent a variable's array. Some variables are so important – for example, wealth, power, status – that we might say their distribution provides a picture of society. Moreover, they work together with mathematical functions to provide seamless passage from the distribution of an independent variable to the distribution of a dependent variable. *Intro* has the distinction of including in the index "probability distribution" together with "binomial distribution" and "Poisson

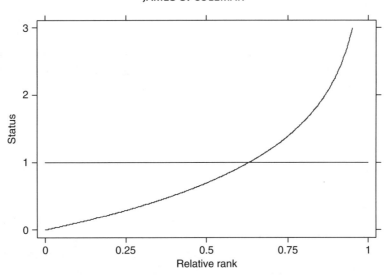

Figure 9.1 The status function. Status increases at an increasing rate with relative rank, as proposed by Sørensen (1979) and satisfying the convexity condition proposed by Goode (1978). The status function is thus also the quantile function of the status distribution. The status distribution has an arithmetic mean of one (indicated by the horizontal line) and a Gini coefficient of 0.5. For further properties and details, see Jasso (2001).

distribution" (1964: 545, 550–551). It gives pride of place to the Poisson distribution, including two eponymous chapters (10 and 11). Further, it provides a wonderful appendix to chapter 10 with the derivation of the Poisson and its mean and variance. It also mentions the normal distribution (1964: 87). *Foundations* mentions the binomial distribution once, but there are no index entries for probability distributions or for any variate.

Note that *Intro* was written – and published – before Haight's (1967) masterly handbook on the Poisson and at a time when there were no compendia or dictionaries of distributions such as we have today, save for Haight's (1961) *Index*. Johnson and Kotz (1969–1972) had not yet written their masterpiece with all the major facts about all the major known distributions. Hastings and Peacock (1974) had not brought out their little handbook. There was no Internet where the US National Institute of Standards and Technology (NIST) could post an *Engineering Statistics Handbook*, with the remarkable Section 1.3.6 on Probability Distributions. The splendid *International Encyclopedia of the Social Sciences*, edited by Sills (1968), was not published until 1968; it had an amazing set of four articles on "Distributions" – including Haight's (1968) article on "Special Discrete Distributions" and Owen's (1968) article on "Special Continuous Distributions" summarizing the properties of ten and nineteen distributions, respectively. As noted above, Bronshtein and Semendyayev (1985) had not yet been translated into English; even its short section on probability theory, with descriptions of three discrete variates – the binomial, hypergeometric, and Poisson – and four continuous variates – the rectangular, normal, exponential, and Weibull distributions – and graphs of most of them would have been a useful starting point for a social scientist intent on finding a good representation for one or another sociobehavioral characteristic.

There were, however, two impressive sources, not coincidentally written by Haight (1961) and Owen (1962), books warmly acknowledged by Johnson and Kotz (1969–1972). As well, there was the first volume of Feller's (1950) foundational textbook, also warmly acknowledged by Haight (1961) – and cited, along with an article on contagious distributions, in *Intro* (1964: 534). And there was still another famous first volume – *Distribution Theory* in the two-volume edition of *The Advanced Theory of Statistics* first published by Kendall in 1943 and the three-volume edition first published by Kendall and Stuart in 1958.[2]

Notwithstanding the welcome citation to Feller, the overall impression in *Intro* is of an environment not quite rich in resources pertaining to probability distributions.

As in the preceding section, it is interesting to speculate whether availability of a dictionary of distributions might have accelerated analytic advances. Consider again Coleman's (1964: 14, 28–30) discussion in *Intro* of rank and of Stephan and Mishler's (1952) work. Familiarity with continuous distributions in general would have provided the clue that any nondecreasing function of relative rank is a quantile function (one of the three major associated functions of probability distributions, the other two being the cumulative distribution function and the probability density function); and a quantile function in which the variate increases at an increasing rate with relative rank would have narrowed the field of possible candidate-distributions for the status distribution. Moreover, Stephan and Mishler's (1952) article actually had the word "exponential" in the title.

In point of fact, it would be 15 years after *Intro* that Sørensen (1979) discovered the exponential distribution as a model for status. The function that he proposed for status – the status function given in (6) – is immediately identifiable as the quantile function associated with an important family of probability distributions, the exponential. This formula is instantly available in any dictionary of distributions, such as Hastings and Peacock (1974: 56).

Look again at Figure 9.1. In the preceding section on mathematical functions, the graph was interpreted as the graph of the status function. Which it is. Now it can also be interpreted as the graph of the quantile function of the status distribution. The status distribution provides a picture of society and, in particular, a vivid picture of the society's status inequality. Applying to status Pen's (1971) evocative imagery about income, imagine an hour-long parade of all members of society, with each person passing at an equal pace (visible for 1/Nth of the hour) and each person's height proportional to his or her status. Pen's Parade would start with dwarfs and end with giants.

Now that status is explicitly viewed as a distribution, interest arises naturally in the distribution's principal parameters, such as its arithmetic mean and its inequality, parameters in which Coleman showed great interest.

Average status in a small group is easily shown to be given by:

$$E(S) = \ln\left(\frac{N+1}{\sqrt[N]{N!}} \right). \tag{8}$$

As group size N increases, average status increases, reaching its limit of unity as N goes to infinity (Jasso, 2001). For example, average status equals 0.752 in a dyad, 0.789 in a triad, and 0.899 when N is 12. Further, the proportion below the mean in the large-N case is $1-1/e$, or approximately 0.632. Thus, almost two-thirds of the population have status below the average, and a few "giants" have very high status.

The Gini coefficient – one of several inequality measures that can be calculated for the status distribution – also increases as group size N increases, reaching its limit of 0.5 as N goes to infinity. Among the questions that immediately arise is the question whether inequality is greater in status or in the good which generates it (Jasso and Kotz, 2007; Jasso, 2008). A Gini coefficient of 0.5 is quite high, higher than the Gini for earnings inequality among full-time year-round workers in the United States in 2008 – 0.403 for both sexes combined, and 0.416 and 0.356 for men and women, respectively (US Census Bureau, Table IE-2). Social cohesion will be greater if people care about earnings than if they care about status.

Of course, the real payoff comes from using the status distribution in theories, deriving testable predictions about the effects of subgroup structures (as will be seen below), about the effects on identity, inequality, and social cohesion of valuing several goods (for example, not only wealth but also beauty, or not only statesmanship but also horsemanship) and of the goods' intercorrelations, and about the differences between societies which care about status and societies which instead care about justice or power.[3]

COLEMAN AND THE ADOLESCENT SOCIETY

Coleman's work on the high school world – *The Adolescent Society* (1961) and several papers – is extraordinarily insightful and imaginative. It is fresh and appealing. Reading it is like reading the screenplay or seeing the 1961 movie of Inge's *Splendor in the Grass*. We are drawn into that world, and as if by instinct go to the garage or the attic and reach for our own high school yearbooks and graduation programs, for the boxes of ribbons and buttons from student government campaigns and medals from interscholastic competition.

Consider these passages:

> The high performers, those who receive good grades, will not be the boys whose ability is greatest but a more mediocre few. Thus the "intellectuals" of such a society, those defined by themselves and others as the best students, will not in fact be those with most intellectual ability. The latter, knowing where the social rewards lie, will be off cultivating other fields which bring social rewards. (Coleman, *AJS*, 1960)

> [A]n innocent visitor ... entering a school would likely be confronted, first of all, with a trophy case ... The figures adorning these trophies represent men passing footballs, shooting basketballs, holding out batons; they are not replicas of "The Thinker." ... Altogether, the trophy case would suggest to the innocent visitor that he was entering an athletic club, not an educational institution. (Coleman, *Annals*, 1961)

> [G]rades are a poor motivating mechanism, because they are unique to the school and useful only in comparison with grades of fellow students. This generates invidious comparisons, sets each student in competition with his fellows, and is a powerfully divisive force among the students. Direct incentive pay, or piecework, in factories produces the same effect and has sometimes been consciously used by employers to keep employees divided against each other ... In the long run, this is a dangerous mechanism, as the history of incentive pay has shown. (Coleman, *Annals*, 1961)

[C]lassroom activities are embedded within a powerful culture whose interests are diverse. The sweater a girl wears to class takes on great significance, overshadowing the significance of the algebra lesson to be learned; apparently casual conversations become loaded with the significance of getting into a certain clique; a boy's response to a teacher is fashioned with regard for the impression it makes upon other boys in his group; between-class conversation centers around recent social events. (Coleman, *PDK*, 1961)

Coleman raises themes of profound importance for social science in these pages – the sources of rewards, how persons choose the valued goods, the sources of happiness and of social cohesion. The adolescents are producing status, and status has a hand in happiness and in social cohesion. Group cohesiveness would return in *Intro* (1964: 76, 87) and in *Resources for Social Change: Race in the United States* (1971: 18–22).

No matter if one disagrees with Coleman's premise on the importance of scholastic achievement in high school – perhaps finding intellectual stimulation outside the classroom, perhaps viewing high school as a gracious interlude between the foundational mental formation of childhood and the intellectual ferment of freshman year in college. For one of those long winter weekends – indeed, for developing basic sociological theory – one can do no better than to read, slowly and savoring deeply, Coleman's work on the high school world.

Such a masterwork reflects deep and long, uninterrupted concentration. And Coleman (1964: 235–236) himself observes:

This analysis and writing, during the months of July and August 1959, were probably the most extended period of intensive, uninterrupted, intellectual concentration I have sustained – a period of complete asceticism. My family was in Baltimore; I was staying in a room at International House in Chicago. (Coleman, 1964)

COLEMAN AND RACIAL INEQUALITY

Resources for Social Change: Race in the United States (1971) may be viewed as an extended meditation on the process by which "freedom of social action" is produced. This work (henceforth *Race*) focuses on Blacks in the United States and the deficits relative to Whites in many outcomes, including schooling, income, and access to good housing and secure neighborhoods. The goal is to discover the production function for these and other desired outcomes and, in particular, the production process for a society free of ethnic- or race-based gaps. Coleman observes (1971: 6):

Conceptually, the process is similar to that of economic production: certain resources – raw material, labor, knowledge – are converted into products that are either desired consumption goods or may in turn be used as resources to produce those goods. The arenas within which this conversion takes place in economic production are factories and other business firms; in social resource conversion the arenas are the institutions of society. It is these institutions within which the "productive process" that generates social change occurs – paradoxically so because the institutions are themselves often changed and sometimes torn down as a consequence of the changes they create. This, too, is no different from economic production. The products of an industry may constitute technological developments that make that or another industry's firms and factories obsolete.

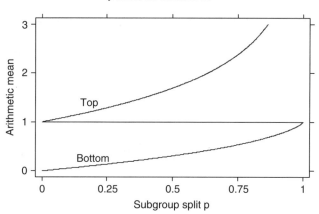

Figure 9.2 Arithmetic mean in the top and bottom subgroups of the status distribution, by the subgroup split. The horizontal line indicates the arithmetic mean of 1 for the entire group.

Along the way, all the inputs in the production function for "freedom of social action" are examined – family structure, the legacy of slavery, school conditions, and, importantly, the law and the actions of other people in the society. *Race* is an early herald for the centrality of the production function in analysis of purposive action and for the "social capital" that Coleman would later explore.

Race is also an early herald for the systematic study of subgroups within a group or population. To elucidate, consider again a situation in which persons have relative ranks, and their relative ranks generate a magnitude of status, as shown in Figure 9.1. Suppose now that the society includes subgroups (e.g. based on race). In this case, it is natural to calculate both the average and also measures of inequality within the subgroups and to explore how a variety of phenomena are related to within-subgroup mean and inequality.

In general, the members of each subgroup may be drawn from anywhere in the distribution; indeed, they may be so interspersed that subgroups are indistinguishable or almost so. At the other extreme, a particularly interesting case pertains to non-overlapping subgroups. For example, a society may be so organized that two races, or the two sexes, occupy disjoint segments of the status distribution, with the lowest-status member of the top subgroup having higher status than the highest-status member of the bottom subgroup.

In this very simple case of two non-overlapping subgroups, a critically important feature is the subgroup split, that is, the proportion of the group in each subgroup, represented by the proportion p in the bottom subgroup. As the proportion p in the bottom subgroup increases, average status in both subgroups increases, as shown in Figure 9.2. Average status increases in the bottom subgroup because higher-status individuals are progressively drawn in; and it increases in the top subgroup because lower-status individuals are progressively eliminated. Figure 9.3 provides examples of societies with two non-overlapping subgroups with different subgroup splits – 0.25–0.75, 0.50–0.50, 0.632–0.368, and 0.75–0.25.[4]

Meanwhile, the inequality within each subgroup – measured by the Gini coefficient – has an interesting dynamic, and this is depicted in Figure 9.4. As the proportion p in the bottom subgroup increases, the bottom-subgroup Gini decreases

A. Subgroup split equals 0.25–0.75.

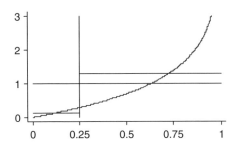

B. Subgroup split equals 0.50–0.50.

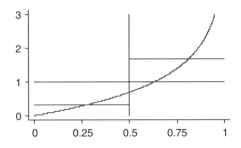

C. Subgroup split equals 0.632–0.368.

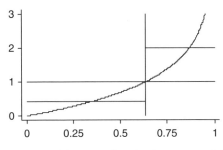

D. Subgroup split equals 0.75–0.25.

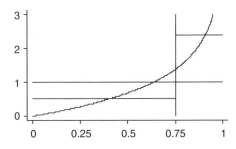

Figure 9.3 The status function in a group with two non-overlapping subgroups of varying relative sizes. As in Figure 9.1, the long horizontal line indicates the arithmetic mean of unity for the entire group. The short horizontal lines indicate the arithmetic means in each subgroup.

(though with a nonmonotonic twist as p approaches 1) and the top-subgroup Gini increases. The two subgroup-specific Ginis equal each other when p is approximately 0.534.

Thus, if subgroup cohesiveness is reduced by inequality, then the bottom subgroup is more cohesive than the top subgroup when its proportion of the population exceeds about 53 percent. Applied to gender, the low-status sex is more cohesive than the high-status sex when its proportion is greater than about 53 percent. In societies in which women are the low-status sex, a small numerical advantage can make them more cohesive than men.

COLEMAN AND RESPONSIVE VERSUS PURPOSIVE BEHAVIOR

In the opening paragraph of *The Mathematics of Collective Action* (1973: 1), Coleman distinguished between responsive and purposive behavior, elevating these from two types of behavior to two conceptions of human behavior:

> There are two quite different streams of work in the study of social action…[They] represent fundamentally different conceptions of man…Where the ordinary lay conception of man is as a person responding to his environment in pursuit of some goal, these conceptions each recognize half of that description. The first conception explains man's behavior as response to his environment; the second explains his behavior as pursuit of a goal.

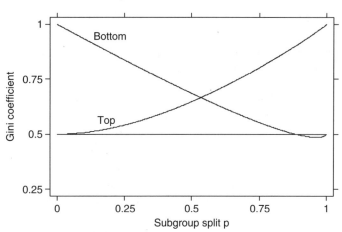

Figure 9.4 Gini coefficient in the top and bottom subgroups of the status distribution, by the subgroup split. The horizontal line indicates the Gini coefficient of 0.5 for the entire group.

Coleman noted that Durkheim's work was based on the first conception, Weber's on the second. And Coleman would set out to develop "a branch of purposive action theory" (1973: 29–31) – now known as the rational action paradigm or rational choice theory.

Of course, it is difficult to develop one without the other – as intimated in the opening paragraph quoted above. And early in the second chapter, Coleman (1973: 32–33) elaborates:

> [I]f an individual acts purposively, then this implies two things: that he expects various possible outcomes of an event to have differing consequences for him, and that the actions available to him must have some effect on the outcomes … [H]is anticipation of future consequences is certainly based on past experience with similar action in similar circumstances.

Today we would say that behavior may be purely responsive – as when someone literally jumps for joy upon hearing some wonderful news or, in a famous incident, kisses strangers upon learning that the Second World War has ended (Goldstein, 2010) – or it may be purposive, but if purposive will include information about a responsive relation. For example, a parent celebrating the birthday of one of two children may decide to give both of them presents so that the non-birthday child does not feel sad and unhappy. The parent's behavior is purposive, but it is designed on the basis of information (or intuition) about a responsive relation – namely, the child's behavior and the causes of a child's unhappiness.

There is indeed a large set of such responsive relations that humans learn over time. They learn how to achieve healthiness, how to achieve good grades, how to achieve status, how to feel happy, how to make others feel happy. In economics these relations are modeled by production functions. The production function specifies the outcome that results from a mix of inputs.

Look again at this gem from Coleman's (1960: 341) work on adolescents:

> Those with most intellectual ability … knowing where the social rewards lie, will be off cultivating other fields which bring social rewards.

The responsive relation pertains to the production of status. If attractiveness and athletic skill are what produce status, then the young purposive actors will choose to develop these, rather than sharpening their intellectual tools.

To illustrate, consider the model for the production of status proposed by Sørensen (1979) and introduced above. In this model, the input is the individual's relative rank on a socially valued good (which may be an attribute like attractiveness or athletic skill or a possession like wealth), and the outcome is status – as shown in expression (6) and Figure 9.1.

The individual both gives and receives status according to this relation. It is in fact the production function for status. The goal for each individual is to improve own status. How can this be done?

In the high school environment studied by Coleman, there is school-wide status as well as sub-school status. The goods on which school-wide status is based usually pre-exist any given cohort of students. Depending on what those goods are, there may be many or few options for improving status. For example, if the valued good, set in concrete, is prowess on the football field, then for most male students there is little chance for improving status, the competition confined to the confirmed athletes. On the other hand, if the valued good is leadership in student government, then for both male and female students, the competition may be wide open.

Sub-school status is always attainable. In most high schools, there is a proliferation of extracurricular activities – editing the yearbook, editing the school newspaper, drama club, dance club, band, poetry reading, math club, tennis, and so on. Applying Coleman's purposive model and Sørensen's status function, each student will choose the activity with the most promise of securing status. For given endowments, different levels of effort are forecast to produce different rank, and hence different status. Thus, the choice is made. And similarly for school-wide status when it is based on open competition.

Put differently, in the case of status, the responsive part of behavior is the way that status follows on relative rank (the status function), and the purposive part of behavior is the individual's choice of the good and group with respect to which a relative rank is acquired.

Of course, purposive action does not end there. Students will spend more time in situations where their status is highest. For most students, this may be in an extracurricular activity. School-wide events will be few and reluctantly attended.

Even when school-wide events are attended, the student who derives higher status from a sub-school activity will display the insignia or paraphernalia of that activity – the newspaper reporter carrying a little notebook, the yearbook photographer a camera, the math enthusiast a slide rule or, nowadays, a calculator watch, and the others an assortment of T-shirts, pins, and buttons all proclaiming allegiance to the status-enhancing activity.

If the highest status attainable is low, the student may withdraw from social activity – reading alone or socializing with a small group on the periphery of school life.

Of course, status is never final. There is always next year. Many students return in September with new skills, new attributes, and, hopefully, new ranks – and higher status.

Then comes senior year and application for college. Depending on the high school context, the new status pursuit may focus on college. A new set of ranks is generated with the admission letters on April 1st of each year (with a status scrimmage or two earlier due to rolling admissions and early admissions). This time, it is the college rankings which determine the student's rank.

Again, the students whose new college-based rank confers higher status than they previously had will quickly sport their new college's insignia. Indeed, the rapidity with which the new paraphernalia is acquired reflects the jump in status.

As Coleman saw, the college world and the adult world will have many more status-conferring hierarchies, now including earnings. And there will be many more choices to be made. Thereafter, the high school world will become salient only periodically during reunions. At such occasions, the principal dynamic centers on the conflict between activating the old high school status or injecting the new status.

By the time of *Foundations* (1990: 13, 941–946, 989) and with the experience of *Race*, discussed in the previous section, "production function" appears explicitly in the index and is used in an example of allocation of resources by a corporate actor, the Ford Motor Company. Thus, even though no link is made to the old responsive action, which is now called "expressive action," it is clear that Coleman was on the way to integrating the two types of behavior, with information about the production of desired outcomes – health, happiness, and so on – an important element in purposive action.

Distinguishing between responsive/expressive and purposive behavior in theories is easy enough. However, it can be challenging in empirical work. Consider the recent incident in which General Stanley A. McChrystal, while serving as Commander of US Forces Afghanistan, together with members of his staff, made derisive and mocking comments about senior US government officials (Rich, 2010). How did this happen? There are two conjectures, one responsive/expressive, the other purposive. The responsive/expressive speculation is that they were under a lot of stress and lost their usual self-control and tact. The purposive speculation is that the comments were highly calculated and goal-directed, either to call attention to a questionable policy or to be dismissed so as to avoid blame for the failure of the policy.

Perhaps much insight may be gained from work in criminology, which attempts to distinguish between crimes of passion and premeditated crimes.

COLEMAN AND THE MICRO–MACRO LINK

As all commentators have noted, the micro-macro link is an important theme in Coleman's work. It is evident in *Intro* and gains momentum across his lifetime. Although the words "micro" and "macro" do not appear in the index to *Intro*, they are implicit in Coleman's (1964: 8) introduction to "the various units of social science, whether they be individuals, groups, organizations, or other units." From then on, he distinguishes between individuals and groups in such subsections of the first chapter as "Characterization of individuals" (1964: 10), "Characterization of groups or other social units" (12), "Disposition properties of individuals" (1964: 17), and "Disposition properties of groups" (1964: 21). By chapter 2, he discusses "aggregation," which does appear in the index to *Intro*, and has a major subsection on "Group and Individual Variables" (1964: 84) with the following remarkably succinct description of the micro-macro problem:

> One important measurement problem in sociology concerns the two levels on which sociologists must work: the level of the individual and that of the group. We have *observations* at two levels, *concepts* at two levels, and *relationships* at two levels. Furthermore, it is often necessary to shift back and forth: measuring group-level concepts from individual data; or inferring individual relationships from group-level relations.

Twenty-six years later, in *Foundations*, "aggregation" has disappeared from the index, but there are now seven entries for various aspects of "micro" and "macro." Moreover, one thing has not changed – the primacy Coleman accords the micro-macro problem. Again, there is a remarkable passage very early (1990: 6), under the heading, "The Major Problem":

> The major problem for explanations of system behavior based on actions and orientations at a level below that of the system is that of moving from the lower level to the system level. This has been called the micro-to-macro problem, and it is pervasive throughout the social sciences. In economics, for example, there is microeconomic theory and there is macroeconomic theory; and one of the central deficiencies in economic theory is the weakness of the linkage between them, a weakness papered over with the idea of "aggregation" and with a ubiquitous concept in macroeconomic theory, that of the "representative agent."

Coleman deploys in *Foundations* a theoretical apparatus with three components, individual purposive action, macro-to-micro transitions, and micro-to-macro transitions. Not surprisingly, these cross-level connections appear throughout the book, inclusive of the title of chapter 29, "Power, the Micro-to-Macro Transition, and Interpersonal Comparison of Utility."

As noted, prestige and status are central themes in Coleman's work, and it is illuminating to consider how the operation of status puts on display a variety of micro-macro dynamics. We begin with the status function (expression (6) and Figure 9.1), proceed to consider the status distribution (whose quantile function is also given in expression (6) and Figure 9.1), together with its mean and inequality, and finally consider status in the case in which the group has subgroups (Figures 9.2–9.4).

Consider first the individual's relative rank, given in expression (7). As shown, though relative rank inheres in the individual, it requires a group before it can be specified or measured. Specifically, the formula for relative rank requires the individual's absolute rank i and the group size N, both of which require a group. It would be impossible to construct a relative rank without a group of given size and in which the measurements are ordered. Thus, relative rank has already gone beyond a pure micro variable, becoming what may be called a hybrid micro variable.

The status distribution spawns many new macro variables, including average status and status inequality. Average status recurs in Coleman, and status inequality is now often considered the basis for group cohesiveness, another group variable of great interest to Coleman.

It is tempting to think of average status as a pure macro variable – and, indeed, the formula in (8) appears to lend support to that view, given that its only argument is group size N. However, that formula embeds a sum of the individuals' status scores, which in turn embed the rank i for each individual. Thus, it must be concluded that average status is a hybrid macro variable.

Similarly, the Gini coefficient, as all the measures of inequality, embeds the sum of individual status, and thus is a hybrid macro variable.

Importantly, the many levels of behavior include not only the level of the individual and the level of the group but also the level of subgroups. As exemplified by the status subgroups portrayed in Figures 9.2, 9.3, and 9.4, the mathematical revolution of *Intro* enables exploration and analysis of this new subgroup level. Accordingly, the hybrid macro variables include not only the average and the Gini for the whole group but also the average and the Gini for each subgroup (for fuller detail, see Jasso, 2008, 2010).

Coleman's pioneering exploration of micro-macro links thus continues to a new territory in which pure and hybrid micro and macro variables are often embedded together, and there are several levels of analysis, leading to distinctive new forms of postulates and predictions in theories.

TALKING TO COLEMAN

When evening comes I return to the house and enter my writing-room, and on the threshold I take off my everyday clothes full of mud and mire and put on royal and curial robes, and properly reclothed I enter the ancient courts of the men of antiquity where affectionately received by them I pasture on that food that alone is mine and for which I was born, where I am not too timid to speak with them and ask them about the reasons for their actions; and they in their courtesy answer me; and for four hours of time I feel no weariness, I forget every trouble, I do not fear poverty, death does not dismay me: I transfer all of myself into them. (Machiavelli, Letter to Vettori, December 10, 1513)

We, too, may make bold and ask Coleman some of the questions there was no time to ask and which no doubt would lead to insightful discussions.[5] But we do so deeply aware that our questions reflect what Smith (2006: xxvii) describes as "current standards that…stemmed from his earlier contributions." Without that watershed *Intro* moment, it would be impossible even to pose these questions.

What were your favorite mathematics books – the ones you returned to again and again?

What were your favorite books on probability distributions – the ones you returned to again and again?

What was your high school like, and what were you like in high school?

Were you one of those (doubly) smart high school students who rather than work hard to get good grades were "off cultivating other fields which bring social rewards"?

Did you take any economics courses in college?

When did you discover that you loved economics?

Did you really love economics, or did you mainly love the formalization?

Were you satisfied describing racial gaps by simply comparing means, or did you yearn for better tools that would enable comparing the whole distributions?

Did you ever calculate a Gini coefficient?

What insights and tips do you have for distinguishing between responsive/expressive behavior and purposive behavior in empirical work?

Did you ever cite Sørensen's (1979) paper proposing the status function?

When Sørensen went to Harvard in 1984 did you suggest he contact Elliot Mishler and explore the possibility of using Sørensen's new tools to analyze Stephan and Mishler's (1952) classic data?[6]

Are there papers you wrote that you wish we would find and read?

Did you like Bach?

Reader's Guide to James Coleman

A good way to simultaneously appreciate the breadth of Coleman's contributions and observe his intellectual development is to read in chronological order *The Adolescent Society* (1961), *Introduction to Mathematical Sociology* (1964), *Equality of Educational Opportunity* (1966), *Medical Innovation* (1966), *Resources for Social Change: Race in the United States* (1971), *The Mathematics of Collective Action* (1973), and *Foundations of Social Theory* (1990). Because many of his contributions were in the form of articles, further depth requires a chronological list of them. As well, his replies to critics are deeply insightful. And no reading would be complete without what may be his intellectual testament – Coleman's introduction to the journal he founded in 1989, *Rationality and Society*.

For insightful commentary, see Sørensen and Spilerman (1993), Clark (1996), Lindenberg (2000), Marsden (2005), and Smith (2006).

Acknowledgments

I am grateful to Lynne C. Burkhart, Jeffrey Stepnisky, and Murray Webster for their valuable comments and suggestions. I also gratefully acknowledge the intellectual and financial support provided by New York University.

Notes

1 Samuel Kotz (Nadarajah 2002: 222) recalls trying to study the Russian 1945 edition "from cover to cover" in his youth and still using it decades later.
2 Note that Abramowitz and Stegun (1964) was a government project and that Haight (1961) was published in a government journal, evoking other work published by civil servants.

Two celebrated classics come immediately to mind – Natrella's (1963) *Handbook 91* on statistical methods and Shryock and Siegel's (1971) *The Methods and Materials of Demography*.

3 For example, Berger, Cohen, and Zelditch (1966) noted in their pioneering exploration that negatively associated goods would reduce status inequality, and Jasso and Kotz (2007), using a method proposed by Berger, Fisek, Norman, and Zelditch (1977), derived the effects on status inequality of the number of goods and their intercorrelations.

4 Figure 9.3 is based on Jasso (2008:422). The subgroup split 0.632–0.378 is included because it has a special significance in the exponential variate, occurring when the proportion in the lower subgroup p is equal to $[1–(1/e)]$, where e is the transcendental number equal to approximately 2.718.

5 Translation of Machiavelli's letter from the Italian is by de Grazia (1984).

6 For a recent example of using new tools to reanalyze old data – an extremely useful practice throughout the history of science – see Dreifus's (2010) interview with marine chemist Jeffrey L. Bada.

Bibliography

Select writings of James S. Coleman

1960. The adolescent subculture and academic achievement. *American Journal of Sociology*, 65: 337–347.

1961. Athletics in high school. *Annals of the American Academy of Political and Social Science*, 338: 33–43.

1961. *The Adolescent Society*. New York, NY: Free Press.

1961. The competition for "Adolescent Energies." *The Phi Kappa Deltan*, 42: 231–236.

1964. *Introduction to Mathematical Sociology*. New York, NY: Free Press.

1964. Research chronicle: The adolescent society. In Phillip E. Hammond (ed.), *Sociologists at Work: Essays on the Craft of Social Research*. New York, NY: Basic Books, pp. 213–243.

1966 (with E. Q. Campbell, C. J. Hobson, J. McPartland, A. M. Mood, F. D. Weinfeld, and R. L. York). *Equality of Educational Opportunity*. Washington, DC: US Government Printing Office.

1966 (with Elihu Katz and Herbert Menzel). *Medical Innovation*. Indianapolis, IN: Bobbs-Merrill.

1971. *Resources for Social Change: Race in the United States*. New York, NY: John Wiley & Sons.

1973. *The Mathematics of Collective Action*. London, UK: Heinemann.

1989. Rationality and society: Editor's introduction. *Rationality and Society*, 1: 5–9.

1990. *Foundations of Social Theory*. Cambridge, MA: Harvard Belknap.

2006. *The Mathematics of Collective Action*. Reprinted with a new introduction by Robert B. Smith. New Brunswick, NJ: Aldine Transaction.

Further Reading

Abramowitz, Milton and Stegun, Irene A. (eds) (1964) *Handbook of Mathematical Functions, With Formulas, Graphs, and Mathematical Tables*. National Bureau of Standards, Applied Mathematics Series, # 55. Washington, DC: US Government Printing Office.

Allen, R. G. D. (1938) *Mathematical Analysis for Economists*. New York, NY: St. Martin's Press.

Berger, Joseph, Cohen, Bernard P., and Zelditch Jr., Morris (1966) Status characteristics and expectation states. In Joseph Berger, Zelditch Jr., Morris, and Anderson, Bo (eds) *Sociological Theories in Progress*, vol. 1. Boston: Houghton Mifflin, pp. 29–46.

Berger, Joseph, M., Fisek, Hamit, Norman, Robert Z., and Zelditch Jr., Morris (1977) *Status Characteristics and Social Interaction*. New York: Elsevier.

Bronshtein, I. N. and Semendyayev, K. A. (1985) *Handbook of Mathematics*. English translation edited by K. A. Hirsch. Leipzig edition. Based on the original 1945 Russian edition and the 1957 translation into German. New York, NY: Van Nostrand Reinhold.

Clark, Jon (ed.) (1996) *James S. Coleman*. Washington, DC: Falmer.

Courant, Richard ([1934]1937) *Differential and Integral Calculus*, 2 vols. Translated by E. J. McShane. New York, NY: John Wiley & Sons.

Danto, Arthur C. (1967) Philosophy of science, Problems of. In Paul Edwards (ed.) *Encyclopedia of Philosophy*, vol. 6. New York: Macmillan, pp. 296–300.

Dreifus, Claudia (2010) A marine chemist studies how life began. *New York Times*, May 17.

Feller, William (1950) *An Introduction to Probability Theory and Its Applications*, vol. 1. New York, NY: John Wiley & Sons.

Goldstein, Richard (2010) Edith Shain, who said famous kiss came her way, dies at 91. *New York Times*, June 26.

Goode, William J. (1978) *The Celebration of Heroes: Prestige as a Control System*. Berkeley, CA: University of California Press.

Gradshteyn, I. S. and Ryzhik, I. M. (1965) *Table of Integrals, Series, and Products*. Fourth edition prepared by Yu. V. Geronimus and M. Yu. Tseytlin. Translation edited by Alan Jeffrey. New York, NY: Academic Press.

Grazia, Sebastian de (1984) Crossings to another world: Machiavelli and others. *Journal of the History of Ideas*, 45: 145–151.

Haight, Frank A. (1961) Index to the distributions of mathematical statistics. US National Bureau of Standards, *Journal of Research*, Series B: Mathematics and Mathematical Physics 65B-23-60.

Haight, Frank A. (1967) *Handbook of the Poisson Distribution*. Number 11 in Publications in Operations Research. New York, NY: John Wiley & Sons.

Haight, Frank A. (1968) Distributions, statistical: Special discrete distributions. In David L. Sills (ed.) *International Encyclopedia of the Social Sciences*, vol. 4. New York, NY: Macmillan, pp. 217–223.

Hastings, N. A. J. and Peacock, J. B. (1974) *Statistical Distributions*. London: Butterworths.

Hoel, Paul G. ([1947]1971) *Introduction to Mathematical Statistics*. New York: John Wiley & Sons.

Jasso, Guillermina (2001) Studying status: An integrated framework. *American Sociological Review*, 66: 96–124.

Jasso, Guillermina (2008) A new unified theory of sociobehavioral forces. *European Sociological Review*, 24: 411–434.

Jasso, Guillermina (2010) Linking individuals and societies. *Journal of Mathematical Sociology*, 34: 1–51.

Jasso, Guillermina and Kotz, Samuel (2007) A new continuous distribution and two new families of distributions based on the exponential. *Statistica Neerlandica*, 61: 305–328.

Johnson, Norman L. and Kotz, Samuel (1969–1972) *Distributions in Statistics*, 4 vols. New York, NY: John Wiley & Sons.

Kendall, Maurice G. (1943) *The Advanced Theory of Statistics, Volume 1, Distribution Theory*. Original two-volume edition. London, UK: Charles Griffin.

Kendall, Maurice G. and Stuart, Alan (1958) *The Advanced Theory of Statistics, Volume 1, Distribution Theory*. First three-volume edition. New York, NY: Hafner.

Lindenberg, Siegwart (2000) Coleman, James. In George Ritzer (ed.) *The Blackwell Companion to Major Social Theorists*. Malden, MA: Blackwell, pp. 513–544.

Marsden, Peter V. (2005) The sociology of James S. Coleman. *Annual Review of Sociology*, 31: 1–24.

Nadarajah, Saralees (2002) A conversation with Samuel Kotz. *Statistical Science*, 17: 220–233.

National Institute of Standards and Technology. *Handbook of Engineering Statistics*. Available online at www.itl.nist.gov/div898/handbook/ (accessed November 25, 2010).

Natrella, Mary G. (1963) *Experimental Statistics*. National Bureau of Standards: Handbook 91. Washington, DC: US Government Printing Office.

Owen, Donald B. (1962) *Handbook of Statistical Tables*. Reading, MA: Addison-Wesley.

Owen, Donald B. (1968) Distributions, statistical: Special discrete distributions. In David L. Sills (ed.) *International Encyclopedia of the Social Sciences*, vol. 4. New York, NY: Macmillan, pp. 223–230.

Pen, Jan (1971) *Income Distribution*. London, UK: Allen Lane.

Popper, Karl R. (1963) *Conjectures and Refutations: The Growth of Scientific Knowledge*. New York: Basic Books.

Rich, Frank (2010) The 36 Hours that shook Washington. *New York Times*, June 25.

Shryock, Henry S. and Siegel, Jacob S. (1971) *The Methods and Materials of Demography*, 2 vols. Prepared at the US Bureau of the Census. Washington, DC: US Government Printing Office.

Sills, David L. (1968) *International Encyclopedia of the Social Sciences*, 17 vols. New York: Macmillan.

Smith, Robert B. (2006) Aldinetransaction introduction. In J. S. Coleman, *The Mathematics of Collective Action*. Brunswick, NJ: Aldine Transaction, pp. vii–Li.

Sørensen, Aage B. (1971) Equality of educational opportunity in an expanding educational system. *Acta Sociologica*, 14: 151–161.

Sørensen, Aage B. (1979) A model and a metric for the analysis of the intragenerational status attainment process. *American Journal of Sociology*, 85: 361–384.

Sørensen, Aage B. and Spilerman, Seymour (1993) *Social Theory and Social Policy: Essays in Honor of James S. Coleman*. Westport, CT: Praeger.

Spilerman, Seymour (1970) The causes of racial disturbances: A comparison of alternative explanations. *American Sociological Review*, 35: 627–649.

Spilerman, Seymour (1971) The causes of racial disturbances: Tests of an explanation. *American Sociological Review*, 35: 427–442.

Stephan, Frederick F. and Mishler, Elliot G. (1952) The distribution of participation in small groups: An exponential approximation. *American Sociological Review*, 17: 598–608.

Stuart, Alan and Ord, J. Keith (1987) *Kendall's Advanced Theory of Statistics, volume 1, Distribution Theory*. 5th edn. Originally by Sir Maurice Kendall. New York, NY: Oxford University Press.

Thompson, Silvanus P. ([1910]1946) *Calculus Made Easy*. 3rd edn. New York: St. Martin's Press.

Toulmin, Stephen E. (1978) Science, Philosophy of. In *The New Encyclopaedia Britannica, Macropaedia 16*. 15th edn. Chicago: Britannica, pp. 375–393.

US Bureau of the Census (2010) *Historical Income Tables*. Available online at www.census.gov (accessed November 25, 2010).

10

Michel Foucault

COUZE VENN

Introduction

Michel Foucault is probably the most productive philosopher for the social sciences in the last hundred years or so. Whilst many other philosophers, such as Jacques Derrida, Martin Heidegger, Jürgen Habermas, or Giorgio Agamben have invented ideas that have become the vocabulary of theoretical work in the social sciences and the humanities, the work of Foucault has had the greatest impact on how intellectuals think about power, discourse, governance, subjectivity, knowledge, and the place and role of the intellectual in society. Amongst the general public, more people are likely to have heard of Foucault than of other contemporary philosophers. The reason is that Foucault addressed issues which are of concern to most of us, such as sexuality, the interrelationship of power and knowledge, governmentality, disciplinary societies, an ethos of the self, and he did so in such a way that his ideas have struck a chord amongst a large range of intellectuals. In a sense Foucault is the modern philosopher of the people.

It is worth pointing out that far from being the typical ivory tower academic, he was constantly involved in political struggles of one kind or another, alongside other well-known thinkers such as Sartre, de Beauvoir, Althusser, Deleuze, Derrida, Barthes, Serres, Lévi-Strauss, Bourdieu, Canguilhem, Castel, etc., who were friends and supporters – though a number of notable quarrels did occur, with Derrida, and Deleuze amongst others. These activities, at a time when public attention could still be galvanized by the positions taken by the "master thinkers" in times of turbulence – the 1960s and 1970s – helped to propel Foucault into the limelight. The brilliance of his books from early on, and their challenge to orthodoxy, added to the aura of Foucault as one of those "universal intellectuals" whose demise he himself predicted.

The Wiley-Blackwell Companion to Major Social Theorists, First Edition.
Edited by George Ritzer and Jeffrey Stepnisky.
© 2011 Blackwell Publishing Ltd. Published 2011 by Blackwell Publishing Ltd.

The other reason for the appeal of his work is probably to be found in the historical dimension of his thinking, developed in terms of what he calls genealogy, illuminated by striking examples such as the gory execution of Damiens in 1757 at the start of *Discipline and Punish*, the pathologization of particular sexual practices in Victorian times in the *History of Sexuality*, or the panopticon as an ideal structure for surveillance and the gaze of power. So, Foucault is a philosopher of practice, and that focus brings his work and his approach closer to the issues people discuss and scholars research.

The concern with practice will serve as guide for this chapter, which will therefore provide an account from the point of view of a user's guide to his work. In order to help readers make judicious use of the concepts and approach he developed, the chapter will locate the broader framework of debate out of which his work emerged, then present his method, before devoting sections to the key concepts which continue to inform the analysis of contemporary societies. It is appropriate to start with his formation as an intellectual, since so much of his theoretical and political engagements and the line of development of his work find a point of support in that formation.

FOUCAULT: INTELLECTUAL AND POLITICAL JOURNEY

Paul-Michel Foucault was born in Poitiers in October 1926, the son of a doctor whose father was also a doctor. He was thus brought up in a well-established bourgeois family, and was expected to follow the family tradition and in turn join the medical profession. His education followed a course appropriate for such a destiny, and it was with great difficulty that he managed to resist his father's wishes and choose instead the path leading to an academic life. Foucault studied in Poitiers and Paris and early in his career taught in Europe and North Africa. He traveled and lectured widely – Brazil, Japan, Canada – and frequently spent time teaching in the USA from 1972, particularly at the Universities of Stanford, Buffalo, California-Berkeley, in the course of which his influence, especially from the 1980s, grew immensely. He died in Paris in 1984.

From the beginning Foucault had the best education that was on offer in the French provinces; he was a brilliant if erratic student. He managed to get through the arduous French educational system, punctuated by competitions to eliminate all but a handful of students, to end up in a lycée in Paris in 1945 to prepare for the Ecole Normale Supérieure (ENS), which was the prescribed route for the intellectual elite. His favorite disciplines from secondary school were history and philosophy, interests that remained central in all his work, developed in terms of notions of genealogy and critique, and exemplarily materialized in the title of his professorship at the Collége de France when he finally reached that pinnacle of the French academic career, namely the Chair of History of Systems of Thought, to which he was elected in 1969. These interests, and the approach, are central to his early great works, those which established his reputation, namely, *Madness and Civilization* (1967[1961]), *The Order of Things* (1971a[1966])and *Discipline and Punish* (1977a[1975]). Another interest, tied to his background, is that of the sciences of life, particularly medicine, psychology, psychiatry, which motivated his early research and teaching. The texts which play out this ambivalent fascination with and suspicion of medicine and psychiatry are *Mental Illness and Psychology* (orig. 1962) which is the revised version of *Maladie mentale et personalité*, a text written in 1954, *The Birth of the Clinic* ([1963]), *Abnormal* (2003a), volume 1 of the *History of Sexuality* (1978[1976]), and *Madness and Civilization*. In part this was his way of "killing the father," whom he detested, according to Eribon (1989), and in part it is the product of his way of dealing with his mental breakdown whilst at ENS – evidence of the difficulties he had in coming to terms with his homosexuality – and his subsequent work in psychiatric clinics and with psychoanalysts (particularly Ludwig Binwanger).

Foucault acknowledges the debt to some of the teachers at ENS who left a lasting impact on his thought, particularly Jean Hyppolite, whose critical engagement with Hegel's corpus marked the whole generation of Left intellectuals in France in the 1940s and 1950s, Louis Althusser, who became a close friend and whom he followed in joining the Communist Party in 1950 (though there is dispute about the extent of his involvement and he left between 1954 and 1955). It must be said that at the time, and in the context of the Cold War, and wars of decolonization in Vietnam and Algeria, many others followed that path, for example, Jean-François Lyotard, Jean Laplanche, Jean-Pierre Faye amongst those closest to Foucault (See Eribon, 1989 for details). Other notable thinkers who are of great importance for an understanding of his work are Gaston Bachelard, Georges Canguilhem, the historian and philosopher of science who was his research supervisor, and Maurice Merleau-Ponty, whose lectures he followed closely, and Jean Hyppolite. He often acknowledged his debt to them, particularly, Hyppolite in *The Order of Discourse* (1971b), and Canguilhem and Bachelard in *The Archaeology of Knowledge* (1972[1969]) and *The Birth of the Clinic* (1973[1963]). He also read voraciously as a student, notably Marx, Husserl, Heidegger, Freud, Lacan, Saussure, Lévi-Strauss, and Nietzsche, amongst the better known names. Many would claim that the latter left the most indelible mark, say, in the essay *Nietzsche, Genealogy, History* (1991[1971]) but also in *Archaeology of Knowledge* and *The Order of Things* (1971a[1966]) both in relation to the critique of the subject and of power and by reference to methodology. Heidegger and Saussure, in their different ways, influenced his critique of the cogito and the privilege of the subject – and "man" – as the origin of thought and reason, and as the foundation of knowledge and history.

It is interesting that after his philosophy degree (license, 1948), he embarked on a psychology degree, gaining a diploma in psychopathology in 1952. During that period he was attracted to the "phenomenological psychiatry" of Ludwig Binswanger who was trying to cross-fertilize psychoanalysis and philosophy via Heidegger. He also worked at Sainte-Anne Hospital with psychiatric patients, whilst teaching psychology at ENS in 1951–1952, courses which, incidentally, Jacques Derrida attended. These engagements fed into *Mental Illness and Psychology*, and later all the works which take subjectivity and the formation of the subject to be their object, as in the histories of sexuality and the self, the studies of the abnormal, and the hermeneutics of the subject.

In terms of intellectual formation and history, several important stages should be picked out. These relate to political engagement, the critique of orthodoxy in epistemology, and the history of modernity. Apart from the interlude when he was in the Communist Party, Foucault was in Uppsala in Sweden as director of the Maison de France from 1955–1958, then in Warsaw and Hamburg, before returning to

France in 1960. It is a strange period during which he writes his thesis (which became *Madness and Civilization*, Macey, 1993: 88), presented in May 1961. Its subsequent publication established Foucault as a leading thinker in France. The book was much commented upon, including by friends and supporters like Barthes, Bachelard and Serres as well as critics like Derrida who despite regarding Foucault as a friend and teacher took exception to some passages – (see Derrida, 1967, and Foucault's response in the 1972 edition of *l'Histoire de la folie*; the two fell out after this, until 1981). In the early 1960s, Foucault taught at the University of Clermont and took part in the planning of the reform of the university in France, before taking a post teaching philosophy at the university of Tunis in 1966. This was shortly after the publication of *The Order of Things*, a book which firmly established Foucault as a new intellectual master, and thus shaped his subsequent political and theoretical engagements. This period before he returned to France in 1969 is notable for his dissatisfaction with the kind of Marxist discourse that framed French left politics up to May 1968. Instead, he preached a Nietzschean critical skepticism and wrote the *Archaeology of Knowledge (AK)* which appeared in 1969.

His return to political engagement was not around the May events – though he returned briefly to Paris that month – but with involvement in earlier student struggles in Tunisia. These included the Palestinian question from 1967, and wider problems of social transformation. He covertly helped students, many of his own, against the repressive measures put in place during that whole period to subdue the protests. For Foucault, it was a turn to a new politics, focused not on broad goals and ideologies, but concrete specific campaigns and objectives. It is precisely this kind of engagement which he was to throw himself into after returning to France at the end of 1968, when he was appointed as the "director" of the philosophy department at the new and experimental university of Vincennes in January 1969 (recruiting Rancière, Balibar, Badiou, Serres, Judith Miller, Deleuze, Lyotard, amongst others) and as professor at the Collège de France at the end of 1969. He immediately found himself in a similar situation to that in Tunisia, with militant students of all shades in struggle against the "authorities," frequently set upon by special police forces (the notorious CRS). Foucault, who was regarded before as politically soft, emerged as a central figure in organizing struggles, not only in defense of students, but for the reform of prisons (with the GIP or Groupe d'Information sur les Prisons), in anti-racist campaigns and in defense of democratization in Eastern Europe (Hungary, Poland). He was often at the head of marches, with colleagues like Sartre, de Beauvoir, Deleuze, Althusser, Barthes, Genet, Cixous, Deleuze, and many others, and was occasionally arrested or beaten. He also contributed to the founding of the radical newspaper, *Libération*, which first appeared in April 1973. So, Foucault the committed intellectual, emerges out of the Vincennes moment of radical engagement against the establishment (Eribon, 1989: 222). A different theorization of power is developed out of these activities, feeding into the analysis of the state, of governmentality, of sexuality, and linking with the earlier analysis of discourse in terms of the concept of power/knowledge. One key text which exemplifies many of the concerns and shifts is *Discipline and Punish* (1977a[1975]), though numerous interviews and articles and lectures expand on both his thinking and political views.

The broad theoretical lines of this development is described in the statement – Titres et Travaux, November 1969 – submitted in support of the post at the College de France and the sketch of the programme of research which he was proposing to pursue. Two aspects are worth highlighting from this statement. On the one hand, one finds his interpretation of what his previous work had dealt with, in particular the study of the process whereby knowledge comes to be inscribed in complex institutional settings, affecting practices such as the constitution of categories like madness. In this view discourses, practices, and institutions form a dynamic and mobile system determining what can be thought or said and done at any particular point. For Foucault, to analyze the systematic relations amongst them requires an archeology, that is, a focus on the questioning of the document and on the transformation of documents into "monuments," as he was to put it in *AK* (6, 7).

On the other hand, he proposes to undertake research into concrete cases – he cites heredity, though this is a topic which is abandoned in favor of the analysis of carceral institutions – within the frame of a history of systems of thought. This programme is given greater specificity in his inaugural lecture, *The Order of Discourse* (December 1970), in which he describes the themes he would like to investigate, based on the view that "in any society the production of discourse is at once controlled, selected, organized and redistributed by means of a number of procedures whose role is to conjure its powers and dangers, to overcome its unpredictability as event, to escape its burdensome and frightening materiality" (1971b: 10, 11). This is because discourse "is not only what translates struggles and systems of domination, but that through which and for which one struggles, the power which one attempts to seize" (12). For these reasons, a will to know drives the production of discourse, doubled with a will to truth, which is part of a system of exclusion – say, reason from madness – supported by institutions, for example pedagogy, libraries, learned societies, and so on. Equally, internal rules for the formation of statements regulate what can be said, who has authority to speak, which discourses shall be granted the authority of truth. Such a view implies the rejection of the principle of the author as agent of discourse, foregrounding instead the role of disciplines, paradigms, and rules of access. And it is in specifying the method adequate for the analysis of the production and change of discourse that he describes a method in which critique is allied to genealogy: "Critique analyses the process of limitation of discourses, but also the process of their recombination and unification; genealogy studies their at once dispersed, discontinuous and regular formation. In fact, these two tasks are never quite separable" (67). It is a method which is put to work in all the research to follow.

METHOD: GENEALOGY, ARCHEOLOGY, CRITIQUE

One of the key innovations of Foucault which has been extensively taken up by researchers has been in the field of method, particularly the concept of genealogy. It is important to bear in mind that the methodological apparatus was developed as part of the critique of orthodox epistemology, which privileged the subject as author, and as part of the rejection of the "history of ideas" approach that assumed and searched for continuities rather than discontinuities, and that supported the paradigm of history as linear progression. So, inventing new concepts, or redefining familiar ones such as genealogy was essential for his overall project. To be faithful to Foucault's own method, one must not attribute such departures to Foucault as the isolated author or great mind. Indeed, when we take account of the background sketched above, and the many occasions when Foucault has spoken about his intellectual debts, we realize that in terms of method, the work of Canguilhem, Bachelard, Nietzsche, Saussure, Hyppolite, Lévi-Stauss, and Braudel have the heaviest presence in the elaboration of his arguments. I should add that particular literary figures, such as Samuel Beckett, served to incite or confirm Foucault's search for an approach to discourse that refuses the privilege of the author principle. In this respect, the quote from Beckett at the beginning of *The Order of Discourse* – stressing the recognition that one's own speech is located in an already-existing stream of discourse which one simply relays by adding one's voice – is an apt homage to his mentors and a recognition of the collective and dialogical production of knowledge.

An argument made in *AK* will point us in the direction for examining the work which genealogy is meant to do. After developing a critique of the linguistic approach to discourse and the "dubious unities" which it assumes – unities of the oeuvre, the author, disciplines, etc. – he says "The description of the events of discourse poses a quite different question: how is it that one particular statement appeared rather than another?" (1972: 27). What is put on the agenda is the recognition of conditions of possibility determining particular discourses, conditions that refer to relations that any discourse or group of statements have with the field in which they appear and "events of a quite different kind (technical, economic, social, political)" (29). The problematization of unities thus foregrounds the point of view of discourse as event, as interruption and irruption; this means that we are led to consider a statement in its emergence. The analysis of the "statement/event" turns attention to the space in which it occurs and thus to "the interplay of relations within it and outside it" (29), so that we can bring to light the strategies that go into its production, and the effects statements have within discourse and on practices.

The elements which have fed into this approach are signaled in the introduction to *AK*, when Foucault mentions Bachelard and Canguilhem to speak about "epistemological acts and thresholds" that "suspend the continuous accumulation of knowledge" (Bachelard), and "the displacements and transformations of concepts" for which "the analyses of G. Canguilhem may serve as models" (4). We need to note that Bachelard, in his studies of physics, argued for "epistemological breaks" occurring at the threshold between paradigms and between everyday knowledge and a rational science – for instance when he points out that the atom of Democritus is not the same as that of modern physics, or that the common sense understanding of mass is epistemologically opposed to its meaning in physics. Bachelard also emphasized the technically constructed character of the objects of scientific practice, that is, concepts are "technically normed" (See Venn, 1982 for elaboration). Canguilhem, in part as an engagement with the work of Bachelard, focused on the history of the sciences of life, studying the process of establishing categories like the normal and the pathological in biology and medicine. He stressed that the history of any science is punctuated by errors (which are just as productive for the development of a science), by uncertainty, by conditions of possibility that include those outside particular disciplines.

The effects on Foucault's analytical approach and methodology are crucial, for instance, in terms of searching for conditions of possibility and emergence in contiguous disciplines and in the wider cultural milieu of theory (as exemplified in Canguilhem's work). He emphasizes the role of documents as part of the "mass of

elements that have to be grouped, made relevant, placed in relation to one another...
[such that] history aspires to the condition of archaeology" (7). The consequences are
that his archeological approach constructs series, detects discontinuities, produces a
"general history" (as opposed to "total history" (8, 9)), and introduces new methodological problems in terms of building coherent bodies of documents, delimiting
and grouping relevant elements, and interpreting relations amongst all the elements.
These relate to problematizations, including about structural components of events –
Foucault has consistently rejected the label structuralism – that nevertheless seek new
coherences, to be found later in the idea of genealogy as a history of the present.

In *AK* the notion of episteme can be seen as an early formulation of this search for
a coherence, bringing together many of the key elements:

> By episteme, we mean, in fact, the total set of relations that unite, at a given period, the
> discursive practices that give rise to epistemological figures, sciences, and possibly for-
> malized systems; the way in which, in each of these discursive formations, the transi-
> tions to epistemologization, scientificity, and formalization are situated and operate; the
> distribution of these thresholds, which may coincide, be subordinated to one another,
> or be separated by shifts in time; the lateral relations that may exist between epistemo-
> logical figures or sciences in so far as they belong to neighbouring, but distinct, discur-
> sive practices. The episteme is not a form of knowledge (*connaissance*) or type of
> rationality which, crossing the boundaries of the most varied sciences, manifests the
> sovereignty of a subject, a spirit, or a period; it is the totality of relations that can be
> discovered, for a given period, between the sciences when one analyses them at the level
> of discursive regularities. (*AK*: 191)

I have quoted this definition at length to point to the affinities, and differences,
with Canguilhem and Bachelard's work, and to signal the point that, when Foucault's
theorization of discourse is viewed in the light of these authors' approach to the mutation of concepts, episteme no longer has the structuralist inflection often attributed to
Foucault's work of that period. Instead one can locate the concept within the project
of an archeology and genealogy, that is, the search for the effects of submerged or
unacknowledged discourses and historical events, the search for "lines of descent"
and dispersion. It is the recognition that discourses constitute series which intersect,
feed off each other, or oppose each other, and that these series, in their dispersion
and development, constitute a history of the present that one can understand why
"one particular statement appeared rather than another." One would need to relate
this process of production of discourse to the effects of power, examined by reference
not to the intra-discursive process alone, but to the relation amongst elements belonging to a wider set of discourses and to the historical context, that is, to inter-discursive,
institutional and material elements that genealogy brings to the surface.

This analytical apparatus began to really emerge in Foucault's studies based on
concrete practices relating to problems in the present and to his own political engagements, notably his genealogies of the prison and of sexuality, where he shows the
effects of power and specific discourses in constituting these categories through
apparatuses put in place to achieve this. The approach is concretized in the idea of
governmentality, that is, the theory relating types of power to apparatuses of constitution and regulation of populations and individuals (Foucault, 1979; see below).

It suggests that one should be looking at the intersections of a number of broader fields and processes, for example, when he argues that "studying penal institutions meant studying them first of all as sites" of such intersections (2008: 34). Similarly, the genealogy of "sexuality" meant trying to reconstruct through what is involved in activities like confessional practices, spiritual direction, and their inscription in, for example, the medical and familial relationship, "the moment when the exchange and cross-over took place between a jurisdiction of sexual relations, defining the permitted and the prohibited, and the veridiction of desire, in which the basic arma-ture of the object 'sexuality' currently appears" (2008: 35).

This is consistent with his "general project" of governmentality as a particular kind of analysis that proceeds according to the following three displacements or ways of "moving outside the institution … This kind of method entails first of all going behind the institution and trying to discover in a wider and more overall perspective what we can broadly call a technology of power" (2007: 117). Such an analysis, he argues, "allows us to replace a genetic analysis … with a genealogical analysis … which reconstructs a whole network of alliances, communications, and points of support" (117). We can see this at work in *Discipline and Punish* (1977), where he tried to understand the role of the prison by looking at the functioning of the body, the role of crime, the remaking of the family, the regulation of population, and in this way relocate the prison not so much in terms of the conventional discourse of crime and punishment, but by reference to the emergence of the form of power he calls governmentality. Similarly the study of the medicalization of the "abnormal" uncovers the constitutive links between concepts of crime, "degeneration," heredity, and social defense (2003a).

The second displacement, relating to the first, concerns the problematization of the function of institutions like the prison to make visible an "external point of view of strategies and tactics" instead of focusing on "the internal point of view of the func-tion" (2007: 118). This is because "the prison is undoubtedly not governed by the successes and failures of its functionality" since the wider strategies framing governmentality as "a general economy of power" are more important (117, 118). His explanation is that "By de-institutionalizing and de-functionalizing relations of power we can grasp their genealogy, i.e., the way they are formed, connect up with each other, develop, multiply, and are transformed on the basis of something other than them-selves, on the basis of something other than relations of power" (119). Later, he speci-fies this other parameter as political economy (2009[1976]). The third shift is central to the idea of conceptual problematization for it means "refusing to give oneself a ready-made object, be it mental illness, delinquency, or sexuality" (118). For, the ques-tion is: how did these objects come to be constituted, under what circumstances, what were the stakes, and what effects did they have on subsequent developments?

We find the earliest formulations of the genealogical method in Foucault's impor-tant essay, "Nietzsche, Genealogy, History" (1991[1971]) which emphasizes geneal-ogy as the open-ended search for conditions of possibility grounded in archival and archeological explorations. Genealogy he says "is gray, meticulous, and patiently documentary. It operates on a field of entangled and confused parchments, on docu-ments that have been scratched over and recopied many times" (76). The implication for research is that genealogy requires "patience and a knowledge of details, and it depends on a vast accumulation of source material. Its 'cyclopedian monuments' are constructed from 'discreet and apparently insignificant truths and according to a rigorous method.' Genealogy … opposes itself to the search for 'origins'" (76, 77). Nietzsche's methodological reflections are clearly evident in Foucault's elaboration of his own approach to the kind of history of the present and historical reconstruction he calls genealogy. Such a history was important for him because he claims it has the value of critique.

The aspects one should bear in mind are the emphasis on emergence and on conditions of possibility and thus the rejection of the idea of origin or simple cause (*Ursprung* in the Nietzschean texts), whereby one assumes one can proceed using the model of the genealogy of the family, namely, by retracing straight lines of descent. Foucault's explanation stresses the view that historical change does not proceed according to a "timeless and essential secret" that a historian is supposed to reveal, but shows that what one takes to be "essences" have in fact been "fabricated"; they are the result of a construction (78). Instead, he constructs a different history, working according to a different understanding of "origin," namely *Herkunft*, and *Entstehung*. The former "is the equivalent of stock or descent," the advantage being that the concept of "descent also permits the discovery, under the unique aspect of a trait or a concept, of the myriad events through which – thanks to which, against which – they were formed. Genealogy does not pretend to go back in time to restore an unbroken continuity that operates beyond the dispersion of forgotten things" (81). By contrast, "*Entstehung* designates emergence, the moment of arising" (83), and "Emergence is always produced through a particular stage of forces" (83). It occurs in the context of an event, which Foucault explains "is not a decision, a treaty, a reign, or a battle, but the reversal of a relationship of forces, the usurpation of power, the appropriation of a vocabulary turned against those who once used it … the entry of a masked 'other'" (88). From such a perspective, the world "is a profusion of entangled events" (89). Each of his major texts demonstrates this entanglement through the intersection of broader fields in the historical process whereby significant transformations occur, such as those that announced the emergence of "high modernity" and biopolitics in terms of the co-emergence of industrialization, liberal capitalism, and the nation-state.

So, basically, genealogy inscribes the idea of a method based on the concepts of emergence, descent, the event, and conditions of possibility that include the effects of dispersed and indeterminate changes and developments. Nevertheless, in spite of the profusion of events, genealogy must search for exemplary cases, documents, or developments, etc., that can act as point of entry for genealogical reconstruction. In *Discipline and Punish* it was the torture and execution of Damiens in 1757 which Foucault uses as entry point to illustrate in a stark manner the shift in the form of power from sovereignty to disciplinary power, that is, from power vested in the right of the sovereign to own and dispose of the body of his subjects as he pleases, as proof of the absolute character of his power, to a form of power vested in the ability to form and regulate subjects according to norms that inscribe normative and juridical ways of acting, that is, a disciplinary form of power. Similarly, as part of his genealogical approach to the modern form of state power, he presents the panopticon as the ideal device for a perfect technology of surveillance consistent with the shift towards governmentality (Foucault, 2007). The panopticon stands as the exemplary apparatus of disciplinary society, the all-seeing, pervasive yet in a sense invisible operation of power; it still operates today as the ideal of surveillance, even if through different devices such as CCTVs. As exemplar, the panopticon gives the archive its meaning and justifies the work of genealogy as a history of the present, that is, it shows at what point and under what circumstances a shift occurs and a new regime of power emerges, here a disciplinary one, that continues to have effects in the present, even if operating through different institutions which have been put in place since.

To summarize, the aspects which are relevant for genealogical explorations are the following: at the general level, an analytical framework that works as the broader theoretical context that provides the coherence for the genealogical account, for example, by reference to problematics such as those of governmentality, biopolitics, disciplinary society, thus inscribing forms of power such as biopolitics. Second, a set of methodological concepts, specifically, emergence, descent or line of descent from the present, conditions of possibility, the event, heterogeneity. Their application requires an archeological excavation of the archive to search for specific events or cases or discourses which work as points of entry, or points at which crucial shifts happened or decisions made that can be presented as key conditions for later developments. Third, genealogy also requires the researcher to establish both intra and inter-discursive relations through detailed analyses of specific documents, texts, archival material, so that the less visible traces of discursive events and shifts can be reconstructed by reference to a discursive formation and the power relations inscribed in discourses.

Finally, Foucault's indications in *Nietzsche, Genealogy, History* point to the need to produce a corpus of material from a dispersed archive, involving wide-ranging archival work, including neglected sources such as biographies and diaries (say, Pierre Rivière, 1975[1973]; or Herculine Barbin in Foucault, 1980). The important lesson in constructing genealogies is that one must be sensitive to the tactical functions that groups of statements have, because of the power effects invested in them, and sensitive to the heterogeneity of discourses and the mobile, contextually dependent character of their effects. It means always having in the background a broad analytical framework which enables choices to be made and lines of descent constructed to reflect a history of shifts in power relations.

The analytical framework is important for establishing the critical dimension of genealogy as a history of the present. It enables archeology to recognize and deploy "the insurrection of subjugated knowledges" through the reactivation of "knowledges from below" (Foucault, 2003b: 7). The relaying of genealogy to critique is explained in Foucault's argument linking "the local character of critique" to "a historical knowledge of struggles" and to genealogy as a project (6, 8, 9). He says:

> When I say "subjugated knowledges" I mean…historical contents that have been buried or masked in functional coherences or formal systematizations…[S]ubjugated knowledges are, then, blocks of historical knowledges that were present in the functional and systematic ensembles, but which were masked, and the critique was able to reveal their existence. (7)

He adds that they also refer to

> a whole series of knowledges that have been disqualified as nonconceptual knowledges, as insufficiently elaborated knowledges: naïve knowledges, hierarchically inferior

knowledges…below the required level of erudition or scientificity. And it is thanks to the reappearance of these knowledges from below, of these unqualified or even disqualified knowledges…the knowledge of the psychiatrized, the patient, the nurse, the doctor, that is parallel to, marginal to, medical knowledge, the knowledge of the delinquent,…what people know…a knowledge that is local, regional, or differential, incapable of unanimity…it is the reappearance…of these disqualified knowledges, that made the critique possible. (7, 8)

This passage highlights the effect of "scientific" discourse in marginalizing knowledges and discourses which in fact played a constitutive role in the emergence of historical practices, and thus the possibility that, by constructing a different account of the historical conditions of possibility of discourses that have become dominant, one can gain a new critical angle on them. The idea of knowledges from below underline the importance of marginal and marginalized discourses to counter the weight of "elite" or "scientific" discourses; it echoes the idea of "history from below," and thus suggests the idea of a genealogy from below. This is a genealogy which focuses on "minor" events and stories and memories that yet feed into a different or "counter history" (73) of alternative practices, dissident discourse, movements of resistance and so on which could inform problematization or counter practices today. Indeed, Foucault says that what is at stake in the genealogies he is theorizing is the recovery of a "historical knowledge of struggles [and] a memory of combats…that had until then been confined to the margins" (8). The connection with critique is clear when he concludes that "we can give the name 'genealogy' to this coupling together of scholarly erudition and local memories, which allows us to constitute a historical knowledge of struggles and to make use of that knowledge in contemporary tactics" (8). It is in that sense that one can understand genealogy as a history of the present, that is, as a specific combination of critique and "desubjugated historical knowledges" (10) that support "an insurrection against the centralizing power-effects that are bound up with the institutionalisation and working of any scientific discourse organized in a society such as ours" (9).

Key Concepts

We are now in a position to examine the key concepts with which the work of Foucault is associated. The trouble is that there are many and they interconnect, and one could compose different combinations. Foucault himself highlighted those of power and the subject, though the latter is foregrounded: "Thus, it is not power, but the subject, which is the general theme of my research" (1982: 209). Nevertheless, he prescribed "a new economy of power relations" which would study the "transversal struggles" that traverses "oppositions which have developed over the last few years: opposition to the power of men over women, of parents over children, of psychiatry over the mentally ill, of medicine over the population, of administration over the ways people live" (211). These are struggles over the "government of individualization" and "regimes of knowledge" (*régimes du savoir*), that is, the way knowledge/know-how "circulates and functions, its relations of power" (212). For Foucault, power is foregrounded because these struggles against forms of domination, exploitation and subjection "revolve around the question: Who are we?" This questioning in his work has two inter-connected sides: one to do with what he calls an ethics and aesthetics of the self or becoming (1991[1984]), and the other to do with the interrogation and challenge to the new political form of power we know as the state (1982: 213). Both themes form the backbone of his last researches, around the analysis and critique of governmentality, biopolitics, and political economy, and around the problematization of the process of subjective becoming. They are presented in the lectures given from 1975 until his death, that we could sub-divide into two series: the political economy of biopolitics series (or governmentalization of biopower series) (1975–1980) and the ethics and aesthetics of the self series (1980–1984). An underlying project connects them: "to liberate us both from the state and the type of individualization which is linked to the state. We have to promote new forms of subjectivity through the refusal of this kind of individualization which has been imposed on us for several centuries" (1982: 216).

This way of making sense of his overall project may allow us to organize further the concepts of power and the subject deployed in his writings around two terms, namely biopolitics and subjectivity. The first would provide the framework for locating concepts like disciplining, normalization, and governmentality, whilst the second enables us to group fields of experience such as madness, crime, sexuality, illness, hermeneutics and ethics of the self. Power/knowledge, and thus the analysis of discourse and discursive relations through genealogy as method, relays the one term to the other.

Power

The concept of power/knowledge is important since it relays the analytical and methodological apparatus to the two central themes of power and subjectivity. Foucault develops the idea in many places, but a number of key propositions or rules frame the gist of what is meant. Describing the rules for analyzing mobile power relations in History of Sexuality I, he says: "Between techniques of knowledge and strategies of power, there is no exteriority, even if they have specific roles" (1998: 98). Power/knowledge is invested in "local centers," such as in the relation between patients and confessors or doctors, or the relation between the child and parents, nurses, educators, etc. Power/knowledge is subject to constant variations, since the "distributions of power" and the "appropriations of knowledge" are not static but are "matrices of transformations" (99). Power/knowledge is conditioned by "over-all strategy," for example, when in the nineteenth century "family organization" and thus sexuality was framed within political economy, including the Malthusian call to control the birth rate (100). Finally, since "it is in discourse that power and knowledge are joined together" (100), the mobility of relations of force means that there are a "multiplicity of discursive elements that come into play in various strategies. It is this distribution that we must reconstruct" (100), thus emphasizing the strategic and dynamic nature of the co-constituting relationship between knowledge and power.

The theoretical arguments for his "nominalist" approach to power is developed throughout the *Archaeology of Knowledge* at the level of principles and method, as I have sketched, though they are present from the beginning, for instance by reference to the analysis of discourse or knowledge in terms of what he calls the "positivities" (1972: 181ff.). The rules summarized above are more clearly at work in the studies of sexuality, the clinic, the prison, where the practices associated with these experiences or institutions are referred to specific fields of knowledge – concerning sex, illness, madness, criminality – knowledges that establish the norms of the normal, and so inform processes of constitution of subjects and the technologies for the regulation of conduct, that is, disciplinary practices. Power in all these studies does not refer, in the first instance, to institutions that ensure conformity through prohibitions or force and so seek domination and subjugation, for these "are only the terminal forms power takes" (1998: 92). Foucault instead wants to stress that

> power must be understood in the first instance as the multiplicity of force relations immanent in the sphere in which they operate and which constitute their own organization; as the process which, through ceaseless struggles and confrontations, transforms, strengthens, or reverses them; as the support which these force relations find in one another, thus forming a chain or a system, or on the contrary, the disjunctions and contradictions which isolate them from one another; and lastly, as the strategies in which they take effect. (92, 93)

It is as part of developing this view that he says "Power is everywhere; not because it embraces everything, but because it comes from everywhere ... 'Power' ... is simply the over-all effect that emerges from these mobilities ... [power is] the name that one attributes to a complex strategical situation in a particular society" (93). The importance of the concept of norm – and thus the normal and the normative – is linked to this objective, since it is a matter of setting the limits within which the individual is able and is allowed to act, and within which a population can be kept within the bounds of the calculable. The concept of discipline in this context relates to the techniques and means – including institutions, laws, forms of punishment and reform, etc. – whereby relations of force bend or incite subjects to conform to the norm. The concept of power is further elaborated in the series of lectures which has biopolitics as a focus, where the concept of power comes to be framed within political economy; this is a phase in the development of his thoughts which I will address more fully below.

Subjectivity

For now I want to locate the discourse of subjectivity in the Foucauldian apparatus, as this is the aspect which has been most fruitful in research in the human sciences and the humanities. The volumes on the history of sexuality are the most sustained investigation of the ways whereby we are made subjects, although the earlier research in *The Order of Things* reconstructs the discursive conditions and the epistemological shifts which gave birth to the conceptualization of the subject as "man," that is, the ontological and epistemological figure which is seen as the originary center in relation to which history, knowledge and meaning, and life, language, and labor, are to be understood. These shifts from the "Classical age" to the beginning of modernity announced the birth of the modern subject, that is, the birth of the idea of the subject as the unitary, self-sufficient, autonomous agent of action and meaning, theorized in Descartes's concept of the cogito, and which was and has remained central in Western modernity. It is this subject whose end Foucault predicts at the end of the book. Foucault was not alone in this critique of this central figure of modernity, variously conceptualized as the bourgeois individual, the cogito, the "logocentric" subject, Man, the Subject. Indeed, the quarrel around structuralism, often most intense around the agency-structure dualism, with "humanism" positioned on the side of the subject and "anti-humanism" on the opposite side, has at stake the questions of individual autonomy, freedom, responsibility, and, at the grander level, the question of who makes history. Foucault tried to avoid the more frustrating aspects of these debates, especially around structuralism, by rejecting the label and insisting that the problem for him is about accounting for the process of emergence of the concept of the subject/man itself (Eribon, 1989: 223).

The emphasis on emergence points to the contribution which Foucault has made to the problematic of the subject. For, in searching for conditions of possibility and for the discursive and institutional "positivities" in enacting various aspects of "society," he was drawing attention to the constructed character of subjectivity, and demonstrating the mechanisms whereby particular forms of the subject are constituted according to specific norms, subjects whose conduct can then be brought within the sphere of regulation and statistical calculation, especially with the emergence of governmentality as a form of power that takes this constitution and regulation of individuals and populations to be its prime objective (Foucault, 1979, 2007[2004]; Henriques *et al.*, 1998, 1984). Studies in the wake of Foucault's advances have focused on problems of normalization, disciplining, surveillance, and regulation in which subjects are both the target and the stake. And, given that the mechanisms of normalization and constitution take individual bodies and populations of living beings as the site of intervention, as with sexuality, Foucault's work has encouraged a great deal of work addressing the body and life (Rose, 1985, 1999[1989]; Butler, 1990, 1993).

An account of Foucault's thinking about the subject would leave out an important element if one were to miss the essay "What is Enlightenment?" (in Rabinow, 1991[1984]), where he speaks of an ethics and aesthetics of being, and the lectures on the hermeneutics of the subject. In the essay, he returns to the problem posed by Kant in 1784 in order to propose an answer for contemporary times. Kant's main concern was the process whereby humanity could "progress" from a state of "immaturity" to one of "maturity," that being the core Enlightenment project He also wanted to work out what signs there could be to indicate that such progress was happening. Kant's arguments leads him to shift the terrain of the problem from one of judging the state of society at any particular time to one about the free use of reason, and the conditions that would optimize its deployment in pursuit of the "project" of the Enlightenment. He reasoned that maturity could be achieved only if one could freely critique the present, that is, if one could use reason to reflect on history and on existing conditions in order to make a difference between the present and the future. Foucault concludes from this: "I wonder whether we may not envisage modernity rather as an attitude than as a period of history. And by 'attitude,' I mean a mode of relating to contemporary reality; a voluntary choice made by certain people; in the end, a way of thinking and feeling; a way, too, of acting and behaving that at one and the same time marks a relation to belonging and presents itself as a task" (1984: 39). It is, he adds, an attitude that has found itself in a struggle with other attitudes that can be thought of as "countermodernity."

This emphasis on attitude, feeling and a way of thinking underlie the direction of his own take on Enlightenment and its contemporary reconfiguration. The making of a difference, and the anticipation of different futures for society – rather than the repetition of the same that we encounter in both "totalising" and so-called "traditional" societies – sets itself two tasks: transforming oneself at the same time as society through the "permanent critique of our historical era" and ourselves (42). This critique must, he says, recognize the limits that are imposed on us because of the contingencies of history, yet its stake joins with the difficult work of freedom because of the risks one runs in asserting one's freedom despite power's interest in limiting it. What is emphasized instead is "the possibility of no longer being, doing, or thinking what we are, do, or think" (46). This is to be achieved through a work "carried out by ourselves upon ourselves as free beings" (47). The stakes involved in this task include how "the growth of capabilities [can] be disconnected from the intensification of power relations" (48), that is, the refusal to acquiesce in the disciplining and normalizing technologies that power/knowledge supports as part of the amplification of capabilities and government of conduct which constitute the goals of political economy. The task of liberation as reconfigured by Foucault needs to take account of "the axis of knowledge, the axis of power, the axis of ethics" (48). In practice, this means modes of problematization through archeological and genealogical studies of practices, and a "critical ontology of ourselves" which is an ethos or "a philosophical life in which the critique of what we are is at one and the same time the historical analysis of the limits that are imposed on us and an experiment with the possibility of going beyond them" (50).

This view of an ethics and aesthetics of ourselves has been emerging in the lectures he gave between 1980 and 1984 on the hermeneutics of the subject, on the government of oneself and others, and on the courage to speak the truth – the theme of *parrhesia* in ancient Greek thought (Foucault, 2001, 2005). In the course of these studies, Foucault rereads a number of Greek meditations on the art of living or technique of existence (*tekhne tou biou*) in order to tease out the principles and protocols that provide indications of what may be involved in the "critical ontology of ourselves." The Greek texts were concerned with the care of oneself (*epimeleia heautou*) that involved a concern both for the life of the body and the life of the spirit. Foucault examines the different levels of this art of living, paying attention to *ascesis*, *parrhesia*, the relation to the other, and the modalities of care. What he retains from his close reading of Greek philosophy is the idea that one must labor upon oneself in order to know oneself, in the form of self-inspection, guided by an apprenticeship with a master, and performed through practices of meditation and truth-telling or frank speaking. It combined a therapeutics with a medical practice (a *pharmakon*), and a hermeneutics. I would highlight the relation to the other, in that it is by speaking about oneself to another, usually a tutor, and listening to his discourse that one learns to inspect one's thoughts and motives. So, what is required is this critical discourse and the accumulated knowledge which is invested in this relationship, and of course the willingness to listen and to question.

I would also highlight this matter of truth-telling or *parrhesia*, which is "both a technique and an ethics, an art and a morality" (2005: 368); it "refers to a type of relationship between the speaker and what he says" (2001: 12). It involves speaking freely so that truth would be the basis upon which the relationship to the other and to oneself can be grounded. But to be able to speak the truth is both the product of the work one does upon oneself as part of the care of the self, as well as evidence of a kind of virtue that the art of existence cultivates. One important element of *parrhesia* is that "the *parrhesiastes* says something which is dangerous to himself and thus involves a risk" (2001: 13). This courage to speak the truth in spite of the risks implies that "the *parrhesiastes* primarily chooses a specific relationship to himself: he prefers himself as a truth-teller than as a living being who is false to himself" (2001: 1); it is a virtue. It is thus a form of criticism directed at oneself or at particular persons, especially those more powerful than oneself: "The *parrhesia* comes from 'below' as it were, and is directed towards 'above,'" such as when a philosopher criticizes a tyrant or the citizen criticizes those in power (2001: 18). The courage to speak the truth is itself an expression of this freedom to speak, avoiding rhetoric and dissembling. The Greeks thought of this aspect of truth-telling as a duty (2001: 19). It is for all these reasons that this courage has been thought in terms of speaking truth to power. And it is in this that the function of critique can be associated with the critical ontology of ourselves. For, without that, there is neither the space nor the will to "make a difference." It can be seen from this interpretation that the link between subjectivity and power remained a constant one in his work from the earliest to his later work on the care of the self; indeed, he himself said: "I have tried to analyse how areas such as madness, sexuality, and delinquency may enter into a certain play of truth, and also how, through this insertion of human practice, of behaviour, in the play of truth, the subject himself is affected" (1990: 48). What is added is the sense of a spiritual dimension to the work one does upon oneself to ready oneself for death and to bring about new ways of life (see also Rabinow, 2009).

POLITICAL ECONOMY AND THE ANALYSIS OF THE PRESENT

It is interesting that the work on a critical ontology comes after the series of lectures from 1975 to 1979 which had established the parameters for analyzing biopolitical power. The recent transcription, editing and translation of his lecture notes provide us with his most detailed analysis of the modern form of power, a form which he tied to the nation-state as the territorialized arena of this power over individuals and populations. It is worth spending some time on the arguments he developed in these lectures because it is the place where he fully addresses the question of political economy, a question that seemed neglected in his earlier work. Indeed, the location of political economy as the form which the exercise of state power increasingly took in Western modernity provides us with a handle on contemporary relations of power. For this reason, this newly available corpus of his work enables us to fully appreciate the importance of his contribution for our understanding of our own times.

The series begins with *Society Must be Defended* (2003 (Lectures, 1975/1976)), in which the strategies whereby power authorizes itself are explored, particularly with reference to the form of power he calls sovereignty, exemplified in "the right to kill" which the sovereign attributes to himself as proof of his might – we are largely concerned with patriarchical societies (240). This right over life, which we can see as the first form of biopower, is authorized by appeal to a juridico-theological or juridico-political discourse, for example, the claim of a divine right to rule, backed by a narrative of history which presents the victors as guarantors of order and justice. An important aspect of this narrative is the recourse to "the discourse of race war," which claims history to be one of a struggle between friend and enemy that can only end with the subjugation (or elimination) of one group or "race" by the other. It is basically a military discourse, legitimizing conquest and a zero-sum game of winners and losers whereby violence is seen as the origin of order as well as of inequalities of wealth and power. This essentially colonial discourse later takes the form of racism, that is, a discourse which "makes it possible to establish a relationship between my life and the death of the other that is not a military or warlike relationship of confrontation, but a biological-type relationship" (255). I should note that Foucault adds that by "killing" he means also "every form of indirect murder: the fact of exposing someone to death, increasing the risk of death for some people, or quite simply, political death, expulsion, rejection, and so on" (256). Political economy here is a matter of dispossession, of legitimizing the zero-sum game locking rich and poor in a fatal struggle; it works by appeal to an idea of natural necessity or to some claim such as the survival of the fittest; equally, political economy has the task of linking the power of the sovereign – the prince, the emperor – with the size of his possessions.

The next step in Foucault's genealogy reconstructs the developments whereby in Europe after Westphalia (1648) and the consequent birth of the nation-state as a fixed and territorialized political entity, the wealth/power of the sovereign comes to be tied to the capabilities of the population over which he rules. So territory, population, and security – the latter understood in the wider sense of the maximization of trust (in the law, in rules of exchange, in public institutions) and the minimization of risks – emerged as the new parameters of wealth creation (2007[1977–1978]). This is the place where Foucault examines in detail the apparatuses of normalization and disciplining which were put in place as part of biopolitical governmentality. We can therefore understand biopolitics as the governmentalization and economization of biopower. In relation to this form of power, the political economy of the time addresses problems of how to increase the wealth of the state, how to improve productivity – hence the importance of improving the health, the skills and "happiness" of the population, particularly through the "science of police" – how to regulate a market economy, and the place of colonial economies for the accumulation of wealth in Europe (though this latter theme is underdeveloped in Foucault generally; see Venn, 2009).

I focus on *The Birth of Biopolitics* (2008[1978–1979]) because it is in this text that he elaborates a perspective which provides the basic arguments for interrogating the world we live in from the standpoint of the possibility of overcoming present conditions. As such Foucault's analysis is prescient whilst offering a challenging renewal of critical theory at a moment when contemporary societies face fundamental crises arising from the limits that are inherent in capitalist economies based on perpetual growth. The background argument here is that historically the development of liberal capitalism, supported by colonialism and particular ontologies that privilege individual interest over the general good, have authorized ways of life that are destructive for social cohesion, psychological well-being and the environment (see Venn, 2009, 2010). These crises include the limits to growth determined by the depletion of basic resources like arable land, minerals, oil, natural gas, plants, biodiversity, etc., environmental damage, species extinction, inappropriate and destructive technologies, and the globalization of self-interested lifestyles which harm the common good. Foucault does not discuss these aspects, at least not sufficiently, except for the question of ontology, as we saw, and even then his critique of the subject does not include a critique of anthropocentrism. His genealogy is an integral part of his analyses of the co-constituting relationships between power, governmentality, politics, and the economy, relationships which he recasts in terms of the multiplicity of the relations of force that can be coded as "war" or "politics," a grid of power which political economy from the nineteenth century reconstituted in terms of biopolitics.

Foucault's approach to the location of political economy as an integral aspect of biopolitical governmentality and contemporary society is to uncover continuities and discontinuities in the rationality underlying government in the period from the end of the eighteenth century to the end of the twentieth. At the start of his detailed interrogation of neo-liberalism, he asserts that "Neo-liberalism is not Adam Smith; neo-liberalism is not market society; neo-liberalism is not the Gulag on the insidious scale of capitalism" (2008: 131). This assertion is meant to distinguish his position from three approaches to neo-liberalism, namely, the economic point of view that it is "no more than the reactivation of old, secondhand economic theories," the sociological point of view that "it is just a way of establishing strictly market relations in society," and the political point of view which claims neo-liberalism to be "no more than a cover for a generalized administrative intervention by the state" (130). This distinction marks a point of departure from conventional left analyses whilst opening up a position that shifts the gaze to genealogy, to conditions of possibility and to the practices constitutive of existing institutions and subjectivities, and inscribing power relations. So, for him "The problem of neo-liberalism is rather how the overall exercise of political power can be modeled on the principles of a market economy … to discover how far and to what extent the formal principles of a market economy can index a general art of government" (131). The answer leads Foucault to a study of the transformations in classical liberalism that were necessary for neo-liberalism to become the new framework for this reordering of modern society.

The first of these was "that of dissociating the market economy from the principle of laissez-faire" (131). Much is at stake here which is unpacked in the lectures partly through a genealogical analysis of the emergence of classical political economy towards the end of the eighteenth century and its role in the reconstitution of the rationality underlying governmental action, and partly through reconstructing the steps whereby ordo-liberals in Germany, then neo-liberalism in America and in Britain and France, depart from key aspects of the discourse of liberalism. The first of these shifts to neo-liberalism for Foucault was the foregrounding of competition, rather than exchange and laissez-faire, as organizing principle framed by the recognition that competition was not a "primitive and natural given, [but] … a structure with formal properties … that assured, or could assure, economic regulation through the price mechanism" (131). The thinking for early neo-liberals and German ordo-liberals of the Freiburg School was that laissez-faire "naturally" lead to monopolies and thereby the elimination of competition, a situation which introduces distortions that disrupt the price mechanism as theorized by classical political economy (134). So, on the one hand, a permanent vigilance was needed, and, on the other hand, related to vigilance, the need to establish the "rules of the game" to ensure that competition could operate as regulating mechanism allowing the market to determine the "true" price and the rational allocation of resources. In any case the argument was that for concentration to turn into monopoly, there needed to be "the support of the state, laws, courts, public opinion" (Foucault, citing Rustow, 2008: 136). An important point is made here, taken up on several occasions, which underlines the fact that "laissez-faire" itself is not "natural" but requires conditions which a state must put into place, including laws, say about property and ownership, the framework of transactions, the regulation of labor through legislation and codes, and so on. Foucault's analysis refers to the Walter Lippmann Colloquium of 1939 at which key thinkers of ordo-liberalism, associated with the Freiburg School (Ropke, Rustow, Hayek, von Mises in particular), debated the way forward for liberal capitalism in the light of the failures of laissez-faire exemplified in the great crash of 1929 and the critiques of liberal capitalism which people like Schumpeter had been elaborating; one could see this Colloquium as a methodological entry point for Foucault's genealogy.

In the background to this shift one finds the attempt by the physiocrats in the eighteenth century to ground state rationality in the economy rather than in a notion of the power of the Prince and Adam Smith's arguments against the assumptions of the physiocrats. The debate therefore was about the role of the state, a topic which has remained central for political economy ever since. For Smith, only the market itself could regulate itself, as if naturally, through the principle of the "invisible hand," that is to say, a process whereby although the individual decisions of participants in the market are motivated by private interest alone, unconcerned by the common interest or the general good, nevertheless things work out for the benefit of all, as if an invisible hand were guiding the transactions to ensure this outcome (Smith, 1812: 352, 354; Foucault, 2008: 278; see Venn, 2009). It is the validity of this laissez-faire assumption of naturalism – which can be thought of as the theological underside of liberalism – that ordo-liberals reject, though neo-liberals, especially in the USA, continue to uphold the principle of non-intervention by the state, and at most advocate the idea of the minimal state, on the assumption that the market will naturally arrange things for the best. The market becomes a transcendent force, with invisibility as its unavowed secret, a point Foucault develops at length (2008: 267–286). The affinity between this naturalism, fundamentalist theologies, and laissez-faire attitude is worth noting. One important aspect of the doctrine upholding the priority of private interest is the identification of the general good with private benefit; yet many would see this as a contradiction, indeed, as the basis for the corruption of both public life and democratic principles, as Arendt (2000) has argued. By the same token, this politico-economic imaginary makes invisible the hand of power, vested in inequalities of wealth, and, importantly, in a vocabulary of management and in technologies for the government of conduct that claim the rationality of efficient action. The whole system itself has been the subject of considerable critique recently, for instance Stiglitz (2001, 2010), Roubini and Mihm (2010), Jackson (2009), and many others, adding to earlier critiques such as those of Arrighi (1994) and Polanyi (2001).

For the early neo-liberals and ordo-liberals, the recognition that the state has a role to play, if qualified and reconstituted, limited to the crucial task of establishing the "framework" for economic process, consistent with the rationality of the market, focused attention on social policy. The state for European neo-liberals must intervene at the level of civil society, not as "counterweight" to the effects of inequality (2008: 142), but to socialize some elements of consumption, such as medical and cultural goods, or to effect transfers in the form of family allowances and thus to prevent open conflict and ensure growth, which would finance more generous social policy. So, the principle limiting state intervention is that there should be "no transfer of income from some to others" (143), that is, no redistribution strategy – in opposition to what they call a "socialist social policy" – because "privatized social policy" should aim for a "vital minimum" and must operate through "privatization" and the individualization of risk (145, 144). Foucault then remarks that for this "social market economy" there is "only one true and fundamental social policy: economic growth" (144). I shall return to this at the end, regarding the implications for a future economy that would need to be based on no aggregate growth, that is, on steady state, because of the limits I noted above.

Enterprise society

The claim about the institution of an enterprise society based on competition rather than exchange is quite central in his analysis, though the dichotomy which he inserts between enterprise on the one hand and consumer society presents some problems in the light of what has developed since 1979. It is clear that this dichotomy fails to take account of the affiliations and trade between consumer society and enterprise society, exemplified in Fordism. For instance, such a polarity cannot consider the underlying forces at work in what Stiegler (2008) characterizes as the "libidinal economy of capitalism," that is to say, the idea that "Capitalism needs to control conducts and in order to achieve this, it develops techniques of capture or captation (*captation*)" (2008: 12). These are the whole series of techniques that include the recruitment of libidinal energies for the satisfaction of basic drives – again Fordism and the car industry in America nicely illustrate the point. Stiegler explains that this capture of the individual requires the aestheticization of objects of consumption and the reduction of humans to commodities through new mechanisms of individuation (Stiegler, op. cit.: 33ff.). So, consumption does not become secondary, but cashes out an economy of desire that underlies both enterprise man and "consumer culture." This is a complex issue that I cannot pursue here, though it is important to note that it connects with the question of a critical ontology of ourselves.

One other connection though can be highlighted: it is the conceptualization of the human individual in terms of *homo oeconomicus*, or enterprise man, that is, the idea that the new "economic man" is the individual who, in Gary Becker's view, "accepts reality" by modulating his conduct so that it is "sensitive to modifications in the variables of the environment and which responds to this in a non-random way," that is, according to calculations of an economic kind (2008: 269). Neoliberal *homo oeconomicus* is man as entrepreneur of himself, and also as "human capital," someone who can convert the "human capital" into an income stream; the worker in this vocabulary becomes a "machine-stream ensemble" (225). This essential figure of neoliberal doctrine is intelligible if one "absolutizes a certain notion of economic interest or choice" (McNay, 2009: 61); furthermore, he is "the author of irreducible, atomistic and non-transferable choices that first emerges in English empiricist philosophy … it is distinct, for example, from the subject of rights who lies at the heart of the social contract" (McNay, 2009: 61). Foucault's conclusions from Becker's and other neoliberal universalization of liberal capitalist market rationality is that behavioral techniques can be devised, using the psychological sciences, to observe, analyze and control individual responses to changes in the environment. Thus, "*Homo oeconomicus* is someone who is eminently governable" (Foucault, 2008: 270). This government of conduct has increasingly been institutionalized in a host of changes aimed at reconstituting the "environment," a strategy which includes the financialization of social insurance systems, savings, and social welfare (Lazzarato, 2009). Foucault interestingly speaks of this politics as an "environmental technology" (Foucault, 2008: 261; see also Massumi, 2009). Furthermore, the "generalization of forms of 'enterprise' by diffusing and multiplying them as much as possible" throughout the social body (Foucault, 2008: 148), is congruent with the marketization of social policy through an "audit culture." The latter reduces social goods to the calculable, that is, it reduces them to the status of commodities whose value is circumscribed within the accounting practices developed to suit business rationality and calculation. This amounts, on the one hand, to the elimination of an autonomous public sphere, and, on the other hand, to the reconstitution of civil society as part of the market (Lazzarato, 2009; Venn, 2009). Incalculable values like generosity, friendship, conviviality, the dignity of life, hospitality, that is, everything that makes life worth living, simply do not compute within this system; they are left to the domain of the private, although the latter is itself "colonised" by what Stiegler (2008) calls "capitalist libidinal economy." One could well speak of a new totalitarian or fundamentalist society, recalling Foucault's constant struggles against such a form of society.

A juridical-economic order

One of the key transformations in the aims of governmentality that neo-liberalism introduces is the downgrading of the strategy of normalization and disciplining which had been central for liberal biopolitics; instead, government seeks to control conduct through "environmental technologies," the establishment of the "framework," and the control of the "rules of the game." One could argue here that Foucault neglects the role of the media in relaying or taking over the objectives of normalization previously ensured by different governmental mechanisms (see Stiegler's work generally). Nevertheless, Foucault's analysis points to an important displacement in the technologies that frame the behavior of individuals and agents once it is recognized that liberal capitalism and the so-called laissez-faire economy are not the result of a natural order, but "the result of a legal order that presupposes juridical intervention by the state" (2008: 161). This means that the economic must be recognized as a set of regulated activities from the beginning. The apparatus for this regulation is an "economic-juridical ensemble" (163). So, law comes to occupy a new place within the rationality of government, not as principle of limitation of state power, as with the tradition of the Rule of Law or *l'Etat de droit* as it was understood in the nineteenth century. Law instead establishes the "rules of the game" consistent with idea that "the economy must be a game…a set of rules which determine the way in which each must play a game whose outcome is not known by anyone…[whilst] the legal institution which frames the economy should be thought of as the rules of the game" (173). It is a position advocated by F. Hayek in *The Road of Serfdom*, that key figure in American neoliberal thought, associated both with the Chicago School and Freiburg, who opposed the model of state planning in its various forms – as the Welfare State, the New Deal, or socialism. One could reconstitute the notion of security which was a central element of liberal or biopolitical governmentality (Foucault, 2007) within this different logic, such that technologies like surveillance, prohibitions, drastic punishments and so on can be seen as mechanisms to increase the cost of criminal acts.

This new functioning of law as part of a juridico-economic complex has another crucial implication which I would like to highlight, namely, the devaluation of the subject of rights. For instance, current neoliberal and the new right's campaign against human rights and legislation introduced to protect them is perfectly consistent with the universalization of market rationality and the fact that the principles underlying human rights radically undermine the primacy of the market and economistic calculations of gains and losses. There is a fundamental, quasi ontological, incompatibility at the level of universal principles and visions of social order between the two positions; this issue raises complex political and ethical issues that require careful clarification.

Zero-sum games, growth, invisibility

Foucault's analysis of neo-liberalism makes better sense when one considers it in the light of the genealogy of power which he develops through *Society Must be Defended* and *Security, Territory, Population*. The points I would like to highlight focus on the question of the interrelationships linking inequality, zero-sum games, growth and the assumed "invisibility" of the general interest. Together these linkages throw a new light on neoliberal capitalism as it operates on the global scale. Foucault makes it clear in these texts that economies generally are zero-sum games, that is, games of winners and losers whereby the rich become richer by dispossessing others of the wealth the rich accumulate. This game of inequality had been taken for granted almost as an inevitable condition of existence in most societies; in Europe its rejection finds a basis in principles of equality and liberty asserted in radical Enlightenment thought – say, the assertion of the fundamental equality of all in Revolutionary France and in revolutionary thought (e.g. Tom Paine's *The Rights of Man*). As I pointed out earlier, for Foucault, inequality typically arises from an original dispossession through conquest and/or subjugation; it was legitimated by appeal to the "discourse of race war" (Foucault, 2003) supporting an "us" versus "them" situation whereby the "other" – usually the subjugated groups – is placed outside the responsibility or concern of the sovereign (2003: 70–74); its other side is a "counter-history of dark servitude and forfeiture" (2003: 73). Foucault argues that the post-Westphalian settlement which constituted a new Europe after 1648, and the territorialization of the state as nation-state which followed, together with shifts in state power from being grounded in the wealth of the sovereign to the wealth of the nation and population, made possible a different discourse about wealth and its growth. In this new model of the state and its economy, these transformations conditioned the emergence of a "science of police" as an ensemble of techniques for the amplification of the productive capacities of the population, and which was thus a condition for political economy (Foucault, 2007). After the physiocrats, Adam Smith could think of the possibility of a non-zero-sum economic game in Europe, provided there be a "globalization of the market" and provided the enrichment of Europe be "brought about as a collective and unlimited enrichment" (2008: 55). Europe as economic subject on a world scale required "the world for its unlimited market"; it is on this condition that "Europe is now in a state of permanent and collective enrichment through its own competition" (55). The fact of colonial possessions and dispossessions is absolutely vital for this new economy, as Smith recognized (see Venn, 2000, 2009; also Polanyi, 2001; Arrighi, 1994) – though Foucault does not pursue this aspect of the shifts that prepare the ground for liberal capitalism in the nineteenth century, and neo-liberalism in the twentieth century. When we take account of these conditions for the triumph of liberal capitalism, we discover that the economic game globally remained a zero-sum game, and, one could argue, has remained so ever since (Venn, 2009; Stiglitz, 2002; Sen, 2004).

The other aspect of liberal political economy which has remained a central determinant of its success in spite of liberal capitalism being a zero-sum game is the necessity of growth to sustain its social policy, as Foucault pointed out. For neo-liberalism, growth, and not redistribution or state investments in social capital, is envisaged as the only mechanism that "should enable all individuals to achieve a level of income that will allow them the individual insurance, access to private property, and individual or familial capitalization with which to absorb risks" (Foucault, 2008: 144). Growth was supposed to allow a wider section of the population to become relatively "affluent" and partake in a "consumer culture." Keynesian economic management, the Welfare State and the New Deal for a while realized this ambition. Structural imbalances in the 1970s, arising from complex factors and historical conditions, provided the neo-liberals with the occasion to re-assert the primacy of free market rationality against interventionist social and economic policy.

Studies based on Foucault's analysis have shown that the consolidation of neo-liberalism over the last thirty years has proceeded through new dispositifs constituting the framework, namely, new technologies of the social, financial technologies working in tandem with the latter, and the alignment of state apparatuses with the objectives and vocabulary circumscribing the neoliberal worldview (Lazzarato, 2009). This development has ensured that prosperity, well-being, growth and capitalism have become correlated in most policy-makers and people's minds; this association or equivalence has acquired the status of an unquestionable and fixed truth for conventional economic discourse. The market is assumed to be a kind of self-regulating mechanism equipped with a built-in, immanent ability to correct itself and ensure prosperity for the greatest number; the assumption is that in the long run the market does not fail. For neo-liberalism, then, it is not the system that fails; instead failure has become individualized – itself an aspect of the model of enterprise society and enterprise man (Foucault, 2008: 227, 259, 261) – or pathologized. As such it is subject to new biopolitical techniques of control such as medicalization, psychological reassignment, or punishment for individuals: incarceration, economic fines, insecuritization, precarious lives. On a world scale, failure is attributed to "underdevelopment" and the pathologies of the "rogue" state and kleptocracies. What the model of growth makes invisible is the fact that capitalism is intrinsically a zero-sum game of winners and losers. One could recall in that respect that Foucault's analysis underlined the artificial, constructed character of the market, enframed by dedicated apparatuses and laws, as the ordo-liberals well understood. The implication one can draw from this is that the critique of these assumed "natural" links and the recognition that they are the effects of politico-legal and administrative artifice opens the way for constructing alternative and more equitable models of the economy.

So, it is clear that the appeal to the salutary mediation of something like an invisible hand, or some immanent regulatory power, to argue against the need for state intervention in the economy to ensure more equitable distribution of resources and opportunities is founded on keeping invisible the reality of inequality as being the direct result of a zero-sum economic game. The globalization of neoliberal doctrine by way of privatization and liberalization and trade agreements framed by the Washington consensus – that is, agreement on a neoliberal market-determined economy and society, or "enterprise society," capitalism as default position for economies, and Bretton Woods as framework for regulating the global economy – the intensification of dispossession through new financial instruments such as derivatives and the futures market, hedge funds acquisitions, "vulture" funds (which are a variation on hedge funds), virtual capital creations through electronic technologies and the mathematics of chaos and probabilities (a technological aspect of current economic transactions that has been greatly neglected in the analysis of the financial crisis), and through the inflation of managerial discursive capital and so on, has widened the gap between rich and poor, within and between states (Fan *et al.*, 2009; Stiglitz, 2001; Wilkinson and Pickett, 2009; Jackson, 2009; Collins *et al.*, 2008; Wang Hui, 2009; Venn, 2006).

The doctrine of growth has also been the source of serious damage to the environment threatening the life-support system of the planet, whilst the drive for "unlimited enrichment" can only result in the exhaustion of limited basic resources. The model furthermore reduces all value to only the values recognized by business accounting practice. The latter in any case cannot take account of the value of the collective wealth or commons which is eroded or depleted in the pursuit of unlimited growth based on the privilege of business interests. Were such costs to the common wealth to be taken into account, one would have to reject both conventional (hegemonic) accounting practice and the model of growth, as Jackson (2009) establishes. Indeed, it would become clear that most existing practices of production and ways of life in wasteful economies are unsustainable in the medium term and catastrophic eventually. One could add that alternative models of prosperity exist, for instance by reference to the idea of capabilities as in the work of Amartya Sen and Martha Nussbaum which prioritize other values vital for human well-being: "physical and mental health," "educational and democratic entitlements," "trust, security, and a sense of community," "ability to participate in the life of society" (Jackson, 2009: 47; see also Venn, 2006). One could also propose other models based on the radical re-organization of ownership and the redefinition of the idea of property, recalling Arendt's (2000) distinction between wealth and property, coupled to a non-anthropocentric and non-individualistic view of humans in relation to the rest of the living world (Venn, 2010). One may well ask: what happens when the limits of the useable world are reached? Foucault's genealogy of neo-liberalism provides us with the historical perspective from which to view our situation as contingent, recent, particularistic, and destined to come to an end, one way or another.

CONCLUDING REMARKS

In this short conclusion, it would be useful to note the kinds of critiques which have been raised about Foucault's work. For instance, many have followed Edward Said (1984) in claiming that there is no theory of power in his work. However, Foucault himself has argued that he is "nominalist" about power, finding it sufficient to recognize its existence, and seeking instead to produce an analysis of its exercise. Many of the criticisms in this regard find an answer in the lectures I have discussed, since there we encounter a genealogy of power which broadens the scope of the earlier analyses by linking it more carefully with a long history of the relation of power to forms of rule and to economies, particularly by reference to biopower and biopolitics.

The concept of genealogy has given rise to objections from historians who argue that Foucault's analytical and long-term view ignores historical detail or is undermined when one takes account of historiographical realities, many of which do not fit Foucault's interpretation. It is true that much is glossed in Foucault, or signaled in broad claims which by-pass evidence that do not quite fit. But it could be countered that genealogy opens up a new vista, more politically pertinent in that it starts with problems in the present and attempts to understand the forces at work in conditioning that events followed this rather than that line of development. Genealogies are about potentialities and limits and not historical "truths" in the conventional sense; they enable us to have a better grasp of historical shifts whilst keeping in view the relation to power, as I explained above.

There are however relative neglects in his accounts, particularly with regard to the effects of colonialism and a global economy on political economy and a history of capitalism (Venn, 2009), and with regard to race in the earlier work. *Society Must be Defended* corrects the latter neglect from an analytical point of view, though the focus on Europe may encourage accusations of Eurocentrism. Whilst his own involvement in anti-racist struggles in France shows his awareness of the problems, it is difficult to avoid regretting the fact that had he taken fuller account of the effects of race in his studies of sexuality, modernity, self-becoming and so on, they would have benefited from this more global perspective.

In spite of these points of criticism, the many insights and innovations in Foucault's oeuvre mark it out as a resource of incomparable richness for the understanding of our own times.

Reader's Guide to Michel Foucault

For an overall view of Foucault's panoramic work, one could begin with *The Foucault Reader*, edited by Paul Rabinow. It contains a number of key essays such as "What is Enlightenment?," as well as extracts from most of the key works. Those who wish to contextualize his thought before reading the texts should check out David Macey's intellectual biography, *The Lives of Michel Foucault*, which is knowledgeable and perceptive about the French intellectual life in which Foucault was located. A good introduction is Clare O'Farrell's *Michel Foucault*, which brings a sharp critical view to make sense of his overall work and provides very good explanations of the key terms and concepts for those who wish to use Foucault. It is important to tackle a number of primary texts, beginning with *The History of Sexuality*, Volume 1 and *Discipline and Punish*, the two texts of Foucault which together present his approach to the question of power in modern times and establish the point of view of the subject, or subjectivity, as constructed. They also clarify concepts like normalization, discipline, regulation, surveillance, and biopolitics and governmentality, concepts which make up Foucault's analytic apparatus. Equally they are illustrations of genealogy in practice, which is the central methodological foundation for his research. For a fuller picture of how far Foucault has problematized conventional histories and has enriched analysis in the human sciences, one needs to add *Madness and Civilization*, *The Order of Things* and *The Birth of Biopolitics*. Finally, since important developments of his thought occur in the many interviews and essays, Colin Gordon's edited collection *Power/Knowledge: Selected Interviews and Other Writings* is essential. For a critical application of Foucault's more recently translated Lectures, the papers in the special issue of the journal *Theory, Culture & Society* (2009) are invaluable.

Bibliography

Writings of Michel Foucault

1967[1961]. *Madness and Civilization: A History of Insanity in the Age of Reason*. Trans. Richard Howard. London: Tavistock.

1971a[1966]. *The Order of Things: An Archaeology of the Human Sciences*. Trans. Alan Sheridan. London: Tavistock.

1971b. *The Order of Discourse*. Trans. Rupert Swyers. Social Sciences Information, April 1971.

1972[1969]. *The Archaeology of Knowledge*. Trans. Alan Sheridan. London: Tavistock.

1973[1963]. *Birth of the Clinic: An Archaeology of Medical Perception*. Trans. Alan Sheridan. London Tavistock.

1975[1973]. *I, Pierre Rivière, Having Slaughtered my Mother, my Sister and my Brother...* Trans. Frank Jellinek. New York: Pantheon.

1976[1962]. *Mental Illness and Psychology*. Trans. Alan Sheridan. New York: Harper & Row.

1977[1975]. *Discipline and Punish*. Trans. Alan Sheridan. London: Allen Lane. Reprinted in 1979 by Peregrine Books.

1977. *Language, Counter-memory, Practice: Selected Essays and Interviews by Michel Foucault*. Edited by Donald F. Bouchard. Oxford: Blackwell.

1978[1976]. *The History of Sexuality I: An Introduction*. Trans. Robert Hurley. New York: Pantheon.

1979. *Michel Foucault: Power, Truth, Strategy*. Edited by Meaghan Morris and Paul Patton. Sydney: Feral Publications.

1979. On governmentality. *Ideology & Consciousness*, 6: 5–21.

1980. *Power/Knowledge: Selected Interviews and Other Writings 1972–1977*. Edited Colin Gordon. New York: Pantheon.

1982. The subject and power. In Michel Foucault, *Beyond Structuralism and Hermeneutics*. Hubert L. Dreyfus and Paul Rabinow (1992) (eds). Brighton: Harvester Press.

1984. *The Foucault Reader*. Edited by Paul Rabinow. New York: Randon House, and (1986) Peregrine Books.

1985[1984]. *The Use of Pleasure*. Trans. Robert Hurley. New York: Pantheon.

1985[1984]. *The Care of the Self*. Trans. Robert Hurley. New York: Pantheon.

1990. An Aesthetics of Existence, interview with Alessandro Fontana. In Michel Foucault, *Politics, Philosophy, Culture*. Edited by Lawrence D. Kritzman. London: Routledge.

1990. *Politics, Philosophy, Culture: Interviews and Other Writings 1977–1984* Edited by Lawrence Kritzman. New York and London: Routledge.

1991[1971]. *Nietzsche, Genealogy, History*. In Paul Rabinow (ed.) *The Foucault Reader*. London: Penguin.

1994. *Dits et Ecrits 1954–1988*. Edited by Daniel Defert and François Ewald, 4 vols. Paris: Gallimard.

1998[1976]. *The Will to Knowledge. The History of Sexuality: 1*. London: Penguin Books.

2001. *Fearless Speech*. Edited by Joseph Pearson. Los Angeles: Semiotext(e).

2003a[1999]. *Abnormal*. Trans. Graham Burchell. New York: Picador.

2003b[1975–1976]. *Society Must Be Defended*. Trans. David Macey. New York: Picador.

2005. *The Hermeneutics of the Subject*. Trans. Graham Burchell. Houndsmills: Palgrave Macmillan

2007[1977–1978]. *Security, Territory, Population*. Trans. Graham Burchell. Houndmills: Palgrave Macmillan.

2008[1978–1979]. *The Birth of Biopolitics*. Trans. Graham Burchell. Houndmills: Palgrave Macmillan.

2009[1976]. Alternatives to the prison: Dissemination or decline of social control? Trans. Couze Venn, *Theory, Culture & Society*, 26(6): 12–24.

Further Reading

Arendt, Hannah (2000) The Social Question. In *The Portable Hannah Arendt*. Edited by Peter Baehr. Harmondsworth: Penguin.

Arrighi, G. (1994) *The Long Twentieth Century*. New York: Verso.

Burchell, G., Gorgon, Colin, and Miller, Peter (eds) (1991) *The Foucault Effect: Studies in Governmentality*. Chicago: Chicago University Press.

Butler, J. (1990) *Gender Trouble: Feminism and the Subversion of Identity*. New York: Routledge.

Butler, J. (1993) *Bodies That Matter*. New York: Routledge.

Collins, L., Di Leonardo, M., and Williams, B. (2008) *New Landscapes of Inequality: Neoliberalism and the Erosion of Democracy in America*. Santa Fe: SAR Press.

Derrida, Jacques (1967) *Cogito and the History of Madness in* Ecriture et la différence. Paris: Editions du Seuil.

Dreyfus, H. L. and Rabinow, P. (1982) *Michel Foucault: Beyond Structuralism and Hermeneutics*. With an afterword by Michel Foucault. Brighton: Harvester Press.

Deleuze, G. (1988) *Foucault*. London: Athlone Press.

Eribon, D. (1989) *Michel Foucault*. Paris: Flammarion.

Fan, S., Kanber, R., and Zhang, X. (2009) *Regional Inequality in China*. London: Routledge.

Henriques, J., Holloway, W., Urwin, C., Venn, C., and Walkerdine, V. (1998[1984]) *Changing the Subject*. London: Routledge.

Jackson, Tim (2009) *Prosperity Without Growth*. London: Earthscan.

Lazzarato, M. (2009) Neoliberalism in action: Inequality, insecurity and the reconstitution of the social. *Theory, Culture & Society*, 26(6): 110–134.

Macey, David (1993) *The Lives of Michel Foucault*. London: Vintage.

Massumi, Brian (2009) National enterprise emergency. Steps toward an ecology of powers. *Theory, Culture & Society*, 26(6): 153–185.

McNay, Lois (2009) Self as enterprise: Dilemmas of control and resistance in Foucault's *The Birth of Biopolitics*. *Theory, Culture & Society*, 26(6): 187–206.

O'Farrell, Clare (2005) *Michel Foucault*. Thousand Oaks, CA: Sage.

Polanyi, Karl (2001[1944]) *The Great Transformation: The Political and Economic Origins of Our Time*. Boston: Beacon Press.

Rose, Nikolas (1985) *The Psychological Complex*. London: Routledge & Kegan Paul.

Rabinow, Paul (2009) Foucault's untimely struggle: Toward a form of spirituality. *Theory, Culture & Society*, 26(6): 25–44.

Rose, Nikolas (1999[1989]) *Governing the Soul: On the Private Self*. London: Free Association Books.

Roubini, Nouriel and Mihm, Stephen (2010) *Crisis Economics. A Crash Course in the Future of Finance*. London and New York: Allen Lane.

Said, Edward (1984) *The World, The Text and The Critic*. London: Faber & Faber.

Sen, Amartya (2004) *Inequality Re-examined*. Cambridge MA: Harvard University Press.

Smith, Adam (1812[1776]) *The Wealth of Nations*. London: Bradbury, Agnew and Co.

Stiegler, Bernard (2008) *Economie de l'hypermatériel et psychopouvoir*. Paris: Mille et Une Nuits.

Stiglitz, Joseph (2001) Foreword. In Karl Polanyi, *The Great Transformation*. Boston: Beacon Press, pp. vii–xvii.

Stiglitz, J. (2002) *Globalization and its Discontents*. London: Penguin.

Stiglitz, J. (2010) *Freefall: Free Markets and The Sinking of the Global Economy*. London: Allen Lane.

Venn, Couze (1982) Beyond the Science-Ideology Relation. Unpublished PhD Thesis. University of Essex.

Venn, Couze (2000) *Occidentalism: Modernity and Subjectivity*. London: Sage.

Venn, Couze (2006) *The Postcolonial Challenge: Towards Alternative Worlds*. London: Sage.

Venn, C. (2009) Neoliberal political economy, biopolitics, and colonialism: A transcolonial genealogy of inequality. *Theory, Culture & Society*, 26(6): 207–344.

Venn, C. (2010) Individuation, relationality, affect: Rethinking the human in relation to the living. *Body & Society*, 16(1): 1–33.

Venn, C. and Terranova, T. (2009) Michel Foucault: Special issue. *Theory, Culture & Society*, 26(6).

Wang Hui (2009) *The End of the Revolution: China and the Limits of Modernity*. London: Verso.

Wilkinson, R. and Pickett, K. (2009) *The Spirit Level*. London: Allen Lane.

11

Dorothy E. Smith

MARIE L. CAMPBELL AND MARJORIE L. DEVAULT

Dorothy Smith: The Person in Social Context

Dorothy Smith's early education was in Britain where she attended a private school for girls during the Second World War, and then the University of London (London School of Economics) where in 1955 she earned a degree in sociology with a specialization in social anthropology. She emigrated with her American husband from Britain to the US where they both studied sociology at the University of California, Berkeley, and she received her PhD in 1963. During this time she gave birth to two sons and her marriage broke up. She worked in California as a research associate in Berkeley's Institute of Human Development and lectured in the Sociology Department, returning to England in 1966 to take a position as a lecturer in the Sociology Department at the University of Essex. In 1968 she moved to Vancouver, Canada joining the Faculty of Sociology and Anthropology at the University of British Columbia. In 1977, she was hired as Professor of Sociology in Education at the Ontario Institute for Studies of Education at the University of Toronto, and she continued her academic career there until her retirement in 2000. Since then, she continues to write and frequently teaches at the University of Victoria where she is Adjunct Professor and elsewhere.

As a graduate student in Berkeley prior to and during the Free Speech movement, Smith saw the rough application of public authority over those who deviated from accepted ideas and behavior. She and other students had followed the San Francisco hearings of the House Un-American Activities Committee, and protested the treatment by police of people who were demonstrating against them. She noted these as among the many public and private troubles that sociology was not addressing in a useful manner. She reports that "the real education I got [at Berkeley] was lessons in recognizing – in society, the university, my life, my marriage, and myself – the

The Wiley-Blackwell Companion to Major Social Theorists, First Edition.
Edited by George Ritzer and Jeffrey Stepnisky.
© 2011 Blackwell Publishing Ltd. Published 2011 by Blackwell Publishing Ltd.

institutional imaginary ... [that] I participated in and sustained" (1994: 52).
It became her life's work to help unveil that "sustained pretense masquerading as
reality, and power masquerading as justice and neutrality, and to understand the difficult but compelling importance of telling the truth" (1994: 52). Smith's experiences
in Berkeley prepared her to step as a scholar into a knowledge revolution that was
integral to the social upheavals of the 1960s and 1970s – the anti-war and the student protest movement, the civil rights movement, the women's movement, and all
the subsequent social justice movements. All of them contained critiques of taken-
for-granted realities and insisted on a different basis for knowing.

Smith's own critique of sociology, her struggle against abstraction in scholarly
work and how it leads away from addressing social life as people lived it, had its
beginnings in her experiences inside and outside the academy of the 1950s and
1960s. She had been taught sociology's imperative – to go "out" from one's location
equipped with concepts in order to find empirical material that would fit the abstractions of academic theory. Even though she was unable to see a different course of
action at that time, she began to query the sociological practice that required her to
leave aside any consideration of the world where people, including scholars themselves, were living. This peculiarly distanced approach to knowing permeated and
constrained her personal life as a student, as it did her academic work. For Smith,
completing her PhD combined the experiences of being known and marginalized as
a woman in academia with her mounting insights about sociology's failures. Smith's
dissertation was a study of front-line authority in a mental hospital. Despite its focus
on the organizational features of the institution, she may have been drawn to the
field of mental health – like other writers of the era (including novelists such as
Sylvia Plath and Doris Lessing) – because of the contribution of psychology and
psychiatry in maintaining the conformist regime of the time. Later, writing about
that period, she recognized how being a woman had established the socially accepted
boundaries of a proper life, in which her yearnings for intellectual growth made her
transgressive (Smith, 1994). She was expected to accept as given that it was men
who did academic work and that their women would take a supportive role. The
guilt she had experienced around her own imperfect conformity reinforced her
acceptance and participation in this trap – that only later (Smith, 1977) – she saw as
a feature of how women's lives are organized.

The sexism she experienced as a student, at a time when the word wasn't yet
invented, brought her to the women's movement of the 1960s and 1970s, in which
she was active in Vancouver and on the campus of the University of British Columbia.
It also brought the women's movement to her – in the sense of providing an audience
hungry for precisely the kind of critique and theoretical work she was already doing.
Early in this period, Smith had begun to explore disjunctures between "official" versions of normalcy and the actualities of the lives women were living. In these works
she pointed to alternative readings of women's lives but also demonstrated the
authority that reached from professional understandings into everyday interpretation, judgments, and sanctions on "unacceptable" behavior (see Smith and David,
1975). In time, these ideas would appear in Smith's distinctive use of "experience"
in her alternative sociology.

Smith's persistence in following her course of intellectual development had gained
her an academic career, but becoming a faculty member did not alter her experience

of a gender regime within academia. As faculty members, women were overlooked, resented, and at least as women, excluded. Here is how she has expressed that sense of exclusion: "My world with children and my work in the house was where I was as a woman. The embodied woman disappeared from view when I went to work in the text-based world of sociology" (2007: 410). What this meant for her and for other women in the institution fueled her enthusiasm to formulate a "sociology *for* women" (rather than, as she saw the social sciences doing, generating inadequate and oppressive knowledge *about* women). Once she began to work out the implications of her early insights in the context of a broad social movement, the work really took off. The new movement of feminist scholars made the critique broadly consequential, gave it fuel, and provided many colleagues who were beginning to develop their own responses to the discovery of sexism – responses that fed and supported Smith's work (as we discuss later) even when they differed in the particulars.

Her commitment to making the exigencies of everyday life understandable to people had inspired the direction of Smith's scholarship that, in the 1970s, she began calling "the social organization of knowledge." By the 1980s, she was recognizing how her feminist scholarship was integral to learning how to tell the truth. The drawing together of these two strands of scholarship fueled her work throughout a long career in which she has made a fundamental critique of conventional sociologies and developed an alternative way to conduct social inquiry. Beginning with the knowing subject, this form of inquiry, now known as institutional ethnography, opens up for empirical discovery – to use Smith's words – "how things actually work."

THE SCHOLARLY WORK

Smith's own contention, in the face of being increasingly recognized as a social theorist, is that her work – her "alternative sociology" – is *not* a project of theorizing, certainly not of theory building. Smith's resistance to being labeled a theorist arises from her critique of the theory building that was central to the conventional sociologies of her day (as it is of ours).

She had chafed against the standard disciplinary procedures which transform people's activities into mere instances that "fill out" the conceptual "shells" of sociological theory. She found support for her critique of contemporary social science in Marx and Engels's (1976) analysis of ideology in which concepts "that interpret the social are treated as if they were its underlying dynamic" (Smith, 2004: 448). This inversion of the relation of concepts to actuality, Smith began to argue beginning in 1972, was also at work in sociology: sociology's methodological practices of objectivity separate ideas from active subjects and from the relations in which those ideas are embedded. This process of abstraction contrasted with Marx's "new materialism" which insisted that science, as opposed to ideology, required the discovery of relations and processes that arise in and only in the actual activities of actual people.

Moving forward from this critique, Smith began to analyze contemporary instances of the social organization of ideological practices to discover how they routinely produce authoritative but misleading versions of "what actually happens." "Ideology," Smith insists, is "a practice of reasoning about society and history, [that] elaborates on [the ideologist's] experience of working in language as an 'independent realm'" (Smith, 2004: 451). Her 1974 paper "The Social Construction of Documentary Reality" is a classic in her repertoire of micro-analyses of how "facts" (whether of social science, demographic information, or professional expertise) are built up in various conceptual practices, leaving behind the actualities of their origins and gaining a new and for Smith a dubious character. She proposed an "ideological circle" (1990a: 93–96) to illustrate how processes of reading and writing, beginning perhaps in organized record-keeping, *constitute events* in language, as ideological accounts that carry institutionally authorized meanings and implications. Her work of explication shows that ideology is integral, not only to the practices of knowledge-based organizational activity, but also to the authoritative understandings being generated.

Investigating such processes empirically, Smith began to show the broad reach and diverse application of these ideological forms of knowledge – indeed showing their integration into widely accepted technologies of coordination and control. She saw how settings can be virtually invented in this manner. For example, Vietnam-era casualty counts, constructed in the field and reported to US military commanders, became a factual basis of the apparently successful prosecution of an unwinnable war (Smith, 1974b). She went on to identify and write about the knowledge processes through which an act of self-killing becomes "suicide" (1990a: 141–173); and observations that someone is "bathing religiously every night ... but leaving the tub dirty" become "mental illness" (1990b: 36). In all these writings, Smith was identifying conceptual schemas through which people accomplished the transformation of "what happened" into organizationally actionable categories: a "patient" presenting "symptoms," or a "juvenile" who is "in need of supervision" (1974b, 1990a). She also began to point to the discourses that such schemas added up to: a discourse of psychiatry, for example, that could organize the diverse elements of Virginia's Woolf's last months of life into a persuasive account of "depressive illness" (1990a). In making visible the social organization of a constructed reality, these early analyses show how the conceptual frames and schemas are essential to authorized knowing and to specific administrative or professional action, and importantly, how these (ideological) forms of knowledge miss much about the actualities being lived.

Inspired by Marx's new materialism (discussion of which appears in her writings in 1974c, 1990a, 1999, and 2004), Smith was approaching the foundational problem for sociology by querying how a society can be said to exist and be made examinable. Rather than employing the ideological practices which cut the social categories from their ground in everyday life to elaborate theory on that basis, the materialist method insists on returning to and investigating the actual activities in which social (and sociological) categories arise. It was from Marx (his analysis of the activities of people concealed in the concept "commodity," for instance), that she learned to see social relations as "opening up a universe for exploration that is 'present' in them but not explicated" (Smith, 1990a: 37). Similarly, the analytic approach Smith began to develop offered the possibility of recovering the activities of the participants that are systematically obscured when an ideological process takes the form of facts, social science findings, or institutionally based information. People's activities or social relations are "the form in which the object of (social) inquiry exists ... in which it can be known, and with reference to which statements made about it can be checked out" (Smith, 2004: 447).

This re-reading of Marx was part of a line of thinking about social inquiry that Smith was developing and sharing with feminist colleagues, and publishing in various journals between 1974 and 1984. It was introduced to a wider audience in her 1987 book, *The Everyday World as Problematic*. That book articulates the feminist discoveries about the gender-biased nature of the social world in whose making, Smith argues, the social sciences are thoroughly implicated. She had recognized and written in 1974 (reprinted in Harding, 1987) that "sociologists have learned to treat the world as instances of a sociological body of knowledge" (1974a: 8) and that the sociologist, like others working in "the governing mode" (9), enters a "conceptually ordered society when he goes to work" (9). While completely at home in this conceptual world, the sociologist (a man, by tradition and, in the early 1970s, still an occupational actuality) nevertheless has a body from whose needs he must be liberated, if he is to participate fully in the abstract conceptual mode. Here is where women, and their particular place, knowledge, and work are essential. Their subservience is a necessary feature of the governing mode; women's work underpins the conditions which facilitate it. A terrible contradiction occurs. As Smith argues, the harder women work, "the more complete the dichotomy between the two worlds, and the estrangement" between men and women (10).

Beyond this feminist critique, but based on its insights Smith framed a more adequate conception for "a sociology as a systematically developed consciousness of society and social relations" (1987: 2). She moved from talking about "governing" to positing "ruling" as a dominant form of knowing both "ourselves and society," and making ruling researchable as actual practices in which people participate knowledgeably, accomplishing the interrelation of capitalist society and patriarchy. She argued that ruling relations are "*extralocal*, producing modes of consciousness that are objectified and impersonal, governed by organizational logics and exigencies ... and constituted externally to particular individuals and their personal and familial relationships" (1987: 3).

In contrast to this extralocal form of knowing, Smith posited women's standpoint – an experiential basis of a woman's (embodied) knowing arising from "outside" the positions where ruling knowledge is produced and deployed. The historical exclusion of women had been well researched and Smith compiled accounts of how women had been ejected from all positions where ruling was exercised in industrial societies since the mid-nineteenth century. In several essays (which are less often read and discussed than other pieces of Smith's work), she detailed the relations that rule women, historical developments which were to become central to her alternative sociology. In "Women, Class, and Family"(1983) and again in *Mothering for Schooling* (with Griffith, 2005), she explores the distinctive place constructed for working- and middle-class women as agrarian forms of life were supplanted by industrial work and the organization of the family household became a space of reproduction rather than productive work. In these writings, she is showing ruling relations to be gender-specific, but she also recognized that ruling relations coordinate the lives of men as well as of women. In what they do every day, both men and women become involved in shifting, evolving, modes of knowledge, continually transcribing "the local and particular activities of [their] lives into abstracted and generalized forms ... and [creating] a world in texts as a site of action" (Smith, 1987: 3).

Smith's analytic moves from people's actions to their coordination through ruling relations. At first, she had formulated the social organization of ruling in relation to a "ruling apparatus." This term (borrowed, perhaps, from Althusser) allowed her to ground the conceptual practices of sociology and to identify *as ruling practices* conducted by institutional actors the everyday activities and the associated uses of knowledge through which administration and government were accomplished in functional areas such as health care, social welfare, education, the law, and so on. In later work, such as her essay entitled "The Ruling Relations" in *Writing the Social* (Smith, 1999: ch. 5), she offers a more contemporary and organizationally focused account of ruling – as management – evolving from personalized control into the modern corporate forms of organization, where coordination is exercised through text and document.

Coordination, specified as people's activities *being coordinated with those of others*, has now become a central feature of the social to be explicated in Smith's alternative sociological inquiry. Coordination, in this context, is not a phenomenon distinct in itself but an aspect of the social relations that connect individual actors to each other, to society, and to history. Smith explains: "Coordination isn't isolated as a phenomenon that can be differentiated from people's activities ... The focus of research is never the individual, but the individual does not disappear; indeed, she or he is an essential presence. Her or his doings, however, are to be taken up relationally" (2005: 59). From an ethnographic account of people's activities being coordinated purposively, it is possible to discover the ruling relations and explicate their accomplishment of distinctive purposes and connections among actual people.

Smith's feminist insistence on learning from women's experience and designing an inquiry to address puzzles arising there was the key to her alternative sociology that in 1987 she began to call institutional ethnography. While mainstream sociology could use people's experiences "as data interpreted to fit its frameworks," it could not use "people's own experiences as its starting point" (Smith, 2007: 411). With the understanding that people's actions coordinate settings and thus shape people's experiences, institutional ethnographers ask the question "how does this setting work?" Happenings in specific sites become the basis for ethnographic description, and subsequently, for analysis of the actual processes coordinating that setting, including what people experience there. Conceptualizing the social as being accomplished and available for analysis "in process," Smith's method of inquiry offers access to the "extended or macro-relations organizing society through analysis of the micro-social" (Smith, 1990b: 10). Making such an analytic account does not displace and transcend people's own knowledge, but rather aims to extend what they can see and understand *from their particular place in the world*. Here is how Smith expresses the goal of institutional ethnography: "The idea is to discover and map that world so that how it is being put together [in people's activities and doings] can be made observable from the point of view of those caught up in it" (Smith, 2007: 411).

While working with people's experiential accounts of actualities always presents certain strictures on analysis in institutional ethnography – because such an account can never be a "pure representation of some original" (Smith, 2005: 123) – it supports an empirical approach. That approach negates the need to theorize and speculate in the process of explanation, the procedure ordinarily accepted as how findings are made and conclusions drawn in social science. According to Smith, as the research subject disappears in the process of sociological theorizing and in related practices of constituting findings as objective, so do the social relations. The result is that "who is acting on whose behalf?" also becomes invisible. By contrast, in institutional ethnography, research is never considered to be neutral but, like knowledge itself, is inevitably "located" *vis-à-vis* particular knowers. Taking the standpoint of those for whom the knowledge might be libratory, institutional ethnographic practice enables scientific research to be political, in the sense that its knowledge product reveals not just the ruling practices but their enactment, and the different consequences of this activation for different actors.

While Smith's early commitment as a feminist researcher had been to take "the standpoint of women" in knowledge construction, any institutional ethnography is likewise "interested" – in discovering how ruling relations coordinate the lives of those who are subject to them. This helps make its knowledge product useful to the people whose standpoint the research takes. McCoy sharpens the point of institutional ethnography being a basis for action, including collective activism, by explaining that "the doings of people organized into extended, translocal chains of action ... bring about similar forms of practice and subjectivity in multiple settings while also generating characteristic forms of inequality" (2007: 701). It is the claim of Smith's *Institutional Ethnography* (2005) that understanding social relations and their consequences, in this sense, can provide a basis for action. Institutional ethnography is a sociology *for* people whose actions are being coordinated purposively by the ruling relations of institutions.

The Intellectual Context and Impact of the Work

In her early scholarship, Smith drew upon the theoretical resources she encountered in the formative period of her education. She made use of her readings of Marx and her experience in left-wing politics, an interpretation of the sociology of George Herbert Mead that came from her teacher, Tomatsu Shibutani, and the work of phenomenologists and ethnomethodologists encountered in her Berkeley education. The abstracted functionalist sociology that held ascendancy in the discipline in the 1950s and early 1960s was also important, in the sense that Smith's intellectual goals took shape in her strongly felt sense of the errors of that approach. She saw her advisor, Erving Goffman, as one who resisted conventional positivist approaches, finding creative ways to examine what people were doing in their everyday lives (Campbell, 2003). She found in these existing theoretical currents some resources for working in a different way, and she began to develop a materialist sociology of knowledge; but she worked in relative isolation in this period, in part because of the sexism that kept her on the margins of the academic world, in part because of her family responsibilities, and in part because critiques of the functionalist orthodoxies of the time were gathering momentum only slowly and in the margins of the discipline.

Feminism and "women's standpoint"

By the mid-1970s, women scholars were developing new feminist perspectives and Smith began to be recognized as a central figure in a burgeoning intellectual movement. She describes her own experience during that period as "a dialogue with and within an extraordinary political process, a late – and it now sometimes seems final – coming-to-fruit of the Enlightenment" (1994: 55). In nearly every discipline, women writers, artists, and scholars were recognizing and analyzing their exclusion from canons of creative and intellectual work. In philosophy and the social sciences, much of this work dealt with the epistemologies that produced such exclusions; Smith made important contributions to that critique, developing the idea of a distinctive "perspective" associated with women's subjugated knowledge (1974a). Along with philosophers Sandra Harding and Donna Haraway, political theorist, Nancy Hartsock, and sociologist Patricia Hill Collins, Dorothy Smith began to be discussed as a "standpoint feminist." Harding had introduced that term (1987) to identify a move more far-reaching than the "empiricist" feminism that would locate the problem of exclusion in failures of "good science," and the solution in closer attention to gender difference. Harding argued that the "standpoint" feminist would reject the positivist view from nowhere – no matter how ostensibly complete – in favor of a fuller and therefore stronger view derived from women's standpoint.

Despite this common project, Smith chafed at being labeled a "standpoint theorist," and in the introduction to her 2005 explication of institutional ethnography, she wrote about how she understood her own work in relation to these feminist colleagues. There, she points to the origin of the concept of women's standpoint in "an active and shared process of speaking from our [women's] experience" (2005: 8) in a period when "talking our experience was a means of discovery" (7). She acknowledges that "white middle-class heterosexual women dominated" in this early theorizing (8). But responding to critiques based in the "alleged essentialism" of the notion of women's standpoint, she offers the idea that women's standpoint functioned for feminists as a political concept, creating a subject position from which to speak, rather than defining shared attributes or experiences. Smith used women's standpoint as an entry point for investigation, a resource that would enable her to "explore what it might mean to think sociologically from the place where I was in-body, living with my children in my home and with those cares and consciousness that are integral to that work" (11). Used in this way, and set against her work in the university, the notion of a bodily standpoint and consciousness brought into view for Smith a disjuncture between everyday, local particularities and the ostensible universality of academic work. The strategy of beginning from everyday life (or "women's standpoint") is meant to "collapse" (25) that distinction, to insist that concepts and discourses also depend on people's doings and exist in the same world in which mothers care for children. Thus, as Harding suggests, Smith's notion of standpoint provides the basis for stronger knowledge, and Smith has deployed it expansively in developing her alternative sociology. What began as "women's perspective" (1974a) she writes of in 2005 as "pulling mind back into body" (25).

We suggest that the scholarship that labeled Dorothy Smith as a "standpoint feminist" was at least in part a function of the need to establish and organize the feminist theory of that period. It highlights some aspects of her scholarship but obscures other strands of her thought. Given her interests in institutional coordination, Smith might have been located alongside scholars (such as Joan Acker and Sally Hacker) who saw that the key questions are not only about women, but about the ways that social institutions and technologies are gendered. Smith's development of a Marxist epistemology that was also central to her writing during this period, and her analyses of the "ruling relations" might have located her in the general terrain of "political economy," despite her resistance to orthodox formulations there (1989). Smith was brought into the canon of sociological theory as a standpoint feminist who emphasized "starting from women's experience," but all of the elements in her thinking that we mention here were significant in the subsequent development of her work.

The linguistic turn

Through the 1980s, a fierce debate raged over the status of experience, especially among feminist scholars for whom the concept had been so generative. These debates arose out of the "linguistic turn," an expansive scholarly movement with reverbera- tions across the humanities, social sciences, and their allied fields of professional practice, and scholars in these fields have built upon the linguistic turn in many different ways. Some followed historian Joan Scott (1991) who argued that experi- ence is always discursively constituted, and that it would be incorrect to take an account of experience as evidence of "what happened" without recognizing the situ- ated and structuring character of vision, language, discourse, and history. Expecting to learn about experience from people's accounts, in this view, might seem hopelessly naïve, and for some social scientists and feminist scholars it suggested that an empir- ically based account of the social was an impossibility (see Clough 1993 and Smith 1993 for a sharp exchange on this issue).

While many theorists in the humanities and some social scientists adopted the new emphases on language and discourse in antifoundationalist projects – arguing that experience could never be conceived outside of discourse – Smith appreciated and mined ideas about the power and consequence of language and discourse but retained a commitment to recognizing pre-discursive aspects of experience and con- sciousness. From her earliest writing, Smith's interests in texts and discourses had focused on their uses, in people's work in and outside of ruling organizations. She saw that people activate texts and in doing so they organize courses of action around the logics of those texts. Such embodied, situated activity is missing from poststruc- turalist theorizing, but central to Smith's. This key distinction can be seen most clearly by locating Smith's work (2005) in relation to Foucault's (1972, 1997).

In her attention to and analysis of "discourse" and the ruling relations, Smith acknowledges Foucault's originality (e.g. Smith, 2005: 224) but draws distinctions between her usage of the term and his. She says, "[Foucault] used the term [dis- course] to pry thinking away from that of the traditional history of ideas that inter- preted works in terms of the intentional thought of their authors. The concept of discourse located systems of knowledge and knowledge making independent of par- ticular individuals." This use of the concept of discourse accords to some degree with Smith's notion of ruling relations whose operation in people's lives is experi- enced as impersonal, abstract, and general. Smith notes how Foucault "directed inquiry to discursive events – that is, spoken or written effective statements that happen and have happened (1972: 28) – and to the distinctive forms of power that discourse represents" (2005: 17). He "describes (the order of discourse) as regulat- ing how people's subjectivities are coordinated," imposing that order on the one who knows, reads, or hears something said. Smith, however, takes care to avoid what she sees as a potential problem in Foucault's concept of discourse – according discourse an overpowering role (Smith, 2005: 127).

Smith finds a more fruitful conceptualization of language and its coordinative power in the writing of Mikhail Bakhtin (1981, 1986) and his dialogic approach to discourse. That approach accords with Smith's respect for the subject's experience as the basis of inquiry into social life. She points to Bakhtin's attention to the situated use of language:

> In Bakhtin's view, every utterance is a dialogue between the givens of language or discourse and the speaker's intentions, the hearer, the situation, and so on. The speaker's or writer's part in the dialogue is that of finding in discourse the resources she or he needs; the part of discourse is to make the speaking/writing of intention possible and at the same time to constrain its utterance. (Smith, 2005: 127)

According to Bakhtin, Smith tells us, experience is dialogic, but that does not imply that discourse *determines* the interchange between what is recollected and whatever was happening that is being expressed as the speaker's experience (as she suggests is the view of poststructuralists such as Butler, Scott, Moya, and others "following in Foucault's footsteps" (2005: 127)). At issue, Smith argues (126), is how "discourse, in the poststructuralist view, speaks over our intentions; they are subordinated and displaced."

Smith's own form of inquiry relies on the dialogic character of experience, as Bakhtin recognizes it in his writings. Thus, the institutional ethnographer, Smith says, is not looking for the truth in informants' accounts of what happened or what was *really* going on but is oriented, rather, to what the informant knows. In the talk between them, the informant's doings and how they are coordinated with those of others become visible to the ethnographer (Smith, 2005: 129). "The dialogue between the interviewer and informant brings the latter's experience into being as an interchange between what she remembers and the interviewer's interest and attention" (Smith, 2005: 128). Smith has also found resources in scholarship on the development of print culture and the work of contemporary writing theorists such as Charles Bazerman (1988), who emphasize the social context of writing and discourse, and offer to social scientists productive ways of thinking about genre and format (Smith and Schryer, 2007). Rather than cleaving to a particular theory of discourse, Smith has drawn from across disciplines perspectives that are of use in the project of inquiry she envisions.

In a 1996 essay, boldly titled "Telling the Truth after Postmodernism," Smith offered an extended response to poststructuralist critics of her grounded epistemology. Her essay is not a repudiation of postmodernism or of the linguistic turn; Smith recognizes her own location as one of many scholars navigating the currents of that intellectual moment. Indeed, more than any other social scientist we can think of, she wished to incorporate language, talk, text, and discourse into a conception of the social. She read widely in literary theory, using what made sense to her as an empirically oriented social scientist and learning as well from work that she regarded as missing the mark. But she also returned to the work of George Herbert Mead, finding there a way to recover the idea of pre-linguistic experience. Her argument in "Telling the Truth" is anchored in the fundamental human task of learning both language and collective consciousness. Think, she suggests, of the way that mothers and infants experience a world together, pointing and labeling in ways that provide a vocabulary and a language. Of course, she acknowledges, language taken up by the infant begins immediately to mediate direct experience. Smith draws on the infant's predicament to remind us that language anchors us not only within a social world but also a physical, material, and socially organized one.

Smith's 2005 book, *Institutional Ethnography: A Sociology for People*, reprises her attention to such issues and offers tools for the analysis of textual mediation that Smith and followers of her approach continue to develop. Making the "generous concept of work" (1987: 165–166) central to institutional ethnography allows Smith to point to "work knowledges" (2005: ch. 7) associated with people's doings (paid or not) and the things they know that direct their doings. Language, and its use, is of course central to people's work. The idea of work knowledge, then, allows the analyst to examine closely how work is accomplished, looking for "text–reader conversations" that are integral to the conduct of work. Such text–reader conversations are constituents of organizationally coordinated courses of action, and they are often meant to lead to "processing interchanges" (Pence, 2001: 215), which link organizationally relevant aspects of activities in one site with those that are to be taken in another. A battered woman, for example, calls the 911 operator, who enters information into a computer program that will dispatch an emergency responder. Police go to the scene and later submit a report that will become the official record of "what happened" if the incident becomes a case and someone is arraigned. The language of the report generated knowledgeably and correctly, will advance the action, coordinating the efforts of institutional actors.

Building on feminism

As feminist scholarship has flourished since the 1980s (producing, in most of the disciplines, influential scholarly frameworks and discourses), feminist ideas and approaches have been picked up and adapted for use by other scholarly movements and concerns (just as the early feminist scholars borrowed and adapted ideas from the anti-colonialist, anti-racist, and other radical scholarly movements that preceded them). In this period of borrowing, Smith's work was developed in the applied fields of human services and education and taken up by advocates and activists working not only on feminist projects but also in areas such as gay and disability rights. Accordingly, she began to describe her approach as a "sociology for people."

Smith's work with others – especially at the Ontario Institute for Studies in Education (now a part of the University of Toronto, but earlier a freestanding graduate institution and a center of academic feminist activism in Canada) – has reflected her conception of institutional ethnography as necessarily a collective project, and she has often acknowledged the contributions of her doctoral students to the development of her approach. As a first generation of students matured, they produced a collection of studies that had their beginnings in Smith's "social organization of knowledge" seminars (Campbell and Manicom, 1995). Several early students produced monographs (Ng, Walker, de Montigny, Townsend, Swift). Other students become research collaborators. For instance, Smith worked with Nancy Jackson in the 1970s, developing analysis that would become increasingly important as Smith

(1990b) refined her understanding of how texts are activated within social relations; George Smith (1990) was a close research collaborator on many joint inquiries until his untimely death in 1994; and Smith continues to collaborate with Alison Griffith on research on mothers' work and schooling (2005) and new modes of public sector governance (discussed below). She has worked with domestic violence activist, Ellen Pence, who built on institutional ethnography to develop a "community audit" method of improving local responses to domestic violence (2001); Smith and Pence also worked with a Native women's group to meld elements of an indigenous research methodology with an institutional ethnographic approach (Wilson and Pence, 2006). And Susan Turner's dissertation research on municipal land-use planning (2003, 2006) involved the development of tools for mapping institutional processes, which have served as a model for other institutional ethnographers. During the 1990s, institutional ethnographers in Canada and the United States began to organize occasional conferences, often focused on topics such as economic restructuring (York University in 1998) or activism (Arizona State University in 1999), and Smith's work was featured in a 2003 session of the International Sociological Association in Brisbane, Australia. Later in that decade, an Institutional Ethnography Division in the US-based Society for the Study of Social Problems became an important site for exchange among institutional ethnographers, and it remains so as of this writing.

Institutional ethnography has a particular appeal to front-line professionals and activists for whom its "standpoint" or grounding in the actualities of practical experience offers practical guidance for explication of troubles in people's lives. The analysis offers "a way to go" (1977), which was Smith's original concern for sociology: it has a social/educational mission. It is "interested" and connected, in contrast to simply being an (individual) intellectual pursuit, and it is meant to be of use to those who are subject to ruling relations. Examples include Ellen Pence's work for battered women's safety within criminal justice systems, George Smith's on accessing AIDS treatments (extended to broader issues related to health care for those with HIV/AIDS in a participatory research project developed by Eric Mykhalovskiy and Liza McCoy), Marie Campbell's on home care for people with disabilities, and Susan Turner's in research projects undertaken with rural Canadian women's groups.

The practical and necessarily collective character of institutional ethnography is related to its ontology, and that ontology also distinguishes it from other critical, reflexive sociologies of the period, such as those put forward by Anthony Giddens and Michael Burawoy. As discussed above, in the institutional ethnographic approach, people's activities are always the ground for analysis, never glossed with the conceptual schemata of sociological theory. Keeping the active character of ruling always in play allows institutional ethnographers to link their studies. The ruling relations thus come into view not as a theoretical construct, but as a material social formation, continually enacted and re-enacted in time and place. Ruling, in this account, is not synonymous with "structure" or "power" or "control" – or for that matter, with any such abstraction. Instead it is, like "everyday life" or "what happens," a matter of people doing things. While some critical sociologists worry that people's "agency" is missing in contemporary theory, Smith does not theorize agency apart from other doings; in her thinking, it would be a mistake to excise a portion of someone's activity and label it as such, because people are always acting "artfully" (as the ethnomethodologists would have it). People are engaged in "courses of action" – an idea from the phenomenological perspective that implies at least some degree of intentionality, if not the capacity to know, predict, and control the outcomes of action. For Smith, those courses of action are linked to the activities of others and coordinated through their alignment with ruling discourses: people act in ways they expect will achieve their intentions, and often, in ways organized for the accomplishment of intentions that are not theirs. This account of action and coordination sidesteps a debate over agency and structure. She comments as follows on her approach to this question, and its implications for the kind of knowledge that can be produced (2008: 421):

> A sociology that stays with people's everyday life experience, as they know and report it (including how they read and take up the texts that enter into the organization of their work) does not even have to attribute agency to people. People never lost it and hence don't have to rely on the sociologist to replace it conceptually – as is proposed, for example, by Anthony Giddens ... Institutional ethnography's research findings offer to people something like a map that extends what they know of their everyday world.

The metaphor of "mapping" has become increasingly important in institutional ethnography as it has developed, in part because of the accumulation of knowledge that has resulted from the shared ontology of its practitioners. As institutional ethnographic studies proliferate, their findings increasingly and more thoroughly map the complex interpenetration of the ruling relations across academic disciplines, professions, organizations, sectors, and jurisdictions.

CURRENT DIRECTIONS: ECONOMIC RESTRUCTURING AND GOVERNANCE

During the past 15–20 years, Smith and other institutional ethnographers have increasingly focused on the economic transformations underway under a banner of neo-liberal globalization. Just as an earlier generation of scholars grappled with a "great transformation" in the global economy (Polanyi, 1957[1944]), so too, this generation is working to understand an economic order undergoing profoundly significant changes. This strand of Smith's work has developed, as have other critical sociologies of the late twentieth and early twenty-first centuries, in response to global economic restructuring and the social transformations associated with it. For institutional ethnographers, this emergent project involves the mapping of a next stage in the complex of institutional power that Smith has labeled "ruling relations." Many of Smith's master's-level and doctoral students during the 1980s – often working in human services or other public sector professions and feeling unsettled by changes in their workplaces – took up questions related to those changes. They were noticing not only new demands for accountability, but new technologies for measuring and reporting outcomes, often borrowed from or administered by private-sector organizations. They saw new forms of budgeting and scheduling, and strategies of outsourcing that were reorganizing front-line work (DeVault, 2008). Together, these studies brought into view an ensemble of "institutional technologies" operating across institutions (Griffith and André-Bechely, 2008).

Many other social scientists have also been exploring and critiquing the develop-ments collected under terms such as globalization or neoliberalism. What is most distinctive about Smith's work in this area is its insistent adherence to a method of inquiry that keeps people and their activities constantly visible, focusing on how those activities are coordinated. That focus brings into view what Smith's institu-tional ethnography emphasizes and that she has called the ontological shift (2005: 4). Its significance is to make central to knowledge production and the accumulation of research findings how people constitute the world and in the process find their expe-riences organized outside of their own intentions. This shift makes it possible to investigate economic restructuring as it happens translocally, in multiple sites, and always as activity, undertaken by actual people working together. These analyses show how institutional regimes are interconnected, but there is no move away from the empirical, back into abstraction.

In that her goals are not fitted to the abstractions of extant disciplinary knowl-edge, Smith's approach departs from the theory-building projects of other enterprises in sociological theory, including the widely employed grounded theory approach and also more contemporary projects such as Michael Burawoy's extended case method. Perhaps closer to Smith's approach are the analyses of governmentality that have developed from Foucault's lectures on that topic. For Foucault, analysis of govern-mentality is a way of exploring power and its uses; he deployed the concept in order to direct attention to the ways that state power has come to operate through the constitution of a subject or self that engages in self-governance. As with Smith's institutional ethnography, Rose, O'Malley, and Valverde (2006) note that governmentality is not meant to provide "a theory of power, authority, or even governance" but instead "asks particular questions of the phenomena that it seeks to understand, questions amenable to precise answers through empirical inquiry" (85). However, where Foucault and the scholars of governmentality who continue to develop his ideas begin with the idea of "biopower" (Foucault, 1997) and the tech-nologies of governing associated with new population-oriented modes of knowl-edge, Smith and her followers ground their analyses in whatever they find happening in particular sites and set as their goal the discovery of "how things work."

Just as the earlier work of both Smith and Foucault made discourse a central point of interest, each has taken an approach toward contemporary forms of power that focuses attention on technologies of domination that are textual and reach into the lives and consciousness of those who are governed. For both Smith and Foucault, the constitution of knowledge and its dissemination provide an orientation to the topic of interest and instructions as to how the analyst should find it. For both gov-ernmentality studies and institutional ethnography, "how" questions have replaced "why" questions. As in their conceptualizations of discourse, however, Foucault's governmentality approach is weighted toward the discursive, while Smith's analysis emphasizes knowledge in use and the actions – the work, broadly conceived – of all those involved in the activation of a particular governing regime. While Foucault's thought is focused on government's production of the subject, Smith's approach assumes that consciousness arises out of people's interactions with others and the work they do together. In keeping with her deeply theorized mistrust of abstraction, Smith insists that an analysis beginning with a notion such as power or structure or even "governing at a distance" (Rose, 1999) will usually hide as much as it discloses.

She uses colloquial phrases such as "what's happening" or "how things work" not as foundational concepts with fixed definitions, but as anchors for a thoroughly grounded, empirical investigation, built upon and meant to extend the researcher's and research participants' own lived knowledge.

Governmentality theorists seem divided on the political implications of their work. Foucault himself rejected any notion of progress toward liberatory knowledge. Some of his followers resist analyses that are directed toward political critique, pointing out that not only subject populations, but also the analyst is captured by discourse; some see in Foucault's work the possibility to provoke creative resistance while others accept that "resistance" itself is an integral feature of government (O'Malley, 1996). Again, this diversity points to governmentality's ontology, where "the subject" is being formed by forces outside and acting on her or him. Institutional ethnography, while attentive to the technologies and knowledge that governmentality also analyzes, keeps the experiencing subject at the center of the analysis and in discovering how ruling enters research settings through people's work knowledges and activities, it identifies how local actors perform thereby the ruling of their own lives.

For Smith, the political usefulness of an institutional ethnographic analysis derives from the reorganization of the relations of knowledge production that we have emphasized throughout the chapter. In taking the standpoint of the experiencing, knowing actor in the everyday world, an institutional ethnography focuses on a problematic that appears in his or her world. Any discoveries of what happens and how that setting is being put together are relevant in so far as they extend knowledge beyond what is available to be known by the experiencing subject from within that local site. Smith's goal for institutional ethnography, of reorganizing the relations of knowledge of the social, is an achievement both ontologically and epistemologically specific, whose generating of *knowledge for people* makes it useful by them. As institutional ethnographers stand with those whose lives are caught up in ruling relations, the research becomes part of the enactment of the politics of everyday life.

CONCLUSION

We have highlighted in this chapter the work of Dorothy Smith that was aimed, she said, at reorganizing the relations of knowledge production in what she has called "an alternative sociology." She was motivated initially by her dissatisfaction with sociological abstraction – by her desire to produce knowledge of the social as she lived it, rather than knowledge driven by the abstractions of existing theory. With that goal in mind, she began in the 1960s and early 1970s to explore the ways that people's embodied experiences were fitted to the conceptual schemas of a ruling apparatus, comprised of concepts, discourses, and the work that activated them. Along with others who insisted on bringing women's varied experiences into view, Smith called sociology to account for its distortion and neglect of women's work and lives. A woman was not to be studied as "subject" but was to remain visible as the agent of the action being inquired into, and the analysis would be reportable to that subject/actor whose life, actions, decisions, experiences, and troubles it would help illuminate. The researcher who adopts Smith's approach must grasp the happenings that occur in the local setting and describe them sufficiently fully to be able to expli-cate their social organization, learning to convey "how the setting works," and building findings into a map of the relations of ruling that coordinate those people's doings.

Even as Smith was making her feminist contributions to a revitalization of the academic disciplines, she perceived the imminent threat of institutionalization of feminist scholarship. She recognized, as early as 1987 that exclusions from the acad-emy and from scholarly topics, organized similarly to those the early feminists had exposed, were now happening to other women whose voices would not be heard in ruling institutions. And feminist *critique* was being marginalized or inhibited as it was streamed toward ruling purposes. Smith (1987) cautioned that separating out for attention the topics that appealed to some feminists, those now in ruling posi-tions themselves, would, she thought, have the effect of restricting the analysis. Smith's own success in applying her approach to "learning from women's experience" encouraged her to see that discovering how women were ruled and oppressed – building knowledge for their benefit – could and should be applied for the benefit of anybody who is ruled, whose own interests are thereby submerged.

The logic of Smith's approach made it relevant beyond feminist scholarship, and institutional ethnography is now claimed as a "sociology for people." Smith's social organization of knowledge approach had begun to make apparent how the knowl-edge industries, including the work of academics, were implicated in ruling (and how academics participate in and benefit from their ruling positions in society). Concepts, discourses, information technologies, and accountability practices are among the material elements of the practices through whose competent operation the ruling of society is accomplished. Her alternative sociology was (to be) commit-ted to reorganizing the relations of knowledge of the social as a research practice. Instead of conceptualizing, building and testing the discourses and instruments that would be deployed in the interests of ruling, with researchers playing a seemingly neutral role, institutional ethnographers would seek a problematic for inquiry in the activities of those whose lives are coordinated by ruling relations.

Smith's approach has been taken up by activists, as well as by those working within ruling institutions, because its form of analysis has the capacity to extend people's ordinary knowledge, locating relations of power and activities of transforma-tion that (dis)organize their lives. It has become clear from Smith's re-interpretation of Marx's epistemology that the social relations that rule from beyond the local and everyday sites of people's lives are relations in which we all participate and there-fore there is no "outside" of ruling relations. In contemporary society ruling prac-tices continually take on new forms, many of them technological, textual, and discursive. And as new forms of governance develop in an increasingly integrated global economic regime, institutional ethnography provides tools for mapping those transformations from local points of view, with people's everyday interests in the forefront. This moves institutional ethnography's focus to what Smith's life work makes increasingly central – discovery of the everyday operation of linkages between people's life conditions and the actualities of how their knowing and acting are being framed.

Reader's Guide to Dorothy Smith

Dorothy Smith's writings may be challenging for readers new to her work. She makes no bones about the need to rethink sociology in order to begin the production of knowledge from a different location – the standpoint of people. So, a reader must be prepared to feel confused at first, and to read on, getting a "feel for" Smith's work and for the different position as knower that her writing requires sociologists to take.

One can track the development of Smith's ideas by beginning with two early books, *The Everyday World as Problematic* (1987) and *The Conceptual Practices of Power* (1990a) – which contain versions of important early essays – and then studying her 2005 *Institutional Ethnography: A Sociology for People*. In addition, the writings of students and colleagues contribute to understanding Smith's approach. The Campbell and Manicom (1995) edited collection *Knowledge, Experience and Ruling Relations* offers research conducted by a "first generation" of students; other collections appear in special issues of several journals (*Human Studies* 21(4) 1998; *Studies in Cultures, Organizations and Societies* 7(2) 2001; *Sociology and Social Welfare* 30(1) 2003; *Social Problems* 53(3) 2006). Campbell and Gregor's (2002, 2004) *Mapping Social Relations* is "a primer in doing institutional ethnography" written for newcomers. Smith selected research accounts that she considered exemplary for her edited collection *Institutional Ethnography as Practice* (2006). To get more deeply into the "theorized" understandings of a world constituted in language, and put together in people's activities, we recommend George Smith's (1990) article, "Political activist as ethnographer," Liza McCoy's (2007) chapter on Institutional Ethnography in *Handbook of Constructionist Research*, and Smith's own essay "Telling the truth after postmodernism," in her 1999 book *Writing the Social: Theory, Critique, and Investigations*.

Bibliography

Writings of Dorothy Smith

1974a. Women's perspective as a radical critique of sociology. *Sociological Inquiry*, 44: 1–13; reprinted in S. Harding (ed.) (1987) *Feminism and Methodology*. Milton Keynes: Open University Press, pp. 84–96.

1974b. The social construction of documentary reality. *Sociological Inquiry*, 44: 257–268.

1974c. The ideological practice of sociology. *Catalyst*, 8: 39–54.

1975 (with S. David) (eds). *Women Look at Psychiatry*. Vancouver: Press Gang.

1977. *Feminism and Marxism: A Place to Begin; A Way to Go*. Vancouver: New Star Books.

1983. Women, class and family. In R. Milliband and J. Saville (eds) *Socialist Register, 1983: A Survey of Movements and Ideas*. Merlin Press, London, pp. 1–44.

1987. *The Everyday World as Problematic: A Feminist Sociology*. Boston: Northeastern University Press and Toronto: University of Toronto Press.

1989. Feminist reflections on political economy. *Studies in Political Economy*, 30: 37–59.

1990a. *The Conceptual Practices of Power: A Feminist Sociology of Knowledge*. Boston: Northeastern University Press.

1990b. *Texts, Facts, and Femininity: Exploring the Relations of Ruling*. London: Routledge.

1993. High noon in Textland: A critique of Clough. *Sociological Quarterly*, 34: 183–192.

1994. A Berkeley education. In K. P. Meadow-Orlans and R. A. Wallace (eds) *Gender and the Academic Experience: Berkeley Women 1952–1972*. Lincoln: University of Nebraska Press, pp. 45–56.

1996. Telling the truth after postmodernism. *Symbolic Interaction*, 19: 171–202.

1999. *Writing the Social: Critique, Theory, and Investigations*. Toronto: University of Toronto Press.

2004. Ideology, science, and social relations: A reinterpretation of Marx's epistemology. *European Journal of Social Theory*, 7: 445–462.

2005. *Institutional Ethnography: A Sociology for People*. Lanham, MD: AltaMira Press/ Rowman and Littlefield.

2005 (with A. I. Griffith). *Mothering for Schooling*. New York: Routledge.

2006 (ed.). *Institutional Ethnography as Practice*. Lanham, MD: Rowman and Littlefield.

2007. Institutional ethnography: From a sociology for women to a sociology for people. In S. N. Hesse-Biber (ed.) *Handbook of Feminist Research*. Thousand Oaks, CA: Sage, pp. 409–416.

2007 (with C. F. Schryer). On documentary society. In C. Bazerman (ed.) *Handbook of Research on Writing: History, Society, School, Individual, Text*. New York: Lawrence Erlbaum/Taylor and Franci, pp. 136–155.

2008. From the 14th floor to the sidewalk: writing sociology at ground level. *Sociological Inquiry*, 78: 417–422.

Further Reading

Bakhtin, M. M. (1981) *The Dialogic Imagination: Four Essays*, trans. C. Emerson and M. Holquist. Austin: University of Texas Press.

Bakhtin, M. M. (1986) *Speech Genres and Other Late Essays*, trans. V. W. McGee. Austin: University of Texas Press.

Bazerman, C. (1988) *Shaping Written Knowledge: The Genre and Activity of the Experimental Article in Science*. Madison: University of Wisconsin Press.

Campbell, M. (2003) Dorothy Smith and knowing the world we live in. *Journal of Sociology and Social Welfare*, 30: 3–22.

Campbell, M. and Gregor, F. (2002) *Mapping Social Relations: A Primer in Doing Institutional Ethnography*. Aurora, ON: Garamond, republished by AltaMira Press, Walnut Creek, CA, 2004.

Campbell, M. and Manicom, A. (eds) (1995) *Knowledge, Experience, and Ruling Relations: Studies in the Social Organization of Knowledge*. Toronto: University of Toronto Press.

Clough, P. T. (1993) On the brink of deconstructing sociology: Critical reading of Dorothy Smith's standpoint epistemology. *Sociological Quarterly*, 34: 169–182.

De Montigny, G. A. J. (1995) *Social Working: An Ethnography of Front-Line Practice*. Toronto: University of Toronto Press.

DeVault, M. (ed.) (2008) *People at Work: Life, Power, and Social Inclusion in the New Economy*. New York: New York University Press.

Foucault, M. (1972) *The Archeology of Knowledge*. London: Tavistock.

Foucault, M. (1997) *Ethics: Subjectivity and Truth; Essential Works of Michel Foucault, 1954–1984*. New York: New Press.

Griffith, A. and André-Becheley, L. (2008) Institutional technologies: Coordinating families and schools, bodies and texts. In M. DeVault (ed.) *People at Work: Life, Power and Social Inclusion in the New Economy*, New York: New York University Press, pp. 74–96.

Harding, S. (1986) *The Science Question in Feminism*. Ithaca, NY: Cornell University Press.

Harding, S. (ed.) (1987) *Feminism and Methodology*. Bloomington: Indiana University Press.

Hartsock, N. (1987) The feminist standpoint: Developing the ground for a specifically feminist historical materialism. In Harding, S. (ed.) *Feminism and Methodology*. Bloomington: Indiana University Press, pp.181–190.

Marx, K. and Engels, F. (1976) *The German Ideology*. Moscow: Progress Publishers.

McCoy, L. (2007) Institutional ethnography. In J. Holstein and J. Gubrium (eds) *Handbook of Constructionist Research*. New York: Guilford, pp. 701–714.

Ng, R. (1986) *Politics of Community Services: Immigrant Women, Class and State*. Toronto: Garamond.

O'Malley, P. (1996) Indigenous government. *Economy and Society*, 25(3): 310–326.

Pence, E. (2001) Safety for battered women in a textually mediated legal system. *Studies in Cultures, Organizations and Societies*, 7: 199–229.

Polanyi, Karl (1957[1944]) *The Great Transformation: The Political and Economic Origins of Our Time*. Boston: Beacon Press and New York: Rinehart & Company.

Rose, N. (1999) *Powers of Freedom: Reframing Political Thought*. Cambridge: Cambridge University Press.

Rose, N., O'Malley, P., and Valverde, M. (2006) Governmentality. *Annual Review of Law and Society*, 2: 83–104.

Scott, J. W. (1991) The evidence of experience. *Critical Inquiry*, 17: 773–797.

Smith, G. W. (1990) Political activist as ethnographer. *Social Problems*, 37: 401–421.

Swift, K. J. (1995) *Manufacturing "Bad Mothers": A Critical Perspective on Child Neglect*. Toronto: University of Toronto Press.

Townsend, E. (1998) *Good Intentions Overruled: A Critique of Empowerment in the Routine Organization of Mental Health Services*. Toronto: University of Toronto Press.

Turner, S. M. (2003) *Municipal Planning, Land Development and Environmental Intervention: An Institutional Ethnography*. PhD dissertation. Toronto: University of Toronto.

Turner, S. M. (2006) Mapping institutions as work and texts. In D. E. Smith (ed.) *Institutional Ethnography as Practice*. Lanham, MD: Rowman and Littlefield, pp.139–161.

Walker, G. A. (1990) *Family Violence and the Women's Movement: The Conceptual Politics of Struggle*. Toronto: University of Toronto Press.

Wilson A. and Pence, E. (2006) US Legal interventions in the lives of battered women: An indigenous assessment. In D. E. Smith (ed.) *Institutional Ethnography as Practice*. Lanham, MD: Rowman and Littlefield, pp. 199–225.

12

Niklas Luhmann

RUDOLF STICHWEH

THE PERSON

Niklas Luhmann was born on December 8, 1927, in Lüneburg, the son of a brewer (Wilhelm Luhmann). His mother (Dora Gurtner) came from the Swiss hotel industry. From 1937 he attended a well-known humanist *Gymnasium* at Lüneburg, the Johanneum. This *Gymnasium* was pervaded by national socialist thinking, but Luhmann's family cultivated a distance towards the regime. Niklas Luhmann spent his summer holidays in Switzerland which had an influence on the opinions and attitudes he acquired. Luhmann was an assiduous student and one of his classmates remembered his "forbidding reading mania." In spring 1943, at only 15, Luhmann was obliged, along with his entire class, to help the German air force with the flak at air bases nearby. School hours continued irregularly at these locations. In autumn 1944 he had to leave school, received a brief military training and became a regular soldier in south Germany. In spring 1945 the American army took him as a prisoner of war and transported him first to Ludwigshafen and then to a labor camp near Marseille. The treatment was harsh and he later remembered beatings.

As Luhmann was still not 18, he was released from the camp in autumn 1945. His secondary school qualifications were not accepted. Therefore Luhmann went back to the Johanneum in Lüneburg and took a special class which led to the "Abitur" at Easter 1946. He decided to study law which was obviously motivated by his supposition that law is the kind of knowledge system that can help with the breakdowns of order he had experienced. From 1946 to 1949 he was a law student at Freiburg and had a strong interest in Roman law and in historical and comparative aspects of law. Luhmann went back to Lüneburg, became a trainee lawyer with a legal practitioner in the city, and prepared a legal dissertation which was never finalized. He only

The Wiley-Blackwell Companion to Major Social Theorists, First Edition.
Edited by George Ritzer and Jeffrey Stepnisky.
© 2011 Blackwell Publishing Ltd. Published 2011 by Blackwell Publishing Ltd.

finished his second state examination in 1953 and started his first job in 1954. We do not know much about the years from 1949 to 1954. But because he probably started his famous file-card box at the end of his studies at Freiburg it will some day be possible to reconstruct his intellectual agenda during these years using this source.

In working with a private legal practitioner Luhmann acquired a certain dislike of what he perceived as dependence on clients. As a result he preferred public service, when finally looking for a job. First he worked at a higher administrative court in Lüneburg (1954–1955) and then he switched to the Ministry of Culture in the federal state Lower-Saxony in Hannover (1955–1962). During this period, through private study he slowly became a sociologist. His first two papers were published in 1958 and 1960 in a journal for the sciences of administration. Then Luhmann applied for a stipend at the Littauer Center for Public Administration (Harvard). He received it and went there, but he studied primarily at the Department of Social Relations with Talcott Parsons (1960–1961).

On returning to Germany he switched from administration to research. In 1962 Luhmann took a job at the research institute of the University for Public Administration at Speyer (a school for the continuing education of public officials). In the same year he published his classical essay on "Function and Causality" in the *Kölner Zeitschrift für Soziologie und Sozialpsychologie*. In 1964 he gave a talk at the University of Münster on the same subject. On this occasion, Helmuth Schelsky, at this time probably the most influential German sociologist, asked him if he wanted to become a professor of sociology at the planned University of Bielefeld, of which Schelsky was one of the main initiators. Luhmann accepted after some hesitation, then in 1965 switched as a departmental head to the Institute of Social Research at Dortmund, affiliated with the University of Münster. He received his Doctor of Philosophy and his Habilitation in 1966, taught in Münster and in 1968 taught in Frankfurt (as a substitute for Theodor W. Adorno). Also in 1968 he became the first professor of the University of Bielefeld, two years before the first students matriculated there. He stayed in Bielefeld until his retirement in 1993, and even afterwards had his main institutional address there. Luhmann liked traveling, but otherwise he preferred a rather uneventful life, during which he produced the most impressive publication record of twentieth-century sociology. He lived in Oerlinghausen near Bielefeld with his wife, who died in 1977, and his three children. Only a few years after retirement Luhmann contracted a severe illness which cut short his life in a way that he probably had not expected. He died on November 6, 1998.

THE SOCIAL CONTEXT

National Socialism and the war experience were very important events in the development of Niklas Luhmann's thought, but in a much more indirect way than it was for other German theorists of his generation. His choice of law as his first concentration of intellectual interest was motivated by the decay of social order in the 1930s and 1940s. But he never wrote about National Socialism directly. He eventually left law, becoming a general sociologist. As a sociologist he never made the mistake of ascribing to the system of law an exalted position in his social theory, although it was easily perceived up to his last publications that this was the field he knew most about.

Another important social condition of Luhmann's work was that in his first professional career he did not opt for the private practice of law but for public administration. Both options Luhmann chose, law as a paradigm of social order (and not political democracy) and public administration as a paradigm of doing work on societal problems (and not the private practice of the professions) are strongly rooted in German traditions observed since at least the eighteenth century (Stolleis, 2002; Stichweh, 1994: ch. 15). As an indirect result of the second decision Luhmann never wrote a sociology of the professions (on which Talcott Parsons worked for decades) but instead had, from his first writings, a strong interest in public administration, and in a more general sense in the sociology of organizations. For his work on organizations Herbert Simon (1950) was a much more important influence than Parsons.

Besides these important social influences Niklas Luhmann really tried not to be a product of his times, and this strong preference in itself probably has a social background. In his own life experience he was very much impressed by the complete switch, in Germany, in such a short time from the ideology of national socialism to the belief in liberal democracy. Luhmann seems to have decided not to become a believer and propagandist of any ideology. Instead he cultivated an ironical detachment that even included his appreciation of his own writings.

When Luhmann became a professor in the late 1960s Germany was very much agitated by the students' movement. Luhmann had no sympathies for it and at some points was possibly hurt by personal experiences. But he never embroiled himself in the kind of conservative resistance some German professors tried to organize. Later in the 1980s and 1990s he did some work on a theory of social movements and social protest (Luhmann, 1996a). He did not have any sympathies for the variants of Marxism and Critical Theory rampant in the 1960s and 1970s. He considered these currents either intellectually outdated, or as moralizations of complex issues which had to be analyzed by conceptual means. Again his intellectual energies were not much absorbed by Marxism or Critical Theory as he was never interested in polemical work on other intellectual and scientific ventures. Luhmann had a strong sociological argument against moralization. He thought that it was divisive and not a constructive social force. From this he developed a general sociology of morale which looks at morale as a communication about the respect another person does or does not deserve (Luhmann, 2008a).

Niklas Luhmann cultivated some contacts with political parties but he never became identified with any of them. He was not the kind of public intellectual who regularly commented on public controversies. By birth and by education he was a Lutheran protestant. For him the sociology of religion became an important part of his work. But again this was done from a significant distance. There are no indicators which point to a personal religious belief. And his extensive readings in the theological tradition are mostly focused on Catholic thinkers, as his interests in the history of concepts mainly motivated readings in the medieval theological tradition.

Whereas many American and British university teachers cultivate a strong belief in the university systems in which they do their work this was never the case with Luhmann. In the beginning he did not want to become a university teacher. In the

1950s as part of his ministerial duties he had to deal with academics who had been professors in the Third Reich, had afterwards lost their jobs and now claimed reinstatement or damages. This experience did not raise his esteem for university people. Schelsky in recruiting him for Bielefeld had promised him a reformed university. But these promises did not materialize, and people who studied with him in Bielefeld very much came to know a person who somehow was an outsider in his own university although he was by far the most important scholar who ever taught there and he obviously liked to teach. Once more the difference from Parsons is instructive. Whereas for Parsons, among the professions he studied, the academic profession somehow had an extraordinary status (the university was described as "the most important structural component of modern societies that had no direct counterpart in earlier types of society" – Parsons, 1961: 261) and became the subject of the last great theoretical book finished in his lifetime (Parsons and Platt, 1973), Luhmann never wrote or even intended to write a sociology of universities as he understood the university to be a "small institution" (Luhmann, 1992). Instead he conceived and published a sociology of science with an epistemological focus in which he conceded only a second-class place for the institutional infrastructures of science (Luhmann, 1990a). Around 1975 Luhmann also began a multi-volume study of education (which for him primarily meant school education and secondly family education), but this is unfinished and has only partially been published (Luhmann, 1979, 2002a).

Another societal sphere towards which Luhmann kept his distance was the mass media. He rarely appeared in the mass media and never became a public intellectual. He sometimes advised his students not to spend their time with newspapers and personally never owned a TV. But this did not hinder him in understanding the social power of mass media. The sentence with which he opens his *The Reality of the Mass Media* (1996b: 9) is among the most famous sentences he ever wrote: "Everything we know about our society, even the world in which we live, we know from the mass media."

In his last fifteen years there were two contexts to which Luhmann conceded a certain influence on his theory. The first are ecological concerns. Luhmann was impressed by arguments regarding the ecological self-endangerment of mankind, and early on he reacted with a book called *Ecological Communication* (1986) which is often and rightly recommended as a good elementary introduction to systems theory. At the same time however, it is a rather pessimistic diagnosis of a society which has to decompose any problem situation into diverging functional perspectives and therefore will never deal with ecological concerns in the concerted way which might be necessary.

The other case regards inequality. Through travel Luhmann came to know cases of extreme societal inequality especially in slums and ghettos in third world metropolises. He focused especially on the seemingly complete separation of whole city quarters which are "in" the metropolis but otherwise completely disconnected from it in terms of chances of participating in the options and life chances of a modern society. Luhmann called this phenomenon "exclusion" in consonance with usages to be found in Parsons and Foucault among others (Luhmann, 1995b: ch. 13). He formulated a very general hypothesis which thematized "inclusion" and "exclusion" as a kind of metadifference which effects separations before the functional differentiation characteristic of the regions of inclusion begins its work. This hypothesis by the late Niklas Luhmann, in a way untypical for Luhmann, directly transfers visual evidences he believed to have seen (for example in "favelas" in Brazilian cities) into very general hypotheses. In some of these observations one gets the impression not of Luhmann the scientist analyzing the various couplings and uncouplings of slums within the function systems of world society, but rather one hears the voice of a visitor experiencing danger and fear.

THE INTELLECTUAL CONTEXT

We do not know much about early intellectual influences on Luhmann's thinking. A relevant fact is that he was a private scholar for a number of years between the end of his law studies (1949) and the onset of his academic work (ca. 1956–1957). Today this is unusual for someone who later becomes a famous scientist. It will be possible to reconstruct this period of Luhmann's intellectual biography as it is probably well documented in Luhmann's file-card box. But this file-card box will only become available in the next few years (after years of litigation a Niklas-Luhmann-Archive is going to be established at the University of Bielefeld). What we will surely learn from this is that the intellectual education of Luhmann was much broader than is usually the case even for extraordinary scientists. From brief forays we know about some of his readings: Camus, Dostoevsky, Hölderlin, Jean Paul, Thomas Mann, and many more names will have to be added to this. For some years he had no plausible reason to become a disciplinary specialist.

But in reconstructing this intellectual education the names of those who had lasting significance for the genesis and structure of Niklas Luhmann's theories will also appear. Two of them will stand out: Edmund Husserl (1859–1938) and Talcott Parsons (1902–1978). Both of them, as soon as Luhmann got to know their writings, induced a cognitive shift in his plans, both of them via key concepts deeply embedded in the structures of the theories Luhmann built. It is an interesting indicator that Luhmann who had a strong tendency to relativize the relevance of persons and names and not to give much weight in intellectual reconstructions to persons (he regularly maintained "it is only by accident that a person has a theory" and, of course, he included himself in this diagnosis) made two exceptions. Husserl and Parsons were the only two authors on whom he sometimes offered lectures: only in these two cases he made use of the construct of a person to systematize ideas. From this dual influence arose the synthesis of phenomenology and systems theory which is historically unique: From Husserl Luhmann took the strict separation of psychic systems (consciousness) and social systems (communication) which he radicalized in a way nobody had done before. He also received from Husserl the core mechanism of which is made use on both sides of the gulf of psychic and social systems: meaning as a mode of selectivity which builds complexity by remembering even those possibilities which were not chosen. Such a system built on meaning as its way of dealing with selections will incessantly oscillate between references towards its own states and references towards things external to it, a distinction which is akin to the Husserlian concept of intentionality.

From these few examples we can infer the originality of the strategy. On the one hand the distinction psychic/social is radicalized which implies a negation of inter-subjectivity, as subjectivity is a concept suitable only for psychic systems. On the other hand – as meaning is used in social systems, too – the rich vocabulary of the European philosophy of consciousness becomes instructive for the understanding of mechanisms and structures of social systems. This is what Luhmann was finally interested in: to develop an ever more differentiated vocabulary for the description and analysis of social systems.

The concept of social system is taken from Talcott Parsons and this process of taking stock of Parsons and reintegrating his conceptual structures into a completely reformulated systems theory is a still more influential cognitive undertaking than the interdisciplinary discourse with Husserl. The logic in Luhmann's way of dealing with Parsons consists in making use of nearly everything Parsons invented and in doing this to recontextualize every concept, a strategy which maximizes as well integrative continuity as it favors building completely new conceptual structures. As this was the core process of what Luhmann did for decades it will only become sufficiently visible in the presentation of his theories.

There are many more authors and thinkers who have to be included as important parts of the intellectual context of Luhmann's writings. I already mentioned Herbert Simon, the earliest influence on Luhmann's organization theory and near to Luhmann's preferences especially in his writings on bounded rationality (Simon, 1983). There is an early and extensive reception of the many authors of General Systems Theory. Among others Ludwig von Bertalanffy and Ross Ashby were important for Luhmann on the prominence of the system/environment distinction respectively the law of requisite variety which relates the complexity of a system to the turbulence of the successive states in the environment. To this one can add a long list of authors who contributed significant insights which Luhmann made use of for decades: Kenneth Burke ("perspective by incongruity"), Gaston Bachelard ("obstacles épistémologiques"), Robert K. Merton ("functional equivalents"), Donald T. Campbell ("variation, selection, retention"), Reinhart Koselleck ("historical semantics"), Erving Goffman ("interaction order"), Humberto Maturana ("autopoiesis"), Henri Atlan ("order from noise"), Gregory Bateson ("difference that makes a difference"), George Spencer Brown ("distinction and indication"), Franz Heider ("medium and form"), and many others.

There are patterns to be observed in these ways of absorbing influences. Luhmann had encyclopedic reading interests which were not limited by likes and dislikes towards other specific disciplines. Whereas even in intelligent sociologists you sometimes find a kind of disapproval towards economics which hinders them from learning from this neighboring discipline; such a kind of judgment would have been very improbable from Luhmann. His main dislike applied to authors who were stronger in normative than in cognitive arguments. Luhmann had no preference for establishment figures. Even in other disciplines he was willing to be inspired by outsiders. What in legal discourse is called the "prevailing opinion" did not impress him. And he liked very much to raise nearly forgotten authors from obscurity and to attribute to them a central role in theory building (as an example Luhmann, 1981a: ch. 7, on Vauvenargues and action theory). Furthermore and perhaps most importantly, Luhmann had an uncanny talent for finding just the right and promising interpretation for strange ideas from other disciplines. There were numerous social scientists who experimented with applications of Maturana's concept of "autopoiesis" on the analysis of social systems. But only Luhmann's interpretation did the trick and did it in a way such that it is the only one that survives today.

THE THEORY

Systems theory

From his beginnings in the early 1960s Luhmann called his contribution to sociological theorizing "Systems Theory" (early papers in Luhmann, 1970). By this he formulated the continuity to General Systems Theory and to Talcott Parsons, and in the decades since there never arose a need to change this theory name. Systems theory is still one of the most influential paradigms of sociological thinking and research with a global community of participants (*Soziale Systeme. Zeitschrift für soziologische Theorie* is probably besides cybernetics journals the core sociological journal for systems theory), and it is held together by the fact that the concept of social system which is used in an informal way in most sociologies, for this paradigm functions as *the core concept* which is in itself the object of incessant reformulation and interdisciplinary renewal.

Function and causality

There was one alternative self-designation Luhmann made use of in the 1960s. That was "functional-structural theory" which was meant as an inversion and as an alternative to the Parsonian "structural-functional theory." By this Luhmann intended to say that his theorizing does not start with given social structures which are subsequently analyzed in their functionality (a *modus operandi* he attributed to Parsons). Instead the sociologist is supposed to begin with social problems which are understood as functional references – for example, how to ensure future need fulfillment by present action; and how to ensure interpersonal consistency in experiencing the world? – and real social structures are analyzed in their capability to contribute to the resolution of these problems. In the next step one will then compare alternative social structures in their problem-solving capabilities and in such a comparison what matters is that they are functional equivalents towards one another regarding a specific functional reference problem. What becomes visible here is Luhmann's preference for a historical and comparative functionalism which always compares alternative structural or institutional patterns in their ability to contribute to the solution of relevant social problems. This is near to Darwinian evolutionary biology or to certain types of evolutionary economic institutionalism (the Veblenian tradition) and articulates a preference for comparative studies against a conventional preference for the causal reduction of observed events. The methodology of this kind of equivalence functionalism was the subject of Luhmann's first extended sociological essay (Luhmann, 1970: ch. 1), and he always remained true to this comparative and evolutionary interpretation of the methodological tendencies of sociological systems theory although he did not write much about functionalism in later years.

System and environment

As soon as the differentiation from Parsons lost its symbolic relevance, Luhmann only occasionally used "functional-structural theory" as a self-description of the theory. Then and afterwards "systems theory" was the only adequate term. In the early years "cybernetic" was sometimes added by Luhmann to the words "systems theory" (Luhmann, 1970: 132, n. 16), and "cybernetic" here means selectivity of the relations of the system to its environments. There are three interesting implications in such a definition. First, selectivity becomes a universal attribute of any event which ever happens in a system. Second, the environment becomes relevant as a circumstance which impacts on any selection event in the system. And, third, in choosing *its* selection events and observing *its* environments the system acquires a self-referential character. Therefore Luhmannian systems theory is emphatically a system/environment theory, but as such it is from its beginnings specified by its cybernetic (i.e. self-referential selectivity) character. From the relevance of the concept of "environment" follows one more methodological postulate for systems theory. Systems theory not only needs to be comparative in all its cognitive operations; it must also, in observing alternative strategies and trajectories of social systems, explain these operations on the basis of the system's observation of its environments.

Another central term for the analysis of a system and its environments is complexity. A system consists of certain elements and realizes in a selective way relations among them. Luhmann called this property of a system "complexity." The complexity of a system seems to be related to the demands its environments place on it. Ross Ashby coined for this interrelation of system complexity and environmental demands the term "requisite variety" (Ashby, 1952). Luhmann added the formula "reduction of complexity" and by this he claimed reductive relations towards multiple environmental concerns as the basis of system autonomy. Luhmann later realized that one should not call this achievement a "reduction of complexity" as only a system can be complex (we only find elements and relations among elements in a system) and its environments consist in unspecified demands. As a result it is better to call it a "constitution of complexity" which is to be observed in the process of the formation of a system.

Meaning and social systems

Up to this point we have not specified which kind of system we are speaking about. In the case of Luhmann the primacy of social systems is very obvious. As much as Luhmann was an interdisciplinary thinker with broad interests in cybernetics, biological theory and numerous other disciplines, there was no doubt that he only intended to contribute to the theory of social systems.

What is the basis of the specificity of social systems? The answer Luhmann proposed is "meaning" (Luhmann, 1971a). Meaning can be described as a special case of a theorem in General Systems Theory which says that in any system one observes a production of surplus possibilities and mechanisms reducing these surpluses. Meaning is that way of dealing with surpluses in which the possibilities not chosen are not eliminated but are remembered and virtualized and thereby stored for future use. It is easy to see that meaning systems which consist of a mix of realities (realized possibilities) and virtualities (as yet unrealized possibilities) need more sophisticated mechanisms for dealing with the kind of complexity they produce. All of them are historical systems, remembering their choices, and being able to come back on earlier decisions by reactivating virtualized possibilities.

Social systems and psychic systems

Meaning allows us to distinguish social systems from biological systems, physio-chemical systems and machines, all of which are not able to produce and to process meaning. But there is one further type of systems – psychic systems – for which meaning is constitutive of its operations.

As it already was the case in Parsons, social and psychic systems are conceived by Luhmann as two different types of systems, separate from one another but coupled via media such as meaning and language. In Parsons this separation was less visible, as the distinction of social and psychic systems was introduced on the level which was called "action frame of reference." On this level they represent two of the four types of action systems which contribute to the emergence of action as a phenome-non constitutive of the human condition. Therefore besides the separation of two types of systems their cooperation in the production of action is emphasized. In Luhmann we have a different constellation. All the hierarchical levels we have in Parsons, of systems always being subsystems of higher levels of the emergence of action, disappear in the strictly non-hierarchical theory of Luhmann. Instead we have a clear disjunction of social and psychic systems, both of them being environ-ments for the other type of system. This way it is articulated much more explicitly that persons and their psychic systems are *only* environments of social systems (and social systems *only* environments of psychic systems). This diagnosis in its clarity was perceived as anti-humanist by some observers and therefore aroused numerous controversies with arguments to be heard even today. Luhmann liked to turn these arguments around and to insist that for a person the autonomy from the structures of social systems is a kind of freedom.

But how is this strict separation of two system types both of which operate on the basis of "meaning" and which are connected by language towards one another to be explained? Luhmann developed a theory which postulates the emergence of a system by the self-specification of the elements which are constitutive of the system. The dif-ferentiation of social and psychic systems is then explained by the differentiation of elements characteristic of these two systems.

In looking at psychic systems Luhmann developed a conception akin to Edmund Husserl. Psychic systems consist of thoughts as their elementary basis. Thoughts are obviously connected with one another, referring to earlier thoughts and preparing ongoing considerations (Luhmann, 1995b: ch. 1–4). Conceived in this way, Luhmann calls psychic systems systems of consciousness. From this follows the implication that in his theory there is no systematic place for a concept of the unconscious, except in an understanding which postulates an observer who ascribes latencies to a psychic system which are unobservable for the system itself. There are other formu-lations in which Luhmann seems to perceive the identification of psychic systems with thought processes as too restrictive. He looks at other elementary constituents such as feelings, acts of will, perceptions – and then proposes "intentional acts" as a name for the elements of consciousness.

Action and experience

What are the elementary constituents of social systems? In a classical sociological understanding one probably would have opted for "actions," e.g. the "unit acts" of Talcott Parsons, and for some years Luhmann described the basic social elements in this way, making use of terms such as "communicative action." But he complicated the understanding of action by introducing a distinction between "action" and "experience" for which there were no antecedents in the sociological tradition (Luhmann, 1981a: ch. 5). Social systems are thought to process selections for which there exist two alternatives: They are either causally attributed to one of the social systems involved and then they are thought to be one of the actions of the system. Alternatively the selections are seen as representing objective circumstances in the world which implies that one only "experiences" these selective events and is unable to influence them in the present situation. This distinction of action and experience is not an ontological distinction which identifies ontological properties of the selection events. It is only based on attributions which are produced by the social systems and which can be disputed and reversed. Once more this argument demonstrates how much social systems exist in a social world entirely produced by themselves and how much objectivity (information about states of the world) and subjectivity (selections for which actors can be held responsible) can reverse their roles. But what does this say about the constitutive element of social systems? We cannot point to "selection" as a candidate since selection is a much more general phenomenon which is at the basis of natural as well as social systems. And there is a clear argument against "action," since the concept of "action" is one part of the distinction of action and experience both sides of which are in the realm of the social. Therefore we have to look for another concept which allows us to identify the boundaries of the social domain.

Communication and action

Until the late 1970s Luhmann sometimes said that he hesitated about whether he should designate "actions" or "communications" as the most elementary constituents of social systems. One could perceive a rhetorical component in these remarks as Luhmann had already established the thesis that in social systems only some selections are attributed to a social system as its actions and therefore the concept of social action cannot claim the universal status needed for *the* constitutive element of a social system.

The other candidate for elemental status is obviously communication, a concept which until that point sociologists mainly used casually. For example, among others one can study this in Parsons in whose writings one frequently finds the concept of communication but who never formulated a theory of communication. On the other hand, since the information theory of the 1940s, in for example Norbert Wiener (1948), or Claude E. Shannon and Warren Weaver (1949), communication was a probable candidate for a general sociological theory. For any social theory that would try to understand the fundamental character of information transfer in social processes the concept of social action always would have been a counterintuitive choice. Already in 1951 there was a book by Jürgen Ruesch and Gregory Bateson *Communication: The Social Matrix of Psychiatry* which gave a good idea of how to base a social science discipline on the concept of communication.

For these reasons one should not be surprised that Luhmann in the theoretical treatise he finally published in 1984 resolutely established his theory of social systems as a theory of communication systems (Luhmann, 1984: ch. 4). Communication is the foundational element of social systems and as such it even constitutes the boundaries of social systems. Social systems only consist of communications and there is no communication outside of social systems which means there is a sharp boundary separating social systems from those environments which do not consist of communications.

In his theory of communication Luhmann regards communication not as *one* specific type of selection. Instead communication is based on three selections which are indispensable components of any communication and are necessarily intertwined. These three selections are called "information," "utterance" and "understanding." Information can be interpreted and has often been interpreted by Luhmann himself in the way Bateson proposed. Information is "a difference which makes a difference" (Bateson, 1973). For this concept of information, already, one needs a kind of minimum sociality. There must be an entity at which the first difference occurs (as a change of one of its states). And there is a second entity which registers or observes the first difference and attributes informative relevance to it. Of course, the first and the second entity can be identical (I observe the change of my bodily states and ascribe informative relevance to them). But even in this interpretation there exists a kind of internal division in the entity which establishes some "internal sociality." It is easily seen that information in the interpretation given to it here is not at all communication. There is a kind of subjectivity involved. This is caused by the second system which by its own states infers the informative relevance of the differences to be observed. But for communication to arise there must be further components in the communication process. There always has to be a system which explicitly decides to *utter* the informative difference. In other words it needs a communicative intention which is not yet there as long we only presuppose a system which produces information by the observation of state changes. Besides these intentional utterances we can concede the possibility of utterances not completely controlled – and therefore being non-intentional – by the system to which they are ascribed as its utterances. For example, I may change my clothing or other aspects of my behavior in a way which is perceived by others as a kind of utterance which informs them about changes of my mind. In any case this second component in a communication process, the utterance, may be called the action component since there always will be an attribution which classifies the utterance as the action of a specific system. Information and utterance still do not suffice to produce an elementary communication. To realize a communication one finally needs *a second system which understands the information uttered by the first system*. Therefore the third component is called by Luhmann "understanding." The concept of understanding presupposed here is a rather formal one which does not demand that "understanding" is a correct or good understanding. It includes the possibility of "misunderstanding" as a case of understanding. Even if I grin in listening to sad news it is obvious that this counts as indicator for understanding, and my grin, surprising and irritating as it may be to other participants and probably pointing to the acceptance or rejection of the news (perhaps I don't believe the news or for me it is good news or I am simply sardonic), has to be seen as a fourth component of communication and at the same time as an utterance which already is part of the next elementary communication.

Communication theory and double contingency

The three-component theory of communication invented by Luhmann is related to theories proposed by Karl Bühler (1934) and John Searle (1969). It is important to bring to mind the most important sociological understandings assumed by Luhmann's theory: (1) Communication is not dependent on the intention to communicate. Utterances can be intentional; but they need not be. There are always two systems (processors) involved; for communication it suffices that the second system observes a difference of information and utterance. (2) Communication can be realized on the basis of language as its medium. But communication can also occur as nonverbal communication; in this case what can be done with it obviously differs (on this difference see Tomasello, 2008). (3) For the competition between "action" and "communication" Luhmann found an elegant solution. The primacy of communication is obvious. But among the components of elementary communications there is one – the utterance – which functions as the action component in each communication. This allows a more general understanding regarding the concept of action. Actions are always constituted by attributions. If for a selection one looks for someone whose responsibility for this selection one wants to claim one will attribute this selection to this system as its action. (4) As we already saw, understanding as the third component of an elementary communication can immediately pass into the fourth component acceptance/rejection which is already part of the next communication. This argument makes visible communication as a flow, the recursivity built into this flow of communications, and the possibilities of the formation of new system/environment distinctions always implied in recursive communications, that is communications coming back to or referring to earlier communications. (5) A precondition of any communication is that at least two systems or processors (or "alter" and "ego" in the terminology taken from phenomenology) participate in it. Parsons as well as Luhmann thematize this condition in terms of a theory of "double contingency" which Parsons invented in *Toward a General Theory of Action* (Parsons and Shils, 1951: 16). Double Contingency means the paradoxical reciprocity of both systems being oriented in their actions and expectations towards what the other system is probably going to do (Luhmann, 1984: ch. 3). Furthermore it means the uncertainty arising from this situation. Double Contingency points to the improbability of communication and the improbability of order in a situation in which each of the participants might be disposed to wait for the decisions of the other one. Theories of double contingency then have to demonstrate – and both Parsons and Luhmann tried to solve this problem – how communication, order and system formation happen to arise in a situation in which at the beginning a reciprocal blockade seems the most probable outcome.

Communication elements as events and operations

Are there plausible arguments against the status of communications as elementary constituents of social systems? One should not adduce the complex character of communications – their three-component structure – as an objection. The same objection would be valid against unit acts or atoms as elements, too. All of them have a complex internal structure. But as elements communications do not seem to possess the internal (temporal) stability which one might demand as a condition for element status. Some years before he adopted communication theory Luhmann was already beginning work on the specific temporality of the elements of social systems. This is a question Parsons never asked. In one of his most fascinating essays, "Time and Action – A Forgotten Theory" from 1979, Luhmann proposed a solution he attributed to the French moralist and enlightenment philosopher Vauvenargues (1715–1747) (Luhmann, 1981a: ch. 7).

The elements of social systems – in this essay Luhmann still theorized about actions, but the same is true regarding communications – are "events." An event is something which has only vanishing duration. As soon as they appear they are gone again. From this condition derives for any social system the imperative to produce incessantly new events which connect to earlier events which are just vanishing. Otherwise the system might come to an end, simply for the reason that nothing happens anymore. This is a remarkable interpretation which is separated by a gulf from the equilibrium and stability postulates of social theory in the 1950s.

Luhmann adds one more concept. This is the "reproduction of event-based elements." Reproduction is not to be understood as identical reproduction but means the circumstance that new event-based elements have to relate to earlier elements in the system and that their constructive freedom is restricted by the history of the system. For this phenomenon of the reproduction of event-based elements Luhmann now proposes the name "operation." This is a far-reaching change in social theory which I will illustrate with a relevant quote from Luhmann:

> To accentuate it as clearly as possible that we do not speak about an unchanged maintenance of a system but an occurrence on the level of system elements which is indispensable as well for the maintenance of the system as for its change we will call the reproduction of the event-based elements an operation. (1984: 79)

This operative reformulation of sociological theory necessitates significant changes in systems theory. For example, one can no longer speak about complexity in the way Luhmann introduced this concept in the late 1960s: Complexity as selectivity in the relations between the elements of a system. Now the same structure arises in each individual operation of a system which means that already on the level of the elements the demands are fulfilled which in earlier systems theory were seen as macro-properties of whole systems. This is clearly said in *The Society of Society*:

> In principle the classical concept of complexity is sabotaged by the concept of operation as it transforms the distinction of element and relation into one unitary concept (Operation = selective relationing of elements). (1997: 139, n. 181)

Self-reference, autopoiesis, operational closure

Coordinated with this change-over to an operative understanding of social systems a number of far-reaching rearrangements take place. The first of them, prepared over two decades, is the increasing importance of the concept of "self-reference." This concept is already there in the idea of a cybernetic systems theory. Selectivity in the relations of a system to its environments in cybernetic systems theory means a "self-determined selectivity." From environmental perturbations the system selects those which it needs to stabilize or optimize its *Eigenstates*. The same principle of self-referential control is valid for the reproduction of the event-based elements of the system. This immediately connects to the concept of "autopoiesis" which Luhmann borrowed in the early 1980s from Humberto Maturana and Francisco Varela (Maturana and Varela, 1980). Autopoiesis only means that everything which functions as a unity in a system – element, operation, structure, boundary – is due to the production processes of the system itself. It follows that on this level of the production of the unities constitutive of a system no external elements can be imported and insofar as the system has to be conceived as an operationally closed system. One can interpret autopoiesis as a rather formal description of a specific type of systems without conceding to the theory explanatory power regarding the conditions of the realization of autopoiesis (this point is made in Luhmann, 1993 and 1997).

Immediately related to the hypothesis of the self-referential closure of autopoietic systems is the idea of the "operative" and "structural coupling of autopoietic systems" which we find once more in Maturana. Operative coupling refers to the fact that an observer can get the impression that a certain individual event (which for the observer is the "same" event) seems to belong to two different autopoietic systems at the same time and that it therefore somehow merges these two systems exactly for the duration of this event. Already in *their* next events these two systems separate again as each system connects to the first event according to its own observation perspectives and thereby incorporates this first event completely in its own system process. Structural coupling on the other hand is not the fusion of the structures of two systems. Instead the concept signifies that the structures of one system are formed in contact with the structures of another system, something for which coevolution is another term regularly used in science. The development of the structures of a psychic system coupled to socializing social systems is a case in point.

Operation and observation

A last important addition to the theory of social systems regards the concept of operation. We take from the theory of meaning and from information theory the insight that operations are always based on differences. Operations choose a certain option and they discard other possibilities. That is, there is always a distinction which functions as the basis of the operation. It is known that in social systems or in psychic systems it is often the case that both sides of the distinction are represented. An operation for which this is true Luhmann calls an observation. Under these conditions one can say that each observation is an operation as it depends on its operative performance. On the other hand in social systems there are many operations one could not call an observation as they simply happen without the differences on which they are based being represented.

As with many contemporary social theorists from Harold Garfinkel to Anthony Giddens, Luhmann postulates that modern social systems are based in acts of observation and self-observation. Luhmann gives a more precise version which uses a term introduced by Heinz von Foerster (1984): Observation in modern social systems, especially in function systems is always "second order observation." Through this term he postulates that observers do not have direct access to realities. Rather, they observe other observers and on the basis of these observations of observations decide with which observations they want to connect, and from which they are going to dissociate their understandings. Modern science, which in all its cognitive operations always refers to observations by other scientists already published before, is a good example of this indirectness that is characteristic of the function systems of modern society.

Luhmann's theory of observation is supplemented by a calculus invented by the English logician George Spencer Brown (1972). Luhmann does not use it as a calculus but as a conceptual structure which explicates the logic of distinctions. Observations are based on distinctions which separate two sides of the distinction of which only one can be indicated. Such distinctions are called "forms" in Spencer Brown and in Luhmann. What is important is the unity of distinction and indication. Spencer Brown postulated that making a distinction and indicating one of the two sides of this distinction is something which always happens *uno actu*. This means that the indication does not remain indistinct but is always implemented in making a distinction. A further consequence is that one cannot at the same time make use of a distinction and observe this distinction via another distinction. In this respect observation is "blind" to the distinction that it makes use of. This is an irrefutable latency which allows the reconstruction of classical figures of functional analysis. And only in the next step the observer may be able to observe the distinction just made use of via another distinction.

A last addendum is called "reentry." A distinction may be used for the further internal differentiation of a social space which has been created by the application of the same distinction. As such it "reenters" the social space it has demarcated in the first place. This is another type of recursivity and Luhmann connects it to the concept of rationality. The ability to make use of reentries is one indicator of the rationality of a system.

THEORY OF SOCIETY

The theory of social systems presented up to this point is, in Luhmann's view, the most general social theory sociology can produce. It has a formal similarity to the status of the "action frame of reference" in the Parsonian *oeuvre*. From at least the early 1970s Luhmann planned this theory as one of two core projects in his research agenda. The other theoretical core project was to conceive a theory of society, society being understood as the most extensive social system including all communications and actions. There is again a formal similarity to the status of the theory of social systems (one of the four boxes in the "action frame of reference") in Parsons.

Interaction, organization, society

To understand the theory of society one has to know that among the immeasurable multitude of social systems there are three types or – as Luhmann calls it – three levels of system formation to which he ascribes special prominence. Luhmann speaks of "interaction," "organization" and "society."

In the case of interaction Luhmann's theory is very close to Erving Goffman's theory of the interaction order (Goffman, 1983; Luhmann, 1975a: ch. 2). Interaction systems only demand physical presence of the participants and a reciprocity of perception. If these conditions are fulfilled a social system among attendant persons will necessarily arise as under these conditions as Watzlawick (1967) demonstrated it is impossible not to communicate. Interaction systems are limited in what they can do and in their duration. They can only process one subject-matter at a time and when the co-presence of participants ends the interaction systems ends, too. But they are very common, they are repetitive and this way crystallize social forms. They account for a significant part of our everyday experience.

Organizations, Luhmann called them formal organizations, define an intermediary level of system formation (Luhmann, 1964, 2000a). They are membership organizations which are based on formalized conditions for entry and exit. As a member, one is bound to the rules of an organization. As autopoietic systems organizations are operationally closed on the level of decisions. At the end everything that happens in an organization comes from a decision or leads to decisions and these decisions have to be attributed to the organization itself.

Society is the most extensive social system, including all interactions and organizations in its purview. Luhmann defines society via communicative attainability and on this basis comes to the conclusion that today there is only one societal system on earth which he calls "World Society." That was a provocative thesis, already published in 1971 (Luhmann, 1975a: ch. 4) which for some time neither found much notice nor much disagreement. One may even say that in Luhmann's work despite its early centrality it is somehow underdeveloped (Stichweh, 2000, 2010).

What does the theory of society Luhmann finally published in the year before his death (1997) look like? Over decades Luhmann developed this theory in four big threads. The youngest of these threads which has not primarily been articulated in theoretical terms is related to the subject of self-reference. Society is understood as a system incessantly producing self-observations and self-descriptions. Luhmann has mainly looked at this subject in case studies on the historical semantics of modern society (Luhmann, 1980–1995, 1997: ch. 5).

The other three threads are closely related to Luhmann's theory of meaning (1971a). In this theory Luhmann distinguished a social, a temporal and a material dimension of meaning. To these three dimensions are connected the theory of symbolically generalized media of communication (social dimension), the theory of sociocultural evolution (temporal dimension) and the differentiation theory (material dimension).

Theory of symbolically generalized media of communication

Regarding the social dimension of meaning the most important question seems to be how it is possible to bridge differences of opinion and of interest among participants and on this basis not to aim for consensus but to achieve an acceptance of selections which means at least non-intervention and tolerance. Language, especially language which is made use of in an effective way, is a medium of communication which promises to achieve this. Since Greek and Roman antiquity this was supported by rhetoric as an art, that is as a technique for improving the effectiveness of those intentions which one pursues in communication. The same social function (effectiveness in communication) was reinvented in modern society several times by symbolically generalized media of communication (Luhmann, 1997: ch. 2).

This is a theory which resumes the theory of exchange media by Talcott Parsons (Parsons, 1967: pt. III). In contrast to Parsons who ascribes to exchange media a special function for mediating input/output processes between systems, Luhmann analyzes symbolically generalized communication media as mechanisms internal to systems. Such mechanisms arise primarily in situations where you need additional mechanisms of motivation for especially improbable demands to adopt selections. Why, for example, should I accept that another person buys goods which I would like to have myself. Luhmann gave the following answer: In the economy there is the symbolically generalized medium of money. The buyer of much sought-after goods has to hand over a significant amount of money in return. And this functions as a symbol which signals to all other owners of money that their money gives them, too, the freedom to buy at points of time they choose, goods which are still unspecified and which need not be specified yet as money in its generality can be exchanged against any goods. In a similar way but with changing motivational constellations of the participants Luhmann analyzes the other media: Love – I am motivated by being wholly oriented towards the experienced life-world of another person which allows me improbable kinds of attention; Power – I am motivated by the negative sanctions a power-holder controls and which I want to evade; Truth – I am motivated by reliable ways of experiencing the world which science promises and of which I know that others have to share them. This is the basic argumentative figure which is supplemented in Luhmann by a long catalog of media properties: *binary code structures in media* (beautiful/ugly, true/wrong, lawful/unlawful); *probabilities of inflation and deflation of media symbols; mechanisms which connect the media with body perceptions of participants* (sexuality, physical force, physical needs). There are numerous other properties (Luhmann, 1975a). It is easily observed that in this theory, handled as a comparative theory of very different media constellations, there is a significant wealth of analytical possibilities, and it should be added that this theory which Parsons invented is one of the rare cases of radical innovation in social science as this theory is an innovation for which it is difficult to name precursors in classical sociology.

Theory of sociocultural evolution

The second significant part of the theory of society looks at *changes of social structures in long-term perspective*. Luhmann does not opt for "modernization," "social change" or "development" as relevant theoretical paradigms (1997: ch.3). Instead he early on pleaded for a neo-Darwinist evolutionary theory. In terms of intellectual history this has been a surprising choice as "evolution" was for a long time a discredited position in social theory. Donald T. Campbell, an American psychologist and methodologist, was one of the few who since the 1950s persistently tried to revivify evolutionary interpretations of social science problems (Campbell, 1988). For Luhmann's approach two factors are important. First, he was fascinated by the idea that chance events can become productive for the formation of social structures. He perceived this idea as the conceptual core of evolutionary theories and it is well adapted to other aspects of his theorizing, especially the centrality of the concept of "contingency" (which Luhmann interpreted by going back to Scholasticism as double negation of chance and necessity). Second, Luhmann saw the main task of an evolutionary research program in a theory of evolutionary mechanisms. This resulted in other problems becoming less prominent in his evolutionary theorizing, especially the question, disquieting for many authors, of whether there exists such a thing as a replication (i.e. identical reproduction) of the elements of social systems (see Sperber, 1996 for whom his negative answer becomes the main argument against neo-Darwinism). The catalog of evolutionary mechanisms – variation, selection, stabilization/retention – and the idea of their conceptual centrality Luhmann took from Campbell. His main questions then aimed at the identification of the three mechanisms in different social systems and their sequential interlocking and on the other hand their separation in systems.

On the macrolevel of the theory of society Luhmann locates the variation mechanism in the possibility to say *no* which is given in any communicative situation and which if it is used always implies the possibility of changed impulses in a system. The selection mechanism consists, according to Luhmann, in the binary codes of the media of communication to which he ascribes the role to sort new meaning elements arising on the basis of negations. The stabilization of selected meaning complexes happens via system formation that is by the differentiation of a (new) system which specializes on the material dimensions of meaning becoming prominent in the selection processes. The stabilization of a system has at the same time the effect that it becomes easier to see where further possibilities of negation and change are located in the reorganized system. This retroactive effect from stabilization to variation demonstrates a circular connectedness of the three evolutionary mechanisms (cf. Weick, 1979). In looking at this theoretical construction one perceives that in the internal structural of this evolutionary theory there is an internal representation of the main distinctions of the theory of society. There is one mechanism that stands for the probability of chance, a second mechanism focused on improbable meaning demands, and a third mechanism which reorganizes the material complexity of the world by differentiation processes.

Differentiation theory

Looking at differentiation theory, the third prominent part of the theory of society, we are near the core of the sociological tradition (1997: ch. 4). The main innovation Luhmann adds to differentiation theory is that he interprets it as a theory of *system formation*. Differentiation processes always produce new system/environment-differences. This differs from the binary logic of splitting up in two new systems which was the Parsonian paradigm. And there is no longer any AGIL-logic which for Parsons provided the guarantee that in differentiation there will always arise exactly four systems which fulfill the four functional imperatives the theory stipulated. For this theorem Luhmann substituted the idea that for the formation of systems in systems there exists only a limited number of forms. Therefore the problem of *changing forms of systems differentiation* becomes the conceptual core of his differentiation theory.

There is first of all *segmentary differentiation*. Segments are to be identified by the sameness of their internal structures and by the equality of their societal importance and rank (kinship groups in a tribal society are an example for this kind of structure). As Durkheim's famous argument postulated in a segmentary differentiated society one can add or take away segments without effecting significant changes in the structure of society.

A second form of societal differentiation which Luhmann added as a result of extensive historical and sociological research having been published is the *differentiation of center and periphery*. A classical illustration of this form of differentiation is the differentiation of city and country which postulates systematical and institutionalized differences in the control of resources and information. The exact place of this form of differentiation in the systematics of differentiation theory is not entirely clear in Luhmann. It would be difficult to make the argument that center/periphery is an autonomous form of system formation which brings about new systems with a system/environment-difference of their own. It would be more convincing that center/periphery functions as an internal structuring in an existent system or a form of interconnectedness among systems which remain separate otherwise. Both interpretations support doubts that center/periphery is a differentiation form of its own and perhaps reinforce the conjecture *that center/periphery differences mainly organize historical transfers between forms of differentiation* and/or bridge regions of the world which are characterized by the primacy of different forms of differentiation.

The third form of differentiation is called *hierarchical differentiation or stratification*. It divides society into social systems (estates, castes, strata) which are distinguished by the inequality of rank. Each of these systems defines for its members a complete life form which does not need other contexts of participation. Of course, there are contacts with members of other strata. All of the traditional high cultures of human history were stratified societies which gives an impression of the historical importance of this differentiation form.

Functional differentiation is by Luhmann postulated as the differentiation form of modern world society. This implies the hypothesis that society today consists of macrosystems for economic relations, politics, law, religion, science and numerous other functional contexts. All of these are global macrosystems of worldwide communicative extension. Among one another they are characterized by extreme social and cultural diversity which excludes any possibility of a rank order among them. What differs from segmentary structures is that all these function systems are indispensable. In one formulation Luhmann called them *self-substitutive orders*. That is if a deficit of money or power or any other functional resource arises in society this cannot be substituted for by more religious beliefs or legal decisions. As the hypothesis of the "functional differentiation of world society" is the central empirical hypothesis of Luhmann's theory of society the future impact of this theory will to a considerable amount be dependent on the influence this hypothesis will have on global sociological theorizing and research.

IMPACT AND ASSESSMENT

When Niklas Luhmann started publishing in the 1960s the separation and isolation of sociological schools was not as prevalent as it is today. Therefore there arose an immediate early reception by experts who realized that Luhmann was a new voice with an unusual independence and authority. From the first publications there became visible a breadth of interdisciplinary knowledge and an overview of disparate literatures which nobody else had mastered at this time. And Münster, his first university, was in the midst of the 1960s an excellent place to which the careers of figures as diverse as Niklas Luhmann, Norbert Elias, Hans Blumenberg and of numerous others were tied in significant ways.

In 1971 Luhmann published together with Jürgen Habermas *Theorie der Gesellschaft oder Sozialtechnologie*. Strangely, this book is still not translated into English, but without doubt it is one of the most important books published in German in the last 50 years. Ever since this book appeared Luhmann became famous in German-speaking countries and his very broad theoretical canvas was attractive to sensibilities very common in Germany. His appeal until today has much to do with the fact that nobody could ever assign him to the political "right" or the political "left." Luhmann's career is a good case study to demonstrate how important this kind of incalculability is for a scholar.

The international reception of Luhmann's writings began after 1971. One can distinguish between Luhmann the sociological theorist and Luhmann the legal scholar. Early on it was often the legal scholar who became well known in other countries, rather than the sociological theorist. There was an early reception in Italy and Spain and in some Latin American countries (Chile, Mexico, Brazil) and in some Asian countries (Japan, Korea, Taiwan, China). The Scandinavian and the Benelux countries came a little bit later but today one finds in most of them an important influence of sociological systems theory. France proved to be a difficult terrain as the sociology of Pierre Bourdieu was always coupled to a strong territorial imperative. The most interesting case is the delayed reception of Luhmann's writings in England and the United States. The most probable reason for this is that in these countries he was perceived as a late follower of Talcott Parsons, and Parsons was thought to have been refuted decisively. In the early twenty-first century the situation is changing again. Now we observe a much broader diffusion of systems theory in many countries, even the English-speaking ones, and the main factor seems to be the ongoing internationalization of the careers of young social scientists which enhances the diffusion of theories if they are prominent in countries from which a significant number of migrants are recruited. Therefore we are still at the beginning of the global impact of the theories of Niklas Luhmann.

There is no place here for an extensive assessment of Niklas Luhmann's works and perhaps this can only be done in detailed discussions of many research problems. Systems theory such as Luhmann took it from Parsons and the cybernetic tradition and gave it a new twist as a non-hierarchical theoretical landscape in a non-hierarchical society today stands out among sociological paradigms because of its sociological universalism, that is not being tied to specific problem situations but trying to be applicable to the whole range of sociological problems from minuscule micro-contexts to world society, and from long-term historical interpretations of the evolution of human society to the most recent developments in communication practices and technologies. This universalism which is not achieved via a rigorous simplification of the conceptual apparatus (as may be the case in rational choice sociology) but by an inclusive, interdisciplinary and historically informed network of sociological theories which are only loosely coupled under the umbrella of systems theory is probably the greatest attraction of present-day systems theory.

Reader's Guide to Niklas Luhmann

In English translation, a good introduction to Luhmann's thinking is *Ecological Communication* (1990). Some of his early and classical essays from *Soziologische Aufklärung* have been published in *The Differentiation of Society* (1982). Other introductory works are *A Sociological Theory of Law* (1985) which is an excellent introduction to general sociology from the point of view of sociology of law and *Political Theory in the Welfare State* (1990). The two major formulations of his theory are in *Social Systems* (1995) and in *Die Gesellschaft der Gesellschaft* (1997), for which an English publication is currently in preparation through Stanford University Press. For those interested in Luhmann's later focus on self-reference and observation see *Theories of Distinction* (2002c). A complete bibliography until 1998 is provided in the journal *Soziale Systeme* (Volume 4, 1998: 233–263).

Bibliography

Writings of Luhmann

1964. *Funktionen und Folgen formaler Organisationen*. Berlin: Duncker & Humblot.

1965. *Grundrechte als Institution*. Berlin: Duncker & Humblot.

1968[1973]. *Zweckbegriff und Systemrationalität*. Frankfurt: Suhrkamp.

1969[1973]. *Vertrauen*. Stuttgart: Enket. Translated in *Trust and Power* (1979). Wiley, Chichester.

1969. *Legitimation durch Verfahren*. Neuwied: Luchterhand.

1970. *Soziologische Aufklärung 1. Aufsätze zur Theorie sozialer Systeme*. Opladen: Westdeutscher Verlag.

1971a. Sinn als Grundbegriff der Soziologie. In J. Habermas and N. Luhmann, *Theorie der Gesellschaft oder Sozialtechnologie?* Frankfurt: Suhrkamp, pp. 25–100.

1971b (with Jürgen Habermas). *Theorie der Gesellschaft oder Sozialtechnologie?* Frankfurt: Suhrkamp.

1971c. *Politische Planung*. Opladen: Westdeutscher Verlag.

1972. *Rechtssoziologie*, 2 vols. Rowohlt: Reinbek. Translated as *A Sociological Theory of Law* (1985). London: Routledge & Kegan.

1975a. *Soziologische Aufklärung 2. Aufsätze zur Theorie der Gesellschaft*. Opladen: Westdeutscher Verlag.

1975b. *Macht*. Stuttgart: Enke. Translated in *Trust and Power* (1979). Chichester: John Wiley & Sons, Ltd.

1977. *Funktion der Religion*. Frankfurt: Suhrkamp. Chapter 2 translated as Religious dogmatics and the evolution of societies (Edwin Mellen (1984). New York).

1979 (with Karl-Eberhard Schorr). *Reflexionsprobleme im Erziehungssystem*. Stuttgart: Klett-Cotta.

1980–1995. *Gesellschaftsstruktur und Semantik*, 4 vols. Frankfurt: Suhrkamp.

1981a. *Soziologische Aufklärung 3. Soziales System, Gesellschaft, Organisation*. Opladen: Westdeutscher Verlag.

1981b. *Politische Theorie im Wohlfahrtsstaat*. München: Olzog. Translated as *Political Theory in the Welfare State* (1990). Berlin: De Gruyter.

1981c. *Ausdifferenzierung des Rechts*. Frankfurt: Suhrkamp.

1982. *The Differentiation of Society*. New York: Columbia University Press.

1982. *Liebe als Passion*. Frankfurt: Suhrkamp. Translated as *Love as Passion* (1986). Cambridge: Polity Press.

1984. *Soziale Systeme*. Frankfurt: Suhrkamp. Translated as *Social Systems* (1995). Standford: Stanford University Press.

1986. *Ökologische Kommunikation*. Opladen: Westdeutscher Verlag. Translated as *Ecological Communication* (1990). Chicago: Chicago University Press.

1988. *Die Wirtschaft der Gesellschaft*. Frankfurt: Suhrkamp.

1990a. *Die Wissenschaft der Gesellschaft*. Frankfurt: Suhrkamp.

1990b. *Essays on Self-Reference*. New York: Columbia University Press.

1991. *Soziologie des Risikos*. Berlin: De Gruyter. Translated as *Risk: A Sociological Theory* (1993). Berlin: De Gruyter.

1992. *Universität als Milieu*. Bielefeld: Haux.

1992. *Beobachtungen der Moderne*. Opladen: Westdeutscher Verlag. Translated as *Observations on Modernity* (1998). Stanford: Stanford University Press.

1993. *Das Recht der Gesellschaft*. Frankfurt: Suhrkamp. Translated as *Law as a Social System* (2004). Oxford: Oxford University Press.

1995a. *Die Kunst der Gesellschaft*. Frankfurt: Suhrkamp. Translated as *Art as a Social System* (2000). Standford: Stanford University Press.

1995b. *Soziologische Aufklärung 6. Die Soziologie und der Mensch*. Opladen: Westdeutscher Verlag.

1996a. *Protest. Systemtheorie und soziale Bewegungen*. Frankfurt: Suhrkamp.

1996b. *Die Realität der Massenmedien*. Opladen: Westdeutscher Verlag. Translated as *The Reality of the Mass Media* (2000). Stanford: Stanford University Press.

1997. *Die Gesellschaft der Gesellschaft*, 2 vols. Frankfurt: Suhrkamp.

2000a. *Organisation und Entscheidung*. Opladen: Westdeutscher Verlag.

2000b. *Die Politik der Gesellschaft*. Frankfurt: Suhrkamp.

2000c. *Die Religion der Gesellschaft*. Frankfurt: Suhrkamp.

2002a. *Das Erziehungssystem der Gesellschaft*. Frankfurt: Suhrkamp.

2002b. *Einführung in die Systemtheorie*. Heidelberg: Carl-Auer.

2002c. *Theories of Distinction*. Stanford: Stanford University Press.

2005. *Einführung in die Theorie der Gesellschaft*. Heidelberg: Carl-Auer.

2008a. *Die Moral der Gesellschaft*. Frankfurt: Suhrkamp.

2008b. *Ideenevolution*. Frankfurt: Suhrkamp.

2008c. *"Tragic Choices." Luhmann on Law and States of Exception*. Stuttgart: Lucius & Lucius.

2008d. *Liebe. Eine Übung*. Frankfurt: Suhrkamp. Translated as *Love: A Sketch* (2010). London: Polity Press.

2010. *Politische Soziologie*. Berlin: Suhrkamp.

Further Reading

Ashby, W. R. (1952) *Design for a Brain*. London: Chapman & Hall.

Bateson, G. (1973) *Steps to an Ecology of Mind*. London: Paladin.

Bühler, K. (1934) *Sprachtheorie*. Stuttgart: Gustav Fischer.

Campbell, D. T. (1988) *Methodology and Epistemology for Social Science*. Chicago: Chicago University Press.

Foerster, H., von (1984) *Observing Systems*. Seaside, CA: Intersystems.

Goffman, E. (1983) The interaction order. *American Sociological Review*, 48: 1–17.

Maturana, H. R. and Varela, F. J. (1980) *Autopoiesis and Cognition*. Dordrecht: Reidel.

Parsons, T. (1961) Introduction to Part Two. In T. Parsons *et al.* (eds) *Theories of Society*. Glencoe: Free Press, pp. 239–264.

Parsons, T. (1967) *Sociological Theory and Modern Society*. New York: Free Press.

Parsons, T. and Platt, G. M. (1973) *The American University*. Cambridge, MA: Harvard University Press.

Parsons, T. and Shils, E. (1951) *Toward a General Theory of Action*. New York: Harper.

Ruesch, J. and Bateson, G. (1951[1968]) *Communication: The Social Matrix of Psychiatry*. New York: Norton.

Searle, J. R. (1969) *Speech Acts*. Cambridge: Cambridge University Press.

Shannon, C. E. and Weaver, W. (1949[1969]) *The Mathematical Theory of Communication*. Urbana: University of Illinois Press.

Simon, H. A. (1950[1970]) *Public Administration*. New York: Knopf.

Simon, H. A. (1983) *Reason in Human Affairs*. Stanford: Stanford University Press.

Spencer Brown, G. (1972) *Laws of Form*. New York: Julian Press.

Sperber, D. (1996) *Explaining Culture*. Oxford: Oxford University Press.

Stichweh, R. (1994) *Wissenschaft, Universität, Professionen*. Frankfurt: Suhrkamp.

Stichweh, R. (2000) *Die Weltgesellschaft*. Frankfurt: Suhrkamp.

Stichweh, R. (2010) *Der Fremde*. Berlin: Suhrkamp.

Stolleis, M. (2002) *Geschichte des öffentlichen Rechts in Deutschland*, 3 vols. München: Beck.

Tomasello, M. (2008) *Origins of Human Communication*. Cambridge: MIT-Press.

Watzlawick, P. (1967) *Pragmatics of Human Communication*. New York: Norton.

Weick, K. E. (1979) *The Social Psychology of Organizing*. Reading: Addison-Wesley.

Wiener, N. (1948) *Cybernetics or Control and Communication in the Animal and the Machine*. Cambridge: MIT-Press.

13

Jean Baudrillard

DOUGLAS KELLNER

French theorist Jean Baudrillard, who on March 6, 2007 died in Paris at the age of 77 after a long fight with cancer, has long been one of the foremost critics of contemporary society, politics, and culture. A professor of sociology at the University of Nanterre from 1966 to 1987, Baudrillard was for some years a cult figure of postmodern theory. Baudrillard moved beyond the discourse of the postmodern from the early 1980s to his death in 2007, and has developed a highly idiosyncratic mode of theoretical and sociocultural analysis that went beyond the confines of modern social theory.[1]

In retrospect, Baudrillard can be seen as an important critic of modern society and theory who claims that the era of modernity and the tradition of classical social theory is obsolete, and that we need novel modes of theory and social analysis adequate to the emerging era of postmodernity.[2] Associated with postmodern and poststructuralist theory, Baudrillard is difficult to situate in relation to classical and contemporary social theory. His work combines philosophy, social theory, and a highly original form of cultural metaphysics that reflects on key events and social, political, cultural, and other phenomena of the epoch. Baudrillard combines theory and social and cultural criticism in original and provocative ways and has developed his own style and forms of writing. He is an extremely prolific author who published over fifty books and commented on some of the most salient cultural and sociological phenomena of the contemporary era, including the erasure of the distinctions of gender, race, and class that structured modern societies in a new postmodern consumer, media, and high-tech society; the mutating roles of art and aesthetics; fundamental changes in politics, culture, and human beings; and the impact of new media, information, and cybernetic technologies in the creation of a qualitatively different social order, providing fundamental mutations of human and social life.

The Wiley-Blackwell Companion to Major Social Theorists, First Edition.
Edited by George Ritzer and Jeffrey Stepnisky.
© 2011 Blackwell Publishing Ltd. Published 2011 by Blackwell Publishing Ltd.

This chapter focuses on the development of Baudrillard's unique modes of thought and how he moved from social theory to postmodern theory to a provocative type of theoretical and sociocultural analysis. In particular, I discuss Baudrillard's thought in relation to the problematic of classical social theory and the debates concerning modern and postmodern societies and theories. Baudrillard's 1960s and early 1970s studies of the consumer society and its system of objects drew on classical sociological theory and provided critical perspectives on everyday life in the post-Second World War social order, organized around the production, consumption, display, and use of consumer goods. His work on the political economy of the sign merged semiological and neo-Marxian perspectives, to provide deep insights into the power of consumption and how it was playing a crucial role in organizing contemporary societies around objects, needs, and consumerism. His 1970s studies of the effects of the new communication, information, and media technologies blazed novel paths in contemporary social theory and challenged regnant orthodoxies. Baudrillard's claim of a radical break with modern societies was quickly appropriated into the discourse of the postmodern, and he was received as the prophet of postmodernity in avant-garde theoretical circles throughout the world.

During the period from the middle 1970s until the end of his trajectory, Baudrillard proclaimed the disappearance of the subject, political economy, meaning, truth, the social, and the real in contemporary postmodern social formations. This process of dramatic change and mutation, he argued, required radically new theories and concepts to describe the rapidly evolving social processes and novelties of the present moment. Baudrillard undertook to explore this new and original situation and to spell out the consequences for contemporary theory and practice. For some years, Baudrillard was a cutting-edge, critical social theorist, one of the most stimulating and provocative contemporary thinkers. He became a cult figure and media celebrity of the postmodern during the 1980s, and while he continued to publish books at a rapid rate, a noticeable decline in the quality of his work was apparent. In retrospect, Baudrillard can be seen a theorist who has traced in original ways the life of signs and impact of technology on social life, and who has systematically criticized major modes of modern thought, while developing his own theoretical perspectives and corpus of distinctive writings.

EARLY WRITINGS: FROM THE SYSTEM OF OBJECTS
TO THE CONSUMER SOCIETY

Jean Baudrillard was born in the cathedral town of Reims, France, in 1929. He told interviewers that his grandparents were peasants and his parents became civil servants (Gane, 1993: 19). He also claims that he was the first member of his family to pursue an advanced education and that this led to a rupture with his parents and cultural milieu. In 1956, he began working as a professor of secondary education in a French high school (*lycée*) and in the early 1960s did editorial work for the French publisher Seuil. Baudrillard was initially a Germanist who published essays on literature in *Les temps modernes* in 1962–1963 and translated works of Peter Weiss and Bertolt Brecht into French, as well as a book on messianic revolutionary movements by Wilhelm Mühlmann. During this period, he met Henri Lefebvre, whose critiques of everyday life impressed him, and Roland Barthes, whose semiological analyses of contemporary society had lasting influence on his work.

In 1966, Baudrillard entered the University of Paris, Nanterre, and became Lefebvre's assistant, while studying languages, philosophy, sociology, and other disciplines. He defended his "Thèse de Troisième Cycle" in sociology at Nanterre in 1966 with a dissertation on "Le système des objects," and began teaching sociology in October of that year. Opposing French and US intervention in the Algerian and Vietnamese wars, Baudrillard associated himself with the French left in the 1960s. Nanterre was the center of radical politics and the "March 22 movement," associated with Daniel Cohn-Bendit and the *enragées*, began in the Nanterre sociology department. Baudrillard said later that he was at the center of the events of May 1968, which resulted in massive student uprisings and a general strike that almost drove de Gaulle from power.

During the late 1960s, Baudrillard published a series of books that would eventually make him world famous. Influenced by Lefebvre, Barthes, Georges Bataille, and the French situationists, Baudrillard undertook serious work in the field of social theory, semiology, and psychoanalysis in the 1960s, and published his first book, *The System of Objects*, in 1968, followed by *The Consumer Society* in 1970, and *For a Critique of the Political Economy of the Sign* in 1972. These early publications are attempts, within the framework of critical sociology, to combine the studies of everyday life initiated by Lefebvre (1971, 1991) and the situationists (Debord, 1970) with a social semiology that studies the life of signs in social life. This project, influenced by Barthes (1967, 1972, 1983), centers on the system of objects in the consumer society (the focus of his first two books), and the interface between political economy and semiotics (the nucleus of his third book). Baudrillard's early work was among the first to appropriate semiology to analyze how objects are encoded with a system of signs and meanings that constitute contemporary media and consumer societies. Combining semiological studies, Marxian political economy, and sociology of the consumer society, Baudrillard began his lifelong task of exploring the system of objects and signs which form our everyday life.

The early Baudrillard described the meanings invested in the objects of everyday life (e.g. the power accrued through identification with one's automobile when driving) and the structural system through which objects were organized into a new modern society (e.g. the prestige or sign value of a new sports car). In his first three books, Baudrillard maintained that the classical Marxian critique of political economy needed to be supplemented by semiological theories of the sign. He argued that the transition from the earlier stage of competitive market capitalism to the stage of monopoly capitalism required increased attention to demand management, to augmenting and steering consumption. At this historical stage, from around 1920 to the 1960s, the need to intensify demand supplemented concern with lowering production costs and with expanding production. In this era of capitalist development, economic concentration, new production techniques, and the development of new technologies, accelerated capacity for mass production and capitalist corporations focused increased attention on managing consumption and creating needs for new prestigious goods, thus producing the regime of what Baudrillard has called "sign value."

The result was the now familiar consumer society, which provided the main focus of Baudrillard's early work. In this society, advertising, packaging, display, fashion, "emancipated" sexuality, mass media and culture, and the proliferation of commodities multiplied the quantity of signs and spectacles, and produced a proliferation of "sign value." Henceforth, Baudrillard claims, commodities are not merely to be characterized by use value and exchange value, as in Marx's theory of the commodity; sign value – the expression and mark of style, prestige, luxury, power, and so on – becomes an increasingly important part of the commodity and consumption.

From this perspective, Baudrillard argues that commodities are bought and displayed as much for their sign value as their use value, and that the phenomenon of sign value has become an essential constituent of the commodity and consumption in the consumer society. This position was influenced by Veblen's notion of "conspicuous consumption" and display of commodities, analyzed in his *Theory of the Leisure Class*, which, Baudrillard asserted, has become extended to everyone in the consumer society. For Baudrillard, the entire society is organized around consumption and display of commodities through which individuals gain prestige, identity, and standing. In this system, the more prestigious one's commodities (houses, cars, clothes, and so on), the higher one's standing in the realm of sign value. Thus, just as words take on meaning according to their position in a differential system of language, so sign values take on meaning according to their place in a differential system of prestige and status.

In developing his own theory, Baudrillard criticizes the mainstream view, which conceptualizes consumption in terms of a rational satisfaction of needs, with the aim of maximizing utility. Against this view, he contrasts a "sociocultural" approach which stresses the ways that society produces needs through socialization and conditioning, and thus manages consumer demand and consumption. For Baudrillard, the system of objects is correlated with a system of needs. Although he shares with American theorists such as Packard, Riesman, and Galbraith a critique of the assumption of a free, rational, autonomous ego which satisfies "natural" needs through consumption, he criticizes Galbraith's model of the production of artificial needs and management of consumer demand.

Baudrillard's argument is that critics of the "false," or artificial, needs produced by the consumer society generally presuppose something like true human needs, or a stabilizing principle within human nature that would maintain a harmonious balance and equilibrium were it not for the pernicious artificial needs produced by advertising and marketing. Yet there is no way, Baudrillard claims, to distinguish between true and false needs – at least from the standpoint of the pleasure or satisfaction received from varying goods or activities of consumption. In addition, he maintains that:

> What Galbraith does not see – and this forces him to present individuals as mere passive victims of the system – is the whole social logic of differentiation, the distinguishing processes of class or caste distinctions which are fundamental to the social structure and are given free rein in "democratic" society. In short, there is a whole sociological dimension of difference, status, etc., lacking here, in consequence of which all needs are reorganized around an objective social demand for signs and differences, a dimension no longer grounding consumption in a function of "harmonious" individual satisfaction. (Baudrillard, 1998: 74)

Baudrillard's focus is on the "logic of social differentiation" whereby individuals distinguish themselves and attain social prestige and standing through the purchase and use of consumer goods. He argues that the entire system of production produces a system of needs that is rationalized, homogenized, systematized, and hierarchized. Rather than an individual commodity (or advertisement) seducing a consumer into purchase (which Baudrillard equates with the primitive notion of mana), individuals are induced to buy into an entire system of objects and needs through which one differentiates oneself socially but is integrated into the consumer society. He suggests that this activity can best be conceptualized by seeing the objects of consumption as *signs* and the consumer society as *a system of signs*, in which a specific object, such as a washing machine or a car, serves as an appliance and acts as an element of prestige and social differentiation. Hence, "need is never so much the need for a particular object as the 'need' for difference (the *desire for social meaning*)" (Baudrillard, 1998: 77–78).

In *The Consumer Society*, Baudrillard concludes by valorizing "multiple forms of refusal" which can be fused in a "practice of radical change" (ibid.: 183), and he alludes to the expectation of "violent eruptions and sudden disintegration which will come, just as unforeseeably and as certainly as did May 68, to wreck this white mass" of consumption (ibid.: 196). On the other hand, Baudrillard also describes a situation where alienation is so total that it cannot be surpassed, because "it is the very structure of market society" (ibid.: 190). His argument is that in a society where everything is a commodity that can be bought and sold, alienation is total. Indeed, the term "alienation" originally signified "for sale," and in a totally commodified society where everything is a commodity, alienation is ubiquitous. Moreover, Baudrillard posits "the end of transcendence" (a phrase borrowed from Marcuse), where individuals can perceive neither their own true needs nor another way of life (ibid.: 190ff.).

BAUDRILLARD AND NEO-MARXISM

By 1970, Baudrillard had distanced himself from the Marxist theory of revolution and instead postulated only the possibility of revolt against the consumer society in an "unforeseeable but certain" form. In the late 1960s, Baudrillard had associated himself with a group of intellectuals around the journal *Utopie*, which sought to overcome disciplinary boundaries and, in the spirit of the Situationist International, to combine reflections on alternative societies, architecture, and modes of everyday life. Bringing together individuals on the margins of architecture, city planning, cultural criticism, and social theory, Baudrillard and his associates distanced themselves from other political and theoretical groupings and developed idiosyncratic and marginal discourse beyond the boundaries of established disciplines and political tendencies. This affiliation with *Utopie* only lasted into the early 1970s, but it may have helped to produce in Baudrillard a desire to work on the margins, to stand aside from current trends and fads, and to develop his own theoretical positions – although, ironically, Baudrillard became something of a fad himself, especially in the English-speaking world (his articles from this project have been collected in English translation in *Utopia Deferred*, 2006).

Baudrillard thus had an ambivalent relation to classical Marxism by the early 1970s. On one hand, he carried forward the Marxian critique of commodity production which delineates and criticizes various forms of alienation, reification, domination, and exploitation produced by capitalism. At this stage, it appeared that his critique came from the standard neo-Marxian vantage point, which assumes that capitalism is blameworthy because it is homogenizing, controlling, and dominating social life, while robbing individuals of their freedom, creativity, time, and human potentialities. On the other hand, he could not point to any revolutionary forces and in particular did not discuss the situation and potential of the working class as an agent of change in the consumer society. Indeed, Baudrillard has no theory of the subject as an active agent of social change whatsoever (thus perhaps following the structuralist and poststructuralist critique of the subject popular at the time). Nor does he have a theory of class or group revolt, or any theory of political organization, struggle, or strategy.

Baudrillard's problematic here is particularly close to the work of the Frankfurt School, especially that of Herbert Marcuse, who had already developed some of the first Marxist critiques of the consumer society (see Kellner, 1984, 1989). Like Lukács (1971) and the Frankfurt School, Baudrillard employs a mode of thought whereby the commodity and commodification become a totalizing social process that permeates social life. Following the general line of critical Marxism, Baudrillard argues that the process of homogenization, alienation, and exploitation constitutes a process of *reification*, in which objects come to dominate subjects, thereby robbing people of their human qualities and capacities. For Lukács, the Frankfurt School, and Baudrillard, reification – the process whereby human beings become dominated by things and become more "thinglike" themselves – comes to dominate social life.

In a sense, Baudrillard's work can be read as an account of a higher stage of reification and social domination than that described by the Frankfurt School. Baudrillard goes beyond the Frankfurt School by applying the semiological theory of the sign to describe the world of commodities, media, and the consumer society, and in a sense he takes their theory of "one-dimensional society" to a higher level. Eventually, Baudrillard will take his analysis of domination by signs and the system of objects to even more pessimistic conclusions, where he concludes that the problematic of the "end of the individual" sketched by the Frankfurt School has reached its fruition in the total defeat of the subject by the object world (see below). Yet in his early writings, Baudrillard has a somewhat more active theory of consumption than that of the Frankfurt School's, which generally portrays consumption as a passive mode of social integration. By contrast, consumption in Baudrillard's early writings is itself a kind of labor, "an active manipulation of signs," a way of inserting oneself within the consumer society, and working to differentiate oneself from others. Yet this active manipulation of signs is not equivalent to postulating an active subject which could resist, redefine, or produce its own signs. Thus Baudrillard fails to develop a genuine theory of agency.

Baudrillard's first three works can thus be read in the framework of a neo-Marxian critique of capitalist societies. One could read Baudrillard's emphasis on consumption as a supplement to Marx's analysis of production, and his focus on culture and signs as an important supplement to classical Marxian political economy that adds a cultural and semiological dimension to the Marxian project. But in his 1973 provocation, *The Mirror of Production* (translated into English in 1975), Baudrillard carries out a systematic attack on classical Marxism, claiming that Marxism is but a mirror of bourgeois society, placing production at the center of life, and thus naturalizing the capitalist organization of society.

Although Baudrillard participated in the tumultuous events of May 1968, and was associated with the revolutionary left, he broke with Marxism in the early 1970s, but remained politically radical, though unaffiliated, for the rest of the decade. Like many on the left, Baudrillard was disappointed that the French Communist Party did not support the radical 1960s movements, and he also distrusted the official Marxism of theorists like Louis Althusser, whom he found dogmatic and reductive. Consequently, Baudrillard began a radical critique of Marxism, one that would be repeated by many of his contemporaries, who would also take a postmodern turn (see Best and Kellner, 1991, 1997).

Baudrillard argues that Marxism, first, does not adequately illuminate premodern societies, which were organized around symbolic exchange and not production. He also argues that Marxism does not radically enough critique capitalist societies, and calls for a more extreme break. At this stage, Baudrillard turns to anthropological perspectives on premodern societies for hints of more emancipatory alternatives. It is important to note that this critique of Marxism was taken from the left, arguing that Marxism did not provide a radical enough critique of, or alternative to, contemporary productivist societies, capitalist and communist. Baudrillard concluded that the French communist failure to support the May 1968 movements was rooted in part in a conservatism that had roots in Marxism itself. Hence, Baudrillard and others of his generation began searching for more radical critical positions.

The Mirror of Production and his next book, *Symbolic Exchange and Death* (1976), a major text finally translated in 1993, are attempts to provide ultra-radical perspectives that overcome the limitations of an economistic Marxist tradition. This ultra-leftist phase of Baudrillard's itinerary would be short-lived, however, though in *Symbolic Exchange and Death* Baudrillard produces one of his most important and dramatic provocations. The text opens with a preface that condenses his attempt to provide a significantly different approach to society and culture. Building on Bataille's principle of excess and expenditure, Marcel Mauss's concept of the gift, and Alfred Jarry's pataphysical desire to exterminate meaning, Baudrillard champions "symbolic exchange" and attacks Marx, Freud, and academic semiology and sociology. Baudrillard argues that in Bataille's claim that expenditure and excess are connected with sovereignty, Mauss's descriptions of the social prestige of giftgiving in premodern society, Jarry's theater, and Saussure's anagrams, there is a break with the logic of capitalist exchange and production, or the production of meaning in linguistic exchange. These cases of "symbolic exchange," Baudrillard believes, break with the logic of production and describe excessive and subversive behavior that provides alternatives to the capitalist logic of production and exchange.

The term "symbolic exchange" was derived from Georges Bataille's notion of a "general economy," where expenditure, waste, sacrifice, and destruction were claimed to be more fundamental to human life than economies of production and utility (Bataille, 1988). Bataille's model was the sun which freely expended its energy without asking anything in return. He argued that if individuals wanted to be truly sovereign (i.e. free from the imperatives of capitalism), they should pursue a "general economy" of expenditure, giving, sacrifice, and destruction to escape determination by existing imperatives of utility.

For Bataille, human beings were beings of *excess*, with exorbitant energy, fantasies, drives, needs, and so on. From this point forward, Baudrillard presupposes the truth of Bataille's anthropology and general economy. In a 1976 review of a volume of Bataille's *Complete Works*, Baudrillard writes: "The central idea is that the economy which governs our societies results from a misappropriation of the fundamental human principle, which is a solar principle of expenditure" (Baudrillard, 1987: 57). In the early 1970s, Baudrillard took over Bataille's anthropological position and what he calls Bataille's "aristocratic critique" of capitalism, which he now claims is grounded in the crass notions of utility and savings, rather than the more sublime "aristocratic" notion of excess and expenditure. Bataille and Baudrillard presuppose here a contradiction between human nature and capitalism. They maintain that humans "by nature" gain pleasure from such things as expenditure, waste, festivities, sacrifices, and so on, in which they are sovereign and free to expend the excesses of their energy (and thus to follow their "real nature"). The capitalist imperatives of labor, utility, and savings by implication are "unnatural," and go against human nature.

Baudrillard argues that the Marxian critique of capitalism, by contrast, merely attacks exchange value, while exalting use value and thus utility, instrumental rationality, and so forth, thereby

> seeking a *good use* of the economy. Marxism is therefore only a limited petit bourgeois critique, one more step in the banalization of life toward the "good use" of the social! Bataille, to the contrary, sweeps away all this slave dialectic from an aristocratic point of view, that of the master struggling with his death. One can accuse this perspective of being pre- or post-Marxist. At any rate, Marxism is only the disenchanted horizon of capital – all that precedes or follows it is more radical than it is. (Baudrillard, 1987: 60)

This passage is highly revealing, and marks Baudrillard's switch to an "aristocratic critique" of political economy, deeply influenced by Bataille and Nietzsche. For Bataille and Baudrillard are presenting a version of Nietzsche's "aristocratic," "master morality," where value articulates an excess, overflow, and intensification of life energies. For some time, Baudrillard would continue to attack the bourgeoisie, capital, and political economy, but from a perspective which valorizes "aristocratic" expenditure and sumptuary, aesthetic, and symbolic values. The dark side of his switch in theoretical and political allegiances is a valorization of sacrifice and death which informs *Symbolic Exchange and Death*. Throughout his life Nietzsche was a major influence (see Kroker, 2007), and especially in the last decades of his work, Nietzschean motifs, modes of thought, and writing practices increasingly informed his work. Baudrillard became increasingly radical and "un-contemporary," standing alone against current trends and fashions, in a fiercely individualistic mode of thought. Nietzschean categories like fate, reversal, uncertainty, and an aristocratic assault on conventional wisdom began to shape his writings that often, à la Nietzsche, took the form of aphorisms or short essays.

On the whole, in his mid-1970s work, Baudrillard was extricating himself from the familiar Marxian universe of production and class struggle into a quite different neo-aristocratic and metaphysical worldview. Baudrillard seems to assume at this point that precapitalist societies were governed by forms of symbolic exchange similar to Bataille's notion of a general economy. Influenced by Mauss's theory of the gift and counter gift, Baudrillard claimed that precapitalist societies were governed by laws of symbolic exchange rather than production and utility. Developing these ideas, Baudrillard sketched a fundamental dividing line in history between symbolic societies – i.e. societies fundamentally organized around symbolic exchange – and productivist societies – i.e. societies organized around production. He thus rejects the Marxian philosophy of history, which posits the primacy of production in all societies, and rejects the Marxian concept of socialism, arguing that it does not break radically enough with capitalist productivism, offering itself merely as a more efficient and equitable organization of production rather than as a completely different sort of society, with a different logic, values, and life activities.

THE POSTMODERN BREAK

Henceforth, Baudrillard would contrast – in one way or another – his ideal of symbolic exchange to the logic of production, utility, and instrumental rationality which governs capitalist (and socialist) societies. "Symbolic exchange" thus emerges as Baudrillard's "revolutionary" alternative to the values and practices of capitalist society, and stands for a variety of heterogeneous activities in his 1970s writings. For instance, he writes in the *Critique*: "The exchange of looks, the present which comes and goes, are like the air people breathe in and out. This is the metabolism of exchange, prodigality, festival – and also of destruction (which returns to non-value what production has erected, valorized). In this domain, value isn't even recognized" (Baudrillard, 1981: 207). He also describes his conception of symbolic exchange in *The Mirror of Production*, where he writes: "The symbolic social relation is the uninterrupted cycle of giving and receiving, which, in primitive exchange, includes the consumption of the 'surplus' and deliberate anti-production" (Baudrillard, 1975: 143). The term therefore refers to symbolic or cultural activities which do not contribute to capitalist production and accumulation and which therefore constitute the "radical negation" of productivist society.

At this stage of his thought, Baudrillard stood in a classical French tradition of extolling the "primitive" or premodern over the dissected rationalism of modern society. Baudrillard's defense of symbolic exchange over production and instrumental rationality thus stands in the tradition of Rousseau's defense of the "natural savage" over modern man, Durkheim's posing mechanical solidarities of premodern societies against the abstract individualism and anomie of modern ones, Bataille's valorization of expenditure and the "accursed portion" of premodern societies, or Mauss's or Lévi-Strauss's fascination with the richness of "primitive societies" or "the savage mind." But after deconstructing the modern master thinkers and his own theoretical fathers (Marx, Freud, Saussure, and other French contemporaries) for missing the richness of symbolic exchange, Baudrillard will eventually question this apparent nostalgia for premodern culture and social forms.

In his mid-1970s work, however, Baudrillard posits another divide in history as radical as the rupture between premodern symbolic societies and modern capitalism. In the mode of classical social theory, he systematically develops distinctions between premodern societies organized around symbolic exchange, modern societies organized around production, and postmodern societies organized around simulation. Against the organizing principles of modern and postmodern society, Baudrillard valorizes the logic of symbolic exchange, as an alternative organizing principle of society. Against modern demands to produce value and meaning, Baudrillard calls for their extermination and annihilation, providing, as examples, Mauss's gift-exchange, Saussure's anagrams, and Freud's concept of the death drive. In all of these instances, there is a rupture with the logic of exchange (of goods, meanings, and libidinal energies) and thus an escape from the logic of production, capitalism, rationality, and meaning. Baudrillard's paradoxical logic of symbolic exchange can be explained as the expression of a desire to liberate himself from modern positions and to seek a revolutionary position outside of modern society. Against modern values, Baudrillard advocates their annihilation and extermination.

It should be noted that Baudrillard's distinction between the logic of production and utility that organized modern societies and the logic of simulation that he believes is the organizing principle of postmodern societies postulates a rupture between modern and postmodern societies as great as the divide between modern and premodern ones. In theorizing the epochal postmodern rupture with modernity, Baudrillard declares the "end of political economy" and of an era in which production was the organizing principle of society. Following Marx, Baudrillard argues that this modern epoch was the era of capitalism and the bourgeoisie, in which workers were exploited by capital and provided a revolutionary force of upheaval. Baudrillard, however, declared the end of political economy and thus the end of the Marxist problematic and of modernity itself:

> The end of labor. The end of production. The end of political economy. The end of the signifier/signified dialectic which facilitates the accumulation of knowledge and of meaning, the linear syntagma of cumulative discourse. And at the same time, the end simultaneously of the exchange value/use value dialectic which is the only thing that makes accumulation and social production possible. The end of the linear dimension of discourse. The end of the linear dimension of the commodity. The end of the classical era of the sign. The end of the era of production. (Baudrillard, 1993a: 8)

The discourse of "the end" signifies his announcing a postmodern break or rupture in history. We are now, Baudrillard claims, in a new era of simulation, in which social reproduction (information processing, communication, knowledge industries, virtual reality, and so on) replaces production as the organizing principle of society. In this era, labor is no longer a force of production but is itself a "one *sign* amongst many" (Baudrillard, 1993a: 10). Labor is not primarily productive in this situation, but is a sign of one's social position, way of life, and mode of servitude. Wages too bear no rational relation to one's work and what one produces but to one's place within the system (ibid.: 19ff.). But, crucially, political economy is no longer the foundation, the social determinant, or even a structural "reality" in which other phenomena can be interpreted and explained (ibid.: 31ff.). Instead, we live in the "hyperreality" of simulations, in which images, spectacles, and the play of signs replace the logic of production and class conflict as key constituents of contemporary societies.

From now on, capital and political economy disappear from Baudrillard's story, or return in radically new forms. Henceforth, signs and codes proliferate and produce other signs and new sign machines in ever-expanding and spiraling cycles. Technology thus replaces capital in this story, and semiurgy, the proliferation of images, information, and signs, replaces production. His postmodern turn is thus connected to a form of technological determinism and a rejection of political economy as a useful explanatory principle – a move that many of his critics reject (see the studies in Kellner, 1994).

Symbolic Exchange and Death and the succeeding studies in *Simulation and Simulacra* (1994a) articulate the principle of a fundamental rupture between modern and postmodern societies and mark Baudrillard's departure from the problematic of modern social theory. For Baudrillard, modern societies are organized around the production and consumption of commodities, while postmodern societies are organized around simulation and the play of images and signs, denoting a situation in which codes, models, and signs are the organizing principles of a new social order where simulation rules. In the society of simulation, identities are constructed by the appropriation of images, and codes and models determine how individuals perceive themselves and relate to other people. Economics, politics, social life, and culture are all governed by the logic of simulation, whereby codes and models determine how goods are consumed and used, politics unfold, culture is produced and consumed, and everyday life is lived.

Baudrillard's postmodern world is also one of radical *implosion*, in which social classes, genders, political differences, and once autonomous realms of society and culture collapse into each other, erasing previously defined boundaries and differences. If modern societies, for classical social theory, were characterized by differentiation, for Baudrillard postmodern societies are characterized by dedifferentiation, or implosion. For Baudrillard, in the society of simulation, economics, politics, culture, sexuality, and the social all implode into each other, such that economics is fundamentally shaped by culture, politics, and other spheres, while art, once a sphere of potential difference and opposition, is absorbed into the economic and political, and sexuality is everywhere. In this situation, differences between individuals and groups implode in a rapidly mutating dissolution of the social and the previous boundaries and structures upon which social theory had once focused.

In addition, his postmodern universe is one of *hyperreality*, in which entertainment, information, and communication technologies provide experiences more intense and involving than the scenes of banal everyday life, as well as the codes and models that structure everyday life. The realm of the hyperreal (media simulations of reality, Disneyland and amusement parks, malls and consumer fantasylands, TV sports, virtual reality games and digital sites, and other excursions into ideal worlds) is more real than real, so that the models, images, and codes of the hyperreal come to control thought and behavior. Yet determination itself is aleatory in a nonlinear world where it is impossible to chart causal mechanisms and logic in a situation in which individuals are confronted with an overwhelming flux of images, codes, and models, any of which may shape an individual's thought or behavior.

In this postmodern world, individuals flee from the "desert of the real" for the ecstasies of hyperreality and the new realm of computer, media, and technological experience. In this universe, subjectivities are fragmented and lost, and a new terrain of experience appears, which for Baudrillard renders previous social theories and politics obsolete and irrelevant. Tracing the vicissitudes of the subject in contemporary society, Baudrillard claims that contemporary subjects are no longer afflicted with modern pathologies like hysteria or paranoia, but exist in "a state of terror which is characteristic of the schizophrenic, an over-proximity of all things, a foul promiscuity of all things which beleaguer and penetrate him, meeting with no resistance, and no halo, no aura, not even the aura of his own body protects him. In spite of himself the schizophrenic is open to everything and lives in the most extreme confusion" (Baudrillard, 1988: 27). For Baudrillard, the "ecstasy of communication" means that the subject is in close proximity to instantaneous images and information, in an overexposed and transparent world. In this situation, the subject "becomes a pure screen, a pure absorption and resorption surface of the influence networks" (ibid.).

Thus, Baudrillard's categories of simulation, implosion, and hyperreality combine to create a new postmodern condition that requires entirely new modes of social theory and politics to chart and respond to the novelties of the contemporary era. His style and writing strategies are also implosive, combining material from strikingly different fields, studded with examples from the mass media and popular culture in a new mode of postmodern theory that effaces all disciplinary boundaries. His writing attempts to simulate the new conditions, capturing its novelties through inventive use of language and theory. Such radical questioning of contemporary theory and the need for new theoretical strategies are thus legitimated for Baudrillard by the radicality of changes in the current era.

For instance, Baudrillard claims that modernity operates with a logic of representation in which ideas represent reality and truth, concepts which are key postulates of modern theory. A postmodern society explodes this epistemology by creating a situation in which subjects lose contact with the real and themselves fragment and dissolve. This situation portends the end of modern theory, which operated with a subject–object dialectic in which the subject was supposed to represent and control the object. In the story of modern philosophy, the philosophic subject attempts to discern the nature of reality, to secure grounded knowledge, and to apply this knowledge to control and dominate the object (nature, other people, ideas, and so on). Baudrillard follows here the poststructuralist critique that thought and discourse could no longer be securely anchored in *a priori* or privileged structures. Reacting against the logic of representation in modern theory, French thought, especially some deconstructionists (Rorty's "strong textualists"), moved into the play of textuality, of discourse, which allegedly referred only to other texts or discourses in which "the real" or an "outside" were banished to the realm of nostalgia.

In a similar fashion, Baudrillard, a "strong simulacrist," claims that in the media and consumer society, people are caught up in the play of images, spectacles, and simulacra, which have less and less relationship to an outside, to an external "reality," to such an extent that the very concepts of the social, political, or even "reality" no longer seem to have any meaning. And the narcoticized and mesmerized (some of Baudrillard's metaphors) media-saturated consciousness is in such a state of fascination with image and spectacle that the concept of meaning itself (which depends on stable boundaries, fixed structures, shared consensus) dissolves. In this alarming and novel postmodern situation, the referent, the behind, and the outside, along with depth, essence, and reality, all disappear, and with their disappearance, the possibility of all potential opposition vanishes as well. As simulations proliferate, they come to refer only to themselves: a carnival of mirrors reflecting images projected from other mirrors onto the omnipresent television screen and the screen of consciousness, which in turn refers the image to its previous storehouse of images, also produced by simulatory mirrors. Caught up in the universe of simulations, the "masses" are bathed in a media massage without messages or meaning, a mass age where classes disappear, and politics is dead, as are the grand dreams of disalienation, liberation, and revolution.

Baudrillard claims that henceforth the masses seek spectacle and not meaning. They implode into a "silent majority," signifying "the end of the social" (Baudrillard, 1983b). Baudrillard implies that social theory loses its very object as meanings, classes, and difference implode into a "black hole" of non-differentiation. Fixed distinctions between social groupings and ideologies implode and concrete face-to-face social relations recede as individuals disappear in worlds of simulation – media, computers, and virtual reality itself. Social theory itself thus loses its object, the social, while radical politics loses its subject and agency.

Nonetheless, he claims, at this point in his trajectory (i.e. the late 1970s and early 1980s), that refusal of meaning and participation by the masses is a form of resistance. Hovering between nostalgia and nihilism, Baudrillard at once exterminates modern ideas (the subject, meaning, truth, reality, society, socialism, and emancipation) and affirms a mode of symbolic exchange which appears to manifest a nostalgic desire to return to premodern cultural forms. This desperate search for a genuinely revolutionary alternative was abandoned, however, by the early 1980s. Henceforth, he develops yet more idiosyncratic perspectives on the contemporary moment, vacillating between sketching out alternative modes of thought and behavior and renouncing the quest for political and social change.

In a sense, there is a parodic inversion of historical materialism in Baudrillard. In place of Marx's emphasis on political economy and the primacy of the economic, for Baudrillard it is the model, the superstructure, that generates the real in a situation he denominates the "end of political economy" (Baudrillard, 1993a). For Baudrillard, sign values predominate over use values and exchange values; the materiality of needs and commodity use values to serve them disappear in Baudrillard's semiological imaginary, in which signs take precedence over the real and reconstruct human life. Turning the Marxist categories against themselves, masses absorb classes, the subject of praxis is fractured, and objects come to rule human beings. Revolution is absorbed by the object of critique and technological implosion replaces the socialist revolution in producing a rupture in history. For Baudrillard, in contrast to Marx, the catastrophe of modernity and the eruption of postmodernity is produced by the unfolding of technological revolution. Consequently, Baudrillard replaces Marx's hard economic and social determinism, with its emphasis on the economic dimension, class struggle, and human praxis, with a form of semiological idealism and technological determinism where signs and objects come to dominate the subject.

Baudrillard thus concludes that the "catastrophe has happened," that the destruction of modernity and modern theory, which he noted in the mid-1970s, has been completed by the development of technocapitalist society itself, that modernity has disappeared and a new social situation has taken its place. Against traditional strategies of rebellion and revolution, Baudrillard begins to champion what he calls "fatal strategies" that push the logic of the system to the extreme in the hopes of collapse or reversal, and eventually adopts a style of highly ironic metaphysical discourse that renounces opposition and the discourse and hopes of progressive social transformation.

From Pataphysics to Metaphysics and the Triumph of the Object

Baudrillard's thought from the mid-1970s to his death in 2007 revolves in its own theoretical orbit and provides a set of challenging provocations to modern social theory. During the 1980s, Baudrillard's major works of the 1970s were translated into many languages, and each new book of the 1980s was in turn translated into English and other major languages in short order. Consequently, he became world renowned as one of the master thinkers of postmodernity, one of the major avatars of the postmodern turn. Hence, he became something of an academic celebrity, traveling around the world promoting his work and winning a significant following, though more outside the field of academic social theory than within the discipline of sociology.

At the same time that his work was becoming extremely popular, Baudrillard's own writing became increasingly difficult and obscure. In 1979, Baudrillard published *Seduction* (1990c), a curious text that represented a major shift in his thought. The book marks a turning away from the more sociological discourse of his earlier works to a more philosophical and literary discourse. Whereas in *Symbolic Exchange and Death* (1993a) Baudrillard sketches out ultra-revolutionary perspectives as a radical alternative, taking symbolic exchange as his ideal, he now valorizes seduction as his alternative to production and communicative interaction. Seduction, however, does not undermine, subvert, or transform existing social relations or institutions, but is a soft alternative, a play with appearances, and a game with feminism that provoked a sharp critical response (see Goshorn in Kellner, 1994).

Baudrillard's concept of seduction is idiosyncratic, and involves games with signs, which oppose seduction as an aristocratic "order of sign and ritual" to the bourgeois ideal of production, while valorizing artifice, appearance, play, and challenge against the deadly serious labor of production. Baudrillard interprets seduction primarily as a ritual and game with its own rules, charms, snares, and lures. His writing at this point becomes dedicated to stylized modes of thought and writing, which introduce a new set of categories – reversibility, the challenge, the duel – that move Baudrillard's thought toward a form of aristocratic aestheticism and metaphysics.

Baudrillard's new metaphysical speculations are evident in *Fatal Strategies* (1983, translated in 1990), another turning point in his itinerary. This text presented a bizarre metaphysical scenario concerning the triumph of objects over subjects within the "obscene" proliferation of an object world so completely out of control that it surpasses all attempts to understand, conceptualize, and control it. His scenario concerns the proliferation and growing supremacy of objects over subjects and the eventual triumph of the object. In a discussion of "ecstasy and inertia," Baudrillard discusses how objects and events in contemporary society are continually surpassing themselves, growing and expanding in power. The "ecstasy" of objects is their proliferation and expansion to the Nth degree, to the superlative; ecstasy as going outside of or beyond oneself; the beautiful as more beautiful than beautiful in fashion, the real more real than the real in television, sex more sexual than sex in pornography. Ecstasy is thus the form of obscenity (fully explicit, nothing hidden) and of the hyperreality described by Baudrillard earlier taken to a higher level, redoubled, and intensified. His vision of contemporary society exhibits a careening of growth and excrescence (*croissance et excroissance*), expanding and excreting ever more goods, services, information, messages, or demands – surpassing all rational ends and boundaries in a spiral of uncontrolled growth and replication.

Yet growth, acceleration, and proliferation have reached such extremes, Baudrillard suggests, that the ecstasy of excrescence is accompanied by inertia. For as the society is saturated to the limit, it implodes and winds down into entropy. This process presents a catastrophe for the subject, for not only does the acceleration and proliferation of the object world intensify the aleatory dimension of chance and non-determinacy, but the objects themselves take over in a "cool" catastrophe for the exhausted subject, whose fascination with the play of objects turns to apathy, stupefaction, and an entropic inertia.

In retrospect, the growing power of the world of objects over the subject has been Baudrillard's theme from the beginning, thus pointing to an underlying continuity in his project. In his early writings, he explored the ways that commodities were fascinating individuals in the consumer society and the ways that the world of goods was assuming new and more value through the agency of sign value and the code – which were part of the world of things, the system of objects. His polemics against Marxism were fueled by the belief that sign value and the code were more fundamental than such traditional elements of political economy as exchange value, use value, production, and so on in constituting contemporary society. Then, reflections on the media entered the forefront of his thought: the TV object was at the center of the home in Baudrillard's earlier thinking and the media, simulations, hyperreality, and implosion eventually came to obliterate distinctions between private and public, inside and outside, media and reality. Henceforth, everything was public, transparent, ecstatic, and hyperreal in the object world, which was gaining in fascination and seductiveness as the years went by.

So ultimately the subject, the darling of modern philosophy, is defeated in Baudrillard's metaphysical scenario and the object triumphs, a stunning end to the dialectic of subject and object which had been the framework of modern philosophy. The object is thus the subject's fatality and Baudrillard's "fatal strategies" project an obscure call to submit to the strategies and ruses of objects. In "banal strategies," "the subject believes itself to always be more clever than the object, whereas in the other [fatal strategies] the object is always supposed to be more shrewd, more cynical, more brilliant than the subject" (Baudrillard, 1990b: 259–260). Previously, in banal strategies, the subject believed itself to be more masterful and sovereign than the object. A fatal strategy, by contrast, recognizes the supremacy of the object and therefore takes the side of the object and surrenders to its strategies, ruses, and rules.

In *The Fatal Strategies* and succeeding writings, Baudrillard seems to be taking social theory into the realm of metaphysics, but it is a specific type of metaphysics, deeply inspired by the pataphysics developed by Alfred Jarry. For Jarry:

pataphysics is the science of the realm beyond metaphysics ... It will study the laws which govern exceptions and will explain the universe supplementary to this one; or, less ambitiously, it will describe a universe which one can see – must see perhaps – instead of the traditional one.

Definition: pataphysics is the science of imaginary solutions, which symbolically attributes the properties of objects, described by their virtuality, to their lineaments. (Jarry, 1963: 131)

Like the universe in Jarry's *Ubu Roi, The Gestures and Opinions of Doctor Faustroll*, and other literary texts – as well as in Jarry's more theoretical explications of pataphysics – Baudrillard's is a totally absurd universe where objects rule in mysterious ways, and people and events are governed by absurd and ultimately unknowable interconnections and predestination (the French playwright Eugène Ionesco is another good source of entry to this universe). Like Jarry's pataphysics, Baudrillard's universe is ruled by surprise, reversal, hallucination, blasphemy, obscenity, and a desire to shock and outrage.

Thus, in view of the growing supremacy of the object, Baudrillard wants us to abandon the subject and to side with the object. Pataphysics aside, it seems that Baudrillard is trying to end the philosophy of subjectivity that has controlled French thought since Descartes by going over completely to the other side. Descartes's *malin génie*, his evil genius, was a ruse of the subject which tried to seduce him into accepting what was not clear and distinct, but over which he was ultimately able to prevail. Baudrillard's "evil genius" is the object itself which is much more malign than the merely epistemological deceptions of the subject faced by Descartes and which constitutes a fatal destiny that demands the end of the philosophy of subjectivity. Henceforth, for Baudrillard, we live in the era of the reign of the object.

INTO THE 1990S

In the 1980s, Baudrillard posited an "immanent reversal," a flip-flop or reversed direction of meaning and effects, in which things turn into their opposite. Thus, according to Baudrillard, the society of production was passing over to simulation and seduction; the panoptic and repressive power theorized by Foucault was turning into a cynical and seductive power of the media and information society; the liberation championed in the 1960s was becoming a form of voluntary servitude; sovereignty had passed from the side of the subject to the object; and revolution and emancipation had turned into their opposites, snaring one more and more in the logic of the system, thus trapping individuals in an order of simulation and virtuality. Baudrillard's concept of "immanent reversal" thus provides a perverse form of Horkheimer and Adorno's "dialectic of Enlightenment" (1972[1947]), where everything becomes its opposite. For Adorno and Horkheimer, within the transformations of organized and hi-tech capitalism, modes of Enlightenment become domination, culture becomes culture industry, democracy becomes a form of mass manipulation, and science and technology form a crucial part of an apparatus of social domination.

Baudrillard follows this concept of reversal and his paradoxical and nihilistic metaphysical vision into the 1990s where his thought becomes ever more hermetic, fragmentary, and difficult. During the decade, Baudrillard continued playing the role of academic and media superstar, traveling around the world lecturing and performing in intellectual events.

Retiring from the University of Nanterre in 1987, Baudrillard subsequently functioned as an independent intellectual, dedicating himself to caustic reflections on the contemporary moment and philosophical ruminations that cultivated his distinct and always evolving theory. From June 1987 through May 1997, he published reflections on events and phenomena of the day in the Paris newspaper *Libération*, a series of writings collected in *Screened Out* (2002b[2000]) and providing access to a laboratory for ideas later elaborated in his books.

During the 1990s and up until his death, Baudrillard continued to write short journal entries and by 2007 had published five volumes of his *Cool Memories*. These texts combine reflections on his travels and experiences with development of his ideas and perceptions. Baudrillard's fragmentary diaries often provide revealing insights into his personal life and psychology, as well as capturing experiences and scenes that generate or embody some of his ideas. While often repetitive, his "cool memory" booklets provide direct access to the man and his ideas, as well as validating him as a global intellectual superstar who travels around the earth and whose every diary notation is worthy of publication and attention.

Baudrillard produced as well reflections on contemporary issues like the Gulf War, the 9/11 terror attacks, that he saw as the only real "event" of the past decades, globalization, the US invasion of Iraq, and other occurrences of the day. Baudrillard also continued his metaphysical speculations in works such as *The Transparency of Evil* (1993b[1990]), *The Illusion of the End* (1994b[1992]), *The Perfect Crime* (1996b [1995]), *Impossible Exchange* (2001[1999], *The Intelligence of Evil or the Lucidity Pact* (2005), and *The Conspiracy of Art* (2005b). These texts continue his excursions into the metaphysics of the object and defeat of the subject and ironical engagement with contemporary history and politics. Bringing together reflections that develop his ideas and/or comment on contemporary events, these texts continue to postulate a break within history in the space of a postmodern *coupure*, though Baudrillard himself usually distances himself from other versions of postmodern theory.

Baudrillard's retirement from a sociology faculty seems to have liberated his theoretical impulses and in addition to his diary collections and occasional forays into engagement of issues of the day, Baudrillard turned out a series of increasingly dense theoretical texts. The post-1990 texts continued the fragmentary style and use of short essays, aphorisms, stories, and aperçus that Baudrillard began deploying in the 1980s. While the books develop the quasi-metaphysical perspectives of the 1980s, they also generate some new ideas and positions. They are often entertaining, although they can also be outrageous and scandalous. These writings can be read as a combination of cultivation of original theoretical perspectives along with continual commentary on current social conditions, accompanied by a running dialogue with Marxism, poststructuralist theory, and other forms of contemporary thought. Yet after his fierce and focused polemics of the 1970s against competing models of thought, Baudrillard's dialogue with theory now consists mostly of occasional asides and recycling of previous ideas, a retro-theory that perhaps ironically illustrates Baudrillard's theses about the decline of theory and politics in the contemporary moment.

In *The Transparency of Evil* (1993b), Baudrillard described a situation in which previously separate domains of the economy, art, politics, and sexuality, collapsed into each other. He claims that art, for instance, has penetrated all spheres of existence, whereby the dreams of the artistic avant-garde for art to inform life has been realized.

Baudrillard calls this situation "transaesthetics" which he relates to similar phenomena of "transpolitics," "transsexuality," and "transeconomics," in which everything becomes political, sexual, and economic, so that these domains, like art, lose their specificity, their boundaries, and their distinctness. The result is a confused condition where there are no more criteria of value, of judgment, or of taste, and the function of the normative thus collapses in a morass of indifference and inertia. And so, although Baudrillard sees art proliferating everywhere, and writes in *The Transparency of Evil* that "talk about Art is increasing even more rapidly" (14), the power of art – of art as adventure, art as negation of reality, art as redeeming illusion, art as another dimension and so on – has disappeared. Art is everywhere but there "are no more fundamental rules" to differentiate art from other objects and "no more criteria of judgment or of pleasure" (14). For Baudrillard, contemporary individuals are indifferent toward taste and manifest only distaste: "tastes are determinate no longer" (72).

And yet as a proliferation of images, of form, of line, of color, of design, art is more fundamental then ever to the contemporary social order: "our society has given rise to a general aestheticization: all forms of culture – not excluding anti-cultural ones – are promoted and all models of representation and anti-representation are taken on board" (16). Thus Baudrillard concludes that: "It is often said that the West's great undertaking is the commercialization of the whole world, the hitching of the fate of everything to the fate of the commodity. That great undertaking will turn out rather to have been the aestheticization of the whole world – its cosmopolitan spectacularization, its transformation into images, its semiological organization" (16).

In the postmodern media and consumer society, everything becomes an image, a sign, a spectacle, a transaesthetic object – just as everything also becomes transeconomic, trans-political, and trans-sexual. This "*materialization* of aesthetics" is accompanied by a desperate attempt to simulate art, to replicate and mix previous artistic forms and styles, and to produce ever more images and artistic objects. But this "dizzying eclecticism" of forms and pleasures produces a situation in which art is no longer art in classical or modernist senses but is merely image, artifact, object, simulation, or commodity (Baudrillard is aware of increasingly exorbitant prices for art works, but takes this as evidence that art has become something else in the orbital hyperspace of value, an ecstasy of skyrocketing values in "a kind of space opera" (19)).

Examples of the paradoxical and ironic style of Baudrillard's philosophical musings abound in *The Perfect Crime* (1996b). Baudrillard claims that the negation of a transcendent reality in the current media and technological society is a "perfect crime" which involves the "destruction of the real." In a world of appearance, image, and illusion, Baudrillard suggests, reality disappears although its traces continue to nourish an illusion of the real. Driven toward virtualization in a hi-tech society, all the imperfections of human life and the world are eliminated in virtual reality, but this is the elimination of reality itself, the Perfect Crime. This "post-critical" and "catastrophic" state of affairs render our previous conceptual world irrelevant, Baudrillard suggests, urging criticism to turn ironic and transform the demise of the real into an art form.

Before 9/11, in Baudrillard's musings of the past two decades, the global post-modern condition had been one of absorbing otherness, of erasing difference, of assimilating and imploding all oppositional or negative forces into a viral positivity and virtuality. That is, Baudrillard saw globalization and technological development producing standardization and virtualization that was erasing individuality, social struggle, critique and reality itself as more and more people became absorbed in the hyper and virtual realities of media and cyberspace and virtue culture. In his view, the positive and the virtual radiate throughout every interstice of society and culture, irradiating into nullity any negativity, opposition, or difference. It is also an era in which reality itself has disappeared, constituting the "perfect crime."

Baudrillard presents himself here as a detective searching for the perpetrator of the "perfect crime," the murder of reality, "the most important event of modern history." His recurrent theme is the destruction and disappearance of the real in the realm of information and simulacra, and the subsequent reign of illusion and appearance. In a Nietzschean mode, he suggests that henceforth truth and reality are illusions, that illusions reign, and that therefore we should respect illusion and appearance and give up the illusory quest for truth and reality.

Obviously, Baudrillard has entered a world of thought far from academic philosophy, one that puts in question traditional modes of thought and discourse. His search for new philosophical perspectives has won him a loyal global audience, but also criticism for his excessive irony, word play, and intellectual games. Yet his work stands as a provocation to traditional and contemporary philosophy that challenges thinkers to address old philosophical problems like truth and reality in new ways in the contemporary world.

Indeed, Baudrillard produced an attempt at a philosophical chef d'oeuvre in his 1999 text *Impossible Exchange* (2001). In three parts containing a series of short essays, Baudrillard first develops his concept of an "impossible exchange" between concepts and the world, theory and reality, and subject and object. In his most elaborate attempt at philosophical thought, Baudrillard attacks philosophical attempts to capture reality, arguing for an incommensurability between concepts and their objects, systems of thought and the world. For Baudrillard, the latter always elude capture by the former, thus philosophy is an "impossible exchange" in which it is impossible to grasp the truth of the world, to attain certainty, to establish a foundation for philosophy, and or produce a defensible philosophical system.

In retrospect, Baudrillard's philosophical play with the subject/object distinction, his abandonment of the subject, and going over to the side of the object is a key aspect of his thought. He identifies this dichotomy with the duality of good and evil in which the cultivation of the subject and its domination of the object is taken as the good within Western thought, while the sovereignty and side of the object is interwoven with the principle of evil. Baudrillard's thought is radically dualistic and he takes the side of the pole within a series of dichotomies of Western thought that has generally been derided as inferior, such as siding with appearance against reality, illusion over truth, evil over good, and woman over man. In *The Perfect Crime*

(1996b), Baudrillard has declared that reality has been destroyed and henceforth that we live in a world of mere appearance, a situation that Baudrillard affirms and positively valorizes. In this universe, certainty and truth are impossible and Baudrillard takes the side of illusion, arguing in *Impossible Exchange* (2001) that: "Illusion is the fundamental rule" (6).

Baudrillard also argues that the world is without meaning and that affirming meaninglessness is liberating: "If we could accept this meaninglessness of the world, then we could play with forms, appearances and our impulses, without worrying about their ultimate destination ... As Cioran says, we are not failures until we believe life has a meaning – and from that point on we are failures, because it hasn't" (2001: 128). Most controversially, Baudrillard also identifies with the principle of evil defined as that which is opposed to and against the good. There is an admittedly Manichean and Gnostic dimension to Baudrillard's thought, as well as deep cynicism and nihilism. Deconstruction, however, takes apart the subject/object dichotomy indicating the impossibly of taking the side of subject or object, or of good and evil as both are interconnected with each other and there can be no pure object without subject and vice versa, an argument Adorno has made. Baudrillard's thought is intrinsically dualistic and not dialectical. His thought is self-avowedly agonistic with the duel presented in tandem with his dualism, taking on and attacking rival theories and positions. Contradictions do not bother Baudrillard, for indeed he affirms them. It is thus tricky to argue with Baudrillard on strictly philosophical grounds and one needs to grasp his mode of writing, his notion of theory fictions, and to engage their saliency and effects.

Theory Fictions: Baudrillard in the Contemporary Moment

Baudrillard develops what he terms "theory fiction," or what he also calls "simulation theory" and "anticipatory theory." Such "theory" intends to simulate, grasp, and anticipate historical events, that he believes are continually outstripping all contemporary theory. The current situation, he claims, is more fantastic than the most fanciful science fiction, or theoretical projections of a futurist society. Thus, theory can only attempt to grasp the present on the run and try to anticipate the future. However, Baudrillard has had a mixed record as a social and political analyst and forecaster. As a political analyst, Baudrillard has often been superficial and off the mark. In an essay "The Anorexic Ruins" published in 1989, he read the Berlin Wall as a sign of a frozen history, of an anorexic history, in which nothing more can happen, marked by a "lack of events" and the end of history, taking the Berlin Wall as a sign of a stasis between communism and capitalism. Shortly thereafter, rather significant events destroyed the wall that Baudrillard took as permanent and opened up a new historical era.

The Cold War stalemate was long taken by Baudrillard as establishing a frozen history in which no significant change could take place. Already in his mid-1970s reflections, he presented the Vietnam war as an "alibi" to incorporate China, Russia, and eventually Vietnam into a more rationalized and modernized world economic and political order (Baudrillard, 1983a: 66f.), and in his book on the Gulf war he repeats this claim (1995: 85), thus failing to see the actual political stakes and reasons for the Vietnam war, as well as the significance of the struggles between capitalist and communist blocs.

For Baudrillard, the twin towers of the World Trade Center in New York also symbolized the frozen history and stasis between the two systems of capitalism and communism. On the whole, Baudrillard sees history as the unfolding of expanding technological rationality turning into its opposite, as the system incorporates ever more elements, producing an improved technological order, which then becomes irrational through its excesses, its illusions, and its generating unforeseen consequences. This mode of highly abstract analysis, however, occludes more specific historical determinants that would analyze how technological rationality is constructed and functioned and how and why it misfires. It also covers over the disorder and turmoil created by such things as the crises and restructuring of global capitalism, the rise of fundamentalism, ethnic conflict, and global terrorism which were unleashed in part as a response to a globalized rationalization of the market system and to the breakup of the bipolar world order.

Baudrillard's reflections on the Gulf war take a similar position, seeing it as an attempt of the New World Order to rationalize the world further, arguing that the Gulf war really served to bring Islam into the New World Order (1995: 19). The first study titled "The Gulf war will not take place" was initially published a few days before the actual outbreak of military hostilities and repeats his earlier concept of "weak events" and frozen history. Baudrillard to the contrary, the Gulf war took place, but this did not deter him from publishing studies claiming during the episode that it was not "really taking place" and after the war asserting that it "did not take place." Although I have also argued that the "Gulf war" was a media spectacle and not a genuine war (see Kellner, 1992), Baudrillard does not help us to understand much about the event and does not even help us to grasp the role of the media in contemporary political spectacles. Reducing complex events like wars to categories like simulation or hyperreality illuminates the virtual and high-tech dimension to media events, but erases all their concrete determinants. And yet Baudrillardian postmodern categories help grasp some of the dynamics of the culture of living in media and computer worlds where people seem to enjoy immersing themselves in simulated events (witness the fascination of the Gulf war in 1991, the O.J. Simpson trials during 1994–1996, the Clinton sex scandals, various other media spectacles throughout the 1990s, and the 9/11 terror attacks in the early days of the third millennium).

In *The Illusion of the End* (1994b), Baudrillard attacks head-on what he sees as current illusions of history, politics, and metaphysics, and gamely tries to explain away his own political misprognoses that contemporary history appeared in a frozen, glacial state, stalemated between East and West, that the system of deterrence had congealed, making sure that nothing dramatic could henceforth happen, that the Gulf war could not take place, and that the end of history had occurred. Baudrillard unleashes his full bag of rhetorical tricks and philosophical analysis to attempt to maintain these hypotheses in the face of the dramatic events of 1989–1991, which he claims are in fact "weak events," that events are still on strike, that history has indeed disappeared. He continues to argue that modernity as a historical epoch is over, with its political conflicts and upheavals, its innovations and revolutions, its autonomous and creative subject, and its myths of progress, democracy,

Enlightenment, and the like. These myths, these strong ideas, are exhausted, he claims, and henceforth a postmodern era of banal eclecticism, inertial implosion, and eternal recycling of the same become defining features.

For Baudrillard by the end of the 1990s with the collapse of communism, the era of the strong ideas, of a conflicted world of revolution and universal emancipation, is over. Communism, in Baudrillard's reading, collapsed of its own inertia, it self-destructed from within, it imploded, rather than perishing in ideological battle or military warfare. With the absorption of its dissidents into power, there is no longer a clash of strong ideas, of opposition and resistance, of critical transcendence. With the embedding of the former communist regimes into the system of the capitalist world market and liberal democracy, the West no longer has an Other to battle against, there is no longer any creative or ideological tension, no longer any global alternative to the Western world.

Baudrillard celebrated the coming of the new millennium with some of his old ideas on cloning, the end of history, and the disappearance of the real in a series of lectures collected as *The Vital Illusion* (2000). For Baudrillard (2000), cloning is connected to the fantasy of immortality, to defeating the life cycle. Thus, its no surprise that cryogenics – the freezing of dead human beings in the hope they might be regenerated in the future through medical advances – is a booming global industry. Likewise, in a digital era, Baudrillard claims that history has come to an end and reality has been killed by virtualization, as the human species prepares itself for a virtual existence.

The Vital Illusion is one of Baudrillard's most derivative and unoriginal works and shows the stasis that infected his thought by the year 2000. Baudrillard had earlier made fun of the speculations on the coming millennium, argued in the 1990s that the new millennium had already happened, and once it did occur Baudrillard had nothing of particular interest to say about its emergence. For years, Baudrillard had complained that the contemporary era was one of weak events, that no major historical occurrences had happened, and that therefore life and thought were becoming increasingly boring.

Shortly after the 9/11 terrorist attacks, Baudrillard wrote a paper "L'esprit du terrorisme" published November 2, 2001, in *Le Monde*. He argued that the assaults on the World Trade Center and Pentagon constituted a "strong event," that the attacks were "the ultimate event, the mother of all events, the pure event uniting within itself all the events that have never taken place." The "event strike," Baudrillard declared, was over and since this time he has continued to focus intensely on the dynamics and happenings of contemporary history.

Hence, Baudrillard's thought has been reignited by 9/11 and the subsequent Terror War which demonstrates the continuing relevance of some of his key categories and that have produced some of his most provocative recent work. In the 9/11 attacks and subsequent Terror War, difference and conflict have erupted upon the global stage and heterogeneous forces that global capitalism appears unable to absorb and assimilate have emerged that have produced what appears to be an era of intense conflict. Ideological apologists of globalization such as Thomas Friedman have been forced to acknowledge that globalization has its dark sides and produces conflict as well as networking, interrelations, and progress. It remains to be seen, of course, how the current Terror War and intensified global conflicts will be resolved.

In any case, Baudrillard had long written on terrorism and was focusing reflection on globalization when the 9/11 attacks occurred. He quickly responded with the *Le Monde* article, soon after translated and expanded into one of the more challenging and controversial books on the terror spectacle, *The Spirit of Terrorism: And Requiem for the Twin Towers* (2002a). For Baudrillard, the 9/11 attacks represent a new kind of terrorism, exhibiting a "form of action which plays the game, and lays hold of the rules of the game, solely with the aim of disrupting it … they have taken over all the weapons of the dominant power." That is, the terrorists in Baudrillard's reading used airplanes, computer networks, and the media associated with Western societies to produce a spectacle of terror. The attacks evoked a global specter of terror that the very system of globalization and Western capitalism and culture were under assault by "the spirit of terrorism" and potential terrorist attacks anytime and anywhere.

Baudrillard perceived that the terrorists hope that the system will overreact in response to the multiple challenges of terrorism and, indeed the Bush administration (2000–2008) responded with an excess of unilateral militarism in Afghanistan and Iraq, and made a "war against terror" the fundament of its domestic and foreign policy, and infamously declared that "you are with us or against us," in effect saying that anyone who did not support Bush's "war on terror" was aiding and abetting "the enemy" and terrorism itself. For many of us, the Bush administration did what Baudrillard said the terrorists would want them to do, in terms of overreaction to the 9/11 attacks that would melt the initial sympathy for the US and that would win recruits for the terrorists reacting against the excess violence and aggression of the US response. Immediately after 9/11, *Le Monde* headlined a commentary "Nous sommes tous les Americains," but after the rancorous debate over Bush's Iraq intervention, the US found itself alienated from longtime allies, facing a proliferation of new enemies, and engaged in what the Bush administration described as a new era of "war on terror," with no end in sight.

Upon the initial publication of his response in French newspapers and its immediate translation into English and other languages, Baudrillard himself was accused of justifying terrorism when he stated in *The Spirit of Terrorism*: "Because it was this insufferable superpower [i.e. the US] that gave rise both to the violence now spreading throughout the world and to the terrorist imagination that (without our knowing it) dwells within us all. That the entire world without exception had dreamed of this event, that nobody could help but dream of the destruction of so powerful a Hegemon – this fact is unacceptable to the moral conscience of the West. And yet it's a fact nevertheless, a fact that resists the emotional violence of all the rhetoric conspiring to cover it up. In the end, it was they who did it, but we who wished it (Baudrillard, 2002a)."

Baudrillard defended himself from accusations that such reflections constituted a virulent anti-Americanism or legitimation of terrorism, claiming: "I do not praise murderous attacks – that would be idiotic. Terrorism is not a contemporary form of revolution against oppression and capitalism. No ideology, no struggle for an objective, not even Islamic fundamentalism, can explain it … I have glorified nothing, accused nobody, justified nothing. One should not confuse the messenger with his message. I have endeavored to analyze the process through which the unbounded expansion of globalization creates the conditions for its own destruction" (Baudrillard, 2002a)

Indeed, Baudrillard has also produced some provocative reflections on globalization. In "The Violence of the Global," he distinguishes between the global and the universal, linking globalization with technology, the market, tourism, and information contrasted to identification of the universal with "human rights, liberty, culture, and democracy." While "globalization appears to be irreversible ... universalization is likely to be on its way out." Elsewhere, Baudrillard writes: "the idea of freedom, a new and recent idea, is already fading from the minds and mores, and liberal globalization is coming about in precisely the opposite form – a police-state globalization, a total control, a terror based on 'law-and-order' measures. Deregulation ends up in a maximum of constraints and restrictions, akin to those of a fundamentalist society" (Baudrillard, 2002d).

Most theorists, including myself, see globalization as a matrix of market economy, democracy, technology, migration and tourism, and the worldwide circulation of ideas and culture. Baudrillard, curiously, takes the position of those in the anti-globalization movement who condemn globalization as the opposite of democracy and human rights. For Baudrillard, globalization is fundamentally a process of homogenization and standardization that crushes "the singular" and heterogeneity. This position, however, fails to note the contradictions that globalization simultaneously produces homogenization and hybridization and difference, and that the anti-corporate globalization movement is fighting for social justice, democratization, and increased rights, factors that Baudrillard links with a dying universalization. In fact, the struggle for rights and justice is an important part of globalization and Baudrillard's presenting of human rights, democratization, and justice as part of an obsolete universalization being erased by globalization is theoretically and politically problematical.

Concluding Reflections

Baudrillard has never been as influential in France as in the English-speaking world and elsewhere – a point made in many French obituaries and blogs upon his death. He is an example of the "global popular," a thinker who has followers and readers throughout the world, though, so far, no Baudrillardian school has emerged. (The inauguration in 2003 of an *International Journal of Baudrillard Studies*, however, indicates that there is a global coterie of Baudrillard scholars continuing to produce publications and reflections on his work; see www.ubishops.ca/baudrillardstudies/contents.htm)

Baudrillard's influence has been largely at the margins of a diverse number of disciplines ranging from social theory to philosophy to art history, thus it is difficult to gauge his impact on sociology, or the mainstream of any specific academic discipline.

In retrospect, Baudrillard is perhaps most important as part of the postmodern turn against modern society and its academic disciplines. His work cuts across the disciplines and promotes cross-disciplinary thought. He challenges standard wisdom and puts in question received dogma and methods. While his early work on the consumer society, the political economy of the sign, simulation and simulacra, and the implosion of phenomena previously separated can be deployed within critical social theory, much of his post-1980s work quite self-consciously goes beyond the classical tradition and in most interviews of the past decade Baudrillard distances himself from critical theory, claiming that the energy of critique has dissipated.

Baudrillard can be seen as a transdisciplinary theorist of the end of modernity who produces signposts to the new era of postmodernity and is an important, albeit hardly trustworthy, guide to the new era. In my view, Baudrillard exaggerates the break between the modern and the postmodern, takes future possibilities as existing realities, and provides a futuristic perspective on the present, much like the tradition of dystopic science fiction, ranging from Huxley to cyberpunk (Kellner, 1989). Indeed, I prefer to read Baudrillard's post-1970s work as science fiction that antici-pates the future by exaggerating present tendencies, and thus provides early warn-ings about what might happen if present trends continue (Kellner, 1995). It is not an accident that Baudrillard is an aficionado of science fiction, who has himself influ-enced a large number of contemporary science fiction writers and filmmakers of the contemporary era, including *The Matrix* (1999) where his work is cited.

However, in view of his exaggeration of the alleged break with modernity, dis-cerning whether Baudrillard's last two decades of work is best read as science fiction or theory, is undecidable. Baudrillard obviously wants to have it both ways with social theorists thinking that he provides salient perspectives on contemporary social realities, that Baudrillard reveals what is really happening, that he tells it like it is. And yet more cynical anti-sociologists are encouraged to enjoy Baudrillard's fictions, his experimental discourse, his games, and play. Likewise, he sometimes encourages cultural metaphysicians to read his work as serious reflections on the realities of our time, while winking a pataphysical aside at those skeptical of such undertakings. And Baudrillard's theoretical writings provoke theorists to defend their positions against his and to rethink certain tradition questions in the light of contemporary realities.

In retrospect, Baudrillard's early critical explorations of the system of objects and consumer society contain some of his most important contributions to contempo-rary social theory. His mid-1970s analysis of a dramatic mutation occurring within contemporary societies and rise of a new mode of simulation, which sketched out the effects of media and information on society as a whole, is also original and important. But at this stage of his work, Baudrillard falls prey to a technological determinism and semiological idealism which posits an autonomous technology and play of signs generating a society of simulation which creates a postmodern break and the proliferation of signs, spectacles, and simulacra. Baudrillard erases autono-mous and differentiated spheres of the economy, polity, society, and culture posited by classical social theory in favor of an implosive theory that also crosses discipli-nary boundaries, thus dissolving philosophy and social theory into a broader form of social diagnosis and philosophical play.

In the final analysis, Baudrillard is perhaps most useful as a provocateur who challenges and puts in question the tradition of classical social theory and critical theory. He claims that the object of classical social theory – modernity – has been surpassed by a new postmodernity and that therefore alternative theoretical strate-gies, modes of writing, and forms of thought are necessary. While his work on simu-lation and the postmodern break from the mid-1970s into the 1980s provides a paradigmatic postmodern theory and analysis of postmodernity that has been highly influential, and that despite its exaggerations continues to be of use in interpreting present social trends, much of his later work may be of more literary and philosophical than sociological interest.

Baudrillard thus ultimately goes beyond sociology and classical social theory altogether into a new sphere and mode of writing that provides occasionally biting critical insights into contemporary social phenomena and provocative critiques of contemporary and classical social theory. He now appears as a completely idiosyncratic thinker who went his own way and developed his own mode of writing and thought that will continue to provoke contemporary and future students of critical theory.

Reader's Guide to Jean Baudrillard

There are several introductions to Baudrillard including Douglas Kellner (1989), *Jean Baudrillard: From Marxism to Postmodernism and Beyond*; Mike Gane (1991), *Baudrillard. Critical and Fatal Theory*; Rex Butler (1999), *Jean Baudrillard: The Defense of the Real*; and William Pawlett (2007), *Jean Baudrillard: Against Banality*. In *Baudrillard Live. Selected Interviews*, Mike Gane (1993) collects interviews with Baudrillard.

More specialized studies of Baudrillard's work include Julian Pefanis (1991), *Heterology and the Postmodern: Bataille, Baudrillard, and Lyotard*; Mike Gane (2000), *Jean Baudrillard: In Radical Uncertainty*; and Victoria Grace (2000), *Baudrillard's Challenge: A Feminist Reading*. Gary Genosko's (1994) *Baudrillard and Signs* presents Baudrillard in relation to semiotics and communication theory, while William Merrin (2005) focuses on *Baudrillard and the Media*. Alain Sokal and Jean Bricmont (1998) provide a controversial attack on Baudrillard in *Fashionable Nonsense: Postmodern Intellectuals' Abuse of Science*.

Collections on Baudrillard's work include Alan Frankovits (ed.) (1984) *Seduced and Abandoned: The Baudrillard Scene*, documenting a conference on Baudrillard's work in Australia. Chris Rojek and Bryan Turner's (eds) (1993) *Forget Baudrillard* include critiques of Baudrillard's work emerging in the 1990s and Douglas Kellner (ed.) (1994) *Jean Baudrillard: A Critical Reader* covers the diversity of Baudrillard studies proliferating. William Stearns and William Chaloupka's (eds) (1992) *The Disappearance of Art and Politics* looks at Baudrillard's work in terms of aesthetics and politics, as do the interviews with Baudrillard and studies in Nicholas Zurbrugg (1997) *Art and Artifact*. Recent collections on Baudrillard include Ryan Bishop (ed.) (2009) *Baudrillard Now: Current Perspectives in Baudrillard Studies* and D.B. Clarke, M.A. Doel, William Merrin, and R.G. Smith (eds) (2009) *Jean Baudrillard. Fatal Theories*, collecting papers from a conference on Baudrillard in Swansea, UK

The *International Journal of Baudrillard Studies*, hosted at Bishop's University, provides lively reviews and studies on or related to Baudrillard's work.

Notes

1   For the first book published on Baudrillard and an overview of early stages of his work, see Douglas Kellner, *Jean Baudrillard: From Marxism to Postmodernism and Beyond*. Cambridge, UK and Palo Alto, CA: Polity Press and Stanford University Press (1989). For my later takes on Baudrillard, see Kellner (1989a); Best and Kellner (1991); Kellner (1994, 1995: ch. 8); and Best and Kellner (1997: ch. 3). Other books on Baudrillard include Frankovits (1984); Gane (1991, 1992, 1993); Stearns and Chaloupka (1992); Rojek and

Turner (1993); Genosko (1994); Butler (1999); Gane (2000); Grace (2000); Clarke *et al.* (2009); and Bishop (2009).

2   To those who would deny that Baudrillard is a postmodern theorist and has nothing to do with the discourse of the postmodern (e.g. Gane, 1991, 1993), one might note the positive uses of the concept of the postmodern in his most recent books (Baudrillard, 1994b: 23, 27, 31, 34, 36, 107, *passim*; 1996a: 36, 70, *passim*). *The Perfect Crime* (Baudrillard, 1996b) does not use the discourse of the postmodern per se, but makes ample use of his classic categories of simulation, hyperreality, and implosion to elucidate a new virtual order opposed to the previous order of reality, the murder of which is "the perfect crime" (ibid.: 16, 83, 125, 128, *passim*).

Bibliography

Writings of Jean Baudrillard

1968. *The System of Objects*. London: Verso (1996c).

1970. *The Consumer Society*. Paris: Gallimard (1998).

1973. *For a Critique of the Political Economy of the Sign*. St. Louis: Telos Press (1981).

1975. *The Mirror of Production*. St Louis: Telos Press.

1983a. *Simulations*. New York: Semiotext(e).

1983b. *In the Shadow of the Silent Majorities*. New York: Semiotext(e).

1983c. The ecstacy of communication. In Hal Foster (ed.) *The Anti-Aesthetic*. Washington, DC: Bay Press.

1987. When Bataille attacked the metaphysical principle of economy. *Canadian Journal of Political and Social Theory*, 11(3): 57–62.

1988. *America*. London: Verso.

1989. The Anorexic Ruins. In Dietmar Kamper and Christoph Wulf (eds) *Looking Back on the End of the World*. Foreign Agent Series. Semiotext(e), pp. 29–45.

1990a. *Cool Memories*. London: Verso.

1990b. *Fatal Strategies*. New York: Semiotext(e).

1990c. *Seduction*. Montreal: New World Perspectives.

1993a. *Symbolic Exchange and Death*. London: Sage.

1993b. *The Transparency of Evil*. London: Verso.

1994a. *Simulacra and Simulation*. Ann Arbor: University of Michigan Press.

1994b. *The Illusion of the End*. Oxford: Polity Press.

1995. *The Gulf War Never Happened*. Oxford: Polity Press.

1996a. *Cool Memories II*. Oxford: Polity Press.

1996b. *The Perfect Crime*. London and New York: Verso Books.

1997. *Fragments: Cool Memories III, 1990–1995*. London and New York: Verso Books.

2000. *The Vital Illusion*. New York: Columbia University Press.

2001. *Impossible Exchange*. London: Verso.

2002a. *The Spirit of Terrorism: And Requiem for the Twin Towers*. London: Verso.

2002b. *Screened Out*. London: Verso.

2002c. This is the Fourth World War, an interview with *Der Spiegel*. See the translation online at www.ubishops.ca/baudrillardstudies/spiegel.htm (accessed on November 25, 2010).

2002d. La violence du Mondial, in *Power Inferno*. Paris: Galilée, pp. 63–83; translated into English and available online at www.ctheory.net/text_file.asp?pick=385 (accessed on November 25, 2010).

2005a. *The Intelligence of Evil or the Lucidity Pact*. London: Verso.
2005b. *The Conspiracy of Art*. New York: Semiotext(e).
2006. *Utopia Deferred. Writings from Utopie (1967–1978)*. New York: Semiotext(e).

Further Reading

Barthes, Roland (1967) *Elements of Semiology*. London: Jonathan Cape.

Barthes, Roland (1972) *Mythologies*. New York: Hill and Wang.

Barthes, Roland (1983) *The Fashion System*. New York: Hill and Wang.

Bataille, Georges (1988) *The Accursed Share*. New York: Zone Books.

Best, Steven and Kellner, Douglas (1991) *Postmodern Theory: Critical Interrogations*. London and New York: Macmillan Press and Guilford Press.

Best, Steven and Kellner, Douglas (1997) *The Postmodern Turn*. New York: Guilford Press.

Best, Steven and Kellner, Douglas (2001) *The Postmodern Adventure*. New York: Guilford Press.

Bishop, Ryan (2009) *Baudrillard Now: Current Perspectives in Baudrillard Studies*. Cambridge, UK: Polity Press.

Butler, Rex (1999) *Jean Baudrillard: The Defense of the Real*. London and Thousand Oaks: Sage.

Clarke, D. B., Doel, M. A., Merrin, William, and Smith, R. G. (eds) (2009) *Jean Baudrillard. Fatal Theories*. London and New York: Routledge.

Debord, Guy (1970) *The Society of the Spectacle*. Detroit: Black and Red.

Frankovits, Alan (ed.) (1984) *Seduced and Abandoned: the Baudrillard Scene*. Glebe, New South Wales: Stonemoss.

Gane, Mike (1991) *Baudrillard: Critical and Fatal Theory*. London: Routledge.

Gane, Mike (ed.) (1993) *Baudrillard Live: Selected Interviews*. London: Routledge.

Gane, M. (2000) *Jean Baudrillard: In Radical Uncertainty*. London: Pluto Press.

Genosko, Gary (1994) *Baudrillard and Signs*. London: Routledge.

Grace, V. (2000) *Baudrillard's Challenge: A Feminist Reading*. London: Routledge.

Horkheimer, Max and Adorno, Theodor (1972[1947]) *Dialectic of Enlightenment*. New York: Herder and Herder.

Jarry, Alfred (1963) What Is Pataphysics? *Evergreen Review*, 13: 131–151.

Kellner, Douglas (1984) *Herbert Marcuse and the Crisis of Marxism*. Berkeley: University of California Press.

Kellner, Douglas (1989) *Jean Baudrillard: from Marxism to Postmodernism and Beyond*. Cambridge and Palo Alto, CA: Polity Press and Stanford University Press.

Kellner, Douglas (1992) *The Persian Gulf TV War*. Boulder, CO: Westview Press.

Kellner, Douglas (ed.) (1994) *Jean Baudrillard: A Critical Reader*. Oxford: Basil Blackwell.

Kellner, Douglas (1995) *Media Culture: Cultural Studies, Identity and Politics between the Modern and the Postmodern*. London: Routledge.

Kellner, Douglas (2005) Baudrillard, globalization and terrorism: Some comments on recent adventures of the image and spectacle on the occasion of Baudrillard's 75th birthday. *International Journal of Baudrillard Studies*, 2(1) January. Available online at www.ubishops.ca/baudrillardstudies/vol2_1/kellner.htm (accessed November 25, 2010).

Kroker, Arthur (2007) The spirit of Jean Baudrillard: In memoriam: 1929–2007. C-Theory (posted March 8, 2007) Available online at www.ctheory.net/articles.aspx?id=573.htm (accessed November 25, 2010).

Lefebvre, Henri (1971) *Everyday Life in the Modern World*. New Brunswick, NJ: Transaction Books.

Lefebvre, Henri (1991) *Critique of Everyday Life*. London: Verso.

Lukács, Georg (1971) *History and Class Consciousness*. Cambridge, MA: MIT Press.

Merrin, William (2005) *Baudrillard and the Media*. Cambridge, UK: Polity Press.

Pawlett, William (2007) *Jean Baudrillard: Against Banality*. London: Routledge.

Pefanis, Julian (1991) *Heterology and the Postmodern: Bataille, Baudrillard, and Lyotard*. Durham, NC: Duke University Press.

Rojek, Chris and Turner, Bryan (eds) (1993) *Forget Baudrillard*. London: Routledge.

Sokal, A. and Bricmont, J. (1998) "Jean Baudrillard" in *Fashionable Nonsense: Postmodern Intellectuals' Abuse of Science*. New York: Picador, pp. 147–153.

Stearns, William and Chaloupka, William (eds) (1992) *The Disappearance of Art and Politics*. New York and London: St Martin's Press and Macmillan Press.

Zurbrugg, Nicholas (1997) *Jean Baudrillard, Art and Artifact*. London: Sage.

14

Jürgen Habermas

WILLIAM OUTHWAITE

THE PERSON

Jürgen Habermas, who retired in 1994 from his post as Professor of Philosophy and Sociology at the University of Frankfurt and who celebrated his eightieth birthday in 2009, is the leading representative of the second generation of the neo-Marxist critical theorists often known as the "Frankfurt School" (see Bottomore, 1984; Jay, 1973; Wiggershaus, 1987).

Born in 1929, Habermas grew up in the small town of Gummersbach, near Cologne. He studied philosophy, history, psychology, and German literature at Göttingen, Zürich, and Bonn, where he obtained his doctorate in 1954 with a thesis on Schelling. After some journalistic work he became, in 1956, Theodor Adorno's research assistant at the Institute of Social Research in Frankfurt, newly re-established in Germany and the base of what had come to be called the "Frankfurt School." Here he participated in an empirical study on the political awareness of students (Habermas et al., 1961). From 1959 to 1961 he worked on his *Structural Transformation of the Public Sphere* (1962). After a period as Professor of Philosophy at Heidelberg, Habermas returned to Frankfurt in 1964 as Professor of Philosophy and Sociology, where he delivered the inaugural lecture on "Knowledge and Interest" (reprinted in Habermas, 1968). Also at this time he published the essays entitled *Theory and Practice* (1963), a survey work on *The Logic of The Social Sciences* (1967) and some further essays grouped under the title *Technology and Science as Ideology* (1968).

In 1971 Habermas left Frankfurt for Starnberg, Bavaria, to take up, along with the physicist C. F. von Weizsäcker, the directorship of the newly created Max Planck Institute for the Study of the Conditions of Life in the Scientific-Technical World. Surrounded by some of the most brilliant younger sociologists in the country, many of whom have since become major theorists in their own right, he began to develop

The Wiley-Blackwell Companion to Major Social Theorists, First Edition.
Edited by George Ritzer and Jeffrey Stepnisky.
© 2011 Blackwell Publishing Ltd. Published 2011 by Blackwell Publishing Ltd.

the theme of communicative action, which had been present but not particularly prominent in his earlier work, into the centerpiece of his theorizing. He published an enormous amount of material, including the well-known *Legitimation Crisis* (1973) and culminating with the *Theory of Communicative Action* (1981). In 1982, he returned to a chair in Philosophy and Sociology at Frankfurt where he taught until his retirement in 1994. Living in Starnberg, he continued to write and speak to a worldwide audience. In 1992 he published a major study of law and democracy, *Between Facts and Norms*, followed by substantial volumes of essays on topics which had concerned him in his earlier work, such as semantics and moral theory, and new ones such as genetics and religion.

The above constitute what Habermas considers his "theoretical" works, but he has also published to date eleven volumes of "political writings," most recently a further volume of essays, *Ach, Europa* (2008), following on and developing themes from *The Postnational Constellation* (1998). Thus his work in social theory is complemented by a volume of writing on contemporary social and political issues which is itself the subject of at least one book-length study (Holub, 1991). Like Max Weber in Imperial Germany, and Karl Jaspers in the early years of the Federal Republic, he has come to be in some sense the intellectual conscience of the country. Like Weber, he is basically a thinker rather than a man of action but one who intervenes in political issues when something, as he often puts it, "irritates" him. And although he rejects Weber's doctrine of the value-freedom of science, he insists, like Weber, on the distinction between scholarly and political discourse (Dews, 1986: 127).

Habermas has been concerned in particular with three sets of issues, past, present, and future. In the past, or more particularly in current uses of the past, he has repeatedly intervened over issues of the responsibility of Germany and of individual Germans for the Third Reich and the Holocaust. One of his earliest essays was concerned with the philosopher Martin Heidegger's refusal in the 1950s to confront his past as an active supporter of Nazism (Habermas, 1953). More recently, in the late 1980s, he initiated what came to be called the Historians' Dispute (*Historikerstreit*) with an attack on what he saw as a concerted attempt by the West German Right to whitewash the past by historicizing it, by relativizing the crimes of the Nazis as one episode among others in a world-historical past which was inevitably often tragic. This "damage settlement" (Habermas, 1987) – an ironic term taken from the insurance industry – was driven by the conservatives' desire to create a new, confident national consciousness. Most recently, Habermas intervened in support of the young North American writer Daniel Goldhagen against virulent attacks in Germany on his controversial attempt to demonstrate how widespread German complicity in the Holocaust was.

Of contemporary events which attracted Habermas's active involvement, undoubtedly the most important were the student protests of 1968. Habermas participated very fully in this movement and, although he came to criticize its extremism and had no sympathy for the desperate terrorism which followed its demise, he welcomed its long-term effect in modernizing the political culture of the Federal Republic. More recently, as noted above, he defended this liberal and enlightened strand of West German thought against attempts to return to a new (conservative) "obscurity" (Habermas, 1985). Finally, the reunification of Germany has led Habermas into extended reflections both on Germany itself and on the future of the European nation-state in general. He has been a critical supporter of the European integration process, which he sees as opening up a possible future for a "postnational" world.

THE SOCIAL CONTEXT

As will be clear from the previous section, Habermas spent the whole of his academic career, with the exception of guest professorships in the US and elsewhere, in his native country, and he has been crucially concerned with the question which the philosopher Karl Jaspers (1966) made into a book title: Where is the Federal Republic going? More concretely, as a member of what has been called the "Hitler Youth generation," drawn as a child into complicity with the most appalling regime of modern times, he was horrified both by the crimes of the Third Reich and by the unwillingness of most of his compatriots to face up to their responsibility for what had happened. For a long time the Nazi period was a taboo subject in schools; major universities conveniently passed over it in their official histories, and the naming of a new university after a leading opponent and victim of Nazism was seen as deeply controversial. Even in communist East Germany, where the history of the Third Reich was at least given the prominence it deserved, issues of personal or collective responsibility were not seriously raised.

The German past is, then, one crucial aspect of the social context of Habermas's life and work (see Turner, 2004). Another was of course something which was common to all the major Western European states in what was called the "thirty glorious years" from the late 1940s to the early 1970s: democratic welfare states, rising prosperity and full employment. Habermas's response, notably in *Legitimation Crisis* (1973), was to reformulate Marxist crisis theory in a suggestive model of the displacement of crisis tendencies from the economic base to the political and cultural sphere. He had earlier taken up and reformulated the critique of "technocracy" which had been fashionable in the fifties and sixties, concerned to construct a socialist response to the technological determinism deriving from the work of Heidegger, Arnold Gehlen, and Helmut Schelsky. In this context, Habermas also looked into the changing nature of political participation, the public sphere and civil society – the latter of course crucially invigorated in the years around 1968 by "citizens" initiatives and new social movements (Habermas, 1963, 1968b).

Soon after the publication of Legitimation Crisis, of course, the age of full employment came to seem lost forever in the aftermath of the first oil price shock of 1973; the political climate shifted to the right, with the rise to power of Ronald Reagan, Margaret Thatcher and, in West Germany, Helmut Kohl. German neoliberalism was a muted affair compared to that in the US and UK, but the political background was a good deal nastier, with political terrorism sparking off a peculiarly violent backlash in the "German Autumn" of 1977 and the following years, in which respectable intellectuals were often accused of sympathizing with terrorists. Habermas, and close associates such as Albrecht Wellmer (in Habermas, 1979), attempted to restore some sense of proportion to public debate on these issues.

The Federal Republic, which had muddled through the 1980s more or less effectively under Helmut Kohl's calm and complacent reign as Federal Chancellor, was surprised in the autumn of 1989 by the collapse of its poor sister-state, the German

Democratic Republic, along with the other Marxist-Leninist dictatorships in Europe. The "national question" ceased to be the preserve of historians and (mostly right-wing) publicists and rapidly moved to the top of the political agenda. As usual with really important agenda items, it was dealt with perfunctorily, in a technical-fix reunification which left all the important issues unresolved. Habermas (1990) was one of many German intellectuals who argued that a crucial opportunity had been missed to rethink the constitution of the Federal Republic, rather than simply incorporating what were delicately referred to as the "five new states" or the "accession territory." These issues now remain to be confronted, as Habermas rightly insists, on a European and global stage.

The Intellectual Context

Habermas's thinking emerges from the flexible and interdisciplinary Marxist tradition of what came to be called the Frankfurt School of Critical Theory, based in the early 1930s and again from 1950 in the Institute for Social Research in Frankfurt. As Habermas showed in detail in his *Theory of Communicative Action*, this tradition draws on both Marx and Max Weber, on another non-Marxist, Weber's contemporary Georg Simmel, and on the father of "Western Marxism" (Anderson, 1976), Georg Lukács. In an autobiographical interview, Habermas recalled reading Lukács for the first time with great excitement but with a sense that his work was no longer directly relevant to post-war societies such as Western Germany. His thinking remained shaped, however, by a Western Marxist agenda emphasizing not just issues of capital and class but the interplay between capitalist exploitation and bureaucratic state rule, and their implications for individual identity and collective political autonomy.

Habermas's relationship to Frankfurt critical theory was somewhat indirect in the early stages of his career. He diverged from the two key members of the Frankfurt School who had returned to Germany, Theodor Adorno and Max Horkheimer, whose interests had become increasingly philosophical, in insisting that a revival of critical theory had once again to engage fully with the social and human sciences. He argued, in other words, for a return to interdisciplinary critical social science of the kind practiced before the Second World War in Horkheimer's Institute of Social Research.

Like Adorno and Horkheimer, Habermas rejected Marxist philosophies of history, in which an account of the development of capitalism and of the rise of the working class is taken to show that the collapse of capitalism and its replacement by socialism are inevitable, or at least extremely probable. Yet he also felt that Adorno and Horkheimer had painted themselves into a pessimistic corner, from which they could only criticize reality, without offering any alternative. He fully shared, however, Adorno and Horkheimer's concern with the way in which Enlightenment, in the form of instrumental rationality, turns from a means of liberation into a new source of enslavement. "Already at that time" (the late 1950s), he has written, "my problem was a theory of modernity, a theory of the pathology of modernity, from the viewpoint of the realization – the deformed realization – of reason in history" (Dews, 1992: 187). This involved a working-through of the classics: Marx and Weber, but also Kant, Fichte, and Hegel – and of course ancient Greek thought.

This theoretical emphasis was however constantly combined, as in his early volume of essays on *Theory and Practice*, with a concern for the conditions of rational political discussion in modern technocratic democracies. Only the social sciences, broadly conceived, could provide the means to construct a genuinely contemporary critical theory of advanced capitalism, but their own positivistic deformation was itself part of the problem to be overcome. Habermas joined in the "positivism dispute" of the early 1960s in which these issues were battled out in Germany (Adorno, 1976), and devoted the following decade to a detailed historical critique of positivist social science and the elaboration of an alternative model of "reconstructive" science, of which his own theory of communicative action is an example. In *Knowledge and Human Interests* (1968), Habermas brilliantly showed how positivism had limited our understanding of the natural and the social world and undermined the possibility of critique; this could however be reconstructed from the work of Kant, Fichte, Hegel, and Marx and shown to inspire, for example, Freudian psychoanalytic theory and practice. "Critical" sciences such as psychoanalysis or the Marxist critique of ideology, governed by an emancipatory interest in overcoming causal obstacles to self-understanding, bridged the gap between the natural or empirical sciences, oriented to the prediction and control of objectified processes and the human sciences, oriented to an expansion of mutual understanding.

Earlier critical theory had distinguished itself from more orthodox variants of Marxism by its intense engagement with non-Marxist thought after Marx. Rather than writing off phenomenology, existentialism, or Heidegger's philosophy as a symptom of capitalist crisis, Adorno devoted major studies to Kierkegaard and Husserl, and a substantial part of *Negative Dialectics* (Adorno, 1966) to a discussion of Heidegger. Similarly, though in a more methodological vein, Habermas worked out his own models of critical and reconstructive science – the former in an engagement with Schutzian phenomenological sociology, Peter Winch's development of Wittgensteinian philosophy into social theory, and Hans-Georg Gadamer's Heideggerian philosophical hermeneutics. These, Habermas argued, could be brought into a complementary relation with one another and could then be further augmented by a more materialist reflection on the way in which our understanding of the social world (the common theme of these three currents of thought) is systematically distorted by relations of power and exploitation. In the 1970s, as noted earlier, he developed an idea of reconstructive science, seen as a systematic attempt to isolate the conditions and implications of practices such as linguistic communication and moral reasoning. Here it is linguistic theories of speech pragmatics which provide the paradigm, and social theory the detailed illustration.

Finally, Habermas's discourse ethics was substantially developed in relation to English-language ethical and political theory. His polemical exchanges with Gadamer and the system theorist Niklas Luhmann have become major documents in their own right. Against Gadamer, he argued that understanding needed to be supplemented by a materialist critique of power and exploitation, which he justified with an appeal to a notion of social theory contrasted with Luhmann's technocratic conception. Habermas has developed his thinking in close contact with others, notably the philosopher Karl-Otto Apel, whose intellectual trajectory in many ways parallels his own. He has also been exceptionally willing to engage with critical discussions of his own work and more recent developments in critical theory in the work of

Axel Honneth, Seyla Benhabib, and others – thus giving practical expression to the theoretical and political importance which he attaches to communication and dialogue.

Habermas's mature theory, as he developed it from the early 1970s, can best be understood as what he would call a "reconstruction" of what is presupposed and implied by human communication, cooperation, and debate. In terms of orthodox academic disciplines, there is a theory of communication (linguistics), a theory of communicative action (sociology) and a theory (both descriptive and normative) of morality, politics (including political communication), and law. At the back of all this are substantial elements of a philosophy of science (including, though not confined to, a critique of positivistic social science) and an account of the development of human societies and in particular of Western modernity which culminates in a diagnosis of what he sees as the central political problems confronting the advanced capitalist democracies and the world as a whole.

THE THEORY

The centerpiece of Habermas's developed theorizing is a theory of communicative action grounded in the analysis of linguistic communication. His basic idea is that any serious use of language to make claims about the world, as opposed, for example, to exclamations or the issuing of orders, presupposes the claims that what we say makes sense and is true, that we are sincere in saying it, and that we have the right to say it. These presuppositions can be questioned by our hearers or readers. As Habermas (1981: vol. 1, 306) shows with the example of a professor asking a seminar participant to fetch a glass of water, even a simple request, understood not as a mere demand but "as a speech act carried out in an attitude oriented to understanding" raises claims to normative rightness, subjective sincerity and factual practicability which may be questioned. The addressee of the request may reject it as illegitimate ("I'm not your servant"), insincere ("You don't really want one"), or mistaken about the facts of the matter (accessibility of a source of water).

Only a rational agreement which excluded no-one and no relevant evidence or argument would provide, in the last resort, a justification of the claims we routinely make and presuppose in our assertions. This idea gives us, Habermas claimed, a theory of truth, anticipated by the American pragmatist philosopher C. S. Peirce, as what we would ultimately come to agree about rationally (Habermas, 1984: 107). Moreover, if Habermas is right that moral judgments also have cognitive content and are not mere expressions of taste or disguised prescriptions, it also provides a theory of truth for issues of morality and of legitimate political authority. Moral norms are justified if they are what we would still uphold at the end of an ideal process of argumentation.

> When I state that one norm should be preferred to another, I aim precisely to exclude the aspect of arbitrariness: rightness and truth come together in that both claims can only be vindicated discursively, by way of argumentation and a rational consensus. (Habermas, 1984: 109)

This consensus is of course an idealization; Habermas at one time described it as resulting from what he called an "ideal speech situation." Yet it is counterfactually presupposed, he argues, by our everyday practice of communication, which is made meaningful by the real or hypothetical prospect of ultimate agreement.

The analysis of language-use, Habermas believes, can thus be expanded into a broader theory of communicative action, defined as action oriented by and toward mutual agreement. In social-theoretical terms, this can be contrasted with the models of instrumental or strategic, self-interested action (the model of *homo economicus* which also largely dominates rational choice theory), normatively regulated action (the model, familiar from functionalism, in which we orient our action to a shared value system) or dramaturgical action, in which our actions are analyzed as a performance, designed to optimize our public image or self-image (Goffman, Garfinkel, and others). All of these types of action, Habermas claims, can be shown to be parasitic upon communicative action, which incorporates and goes beyond each of them (Habermas, 1981: vol. 1, 82–101). The theory of communicative action, then, underpins a communication theory of morality, law, and democracy, and it is these aspects which have dominated Habermas's most recent work.

One of Habermas's best-known books is a short and highly compressed text called in English *Legitimation Crisis* (Habermas, 1973). Here, and in related essays, published in English under the title *Communication and the Evolution of Society* (Habermas, 1979), he advanced a neo-Marxist theory of historical development and a critique of contemporary advanced or "late" capitalism. Habermas argued that historical materialist explanations of the development of the productive forces needed to be augmented by an account of the evolution of normative structures, understood in a wide sense to include, for example, family forms. In late capitalism, again, a traditional Marxist account of capitalist crisis which focuses on the economic contradictions of the capitalist system needs to be modified to account for the role of the modern interventionist welfare state and the resultant displacement of crisis tendencies from the economic sphere to the political and cultural domains. Instead of the economic crises (which remain the fundamental problem), what we experience are incoherent state responses, leading to what Habermas calls rationality crises which weaken state legitimacy; these state interventions also lead to an erosion of individual motivation and a loss of meaning.

In Habermas's subsequent work, grounded in his theory of communicative action, he worked out in more detail both the historical thesis and the diagnosis of contemporary capitalist crises. *The Theory of Communicative Action* (1981) traces the conflict between the rationalization of world-views in early modernity, expressed for example in secularization and formal law and in the erosion of appeals to traditional authority, and, on the other hand, the restriction of this newly attained sphere, open in principle to rational debate, as market and bureaucratic structures come to dominate the modern world.

Thus where Max Weber had seen a single, however diverse, rationalization process working its way through economic, political, legal, and religious structures and world views, Habermas stresses the distinction between two kinds of rationalization process. He borrows and modifies the phenomenological philosopher Edmund Husserl's concept of the "lifeworld," the world as it immediately presents itself to us prior to philosophical or scientific analysis. For Habermas, the lifeworld is less a purely cognitive horizon than an environment made up both of attitudes and of practices – a realm of informal culturally grounded understandings and mutual accommodations. In modernity, the systematization of world-views and the development of formal reasoning in the law and other spheres involve a rationalization of the lifeworld; the autonomous development of markets and bureaucratic systems represents what he called its "colonisation" (Habermas, 1981: vol. 2, 196). In other words, no sooner are human social arrangements opened up to rational discussion with a view to their modification than they are rigidified into the autonomous subsystems analyzed but not criticized by sociological systems theory. In Habermas's model, the "uncoupling" of autonomous market and administrative systems means that the lifeworld becomes "one subsystem among others." As Max Weber realized, these subsystems become like machines, running independently of their original sources in the moral and political structures of the lifeworld: "economic and bureaucratic spheres emerge in which social relations are regulated only by money and power" (Habermas, 1981: vol. 2, 154).

Habermas's reconstructive theory of communicative action includes an account of the changing institutional forms which it takes in Europe and North America from around the eighteenth century. This is a two-sided process. On the one hand, more and more areas of social life are prized out of traditional contexts and subjected to rational examination and argument. On the other hand, the expansion of markets and administrative structures leads to what Habermas calls the colonization or hollowing-out of the lifeworld by autonomous subsystems which are removed from rational evaluation, except within their own highly circumscribed terms. Examples of this process can be found in the attempts by welfare-state systems to extend legal regulation and monetary calculation right into the private sphere, at the cost of those traces of solidarity which remain; and solidarity, Habermas insists, is a resource which cannot be bought or constrained. More broadly, the differentiation, whose analysis goes back to Kant, of what he calls the "value-spheres" of science, morality and art facilitates their individual development, but at the cost of their estrangement from each other and from culture as a whole.

Habermas thus follows the tradition of analysis developed by Marx in his theory of alienation, by Max Weber in terms of rationalization and disenchantment (*Entzauberung*), and in Georg Lukács's concept of reification (*Verdinglichung*). In the early critical theorists' critique of instrumental rationality as something inevitably linked to domination, all these motifs come together (Habermas, 1981: vol. I, 144). In Habermas's view, however, all these models are insufficiently complex. Marx focuses too one-sidedly on the rationalization of the forces and relations of material production; Max Weber sees societal rationalization too narrowly in terms of patterns of individual purposive-rational action. One needs instead to differentiate between "the rationalization of action orientations and lifeworld structures" and "the expansion of the 'rationality,' that is, complexity of action systems" (Habermas, 1981: vol. I, 145). Habermas addresses, in other words, the big question of whether we could have had, or could now have, modernity without the less attractive features of capitalism and the bureaucratic nation-state. More tentatively, in *Between Facts and Norms* (1992) and in more recent volumes of essays, he reformulated elements of his model of advanced capitalist crisis in the language of his more recent theories (Habermas, 1992: 384–387).

I have focused in this discussion on the theoretical model which Habermas developed from the mid-1970s. His earlier work, however, which he now tends to treat somewhat dismissively, also remains in my view of enormous richness and importance. This is particularly true of *Knowledge and Human Interests* (1968), which I shall briefly discuss below (see also Müller-Doohm, 2000), but also of much of the rest of his extremely creative oeuvre. In some ways, indeed, his more recent work on the state and the public sphere returns to concerns which he had addressed at the beginning of his career and which continue to be central to his thinking.

If Habermas had a single target of attack in his early work, it might best be termed technocratic politics. This he attacked from two directions. One was his influential analysis of the rise and fall of the bourgeois public sphere (Habermas, 1962). The partially realized ideal of independent discussion and rational critique of public affairs which developed in the eighteenth century in Europe and North America mutates in the twentieth century, Habermas argued, into a conception of public opinion as something to be measured and manipulated. These operations in turn relied heavily on an ideology and practice of positivistic social science which Habermas (1963, 1968) subjected to a philosophical and historical critique; this critique finally underpinned his conception of critical social theory oriented to the critique of ideology.

What might form the basis of this model of critical social science? Habermas (1963) was initially attracted by the idea of conceiving it as an empirically oriented and falsifiable philosophy of history with an emancipatory purpose. He then defined it in more methodological terms as a critical project combining causal explanation and hermeneutic understanding – a model based on his rather controversial reading of Freudian psychoanalysis as involving, in essence, the removal of causal obstacles to self-understanding and thus resulting in the patient's liberation from avoidable constraints (Habermas, 1968). Once we know the real reason, for example, why we are afraid of spiders which we know at some level to be harmless, a reason typically located in a traumatic childhood experience, we are on the way to overcoming our fear. The same sort of model, Habermas argued, underlay the Marxist critique of ideology: once we understand *why* capitalism appears, misleadingly, as a just system based on agreement and contract, and is presented as such by bourgeois political economy, the way is open to a more accurate and empowering understanding of it as an avoidable system of social exploitation. In other words, Freudian and Marxian thought can be understood as paradigms of critical social science, oriented by and to an interest in emancipation.

Habermas (1973b) then came to feel that the trichotomy of empirical, hermeneutic, and critical sciences was too simplistic, especially in that reflection in the philosophical sense did not necessarily mean emancipation in practice. The truth, in other words, does not necessarily make us free, in the absence of other conditions (this is also, incidentally, the basis of the more orthodox critique of his version of psychoanalysis). And some of the best historical sociology, for example, although it may aid reflection in the first sense, does not really fit Habermas's model of emancipatory science. In place of this model, he developed in the 1970s a more modest account of reconstructive science exemplified, as noted earlier, by his emergent theory of communicative action and his theory of discourse ethics.

Just as some linguistic theories reconstruct in formal terms our competence as speakers, the theory of communicative action provides a theoretical reconstruction of a practice in which we regularly engage, whether or not we reflect explicitly and theoretically on it. As he put it in an interview (Habermas, 1991: 111), he does not say that people *want* to act communicatively, but that *they have to*...When parents bring up their children, when the living generations appropriate the transmitted wisdom of preceding generations, when individuals and groups cooperate, that is, get along with one another without the costly recourse to violence, they all have to act communicatively. There are elementary social functions that can only be satisfied by means of communicative action.

As we saw earlier, Habermas (1981) outlined this model in reference both to the traditions of social theory and to the history of Western modernity. He draws in particular on George Herbert Mead's analysis of self-other relations in interaction, and Durkheim's theorization of intersubjectivity and social solidarity in relation to the secularization of religion, what Habermas calls the "linguistification of the sacred," to illustrate some of the social-theoretical roots of his own model of communicative action. Habermas goes on to show how Max Weber, who, in *The Protestant Ethic and the "Spirit" of Capitalism* and in his work as a whole described the rationalization of the lifeworld in early modernity, also offered an account, complementary to that of Marx, of the re-confinement of human beings in an increasingly rigid and bureaucratized world. As Habermas shows, systematizing the central theme of Western Marxism expressed in Georg Lukács's concept of reification, markets and bureaucratic power relations combine, in varying configurations, to reduce individuals' freedom to act both as individuals and collectively. This means, incidentally, that the postmodern critique of modernity is fundamentally misconceived, since it takes as essential to modernity features found indeed in the capitalist form which it took, but logically separable from it. The task of critical theory, then, is to explore alternative historical and present-day possibilities (Habermas, 1981: vol. 2, 374–403).

Shortly after the publication of *The Theory of Communicative Action*, Habermas returned in his writing to the theme of morality which had concerned him in his theory of social evolution and to systematize the ethical principles which underlay that historical model. The American developmental psychologist Lawrence Kohlberg had traced the advance of children's moral reasoning to what Habermas called a post-conventional stage at which the question of the validity of (often conflicting) moral principles is explicitly addressed. At this point, Habermas argues, ordinary moral reasoning overlaps with philosophical ethics, and this is the situation which confronts us in the contemporary world, in which, as Max Weber put it, mutually opposed "gods and demons" compete for our allegiance. But where Weber leaves us impaled on these existential dilemmas, with nothing to guide us except the imperative to choose in an authentic manner, Habermas insists that one can give compelling reasons in moral argumentation, just as one can in matters of fact.

Once again, it is an ideally informed consensus which would conclusively underwrite, and the more or less conscious pursuit of such a consensus which in practice underwrites our judgments about justice and, to some extent, even our conceptions of the good. Post-conventional moral reasoning is inevitably a matter of dialogue or discourse, in which principles are justified if they can or could find, for the moment at least, the assent of all those who are or might be affected by them. More formally, according to the principle which Habermas labels U, a norm is morally right if "*All* affected can accept the consequences and the side effects its *general* observance can be anticipated to have for the satisfaction of *everyone's* interests (and these consequences are preferred to those of known alternatives)" (Habermas, 1983: 65).

There are strong echoes here, of course, of the Kantian notion of the universalizability of moral judgments, and of John Rawls's modified utilitarian theory of justice, in which inequalities are justified if they are to the benefit of the worst off, but in Habermas's model we also have to choose between alternative bases of moral judgment as well as between alternative applications of them. The same goes, Habermas argues, for the legal principles which abut onto moral ones. Precisely because there are substantial disagreements between alternative legal principles as well as over their interpretation, only the dialogue institutionalized in a functioning democratic state can legitimate the choice between these principles. In Habermas's slogan, "no rational law without democracy," Habermas's moral universalism is not then, the arrogant gesture which it sometimes appears to be in the accounts of post-modern or antifoundationalist critics. It is, rather, intended as the only possible response to a situation of radical diversity of views and in which it is practically essential to be able to offer universalistic defenses of fundamental principles:

> the concrete, particular moralities rooted in specific forms of life are only acceptable today if they have a universalistic kernel. For they must if it comes down to it be able to prevent something like the Shoah happening again. Otherwise they are worth nothing and cannot be justified (Dews, 1986, 2nd edn 1992: 226).

At the same time, however, it is not clear how *much* discussion a discourse ethics commits us to, nor how this might best be institutionalized. Communicative action, Habermas insists, is not the same as argumentation; the latter term denotes specific forms of communication: "islands in the sea of praxis," but the expansion of communicative action at the expense of more authoritarian traditions forms a necessary basis for argumentative discourse to become more widespread. As he put it in another recent work, "What seems to me essential to the degree of liberality of a society is the extent to which its patterns of socialization and its institutions, its political culture, and in general its identity-guaranteeing traditions and everyday practices express a non-coercive form of ethical life in which autonomous morality can be embodied and can take on concrete shape" (Habermas, 1991b: 171). Habermas points to the variety of forums in modern societies, ranging from academic symposia to TV debates and parliamentary assemblies, in which specific moral and ethical issues are argued out.

Discourse ethics does not offer, then, a practical solution to concrete moral or ethical issues, so much as a set of recommended practices within which such solutions may be pursued (Habermas, 1983: 103; Outhwaite, 2009). In this of course it resembles democratic theory, which it has also complemented and enriched – notably in its contribution to the conception of deliberative democracy. This to some extent resolves the issue raised in Germany by Albrecht Wellmer and in the US by a number of critics as to whether discourse ethics should be understood more in relation to politics and the public sphere than in relation to morality in a strict sense. His discourse ethic is, Habermas concedes, necessarily somewhat formal. It is based on a procedure, that of practical discourse, rather than specific ethical prescriptions (Habermas, 1983: 103). It draws a sharp distinction between questions of justice and questions of the "good life"; the latter can only be addressed in the context of diverse cultures or forms of life or of individual life-projects (Habermas, 1983: 108). On the other hand, a universalistic morality can bridge the division between morality and law, in that both are based, in varying ways, on a relation to discourse. In *Between Facts and Norms*, Habermas developed the implications of this model for a theory of law and the democratic state.

Although law and morality are distinct, both moral and legal norms depend implicitly on what Habermas calls the discourse principle, that those affected by them could agree to them as participants in a rational discourse (Habermas, 1992: 107). Modified to fit the three contexts of morality, law, and political democracy, the intuition embodied in the discourse principle, which aims "to explain the point of view from which norms of action can be *impartially justified*" (Habermas, 1992: 108–109) underpins the structural relations between them.

Law, especially constitutional law, is crucial for Habermas's argument because it bridges the gap between moral reasoning on the one hand, which can only exhort and rebuke those who ignore it, and political decision-making on the other, which is always at risk of arbitrariness, even when it is democratically legitimated:

> In less complex societies, socially integrating force inheres in the ethos of a form of life, inasmuch as this integral ethical life binds all the components of the lifeworld together, attuning concrete duties to institutions and linking them with motivations. Under conditions of high complexity, moral contents can spread throughout a society along the channels of legal regulation. (Habermas, 1992: 118)

For Habermas, of course, democracy does not simply mean universal suffrage and majority rule. Although, for example, he accepts the legitimacy of majority voting in a system necessarily operating under time constraints, he insists that procedural rules of this kind must themselves be discursively justified. Habermas is at least as much concerned for the extent and quality of public discussion of political issues as for the details of institutional arrangements. In other words, he has returned to issues of the public sphere and public opinion which were the object of one of his first studies, but now armed with a much more substantial normative and empirical theory of the state:

> The rational quality of political legislation does not depend only on how elected majorities and protected minorities work within the parliaments. It depends also on the level of participation and education, on the degrees of information and the precision with which controversial issues are articulated – in short, on the discursive character of non-institutionalized opinion formation in the political public sphere. (Habermas, 1992: 570; cf. Habermas, 1988: 249)

Anyone advancing a theory of the state in the contemporary world has of course to confront issues of globalization and what Habermas (1998) has termed the "postnational constellation." While Habermas's formal model of the democratic constitutional state (*Rechtsstaat*) was cast very much in traditional nation-state terms, his more informal reflections in interviews and occasional articles have focused on the challenges to state sovereignty posed not simply by the fact of globalization but also by the normative intuitions captured by the notion of a global public opinion or global civil society and political concepts of "cosmopolitan democracy" or "world domestic politics." As Habermas noted, a crucial question is "whether political communities can construct a *collective identity* beyond the limits of a nation and thereby satisfy the legitimacy conditions of a postnational democracy" (Habermas, 1998: 136). His tentative answer is that a European federal state, developing a sense of solidarity on the basis of a common European history, albeit one of tension and division, may serve as a testing ground and a basis for more ambitious experiments in cosmopolitan democracy, just as Europe earlier pioneered a nation-state structure and in large part imposed it on the rest of the world. "Europe's second chance" (Habermas, 1996) should not of course take the form of neocolonial arrogance, but nor should it be missed in a "postcolonial regression into Eurocentrism" (Habermas, 1998: 9).

In the 1980s and 1990s, then, Habermas had developed the implications of his theory of communicative action in three broadly distinct domains. First, he advanced what is generally called a "discourse ethics" or, more precisely, a "discourse theory of morality," in *Moral Consciousness and Communicative Action* (1983), *Justification and Application* (1991) and a number of essays. Second, in the critical history of philosophy, his critique of post-structuralism in *The Philosophical Discourse of Modernity*, based on a series of lectures, was published in 1985, *Postmetaphysical Thinking* in 1988 and *Texte und Kontexte* in 1991. Third, he developed his moral theory into a theory of politics, law and the democratic state, with a series of lectures on "Law and Morality" delivered in 1986, *Between Facts and Norms* (1992), and the essays published as *The Inclusion of the Other* (1996).

In the twenty-first century, Habermas turned his attention to ethical issues concerning science and religion, from essentially two angles. The first, addressed in *The Future of Human Nature* (2001), concerned the implications of genetic engineering for human self-understanding and what forms of intervention we consider legitimate. As he noted in a speech in the autumn of 2001, these issues had "led to a clash between the spokespersons of institutionalized science and those of the churches." By then, however, "the tension between secular society and religion [had] exploded in an entirely different way" (Habermas, 2003: 101). The terrorist attacks on New York and Washington posed these issues more urgently, linking them to questions of racist disparagement of ethnic and religious minorities in Europe and North America. Habermas continued however to pose the issues in terms of a conflict between secular and often scientist "naturalism" and traditional religion. He returned, for example, to questions he had debated with John Rawls about the "translation" of religiously grounded positions into secular political debate, and about the "inspiring, even indispensable semantic contents" to be found in religious language. A published conversation with the intellectual dogmatist Cardinal Ratzinger attracted renewed attention when he became Pope Benedict XVI (Habermas and Ratzinger, 2005).

Habermas has tended to frame these issues in the concept (which he admits is controversial) of "post-secular society," defined as one "which adapts to the fact that religious communities continue to exist in a context of ongoing secularization" (Habermas, 2005: 104). Here the concept of the post-secular is defined in quite a weak sense, but there seems to be lurking a stronger one in which religious ideas have a persisting and indispensable role. This sets limits of principle to secularization and thereby calls into question the secularizing project, rather as the postmetaphysical suggests the need to give up on certain metaphysical projects (see Outhwaite, 2009, chapter 10 and the literature referred to there). In a recent volume of interviews (Funken, 2008: 185), Habermas insists however that he has grown "old, but not pious," and Axel Honneth suggests in the same volume that this direction in Habermas's thinking is motivated by a "sociological realism" about the continued social importance of religion rather than any shift in his personal convictions (Funken, 2008: 42).

He has also continued to argue repeatedly for European integration in what he calls the "postnational constellation" of economic and political globalization and regional integration, and in particular for a European constitution. As Müller-Doohm (2010) notes, his over twenty substantial essays and speeches on this topic since the beginning of the 1980s represent his fullest contribution to any of the political themes which he has addressed in the course of his life. This in part reflects the ongoing character of the European debates, but also the importance he now attaches to a theme which had been prominent in political discussion since the 1950s but had not particularly interested him until much later. The reasons seem to be a combination of practical concerns, that Europe should be able to make a contribution to global discussions and that the European Union should not become a fortress of economic neoliberalism, and more fundamental democratic principles that those affected by political decisions should be able to participate in them at the appropriate levels, which are increasingly those of large regions such as Europe and of the world as a whole. "Governance beyond the national state" becomes an urgent necessity, as does the transcendence of nationally structured public spheres in larger and more cosmopolitan frameworks. Habermas's support of the notion of "constitutional patriotism" makes particular sense at the European level, where it does not seem credible to say that there exists a European "people" as there might be a German or French people, but where the notion of a diverse political community living together under an agreed democratic constitutional framework does not seem an unrealistic aspiration, whether or not it can be said to exist in the European Union as presently constituted (see, for example, Outhwaite, 2010).

On the specific issue of a constitution for the European Union, Habermas's arguments parallel those which he had made at the time of German unification, that this should take place through a formal constitutional process and not, as in the end happened in Germany, through the mere "accession" of the former East German territories to the Federal Republic. The constitutional fudge may have been quicker and easier, especially for a Federal Chancellor in a hurry, but it swept under the carpet issues which no doubt should have been argued through at the time and which continue to plague Germany today in the form of East–West material inequalities and a persisting sense of estrangement between the two parts of the country often described as the "wall in the head."

Habermas was on the losing side on this issue, and the continuing shambles around the ratification of the EU's constitutional treaty may suggest that it would have been better not to attempt to create a formal constitution. (For the two sides of the debate, see the contributions by Habermas and Philippe Schmitter in Rogowski and Turner 2006.) Yet the Constitutional Convention may seem in retrospect to have been a worthwhile exercise in deliberative democracy, even if it did not produce as neat (or brief) a result as the Philadelphia meeting which gave birth to the US constitution. And whether or not the European Union becomes a beacon of cosmopolitan governance (Benhabib, 2006), Habermas's notion of a "postnational constellation" seems a valuable one (see Outhwaite, 2009).

IMPACT

Habermas came to be recognized relatively early in Germany as a major social and political theorist. His standing as a political commentator was helped perhaps by his prominent role in 1968 and the attacks he suffered from both sides of the barricades. Outside the country, he was slower to attract a substantial following, in *milieux* largely ignorant of the Frankfurt School tradition and its characteristic concerns and modes of approach. Even with the turn to social theory and more politicized social science in the UK in the early 1970s, Habermas was perhaps not Marxist enough for the orthodox, who tended to favor structuralist variants of Marxism, and too Marxist or "theoretical" for others. His impact in the UK and France, for example, came largely as a result of growing interest in his work in the more diverse and pluralistic intellectual milieu of the US.

In the 1980s and 1990s, however, and despite the somewhat forbidding character of many of his books, his reputation in the English-speaking world grew rapidly. The German weekly newspaper *Die Zeit* referred to him, in a front-page headline celebrating his birthday, as a "world power." As noted above, Habermas's work has been influential in a whole range of fields, and has become one of the principal reference points for much discussion both in social theory and, for example, moral philosophy, legal theory, and theories of international relations. Historians and theorists of culture have also increasingly been influenced by his conception of the public sphere and other elements of his thought (see Calhoun, 1992). Critical theory in the broadest sense has been carried on by contemporaries such as Albrecht Wellmer and a third generation of thinkers including Axel Honneth, Hans Joas, Thomas McCarthy and Seyla Benhabib – all of whom, in different ways, have responded to issues posed by post-structuralist, postmodernist and feminist theory and shown how Habermas's approach can be usefully developed and extended. Habermas's concern with historical sociology and theorizing states and social movements has been carried forward by, for example, Claus Offe and Klaus Eder. In a more speculative vein, Ulrich Beck's influential analysis of modernity in terms of risk again owes a great deal to Habermas. Finally, his discourse ethics and his more recent theorizing about law and the state have attracted enormous interest in areas of analytic moral and legal philosophy previously untouched by Habermasian concerns. This is currently one of the most active areas of research, and to some extent practical ethical and legal argument, which draw directly on Habermas's work, and Habermas has himself been working very substantially in this field.

His opposition to post-structuralism and post-modernism and his occasional polemics with the French philosopher Jean-François Lyotard and others have marked out one of the systematic lines of division in contemporary social theory, concretized to some extent in positions taken in relation to the Enlightenment. For Habermas, this should essentially be seen as a project, incomplete and ambiguous in many ways but no less worthwhile than when it was first articulated in the seventeenth and eighteenth century. Thus while he accepts some of what has been said by postmodernists and others about a certain rigidity in Enlightenment and, more broadly, liberal thinking – as indicated in the title of one of his recent volumes, "The Inclusion of the Other" (Habermas, 1996) – he remains committed to these values and to a universalistic mode of thought and argumentation; again not despite, but precisely because of, the enormous diversity of values and cognitive orientations found in modern societies.

The rise of social theory since the beginning of the 1970s, and more particularly in the 1990s, as a relatively distinct domain of activity and a source of inspiration to the social sciences as a whole has also been due in considerable part to Habermas's work. He has always been hard to place in disciplinary terms, working on the borders of social theory and philosophy, and always willing to venture into new fields such as the analysis of language or law as required by the development of his own work. In short, he has made it possible both to see the contemporary world differently, and to rethink the relations between theories in the social sciences which are at least one of our main resources in understanding this world.

Assessment

Will people still be reading Habermas at the end of the twenty-first century? My feeling is that they should be, for several reasons. First, and irrespective of the direction to be taken by social theory in the current century, Habermas's work documents, more clearly perhaps than that of any other contemporary thinker, the attempt to revitalize the classic propositions of Western Marxism with the aid of some very diverse themes of mid to late twentieth-century social theory. As such, he will surely attract attention from historians of thought as someone who attempted, in the most ambitious theoretical terms, to bring together some at least of the dominant theoretical paradigms of the age and to confront some of its central problems.

The implicit parallel with Hegel's idea of philosophy's mission to grasp "its time" in thought is deliberate: Habermas's mode of theorizing, even when he seems at his most Kantian and formalistic, is to trace a rational line of development through a set of apparently opposed frameworks. This is nowhere clearer than when he attempts, however cautiously and tentatively, to bridge the gaps between empirical and normative issues. As we have seen, for example, his thoroughgoing critique of positivism and ethical subjectivism feeds into an approach to legal and democratic theory which transcends conventional separations between, on the one hand, so-called positive law, where what counts is merely that it has been enacted according to due process, and, on the other hand, an individualistic morality. These are in turn internally related, he argues, to representative democracy and public communication.

Whether or not Habermas is right that one can formally reconstruct theories of all these domains on the basis of an analysis of the preconditions of communication, his basic notion that communication with others is only meaningful if it is driven by the pursuit of rational agreement, and that such agreement is the only legitimate basis of morality and political authority in the modern world, would be widely shared. And if one of the problems of much contemporary social and political theory is that it has little to say about the practical dilemmas with which we are confronted, Habermas offers at least the outlines of a practical political theory as well as a theory of politics.

This is not to say that Habermas will have anything like the massive impact which Hegel exercised over his contemporaries and immediate successors; no present-day thinker could possibly do this in an intellectual world which has become as disaggregated and pluralistic as our own. On the other hand, if, as I suspect, capitalist market economies and capitalist and state bureaucracies continue to dominate the more developed parts of the world in the twenty-first century, critiques of capitalism which still owe much to Marx will no doubt retain their appeal. Habermas was surely right to argue that an adequate theory of the contemporary world must attend to the distinctiveness of advanced capitalism and, in particular, of the state forms with which it coexists and to the issues of culture and identity to which critical theory has been more sensitive than most other Marxist and non-Marxist traditions in social theory. With the eclipse, in the 1980s and 1990s, of more orthodox variants of Marxism, and a certain fusion of horizons between Marxist and non-Marxist approaches in social theory, Habermas's creative synthesis may seem more attractive than ever.

As I noted earlier, Habermas has continued in his more recent works his analysis of the public sphere and of crisis tendencies in contemporary societies, first addressed in his books of 1962 and 1973. In relation to the public sphere, he has stressed the interplay of public communication at many different levels and the fact that public spheres in modern societies are increasingly mediated and virtual. What this might mean in practice for a political theory of communicative democracy is an issue which clearly requires further exploration. We also badly need a more developed theory of economic, social, and political crises in modern societies which Habermas is extremely well placed to provide.

What do we *not* get from Habermas? Not much about economics or about culture. These were the two areas which earlier critical theory had attempted to relate – no doubt somewhat too fast and easily, as Axel Honneth (1985) has argued. Habermas's attempt to fill out the dimension of social and political theory restores the center that was missing from much of the work of the first generation of critical theorists, but in a way which leaves the analysis of global political economy and contemporary cultural processes, and the crucial interrelations between them, to others. To say that Habermas has not done this, however, is not to say that it cannot be done within a recognizably Habermasian framework, and a good deal of recent work in international relations theory has taken this direction. His own work and that of others using a Habermasian approach has also been particularly illuminating in relation to recent discussion of the post-1989 world; thinkers concerned with, for example, the political consequences of globalization for our conceptions of ethics, democracy, citizenship, and (post-) national identity have drawn significantly on Habermas's insights. Habermas would, I think, be happy to feel that he had set up a set of frameworks for use both by himself and by others.

Reader's Guide to Jurgen Habermas

Two recent short introductions to Habermas's thought are Andrew Edgar's (2006) *Habermas: The Key Concepts* and J. Gordon Finlayson's (2005) *Habermas: A Very Short Introduction*. An earlier book, with a sociological focus that remains useful is Michael Pusey's (1987) *Jürgen Habermas*. Erik O. Eriksen and Jarle Weigård's *Understanding Habermas: Communicative Action and Deliberative Democracy* is also a good entry point into Habermas's work. For more detail, see William Outhwaite, *Habermas* or Jane Braaten, *Habermas's Critical Theory of Society*. Thomas McCarthy's *The Critical Theory of Jürgen Habermas* remains an outstanding guide to his earlier writing.

There are two easy ways into Habermas's work. One is via readers, such as William Outhwaite, *The Habermas Reader* or, in North America, Steven Seidman, *Jürgen Habermas on Society and Politics*. The other is via volumes of interviews, such as *Jürgen Habermas: Autonomy and Solidarity*, edited by Peter Dews, or *The Past as Future*.

Among the best books on specific aspects of Habermas's work are Robert Holub, *Jürgen Habermas: Critic in the Public Sphere*, Maeve Cook, *Language and Reason: A Study of Habermas's Pragmatics*, and Max Pensky, *The Ends of Solidarity. Discourse Theory in Ethics and Politics*. There are good critical discussions of Habermas in Stephen White, *The Cambridge Companion to Habermas* and Peter Dews, *Habermas: A Critical Reader*. Finally, readers of German are well served by the new *Habermas-Handbuch*, edited by Hauke Brunkhorst, Regina Keide and Cristina Lafont.

Bibliography

Writings of Jürgen Habermas

Page references in the text are to the most recent edition cited, and to English translations where these exist.

1953. Mit Heidegger gegen Heidegger denken. *Frankfurter Allgemeine Zeitung*, July 25, 1953. Reprinted in Habermas, 1971, pp. 67–75.

1961 (with L. von Friedeburg, C. Oehler, and F. Weltz). *Student und Politik*. Neuwied, Berlin: Luchterhand.

1962. *Strukturwandel der Öffentlichkeit*. Neuwied, Berlin (2nd edn Frankfurt: Suhrkamp, 1989; 1st edn, trans. T. Burger, *The Structural Transformation of the Public Sphere*. Cambridge: Polity, 1989).

1963. *Theorie und Praxis*. Neuwied, Berlin: Luchterhand (trans. J. Viertel, *Theory and Practice*. London: Heinemann, 1974).

1968a. *Technik und Wissenschaft als Ideologie*. Frankfurt: Suhrkamp (part trans. J. Shapiro, *Toward a Rational Society*. London: Heinemann, 1971).

1968b. *Erkenntnis und Interesse*. Frankfurt: Suhrkamp (trans. J. Shapiro, *Knowledge and Human Interests*. London: Heinemann, 1971).

1971. *Zur Logik der Sozialwissenschaften*, 2nd edn. Frankfurt: Suhrkamp (trans. S. W. Nicholsen and J. A. Stark, *On the Logic of the Social Sciences*. Cambridge: MIT Press, 1988).

1971. *Philosophisch–Politische Profile*. Frankfurt: Suhrkamp (part trans. F. G. Lawrence, *Philosophical–Political Profiles*. London: Heinemann, 1983).

1971 (with N. Luhmann). *Theorie der Gesellschaft oder Sozialtechnologie: Was Leistet die Systemforschung?* Frankfurt: Suhrkamp.

1973. *Legitimationsprobleme im Spätkapitalismus*. Frankfurt: Suhrkamp (trans. T. McCarthy, *Legitimation Crisis*. London: Heinemann, 1976).

1973. *Kultur und Kritik*. Frankfurt: Suhrkamp).

1974. The Public Sphere: An encyclopedia article. *New German Critique*, 3: 49–55.

1976. *Zur Rekonstruktion des historischen Materialismus*. Frankfurt: Suhrkamp (part trans. F. G. Lawrence, *Communication and the Evolution of Society*. Boston: Beacon Press, 1979).

1976 (ed.). *Stichworte zur "Geistigen Situation der Zeit"*. Frankfurt: Suhrkamp (trans. A. Buchwalter, *Observations on the Spiritual Situation of the Age*. Cambridge, MA: MIT Press, 1984).

1981. *Theorie des kommunikativen Handelns*, 2 vols. Frankfurt: Suhrkamp (trans. T. McCarthy, *Theory of Communicative Action*. London: Heinemann, 1984 and Cambridge: Polity, 1987).

1982. The entwinement of myth and enlightenment. *New German Critique*, 26: 13–20.

1982. Objektivismus in den Sozialwissenschaften. In *Zur Logik der Sozialwissenschaften*, 5th edn, p. 549.

1983. *Moralbewußtsein und kommunikatives Handeln*. Frankfurt: Suhrkamp (trans. C. Lenhardt and S. W. Nicholsen, *Moral Consciousness and Communicative Action*. Cambridge, MA: MIT Press, 1989).

1984. *Vorstudien and Ergänzungen zur Theorie des Kommunikativen Handelns*. Frankfurt: Suhrkamp.

1985. Modernity – An Incomplete Project. In H. Foster (ed.) *Postmodern Culture*. London: Pluto.

1985. *Die neue Unübersichtlichkeit*. Frankfurt: Suhrkamp (trans. S. W. Nicholsen, *The New Conservatism*. Cambridge: Polity, 1989).

1985. *Der Philosophische Diskurs der Moderne*. Frankfurt: Suhrkamp (trans. F. G. Lawrence, *The Philosophical Discourse of Modernity*. Cambridge: MIT Press, 1987).

1988. *Nachmetaphysisches Denken*. Frankfurt: Suhrkamp (trans. W. M. Hohengarten, *Postmetaphysical Thinking*. Cambridge: Polity, 1992).

1988. Law and Morality. *The Tanner Lectures on Human Values*, VIII: 217–219.

1990. *Die nachholende Revolution*. Frankfurt: Suhrkamp.

1991a. *Vergangenheit als Zukunft*, ed. M. Heller. Zürich: Pendo (2nd edn. Munich: Piper, 1993; trans. M. Pensky, *The Past as Future*. Lincoln: University of Nebraska Press, 1994).

1991b. *Erläuterungen zur Diskursethik*. Frankfurt: Suhrkamp (trans. C. Cronin, *Justification and Application*. Cambridge: MIT Press, 1993).

1992. *Texte und Kontexte*. Frankfurt: Suhrkamp.

1992. *Faktizität und Geltung*. Frankfurt: Suhrkamp (trans. W. Rehg, *Between Facts and Norms*. Cambridge: Polity, 1996).

1994. *The Past as Future*. Lincoln, University of Nebraska Press.

1996. *Die Einbeziehung des Anderen*. Frankfurt: Suhrkamp (trans. as *The Inclusion of the Other*. Cambridge: Polity, 1998).

1998. *Die Postnationale Konstellation. Politische Essays*. Frankfurt: Suhrkamp (trans. as *The Postnational Constellation. Political Essays*. Cambridge: Polity, 2007).

1998. *On the Pragmatics of Communication*, ed. M. Cooke. Cambridge: Polity.

1999. *Wahrheit und Rechtfertigung*. Frankfurt, Suhrkamp (trans. as *Truth and Justification*. Cambridge, Polity, 2003).

2001. *Die Zukunft der menschlichen Natur*. Frankfurt, Suhrkamp (trans. as *The Future of Human Nature*. Cambridge: Polity, 2003).

2001. *Glauben und Wissen. Friedenspreis des Deutschen Buchhandels.* Frankfurt: Suhrkamp. Reprinted in *The Future of Human Nature*, pp. 101–115.

2001. *Kommunikatives Handeln und detranszendentalisierte Vernunft.* Stuttgart: Reklam.

2001. *Zeit der Übergänge.* Frankfurt: Suhrkamp.

2003. *Zeitdiagnosen. Zwölf Essays 1980–2001.* Frankfurt: Suhrkamp.

2004. *Der gespaltene Westen.* Frankfurt: Suhrkamp (trans. as *The Divided West.* Cambridge: Polity, 2006).

2005. *Zwischen Naturalismus und Religion.* Frankfurt: Suhrkamp (trans. as *Between Naturalism and Religion.* Cambridge: Polity, 2008).

2005 (with J. Ratzinger). *The Dialectics of Secularization. Reason and Religion.* San Francisco, CA: Ignatius Press.

2006. Why Europe needs a constitution. In Ralf Rogowski and Charles Turner (eds) *The Shape of the New Europe.* New York: Cambridge University Press, pp. 25–45

2007. Die Dialektik der Säkularisierung. *Blätter für deutsche und internationale Politik,* 4: 33–46.

2008. *Ach, Europa.* Frankfurt: Suhrkamp (trans. as *Europe: The Faltering Project.* Cambridge: Polity, 2009.)

Further Reading

Adorno, T. W. (1966) *Negative Dialektik*; trans. E. B. Ashton, *Negative Dialectics.* London: Routledge, 1973.

Adorno, T. W. *et al.* (1969) *Der Positivismusstreit in der deutschen Soziologie.* Neuwied (trans. Glyn Adey, *The Positivist Dispute in German Sociology.* London: Heinemann, 1976).

Anderson, P. (1976) *Considerations on Western Marxism.* London: New Left Books.

Benhabib, S. (2006) *Another Cosmopolitanism.* New York: Oxford University Press.

Bottomore, T. (1984) *The Frankfurt School.* Chichester: Ellis Horwood.

Braaten, J. (1991) *Habermas's Critical Theory of Society.* Albany: SUNY Press.

Brunkhorst, H., Kreide, R., and Lafont, C. (eds) (2009) *Habermas-Handbuch: Leben – Werk – Wirkung.* Stuttgart and Weimar: Metzler.

Calhoun, C. (ed.) (1992) *Habermas and the Public Sphere.* Cambridge: MIT Press.

Cooke, M. (1994) *Language and Reason: A Study of Habermas's Pragmatics.* Cambridge, MA: MIT Press.

Cooke, M. (2000) Critical theory and religion. In D. Z. Phillips and T. Tessin (eds) *Philosophy of Religion in the Twenty-First Century.* London: Palgrave, pp. 211–243.

Cooke, M. (2006) *Re-Presenting the Good Society.* Cambridge, MA: MIT Press.

Cooke, M. (2006) Salvaging and secularizing the semantic contents of religion: the limitations of Habermas's postmetaphysical proposal. *International Journal for the Philosophy of Religion,* 60: 187–207.

Cooke, M. (2006) Säkulare Ubersetzung oder Postsäkulare Argumentation? Habermas über Religion in der demokratischen Offentlichkeit. In R. Langthatler and H. Nagl-Docekal (eds), *Jürgen Habermas über Religion.* Vienna and Berlin: Oldenbourg, pp. 342–366.

Dews, P. (ed.) (1986) *Habermas: Autonomy and Solidarity.* London: Verso (2nd edn 1992).

Dews, P. (1987) *Logics of Disintegration: Post-Structuralist Thought and the Claims of Critical Theory.* London: Verso.

Dews, P. (ed.) (1999) *Habermas: A Critical Reader.* Oxford: Blackwell.

Eder, Klaus (2002) Europäische Säkularisierung – ein Sonderweg in die postsäkulare Gesellschaft. *Berliner Journal für Soziologie,* 3: 343.

Edgar, E. (2005) *The Philosophy of Habermas*. London: Acumen.

Edgar, E. (2006) *Habermas: The Key Concepts*. London: Routledge.

Eriksen, E. O. and Weigord, J. (2003) *Understanding Habermas: Communicative Action and Deliberative Democracy*. London: Continuum.

Finlayson, J. G. (2000) Modernity and Morality in Habermas's Discourse Ethics. *Inquiry*, 43(3): 319–340.

Finlayson, J. G. (2005) *Habermas: A Very Short Introduction*. Oxford: Oxford University Press.

Funken, M. (ed.) (2008) *Über Habermas: Gespräche mit Zeitgenossen*. Darmstadt: Wissenschaftliche Buchgesellschaft.

Harrington, A. (2007) Habermas and the post-secular society. *European Journal of Social Theory*, 10(4), November: 547.

Holub, R. C. (1991) *Jürgen Habermas: Critic in the Public Sphere*. London: Routledge.

Honneth, A. (1985) *Kritik der Macht*. Frankfurt (trans. by K. Baynes as *Critique of Power*. Cambridge, MA: MIT Press, 1992).

Honneth, A. and Joas, H. (eds) (1991) *Kommunikatives Handeln*. Frankfurt: Suhrkamp (trans. J. Gaines and D. L. Jones, *Communicative Action*. Cambridge: Polity, 1991).

Honneth, A. *et al.* (eds) (1989) *Zwischenbetrachtungen: Im Prozess der Aufklärung*. Frankfurt: Suhrkamp (trans. W. Rehg, *Philosophical Interventions in the Unfinished Project of the Enlightenment*. Cambridge, MA: MIT Press, 1992; trans. B. Fultner, *Cultural-Political Interventions in the Unfinished Project of the Enlightenment*. Cambridge, MA: MIT Press, 1992).

Jaspers, K. (1966) *Wohin treibt die Bundesrepublik?* Munich: Piper.

Jay, M. (1973) *The Dialectical Imagination: A History of the Frankfurt School and the Institute of Social Research, 1923–1950*. London: Heinemann.

Marinopoulou, A. (2008) *The Concept of the Political in Max Horkheimer and Jürgen Habermas*. Athens: Nissos.

McCarthy, T. (1978) *The Critical Theory of Jürgen Habermas*. Cambridge: Polity.

Müller-Doohm, S. (ed.) (2000) *Das Interesse der Vernunft: Rückblicke auf das Werk von Jürgen Habermas seit "Erkenntnis und Interesse."* Frankfurt: Suhrkamp.

Müller-Doohm, S., Adorno, Theodor W., and Habermas, Jürgen (2005) Two ways of being a public intellectual: Sociological observations concerning the transformation of a social figure of modernity. *European Journal of Social Theory*, 8(3): 269–280.

Müller-Doohm, S. and Bird-Pollan, S. (2010) Nation-state, capitalism and democracy: Philosophical and political motifs in the thought of Jürgen Habermas. *European Journal of Social Theory*, 13(4): 443–457.

Outhwaite, W. (1994) *Habermas: A Critical Introduction*. Cambridge: Polity (2nd edn, 2009).

Outhwaite, W. (ed.) (1996) *The Habermas Reader*. Cambridge: Polity.

Outhwaite, W. (1998) Habermas: Modernity as reflection. In L. Marcus and B. Cheyette (eds) *Modernity, Culture and 'the Jew'*. Cambridge: Polity.

Outhwaite, W. (2009) Discourse Ethics. In Ruth Chadwick (ed.) *The Encyclopedia of Applied Ethics*. Abingdon: Elsevier (in press).

Outhwaite, W. (2010) Legality and Legitimacy in the European Union. In Chris Thornhill and Samantha Ashenden (eds) *Legality and Legitimacy: Normative and Sociological Approaches*. Baden-Baden: Nomos, pp. 279–290.

Pensky, M. (ed.) (1994) *The Past as Future*. Lincoln, University of Nebraska Press.

Pensky, M. (2008) *The Ends of Solidarity: Discourse Theory in Ethics and Politics*. Albany: State University of New York Press.

Pusey, M. (1987) *Jürgen Habermas*. London, Tavistock.

Schmitter, Phillipe C. (2006) Why constitutionalize the European Union. In Ralf Rogowski and Charles Turner (eds) *The Shape of the New Europe*. New York: Cambridge University Press, pp. 46–60.

Seidman, S. (ed.) (1989) *Jürgen Habermas on Society and Politics*. Boston, Beacon Press.

Susen, S. (2007) *The Foundations of the Social: Between Critical Theory and Reflexive Sociology*. Oxford, Bardwell.

Thompson, J. B. and Held, D. (eds) (1982) *Habermas: Critical Debates*. London: Macmillan.

Turner, Charles (2004) Jürgen Habermas: European or German? *European Journal of Political Theory*, 3(3): 293–314.

White, S. K. (ed.) (1994) *The Cambridge Companion to Habermas*. Cambridge: Cambridge University Press.

Wiggershaus, R. (1987) *Die Frankfurter Schule*. Munich (trans. Michel Robertson, *The Frankfurt School*. Cambridge: Polity, 1993).

Wingert, L. and Günther, K. (eds) (2001) *Die Öffentlichkeit der Vernunft und die Vernunft der Öffentlichkeit: Festschrift für Jürgen Habermas*. Frankfurt: Suhrkamp.

15

Pierre Bourdieu

CRAIG CALHOUN

The most influential and original French sociologist since Durkheim, Pierre Bourdieu was at once a leading theorist and an empirical researcher of extraordinarily broad interests and distinctive style. He analyzed labor markets in Algeria, symbolism in the calendar and the house of Kabyle peasants, marriage patterns in his native Béarn region of France, photography as an art form and hobby, museum goers and patterns of taste, modern universities, the rise of literature as a distinct field of endeavor, the reproduction of masculine domination, and the sources of misery and poverty amid the wealth of modern societies. Bourdieu insisted that theory and research are inseparable parts of one sociological enterprise.

In this Bourdieu was more like the great classical sociologists Emile Durkheim, Max Weber, and Karl Marx than are those who write commentaries about them without engaging empirical explanation at the same time. His work reflected a Durkheimian view that human life is all deeply social, Weber's concern for status hierarchies and the differentiation of spheres of social life, and Marx's emphasis on power, domination, and inequalities in the material conditions of life. Bourdieu also learned significantly from Marcel Mauss (who connected Durkheimian sociology to a more critical analysis of historical struggles), Erving Goffman (who approached social life as a matter of social dramas combining performance and communication), phenomenology (particularly through Maurice Merleau-Ponty but also ethnomethodology), structuralism (particularly through Claude Lévi-Strauss), and the history and philosophy of science through Gaston Bachelard, Georges Canguilhem, and Jules Vuillemin (shapers of a distinctive French analysis of the historical character of epistemology – the production and validation of knowledge). Of all Bourdieu's famous contemporaries the one with whom his work has the most affinity is probably Michel Foucault, a friend from his student days and throughout his life.

The Wiley-Blackwell Companion to Major Social Theorists, First Edition.
Edited by George Ritzer and Jeffrey Stepnisky.
© 2011 Blackwell Publishing Ltd. Published 2011 by Blackwell Publishing Ltd.

Bourdieu's most original contributions to sociological theory center on a conceptual framework for bridging the divide between (a) structural theorists like Durkheim, who emphasized that social facts are "external, enduring, and coercive," simply part of objective reality and (b) interactionist or constructivist theorists like George Herbert Mead who focused on subjective perceptions and the way social relations are constructed out of individual action and communication. In line with this approach, he urged sociologists to be "reflexive," to study and analyze the conditions of their own work and how these might shape their perception and even their theories.[1]

Taking Games Seriously

A former rugby player, Bourdieu was drawn to the metaphor of games to convey his sense of social life. But by "game" he did not mean mere diversions or entertainments. He meant the serious athlete's sense of being passionately involved in play, engaged in a struggle with others and with our own limits, over stakes to which we are (at least for the moment) deeply committed. He meant intense competition. He meant for us to recall losing ourselves in the play of a game, caught in its flow in such a way that no matter how individualistically we struggle we are also constantly aware of being only part of something larger – not just a team, but also the game itself. It is worth knowing that rugby is one of the world's most physically intense games. When Bourdieu spoke of playing, he spoke of putting oneself on the line.[2]

Social life is like this, Bourdieu suggested, except that the stakes are bigger. It is always a struggle; it requires constant improvisation; yet it is organized according to an enduring structure. Bourdieu was inspired by the philosopher Ludwig Wittgenstein (1967) who saw language itself as a game since it is structured by rules but using it effectively requires more than just following the rules. Learning a language is constant training in how to improvise "play" in social interaction. The same goes for cultural participation more generally. Play is not simply a diversion from some more basic reality but a central part of the activity by which forms of life are constituted, reproduced, and sometimes transformed. No game can be understood simply by grasping the rules that define it. It requires not just following rules, but having a "sense" of the game, a sense of how to play.[3] This is a social sense, for it requires a constant awareness of and responsiveness to the play of one's opponent (and in some cases one's teammates). A good rugby (or soccer or basketball) player is constantly aware of the field as a whole, and anticipates the actions of teammates, knowing when to pass, when to try to break free. A good basketball player is not simply one who can shoot, but one who knows when to shoot. If sports metaphors don't clarify this for you, think of telling a joke or playing music. Timing is crucial.

This sense of timing is a product of what Bourdieu termed a "habitus," the capacity each player of a game has to improvise the next move, the next play, the next shot – and to do so with intuitive awareness of what other players are doing. We may be born with greater or lesser genetic potentials, but we are not born with a habitus. As the word suggests, this is something we acquire through repetition, like a habit, and something we know in our bodies not just our minds. A professional basketball player has shot a million free throws before he steps to the line. Some of these have come in practice sessions, designed to allow the player to work on technical skills free from the pressure and chance of a game. But the player's practical experience – and learning – also came in real games, in front of crowds, with the hope of victory and the fear of letting down his teammates on his mind. Whether he has developed a relaxed confidence in his shot and an ability to blot out the noise and waving hands of the arena is also a matter of previous experience. It is part of the player's habitus. And the difference between a great athlete and a mediocre also-ran is often not just physical ability but a hard-to-pin-down mix of confidence, concentration, and ability to rise to the occasion.

The confidence that defines greatness is largely learned, Bourdieu suggests. It is learned in a thousand earlier games. On playgrounds, in high school, and in college, basketball players imagine themselves to be Michael Jordan – but they also learn that they are not. They do not jump as high or float as long; their desperate shots miss when his amazingly often went it. Indeed, our very experience of struggling to do well teaches us to accept inequality in our societies. We internalize the experience of not succeeding and avoid those "games" but in some cases – like the "games" of success in school – the result may keep us away from good job options. The reasons some succeed and others don't may not be effort or innate ability but inequalities in the help we get from families. It is not just bank accounts that distinguish the middle class from the poor but often things like whether parents read with children and provide access to educational computer games. Kids with those advantages will tend to do better in school – but they may draw false conclusions that the middle-class kids are just naturally more talented or more self-disciplined.[4] We learn and incorporate into our habitus a sense of what we can "reasonably" expect – even at the level of gauging our chances for a relationship with a man or woman we like. Our desire for the stakes of the game ensures our commitment to it. But we do not invent the games by ourselves; they are the products of history, of social struggles and earlier improvisations, and of impositions by powerful actors with the capacity to say this, and not that, is the right way to make love, create a family, raise children.

To understand any social situation or interaction, Bourdieu suggested, we should ask what game (or games) the actors are playing. This means not just their individual strategies or what they think they are doing, but within what social framework they are pursuing their goals, what unconscious learning informs their actions, what constraints they face, and what others are doing. What is at stake in their play? The stakes determine what will count as winning or losing. The game may be literature, for example, and the players seek reputation and immortality (defined as inclusion in the canon of recognized great works). The game may be business, and the players seek wealth. It may be politics and they pursue power. The stakes of different games also shape the ways in which players who are sometimes competitors also cooperate – for example to make sure their game is respected. Precisely because they care about their literary reputations, therefore, authors of serious books are at pains to distinguish their field from "mere journalism" (Bourdieu, 1996).

Science too is a game, in this only partly metaphorical sense. It is strategic. It has winners and losers. It depends on specific sorts of resources and rules of play. And science has stakes, most notably, truth. Scientists do not pursue truth out of simple altruism. It is an interest, not a disinterest. Commitment to truth – and to the specifically scientific way of pursuing truth (e.g. by empirical research rather than waiting for divine inspiration) – defines the field of science. But the participants in this field do not simply share peacefully in truth; they struggle over it. They seek to control who gets hired in universities and research institutes, which projects get funded by national science foundations, which kinds of work are published in the most famous journals. They advance competing theories; they attempt to advance competing careers. This selfishness and competition is not all bad, according to Bourdieu (2004), because the field of science only allows people to succeed by advancing the truth. Expecting scientists – or anyone else – simply to be altruistic is bound to lead to disappointment and to a misunderstanding of the actual workings of science. Science achieves an effect that is in the general good – advancing truth – by harnessing the self-interests as well as the ideals of scientists. Science works as a field devoted to truth because it provides players with organized incentives for pursuing their rewards – their victories in the game – by discovering and communicating genuine knowledge. It also offers organized disincentives for lying, failure to use good research methods, or refusing to communicate one's discoveries.

The rules of each game are both constraints on the players and the ways in which players get things done. Players usually have to treat them as fixed and unchanging, but in fact they are historically produced. They have origins, and they can change, but most of the time they are reproduced. That is, they are used because that is how things get done, and so they become habitual; they seem necessary; they are even enforced by rulebooks. Think of basic language rules as an analogy: every time we speak we rely on grammar, syntax, and semantics. For example, we expect words to have the same meaning they did yesterday and before that. But there are changes. A computer did not always mean a machine; it previously meant a person who did computational work. A manuscript historically meant a handwritten text; now we use the term for a text printed by a computer. When we improvise actions, we respond both to the social and cultural structures in which we find ourselves and to our own previous experiences. We meet new needs mostly by trying new uses for actions we've tried before (like using an old word for a new computing machine). We are able to act only because we have learned from those experiences, but much of what we have learned is how to fit ourselves effectively into existing cultural practices. We are constrained not just by external limits, in other words, but by our own internalization of limits on what we imagine we can do. We cannot simply shed these limits, not only because they are deep within us, but also because they are part of our sense of how to play the game. In other words, they are part of the knowledge that enables us to play well, to improvise actions effectively, and maintain our commitment to the stakes of the game.

Bourdieu uses the concept of practice to identify the interdependence of structure and action. *Practice* is doing things, practical activity, which always reflects the combination of conscious and unconscious intentions and the interaction of actors with social and material conditions outside themselves. Bourdieu shows action to be always shaped by learning (habitus), social contexts (including fields), and structural conditions (including distributions of capital) as well as choice and creativity. Bourdieu emphasizes that it is an illusion to think of individual action as pure freedom and social structure as pure constraint. Social structure is internalized in what we learn from experience and thus how we generate action as well as an external matter of resources and obstacles. The "logic of practice" calls attention to two paradoxes: (1) doing anything depends on processes of which we are not usually conscious and do not usually rationally control (like the way we move our mouths to make sounds while speaking but also our choices of words and even when to speak); (2) individual actions appear as though they were consciously strategic even when they are not because they are given the effect of direction by the larger social field (as for example kids who go to elite colleges get elite friends and elite artistic tastes that turn out to help them in later careers even if they are not thinking much about how friends become social capital or artistic knowledge becomes cultural capital).[5]

The social structures that enable and constrain our action may seem unchanging, but they are not. What appear to be fixed structures in social life are (a) the product of historical action that creates them, (b) never completely finalized but always subject to either reinforcement or change, and (c) usually more reproduced than changed, even when people try to change them. Those with greater resources have greater capacity to make the structure serve their interests, but even those with minimal resources are usually drawn into reproducing the existing culture and social structure as their only ways of achieving anything and as defenses against various threats.

Bourdieu emphasizes reproduction, partly because he thinks that people often overestimate how easily structures change. Nonetheless, structures are incomplete; at one point Bourdieu ([1971]1991) describes all structures as in fact more or less advanced processes of "structuration" (an idea Anthony Giddens took up and made a cornerstone of his sociological theory). The other side of the coin is, of course, the ways in which tensions and internal contradictions create vulnerabilities to social structures. Bourdieu argues that most of the time, even when people seek change, the forces leading to reproduction are stronger.

Nonetheless, transformation sometimes takes place. Bourdieu's work reflects on four major examples. First, French colonialism and market capitalism disrupted traditional peasant life in Algeria, leading to both violent conflict and a different effort to create new structures. Second, late nineteenth-century authors created a literary field distinct from journalism, protected by its cultural prestige against direct reduction to market forces, and potential a source of intellectual critique of French society more generally.[6] Third, after the Second World War economic growth and the building of European welfare states were expected to bring a more egalitarian society in France. Instead, new forms of inequality arose. More students were able to go to secondary school, thus, but what grades they received, where they went, and what they studied became newly influential. It was harder to inherit social status directly, but family influences on how well children did in school and widespread use of that reinforced such distinctions made education more an agent of reproduction than of change (Bourdieu and Passeron, 1964, 1970). Fourth, in the 1990s the project of freeing market capitalism from state constraints encouraged it to colonize different social fields, reducing their autonomy and undermining social democracy. The second case showed a positive account of social change; the others (reflecting Bourdieu's critical orientation) showed either outright destruction, or the illusion of change in the face of powerful tendencies toward reproduction.

PERSON AND CAREER

Bourdieu was born in 1930 in a rural village in the mountainous Béarn region of Southwest France.[7] This is the rough French equivalent of coming from Appalachia or a remote part of Idaho. The regional dialect was strong and distinctive; the Béarnaise have resisted homogenizing efforts of the French state for generations. Both brilliant and hard-working, Bourdieu gained admission to a special, highly selective regional high school, then to one of Paris's most famous secondary schools, and finally to the École Normale Supérieure (ENS) – the most elite of the Parisian grandes écoles, in 1951. Simply gaining admission to the ENS was a guarantee of membership in France's intellectual power-elite. Students were treated as members of the civil service from the moment they entered, taught to think of themselves as what Bourdieu (1989) later termed "the state nobility." Some who started as outsiders simply assimilated; Bourdieu excelled and also resisted. So did his ENS contemporaries Jacques Derrida (philosopher and literary scholar, founder of "deconstruction") and Michel Foucault (intellectual historian and cultural theorist). All three became famous, but all three also challenged existing intellectual frameworks. Bourdieu's very accent marked him as an outsider in elite Parisian academic life and he resented the status hierarchy. Yet he was so famous that a popular film was made about him (Carles, 2001). When he died in 2001 France's leading newspapers delayed publication to run the story on the first page. Since his death, Bourdieu's work has grown even more influential around the world.

After completing his undergraduate education, Bourdieu briefly taught high school then was ordered to do his military service in the French colony of Algeria. Appointed to a desk job in the air force, he had the time to explore the country. He bought a Leica camera and a number of notebooks to record what he saw. The education was complicated, since Bourdieu had to learn both about Algerian culture and about French colonialism, the brutality and problems of which had not been openly admitted in France. He traveled all over Algeria, eventually writing a book on its different major cultures (Bourdieu, 1960[1958]). Bourdieu's formal education had been in philosophy, but in Algeria he remade himself as a self-taught ethnographer (Honneth, Kocyba, and Schwibs, 1986: 39). He learned to ask questions that would elicit deeper information than surface ideologies, to take copious notes and carefully watch the practices of everyday social life, agricultural production, household organization, and ritual. As an aid to his memory and analysis he took more than a thousand photographs. Bourdieu recorded – with an elegant realist style – ways of life and the sometimes abrupt changes they were undergoing – as in a picture of a veiled woman on a motorcycle or another in traditional dress before a store window showing Western clothes.

Bourdieu initially surveyed Algeria as a whole, but came to concentrate on the region known as Kabylia.[8] Kabyle is the Arabic word for tribe, and the Kabyle were Berber-speaking peasants seen as backward not only by the French but by Algeria's Arabic-speaking urban elite. They were doubly dominated. By itself anti-colonial revolution wouldn't fix this, even though it might get rid of a hated outside power. Kabylia resonated with Bourdieu's knowledge of his own home region, the Béarn, and the limited opportunities the French Revolution and centralizing modernization brought to it. This was a powerful influence as he came to learn how ritual, a sense of mutual obligations, and aspects of traditional culture permeated what were also economic relationships (but never just economic, a reduction at odds with Kabyle culture). He studied participation in the new cash economy advanced by colonial rule and economic development, and he studied both how this threatened and changed Kabyle society and how labor migrants moved between two worlds, using money earned in the cities to pay for weddings back home but feeling they did not fit fully either place (Bourdieu and Sayad, 1964). He studied the difficult situation of those who chose to work in the modern economy and found themselves transformed into its "underclass," not even able to gain the full status of proletarians because of the ethno-national biases of the French colonialists (Bourdieu, 1973; Bourdieu, Darbel, Rivet and Seibel, 1963). And during the time of his fieldwork, Bourdieu confronted the violent French repression of the Algerian struggle for independence. The bloody battle of Algiers was a formative experience for a generation of French intellectuals who saw their state betray what it had always claimed was a mission of liberation and civilization, revealing the sheer power that lay behind colonialism, despite its legitimation in terms of progress.[9]

When Bourdieu left Algeria, he received a fellowship to the Institute for Advanced Study in Princeton and followed it with a stay at the University of Pennsylvania. While in the US, he met the American sociologist Erving Goffman – another theoretically astute sociologist who refrained from abstract system building in favor of embedding theory in empirical practice. Goffman had begun to develop a sociology that followed Durkheim's interest in the moral order, but focused on the ways this was reproduced in interpersonal relations by individuals with their own strategic investments in action. Rather than treating individuals as either autonomous or simply socially constructed, for example, Goffman (1959) introduced the element of strategy by writing of the "presentation of self in everyday life." His point was similar to that Bourdieu would stress: to show the element of improvisation and adaptation, rather than simple rule-following, and to introduce agents as dynamic figures in the social order. Where Bourdieu's favorite metaphor was games, Goffman's was drama, but they shared the sense of social life as a performance that could be played better or worse, and which nearly always tended to the reproduction of social order even when individuals tried to make new and different things happen in their lives.

Goffman encouraged Bourdieu to take a position at the University of Pennsylvania, but Bourdieu felt that if he stayed in the US he would be unable to develop the kind of critical sociology he wanted to create.[10] It was not simply that he wanted to criticize France rather than the US, but that he wanted to benefit from inside knowledge while still achieving critical distance. This would present a challenge, but the challenge was itself a source of theoretical insight:

> In choosing to study the social world in which we are involved, we are obliged to confront, in dramatized form as it were, a certain number of fundamental epistemological problems, all related to the question of the difference between practical knowledge and scholarly knowledge, and particularly to the special difficulties involved first in breaking with inside experience and then in reconstituting the knowledge which has been obtained by means of this break. (Bourdieu, 1988: 1)

Bourdieu returned to France with a sense of the intellectual project that would guide his life's work. This was to grasp the material conditions people faced, the practical strategies they employed, the culture through which they understood their choices and the patterns and limits it imposed, and the ways in which people's pursuit of their own ends nonetheless tended to reproduce objective patterns which they did not choose and of which they might even be unaware.

This project was a profound intervention into Bourdieu's intellectual context. French intellectual life in the 1950s and 1960s produced two powerful but opposed perspectives in the human sciences: structuralism and existentialism. The former emphasized the formal patterns underlying all reality (extending ideas introduced to sociology by Durkheim and his followers); the latter stressed that meaning inhered in the individual experience of being in the world and especially in autonomous action. The two greatest and most influential figures in French intellectual life of the period were Claude Lévi-Strauss (the structuralist anthropologist) and Jean-Paul Sartre (the existentialist philosopher). Bourdieu's theoretical tastes were closer to Lévi-Strauss, but he saw both as one-sided. If existentialism greatly exaggerated the role of subjective choice, structuralism neglected agency. In a sense, Bourdieu developed an internal challenge to structuralism, incorporating much of its insight and intellectual approach but rejecting the tendency to describe social life in overly cognitive and overly static terms as a matter of following rules rather than engaging in strategic practice.

Bourdieu saw theory as best developed in the task of empirical analysis, and saw this as a practical challenge. Rather than applying a theory developed in advance and in the abstract, he brought his distinctive theoretical habitus to bear on a variety of analytic problems, and in the course of tackling each developed his theoretical resources further. The concepts developed in the course of such work could be transposed from one setting to another by means of analogy, and adapted to each. Theory, like the habitus in general, serves not as a fixed set of rules but as a characteristic mode of improvising (Brubaker, 1993). In an implicit critique of the dominance of philosophy over French social science, Bourdieu held that the real proof that a sociological project has value is to be demonstrated in its empirical findings, not in abstract system building.

Back in France Bourdieu took a position in the European Center for Historical Sociology headed by Raymond Aron, then France's leading sociologist. An important early supporter of Bourdieu's, Aron made him a deputy in the administration of the Center and helped him secure a teaching appointment in Section VI of the École Pratique des Hautes Études. Later Aron also helped Bourdieu secure the Ford Foundation funding that enabled the establishment of the Center for European Sociology. The two were never close collaborators, despite initial mutual respect, and they came into increasing conflict as Bourdieu became more critical of French higher education. Aron was a moderate conservative politically, and Bourdieu was aligned with the left. Perhaps more importantly, Aron was a defender of French academia and Bourdieu criticized its role in preserving class inequality (Bourdieu and Passeron, 1964). Things came to a head when student revolt broke out in 1968. Aron suggested that the problem lay primarily with the students and sought to limit – rather than expand – their involvement in the life of the university. Bourdieu was sympathetic to the students, though he thought them naively voluntaristic and inattentive to the deep structures that made for the reproduction of class inequality and the university as an institution (see Bourdieu and Passeron, 1970).[11]

Though Bourdieu's writings on the problems of French higher education influenced the student protests of the 1960s, he was not himself centrally involved in the activism. His approach to politics was more to intervene through producing new knowledge, with the hope that this would help to demystify the way institutions worked, revealing the limits to common justifications and the way in which power rather than simple merit shaped the distribution of opportunities. His views of the educational system reflected the disappointed idealism of one who had invested himself deeply in it, and owed much of his own rise from provincial obscurity to Parisian prominence to success in school. As he wrote in *Homo Academicus*, the famous book on higher education that he began amid the crises of 1968, he was like someone who believed in a religious vocation then found the church to be corrupt. "The special place held in my work by a somewhat singular sociology of the university institution is no doubt explained by the peculiar force with which I felt the need to gain rational control over the disappointment felt by an 'oblate' [a religious devotee] faced with the annihilation of the truths and values to which he was destined and dedicated, rather than take refuge in feelings of self-destructive resentment" (Bourdieu, 1988: xxvi). The disappointment could not be undone, but it could be turned to understanding and potentially, through that understanding, to positive change.

Educational institutions were central to Bourdieu's concern, but both his sense of disappointment and his critical analyses were more wide reaching. All the institutions of modernity, including the capitalist market and the state itself, share in a tendency to promise far more than they deliver. They present themselves as working for the common good, but in fact reproduce social inequalities. They present themselves as agents of freedom, but in fact are organizations of power. They inspire devotion from those who want richer, freer lives, and they disappoint them with the limits they impose and the violence they deploy. Simply to attack modernity, however, is to engage in the "self-destructive resentment" Bourdieu sought to avoid. Rather, the best way forward lies through the struggle to understand, to win deeper truths, and to remove legitimacy from the practices by which power mystifies itself. In this way, one can challenge the myths and deceptions of modernity, enlightenment, and civilization without becoming the enemy of the hopes they offered.

Bourdieu assembled a remarkable group of collaborators including Luc Boltanski, Jean-Claude Passeron, and Monique de Saint Martin. Together, this group (and new recruits) conducted a wide range of empirical studies. Themes ranged from photography as an art form and hobby (Bourdieu *et al.*, [1965]1990), to museum goers and patterns of taste (Bourdieu and Darbel, [1966]1990; Bourdieu, [1979]1984, schooling and social inequality (Bourdieu and Passeron, [1964]1979, 1971), modern universities (Bourdieu, [1978]1988, [1989]1996), the rise of literature and art as a distinct fields of endeavor (Bourdieu, [1989]1993, [1992]1996), and the experience of poverty amid the wealth of modern societies (Bourdieu *et al.*, [1993]2000). These put the perspective Bourdieu had developed to use in analyzing many different aspects of French social life. In 1975 Bourdieu and his collaborators also founded a new journal, *Actes de la Recherche en Sciences Sociales*. In its pages they not only took up different empirical themes but also developed and tried out new ideas and theoretical innovations. *Actes* also translated and introduced work from researchers with cognate interests in other countries.

The approach of the Center was developed simultaneously in research projects and seminars. It is reflected in a kind of manual for doing sociology (Bourdieu, Chamboredon, and Passeron, [1968]1991). This differed from typical textbooks in presenting not a compilation of facts and a summary of theories, but an approach to sociology as an ongoing effort to "win social facts." Entitled *The Craft of Sociology*, it bypassed abstract codification of knowledge and endeavored to help students acquire the practical skill and intellectual habitus of sociologists. Soon after, Bourdieu published his most influential theoretical statement (though characteristically in a book also rich in empirical analyses, *Outline of a Theory of Practice*, [1972]1977). Bourdieu later rewrote this study as *The Logic of Practice*. Soon after, he published his celebrated study of French cultural patterns, *Distinction* ([1979]1984). This remarkable corpus of work was the basis for his election to the chair of sociology in the Collège de France.

In sum, Bourdieu's own educational experience at once gave him fantastic resources – a command of the history of philosophy, multiple languages, and skills in critique and debate – and alienated him from the very institutions that helped, as it were, to make him a star. The resources were not limited to intellectual abilities but included the credentials, connections, and sense of the game that enabled him not just to become famous but also to create new institutions. The alienation gave Bourdieu the motivation and emotional distance to pioneer a critical approach, rather than a simple affirmation of the status quo.

Bourdieu saw critical social science as politically significant, but he was careful to avoid "short-circuiting" the relationship between scholarly distinction and political voice. Until late in his life, he resisted trading on his celebrity, and kept his interventions to topics where he was especially knowledgeable, such as education or the situation of Algerians in France. In the 1990s, he became furious at the ways in which market logic was being introduced into cultural life ([1996]1999) and at the weak response even of the political left. He wrote a best-selling polemic about television ([1995]1998) but began to use it more as he tried to reach a broader public on issues from undocumented workers to funding for education. His typical goal was to demystify the ways in which seemingly neutral institutions in fact make it harder for ordinary people to learn the truth about the state or public affairs. He called for an "internationale" of intellectuals (to replace the old *internationale* of the working class movement). In this spirit, he founded a review of books and intellectual debate, *Libère*, which appeared in half a dozen languages (though, curiously, not English). He also overcame a long-standing resistance to making public declarations of conscience by signing petitions. For example, he worked with other leading figures to suggest in the midst of the Yugoslavian wars that there were other options besides passivity and massive high altitude bombing. The media and the state seemed to suggest, wrote Bourdieu and his colleagues, that there was a simple choice between the NATO military campaign and ignoring the horrors of ethnic cleansing that Milosevic and others had unleashed. Not so, they argued, for there were other possible approaches to stemming the evils, including working more closely with Yugoslavia's immediate neighbors. And it was worth seeing that NATO's intervention had actually increased the pace of ethnic cleansing. As Bourdieu (1999) argued, the categories with which states "think" structure too much of the thinking of all of us in modern society; breaking with them is a struggle but an important one.

More generally, Bourdieu's mode of intervention was to use the methods of good social scientific research to expose misrecognitions that support injustice. A prime example is the enormous collective study of "the suffering of the world" produced under his direction (Bourdieu, 1993). This aimed not simply to expose poverty or hardship, but to challenge the dominant points of view that made it difficult for those living in comfort, and especially those running the state, to understand the lives of those who had to struggle most simply to exist. The book thus included both direct attempts to state the truths that could be seen from social spaces of suffering, and examinations of how the views of state officials and other elites prevented them from seeing these truths for themselves. The misrecognition built into the very categories of official knowledge was thus one of its themes. Bourdieu and his colleagues entered the public discourse not simply as advocates, therefore, but specifically as social scientists.

Not least, Bourdieu worried that the possibilities for free intellectual exchange were being undermined. The work and social value of artists, writers, and intellectuals depends on such free exchange – an unhampered and open creativity and communication. It thus depends on maintaining the autonomy of the artistic, literary, and scientific or intellectual fields. Boundaries need to be maintained between serious intellectual pursuit of truth and discourses – however smart – that seek only to use knowledge instrumentally. In this, he has stood clearly against those who would censor intellectual or cultural life in favor of their standards of morality or political expediency (see Bourdieu and Haacke, [1994]1995).

MISRECOGNITION, SYMBOLIC DOMINATION, AND REFLEXIVITY

Social life requires our active engagement in its games. It is impossible to remain neutral, and it is impossible to live with the distanced, detached perspective of the outside observer. As a result, all participants in social life have a knowledge of it that is conditioned by their specific location and trajectory in it. That is, they see it from where they are, how they got there and where they are trying to go. Take something like the relations between parents and children. As participants, we see these from one side or the other. They look different at different stages of life and other different circumstances – as for example when one's parents become grandparents to one's children. Our engagement in these relationships is powerful, but it is deeply subjective, not objective. We know a lot, but what we know is built into the specific relationships we inhabit and into specific modes of cultural understanding. Much of it is practical mastery of how to be a parent or a child. This is a genuine form of knowledge, but it should not be confused with scientific knowledge.

Bourdieu's perspective and approach were both shaped crucially by his fieldwork in Algeria. In trying to understand Kabyle society he shaped his distinctive perspective on the interplay of objective structures and subjective understanding and action. The experience of fieldwork itself was powerful, and helped to shape Bourdieu's orientation to knowledge. As an ethnographer, Bourdieu entered into another social and cultural world, learned to speak an unfamiliar language, struggled to understand what was going on while remaining necessarily in crucial ways an outsider to it. This helped him to see the importance of combining insider and outsider perspectives on social life. To be altogether an outsider to Kabylia, to try to know it only through "objective" facts, was certainly to fail to understand it, but in order to grasp it accurately the ethnographer also had to break with the familiarity of both his own received categories and those of his informants. His job is neither to impose his own concepts nor simply to translate those of the people he studies. He must struggle, as the philosopher Bachelard put it, to "win" the facts of his study.

One of the most basic difficulties in such research, Bourdieu came to realize, is the extent to which it puts a premium on native's discursive explanations of their actions. Because the anthropologist is an outsider and starts out ignorant, natives must explain things to him. But it would be a mistake to accept such explanations as simple truths, not because they are lies but because they are precisely the limited form of knowledge that can be offered to one who has not mastered the practical skills of living fully inside the culture (1977: 2). Unless he is careful, the researcher is led to focus his attention not on the actual social life around him but on the statements about it that his informants offer.

> The anthropologist's particular relation to the object of his study contains the makings of a theoretical distortion inasmuch as his situation as an observer, excluded from the real play of social activities by the fact that he has no place (except by choice or by way of a game) in the system observed and has no need to make a place for himself there, inclines him to a hermeneutic representation of practices, leading him to reduce all social relations to communicative relations and, more precisely, to decoding operations. (1977: 1)

Such an approach would treat social life as much more a matter of explicit cognitive rules than it is, and miss the ways in which practical activity is really generated beyond the determination of the explicit rules.

In this respect, Bourdieu took the case of anthropological fieldwork to be paradigmatic for social research more generally. The confrontation with a very different way of life revealed the need for both outsider and insider perspectives. Not long after he completed his work in Algeria, Bourdieu challenged himself by applying the method he was developing to research in his own native region of Béarn. The task, as he began to argue didactically and to exemplify in all his work, was to combine intimate knowledge of practical activity with more abstract knowledge of objective patterns, and using the dialectical relation between the two to break with the familiar ways in which people understand their own everyday actions. These everyday accounts always contain distortions and misrecognitions that do various sorts of ideological work. The classic example is gift-giving, which is understood as disinterested, voluntary, and not subject to precise accounting of equivalence, but which people actually do in ways that are more strategic than their self-understanding allows. In the Béarn, Bourdieu analyzed how more and more oldest sons were being forced to become bachelors. Because they inherited the family farms, they had previously been the most prized marriage partners, but as farming declined in economic importance this became a less valuable asset. At the same time, more young women went to work in cities and towns. There they not only met other people, they changed their attitudes and adopted urban standards that made the men at home seem clumsy and out of touch with social change. Even the bachelors themselves accepted this characterization, and by internalizing it undermined still further their chances of finding marriage partners (Bourdieu, 2002a).

Bourdieu makes a similar point in trying to explain how it is that women acquiesce in male domination. It is not that they find this a good thing, nor that they are entirely unaware of it, but they usually grasp their experience of it in biased cultural categories. This amounts to "symbolic violence, a gentle violence, imperceptible and invisible even to its victims, exerted for the most part through the purely symbolic channels of communication and cognition (more precisely, misrecognition), recognition, or even feeling" (Bourdieu, 2001: 1–2).

Our everyday life involvements, Bourdieu suggested, give us a great deal of practical knowledge. But because practical engagements focus our attention only on certain issues and interests and also limit the time we can spend reflecting we typically misrecognize much of what we and other people do. Misrecognition is not simply error; every recognition is also a misrecognition. This is so precisely because we cannot be objective and outside our own relations, we cannot see them from all possible angles. Which aspects of them we understand and how reflects our own practical engagement in them and also the conditions for perpetuating the games in which we are participants. As Bourdieu ([1980]1990: 68) wrote:

Practical faith is the condition of entry that every field tacitly imposes, not only by sanctioning and debarring those who would destroy the game, but by so arranging things, in practice, that the operations of selecting and shaping new entrants (rites of passage, examinations, etc.) are such as to obtain from them that undisputed, prereflexive, naïve, native compliance with the fundamental presuppositions of the field which is the very definition of doxa.

"Doxa" is Bourdieu's term for the taken-for-granted, preconscious understandings of the world and our place in it that shape our more conscious awarenesses. Doxa is more basic than "orthodoxy," or beliefs that we maintain to be correct in the awareness that others may have different views. Orthodoxy is an enforced straightness of belief, like following the teachings of organized religion. Doxa is felt reality, what we take not as beyond challenge but before any possible challenge. But though doxa seems to us to be simply the way things are, it is in fact a socially produced understanding, and what is doxic varies from culture to culture and field to field. In order for us to live, and to recognize anything, we require the kind of orientation to action and awareness that doxa gives. But doxa thus also implies misrecognition, partial and distorted understanding. It was the doxic experience of Europeans for centuries that the world was flat. Thinking otherwise was evidence not of scientific cleverness but of madness.

The ideas of doxa and misrecognition allowed Bourdieu a subtle approach to issues commonly addressed through the concept of ideology. Marxist and other analysts have pointed to the ways in which people's beliefs may be shaped to conform with either power structures or the continued functioning of a social order. Ideology is commonly understood as a set of beliefs that is in some degree partial and distorted and serves some specific set of social interests. Thus it is ideological to suggest that individual effort is the basic determinant of where people stand in the class hierarchy. It is not only false, but it serves both to legitimate an unequal social order and to motivate participants. Common use of the notion of ideology, however, tends to imply that it is possible to be without ideology, to have an objectively correct or undistorted understanding of the social world. This Bourdieu rejected. One can shake the effects of specific ideologies, but one cannot live without doxa, and one cannot play the games of life without misrecognition. Misrecognition is built into the very practical mastery that makes our actions effective.

Nonetheless, symbolic power is exercised through the construction of doxa as well as orthodoxy. Every field of social participation demands of those who enter it a kind of preconscious adherence to its way of working. This requires seeing things certain ways and not others, and this will work to the benefit of some participants more than others. Take the modern business corporation. It seldom occurs to people who work for corporations, or enter into contracts with them, or represent them in court, to question whether they exist. But what is a corporation? It is not precisely a material object and not a person in any ordinary sense. As the Supreme Court Justice Marshall (1819) put it famously, a corporation has "no soul to damn, no body to kick." Yet corporations can own property, make contracts, and sue and be sued in courts of law. Corporations exist largely because they are recognized to exist by a wide range of people, including agents of the legal system and the government. In order to do almost any kind of business in a modern society, one must believe in corporations. Yet, they are also in a sense fictions. Behind corporations stand owners and managers – and for the most part, they cannot be held liable for things the corporation "does." To believe in the corporation is to support a system that benefits certain interests much more than others, and yet not to believe in it makes it impossible to carry out effective practical action in the business world. This is how misrecognition works.

In addition to making misrecognition, and doxa, the objects of analysis, Bourdieu wishes to remind us of their methodological significance. It is because ordinary social life requires us to be invested in preconscious understandings that are at least in part misrecognitions that it is a faulty guide to social research. A crucial first step for every sociologist is to break with familiar, received understandings of everyday life. To "win" social facts depends on finding techniques for seeing the world more objectively. This is always a struggle, and one that the researcher must keep in mind throughout every project. It will always be easy to slide back into ways of seeing things that are supported by everyday, doxic understandings – one's own, or those of one's informants. Some of the advantages of statistical techniques, for example, come in helping us to achieve distance on the social life we study. At the same time, however, we need to work to understand the processes by which misrecognition is produced, to grasp that it is not a simple mistake. It is not enough to see the "objective" facts alone. We need to see the game in which they are part of the stakes.

We seldom grasp the whole truth about anything of importance without attending to the way cultural ideas and values and even language itself can reinforce power relations and produce injuries. Bourdieu includes insults, but he is interested especially in less obvious forms of symbolic domination. He points out, for example, that the root meaning of the word "categorize" is "to accuse" and he points out how putting people in cultural categories can have major effects. This is consistent with other sociological theories like "labeling theory" that shows how being labeled a deviant or an underachiever can have an effect on a person. As Foucault also argued, the very idea of "normal" can be used in a way that prejudices people against whatever is considered not normal. Conversely, whatever is said to be normal is insulated from criticism even if it is unjust. Bourdieu goes further in emphasizing the way categorization works as a tool of state power, whether by classifying people as citizens or not, as eligible to vote or not, as criminals or as people whose names are suspicious enough to get them stopped in airports. When governments say that marriage can only be between men and women they are exerting symbolic domination. The legal categories male and female can be problematic for a transgendered person. So are laws that describe homosexuality as involving "unnatural acts" even if they are not enforced. Children of interracial families may experience questions that demand they choose one race or the other as examples of symbolic violence. So, of course, are stereotypes about different races or genders. When the media rely on prejudicial descriptions they may perpetrate symbolic violence – for example when they say someone who was arrested "looked like a wild animal." Indeed, just choosing a particularly unflattering photograph to publish can have this effect. Bourdieu stresses symbolic violence because it is commonly less obvious than physical violence, because its influence can be pervasive, and because when cultural norms are widely shared they can make people who are the victims of symbolic violence or unfair practices accept them as normal. But symbolic violence is made possible partly by the still more widespread reality of misrecognition, the extent to which all understanding tends to be one-sided, to understand other people or ideas from the perspective of how they might matter to our actions, not simply as objects of scientific contemplation. This is a key reason why "winning the social fact" is a challenge for science, because the everyday understanding of social phenomena is misrecognition as much as recognition.

Reflexivity is achieving the capacity to look analytically at oneself, to take an external view of one's own action. This starts with seeing oneself from the point of view of others, but it also includes seeing how objective conditions and cultural influences shape one's own actions. Sociological research is an effort to help people see how their own actions are produced and what unintended consequences they have. As Bourdieu wrote, "sociology wouldn't merit an hour's trouble … if it didn't give itself the task of restoring to people the meaning of their actions" (2002a: 128). People don't know the full meaning of their own actions partly because of the role of unconscious learning – habitus – in shaping actions; partly because structural factors like inequality of capital may not be readily observed; and partly because habits of cultural understanding not only shape what people do but limit how much they are aware of it. For example, if children are always told that success in school is simply an indication of personal merit – the combination of brains and effort – they may not see the role of class inequality. This has effects through differences in the quality of schools and the size of classes, and in the experiences and expectations that from an early age begin to shape each child's habitus. And it shapes decisions – like whether to stay in school or drop out – which have meanings beyond what is immediately apparent to those involved. These are all dimensions of meaning that sociological research clarifies so that people can better understand their own action and circumstances. But the same goes for social institutions and society as a whole. Sociology helps teachers and superintendents see the implications of the way schools are run, and sociology helps people see the structure of society and the sources and implication of their own actions. This is a bit like a coach using video to help a tennis player see her own swing and kinesiological research to understand the mechanics of bodily motion. The player can then connect this objective information to subjective experience – knowledge won't matter if she cannot change her habits of action. The new knowledge may make her stroke more forceful or reduce the risk of injury. Likewise, better knowledge of how society is organized and what shapes social action can inform the pursuit of social change. But Bourdieu emphasizes also that social research is itself a social process, made possible by specific sorts of resources, organized by the values and hierarchy embedded in a field, and shaped by the experience and previous learning of researchers – including learning of which they are not aware. In order to be a good "objective" researcher, thus, a social scientist needs to understand the factors that shape his or her subjective perception. These include background variables like gender, race, and class, but also ways in which intellectual categories and social institutions are organized – like the distinctions among disciplines that for example make economic issues seem more separate from the social or psychological than they really are. A basic condition of deeper social knowledge is a job that provides time to engage in research and reflection – and this too shapes a view of the world not equally available to those without that opportunity.

Bourdieu did not call for the study of the points of view of individual scientists, or a critical uncovering of their personal biases, so much as for the study of the production of the basic perspectives that operate within intellectual fields more broadly. These are collective products. Identifying them is a source of insight into the unconscious cultural structures that shape intellectual orientations. These may be general to a culture or specific to the intellectual field. We saw an example in considering the ways in which anthropologists may be prone to an intellectualist bias in describing action in terms of following cultural rules. This follows not only from the typical self-understanding of intellectuals, but from reliance on discourse with informants as a way of discovering how practices are organized. Grasping how this bias gets produced is a way to improve the epistemic quality of analyses.

Beyond uncovering such possible biases, reflexivity offers the opportunity to see how the organization of the intellectual or academic field as a whole influences the knowledge that is produced within it. A simple example is the way in which the differentiation of disciplines organizes knowledge. Each discipline is predisposed to emphasize those features that are distinctive to it, reinforce its autonomy, and give it special advantage in relation to others. Topics that lie in the interstices may be neglected or relatively distorted. Bourdieu attempted more systematically to analyze the social space of intellectual work, using a technique called correspondence analysis. This allows him to identify similarities in the products, activities, and relationships of different intellectuals and graphically represent them as locations in a two or more dimensional space. In his major book on the organization of universities and intellectuals, *Homo Academicus*, he uses this technique to produce an overall picture of social space. This is useful for grasping the battle lines over specific intellectual orientations, and also the conflicts over using knowledge to support or challenge the social order. Law professors, for example, are more likely to be products of private schools and children of senior state officials, and not surprisingly also more likely to be supporters of the state and its elites. Social scientists, more likely to be the children of schoolteachers and professionals, and graduates of Parisian public *lycées*, tend towards a more critical engagement with the state. Obviously, these are relatively superficial attributes and Bourdieu offers much more detail. Paying attention to these sorts of differentiations among the different disciplines helps us to understand what is at stake when they struggle over intellectual issues – say, whether a new field of study should be recognized with departmental status – and also when their members engage in intellectual production.

For Bourdieu, reflexivity was not aimed at negative criticism of science, but rather at improving it. He wished social science to be more scientific, but this depends not simply on imitating natural science but on grasping the social conditions for the production of better scientific knowledge. Mere imitation of natural science (as in some economics) produces objectifications which make no sense of the real world of social practices because they treat social life as though it were solely material life with no room for culture or subjectivity. Bourdieu's analysis helps not only to show the limits of such an approach but to show why it can gain prestige and powerful allies, why it attracts recruits of certain backgrounds, and how it in turn supports the state and business elites. A better social science requires, as we saw earlier, breaking with the received familiarity of everyday social practices in order to grasp underlying truths. It requires reflexively studying the objective limits of objectivism. But it also requires maintaining the autonomy of social science, resisting the temptations to make social science directly serve goals of money or power. Just as literature depends on authors gaining the freedom to produce art for art's sake – with other members of the literary field as its arbiters – so science depends on producing truth for truth's sake with other scientists as arbiters. This truth can become valuable for a variety of purposes. But just as there is a difference between basic physics and the use of the truths of physics in engineering projects, there is a difference between producing basic sociological knowledge and using this in business or politics. It is especially easy for social scientists to be drawn into an overly immediate relationship to money or power; it is crucial that their first commitment be to the scientific field, because their most valuable contributions to broader public discourse come when they can speak honestly in the name of science. At the same time, truths that social science discovers are likely to make many upholders of the social order uneasy, because they will force more accurate recognitions of the ways in which power operates and social inequality is reproduced.

HABITUS

Participation in social games is not merely a conscious choice. It is something we do unconsciously or at least pre-reflectively. We are, in a sense, always already involved. From childhood we are prepared for adult roles. We are asked what we want to be when we grow up and learn that it is right to have an occupation. We are told to sit up straight and speak when spoken to. We experience the reverence our parents show before the church – or before money or fame, depending on the parents. Out of what meets with approval or doesn't, what works, or doesn't, we develop a characteristic way of generating new actions, of improvising the moves of the game of our lives. We learn confidence or timidity. But in either case much of the power of the socialization process is experienced in bodily terms, simply as part of who we are, how we exist in the world. This sense is the habitus, a key concept for Bourdieu to which we have been introduced through the idea of the embodied sense of how to play a game.

Habitus (an idea that goes back to Aristotle) refers to the way we intuitively, unconsciously position ourselves in the world and relate to the world. It is formed through a learning process by which experience comes to be embodied so that it shapes our action unconsciously (like having a sense of how close to stand to someone else when having a conversation, or knowing how to swim or speak). Bourdieu stresses how this not only generates repeated behavior but helps produce new actions when people try to fit the habits they have learned into new situations. He shows how culture works not just as an abstract system of values or ideas but through the generation of sensibilities that inform bodily experience and action – as for example the words honor and shame name not only ideas but powerfully orienting experiences that orient what we do (as for example we try both consciously and unconsciously to avoid shame) and how we relate to others (as for example we trust someone who seems honorable). Habitus is shaped by gender, class, and culture because these shape the experiences from which we learn. Habitus can be formed in different ecologies – desert, forest, or city. In modern society our sense of being bodily located in the world is extended by all sorts of media, as for example texting depends both on physical habits involving keys and screens and on having an intuitive mental sense of other people located in other places reading what we transmit. But despite technologies, our physically embodied relationship to the world remains basic, and our actions are shaped not just by conscious choices but by intuitive orientations that are the product of previous experience.

"Habitus" provides the embodied sensibility that makes possible structured improvisation.[12] Jazz musicians can play together without consciously following rules because they have developed physically embodied capacities to hear and respond appropriately to what is being produced by others, and to create themselves in ways which others can hear sensibly and to which others can respond. Or in Bourdieu's metaphor, effective play of a game requires not just knowledge of rules but a practical sense for the game. If this is a challenge to the static cognitivism of structuralism, it is equally a challenge to the existentialist understanding of subjectivity. Sartre created his famous account of the existential dilemma by positing "a sort of unprecedented confrontation between the subject and the world" (Bourdieu, 1977: 73). But this misrepresented how actual social life works, because it leaves completely out of the account the durable dispositions of the habitus. Before anyone is a subject, in other words, they are already inculcated with institutional knowledge – recognition and misrecognition.

The habitus appears in one sense as each individual's characteristic set of dispositions for action. There is a social process of matching such dispositions to positions in the social order (as, in another vocabulary, one learns to play the roles that fit with one's statuses). But the habitus is more than this. It is the meeting point between institutions and bodies. That is, it is the basic way in which each person as a biological being connects with the socio-cultural order in such a way that the various games of life keep their meaning, keep being played.

> Produced by the work of inculcation and appropriation that is needed in order for objective structures, the products of collective history, to be reproduced in the form of the durable, adjusted dispositions that are the condition of their functioning, the habitus, which is constituted in the course through which agents partake of the history objectified in institutions, is what makes it possible to inhabit institutions, to appropriate them practically, and so to keep them in activity, continuously pulling them from the state of dead letters, reviving the sense deposited in them, but at the same time imposing the revisions and transformations that reactivation entails. (Bourdieu, 1990: 57)[13]

Think of an example – say the Christian church, a product of two millennia that still seems alive to members. They experience it as alive, but they also make it live by reinventing it in their rituals, their relations with each other, and their faith. Being brought up in the church helps to prepare members for belief (inculcation), but it is also something they must actively claim (appropriation). The connection between the institution and the person is the very way in which members produce their actions.

> Each agent, wittingly or unwittingly, willy-nilly, is a producer and reproducer of objective meaning. Because his actions and works are the product of a modus operandi of which he is not the producer and has no conscious mastery, they contain an 'objective intention,' as the Scholastics put it, which always outruns his conscious intentions. (Bourdieu, 1977: 79)

To return to an earlier example, each of us reproduces the idea of corporation every time we engage in a transaction with one – owning stock, renting an apartment, going to work – even though that may not be our conscious intention.

Bourdieu emphasized that habitus is not just a capacity of the individual, but also an achievement of the collectivity. It is the result of a ubiquitous "collective enterprise of inculcation." The reason why "strategies" can work without individuals being consciously strategic is that individuals become who they were and social institutions exist only on the strength of this inculcation of orientations to action, evaluation, and understanding. The most fundamental social changes have to appear not only as changes in formal structures but also as changes in habitual orientations to action. Bourdieu sought thus to overcome the separation of culture, social organization and embodied individual existence that is characteristic of most existing sociology.

FIELDS AND CAPITAL

As we saw earlier, one of the ways in which Bourdieu used the metaphor of "games" was to describe the different fields into which social activities are organized. Each field, like law or literature, has its own distinctive rules and stakes of play. Accomplishments in one are not immediately granted the same prestige or rewards in another. Thus novelists are usually not made judges, and legal writing is seldom taken as literature. But, although the fields involve different games, it is possible to make translations between them. To explain this, Bourdieu uses the concept of capital. His analysis of the differences in forms of capital and dynamics of conversion between them is one of the most original and important features of Bourdieu's theory. This describes both the specific kinds of resources accumulated by those who are winners in the struggles of various fields and the more general forms of capital – such as money and prestige – that make possible translations from one to the other. "A capital does not exist and function except in relation to a field" (Bourdieu and Wacquant, 1992: 101). Yet, successful lawyers and successful authors both, for example, seek to convert their own successes into improved standards of living and chances for their children. To do so, they must convert the capital specific to their field of endeavor into other forms. In addition to material property (economic capital), families may accumulate networks of connections (social capital) and prestige (cultural capital) by the way in which they raise children and plan their marriages. In each case, the accumulation has to be reproduced in every generation or it is lost.

Capital is Bourdieu's term for resources that structure what is possible for different individuals or groups to do, and that form the "stakes" of social struggles. Capital comes in different forms – social, symbolic, and cultural as well as materially economic. Who you know can be a resource just like a bank account, and some people network very consciously to build social capital. Material, economic capital is especially important in modern societies – though so are educational credentials. Different forms of capital are convertible, as for example rich parents can buy their children education at expensive universities. Public institutions (like schools or museums) and cultural values (like beauty or justice) work to limit immediate dominance of economic capital over all other kinds. Nonetheless, capitalism (in Marx's sense of a system in which accumulation of wealth based on the conversion of human labor into commodities becomes an end in itself) is for Bourdieu a tendency in modern life that threatens to dominate. But people still accumulate other sorts of capital, sometimes by explicitly rejecting economic values, as an artist may gain symbolic credit for demonstrating devotion purely to aesthetics and popularizing his work for sales. Because of the importance of capital, inequalities are basic to social life. Capital is both necessary for individual action and built into the structure of collective action so that people are embedded in competition and accumulation even without conceptualizing them as such or forming conscious intentions.

Field refers to the organization of modern social life into different spheres of value and activity, each partially autonomous from others. At the same time, the term also refers to the field of play in which social interaction takes place, the action of each player influenced by positions and play of the others, or the field of force in which physical entities are organized by their relations to each other. Each field, like law or literature, has its own distinctive sorts of resources (capital) and hierarchies of prestige and influence. These are related to each other in a larger field of power (shaped especially by the state which both regulates and empowers) and in exchange relationships (largely mediated by markets but not entirely – as members of different fields may do favors for each other). Each field demands a distinctive habitus from its members, sets of skills and predispositions that enable them to work effectively in it but also commit them to its values. Every field is unequal, organized into a hierarchy of both cultural value and material resources or influence. Modern society is distinctive in the extent to which it is organized by a differentiation of fields. Here

Bourdieu develops an insight associated with Max Weber, who called fields "value spheres" because each maintained distinctive values – whether religious, artistic, or economic. This allows modern societies to be diverse and allows members of modern societies to "compartmentalize" their lives (focusing on religion at church or money when at the bank) more than people in less differentiated societies. Bourdieu stresses that the value associated with each field also defines a hierarchy – whether of spiritual purity and wisdom, artistic creativity and judgment, or economic wealth. Within each field members are empowered by connections, credentials, and other sorts of capital – and by habits of action adjusted to their field. They therefore tend to defend the boundaries and autonomy of their field.

There are two senses in which capital is converted from one form to another. One is as part of the intergenerational reproduction of capital. Rich people try to make sure that their children go to good colleges – which, in fact, are often expensive private colleges (at least in the USA). This is a way of converting money into cultural capital (educational credentials). In this form, it can be passed on and potentially reconverted into economic form. The second sense of conversion of capital is more immediate. The athlete with great successes and capital specific to his or her sporting field – prestige, fame – may convert this into money by signing agreements to endorse products, or by opening businesses like car dealerships or insurance agencies in which celebrity status in the athletic field may help to attract customers.

Bourdieu's account of capital differed from most versions of Marxism. It was not backed by a theory of capitalism as a distinct social formation (Calhoun, 1993). Neither was it the basis for an economic determinism. Bourdieu saw "an economy of practices" at work insofar as people must always decide how to expend their effort and engage in strategies that aim at gaining scarce goods. But Bourdieu did not hold that specifically economic goods are always the main or underlying motivations of action or the basis of an overall system. By conceptualizing capital as taking many different forms, each tied to a different field of action, Bourdieu stressed (a) that there are many different kinds of goods that people pursue and resources that they accumulate, (b) that these are inextricably social, because they derive their meaning from the social relationships that constitute different fields (rather than simply from some sort of material things being valuable in and of themselves), and (c) that the struggle to accumulate capital is hardly the whole story; the struggle to reproduce capital is equally basic and often depends on the ways in which it can be converted across fields.

In addition, Bourdieu showed that fields (such as art, literature, and science) that are constituted by a seeming disregard for or rejection of economic interests nonetheless operate according to a logic of capital accumulation and reproduction. It is common to think of religion, art, and science as basically the opposite of economic calculation and capital accumulation. Even fields like law are constituted not simply by reference to economic capital (however much lawyers may treasure their pay) but by reference to justice and technical expertise in its adjudication. This is crucial, among other reasons, as a basis for the claim of each field to a certain autonomy. This, as Bourdieu (1992[1996]: 47ff.) argued, is the "critical phase" in the emergence of a field. Autonomy means that the field can be engaged in the play of its own distinctive game, can produce its own distinctive capital, and cannot be reduced to immediate dependency on any other field.

Bourdieu's most sustained analysis of the development of such a field focused on the genesis and structure of the literary field. He analyzed the late nineteenth-century point at which the writing of "realistic" novels separated itself simultaneously from the broader cultural field and the immediate rival of journalism. His book, *The Rules of Art* ([1992]1996), focused equally on the specific empirical case of Gustave Flaubert and his career, and on the patterns intrinsic to the field as such. The emphasis on Flaubert was, among other things, a riposte to and (often implicit) critical engagement with Sartre's famous largely psychological analysis. *The Rules of Art* contested the view of artistic achievement as disinterested, and a matter simply of individual genius and creative impulses. It showed genius to lie in the ability to play the game that defines a field, as well as in aesthetic vision or originality.

Flaubert was the mid-nineteenth-century writer who, more than anyone else with the possible exception of Baudelaire, created the exemplary image of the author as an artistic creator working in an autonomous literary field. The author was not merely a writer acting on behalf of other interests: politics, say, or money. A journalist was such a paid writer, responsible to those who hired him. An author, by contrast, was an artist. This was the key point for Flaubert and for the literary field that developed around and after him. What the artistic field demanded was not just talent, or vision, but a commitment to "art for art's sake." This meant producing works specifically for the field of art.

When we set out to understand the "creative project" or distinctive point of view of an artist like Flaubert, therefore, the first thing we need to grasp is his place in and trajectory through the field of art (or the more specific field of literature as art). This, Bourdieu recognizes, must seem like heresy to those who believe in the individualistic ideal of artistic genius. It is one thing to say that sociology can help us understand art markets, but this is a claim that sociology is not just helpful for but crucial to understanding the individual work of art and the point of view of the artist who created it. Bourdieu takes on this task in an analysis simultaneously of Flaubert's career, or his own implicit analysis of it in the novel *Sentimental Education*, and of the genesis and structure of the French literary field. In doing so, he accepts a challenge similar to that Durkheim (1897) took in seeking to explain suicide sociologically: to demonstrate the power of sociology in a domain normally understood in precisely antisociological terms.

At the center of Bourdieu's analysis lies the demonstration that Flaubert's point of view as an artist is shaped by his objective position in the artistic field and his more subjective position-takings in relation to the development of that field. For example, it is important that Flaubert came from a family that was able to provide him with financial support. This enabled him to participate fully in the ethic (or interest) of art for art's sake while some of his colleagues (perhaps equally talented) were forced to support themselves by writing journalism for money. This is different from saying simply that Flaubert expressed a middle class point of view. In fact, it suggests something of why middle and upper class people who enter into careers (like art) that are defined by cultural rather than economic capital often become social critics. Their family backgrounds help to buy them some autonomy from the immediate interests of the economy, while their pursuit of distinction in a cultural field gives them an interest in producing innovative or incisive views of the world. In other words, the objective features of an artist's background influence his work not so much directly as indirectly through the mediation of the artistic field.

In this sense, the artist is not so much "disinterested" as "differently interested." The illusion of disinterest is produced by the way economic and cultural dimensions of modern societies are ideologically opposed to each other. The field of cultural production is defined as the economic world reversed (Bourdieu, 1993: ch. 1). It is one of the central contributions of Bourdieu's theory, however, to show that this is a misrecognition and the opposition is really between different forms of capital. Directly economic capital operates in a money-based market that can be indefinitely extended. Cultural capital, by contrast, operates as a matter of status, which is often recognized only within specific fields (here again, Bourdieu follows Weber).

Bourdieu situated his logic of multiple fields and specific forms of capital in relation to a more general notion of "the field of power." The field of art, thus, has its own internal struggles for recognition, power, and capital, but it also has a specific relationship to the overall field of power. Even highly rewarded artists generally cannot convert their professional prestige into the power to govern other institutional domains. By contrast, businesspeople and lawyers are more able to do this. The question is not just who is higher or lower in some overall system, but also how different groups and fields relate to each other. Fields that are relatively high in cultural capital and low in economic capital occupy dominated positions within the dominant elite. In other words, university professors, authors, and artists are relatively high in the overall social hierarchy, but we would not get a very complete picture of how they relate to the system of distinctions if we stopped at this. We need to grasp what it means to be in possession of a very large amount of particular kinds of capital (mainly cultural) that trade at a disadvantage in relation to directly economic capital. This translates into a feeling of being dominated even for people who are objectively well off in relation to society as a whole. College professors, for example, don't compare themselves to postmen so much as to their former university classmates who may have gotten lower grades but made more money in business. Similarly, they experience the need to persuade those who control society's purse strings that higher education deserves their support (whereas the opposite is much less often the case; businessmen do not have the same need to enlist the support of college professors – though sometimes it can be a source of prestige to show connections to the intellectual world). This experience of being what Bourdieu called "the dominated fraction of the dominant class" can have many results. These range from a tendency to be in political opposition to specific tastes that do not put possessors of cultural capital in direct competition with possessors of economic capital. College professors, thus, may prefer old tweed jackets to new designer suits or old Volvos to new Mercedes as part of their adaptation to the overall position of their field.

Bourdieu's most sustained analysis of such issues occurs in *Distinction* ([1979]1984), a book that attempts "a social critique of the judgment of taste." It is a mixture of empirical analysis of the kinds of tastes characteristic of people at different positions in the French class hierarchy and theoretical argument against those who would legitimate a system of class-based classifications as reflecting a natural order. In other words, Bourdieu shows tastes not to reflect simply greater or lesser "cultivation" or ability to appreciate objective beauty or other virtues, but to be the result of a struggle over classification in which some members of society are systematically advantaged. Lower classes, he contends, make a virtue of necessity while elites demonstrate their ability to transcend it. The results include working class

preferences for more "realistic" art and comfortable, solid furniture and elite preferences for more "abstract" art and often uncomfortable or fragile antique furniture.

Analyses of the objective determinants of the tastes of college professors are not
in Bourdieu's view simply an idle form of narcissistic self-interest. Rather, it is vital
for intellectuals to be clear about their own positions and motivations in order to be
adequately self-analytic and self-critical in developing their accounts of the social
worlds at large. This is the necessary basis for both public interventions and the best
social science itself. Just as an analysis can discern the combination of objective and
subjective factors that combine to produce the point of view of an author like
Flaubert, so analysis can establish the grounds on which scientific production rests.
And more generally, social science helps everyone become clearer about institutions
and the sources and results of their own action.

IMPACT AND ASSESSMENT

Bourdieu's work has had an exceptionally broad impact in sociology and this continues to grow since his death.[14] He is one of the few recent shapers of an analytical
and theoretical perspective of wide influence on research in the field and the potential to stand alongside the classics of sociology's early history. Nonetheless, understanding of Bourdieu is very unevenly distributed in sociology, and based usually on
reading fragments of his work and appropriating one or two concepts rather than
grasping his perspective in an integrated way.

Bourdieu's analyses of the educational structure were the first of his studies to
have major impact in sociology, and they have been basic to analysis of the role of
education in the reproduction of social inequality (Grenfell, 2004 is perhaps the best
source). James Coleman assimilated Bourdieu's concept of cultural capital to Gary
Becker's notion of human capital, and to Bourdieu's discomfort called for a social
engineering effort to enhance both (Bourdieu and Coleman, 1991). Bourdieu's
emphasis on networks as social capital is probably most familiar from the work of
Robert Putnam (1995) though in common with many Putnam emphasizes the positive aspects to the near exclusion of Bourdieu's more critical insights.[15] Research in
social stratification has continued to be predominantly highly objectivist, concerned
with descriptions of hierarchies and predictions of patterns of mobility, rather than
taking up Bourdieu's challenge to understand the nature of reproduction. This would
require a more temporally dynamic and historically grounded approach. It would
also require paying attention to cultural as well as material factors, and to the differentiation of fields and problems of the conversion of capital.

Bourdieu's influence on empirical research has been greatest in the sociology of
culture. This stems in large part from the range and power of his own empirical studies of forms of artistic production and consumption, and especially of the pursuit of
distinction. These have, indeed, played a basic role in creating the contemporary
(and highly vibrant) subfield of sociology of culture and have also shaped the broader
interdisciplinary field of cultural studies. *Distinction* is easily the best known of
these works, and it is extremely widely studied and cited. Somewhat surprisingly,
however, there has not been much systematic cross-national research attempting to
replicate the study or establish differences in the organization of tastes in different

settings. Observers (e.g. Swartz, 1997; Fowler, 1997) have remarked that France may have an unusually tightly integrated cultural hierarchy; it remains for Bourdieu's approach to shape a series of similar empirical studies of anything resembling comparable breadth. Bourdieu himself did some comparative research on similar themes. *The Love of Art* (Bourdieu and Darbel, [1969]1990), for example, focused on attendance at museums. It is framed by the paradox that state support (and nonprofit private organizations) makes the great treasures of European art readily accessible to broad populations, most of whom ignore them. The achievement of democratic access is undercut by a widespread perception that the ability to appreciate art is something ineffable, an individual gift, intensely personal. This, Bourdieu and Darbel suggest, is simply a misrecognition underpinning the continued use of art to establish elite credentials in an ostensible democratic but still highly unequal society. Their study (which looked at six European countries) was one of the earliest in a series of research projects that have established in considerable detail the empirical patterns in the appropriation of culture. Bourdieu did not limit himself to high culture, studying as well the "middlebrow" art form of photography, including that of amateurs (Bourdieu *et al.*, [1965]1990). In this and other research, he participated in a broad movement that was basic to the development of cultural studies. This was a challenge to the traditional dichotomy of high vs. popular culture. Along with others, Bourdieu helped to debunk the notion that this represented simply an objective distinction inherent in the objects themselves, the nature of their production, or the capacities required to appreciate them. While Bourdieu and other researchers revealed differences in tastes, they showed these to be created by the system of cultural inequality, not reflections of objective differences.

An overall appreciation of Bourdieu's work must resist reading it in fragments: the work on education separate from that on art and literature, that on power and inequality distinct from that devoted to overcoming the structure/action antinomy. Bourdieu's key concepts, like habitus, symbolic violence, cultural capital, and field are useful in themselves, but derive their greatest theoretical significance from their interrelationships. These are best seen not mechanistically, in the abstract, but at work in sociological analysis. The fragments of Bourdieu's work are already exerting an influence, but the whole will have had its proper impact only with a broader shift in the sociological habitus that lies behind the production of new empirical understandings.

Bourdieu's work has been criticized from various perspectives.[16] Jenkins (1992) grumbles about many points but (aside from complaints about language and French styles in theory) centers on three contentions. First, Bourdieu was somewhat less original than at first appears. This is not an unreasonable point, for Bourdieu's work was indebted to influences (like Weber, Goffman, and Mauss) that are not always reflected in formal citations. Second, Bourdieu's conceptual framework remained enmeshed in some of the difficulties to which he drew attention and from which he sought to escape. His invocations of "subjectivism" and "objectivism," for example, were made in the service of encouraging a less binary and more relational approach. Nonetheless, they tend to reinstitute (if only heuristically) the very opposition they contest. Moreover, Jenkins (1992: 113) suggests, Bourdieu's approach entails reifying social structure while developing an abstract model of it; it becomes too cut and dried, too total a system. Third, for Jenkins Bourdieu remained ultimately and

despite disclaimers, a Marxist and a deterministic one at that. His concept of misrecognition is an epistemologically suspect recourse to the tradition of analyzing ordinary understandings as "false consciousness." This raises the problems that (a) if
ordinary people's consciousness is deeply shaped by misrecognition, their testimony
as research subjects becomes dubious evidence, and (b) the claim to have the ability
to uncover misrecognition privileges the perspective of the analysts (and may even
function to conceal empirical difficulties). Jenkins's reading of Bourdieu is filtered
through English-language concerns, theoretical history, and stylistic tastes; though
his account is dated and partial, many English-language readers share his views.

Despite the "sheep's clothing" of his emphases on culture and action, Bourdieu is
held by many critics to be a reductionist wolf underneath. That is, he is charged with
adhering to or at least being excessively influenced by one or both of two schools of
reductionistic social science: Marxism and rational choice theory. It seems to me
clear, for reasons given above, that he was not in any strict sense a follower of either
of these approaches. He was certainly influenced by Marxism, but also by structuralism, Weber, Durkheim and Durkheimians from Mauss to Goffman, phenomenology, and a variety of other sources. Bourdieu's language of strategy and rational
calculation is a different matter. It does not derive from rational choice theory but
rather from more general – though related – traditions in English philosophy and
economics. Bourdieu does think that action is shaped by interests and strategies, but
he does not think that conscious intentions fully explain either the sources or the
outcomes of action. Structural factors are important not only as external resources
and obstacles but as they are internalized through learning from previous actions.
We generate our actions not only by strategy, thus, but also through improvisation
guided by the habitus. What appear in hindsight to be strategies – say, successful
business careers – are often the effects of a combination of structural factors, habitus, and actual conscious choices.

Nonetheless, Bourdieu is concerned to show that "economizing" shapes action
even in social fields that explicitly deny self-interest, calculation, and economic values. "Economizing" in this sense means acting on the basis of differential resources
to pursue interests. Actors make investments of the resources they have – which
may be time or talent or such field-specific capital as reputation – to try to enhance
their standing in their field. Standing – prestige or relative power for example – is
necessarily distributed unequally. Actors pursue what is valued in different fields –
truth or justice or beauty. But they have unequal resources to use and the distribution of field-specific rewards is unequal. There is a scarcity of positions at the
top, whether one speaks of priests becoming bishops or lawyers becoming judges or
painters getting hung in museums. One does not have to reduce the values people
pursue to money or material goods to see that actions reflect an economic logic.
Whether actors are consciously strategic or not, looking backward one can analyze
their actions and trajectories in strategic terms. This said, many readers still find
Bourdieu's empirical analyses to be reductionistic (despite his theoretical disclaimers) because he leaves little place for disinterested judgment (Jenkins, 1992; Evens,
1999; Sayer, 1999).

One of the harshest critiques of Bourdieu's alleged reductionism came from
Alexander (1995). His vitriolic attack is partly an attempt to underpin Alexander's
own preferred approach to overcoming oppositions of structure and agency, one

that would grant culture more autonomy and place a greater emphasis on the capacity of agents to achieve liberation through "authentic communication." Bourdieu, Alexander suggested, tries to make the sociology of knowledge substitute for the judgment of what knowledge is true or false. That is, he thinks Bourdieu tried to make accounts of how people take positions do the work of analyses of those positions and their normative and intellectual merits. In short, he was a determinist. Moreover, somewhat in common with Jenkins, Alexander sees Bourdieu covertly accepting too much of the rationalism, structuralism, and Marxism he argued against:

> Since the early 1960s, Bourdieu has taken aim at two intellectual opponents: structuralist semiotics and rationalistic behaviorism. Against these perspectives, he has reached out to pragmatism and phenomenology and announced his intention to recover the actor and the meaningfulness of her world. That he can do neither ... is the result of his continuing commitment not only to a cultural form of Marxist thought but to significant strains in the very traditions he is fighting against. The result is that Bourdieu strategizes action (reincorporating behaviorism), subjects it to overarching symbolic codes (reincorporating structuralism), and subjugates both code and action to an underlying material base (reincorporating orthodox Marxism). (Alexander, 1995: 130)

Alexander attempts to substantiate this critique by both theoretical argument and (curiously, because he seems to exemplify in more hostile form the very position he decries in Bourdieu) by an account of Bourdieu's intellectual development and successive enmities. The latter side of the argument amounts to suggesting that Bourdieu was disingenuous about the sources of his work, but carries little theoretical weight in itself.[17] The former side, like Sayers's argument, raises a basic issue.

The strengths of Bourdieu's work lie in identifying the ways in which action is interested even when it appears not to be, the ways in which the reproduction of systems of unequal power and resources is accomplished even when it is contrary to explicit goals of actors, and the ways in which the structure of fields and (sometimes unconscious) strategies for accumulating capital shape the content and meaning of "culture" produced within them.[18] Bourdieu's theory is weaker as an account of creativity itself than of how creativity gains standing in social fields. Though he addresses deep historical changes in the nature of social life and deep differences in cultural orientation he does less to explain these than to show how they work. For example, his study of masculine domination has been criticized as examined not so much the sources of male oppression of women as the reasons for women's acquiescence to it (Bourdieu, 2001; Fowler, 2003; Wallace, 2003). No theoretical orientation provides an equally satisfactory approach to all analytic problems, and certainly none can be judged to have solved them all.

Alexander makes a false start, however, in presenting Bourdieu as simply "fighting against" two specific traditions. His relation to each was more complex, as was his relationship to a range of other theoretical approaches. From the beginning, and throughout his work, Bourdieu sought precisely to transcend simple oppositions, and approached different intellectual traditions in a dialectical manner, both criticizing one-sided reliance on any single perspective and learning from many. It is neither surprise nor indictment, for example, that Bourdieu incorporated a great deal of structuralism; it is important to be precise in noting that he challenged the notion that semiotics (or cultural meanings) could adequately be understood autonomously from social forces and practices. Likewise, Bourdieu labored against the notion that the meanings of behavior are transparent and manifested in purely objective interests or actors' own labels for their behavior. But this does not mean that he ever sought to dispense with objective factors in social analysis.

It is appropriate to close on a note of contention, not just because Bourdieu had critics but also because his theory was and is critical. During his lifetime, it was a contentious, and evolving, engagement with a wide range of other theoretical orientations, problems of empirical analysis, and issues in the social world. Bourdieu's theory remains contentious partly because it unsettles received wisdom and partly because it challenges misrecognitions that are basic to the social order – like the ideas that education is meritocratic more than an institutional basis for the reproduction of inequality, or indeed that if the latter is true this is simply something done to individuals rather than something they – each of us – participates in complex ways. As I have suggested – and indeed, as Bourdieu himself indicated – it is also in a strong sense incomplete. It is not a Parsonsian attempt to present a completely coherent system. It does have enduring motifs and recurrent analytic strategies as well as a largely stable but gradually growing conceptual framework. It does not have or ask for closure.

Bourdieu's work has increasingly wide influence. It is shaping discussions in feminism (Adkins and Skeggs, 2004), journalism (Benson and Neveu, 2005), religious studies (Rey, 2007) and numerous other fields. In some cases this is a matter directly of work in a "Bourdieusian" perspective. But often it is a matter of drawing from Bourdieu new ideas to help in rethinking existing perspectives and conducting new empirical analyses.

Most basically, Bourdieu's theory asks for commitment to the creating knowledge – and thus to a field shaped by that interest. This commitment launches the very serious game of social science, which in Bourdieu's eyes had the chance to challenge even the state and its operational categories. In this sense, indeed, the theory that explains reproduction and the social closure of fields is a possible weapon in the struggle for more openness in social life.

Reader's Guide to Pierre Bourdieu

Bourdieu never wrote a synthesis of his own theory or an introduction to it. This makes starting to learn it a challenge. Bourdieu's most accessible writings appear in short essays. *In Other Words* (1990) contains useful texts of lectures he gave to audiences outside France. *Acts of Resistance* (1998) contains the best known of his political essays; Pierre Carles's film, *Sociology Is a Martial Art* (2001) is also a nice introduction to Bourdieu's political activism. He reflects on key concepts in his work and on influences that shaped his approach in *Pascalian Meditations* (2001). His most general statement on the sociology of culture is *Distinction* (1984); *The Field of Cultural Production* (1993) contains several seminal essays. Bourdieu's most developed text on practice theory is *The Logic of Practice* (1990). Together with his student Loïc Wacquant he turned a seminar into a book that offers a useful general orientation to his work, *Invitation to Reflexive Sociology* (1992), though it is less introductory than the title suggests.

The best general introduction to Bourdieu's work and intellectual context is by Jeremy Lane (2000). Grenfell (2004) and Swartz (1997) and Robbins (1991) are useful complements written with more attention to discussions within sociology. Webb, Scirato, and Danaher (2002) is more elementary. Wacquant has also written several useful articles on Bourdieu, notably (2002, 2004; see also Calhoun and Wacquant, 2002). His edited collection on Bourdieu and democratic politics is also useful (Wacquant, 2005). Fowler (1997) and Robbins (2000) situate Bourdieu in relation to cultural theory. The essays in Calhoun, LiPuma, and Postone (1993); Brown and Szeman (2000) consider several different aspects of Bourdieu's work; Shusterman (1999) remains useful on aesthetics; Adkins and Skeggs contains notable essays connecting Bourdieu to debates in feminism; Gorski (forthcoming) offers several strong essays on Bourdieu generally and especially in relation to historical sociology.

Notes

1 Another of Bourdieu's teachers, Alexandre Koyré (1957), made a similar point about physics. The advances of abstract models, mathematicization, and experimental research mean that first-hand observation and experience and historical tradition no longer provide the crucial data about the physical world. Nonetheless, they do provide crucial data about scientific research itself, in which individual people and social institutions matter a great deal.

2 Perhaps the best recent exemplification of the relationship of habitus and bodily commitment is a study of boxing by Bourdieu's student Wacquant (2003).

3 See Taylor (1993) on Bourdieu's account of the limits of rule-following as an explication of action and its relationship to Wittgenstein.

4 See Paul Willis (1981) for a superb account of how this process works among working class kids in England.

5 Bourdieu's most developed analysis appears in a book entitle *Le Sens Pratique*. The title, a pun in French, could be translated several ways. The notion of "sense" carries, in French as in English both cognitivist and bodily connotations: to "make sense" and to "sense something." In French, "sens" carries the additional meaning of "direction," where a path leads. The English title, *The Logic of Practice*, necessarily sacrifices some of the meaning.

6 See Bourdieu ([1992]1996) and the analysis of the emergence of "intellectuals" as a source of critique by his student, Christophe Charles (1990).

7 Though Bourdieu put himself passionately into his work, he wrote relatively little about his own biography until at the very end of his life he presented a *Sketch for a Self-Analysis* (Bourdieu, 2007). The best available general discussions of Bourdieu's life and work are Lane (2000) and Swartz (1997).

8 Kabylia was also Durkheim's (1893) primary example of a segmentary society and mechanical solidarity.

9 On the war and its impact, see Le Seuer (2002) and Bourdieu's foreword to that book. On the formation of his intellectual approach see the insightful essay by Tassadit Yacine (2004), Bourdieu's former student, herself from Kabylia and Wacquant (2004). Essays in Goodman and Silverstein (2009) also address Bourdieu's work in Algeria.

10 Back in France, Bourdieu was responsible for introducing Goffman's work and arranging the translation of several of his books.

11 In this regard, Bourdieu differed from Alain Touraine, the other most prominent French sociologist of his generation and also a member of Aron's Center. Touraine embraced the student revolt more whole-heartedly and his sociology presented a much more voluntaristic cast. He also broke with Aron and formed his own center (see Colquhoun, 1986).

12 The concept has classical roots, and was revived for sociological use by Norbert Elias as well as Bourdieu; on Elias's version, see Chartier (1988).

13 Writing sentences like this was part of Bourdieu's habitus, his connection to the academic game, not least because their very complexity forces us to make the effort to hold several ideas in mind at once, resisting the apparent simplicity of everyday formations. Nonetheless, they do not translate elegantly or read easily.

14 See Wacquant's (1993) account of American social scientist's readings; also Sapiro and Bustamante (2009). Bourdieu (1998) offers his own complaints about how he has been understood in translation.

15 See the useful review of literature on social capital by Portes (1998).

16 The following describes criticisms, focusing on two more or less hostile analyses. Appreciations also include critique, of course, and there is a growing literature on Bourdieu. Lane (2000) is still the best general introduction; both Swartz (1993) and Robbins (1991) are useful complements emphasizing Bourdieu's importance in sociology; Webb, Scirato, and Danaher (2002) is more elementary. Fowler (1997) and Robbins (2000) situate Bourdieu in relation to cultural theory. The essays in Shusterman (1999); Calhoun, LiPuma, and Postone (1993); Brown and Szeman (2000) consider several different aspects of Bourdieu's work as do Grenfell (2004), Robbins (1991, 2000), Reed-Danahay (2005) and Jenkins (1992). Various articles by Bourdieu's close collaborator Loïc Wacquant provide helpful interpretation; see especially his contributions to the Bourdieu and Wacquant (1992) and his discussion of Bourdieu and democratic politics in Wacquant (2005). I refer here mainly to analyses in English. Several discussions have appeared in French, polarized into attacks and defenses. Lahire (2001) combines appreciation and critique; Mauger (2005) is a major compilation of perspectives from former collaborators, students, and colleagues. See Roos (2000) for a review of the very active Nordic discussions of Bourdieu's work, many influenced by Broady's (1990) monumental study.

17 Alexander's intellectual history is tendentious and his reading of Bourdieu is not deep, but it is nonetheless much more serious that the right-wing ideological attack by Verdès-Leroux, 2001.

18 Alexander (1995: 152) terms "unconscious strategy" an oxymoron. It is true that the notion invites misunderstanding and confusion, since it is hard to distinguish when it means that results fell into place "as if" there had been a strategy at work, and when it means that actors make a million small choices that add up to a strategy of which they are never consciously aware as such. In any case, Alexander fails himself to consider either of these possibilities clearly. The former is basic to modern economic analysis; the latter is at the heart of the idea of "sense of play" which Bourdieu has argued should replace a mechanistic, rule-following approach to the production of action.

Bibliography

Writings of Pierre Bourdieu

1960[1958]. *Sociologie d'Algérie*. Paris: PUF (trans. as *Algeria* in 1960; rev. edn. 1979, Cambridge University Press).

[1963]1973 (with J.-C. Passeron). *The Inheritors*. Chicago: University of Chicago Press.

[1963]1995 (with Alain Darbel, J.-P. Rivet and C. Seibel). *Work and Workers in Algéria*. Stanford, CA: Stanford University Press.

1964 (with Ahmed Sayed). *Le déracinement, la crise de l'agriculture en Algérie*. Paris: Editions de Minuit.

[1964]1979 (with Jean-Claude Passeron). *The Inheritors: French Students and their Relation to Culture*. Chicago: University of Chicago Press.

[1965]1990 (with Luc Boltanski, Robert Castel, J.-C. Chamboredon, and D. Schnapper). *Photography: A Middlebrow Art*. Cambridge: Polity.

[1967]1971 (with J.-C. Passeron). *Reproduction: In Education, Culture, and Society*. Beverly Hills: Sage.

[1968]1991 (with Chamboredon and J.-C. Passeron). *The Craft of Sociology*. Berlin: de Gruyter.

[1969]1990 (with Alain Darbel). *The Love of Art*. Stanford, CA: Stanford University Press.

1970 (with J.-C. Passeron). *La Reproduction. Eléments pour une théorie du système d'enseignement est un ouvrage de sociologie*. Éditions de Minuit, 1967).

[1971]1991. Genesis and structure of the religious field. *Comparative Social Research*, 13: 1–43.

[1972]1977. *Outline of a Theory of Practice*. Trans. Richard Nice. Cambridge: Cambridge University Press.

1973. The Berber house. In M. Douglas (ed.) *Rules and Meanings*. Harmondsworth: Penguin, pp. 98–110.

[1979]1984. *Distinction*. Cambridge, MA: Cambridge University Press.

[1980]1990. *The Logic of Practice*. Stanford, CA: Stanford University Press.

[1983]1993. The field of cultural production, or The economic world reversed. In *The Field of Cultural Production*. New York: Columbia University Press, pp. 29–73.

[1984]1988. *Homo Academicus*. Stanford, CA: Stanford University Press.

1986. The forms of capital. In John G. Richardson (ed.) *Handbook of Theory and Research in the Sociology of Education*. New York: Greenwood, pp. 241–258.

1988. Vive la crise! For heterodoxy in social science. *Theory and Society*, 17(5): 773–788.

[1988]1991. *The Political Ontology of Martin Heidegger*. Stanford, CA: Stanford University Press.

[1989]1993. The historical genesis of a pure aesthetic. In *The Field of Cultural Production*. New York: Columbia University Press, pp 254–266.

[1989]1996. *The State Nobility*. Stanford: Stanford University Press.

1990. *In Other Words: Essays towards a Reflexive Sociology*. Stanford, CA: Stanford University Press.

1991. *Language and Symbolic Power*. Cambridge, MA: Harvard University Press.

[1992]1996. *The Rules of Art: Genesis and Structure of the Literary Field*. Stanford, CA: Stanford University Press.

1992 (with Loïc Wacquant). *An Invitation to Reflexive Sociology*. Chicago: University of Chicago Press.

1993[2000] (ed.). *The Weight of the World: Social Suffering in Contemporary Society*. Stanford: Stanford University Press.

[1994]1995 (with Hans Haacke). *Free Exchange*. Stanford, CA: Stanford University Press.

[1995]1998. *Television*. New York: New Press.

1996 (with J.-C. Passeron, M. de Saint Martin, and R. Teese). *Academic Discourse: Linguistic Misunderstanding and Professorial Power*. Stanford University Press.

1998. *Practical Reason: On the Theory of Action*. Stanford: Stanford University Press.

1998. *Acts of Resistance*. New York: New Press.

[1998]2001. *Pascalian Meditations*. Stanford: Stanford University Press.

1999. Rethinking the state: Genesis and structure of the bureaucratic field. In George Steinmetz (ed.) *State/Culture: State Formation after the Cultural Turn*. Ithaca, NY: Cornell University Press, pp. 53–75.

2001. *Masculine Domination*. Stanford: Stanford University Press.

2002a. *Le Bal des Célibataires*. Paris: Éditions du Seuil.

2002b. *Firing Back*. New York: New Press.

2004. *Science of Society and Reflexivity*. Chicago: University of Chicago Press.

2007. *Sketch for a Self-Analysis*. Cambridge: Polity.

Further Reading

Adkins, Lisa and Skeggs, Beverly (2004) *Feminism after Bourdieu*. Oxford: Blackwell.

Alexander, Jeffrey C. (1995) The reality of reduction: The failed synthesis of Pierre Bourdieu. In *Fin de Siècle Social Theory*. London: Verso, pp. 128–216.

Benson, Rodney and Neveu, Erik (2005) *Bourdieu and the Journalistic Field*. Cambridge: Polity.

Broady, D. (1990) *Sociology and Epistemology: On Pierre Bourdieu's Work and the Historical Epistemology*. Stockholm: HLS Förlag.

Brown, Nicholas and Szeman, Imre (eds) (2000) *Pierre Bourdieu: Fieldwork in Culture*. Lanham, MD: Rowman and Littlefield.

Brubaker, Rogers (1993) Social theory as habitus. In C. Calhoun, E. LiPuma, and M. Postone (eds) *Bourdieu: Critical Perspectives*. Chicago: University of Chicago Press, pp. 212–234.

Calhoun, Craig (1993) Habitus, field, and capital: The question of historical specificity. In C. Calhoun, E. LiPuma, and M. Postone (eds) *Bourdieu: Critical Perspectives*. Chicago: University of Chicago Press, pp. 61–88.

Calhoun, Craig and Wacquant, Loïc (2002) Social science with conscience: Remembering Pierre Bourdieu. *Thesis*, 11(70) August: 1–14.

Calhoun, Craig, LiPuma, Edward, and Postone, Moishe (eds) (1993) *Bourdieu: Critical Perspectives*. Chicago: University of Chicago Press.

Carles, Pierre (2001) *Sociology is a Martial Art* (English subtitles). New York: Icarus Films.

Charles, Christophe (1990) *Naissance des "Intellectuels," 1880–1900*. Paris, Editions de Minuit.

Chartier, Roger (1988) Social figuration and habitus in Cultural History. Ithaca, NY: Cornell University Press, pp. 71–94.

Colquhoun, Robert (1986) *Raymond Aron: The Sociologist in Society, 1955–1983*. Beverly Hills, CA: Sage.

Dosse, Francois (1997) *Structuralism*, 2 vols. Minneapolis: University of Minnesota Press (orig. 1991).

Durkheim, Emile (1897[1988]) *Suicide*. New York: Free Press.

Evens, T. M. S. (1999) Bourdieu and the logic of practice: Is all giving Indian-giving or is "generalized materialism" not enough? *Sociological Theory*, 17(1): 3–31.

Fowler, B. (1997) *Pierre Bourdieu and Cultural Theory: Critical Investigations*. London: Sage.

Fowler, B. (2003) Reading Pierre Bourdieu's masculine domination: Notes towards an intersectional analysis of gender, culture and class. *Cultural Studies*, 17: 468–494.

Goffman, Erving (1959) *The Presentation of Self in Everyday Life*. New York: Doubleday, Anchor Books.

Goodman, Jane E. and Silverstein, Paul A. (eds) (2009) *Bourdieu in Algeria: Colonial Politics, Ethnographic Practices, Theoretical Developments*. Lincoln: University of Nebraska Press.

Gorski, Phil (forthcoming) *Bourdieu and Historical Analysis*. Durham, NC: Duke University Press.

Grenfell, Michael (2004) *Pierre Bourdieu: Agent Provocateur*. New York: Continuum.

Harker, Richard, Mahar, Christian, and Wilkes, Chris (eds) (1990) *An Introduction to the Work of Pierre Bourdieu*. New York: St. Martins.

Honneth, Axel, Kocyba, Hermann, and Schwibs, Bernd (1986) The struggle for symbolic order: An interview with Pierre Bourdieu. *Theory, Culture, and Society*, 3(3): 35–51.

Jenkins, Richard (1992) *Pierre Bourdieu*. London: Routledge.

Koyré, Alexandre (1957) *From the Closed World to the Infinite Universe*. Baltimore: Johns Hopkins University Press.

Lahire, Bernard (2001) *Le Travail Sociologique de Pierre Bourdieu*. Paris: Decouverte.

Lane, Jeremy (2000) *Pierre Bourdieu: A Critical Introduction*. London : Pluto.

Le Seuer, James D. (2002) *Uncivil War: Intellectuals and Identity Politics during the Decolonization of Algeria*. Philadelphia: University of Pennsylvania Press.

Marshall, John (1819) Trustees of Dartmouth College vs. Woodward, 17 US 518 (1819).

Mauger, Gérard (ed.) (2005) *Rencontres avec Pierre Bourdieu*. Broissieux: Éditions du Croquant.

Portes, Alejandro (1998) Social capital: Its origins and applications in modern sociology. *Annual Review of Sociology*, 24: 1–24.

Putnam R. D. (1995) Bowling alone: America's declining social capital. *Journal of Democracy*, 6: 65–78.

Reed-Danahay, Deborah (2005) *Locating Bourdieu*. Bloomington, IN: Indiana University Press.

Rey, Terry (2007) *Bourdieu on Religion: Imposing Faith and Legitimacy*. London: Equinox.

Robbins, Derrick (1991) *The Work of Pierre Bourdieu*. Boulder: Westview.

Robbins, Derrick (2000) *Bourdieu and Culture*. London: Sage.

Roos, J. P. (2000) The "Arctic Bourdieu": Four theses from the Nordic countries, cited on Roos's web page, University of Helsinki, Department of Social Policy.

Sapiro, Giselle and Bustamante, Mauricio (2009) Translation as a measure of international consecration: Mapping the world distribution of Bourdieu's books in translation. *Sociologica*, 2–3, DOI: 10.2383/31374.

Sayer, Andrew (1999) Bourdieu, Smith and disinterested judgment. *The Sociological Review*, 47(3): 403–431.

Shusterman, Richard (ed.) (1999) *The Bourdieu Reader*. Cambridge, MA: Blackwell.

Swartz, David (1997) *Culture and Power: The Sociology of Pierre Bourdieu*. Chicago: University of Chicago Press.

Taylor, Charles (1993) To follow a rule. In C. Calhoun, E. LiPuma, and M. Postone (eds) *Bourdieu: Critical Perspectives*. Chicago: University of Chicago Press, pp. 45–60.

Verdès-Leroux, Jeannine (2001) *Deconstructing Pierre Bourdieu*. New York: Algora Publishing.

Wacquant, Loïc (1993) Bourdieu in America: Notes on the transatlantic importation of social theory. In C. Calhoun, E. LiPuma, and M. Postone (eds) *Bourdieu: Critical Perspectives*. Chicago: University of Chicago Press, pp. 235–262.

Wacquant, Loïc (2002) The sociological life of Pierre Bourdieu. *International Sociology*, 17(4): 549–556.

Wacquant, Loïc (2003) *Body and Soul: Notebooks of an Apprentice Boxer*. New York: Oxford University Press.

Wacquant, Loïc (2004) Following Bourdieu into the field. *Ethnography*, 5(4): 387–414.

Wacquant, Loïc (ed.) (2005) *Bourdieu and Democratic Politics*. Cambridge: Polity.

Wallace, Martin (2003) A disconcerting brevity: Pierre Bourdieu's *Masculine Domination*, *Postmodern Culture*, 13(3); accessed from *Project Muse*.

Webb, Jen, Schirato, Tony, and Danaher, Geoff (2002) *Understanding Bourdieu*. London: Sage.

Willis, Paul (1981) *Learning to Labor: How Working Class Kids Get Working Class Jobs*. New York: Columbia University Press (rev. edn, orig. 1977).

Wittgenstein, Ludwig (1967) *Philosophical Investigations*, 2nd edn. Oxford: Blackwell.

Yacine, Tassadit (2004) Pierre Bourdieu in Algeria at war: Notes on the birth of an engaged ethnosociology. *Ethnography*, 5: 487–509.

16

Immanuel Wallerstein

CHRISTOPHER CHASE-DUNN AND HIROKO INOUE

Immanuel Wallerstein is among the most influential living social theorists despite the fact that he explicitly denies the possibility of general theory in social science. Wallerstein's conceptual approach to world history, what he has called the "world-systems perspective," has had a wide and deep impact in both the social sciences and the humanities wherever scholars and organic intellectuals have tried to penetrate what Giovanni Arrighi called "the fog of globalization." With Terence Hopkins, Wallerstein founded the Fernand Braudel Center for the Study of Economies, Historical Systems, and Civilizations at Binghamton University. He is now a senior research scholar at Yale. Wallerstein is also past president of the International Sociological Association and has published more than 30 books and over 200 articles and book chapters.

Born in New York on September 28, 1930, Wallerstein grew up in the intellectual, political, and cultural center of the world during the *Age of Extremes*[1] and the commencement of *America's Half Century*.[2] He received nearly all his education in New York. He earned his undergraduate BA (1951), graduate MA (1954) and PhD (1959) degrees from Columbia University. He then taught at Columbia until 1971. From 1971 to 1976 Wallerstein professed sociology at McGill University and then he moved to Binghamton to found the Fernand Braudel Center. He retired from Binghamton in 1995 but remained as Director of the Fernand Braudel Center until 2005. Wallerstein was also chair of the international Gulbenkian Commission on the Restructuring of the Social Sciences between 1993 and 1995.

Wallerstein (2000a) describes his intellectual biography as "one long quest for adequate explanation of reality" and "the quest was both intellectual and political." For Wallerstein, intellectual and political projects are two sides of the same coin, and they should not be pursued independently. Wallerstein began this quest at a very early age. He was brought up in a very politically conscious and intellectual family.

The Wiley-Blackwell Companion to Major Social Theorists, First Edition.
Edited by George Ritzer and Jeffrey Stepnisky.
© 2011 Blackwell Publishing Ltd. Published 2011 by Blackwell Publishing Ltd.

The contentious issues of world affairs in the 1930s the 1940s (the depression, Second World War, the labor movement, the rise of fascism, the Hitler-Stalin pact) were frequent topics of conversation at home (Wallerstein, 2000). The cosmopolitanism of his familial and urban environment contributed to his developing interest in the world beyond the United States during his high school years.

Walter Goldfrank (2000) has written the most insightful contextualized summary and critique of Wallerstein's work up until the end of the twentieth century. Goldfrank observed that the three most important locales of Wallerstein's formative years were New York, Paris, and West Africa. While working on his dissertation at Columbia Wallerstein studied in Paris. His mentor there was Georges Balandier, a French sociologist, anthropologist and ethnologist who studied African colonialism. During this period Wallerstein also became acquainted with the work of the Annales School. Paris was a lively center of political and intellectual radicalism among émigré Africans, Asians, and Latin Americans.[3]

For his dissertation Wallerstein conducted research on the voluntary associations that led the West African independence movements, which was later published as *The Road to Independence: Ghana and the Ivory Coast* (1964). The work was based on interviews and surveys conducted in the Gold Coast (later Ghana) and the Ivory Coast. Wallerstein's studies of the rise and demise of colonial regimes in Africa led him to conclude that one could not understand African history and social change without comprehending the historical and contemporary interactions among Africa, Europe, and the Americas.

Wallerstein spent nearly a quarter century of his life at Columbia University (1947–1971). He studied at Columbia occurred during an especially fertile period in which American academia, especially social science and the humanities, was beginning to open up to non-WASPs (White Anglo-Saxon Protestants). Later, he became a faculty member at Columbia. Both Bergesen (2000) and Goldfrank (2000) argue plausibly that the Columbia days were the context that most strongly shaped Wallerstein's intellectual trajectory. Columbia was the home campus of such luminaries as Karl Polanyi, Lionel Trilling, and Richard Hofstadter as well as C. Wright Mills.[4]

As an undergraduate at Columbia Wallerstein took classes from "the radical nomad," C. Wright Mills (Hayden, 2006) who was busy writing *The Power Elite*. In 1968 Wallerstein authored an entry about Mills for the *International Encyclopedia of the Social Sciences* that describes Mills's intellectual trajectory in terms that could easily summarize much of Wallerstein's own (Wallerstein, 1968). Mills was disaffected with the predominant theoretical and methodological approaches in sociology (abstracted empiricism and grand theory) and was moving toward the writing of engaged and topical essays and books that addressed the most salient issues of the day.

Wallerstein described Mills's work as an attempt to open up paths of inquiry and analysis that would enable intellectuals to combat what Mills called the "main drift" of modern society to "rationality without reason" – the use of rational means in the service of substantively irrational ends. Wallerstein says Mills wanted to go beyond Marx and Weber to "a new comparative world sociology that would seek to understand our time in terms of its historical specificity and by so doing renew the possibility of achieving human freedom" (Wallerstein, 1968: 362).

New York was also the home of the *Monthly Review*, still arguably the most important "independent socialist" journal and book publisher in the United States.

The *Monthly Review* branch of "Western Marxism" was moving away from core-centric "workerism" to identify the revolutionary locus of the global working class as being primarily located in the "Third World" (now the Global South). *Monthly Review* published Paul A. Baran's *The Political Economy of Growth* in 1956, an important early study of how dependence on foreign investment and trade stunted economic development in the Global South. C. Wright Mills wrote about colonialism and neo-colonialism in Puerto Rico, and defended the Cuban Revolution when it came in 1959, as did Baran.[5]

Dependency theory, the idea that there is an international hierarchy that underdevelops the Global South, emerged primarily among Latin American scholars such as Raul Prebisch, Teotonio Dos Santos, and Fernando Henrique Cardozo. It was taken up and popularized in the Global North by Andre Gunder Frank (1967, 1969). Wallerstein, Giovanni Arrighi, and Samir Amin applied the idea of an evolving hierarchical global division of labor to Africa (Wallerstein, 1976).

Wallerstein was a faculty member at Columbia during what he would later call "the world revolution of 1968."[6] This was the 1960s, an era of nearly global student revolt, the Civil Rights movement in the United States, the war in Vietnam, and a counter-cultural rebellion that made alliances with radical workers in France and Italy. At Columbia Wallerstein helped to lead a faction of the faculty who were allied with the New Left students. This experience further radicalized him and spurred him to develop his analysis of the history and evolution of the Global Left even more.

In addition to the milieu at Columbia and in New York, Wallerstein's ideas were obviously shaped through collaborations with certain colleagues. Though some think of Wallerstein as the primary creator of the world-systems perspective, it is obvious that quite similar approaches were emerging in the works of several of his colleagues and collaborators, especially Samir Amin, Andre Gunder Frank, Terence Hopkins, and Giovanni Arrighi. Together these seminal thinkers discovered, or rediscovered, and reinterpreted the modern system of national states and the capitalist world-economy that emerged with the rise of Europe. Their vocabularies were slightly different, but this was clearly a single interactive intellectual project. Wallerstein added depth to the analysis of core/periphery relations when he realized that formal colonialism was not the only way in which an unequal international division of labor had been structured. This had already been theorized by the dependency theorists using the idea of neo-colonialism, but Wallerstein discovered a similar case in the way that an unequal division of labor between Poland and Western Europe had underdeveloped Poland in the long sixteenth century (Wallerstein, 1972). Wallerstein's co-founding of the Fernand Braudel Center and the publication of the first volume of *The Modern World-System* in 1974 established his name as synonymous with the world-systems perspective.

The world-systems perspective is a strategy for explaining institutional change that focuses on whole interpolity systems rather than single polities. The tendency in sociological theory to think of single national societies as systems led to many errors, because the idea of a system usually implies closure and endogenous processes. National societies (both their states and their nations) emerged over the last few centuries to become the strongest socially constructed identities and structures in the modern world, but they have never been whole systems. They have always existed in a larger context of important interaction networks (trade, warfare, long-distance communication) that has greatly shaped events and social change. Well before the emergence of globalization in the popular consciousness the world-systems perspective focused on the world economy and the system of interacting polities, rather than on single national societies. Wallerstein defines three kinds of whole systems: mini-systems based on reciprocity and two kinds of world-systems: world empires based on redistribution in which a single state has managed to encompass a whole multicultural division of labor, and world-economies in which a system of competing and allying polities (states) are also linked by trade and a division of labor.[7]

The world-systems perspective is not a single theory, but rather a collection of theories, historical narratives, and bodies of research that explain different aspects of world historical social change. The main insight is that important interaction networks (trade, information flows, alliances, and fighting) have woven polities and cultures together since the emergence of hominids and complex culture. Explanations of patterned institutional change should use whole interpolity systems (world-systems) as the units that evolve. Globalization, in the sense of the expansion and intensification of larger and larger economic, political, military and information networks, has been increasing for millennia, albeit unevenly and in waves.

The intellectual history of Wallerstein's version of the world-systems perspective has its roots in classical sociology (especially Max Weber), Marxian political economy, German historicism, the French Annales School, and geopolitical studies (Goldfrank, 2000). The idea of the whole system means that all the human interaction networks small and large, from the household to global trade, constitute the world-system. It is not just a matter of "international relations" or global-scale institutions such as the World Bank, etc. Rather, at the present time, the world-system includes all the people of the Earth and all their cultural, economic and political institutions and the interactions and connections among them. The whole of humanity is now linked into a single complex network of interactions. The world-systems perspective looks at human institutions over centuries and millennia and employs the spatial scales that are required for comprehending these whole interaction systems. Interaction networks became larger with the development of technologies of transportation and communications, and so small regional world-systems have expanded and merged to become the Earth-wide system of the present.

The modern world-system can be understood structurally as a nested stratification system composed of dominant core societies (themselves in competition with one another) and dependent peripheral and semiperipheral regions, a few of which have been either upwardly or downwardly mobile in the larger core/periphery hierarchy, while most have simply maintained their relative positions. It is also a global class structure with increasingly transnational organizations and ties among farmers and workers as well as among elite groups.

This Wallersteinian perspective on world history allows the analysis of the cyclical features of institutional change and the long-term patterns of development in historical and comparative perspective. The evolution of the modern world-system has been primarily driven by capitalist accumulation and geopolitics in which businesses and states compete with one another for power and wealth. Competition among states and capitals is conditioned by the dynamics of struggle among classes and by the resistance of peripheral and semiperipheral peoples to domination and exploitation from the core. In the contemporary system the semiperiphery is composed of large and powerful countries in the Global South (e.g. Mexico, India, Brazil, China) as well as smaller countries that have intermediate levels of economic development (e.g. the East Asian NICs, Israel, South Africa). It is not possible to understand the history of institutional change without taking into account both the strategies and technologies of the winners and the strategies and forms of struggle of those who have resisted domination and exploitation.

As we have seen, Wallerstein grew up in the pungent broth of the New York Left. The *Monthly Review* scholars were renovating a Global South version of Marxism and Wallerstein took up the political sociology of African nationalism and pan-Africanism. Dependency theory emerged from the efforts of Latin American social scientists and activists to confront US hegemony and sociological modernization theory (Talcott Parsons and his followers) with the realities of five hundred years of European colonialism and US neo-colonialism. Wallerstein saw the relevance of this approach to the history of Africa, and when he read Fernand Braudel's *The Mediterranean* and Marian Malowist's studies of sixteenth-century Poland he realized that core/periphery relations have been fundamental to the rise of capitalism in Europe for centuries. This was not just a phase of "primitive accumulation" that set the motor of capitalism going. It was an evolving system in which new institutional structures of exploitation emerged as earlier structures (like formal colonialism) came to an end. Thus did Wallerstein discover the core/periphery hierarchy as a crucial dimension for understanding the last five hundred years of world history and for comprehending the future.

Wallerstein's metatheoretical stance is signified by his use of the term "historical system," which is meant to collapse radically the separation in the disciplinary structure of the modern academy between social science and history – the contrast between nomothetic ahistoricism and idiographic historicism. His narrative of the history of the modern world-system tells the story of a hierarchical interpolity system in which class relations, state formation, nation-building, race relations, geopolitics, capitalist competition, and core/periphery domination and resistance have constituted the main outlines of social change for centuries.

Wallerstein formulated his version of the modern core/periphery hierarchy as an asymmetrical division of labor between producers of highly profitable core commodities and producers of much less profitable peripheral goods. He also asserted the systemic importance of an intermediate zone, the semiperiphery. This tripartite spatial division of labor, reproduced over the centuries despite some upward and downward mobility, is the most important of the conceptual schemas that Wallerstein's historical-structural analysis of world history has produced.

Wallerstein's big point is that it is impossible to truly understand and explain the development of modern capitalism without attention to the core/periphery hierarchy. The ability of core capitalists and their states to exploit peripheral resources and labor has been a major factor in the competition among core contenders, and the resistance to exploitation and domination mounted by non-core peoples has also played a powerful role in world history because the "great powers" were forced to compete with each other in their abilities to both exploit the non-core and to deal with the powerful challenges that emerged both within core societies and from the non-core of the world-system.

Wallerstein argues that the modern world-system emerged in the long sixteenth century (1560–1640) when Europeans first circumnavigated the globe and began colonizing and exploiting other continents. His focus on agriculture helps his argument that capitalism first became the predominant mode of production in the sixteenth century as a result of a crisis of European feudalism (Wallerstein, 1974). He contends that the Dutch hegemony peaked during the economic and demographic crisis of the seventeenth century. Great Britain and France contended for hegemony in the eighteenth century as the system continued to expand. The nineteenth century was the period of the British hegemony and the incorporation of East Asia into the modern world-system (Wallerstein, 1984). The world-system went through a number of cyclical processes and secular upward trends while continuing to expand. The twentieth century was the period of the US hegemony, which is now in decline. The contradictions of capitalism are becoming unresolvable and a world historical transformation is now occurring in which the world-system will become something other than a capitalist system (see below).

There have been five major critiques of Wallerstein's approach to world-systems analysis:

1 Those who contend that Wallerstein ignores the particularities of different kinds of capitalism within the core and that he reifies the world-system and discounts the importance of processes that are internal to national societies.
2 "Point-of production" Marxists who contend that his approach misconstrues class relations and relies too heavily on exchange relations rather than relations of production.
3 Political sociologists who say that his approach is too "economistic" and that he ignores the crucial role of different kinds of political configurations in different states.
4 "Global capitalism" sociologists who contend that Wallerstein is "state-centric" and ignores qualitatively unique features that distinguish a recent stage of global capitalism from earlier stages of capitalism.
5 Those who contend that Wallerstein largely ignores the very long-run evolution of world-systems before the emergence of the modern system and that his use of mode of production (capitalism) for spatially bounding the modern system is a grave mistake.

REIFICATION OF THE WORLD-SYSTEM

Many critics over the years have alleged that Wallerstein ignores the particularities of different kinds of capitalism within the core and that he reifies the world-system and discounts the importance of processes that are internal to national societies. A fairly recent statement of this criticism is found in Stephen K. Sanderson's 2005 critique of the world-systems perspective. Sanderson's critique differs from most of the others in that he is more knowledgeable about the world-systems literature and the work of Wallerstein than are most of the other critics. Sanderson claims that

Wallerstein's work gives primacy or exclusivity to exogenous over endogenous factors in explaining social change. He says that world-systems analysts privilege the causal importance of intersocietal and system-wide processes and structures. In the contemporary world in which each national society, despite all the hubbub about globalization, is still routinely described by both social scientists and most other commentators as if it were a self-contained entity that is unique and largely unconnected to, and incomparable with, other national societies, this claim of a bias toward world historical explanations seems ironic. That said, Wallerstein and other world-systems analysts nowhere claim that intersocietal or global level processes cause everything that happens. Rather it is argued that world-level processes and patterns are important in their own right and that pretending that each national society is a whole independent system – as if it were on the moon – is an ideological mystification that supports, and is based on nationalism – still a very prevalent institutionalized form of collective identity.

Sanderson says that world-systems analysts privilege exogenous processes. The very distinction between endogenous and exogenous processes is what is being challenged by the world-systems perspective. Sanderson means that societies (meaning modern national societies such as the United States) are systems with endogenous processes, and that forces that impinge from beyond the borders are exogenous. The world-systems perspective sees the whole interpolity system and world economy as the focal system of study and this includes that which is within national societies and their states as well as transnational relations and global institutions and structures. This does not mean that the causes of change only come from global level patterns or structures. Philip McMichael (1990) introduced the explanatory strategy of "incorporating comparison" precisely to deal with the problem of agency in world-systemic social change. Local action not only can have an impact on local outcomes despite larger structural constraints, but sometimes local action or the concatenated or coordinated actions of local agents can change the whole system. Perhaps this is what Sanderson was advocating when he stressed that the locus of causality should be an empirical question that depends on what we are trying to explain. This being said, it is important to study system-level processes and patterns in their own right, and despite all the global-babble there is very little in social science that actually does this.

Wallerstein has never said that national societies are internally homogenous. There have been peripheries within the core, and cores within the periphery all along. It is and always was a nested system. And Wallerstein has contended that semiperipheries are either intermediate forms or are a mix of core and peripheral characteristics.

CLASS ANALYSIS

Some Marxists have alleged that Wallerstein pays too little attention to class relations as the key to capitalist development. The most influential statement of this critique was that by Robert Brenner (1977). Wallerstein's claim that peripheral class relations – serfdom and slavery – have played a fundamental role in shaping the modern world-system was alleged to water down Marx's insistence on wage labor as the *sine qua non* of modern capitalism. These "point of production" Marxists focused almost exclusively on the institutional structures and the processes by which surplus value is extracted in the process of production, as had Maurice Dobb in an earlier critique of Paul Sweezy. Wallerstein was lumped with other "neo-Smithian Marxists" (such as Paul Sweezy and Andre Gunder Frank) because his emphasis on the importance of core/periphery relations was seen to privilege the realm of exchange relations (trade) over production relations (the appropriation of surplus value by capitalist exploitation of wage labor). Wallerstein's broadening of the definition of capitalism to include other forms of commodified labor (capitalist slavery and serfdom) made it possible to include the non-core (and the core before the industrial revolution) as within the scope of the capitalist world economy. These oft-repeated critiques have allowed many Marxists to continue to indulge in an analysis of societal class relations as if national societies were separate and autonomous entities, at least until the allegedly recent emergence of globalization.

BRINGING THE STATE BACK IN

The third main critique came from those who contended that Wallerstein privileged economic factors over and above politics, states and culture. Some political sociologists argued that Wallerstein's focus on the core/periphery division of labor glossed over important differences between the institutional structures of particular state apparatuses, varieties of capitalism within the core and struggles over policy changes that have occurred in the realm of politics (Skocpol, 1977).

Wallerstein's approach can be understood to imply that geopolitics between states, politics within states, and capitalist accumulation compose a single interconnected logic. Many political sociologists support the idea that politics and economics are two distinct and largely unconnected logics. This is, of course, a fundamental claim that justifies disciplinary boundaries within the social sciences. It is also congruent with and reinforces the definition of democracy as polyarchy in which political rights are asserted to be separable from economic rights and economic rights are excluded from the realm of democracy.

Wallerstein has long and loudly proclaimed that the structure of disciplines in the modern university is a historical accident that occurred in the formation of universities during a certain period of world history, and that these distinctions are mythical smoke-screens that stand in the way of true comprehension of a world history in which economics and politics are strongly linked, like wrestlers in a clinch. In response to similar critiques that he ignored culture, Wallerstein took up the analysis of "geo-culture," by which he means the predominant political philosophies that contend with one another within the modern system.

Curiously, both the point-of-production Marxists and the "bring the state back in" political sociologists seem to have missed the specifics of Wallerstein's narrative accounts as presented in the three volumes of *The Modern World-System*. He repeatedly explains how differences in regional or national class structures led to significant world historical outcomes such as Portugal's leading role in fifteenth-century European expansion or the rise of the Dutch and British hegemonies. Wallerstein's insistence on the study of the whole world-system and his resonant avowal of the relevance of historical and comparative knowledge threaten those scholars whose specialized expertise is spatially or temporally narrow.

GLOBAL CAPITALISM

The "global capitalism" school claims that the world-systems perspective is "state-centric" because it conceptualizes the global hierarchy as composed of core, peripheral and semiperipheral states, and because it ignores certain important and unique features that have emerged in the last few decades during which a global stage of capitalism has emerged (Sklair, 2006; Robinson, 2010). Sklair emphasizes the emergence of transnational production by global corporations, world cities that perform important functions for global finance capital, transnational practices carried out by globally oriented and cosmopolitan CEOs. Robinson portrays an emergent global class structure that is allegedly replacing the core/periphery hierarchy in a single world society with a transnational (or global) state that is largely under the control of the transnational capitalist class (2004, 2006).

Wallerstein and other world-systems scholars have long acknowledged the existence and importance of a global class structure and transnational relations. Transnational production has been understood in terms of the idea of "commodity chains" that have existed since the sixteenth century (Hopkins and Wallerstein, 1986). Some of the theorists of global capitalism contended that the nation-state has been made irrelevant by the growing power of transnational corporations. Their early work implied that national economies were largely self-sufficient before the rise of globalization that occurred in the last decades of the twentieth century. More recently they have described how the functions of the nation-state have been reconfigured by global capitalism (Sassen, 2006). Robinson tells how the global division of labor has shifted from a structure of arms-length state-to-state international trade to a system in which transnational production is integrated inside the structure of global corporations and their supply networks and the key players are retailers such as Walmart.

William I. Robinson (2004, 2006) contends that a world society and a global class system are emerging in which the transnational segments of each class in most countries have become predominant. This is a useful idea and it is partly true. But the current reality is that the Westphalian international system of national states, and the realities of global governance by a hegemon are still with us at the same time that the world has been slowly moving toward global state formation and a more transnationalized global class structure since the nineteenth century.

The US government still controls a massive global military apparatus that is a *de facto* world state. But Robinson contends that the U.S. federal government has become an instrument of the transnational capitalist class. He contends that workers in both the core and the periphery have been subjected to similar forces of job blackmail, attacks on the welfare state, withdrawal of legal protections for labor unions and the casualization of labor. This is true, but there are still big differences between being a worker or a citizen in the US or other core states and a worker or citizen in the Global South. These differences may or may not be smaller than they were before the neoliberal "globalization project" rose to hegemony with Reaganism–Thatcherism in the 1980s.

The notions of a more integrated transnational capitalist class and a transnational working class are important ideas. But even though there has been a trend in the direction of global class formation, many capitalists and workers continue to act as if they are members of a national society first, and global actors second. That is likely to be the case for some time to come. It is certainly preliminary to declare, as Robinson and others have done, that there is now no such thing as the core/periphery hierarchy. Global inequalities have not decreased. There is recent mobility in the system – the rise of India and China – but that is nothing new.

Wallerstein also contends that globalization is as much a cycle as a trend and that the wave of global integration that has swept the world in the last few decades is best understood by studying its similarities and differences with the waves of international trade and foreign investment expansion that have occurred in earlier centuries, especially the last half of the nineteenth century. Wallerstein has insisted that US hegemony is continuing to decline. He interpreted the US unilateralism of the Bush administration as a repetition of the mistakes of earlier declining hegemons that attempted to substitute military superiority for economic comparative advantage (Wallerstein, 2003). Most of those who denied the notion of US hegemonic decline during what Giovanni Arrighi (1994) called the "belle epoch" of financialization have now come around to Wallerstein's position in the wake of the current global financial crisis. Wallerstein contends that once the world-system cycles and trends, and the game of musical chairs that is capitalist uneven development, are taken into account, the "new stage of global capitalism" does not seem that different from earlier periods.

Robinson also critiques Wallerstein's redefinition of capitalism as a system-wide mode of production. But Robinson seems unaware of the most important reason why Wallerstein and Samir Amin challenged Marx's definition of capitalism as commodity product, wage labor, and private ownership of the major means of production. Both Wallerstein and Amin broadened the definition of commodified labor to include slave labor used for the production of commodities and coerced cash crop labor (share-cropping, indentured servitude, etc.) because they see the non-core as an essential part of capitalism. Another way to put this is that primitive accumulation and imperialism are necessities of the capitalist mode of production, not just a sideshow in the Global South.

David Harvey's (2003) *The New Imperialism* argues that "accumulation by dispossession" is a central and continuing feature of the logic of capitalism, not just a transition phase of "primitive accumulation." The non-core is not just something that happens out on the edge. The mobilization of peripheral capitalism was essential for successful accumulation in the core as different groups of capitalists and their states contended with one another for wealth and power. And the non-core played an important role in challenging the power of the core from the beginning. The non-core (periphery and semiperiphery) is important and necessary for the whole system of capitalism.

Marx, like Thomas Friedman, assumed that the world was flat – that (core) capitalism would spread evenly everywhere. But it did not and it has not. There are still huge global inequalities. The amount of global inequality has not gone down since it increased in the nineteenth century.

Broadening the definition of commodified labor also allows us to pay attention to the kinds of coercion that may affect wage labor. Protective and enforced labor laws have made a huge difference in most core states. The expansion of wage labor in the non-core has followed the abolition of most slavery and serfdom, but much of the wage labor in the non-core, and some parts of the core, is unprotected by enforced labor law. While labor protection has gotten worse in the core during the recent period of the neoliberal globalization project, it is still better than in most of the non-core. So there is still a meaningful distinction between forms of labor control that corresponds with the core/periphery hierarchy.

Leslie Sklair has said that there is no global in world-systems thinking. Obviously the word "world," means global. But it also allows for whole non-planet-wide regional interaction systems of the sort that existed before Europe incorporated all the Earth into its web. The relevant world is the network of important human interactions (trade, alliances, conflict). So "world" is better than "global." Robinson follows Sklair in cramming Wallerstein into the box of "state-centrism." But Wallerstein is rather less state-centric than most of the other traditional Marxists. Robinson says that "world-system theory views the system of nation-states as an immutable structural feature of the larger world or interstate system." Certainly Wallerstein, who designates world empires as another type of world-system, does not see the system of nation-states as immutable.

PREMODERN WORLD-SYSTEMS

Other scholars who are within the world-systems camp have disagreed with Wallerstein on certain important points. We have already mentioned Wallerstein's typology of "mini-systems," "world empires" and "world-economies" which encourages comparisons between the modern system and earlier systems. Andre Gunder Frank and Barry Gills (1994) claimed that the contemporary system emerged 5000 years ago when states and cities came into being in Mesopotamia. They also contended that this system had a capital-imperialist mode of production that was indistinguishable from the contemporary mode of production, and so capitalism did not emerge in Europe at all. Rather, according to Frank and Gills, the world-system had been capitalist all along.

Chase-Dunn and Hall (1997) proposed a comparative and evolutionary world-systems perspective that contends, *contra* Wallerstein, that pre-agrarian world-systems were not usually culturally homogenous mini-systems, but were often multicultural and multipolity world-systems (see also Chase-Dunn and Mann, 1998). So-called "world empires" were not usually a whole division of labor enclosed within a single polity. Rather there were large core-wide empires that were trading and fighting with other polities. The Roman Empire traded and fought with the Parthian Empire and traded prestige goods with the Han Empire in China. It was never a whole world-system.

Chase-Dunn and Hall agree with Wallerstein that capitalism emerged first as a predominant mode of accumulation in Europe, and that it was this that made the European rise to hegemony possible. But they disagree that a mode of accumulation (capitalism) is a useful way to spatially bound world-systems.[8] Rather they use regular two-way human interaction networks to bound world-systems. With this criterion small systems grew larger and merged as transportation and communications technologies developed. Wallerstein had also discounted the importance of trade in "preciosities" (prestige goods) in order to contend that the long-distance trade across Eurasia that had existed since before the Roman and Han Empires was not systemic. Chase-Dunn and Hall followed Jane Schneider (1991) Janet Abu-Lughod (1989) and many others in arguing that prestige goods are very important in some world-systems.

So Wallerstein's portrayal of the modern world-system maintains that Europe was a separate system because it was capitalist, and that its interactions with other regions were inconsequential before the rise of European hegemony. Europe was linked with the old West Asian/North African core region of states and large cities at least since the early Bronze Age. The story of the modern world-system is about the rising power of a formerly peripheral and semiperipheral world region within an older West Asian/Mediterranean core region that was itself becoming increasingly linked with other distant core regions in South and East Asia. These are not small matters. The story of world-historical social change cannot be told accurately or well explained without getting the spatial systemic boundaries right.

EVOLUTION WITHIN THE MODERN SYSTEM

Giovanni Arrighi's (1994) more evolutionary account of "systemic cycles of accumulation" has solved some of the problems of Wallerstein's notion that world capitalism started in the long sixteenth century and then went through cycles and trends. Arrighi's account is explicitly evolutionary, but rather that positing "stages of capitalism" and looking for each country to go through them (as most of the older Marxists did), he posits somewhat overlapping global cycles of accumulation in which finance capital and state power take on new forms and increasingly penetrate the whole system. This was a big improvement over both Wallerstein's world cycles and trends and the traditional Marxist national stages of capitalism approach.

For Wallerstein capitalism started in the sixteenth century, grew larger in a series of cycles and upward trends, and is now nearing "asymptotes" (ceilings) as some of its trends create problems that it cannot solve. Thus, for Wallerstein the world-system became capitalist and then it expanded until it became completely global, and now it is coming to face a big crisis because certain long-term trends cannot be accommodated within the logic of capitalism (Wallerstein, 2003). The three long-term upward trends (ceiling effects) that capitalism cannot manage are:

1   the long-term rise of real wages;
2   the long-term costs of material inputs; and
3   taxes.

All three upward trends cause the average rate of profit to fall. Capitalists devise strategies for combating these trends (automation, capital flight, job blackmail, attacks on the welfare state and unions), but they cannot really stop them in the long run. Deindustrialization in one place leads to industrialization and the emergence of a labor movements somewhere else (Silver, 2003). The falling rate of profit means that capitalism as a logic of accumulation will face an irreconcilable structural crisis during the next 50 years, and some other system will emerge. Wallerstein calls the next five decades "The Age of Transition."

Part of the difficulty in understanding his point of view is time horizon. Wallerstein's "Age of Transition" is at least 50 years. Most people do not have that kind of time horizon. He also sees recent losses by labor unions and the poor as temporary. He assumes that workers will eventually figure out how to protect themselves against market forces and capitalists. This may underestimate somewhat the difficulties of mobilizing effective labor organization in the era of globalized capitalism, but he is probably right in the long run. Global unions and political parties could give workers an effective instrument for protecting their wages and working conditions from exploitation by global corporations.

Wallerstein is intentionally vague about the new system that will replace capitalism (as was Marx). He sees the declining hegemony of the United States and the crisis of neoliberal global capitalism as strong signs that capitalism can no longer adjust to its systemic contradictions. He contends that world history has now entered a period of chaotic and unpredictable historical transformation. Out of this period of chaos a new and qualitatively different system will emerge. It might be an authoritarian global state that preserves the privileges of global elite or an egalitarian system in which non-profit institutions serve communities (Wallerstein, 1998).

Giovanni Arrighi's (1994, 2006) "systemic cycles of accumulation" are more different from one another than are Wallerstein's cycles of expansion and contraction and upward secular trends. And Arrighi (2006) has made more out of the differences between the current period of US hegemonic decline and the decades at the end of the nineteenth century and the early twentieth century when British hegemony was declining. The emphasis is less on the beginning and the end of the capitalist world-system and more on the evolution of new institutional forms of accumulation and the increasing incorporation of modes of control into the logic of capitalism. Arrighi (2006), taking a cue from Andre Gunder Frank (1998), saw the rise of China as portending a new systemic cycle of accumulation in which "market society" eventually comes to replace rapacious finance capital as the leading institutional form in the next phase of world history.

Wallerstein's version is more apocalyptic and more millenarian. The old world is ending. The new world is beginning. In the coming bifurcation what people do may be prefigurative and causal of the world to come. Wallerstein agrees with the analysis proposed by the students of the New Left in 1968 and large numbers of activists in the current global justice movement that the tactic of taking state power has been shown to be futile because of the disappointing outcomes of the World Revolution of 1917 and the decolonization movements.

Wallerstein has become a leader in the global justice "movement of movements" that has emerged around the World Social Forum. This despite the fact that many, or even most, of the other activists in this latest incarnation of the Global Left profess "horizontalism" and participatory democracy at the grass roots level. Famous intellectuals from New York are supposed to let leadership and ideas "bubble up from below."[9]

Wallerstein has been a foundational figure for the world-systems perspective – perhaps the most important, but the contributions of Frank, Amin, Arrighi, and

Hopkins has also been great. As the body of work has moved in new directions, world-systems analysis has matured, expanded, and diversified such that it can no longer be accurately described solely with reference to Wallerstein's vision or to the seminal works of the other founders. Wallerstein's stellar performances as a brilliant historical sociologist and as a courageous public intellectual demonstrate that social theory is not only for academics.

Reader's Guide to Immanuel Wallerstein

The best collection of Wallerstein's own work, including seminal articles that show the main structure of his overall argument, are contained in *The Essential Wallerstein* (2000b).

Readers seeking a short introduction to Wallerstein should consult Wallerstein's (2004) *World-systems Analysis: An Introduction*. Another useful, but somewhat dated, overview is by Thomas R. Shannon (1996) *An Introduction to the World-System Perspective*. For general overviews of the world-systems perspective readers should consult Hall (2000). This includes specially commissioned overview chapters on archeology, geography, political science, and gender. The first two chapters are excellent broad summaries with extensive bibliographies. Chase-Dunn and Babones (2006) include chapters by Leslie Sklair and Peter Gowan that are critical of the perspective. Wallerstein also provides occasional commentaries on world events at http://fbc.binghamton.edu/cmpg.htm

Notes

1 *Age of Extremes* is the title of Eric Hobsbawm's (1994) insightful world history of the first half of the twentieth century.
2 *America's Half Century* is the title of Tom McCormick's (1989) fine study of diplomatic history during the golden age of US hegemony.
3 Wallerstein has published numerous articles and reviews in French journals and he taught a semester each year in Paris for many years.
4 Bergesen (2000: 211) contends that Wallerstein's penchant for the critical essay as a form of expression was reinforced in this context.
5 Both Mills and Baran had fatal heart attacks (Mills in 1962, Baran in 1964) associated with the pressures of taking unpopular political positions that challenged the triumphalism of American hegemony during the boom years of the 1950s.
6 The concept of "world revolutions" refers to clusters of local rebellions and revolts that occur within the same decades and pose great challenges to the global powers-that-be. Arrighi, Hopkins, and Wallerstein (1989) analyze how clusters of "anti-systemic movements" evolved in the world revolutions of 1789, 1848, 1917, and 1968.
7 Goldfrank (2000) noted that the distinction between different modes of accumulation (reciprocity, redistribution, and market forms of exchange) came from Karl Polanyi (Polanyi, Arensberg, and Pearson, 1957).
8 Chase-Dunn and Hall agree with Wallerstein and Amin that peripheral capitalism has been and still is a fundamental and necessary sector of the modern world-system.
9 Wallerstein and his intrepid spouse Beatrice could be observed trekking between rather spread-out World Social Forum gatherings near the soccer stadium in the heat and humidity of Nairobi in January of 2007.

Bibliography

Select Writings of Immanuel Wallerstein

1964. *The Road to Independence: Ghana and the Ivory Coast*. Paris: Mouton.

1968. C. Wright Mills. *International Encyclopedia of the Social Sciences*, pp. 362–364.

1972. Three paths to national development in 16th century Europe. *Studies in Comparative International Development*, 7(2): 95–101.

1974. *The Modern World-System I: Capitalist Agriculture and the Origins of the European World-Economy in the Sixteenth Century*. New York: Academic Press.

1974. The rise and future demise of the world capitalist system: Concepts for comparative analysis. *Comparative Studies in Society and History*, 16: 387–415.

1976. Three stages of African involvement in the world-economy. In Peter C. W. Gutkind and Immanuel Wallerstein (eds) *The Political Economy of Contemporary Africa*, vol. 1. Beverly Hills, CA: Sage Press.

1979. *The Capitalist World-Economy*. Cambridge: Cambridge University.

1980. *The Modern World-System II: Mercantilism and the Consolidation of the European World-Economy, 1600–1750*. New York: Academic Press.

1983. *Historical Capitalism*. London: Verso.

1984. *The Politics of the World-Economy: The States, the Movements and the Civilizations*. Cambridge: Cambridge University Press.

1984. The three instances of hegemony in the history of the capitalist world-economy. In Gerhard Lenski (ed.) *Current Issues and Research in Macrosociology, International Studies in Sociology and Social Anthropology*, vol. 37. Leiden: E.J. Brill, pp. 100–108.

1986 (with Terence K. Hopkins and Immanuel Wallerstein). Commodity chains in the world-economy prior to 1800. *Review*, 10(1) Summer: 157–170.

1989. *The Modern World System III: The Second Era of Great Expansion of the Capitalist World-Economy, 1730–1840s*. New York: Academic Press.

1991. *Geopolitics and Geoculture: Essays on the Changing World-System*. New York: Cambridge University Press.

1992 (with E. Balibar). *Race, Nation, Class: Ambiguous Identities*. London: Verso.

1995. *After Liberalism*. New York: The New Press.

1995. Hold the tiller firm: On method and the unit of analysis. In Stephen K. Sanderson (ed.) *Civilizations and World-Systems: Two Approaches to the Study of World–Historical Change*. Walnut Creek, CA: Altamira Press, pp. 225–233.

1998. *Utopistics or Historical Choices of the Twenty-First Century*. New York: The New Press.

2000a. The development of an intellectual position. Available online at www.yale.edu/sociology/faculty/pages/wallerstein/ (slightly adapted version of the introductory essay to *The Essential Wallerstein*. New York: New Press. Accessed November 25, 2010).

2000b. *The Essential Wallerstein*. New York: The New Press.

2001. *The End of the World as we Know It: Social Science for the Twenty-first Century*. Minneapolis, MN: University of Minnesota Press.

2001. *Unthinking Social Science: The Limits of Nineteenth-Century Paradigms (Second Edition)*. Philadelphia, PA: Temple University Press.

2003. *The Decline of American Power: The US in a Chaotic World*. New York: The New Press.

2004. *The Uncertainties of Knowledge*. Philadelphia, PA: Temple University Press.

2004. *World-Systems Analysis: an Introduction*. Durham, NC: Duke University Press.

2005. *Africa: The Politics of Independence and Unity*. Lincoln, NE: University of Nebraska Press.

2006. *European Universalism: the Rhetoric of Power*. New York: The New Press.
Forthcoming. *The Modern World-System, Volume IV*. Berkeley: University of California Press.

Websites

Immanuel Wallerstein: www.iwallerstein.com/
Wallerstein's Commentaries on Current Events: http://fbc.binghamton.edu/cmpg.htm
Yale Sociology – Immanuel Wallerstein: www.yale.edu/sociology/faculty/pages/wallerstein/

Further Reading

Abu-Lughod, Janet Lippman (1989) *Before European Hegemony: The World System A.D. 1250–1350*. New York: Oxford University Press.
Amin, Samir (1974) *Accumulation on a World Scale*, 2 vols. New York: Monthly Review Press.
Amin, Samir (1975) *Unequal Development*. New York: Monthly Review Press.
Amin, Samir (1980) *Class and Nation, Historically and in the Current Crisis*. New York: Monthly Review Press.
Amin, Samir (1997) *Capitalism in the Age of Globalization*. London: Zed Press.
Arrighi, Giovanni (1994) *The Long Twentieth Century*. London: Verso.
Arrighi, Giovanni (2006) *Adam Smith in Beijing*. London: Verso.
Arrighi, Giovanni and Goldfrank, Walter L. (eds) (2000) Festschrift for Immanuel Wallerstein. *Journal of World-Systems Research*, 6(2–3).
Arrighi, Giovanni, Hopkins, Terence K., and Wallerstein, Immanuel (1989) *Antisystemic Movements*. London: Verso.
Bergesen, Albert (2000) The Columbia social essayists. In Giovanni Arrighi and Walter L. Goldfrank (eds) Festschrift for Immanuel Wallerstein. *Journal of World-Systems Research*, 2: 198–213.
Brenner, Robert L. (1977) The origins of capitalist development: A critique of neo-Smithian Marxism. *New Left Review*, 104: 25–92.
Chase-Dunn, Christopher and Babones, Salvatore J. (2006) *Global Social Change: Historical and Comparative Perspectives*. Baltimore: Johns Hopkins University Press.
Chase-Dunn, Christopher and Hall, Thomas D. (1997) *Rise and Demise: Comparing World-Systems*. Boulder, CO: Westview Press.
Chase-Dunn, Christopher and Mann, Kelly M. (1998) *The Wintu and Their Neighbors: A Very Small World-System in Northern California*. Tucson: University of Arizona Press.
Collins, Randall (1992) The geopolitical and economic world-systems of kinship-based and agrarian-collective societies. *Review*, 15(3) Summer: 373–389.
Frank, Andre Gunder (1967) *Capitalism and Underdevelopment in Latin America*. New York: Monthly Review Press.
Frank, Andre Gunder (1969) *Latin America: Underdevelopment or Revolution?* New York: Monthly Review Press.
Frank, Andre Gunder (1998) *Reorient: Global Economy in the Asian Age*. Berkeley: University of California Press.
Frank, Andre Gunder and Gills, Barry (1994) *The World System: 500 or 5000 Years?* London: Routledge.
Goldfrank, Walter L. (2000) Paradigm regained? The rules of Wallerstein's world-system method. In Giovanni Arrighi and Walter L. Goldfrank (eds) (2000) Festschrift for Immanuel Wallerstein. *Journal of World-Systems Research*, 6(2): 150–195.

Hall, Thomas D. (ed.) (2000) *A World-Systems Reader: New Perspectives on Gender, Urbanism, Cultures, Indigenous Peoples, and Ecology*. Lanham, MD: Rowman & Littlefield Press.

Harvey, David (2003) *The New Imperialism*. New York: Oxford University Press.

Hayden, Tom (2006) *Radical Nomad: C. Wright Mills and His Times*. Boulder, CO: Paradigm.

Hobsbawm, Eric J. (1994) *The Age of Extremes: A History of the World, 1914–1991*. New York: Pantheon.

McCormick, Thomas J. (1989) *America's Half Century: United States Foreign Policy in the Cold War*. Baltimore : Johns Hopkins University Press.

McMichael, Philip (1990) Incorporating comparison within a world-historical perspective: An alternative comparative method. *American Sociological Review*, 55: 385–397.

Polanyi, Karl, Arensberg, Conrad, and Pearson, Harry W. (eds) (1957) *Trade and Market in the Early Empires*. New York: The Free Press.

Robinson, William I. (2004) *A Theory of Global Capitalism*. Baltimore: Johns Hopkins University Press.

Robinson, William I. (2006) *Latin America and Globalization*. Baltimore: Johns Hopkins University Press.

Robinson, William I. (forthcoming) Globalization and the sociology of Immanuel Wallerstein: a critical appraisal. *International Sociology*, 26(1).

Sanderson, Stephen K. (2005) World-systems analysis after thirty years: should it rest in peace? *International Journal of Comparative Sociology*, 46, June: 179–213.

Sassen, Saskia (2006) *Territory, Authority, Rights: From Medieval to Global Assemblages*. Princeton, NJ: Princeton University Press.

Schneider, Jane (1977) Was there a precapitalist world-system? *Peasant Studies*, VI(1): 20–29. Reprinted in C. Chase-Dunn and T. D. Hall (eds) (1991) *Core/Periphery Relations in Precapitalist Worlds*. Boulder, CO: Westview, pp. 45–66.

Shannon, Thomas R. (1996) *An Introduction to the World-System Perspective*. Boulder, CO: Westview.

Silver, Beverly J. (2003) *Forces of Labor: Workers Movements and Globalization Since 1870*. Cambridge: Cambridge University Press.

Sklair, Leslie (2006) Competing conceptions of globalization. In C. Chase-Dunn and S. Babones (eds) *Global Social Change*. Baltimore: Johns Hopkins University Press, pp. 59–78.

Skocpol, Theda (1977) Wallerstein's world capitalist system: A theoretical and historical critique. *American Journal of Sociology*, 82: 1075–1090.

17

Edward W. Said

PATRICK WILLIAMS

THE PERSON

"For as long as I can remember, I have had the feeling of being part of more than one world." This was the comment of Said in 1992, in his mid-fifties, in a BBC2 programme made to mark the publication of one of his major works, *Culture and Imperialism*. Said was born in Jerusalem and brought up in Cairo, before finishing his education in the United States where he spent the rest of his life, but felt that his was a life characterized by "the many displacements from countries, cities, abodes, languages, environments that have kept me in motion all these years" (Said,1999: 217). In addition, there is the important fact of belonging to a people who are dispossessed, displaced, and dispersed, namely the Palestinians. Beyond this, the idea of multiple worlds is an indication of Said's enduring sense of the interconnectedness of cultures, as well as his opposition to the idea of separate, monolithic, or self-contained identities, whether personal or collective.

The complexity of location and formation contained in the many "worlds" of which he was part mark both Said's personal life and his intellectual output, and the importance of tracing them is indicated in a quote from Gramsci's *Prison Notebooks*, which Said uses in *Orientalism*, as well as the BBC programme: "The starting point of critical elaboration is the consciousness of what one really is, and is 'knowing thyself' as a product of the historical process to date which has deposited you in an infinity of traces, without leaving an inventory. The first thing to do is to make such an inventory" (Gramsci, 1971: 324). The three elements which need emphasis here are, first, the centrality of the individual, something which Said, various influential theories notwithstanding, refused ever to give up on; second, the necessary understanding of historical process; and third, the work of "critical elaboration."

The Wiley-Blackwell Companion to Major Social Theorists, First Edition.
Edited by George Ritzer and Jeffrey Stepnisky.
© 2011 Blackwell Publishing Ltd. Published 2011 by Blackwell Publishing Ltd.

A basic element in the inventory is the familial, something which Said recorded at length in his 1999 memoir *Out of Place*, written during, and as an antidote to, his long fight against leukemia. Said's parents were Palestinian Protestants, Anglicans on his father's side, and Baptists on his mother's, which made them part of a minority even among the minority community of Palestinian Christians. While religion appears not to have played a major role in Said's upbringing, it was something he grew increasingly suspicious of, and even antagonistic towards, in later life. Although Said's mother returned to Jerusalem in 1935 for his birth, the family lived in Cairo, where his father ran a successful business selling stationery equipment. With the family comfortably off, Said was able to attend fee-paying English schools, including the prestigious Victoria College, where, as well as the assumed benefits of a "good" education, he acquired an awareness of the pretentiousness, hypocrisy, and frequent downright racism of his colonial "masters." The same financial background, as well as his father's American citizenship, the result of his attraction to the US which led to his serving in the army during the First World War, saw Said sent to complete his secondary education and go to university in the United States, which became his home for the rest of his life.

A less happy form of the multiple worlds he inhabited is represented by Said's internal divisions. A result in part of the tensions of trying to please an emotionally distant, authoritarian father, and a mother who was both emotionally intimate and manipulative, he developed a sense of a profoundly divided personality, split between the public, outer "Edward" – naughty despite good intentions, who failed to achieve academically or in sports, a permanent source of disappointment to his parents – and an inner self, freer, more complex and cultured. Even at university in Princeton, "the sense of myself as unaccomplished, floundering, split in different parts (Arab, musician, young intellectual, solitary eccentric, dutiful student, political misfit) was dramatically revealed to me" (1999: 281). Although this amounts to a profound self-misapprehension by a brilliant young student and gifted pianist, the mere fact of such misapprehension is significant. While, as we will see later in the chapter, the attempt to bridge divides forms an important part of Said's cultural and political work, it is hard not to see a personal component there also.

The bad "Edward" may have been a problem persona for the young Said, but a certain tendency to transgress – viewed from the position of authorities and orthodoxies for whom he had little time or respect – arguably remained with him throughout his life, ranging from what we might call a minimalist position (just not doing what is expected) to a maximalist one (adopting radical oppositional political positions). He was, for example, transgressive in his unfashionable defense of humanism and the aesthetic; he was transgressive in being political about literature; he was transgressive in being unapologetically Palestinian.

The unwelcome, but formative, intrusion of the political into Said's life constituted a different kind of divide to be bridged. Important examples include 1948, and the *nakba* (disaster) of the expulsion of the Palestinians from their homeland, which meant that henceforth Said's life as one of the millions in the diaspora would inevitably include more "worlds"; 1967, where another Israeli victory, which signaled the loss of the remaining Palestinian territory, was crucial in turning Said from something like a Gramscian "traditional" intellectual to a politicized "organic" one; and the subsequent, endless, process of the dispossession, and oppression, of the

Palestinians by the Israeli state, which became the focus of so much of Said's work, especially in later years, and about which he became such an eloquent spokesman. Given the importance of Palestine, it is perhaps unsurprising to find him expressing deeply divided feelings about it:

> Even now the unreconciled duality I feel about the place, its intricate wrenching, tearing, sorrowful status as exemplified in so many distorted lives, including mine, and its status as an admirable country for *them* (but of course not for us) always gives me pain and a discouraging sense of being solitary, undefended, open to the assaults of trivial things that seem important and threatening, against which I have no weapons. (1999: 142)

For some, the medium of culture offers the possibility of healing certain rifts, and music was particularly important for Said in that respect. An accomplished musician, long-time music critic for the *Nation*, author of several books on music (*Musical Elaborations, Parallels and Paradoxes, Music at the Limits*) he founded the West-Eastern Divan Orchestra with Daniel Barenboim as a deliberate attempt to bridge the Israeli-Palestinian divide, at least at the level of cultural cooperation and mutual understanding. This Arab-Israeli orchestra has rapidly become internationally successful, musically above all, but also in a sense politically, as Barenboim has defied the wishes of the Israeli government and performed in Ramallah on the West Bank. As such, it constitutes an appropriate legacy to Said's lifelong attempt to overcome artificially divisive politics and ideologies.

The last decade and more of Said's life was marked by the leukemia which he fought with remarkable courage but which would eventually kill him. The sense of the preciousness of time in the shadow of the disease galvanized Said, and his output in this period was remarkable. In addition to over a dozen books – more than a lifetime's output for most academics – he produced regular articles for the Arab world, particularly via the newspapers *Al Ahram* and *Al Hayat*, and had a speaking schedule which would have been punishing for someone much younger and in good health. In his 1999 presidential address to the MLA on "Humanism and heroism," Said comments: "One must not only hope, but also do" (2000d: 291). The various modes of his "doing" – theoretical, cultural, political – mark his enduring engagement with the social.

Social Context

Like anyone of his generation, Said lived through the major events of two thirds of the twentieth century – the Second World War, the Holocaust, the nuclear threat, the Cold War, decolonization, the collapse of the Soviet Union, globalization – but the ones which initially moved him were an appropriate combination of the personal and the internationally significant. As someone who grew up in Egypt, Said was aware of, and subsequently enthused by, the epoch-making process of decolonization as it worked itself out through the Nasserite revolution. While the bright promise represented by Nasser was at best only partially realized, Said nevertheless retained a great deal of sympathy for his brand of progressive nationalist politics (notwithstanding the fact that they were precisely nationalist). The other, far more obvious, but in many ways oddly belated, political *prise de conscience* was in relation to Palestine and came with the crushing Israeli victory in the 1967 war, and since then Palestine has, in one form or another, been part of almost everything that Said produced.

In their different ways, these two examples can stand for the questions which have engaged Said ever since. The situation in Palestine/Israel contains a whole complex of issues, including latter-day Israeli colonialism, the dispossession of almost an entire people, the appalling foreign policy of the United States, not least in relation to the oppression carried out by its clients, whether states or dictators, and the awful process by which victims can become, in their turn, cruel victimizers. On the other side of this superpower-supported injustice and oppression stands the example of Nasser: champion of Third World liberation movements, thorn in the flesh of those who aim to perpetrate oppression and injustice; icon of popular resistance. While the fact, and example, of Palestine has remained to provide an enduring social, political, and ethical context, the potential for liberation movements, as well as their nature, has changed drastically from the period of decolonization and the possibilities embodied in charismatic leaders. Different modes of, in Wallerstein's terms, "anti-systemic" protest and popular mobilization, most famously, perhaps, the anti-globalization movement, but including significant moments such as the first Palestinian *intifada* or uprising, now carry the hopes for liberation which mattered so much to Said.

INTELLECTUAL CONTEXT

Said's intellectual and academic context offer once again a divided and contradictory situation. On the one hand, as Said himself commented many times, the modern university provided "an almost utopian space" (1994: 61) – indeed, one of the very few remaining such spaces. On the other, beyond this realm of possibility, the actual facts of the university world could be much less encouraging, whether locally, in Said's own area of literary studies, or more generally. When Said was at Harvard, for example, "Conventional history and a wan formalism ruled the literary faculty" (1999: 289), and in such circumstances, his own formation could hardly escape being conventional. A decade later, things seemed not to have improved, as Said quotes Richard Ohmann's comment that English departments represent "a moderately successful effort by professors to obtain some benefits of capitalism while avoiding its risks, and, yet, a reluctance to acknowledge any link between how we do our work and the way the larger society is run" (1984: 229). Despite that, Said notes with gratitude the intellectual quality of various teachers and colleagues, including substantial figures such as Lionel Trilling and R. P. Blackmur.

One response to that combination of traditionalism, inertia, and disengagement in the university is to promote their opposites, which is what Said did. The 1970s and early 1980s saw the rapid growth of continental theory – structuralism, post-structuralism, feminism, Marxism – in universities in the United States, helped in no small measure by the work of Said and others like him, but, as we will see in more detail later, the promise of theory, its radical renovatory possibilities, were coming to seem to Said as unfulfillable – or at least unfulfilled in the current context. This sense of the rapid rise and even more rapid fall of theory – at least in so far as theory could be seen as carrying out any truly useful function – is one of the things which most marks Said's own use of, and, in different ways and to varying degrees, his distancing himself from, theoretical approaches.

Though one group of contemporary intellectuals appeared not to be delivering on the promises implied by their practice, it was still possible that a different group might yet do so. If the major humanists who were important in Said's intellectual development such as Blackmur and Auerbach could be counted as, in Gramscian terms, traditional intellectuals (whether or not one would wish to include the "failed" contemporary theorists in there is obviously a matter for debate), then the group to whom he increasingly turns are the organic intellectuals, whether that organicism lies in their class location, anti-colonial formation, or something else. These include Marxists such as Lukács, Gramsci, Benjamin, Adorno and Raymond Williams, as well as Third World or postcolonial (in the broad sense) thinkers like C. L. R. James, Aimé Césaire, Frantz Fanon, Amilcar Cabral and Eqbal Ahmad. With this reorientation comes a sharpened sense of the role of the intellectual, something which Said discusses at length in his 1993 Reith Lectures.

Theory

In many ways, Said could appear as the opposite of a social theorist, having a background neither in social science, nor in theory. In addition, his intellectual formation was in an area – traditional literary studies – notorious for its aversion to theory. While there is indeed a sense in which Said's theoretical interventions might be considered modest (in the best sense, as not self-aggrandizing, and displaying an awareness of their limits), and some critics call them modest in a thoroughly derogatory sense (with others even saying they are unoriginal), it is worth asking why, if they are unoriginal, or merely modest, they have proved so remarkably inspiring, as well as controversial, for the last thirty years and more.

In *Out Of Place*, Said notes that as an undergraduate at Princeton he developed "a fascination with complexity and unpredictability" (1999: 277) which remained with him thereafter, with both making their last appearance as among the valorized qualities of the creative artist in the posthumously published *Late Style* (2006). Many would feel that at least the second of these attributes could be held to characterize his performance as theorist, above all as a traditionally formed professor of literature who at one point champions radical theory but subsequently turns away from it, but also as a literary theorist who argues that the point of theory is to engage the experiential and the social. The manner in which theory approaches the world became for Said one of its most important qualities, and the one by which it would, in his eyes, stand or fall. In addition, a form of "unpredictability" as resistant, transgressive, or in Saidian terms "unco-opted," intellectual practice typifies much of his approach to theory.

The un-worlding and re-worlding of theory

Questions of the nature and function of theory have always been important for Said, and his first major theoretical book, *Beginnings: Intention and Method* (1975) is notable for its inclusion of a range of structuralist and poststructuralist theorists – Barthes, Lévi-Strauss, Saussure, Foucault and Derrida, as well as earlier figures such as Freud, Nietzsche, and the unlikely but enormously important Vico – and he was subsequently known as a pioneering advocate and popularizer of continental theory. It therefore came as a surprise to many when, in his 1984 collection *The World, the Text, the Critic,* Said subjected Derrida and Foucault, the most substantial of the theorists in *Beginnings*, and by then two figures with global reputations, to stringent critique in the long essay "Criticism between Culture and System." Of the two, it is Derrida who comes off worse, but even Foucault is seen to epitomize many of the problems which Said had come to regard as vitiating theory. He discusses their work at length – in many ways a more sustained engagement with them than was evident in *Beginnings* – and praises them, for example for their attempts "to devise what is a form of critical openness and repeatedly renewed theoretical resourcefulness, designed to provide first knowledge of a very specific sort" (1984: 191) as well as for their rethinking of techniques (something which, as we will see, is important in Said's own approach); each, nevertheless, espouses theory which insufficiently engages the world. Derrida's theory, as Said says, leads us *into* the text; Foucault's *in* and *out*. While Derrida's approach thus leaves the reader trapped in the realm of the textual, even Foucault's putative re-emergence into the world is insufficient. His theory of power/knowledge, for example, perhaps his most "worldly" in Saidian terms, still fails to display an appropriate sense of historical change or, more significantly, a recognition of what Said, in an echo of Walter Benjamin, calls the "coarse items" (1984: 221): class struggle, military coercion, wealth and privilege.

In addition to what theory does – neglecting the social, "textualizing" itself – there is also the problem of what happens to theory. In a manner which recalls Sartre's theory of praxis and the practico-inert in *Critique of Dialectical Reason* (1960), Said sees a pattern of rise and fall, whereby a dynamic, perhaps opposi-tional, theory emerges, flourishes, but through a process of repetition becomes tame and ineffectual. Part of that repetition may involve a trajectory of transmission, from one theorist and one socio-historical location to another, and the example Said uses, in "Travelling Theory" in *The World, the Text, the Critic*, is the incremental diluting of the radicalism in Lukács's *History and Class Consciousness* (1971) as it passes through the work of Lucien Goldmann in Paris in the 1950s, and that of Raymond Williams in Cambridge in the 1970s. In *Culture and Imperialism,* Said suggests that one of the effects of traveling theory is to make decisions about whether to be a Marxist theorist or a feminist, for example, about as demanding (and perhaps as meaningful) as choosing items from a restaurant menu. A different kind of trajec-tory, but no less negative, is that taken by theory as it loses radical energy, becomes increasingly institutionalized, co-opted, part of the system it originally aimed to oppose. A final element in what Said calls "the systematic degradation of theory" (1984: 243) is the shift from theory as progressive intervention to theory as, in Said's terms, "cult" with its chief priests and hordes of disciples. Theory, according to Said – using a phrase from R. P. Blackmur on modernism of which he is fond – should be "a technique of trouble." The problem with so much contemporary theory is precisely that it is insufficiently troublesome.

One of the questions that arise from this rather depressing picture is whether Said is offering a general account of the (inevitable) problems of theory, or one which is historically specific, particularly to the US academy in the 1970s and 1980s, which he analyses in a number of essays. One of the clearest answers is provided by

"Travelling Theory Reconsidered" in *Reflections on Exile* (2000a), an important example of Said rethinking concepts – in the manner for which he praised Foucault and Derrida – and locating them in appropriate social and historical contexts. Here, despite the ongoing difficulties of theory – "the indeterminacy of deconstructive reading, the airy insouciance of post-axiological criticism, the casual reductiveness of some (but by no means all) ideological schools" (2000a: 383) – all is not lost: the degradation of theory, in over-specialization and professionalization, and as a result of "travelling," is not inevitable. The same Lukácsian theory now goes in the opposite direction, towards a better, more resistant intellectual practice in the person of Adorno, and, most importantly, towards the world and the political in Fanon's anti-colonialism, internationalism and visionary humanism. If theory's journey was previously a marker of its flaws, degradation and decline, now, interestingly, "The point of theory ... is to travel, always to move beyond its confinements, to emigrate, to remain in a sense in exile" (2000a: 451). Rather than suggesting a contradiction with the earlier position, this indicates that even theory is not automatically (to use another of the titles from the collection) one of history's "Lost Causes." Also, the location of theory "in exile" is no coincidence, as exile comes to occupy an increasingly important place in Said's later thought, not least in relation to the figure of the intellectual.

However, one of the results of the perceived failure of theory as a general intellectual and cultural project – the previous example notwithstanding – is that Said increasingly distances himself from it, though this is nothing like the simple, wholesale rejection of theory that some have portrayed it as being: as he comments, "to say that we are against theory ... is to be blind and trivial" (2000a: 383). Nevertheless, he is concerned to rethink and rename his practice, and the term chosen, for a variety of different reasons, is criticism. If theory seems almost doomed to increasing abstraction and specialization, criticism stands for a mode of intellectual activity which is self-reflexive, socially and historically aware, and engaged. Further, "were I to use one word consistently along with *criticism* ... it would be *oppositional*" (1984: 29). Against "religious criticism" – which sounds rather like theory in another guise – Said promotes "secular criticism": humanistic, socially grounded, and embodied in a "critical consciousness." Although the return to "criticism" might look like the retreat of a closet traditionalist to safe ground, it in fact constitutes one of Said's numerous (unpredictable, "transgressive") attempts to reanimate traditional ideas and render them relevant. "In other words, rather than being defined by the silent past, commanded by it to speak in the present, criticism, no less than any text, is the present in the course of its articulation, its struggles for definition" (1984: 51). The secular nature of criticism connects it to the much-quoted notion which he takes from Vico, that human beings can know what they have made, and what they have made is their society and history. The fact that, however much they might deny it, ideas (even the endlessly self-rarifying forms of theory) cannot avoid "worldliness" – both a specific location (historical, social) and a certain materiality (institutional presence; effects in the real world, etc.) – is crucial, though ideas, as well as those who formulate them, acknowledge and engage with that worldliness in very different ways.

The preferred mode for the secular critic is yet another appearance of the unpredictable: in part to distinguish her from the ever-more problematic professionalized intellectual-as-expert, Said offers the critic as amateur. While this represents an example of the "modest" theoretical proposal, it is also a serious proposition for the reformulated role of the intellectual: the amateur does what she does (literally) out of love for the subject; unconstrained by disciplinary boundaries or academic specialisms, she reads widely and analyses those things that matter, rather than the ones she might feel professionally constrained to, her choices, in Said's terms, being broad affiliative ones rather than normative and filiative.

Theory and the world

Orientalism

Although *Orientalism* is often taken as occupying a position of almost isolated pre-eminence in Said's oeuvre, there are good reasons for seeing it as part of a number of textual groupings or continuities. The first of these would be the trilogy of which *Orientalism* formed the first part, the other two being *The Question of Palestine* and *Covering Islam*. Between them they examine a set of distinct but related issues centering on the connections between the modes of representation of actual or constructed entities (the Orient, Islam, Palestine) and the workings of power, especially in the form of international politics. "I have not been able to discover any period in European or American history since the Middle Ages in which Islam was generally discussed or thought about *outside* a framework created by passion, prejudice and political interests" (1981: 24). He then adds "This may not seem a surprising discovery"; perhaps not, but its unsurprising assertion is precisely the kind of claim which makes Said a controversial figure.

Another grouping into which one might place *Orientalism* would be those texts grappling with theory. Several of the essays in *The World, the Text, and the Critic* on the problems of theory were written before *Orientalism*, and it is important to see the latter as tackling the range of failings they expose. Above all, it is a sustained attempt to deploy theory as a "worldly" forensic tool in the production of historically grounded knowledge.

Although questions of the production and circulation of knowledge occupied Said throughout his career, *Orientalism* is perhaps his most extensive examination of the relationship of knowledge and power, even though, as he points out in the 1993 Afterword, that is not how many readers have viewed it: "Nevertheless, *Orientalism* has more often been thought of as a kind of testimonial to subaltern status – the wretched of the earth talking back – than as a multicultural critique of power using knowledge to advance itself" (2003c: 336). Here, the power/knowledge pairing is usually seen as an application of Foucault's "savoir/pouvoir," though it could equally be taken from the book's other important theorist, Gramsci. The presence in the same book of Foucault's post-structuralism and Gramsci's Marxism has been variously seen as a productive theoretical synergy or conclusive proof of Said's lack of awareness of the implications of his theoretical choices (Clifford (1988) and Porter (1993) are two well-known examples of the negative criticisms.) Said was generally unconcerned by this controversy; as he commented in an interview: "*Orientalism* is theoretically inconsistent, and I designed that way" (in Salusinszky, 1987: 36). On the one hand, this is part of Said's negative reaction to theory perceived as all-encompassing, "coherent" system-building; it is also another example of his repeated refusal to do the expected.

Theoretically inconsistent or not, *Orientalism* is a powerful dissection of the relation between the ways in which the West has thought and written about the "Orient," that is, represented it, and the ways in which it has exercised control over it. Most generally, Orientalism operates as an instance of what Said terms "imaginative geography," the universal human propensity to divide the world into "us" and "them," in this case Orient and Occident, and thus participates in the creation of ideas, myths, stereotypes, and the like about the unknown or little-known Orient. More specifically, Orientalism is the ensemble of academic disciplines – sociology, history, linguistics, geography, anthropology, literature, etc. – which have been producing knowledge about the Orient, sometimes for centuries. Finally, Orientalism is "a Western style for dominating, restructuring and having authority over the Orient" (1978: 3). Central to Said's argument is the way in which the types of knowledge – widely divergent, at least as far as their sources are concerned – act to inform and legitimate the political, economic, and military power which is unleashed on the Orient. The supposedly discrete academic disciplines produce astonishingly similar, and mutually reinforcing, "knowledge" about the Orient as deviant, dysfunctional, civilizationally stagnant, technologically backward, socially retrogressive, morally deficient, culturally impoverished, in all senses the Other to the West.

Said draws on Foucault's concept of a discourse as a framework within which "appropriate" knowledge is regulated, produced, and constrained (though arguably he might have been better served by treating it as an ideological formation – which has different theoretical and political implications). As he says: "My contention is that without examining Orientalism as a discourse one cannot possibly understand the enormously systematic discipline by which European culture was able to manage – and even produce – the Orient politically, sociologically, militarily, ideologically, scientifically, and imaginatively during the post-Enlightenment period" (1978: 3). From "hard" science to imaginative literature, the Orient is constructed as inferior, in need of Western intervention, and whether the representations aim to be sympathetic or are unrepentantly derogatory, they are recuperated by Orientalism in the production of its sanctioned forms of knowledge. One result of the operations of Orientalism as a discourse is therefore that the representations it produces are much more concerned with internal consistency than with providing the truth about the Orient (though they nevertheless claim to do that also). That focus on internal consistency helps explain the strength of the discourse and the longevity of Orientalist ideas over several centuries – factual contradiction notwithstanding.

The inferiority of the Orient and Orientals is marked by the fact that, in the phrase from Marx's *The Eighteenth Brumaire of Louis Bonaparte* which Said uses as one of the epigraphs for the book, "They cannot represent themselves; they must be represented" (Said, 1978: xiii). The power, cultural and other, of the West allows it to represent the Orient as it chooses, but in addition there is the legitimating "must": since they are incapable of representing themselves, it falls to us to do it for them. This doubles the power of the West, as it speaks not only in its own voice, but also in that of the Other.

Much critical ink has been spilled on the topic of the process of Orientalist representation, as well as its object, the Orient. Said, for example, argues that there is no such thing as a true representation, only varying degrees of misrepresentation, and also that there is no such thing as a real Orient to be represented. Without entering unnecessarily into the prolonged theoretical debates (see, for example, Young, 1990 for a representative poststructuralist critique), it is important to clarify Said's position. First, a representation cannot provide a perfect copy of the original, and therefore is inevitably to some degree a misrepresentation. Much more important for Said than any question of putative fidelity to the original, however, is what the representation actually does: its power to persuade, to legitimate, to dominate. Second, because the Orient is a Western construct, there is indeed no "real" Orient for Orientalism to produce its "truthful" representations of. As Said comments, "There were – and are – cultures and nations whose location is in the East, and their lives, histories and customs have a brute reality obviously greater than anything that could be said about them in the West" (1978: 5) – and they are not the "Orient."

The truth of knowledge is another of those apparently uncontroversial topics which somehow become controversial when articulated by Said. As he says, "the general liberal consensus that 'true' knowledge is fundamentally non-political (and conversely that overtly political knowledge is not 'true' knowledge) obscures the highly if obscurely organised political circumstances obtaining when knowledge is produced" (1978: 10). Scholars in the humanities, and Orientalists above all, were, however, scandalized at the suggestion that their work was not disinterested, above politics as they claimed (and some like Bernard Lewis still claim). It is, nevertheless, one of the successes of *Orientalism* that it demonstrates so convincingly that not only is Orientalist knowledge not above politics, but it is precisely deeply enmeshed in the very worst sort of politics, namely colonial domination and exploitation.

For Said, writing in 1978 in the phase of US Orientalism, the centuries-long persistence of Orientalist modes of thought and representation was remarkable. Twenty-five years later, in the context of the invasion of Iraq, the situation in terms of representing and understanding Muslims was visibly much worse. While this offers little comfort to those who might hope that critique as powerful as Said's could bring the ideology it is attacking to an end, it does nevertheless demonstrate the accuracy of Said's contention that the knowledge production of Orientalism is intimately linked to the material interests of Western – in this case US – supremacy.

Culture and imperialism

In *Orientalism* Said laments the absence of a general study of the relationship between culture and imperialism. A decade and more later, none had appeared, so he was obliged to write it himself. *Culture and Imperialism* (1993) is in some ways a continuation and extension of *Orientalism*; it is also its opposite, Other, face. For instance, if *Orientalism* is a study in the construction and maintenance of hierarchical and oppressive cultural divisions by means of ideas, images and texts, *Culture and Imperialism* is an argument for recognizing the many possible connections which bridge those divides. One of the sections of the book is entitled "Overlapping territories, intertwined histories," which indicates how far Said is from the conventional view of the gulf separating colonizer and colonized. At the same time, however,

Orientalism's thesis about the material impact of ideas remains central to the new study: "For the enterprise of empire depends upon the *idea* of *having an empire*" (1993: 10).

To a certain extent, *Culture and Imperialism* looks like a more Saidian book than *Orientalism*, since it devotes a great deal of space to discussing the classic European novel, the subject he taught for the whole of his career. The approach adopted is typically modest and iconoclastic: in addition to noting (modestly) the connections between the European novel and imperial expansion, Said argues for the mutually constitutive nature of those connections, which outraged various literary scholars, as well as drawing accusations of "culturalism" from certain, especially Marxist, quarters. At the heart of the analysis is Said's own strategy of "contrapuntal reading." Derived from musical counterpoint, where various themes or voices interweave without dominance or necessarily any overall resolution, the contrapuntal aims to show the "overlapping territories, intertwined histories" in text and world.

The most controversial example of this in the book is Said's discussion of Jane Austen's *Mansfield Park*, where he argues that the pleasant, genteel way of life in the stately home is ultimately dependent on the income from Sir Thomas Bertram's slave holdings and sugar plantations in the Caribbean, and the same system of order and control (if not applied in exactly the same manner) is required to make both worlds function appropriately. Reading the histories and territories contrapuntally produces a fuller understanding of the world of the novel, even if it renders Austen scholars apoplectic at the supposed besmirching of her name. Said, however, is very clear: understanding these connections "does not ... diminish the novels' value as works of art; on the contrary, because of their *worldliness*, because of their complex affiliation with their real setting, they are more interesting and more valuable as works of art" (1993: 13, emphasis in original).

In addition to reading these great assertions of colonial cultural authority in contrapuntal fashion, Said also sets them in a different counterpoint alongside their antithesis, *Orientalism*'s significantly (if appropriately) absent Other: anti-colonial resistance. The opposition of Fanon, Yeats, Césaire, C. L. R. James, Ngugi wa Thiong'o, and others to colonial oppression, as well as their complex relation to colonial culture, is examined. The latter is embodied in the ambivalence of the "Voyage In" to the metropolitan center, which, despite the possibilities it creates for assimilation, more usually functions as "a sign of adversarial internationalism in an age of continued imperial structures" (1993: 295).

One of the facts of resistance – a product in part of the overlaps already noted – is its "partial tragedy": "that it must to a certain degree work to recover forms already established or at least influenced and infiltrated by the culture of empire" (1993: 253). This historically unavoidable circumstance is one answer to the (rather pointless, but nonetheless frequently repeated) earlier criticism: how could Said hope to produce a credible critique of Orientalism using Western theories and from within the heart of the Western academy? No "uncontaminated" theory is available, nor any "pure" position, but that does not thereby render what is available unusable or ineffective.

One of the available forms of resistance – as well as classic expression of colonial power – is narrative, and in *Orientalism* Said had already noted its ability to disrupt the reifying power of the imperial "vision." Here, in terms which echo his essay on the politics of narrative in relation to Palestine, "Permission to Narrate" (in Said, 1995b), he says: "The power to narrate, or to block other narratives from forming and emerging, is very important to culture and imperialism, and constitutes one of the main connections between them" (1993: xiii). In that context, the struggle to tell one's own story has implications, and effects, far beyond the aesthetic.

Humanism

As theories can travel, so can theorists, often in the same unfortunate direction. Said's own trajectory is, predictably or not, different. In his case, it goes from humanism to humanism; from his early formation as a traditional humanist to his final completed book, *Humanism and Democratic Criticism*. In part, this is about Said's unshakeable loyalty to certain important ideas; at the same time, it is about his critical engagement with, and rethinking of, those ideas, in line with Gramsci's comment on the importance of "renovating and making 'critical' an already-existing activity"(1971: 331). Certainly, with the advent of sometimes stridently anti-humanist structuralist and poststructuralist theory, continuing to proclaim oneself a humanist could look like the most reactionary of anti-theoretical stances. However, humanism had also been under fire from positions which might matter more to Said, most famously, perhaps, Fanon's *The Wretched of the Earth*, and Sartre's polemical preface to the book:

> First, we must face that unexpected revelation, the striptease of our humanism. There you can see it, quite naked, and it's not a pretty sight. It was nothing but an ideology of lies, a perfect justification for pillage; its honeyed words, its affectation of sensibility were only alibis for our aggressions … With us there is nothing more consistent than a racist humanism since the European has only been able to become man through creating slaves and monsters. (in Fanon, 1967: 21–22)

Although many conveniently took this as the complete demolition of the edifice of humanism, that was categorically not what Fanon and Sartre had in mind; on the contrary, their aim was to remake humanism, but what was needed first was a thoroughgoing, honest critique of its failings. The same process can be seen at work in Said.

Amidst the theoretical wrangling over whether *Orientalism* was too Foucauldian, or insufficiently Gramscian, few cared to notice Said's insistence that he was writing a humanist book (Clifford is a significant exception here). Part of the problem that Orientalism represented for Said was that it was a humanist discipline, but in the particular form of its worldly involvement, in its structures and practices, it had, as he said, destroyed all of its humanistic values. While Orientalism was busy negating its humanist heritage through over-involvement in colonial politics, however, academics in the humanities were constructing a self-image of "non-interference," as Said terms it, which denied their involvement in any politics whatsoever. Such matters had far more than merely academic import, and Said notes the way in which, as part of the nationalist politics of the period, the Right in the US in the 1980s attempted to claim humanism as its own – but precisely the narrow, exclusivist, ultimately racist, deformation of humanism which Fanon, Sartre, and Said in turn attacked.

Against this, *Humanism and Democratic Criticism* argues for a humanism which in part aims to recapture the universalism claimed by earlier versions, but which more urgently is a humanism for a different world, or at the very least a world understood differently: "In my understanding of its relevance today, humanism is not a way of affirming what 'we' have always known and felt, but rather a means of questioning, upsetting and reformulating so much of what is presented to us as commodified, packaged, uncontroversial and uncritically codified certainties, including those contained in the masterpieces herded under the rubric of 'the classics'" (2004a: 28). In addition, regardless of any sense of cultural centrality, "Humanism ... must excavate the silences, the world of memory, of itinerant, barely surviving groups, the places of exclusion and invisibility, the kind of testimony that doesn't make it onto the reports" (2004a: 81). From comments such as these, it is clear that humanism is being rethought as a strategy for diverse forms of resistance, and that proper pursuit of its intellectual goals will simultaneously involve pursuing ameliorative social ones. In his presidential address to the MLA, Said goes so far as to categorize the truly humanistic enterprise as "heroic" in its aims and efforts, while in the 2003 Preface to *Orientalism*, he talks of humanism as "the final resistance" to injustice and inhuman practices (2000d, 2003c: xxii).

Humanism and intellectuals

Said's final comment in *Orientalism* is, "I consider Orientalism's failure to have been a human as much as an intellectual one" (1978: 328). While the former is the greater failure, the latter matters very much, both in itself and to Said. Explicitly or not, much of what he wrote concerns the nature and function of intellectuals, who have become, as he trenchantly comments, "a class badly in need of moral rehabilitation and social redefinition" (2000a: 120). His own effort in that direction is his 1993 BBC Reith Lectures, published as *Representations of the Intellectual*, an eloquent discussion, even if it does veer somewhat between the descriptive (intellectuals include anyone working in knowledge production or distribution) and the prescriptive ("the intellectual belongs on the same side with the weak and unrepresented" (1994: 17)). Between these, it is the affiliative, ethical stance of the intellectual, rather than their broad social location, which is important.

One result of the affiliative stance of the intellectual is the need, in a phrase which Said takes from Chomsky, to "speak truth to power." This is clearly not any simple or absolute truth, however, as Said's self-questioning makes apparent: "In effect I am asking *the* basic question for the intellectual: how does one speak the truth? What truth? For whom and where?" (1994: 65). These are questions to be tackled with the secular tools available to the intellectual – "revelation and inspiration" are categorically to be avoided.

The ability of the intellectual to distance herself from abuses of power in order to criticize them is the result of her position as exile. In both *Reflections on Exile* and *Representations of the Intellectual*, Said examines the situation of intellectuals as literal, and metaphorical, exiles. The exile's location as insider/outsider creates a "double perspective," which in turn aids the understanding of phenomena relationally, in terms of their networks of relations, and developmentally, in terms of their historical and social becoming, both of which are essential elements in Said's humanist framework.

Humanism and Palestine

One of the questions Said wrestled with for more than thirty years was how to write about and theorize Palestine appropriately. (It has proved a problem for others too: Palestine remains one of the great, inexplicable absences in the field of postcolonial theory which Said's work did so much to inspire.) At one level, the sheer existential fact of the dispossession and continuing oppression of the Palestinian people seems to take the situation beyond theory, and indeed a considerable quantity of Said's writing on Palestine could not be construed as theoretical. At the same time, there is the need to conceptualize and analyze the experience, and theory has a part to play in that. After all that has been said so far, it is no surprise, perhaps, that, above all, Palestine needs to be written about humanistically: rationally (rather than on the basis of ideological mystifications); secularly (instead of drawing on "theological" abstractions); contrapuntally (involving an understanding of the interconnections and entanglements of both sides); with an awareness of the historical and social dimensions of any analysis, as well as a commitment to "speak truth to power," given that the powerful in this situation seem determined to avoid the truth at all costs.

One approach to writing about Palestine is to integrate it into other discussions. Palestine then appears as exemplar of a wide range of variously theorized topics including universalism, human rights, the politics of narrative, lost causes, exile, representation, and nationalism. One of the most important of these concepts is universalism, which takes several forms. In relation to one of these, Said says, "For the intellectual the task, I believe, is explicitly to universalise the crisis, to give greater human scope to what a particular race or nation suffered, to associate that experience with the sufferings of others" (1994: 33). This goes far beyond the already well-established aim of bridging divides or making connections. It has, for example, a flavor of Gramsci's argument that single events must clarify general concepts within an increased general understanding of the world. In this particular context, the specific example of Palestine takes its place in the ongoing, and dreadful, history of oppressed communities (alongside, among others, the Jews), but given due weight, understanding and human sympathy, rather than the routine dismissals or demonizing perpetrated by the media or antagonistic politicians.

Another aspect of the universal is that of (humanistically promoted) universal values – which intellectuals are to fight for and instantiate – as well as universal human rights. Once again, Palestine is central: "Palestine, I believe, is today the touchstone case for human rights, not because the argument for it can be made as elegantly simple as the case for South Africa liberation, but because it *cannot* be made simple" (2000c: 435). In part, that absence of simplicity is the result of the deeply implicated human situation of Israelis and Palestinians, which Said interprets in contrapuntal fashion.

Commenting on the processes of social transformation which follow subaltern action, Gramsci says, "one thus gives a modern and contemporary form to the traditional secular humanism which must be the ethical basis of the new type of State" (1971: 388). While Said's theoretical ambitions do not typically extend to the possibility of affecting state formation (though he obviously tried to play some part in the development of a rational, secular-based model for Palestine), Gramsci's combination is appealing. Older theories rethought and reconfigured appropriately for the contemporary context; secular humanism providing the ethical basis for progressive worldly intervention – there is perhaps not a lot more that Said would have hoped for from theory in general, and humanism in particular.

IMPACT

Said is in the relatively unusual position of being credited with inaugurating an entire new field of academic enquiry in the shape of postcolonial studies, which is now found in university departments around the world. Above all, it is *Orientalism* which many regard as the founding text for the new discipline. If that were correct, then Said's impact would be truly remarkable. However, while it is not the case that Said single-handedly brought postcolonial studies into being, nor that *Orientalism* constitutes the field's one urtext, it is nevertheless true that for a great many scholars in different subject areas, Said's book had a profound effect, opening up new possibilities for theory, changing both the way in which the relationship between text and politics was perceived, as well as, in certain cases, the way in which entire disciplines thought about their practices and principles.

Postcolonial studies, it must be said, represents something of an ambiguous legacy – insofar as it actually constitutes one – for Said. At its worst, it can function as little more than a means of recycling or re-animating a somewhat lifeless segment of English Literature with an uncertain relationship to theory. At its best, however, it offers a mode of transdisciplinary study, historically grounded, politically aware, theoretically informed, radical, and oppositional in the best tradition of the Saidian intellectual. One of the things which academic disciplines and schools of theory constantly need to practice, in Said's view, is self-criticism, and in the case of postcolonial studies this is carried to something of an extreme. Repeated debates about the nature and function of postcolonial studies may sometimes have more the air of self-flagellation than self-criticism, but, as a recent, random example, *Rerouting the Postcolonial* (Wilson *et al.*, 2010) attests, at least the scrutiny continues.

Given the emphasis Said lays on connecting with the social, different, but in some ways not unrelated, kinds of impact were achieved in the world outside the academy. For fifteen years, Said was a member of the Palestine National Council, the Palestinian parliament-in-exile, and was involved in drafting policy documents, most importantly, perhaps, the 1988 Palestinian Declaration of Independence, with its acceptance of a two-state solution; in addition, when he was not being travestied as "Arafat's man in New York," he was being endlessly approached by the media for his opinion on numerous aspects of Middle Eastern politics. In each of these areas, however, impact might be less than hoped for: Arafat was apparently quite capable of ignoring carefully prepared documents, even at moments as crucial as the lead up to the Oslo Accords. Similarly, Said had no illusions about how carefully the opinions of a Palestinian "expert" would be listened to in the US media. Having resigned from the PNC over Arafat's sell-out of the Palestinians at the Oslo negotiations, Said helped form the Palestinian National Initiative with Mustafa Barghouti as a secular and reformist political alternative to the problems posed by Fatah and Hamas. As a different means of engaging an audience in the Arab world, Said took to writing articles for Arab newspapers, in particular *Al Ahram* and *Al Hayat*, which gave his ideas the widest currency they had yet achieved. Through strategies such as these, Said had, as Rashid Khalidi comments, "[a] profound impact on Palestine and the Palestinians" (Khalidi, 2008: 48). In particular, his willingness to talk to potentially hostile audiences on difficult subjects such as the need to recognize the humanity of Israelis, "was one of his greatest and most difficult achievements, and probably one of the most unappreciated by those many people who are ignorant of the impact that Said had on Palestinian public discourse" (ibid.). As an instance of theoretically informed humanistic political practice, this is as good an example as any of Said living out what he believed in.

One result of this combination of the intellectual and the engaged political is that Said's name, his thought, and his impact extend much further than an academic could normally expect. His ideas and his example are invoked in a wide variety of contexts, invariably on the side of the twin values of "enlightenment and emancipation" in whose name he fought so hard.

Assessment

In many ways, "assessing" Said has been standard practice since the publication of *Orientalism*. Particularly in the 1980s, it was something of a rite of passage, especially for younger academics working in theory or in the emergent postcolonial studies, to provide a critique, to go "beyond" Said, as a mark of theoretical rigor, political radicalism, or just generally being ahead of the game. At the same time as this body of notionally fraternal commentary, there was a considerable quantity of straightforwardly antagonistic responses, particularly from more established figures like Ernest Gellner, or those who felt more threatened by the kind of analysis Said was offering, such as the Orientalist Bernard Lewis. One critic who combined both the notionally fraternal and the straightforwardly antagonistic was the Indian Marxist Aijaz Ahmad, who made a long and bitter *ad hominem*, as well as intellectual, attack on Said the centerpiece of his book *In Theory* (1992). Ahmad's argument was in turn subject to stringent criticism by others on the left such as Benita Parry and Neil Lazarus.

Orientalism has been criticized for many things, often in completely contradictory fashion. It has, for example, been accused of being wildly over-theoretical, or of being insufficiently theoretical; of being excessively indebted to Foucault, or of failing to make proper use of the range of insights a Foucauldian perspective offered. It has also been taken to task for not including an examination of the gendered dimensions of Orientalism, as well as for not including any consideration of the resistance on the part of colonized people to Orientalist and colonialist incursions. The first of these, typified by a book like Meyda Yegenoglu's *Colonial Fantasies: Towards a Feminist Reading of Orientalism* (1998), is an example of the slightly better or more accurate criticisms of *Orientalism* – gender was arguably never one of Said's strong points in any of his books – but it hardly constitutes a total omission in the way that is often asserted. The second typifies the way in which Said is criticized for not doing something which he had no intention of doing: *Orientalism* is a study of the forms of power – discursive, textual and ideological, as well as economic, political and military – deployed by the West in its relations with non-Western cultures; indigenous resistance is dealt with elsewhere, particularly in *Culture and Imperialism*. The latter example also typifies an extremely frequent phenomenon: it is remarkable that for someone whose work is not at all difficult to understand (unlike that of many "proper" theorists) Said is so routinely attacked on the basis of – apparently – a very poor comprehension of the substance of his arguments, or his critical practice.

One of the most shocking of these acts of incomprehension is a recent addition to· a new sub-genre – the posthumous attack. *Postcolonial Theory and the Arab-Israel Conflict* (Salzman *et al.*, 2008) joins books such as Robert Irwin's *Dangerous Knowledge* (2006) and Ibn Warraq's *Defending the West* (2007) in mounting critiques which are frequently personalized and trivializing rather than offering any substantive engagement with Said's work, though it far outdoes them as an instance of academic failure. Although its supposed subject is the broad remit offered by its title, its main aim appears to be to discredit Said. Ironically, the discrediting arguably works in entirely the opposite direction, as contributor after contributor fails to display any creditable knowledge either of postcolonial theory or of Said's work. For their part, Irwin and Ibn Warraq typically try to undermine Said through identifying small errors, presumably because his larger arguments, particularly theoretical ones, are beyond their polemical powers.

A different kind of (unsuccessful) undermining of Said occurs in the work of the sociologist Bryan Turner. In *Orientalism, Post-modernism and Globalism*, for example, Turner says, "the book [*Orientalism*] is now obviously outdated" (1994: 4) because, among other things, "It is simply the case that globalisation makes it very difficult to carry on talking about Oriental and Occidental cultures as separate, autonomous or independent cultural regimes" (8). Apart from the fact that Said was at great pains to stress the interrelated and overlapping nature of cultures, the ability to represent the West and the East as indeed separate, if not fundamentally antagonistic, in classic Orientalist fashion, has obviously been one of the defining features of the history of the world in the last decade, in the context of the "War on Terror" and the wars in Iraq and Afghanistan. In a more recent piece, "Orientalism, or the politics of the text," Turner criticizes Said for errors of which he is arguably not guilty, and concludes that, "The traditional game of the Orientalist text appears to have come to an end" (2002: 30). Part of the reason for this is that in a putatively postmodern world, "intellectuals are unwilling or unable to defend grand narratives, since academic intellectuals no longer have the authority to pronounce on such matters" (29). If nothing else, however, Said's life and work provide a powerful example – though by no means the only one from the "postmodern" world – of precisely why Turner's assessment is wrong.

In case this section looks like an attempt to suggest that Said is above reproach, it is important to point out that this is not the case, simply that, as suggested, many of the reproaches are not well made. It is true that Said might have been more systematic as a thinker; he might have been more thoroughgoingly theoretical (however that is understood) – though, as we have seen in this chapter, theory and, above all, system were things which Said found deeply problematic. Positions he adopted were sometimes contradictory, though, as discussed above in relation to his apparent turning away from the field of the postcolonial, the contradictions may be less than they seem. Above all, this is theory with a human focus, theory on what Said would see as a human scale: turning its back on jargon, abstraction, irrelevance, and a lack of concern with the world and its problems. It is theory which not only recognizes worldly connections but tries actively to forge them, in the name, as Said so often said, of knowledge and freedom.

Reader's Guide to Edward W. Said

Perhaps the easiest introduction to the breadth of Said's work is via *The Edward Said Reader*, edited by Moustafa Bayoumi and Andrew Rubin (2000), which covers the three decades from *Joseph Conrad and the Fiction of Autobiography* (1966) to *Out of Place* (1999). In terms of the relations between literature (as well as other forms of writing) and colonial and postcolonial politics, *Orientalism* and *Culture and Imperialism* remain his major achievements. Among his many books on Palestine, *After the Last Sky* (1986), with its wonderful photographs by Jean Mohr, is a personal, and moving, approach to the terrible situation of his people. There are a number of useful collections of interviews with Said. The most substantial of these is *Power, Politics and Culture*, edited by Gauri Viswanathan (2004), while David Barsamian has edited *The Pen and the Sword* (1994) and *Culture and Resistance* (2003). A book of conversations, rather than interviews, *Parallels and Paradoxes*, edited by Ara Guzelimian (2003) is the easiest of Said's music books, as well as offering a fascinating interaction between himself and Daniel Barenboim.

The secondary literature on Said, especially in the form of journal articles, essays and book chapters, is enormous. The largest collection of critical material in one publication is the four-volume *Edward Said*, edited by Patrick Williams (2000). Books with chapters on Said specifically as a postcolonial theorist include Bart Moore-Gilbert, *Post-Colonial Theory* (1997), and Peter Childs and Patrick Williams, *An Introduction to Post-Colonial Theory* (1996). Single volume introductions to his work include Bill Ashcroft and Pal Ahluwalia, *Edward Said: The Paradox of Identity* (1999), and Valerie Kennedy, *Edward Said: A Critical Introduction* (2000). One of the best collections of essays (despite the slightly misleading subtitle) is *Edward Said: A Critical Reader*, edited by Michael Sprinker (1992).

Bibliography

Writings of Edward W. Said

1966. *Joseph Conrad and the Fiction of Autobiography*. Harvard: Harvard University Press.
1975. *Beginnings: Intention and Method*. New York: Basic Books.
1978. *Orientalism*. London: Routledge and Kegan Paul.
1979. *The Question of Palestine*. New York: Vintage Books.
1981. *Covering Islam*. London: Routledge and Kegan Paul.
1984. *The World, the Text, and the Critic*. London: Faber and Faber.
1986. *After the Last Sky: Palestinian Lives*. London: Faber and Faber.
1988 (with Christopher Hitchens (eds)). *Blaming the Victims: Spurious Scholarship and the Palestinian Question*. London: Verso.
1991. *Musical Elaborations*. London: Chatto and Windus.
1993. *Culture and Imperialism*. London: Chatto and Windus.
1994. *Representations of the Intellectual*. London: Vintage.
1995a. *Peace and Its Discontents*. London: Vintage.
1995b. *The Politics of Dispossession*. London: Vintage.

1999. *Out of Place*. London: Granta.

2000a. *Reflections on Exile*. London: Granta.

2000b. *The End of the Peace Process: Oslo and after*. London: Granta.

2000c. *The Edward Said Reader*. Bayoumi and Rubin (eds). London: Granta.

2003a. *Freud and the non-European*. London: Verso.

2003b (with Daniel Barenboim). *Parallels and Paradoxes: Explorations in Music and Society*. London: Bloomsbury.

2003c. *Orientalism* (reissue with Preface and 1993 Afterword). London: Penguin.

2004a. *Humanism and Democratic Criticism*. New York: Columbia University Press.

2004b. *From Oslo to Iraq and the Roadmap*. London: Bloomsbury.

2006. *On Late Style*. London: Bloomsbury.

2008. *Music at the Limits*. London: Bloomsbury.

Essay

2000d. Humanism and Heroism (Presidential Address 1999). *PMLA*, 115(3).

Interviews

1987 (in Salusinszky, Imre). *Criticism in Society*. London: Methuen.

1994. *The Pen and the Sword*. David Barsamian (ed.). Edinburgh: A. K. Press.

2003. *Culture and Resistance*. David Barsamian (ed.). Cambridge, MA: South End Press.

2004. *Power, Politics and Culture*. Gauri Viswanathan (ed.). London: Bloomsbury.

Further Reading

Ahmad, Aijaz (1992) *In Theory*. London: Verso.

Ashcroft, Bill and Ahluwalia, Pal (1999) *Edward Said: The Paradox of Identity*. London: Routledge.

Childs, Peter and Williams, Patrick (1996) *An Introduction to Postcolonial Theory*, Hemel Hempstead: Prentice-Hall.

Clifford, James (1988) On Orientalism. In *The Predicament of Culture: Twentieth Century Ethnography, Literature and Art*. Cambridge, MA: Harvard University Press.

Fanon, Frantz (1967) *The Wretched of the Earth*. Harmondsworth: Penguin.

Gramsci, Antonio (1971) *Selections from Prison Notebooks*. Trans. Nowell Smith and Hoare. London: Lawrence and Wishart.

Hussein, Abdirahman A. (2002) *Edward Said: Criticism and Society*. London: Verso.

Ibn Warraq (2007) *Defending the West: A Critique of Edward Said's Orientalism*. Amherst, NY: Prometheus Books.

Irwin, Robert (2006) *Dangerous Knowledge: Orientalism and its Discontents*. New York: Overlook Press.

Kennedy, Valerie (2000) *Edward Said: a Critical Introduction*. Cambridge: Polity Press.

Khalidi, Rashid (2008) Edward Said and Palestine. In Sökmen and Ertur (eds) *Waiting for the Barbarians*. London: Verso, pp. 44–52.

Lukács, Georg (1971) *History and Class Consciousness*. London: Merlin Press.

Marrouchi, Mustapha (2004) *Edward Said at the Limits*. Albany: SUNY Press.

Moore-Gilbert, Bart (1997) *Post-Colonial Theory: Contexts, Practices, Politics*. London: Verso.

Porter, Dennis (1993) Orientalism and its problems. In Williams and Chrisman (eds) *Colonial Discourse and Post-Colonial Theory*. New York: Columbia University Press, pp. 150–161.

Salzman, Philip Carl and Divine, Donna Robinson (eds) (2008) *Postcolonial Theory and the Arab–Israel Conflict*. London: Routledge.

Sartre, Jean-Paul ([1960] 1976) *Critique of Dialectical Reason*. London: Verso.

Sökmen, Müge Gürsoy and Ertur, Basak (eds) (2008) *Waiting for the Barbarians: A Tribute to Edward W. Said*. London: Verso.

Sprinker, Michael (ed.) (1992) *Edward Said: A Critical Reader*. Oxford: Blackwell.

Turner, Bryan (1994) *Orientalism, Post-modernism and Globalism*. London: Routledge.

Turner, Bryan (2002) Orientalism, or the politics of the text. In Hastings Donnan (ed) *Interpreting Islam*. London: Sage.

Williams, Patrick (2000) *Edward Said*, 4 vols. London: Sage.

Williams, Patrick and Chrisman, Laura (eds) (1993) *Colonial Discourse and Post-Colonial Theory*. New York: Columbia University Press.

Wilson, Janet, Sandru, Cristina, and Lawson Welsh, Sarah (eds) (2010) *Rerouting the Postcolonial: New Directions for the New Millennium*. London: Routledge.

Yegenoglu, Meyda (1998) *Colonial Fantasies: Towards a Feminist Reading of Orientalism*. Cambridge: Cambridge University Press.

Young, Robert (1990) *White Mythologies: Writing History and the West*. London: Routledge.

18

Anthony Giddens

CHRISTOPHER G. A. BRYANT AND DAVID JARY

The British sociologist Anthony Giddens has long since established himself as a social theorist of global stature in each of the three main phases of his work: first, as a major interpreter of the classical tradition and its successors; second, as the author of structuration theory, a very influential treatment of agency and structure in which primacy is granted to neither; third, as a commentator on late modernity and globalization. The third of these has increasingly seen Giddens the theorist with the secure reputation give way to Giddens the public intellectual and political networker of contested repute.

Giddens's social theorizing is distinguished by its comprehensive critical appropriation and imaginative reworking of the main concepts and perspectives of classical and modern theorists. Central to his early and middle work is an incisive critique of functionalism, evolutionism, and historical materialism. His structuration theory is a major achievement that has found countless applications throughout the social sciences. The breadth and flair of his coverage of historical and global issues is no less striking. Having taken issue with once fashionable conceptions of postmodernity, he advanced instead an account of radicalized modernity in which changes others had characterized as postmodern are treated as already implicit in modernity. Latterly, Giddens has explored the implications of changing conceptions of self-identity, and new sources of risk and opportunity, in a globalizing society. He has also done much to define a new "utopian-realist" politics beyond left and right with reference to British, European and global issues.

Giddens's theoretical writings in the 1970s and 1980s and his work on late modernity in the 1990s caught the attention of social scientists the world over. His prominence as a public intellectual began with the British new Labour government of Tony Blair elected in 1997 and quickly spread to the Clinton White House and center-left and progressive political circles in Europe, the Americas, and Asia.

The Wiley-Blackwell Companion to Major Social Theorists, First Edition.
Edited by George Ritzer and Jeffrey Stepnisky.
© 2011 Blackwell Publishing Ltd. Published 2011 by Blackwell Publishing Ltd.

Introduction: A Global Social Theorist

Giddens is remarkable for the number of his publications, including some forty-one authored and edited books between 1971 and 2009 (which have been translated into over forty languages), and around three hundred articles, essays, and reviews in academic journals, books and symposia, and magazines and newspapers. He is also unusual for the scale and scope of his work on three different dimensions. The first has to do with substance. Giddens has written on most developments in the social sciences except research design and methods. He has discussed most leading theorists, both living and dead, and most schools and traditions of social thought; he has worked on the ontology of the social and the self and has articulated the structuration theory with which his name is now everywhere associated; he has focused on class, class societies, and the state; he has paid great attention to features of our own age of late, or "high," modernity and globalization and to their theorization; he has taken up issues of self and self-identity; and he continues to promote a politics beyond left and right that addresses the major challenges of our global age. In short, he is a world-renowned, truly global, social theorist.

The second dimension pertains to disciplinary range. Giddens is a sociologist who has been interested in anthropology and psychology since his undergraduate days, and who has engaged with developments, and prompted responses from critics, in philosophy, history, geography, linguistics, all the social sciences, management, social work, and psychotherapy. The third dimension is one of levels and diverse readerships. Giddens's writings range from discussions of fundamental, often somewhat abstruse, metatheoretical problems – as in *New Rules of Sociological Method* (1976a), *Central Problems in Social Theory* (1979) and *The Constitution of Society* (1984) – to very direct and effective books for students including a textbook, *Sociology*, first published in 1989 and now in its sixth edition, which has sold over a million copies. To all of these can now be added the varied products of a highly active public intellectual: books, manifestos, magazine and newspaper articles, and media appearances in Britain and abroad.[1]

In the 1980s and 1990s Giddens would have figured in most sociologists' lists of the top ten sociologists in the world then alive. He has been described as Britain's best-known social scientist since Keynes. His visibility and influence increased greatly when he moved from a fellowship at King's College, Cambridge, to the directorship of the London School of Economics just four months before the Labour Party's triumph at the general election of May 1, 1997 after eighteen years in opposition. The new Labour government was dedicated to the "modernization" of Britain and sought a politics of the "radical center." Quite what these might mean was still very much open to debate and Tony Giddens was pleased to be one of the voices outside government, but close to it, who was increasingly heard. From the publication of *The Third Way* (1998) onwards his labors were redirected and his readership broadened.

Giddens's Career

We will offer an overall comment on Anthony Giddens's *oeuvre* in due course but first it may be helpful to say something about his career.[2] Giddens was born in 1938 in Edmonton, north London, the son of a clerk with London Transport. He was educated at a local grammar school, and then Hull University, where he read two nonschool subjects – sociology and psychology. At these he excelled, graduating with first-class honors in 1959. On graduation, he went to the London School of Economics, where he completed an MA thesis entitled "Sport and Society in Contemporary England." In 1961 he started as a lecturer in sociology at Leicester University. At Leicester he taught neither the second-year course in classical sociological theory (apart from three lectures on Simmel) – that was Ilya Neustadt's preserve – nor the third-year course on more recent developments in theory – this was given by Percy Cohen, whose *Modern Social Theory* (1968) is derived from it. Instead, he was primarily responsible for the third-year course in social psychology, in which he chose to link "social personality" to a number of other topics, including socialization, language, attitude formation, identity, institutions, and national character. In this and other courses, including lectures on Durkheim and suicide to a large first-year audience, he impressed not just with what he said but also with how he said it – with exceptional fluency and without notes. It was, it should also be emphasized, a significant time and place in which to make an impact. As T. H. Marshall (1982) and John Eldridge (1990) have each pointed out, Leicester in the late 1950s and the 1960s was one of the seedbeds of British sociology.

We do not wish to make too much of this early experience, but some features are worth noting. For a start, Giddens's version of sociology has always been open to developments in anthropology and psychology. Having been introduced to these in Hull, he found at Leicester a sociology department with an interest in developmental sociology and in-house teaching not only in anthropology but also in psychology. Indeed, it was through in-house psychology courses that Leicester sociology undergraduates first encountered Mead, Becker, and Goffman. Giddens also encountered a remarkable collection of teachers, including Norbert Elias – a key figure in the formation of the Leicester approach to sociology.[3]

Giddens mentioned to us in 1989 that he regarded all his work as one continuous project, which we have called "the making of structuration theory." In addition to their merits as commentary, Giddens's writings prior to *New Rules of Sociological Method* (1976a) have thus also to be seen as part of a larger venture, the critical appropriation of earlier traditions in order to secure a base upon which to build theoretical constructions of his own. Many of those with a special interest in, and respect for, the work of Elias argue that Giddens owes more to Elias in the conception and execution of this undertaking than he acknowledges (on Giddens and Elias, see Kilminster, 1991). Elias, after all, had developed a (con)figurational, or process, sociology which, like Giddens's later structuration theory, sought to overcome the dualism of agency and structure. In particular, Eric Dunning (1994), a long-serving teacher at Leicester, has directly challenged our judgment (in Bryant and Jary, 1991) that we had no reason to question Giddens's claim that he never knew enough about Elias's (largely unpublished) work for it to have been a major intellectual influence. Giddens did, however, attend Elias's first-year lecture course, which was organized around the theme of development, in 1961–1962, the last time it was given, and he did read volume 1 of the *The Civilizing Process* both in unpublished translation and later in German (Elias, 1939). Giddens, it should be noted, joined the University of Leicester in 1961 and left in 1969, but, such were their travels, in only four of those eight years were both he and Elias in Leicester at the same time. Having said that, Giddens told us how impressed he was by the personal example of Elias – the single-minded scholar willing to pursue a large-scale personal project, heedless of distractions, over very many years.

Dunning argues that ours is too individualistic an approach to influence. Elias was, he contends, the major contributor to a departmental culture which influenced Giddens more than he is able or willing to admit. As evidence for this claim, Dunning recalls the debates among the staff between the supporters of developmental sociology led by Elias and their opponents led by Cohen. The opponents supposed Elias to be "championing a regressive return to an old-fashioned and outmoded 'evolutionism' rather than arguing, as he was, for the synthesis of classical and modern themes, concepts and concerns" (Dunning, 1994: 4). "To his credit," Dunning continues, Giddens "was one of those who grasped Elias's synthesizing aims." But, of itself, that does not indicate any particular debt to Elias. Indeed, Dunning effectively concedes as much with his next remark that, "while at Leicester, Giddens remained – by choice, I think – essentially an aloof outsider." Dunning thinks this helps to explain Giddens's inadequate grasp of Elias's work; we think it suggests that Giddens was his own man from the start.[4]

Giddens taught at Simon Fraser University, near Vancouver, in 1966–1967. There he saw how difficult it was for a European Marxist head of department, Tom Bottomore, to cope with students whose radicalism far exceeded his own. In 1967–1968 Giddens moved on to the University of California in Los Angeles. Southern California was, he says, a revelation. He tells how a trip to Venice Beach, where he encountered large numbers of strangely attired people engaged in unlikely pursuits, brought home to him how both European structural sociologies and the agenda of the European left had their limitations. Their preoccupations with class, authority, and political party offered little insight into the way of life of the hippies or the course of the anti-Vietnam War movement.

Southern California may have fired his imagination but Giddens would still seem to have felt obliged to take stock of European structural sociologies before moving on intellectually. His *Capitalism and Modern Social Theory* (1971a) and *The Class Structure of the Advanced Societies* (1973) precede the first book to address systematically questions of agency and the microfoundations of social order, *New Rules of Sociological Method* (1976a). Given the early North American experience, however, it is understandable not only that Giddens should, in due course, take up questions of agency, but also that he should eventually seek a politics *Beyond Left and Right* (1994a).

In 1969, Giddens left Leicester for a university lectureship at Cambridge and a fellowship at King's College. He belatedly acquired a doctorate in 1974 and eleven years later became the second holder of the chair of sociology. In 1986, he played a leading role in the establishment of the first new faculty at Cambridge for many decades, Social and Political Sciences, and was appointed its first dean. Giddens remained at Cambridge until 1996, but also made numerous visits to universities and other institutions all over the world. *The Consequences of Modernity* (1990a) originated in lectures given at Stanford University, California, in 1988, and he also greatly valued teaching at the University of California at Santa Barbara before and after the publication of the US edition of his textbook, *An Introduction to Sociology* (1989, 1991).

Between 1975 and 1978, Giddens was the editor for ten books published in the Hutchinson Sociology series, and between 1977 and 1989 he was the editor for over fifty books published in two series by Macmillan. Since 1978, he has been an editor of the journal *Theory and Society*. No doubt this experience stood him in good stead when in 1985 he joined with John Thompson and David Held to found Polity Press. Polity has since become one of the world's leading social science publishers, with a host of prominent authors and hundreds of titles currently in print, and Giddens has been directly involved with commissioning, editing, and promotion throughout, though, he had to scale back somewhat when Director of the LSE.

Giddens's career developed interestingly in the 1990s. From 1989 he had three and a half years with a psychotherapist. The experience deepened his interest in personal life and the emotions, and led to the discussions of the self, identity, love, and sexuality in *Modernity and Self-identity* (1991a) and *The Transformation of Intimacy* (1992b). He has told us how he came to make connections between his personal circumstances and developments in society and culture from the local to the global, and how he came to re-view the latter in light of the former.[5] Giddens's thinking on "dialogic democracy" (presented in *The Transformation of Intimacy* and *Beyond Left and Right*), for example, worked outwards from personal relations to global issues. He also says that therapy gave him the confidence to seek a public role for the first time. It was truly life-transforming; it persuaded him that he could make his future significantly different from his past.

This, then, is the context in which Giddens embarked on the new vein of writing on the human condition in an age of high modernity in the 1990s; increased his intervention in public debates via articles in the press, media appearances, and joint seminars with academics, journalists, politicians, etc.; and in due course, took a new job which would provide both a new challenge and an opportunity to promote the public value of social science, inform government, and influence opinion. The intervention in public debates intensified with *The Third Way* (1998), and his evident closeness to the new Labour British prime minister, Tony Blair, and has continued ever since. His latest book is on *The Politics of Climate Change* (2009). The new job was the directorship of the London School of Economics. Ever the teacher, he began by introducing a weekly director's lecture (with attendances of up to a thousand students in its first year). He proved able to attract some distinguished new staff and the funding for some significant new research centers, one of which – the Centre for the Analysis of Risk and Regulation – reflected a major concern of his. He also had the international connections to secure visits from some of the world's leading politicians, economists, and policy-makers. By the time he stepped down as director in 2003 he had greatly raised the media profile of the school and re-established it as the place where the issues of the age are addressed and debated. His directorship is generally considered to have been a notable success. Since becoming a life peer in 2004 he has been an active, if critical, supporter of the Labour cause in the House of Lords.

THREE PHASES IN THE MAKING OF STRUCTURATION THEORY

It is very generally accepted among sociologists and other social scientists that neither the holy trinity of Marx, Durkheim, and Weber, nor additions to the sainthood like Simmel, provided satisfactory ways of connecting micro- and macro-analysis or agency and structure. The same is generally said about subsequent developments, such as the structural-functionalism and the empirical, even empiricist, inquiry favored by the American mainstream from the 1930s onwards, and the variants of the interpretive tradition which were the principal alternative to the mainstream. The shortcomings of earlier ontologies of the social, and of the self, have thus invited correction, and from the 1970s onwards the numerous writers who have set out to supply it have generated a massive, protracted, and still unconcluded debate (Bryant, 1995, chapter 3). It was in 1976, with the appearance of *New Rules of Sociological Method* (1976a) and "Functionalism: *après la lutte*" (1976b), that Giddens first offered his correction, "structuration theory." In terms of the breadth of the response he has generated in different disciplines and in different countries, Giddens is arguably the single most important figure in the whole debate.

Although structuration theory, as such, was only unveiled in 1976, it is possible to view Giddens's work prior to then as, in many ways, a preparation for it. And although its "summation" was published in 1984, in *The Constitution of Society*, it is possible to treat some of Giddens's subsequent academic work as a further development of it. Indeed, this is how Giddens has presented it himself notwithstanding the transformative consequences of therapy for his writings in the 1990s. It is thus feasible to identify three clear phases in the making of structuration theory. Each is a step in the making of structuration theory but in each works of a particular character predominate.

Phase 1: Exegesis and commentary

Before 1976, most of Giddens's writings offer critical commentary on a very wide range of writers, schools, and traditions. (The main exception is the work on suicide which extends beyond Durkheim and culminates in *The Sociology of Suicide* (1971b) and Giddens's revised theory of suicide (1977b).) The best-known books in this phase are *Capitalism and Modern Social Theory: An Analysis of the Writings of Marx, Durkheim and Max Weber* (1971a) and *The Class Structure of the Advanced Societies* (1973). After publication of *New Rules of Sociological Method* (1976a), commentary is never Giddens's primary activity again – though commentaries continue to appear. He remains, it is generally agreed, a very knowledgeable, perceptive, and stimulating commentator.

In his engagement with the work of others, Giddens is, by his own admission, seeking to go beyond commentary to critical appropriation as a basis from which to develop a long-term project of his own – the making of structuration theory. In this he calls to mind the early Talcott Parsons (see Sica, 1991).

Phase 2: Structuration theory and the duality of structure

There is space here for only a brief account of some of the main features of the theory and an even briefer indication of some of the criticisms, developments and applications it has generated.

Principles

The second period, from 1976 to 1984, is dominated by intensive work on the elaboration of the principles of structuration theory. It opens with *New Rules* (1976a), includes *Central Problems in Social Theory* (1979), and reaches its climax in *The*

Table 18.1 Modes of theorizing structure and agency

	Structuralist theories	Voluntarist theories	Structuration theory
Characterization of structure	Structures and cultures determine, shape, or heavily constrain.	Structures are the revisable products of free agents.	Structure is the medium and outcome of the conduct it recursively organizes.
Characterization of actors/ agents	Actors' choices are illusory, marginal, and/or trivial. Actors are cultural dopes, the victims of circumstances or instruments of history.	Actors make real choices. Actors determine.	Actors are knowledgeable and competent agents who reflexively monitor their action.

Constitution of Society (1984). It involves a disengagement from epistemology, on which Giddens had written penetratingly, and an engagement with ontology.

Giddens picked up the term "structuration" from (the French of) Piaget and Gurvitch, but his usage differs from theirs. With the objective of carrying social theory beyond classical conceptions, structuration theory makes critical appropriations from two main theoretical innovations in mid-twentieth-century sociology. On one front, Giddens engages with developments in action theory and social phenomenology. "The characteristic error of the philosophy of action," according to Giddens (1976a: 121), "is to treat the problem of 'production' only, thus not developing any concept of structural analysis at all," but he is able to take from action theories (especially from Schutz, Garfinkel, and the ethnomethodologists) conceptions of "methodical" or "practical" consciousness, which he then deploys against both Durkheim and Parsons. On the other, Giddens engages with the newer forms of structuralism, with their roots in linguistics, especially the work of Lévi-Strauss and Althusser. Although "the limitation of both structuralism and functionalism ... is to regard 'reproduction' as a mechanical outcome, rather than as an active constituting process, accomplished by, and consisting in, the doings of active subjects" (ibid.), Giddens is able to derive from structuralism the notion of generative rules. Giddens's claims for the distinctiveness of structuration theory are illustrated in Table 18.1.

Structuration theory attempts to supersede these deficiencies by showing how "social structures are both constituted by human agency, and yet at the same time are the very medium of this constitution" (ibid.), and by explaining how "structures are constituted through action, and reciprocally how action is constituted structurally" (Giddens, 1976a: 161). This is what is meant by "duality of structure," the central concept in Giddens's structuration theory, and the means by which he seeks to avoid a dualism of agency and structure. It is also to conceive structures not "as simply placing constraints upon human agency, but as enabling" (ibid.), and to recognize, contrary to Foucault, the omnipresence of a dialectic of control whereby "the less powerful manage resources in such a way as to exert some control over the more powerful in established power relationships" (Giddens, 1984: 374).

"To examine the structuration of a social system is to examine the modes whereby that system, through the application of generative rules and resources, is produced and reproduced in social interaction" (Giddens, 1976b: 353). Systems, for Giddens, refer to "the situated activities of human agents" (Giddens, 1984: 25) and "The patterning of social relations across time-space" (ibid.: 377). They have an *actual* existence (or a real existence, in the economist's sense of real). Systems display structural properties but are not themselves structures. Structures, by contrast, refer to "systems of generative rules and resources" (Giddens, 1976a: 127), or, as Giddens later put it, to "rule-resource sets, implicated in the articulation of social systems" (Giddens, 1984: 377). They have only a *virtual* existence, "out of time and out of space" (Giddens, 1976a: 127). Structure only exists in the memory of knowledgeable agents and as instantiated in action.

Actors, for Giddens, are never cultural dopes, but knowledgeable and capable agents who reflexively monitor their action. In his stratification model of the actor or agent, Giddens distinguishes between the motivation of action which may be partly unconscious but is not necessarily so, the rationalization of action (agents' articulated reasons for action), and the reflexive monitoring of action (agents' knowledge of what they are doing). Rationalization always involves discursive consciousness, or verbalization; reflexive monitoring involves either or both of discursive consciousness and practical consciousness (unverbalized awareness). Giddens claims that many other theories have ignored practical consciousness, or what actors tacitly know but cannot put in words.

For Giddens, "A representation of the duality of structure in social interaction can be given as follows:

INTERACTION	communication	power	morality
(MODALITY)	interpretative scheme	facility	norm
STRUCTURE	signification	domination	legitimation

All processes of the structuration (production and reproduction) of systems of social interaction involve" the three elements in the top line: "the communication of meaning, the exercise of power, and the evaluative judgement of conduct" or morality (Giddens, 1977c: 132–133). Structure has the three analytically separable components in the bottom line. "Structure as signification involves semantic rules; as domination, unequally distributed resources; and as legitimation, moral or evaluative rules" (133). Rules and resources are the properties of communities and collectivities. The modalities of the middle line refer to the modes in which actors can draw upon rules and resources in the production of interaction. " 'Interpretative schemes' are the modes of typification incorporated within actors' stocks of knowledge, applied reflexively in the sustaining of communication" (Giddens, 1984: 29). Facilities include command over people and resources, and norms include normative expectations of actors.

Rules, both semantic and moral, are the "techniques or generalizable procedures applied in the enactment/reproduction of social practices" (ibid.: 21). Resources divide into allocative, or material, and authoritative, or nonmaterial; the former derive from dominion over things, the latter from dominion over people. Both are involved in the generation of power, the capacity to do; there is also, however, a dialectic of control, whereby the controlled, and not just the controllers, can have an effect on the relation between them and the situation they share. "The most deeply embedded structural properties, implicated in the reproduction of societal totalities" (i.e. groups, organizations, collectivities, societies), he calls "*structural principles.* Those practices which have the greatest time-space extension within such totalities can be referred to as *institutions*" (ibid.: 17). Symbolic orders/modes of discourse, political and economic institutions and legal institutions are only separable from each other analytically in that they all draw on structures of signification, domination and legitimation, albeit to different degrees. "We can conceive of the relationships involved as follows:

S-D-L   Symbolic orders/modes of discourse

D (auth)-S-L   Political institutions

D (allc)-S-L   Economic institutions

L-D-S   Legal institutions

Where S = signification, D = domination, L = legitimation" (ibid.: 33).

Concern for time-space is one of the most distinctive features of structuration theory, and it has opened up fruitful exchanges with geographers. Drawing on sources as diverse as Heidegger, Lévi-Strauss and the *Annales* historians, Giddens demands that we avoid the sharp distinction between synchrony and diachrony favored by structuralists and functionalists and that "we ... grasp the time-space relations inherent in the constitution of all social interaction" (Giddens, 1979: 3). Time-space thus refers not to some framework, or set of coordinates, external to social interaction, but to the ways duration and extent enter into the constitution of social practices. Writing, for example, affords communication at a distance and over time, and clock timing affords the commodification of labor power.

Criticisms

Derek Layder (1994) has pointed out that what Giddens means by "structure" when he refers to the dualism of structure and agency which has bedeviled social science is the notion of pre-given objects or patterned realities. And what Giddens means by "structure" in the duality of structure which graces structuration theory are the rules and resources of the virtual order which are implicated in the reproduction of the actual order or social system. In other words, his resolution of the dualism of agency and structure works by discarding structure as conventionally understood by social scientists and substituting something quite different.

In 1982, Margaret Archer complained that structuration theory is unhelpful when trying to account for variations in degrees of voluntarism and determinism and degrees of freedom and constraint. In *The Constitution of Society* (1984), Giddens responds by distinguishing different senses of "constraint" and by reminding us that there are no natural laws of society. He adds that

> The nature of constraint is historically variable, as are the enabling qualities generated by the contextualities of human action. It is variable in relation to the material and institutional circumstances of activity, but also in relation to the forms of knowledgeability that agents possess about those circumstances. (Giddens, 1984: 179)

This, however, does not deal with Archer's complaint. Are all these variations historically so contingent that structuration theory can say nothing further about them? Giddens gives a partial answer in terms of structural principles and structural sets. Structural sets, or structures (in the plural), refer to rules and resources which hang together to make a set. Take, for example, the following, very familiar, case of capitalism.

private property: money: capital: labor contract: profit

The items in the set are internally related. One can also move from the set both to (a) the more abstract structural principle of capitalism, or class societies ("the disembedding, yet interconnecting, of state and economic institutions"; Giddens, 1984: 183), and (b) the less abstract structure, the rules and resources, which, via the dimensions or axes of structuration (signification, domination, and legitimation), are involved in the institutional articulation of capitalist societies. In assessing what options actors have, much depends on the strength of the internal connectives both within the structural set and between it and the rules and resources upon which actors draw. The options which actors perceive/conceive and enact can vary greatly in number and scope.

John Thompson (1989), taking up similar issues, argues that there is more to structures than rules and resources, and the addition is not captured by the notion of structural principles. Instead, it has to do with the connections between, and distributions of, different rules and resources; alternatively, it is about why Giddens's rule-resource sets are set as they are and what agents can do about them, or with them, other than just reproduce them. Thompson takes as an example Marx's analysis of the capitalist mode of production. It attends to the conditions which make possible capitalist production and exchange, from the circumstances which facilitate the formation of a "free" labor force to the principles and processes involved in the constitution of value and the generation of profit. These cannot, Thompson claims, satisfactorily be "forced into the conceptual mould of structure qua rules and resources" (Thompson, 1989: 69).

Both Archer's and Thompson's difficulties are connected to a complex of issues concerning the status of the virtual, voluntarism and determinism, and the nature of constraint. Archer (1982, 1988) has done more than anyone to tease them out. According to Giddens, structure refers to cognitive and moral rules and to allocative and authoritative resources, but it is virtual, not real, in that it exists only in instantiations in action and in memory traces. This amounts to saying structure is real only when it is activated. What Giddens calls rules Archer prefers to call the cultural system. She argues that "since what is instantiated depends on the power of agency and not the nature of the property [of the rule or constituent of the cultural system], then properties themselves are not differentially mutable" (Archer, 1988: 88). In other words, Giddens's rules do not constrain because agents can conform to, modify, or reject them at will. She labels this the "ontological diminution of the cultural system." Giddens's response (1990b) is to say that of course structure, resources, as well as rules, differentially enable and constrain, but it does so only as mediated by agents' reasons. Structural constraint cannot enforce like a causal force in nature. Even Marx's wage laborers, forced to sell their labor power, can, and on occasions do, reject one employer's labor contract for another, go on strike, go slow, and organize politically. Structure is virtual, it turns out, not just because it is out of time and space, but also because it does not alone determine. To this we would counter that structure, or better structures, are real (a) because, by Giddens's own admission, they differentially enable and constrain (it is, after all, a realist axiom that something is real if it has real effects), and (b) because, as Archer has pointed out, the differential potentials for enablement and constraint which structures offer have to do not just with agents' different activations of them but also with different properties which inhere in them. Because this applies to both rules and resources we do not favor Sewell's (1992) differential treatment of the first, rules, as virtual and the second, resources, as material.

There is also an instructive exchange between Nicos Mouzelis (1991) and Giddens (1993). Mouzelis contests the very notion of the duality of structure. "Actors often distance themselves from rules and resources, in order to question them, or in order to build theories about them, or – even more importantly – in order to devise strategies for their maintenance or their transformation" (Mouzelis 1991: 27–28). In other words there *is* a dualism of agency and structure; actors, subjects, confront rules and resources as objects. Giddens's rejoinder is that "It is perfectly obvious that every situated actor faces an environment of action which has an 'objectivity' for him or her in a quasi-Durkheimian sense" (Giddens 1993: 6–7). Mouzelis's objects are, however, never just objects. "Individuals in all forms of society 'distance themselves' from rules and resources, approach them strategically and so forth ... [But] all moments of reflexive attention themselves draw upon, and reconstitute, rules and resources ... there can be no stepping outside the flow of action" (6).

In conclusion, two deficiencies of Giddens's original theory of structuration stand out. On the one hand, it has relatively little to say about the formation and distribution of the unacknowledged and acknowledged conditions of action or about the differential knowledgeability of actors. On the other, it does not elaborate on individual and collective *transformative* projects, and the differential capabilities of actors to see projects through successfully, including the capacity to cope successfully with unintended consequences.

Uses and developments of structuration theory

Critics such as Stinchcombe (1986) and Gregson (1989) have claimed a third deficiency of structuration theory: its uselessness for empirical research. On the face of it, this is a gross misjudgment given the copious evidence of its use throughout the social sciences (Bryant and Jary 1997: vol. 4, 2001: ch. 2). These uses have included reconstituting a discipline (for example, Roberts and Scapens (1985) in accountancy), reconstituting a specialty (for example, Orlikowski (1992) in the sociology of technology), reconstituting an interdisciplinary field (for example, Sydow and Windeler (1996) in management), and facilitating empirical research. Giddens (1991b) has himself commended the use of structuration theory in Burman (1988) on unemployment in Canada, Connell (1987) on gender relations in Australia, and Dandeker (1989) on surveillance, bureaucratic power, and war. A very large number of other examples include: Shotter (1983) in psychology; Carlstein (1981) in geography; Elchardus (1988) on time; Barrett (1988) and Graves (1989) in archeology; Spybey (1984), Whittington (1992), and Yates and Orlikowski (1992) on management and organizations; Lee (1992) and Mellor (1993) on religion; Shilling (1992) on education; and Bastien, McPhee, and Bolton (1995) and Cash (1996) on government and politics.

If all the above and much more had been published by the time *The Constitution of Society* (1984) was little more than a decade old, how could serious commentators on Giddens's structuration theory ever have judged it useless? Giddens has only ever wanted social scientists to adopt a structurationist *perspective* as some had in effect already done before he articulated structuration *theory* – in *The Constitution of Society* he gives the example of Willis's research on working-class children *Learning to Labour* (1977) – and he has resolutely refused to offer a research cookbook. Structuration theory sets forth an orientation to all social life that is intended to sensitize us to all its principal features. For many social scientists it has done this better than any other (meta-)theory available and that has been enough of a spur for them to reshape their inquiries and design their empirical research accordingly. In the process they have made use of many of Giddens's concepts even though he is indifferent to such use, believing it as likely to clutter research as facilitate it. In our judgment, structuration theory has offered researchers concepts, frameworks, and formulations of intermediate complexity – something beyond piecemeal *bricolage* but short of the kind of comprehensive theoretical system which theorists love to interpret and contest. Giddens's resolutions of the dualisms of structure and agency, determinism and voluntarism, and order and change work because they have helped specialists throughout the social sciences to overcome deficiencies in their disciplines and specialties as they perceive them and get their research done.

Notwithstanding the above, structuration theory would be still more effective if it were made easier for researchers to move from ontology in general to particular substantive inquiries. Rob Stones has long argued that what is missing from Giddens's theory of structuration is concern for the strategic context of action (Stones, 1991) or, as he later preferred, agent's context analysis (Stones, 1996). Like Ira Cohen (1989), Stones noted how Giddens inclines either to bracket institutional analysis in his treatment of the strategic conduct of knowledgeable agents, or to bracket strategic conduct in his analysis of institutions as chronically reproduced rules and resources. By reworking Giddens's concept of knowledgeability in terms of strategic context, Stones directed attention to the agent's strategic terrain – "the social nexus of interdependencies, rights and obligations, asymmetries of power and the social conditions and consequences of action" (Stones, 1996: 98) which make up the perceived and perceivable possibilities of action and their limitations. In effect, Stones sought a hermeneutically sensitive version of what Parsons (1937) called the conditions of action in his original voluntaristic theory of action. Strategic, or agent's, context analysis, so conceived, affords a critique of action, an examination of its conditions and limits; or, as Stones averred, it allows examination of counterfactual claims that agents could have acted other than they did by treating contexts as neither entirely fixed nor entirely fluid.

In his subsequent *Structuration Theory* (2005), Stones sets out the most important development of structuration theory since Giddens himself turned to other matters. Giddens's structuration theory is, he says, about ontology in general and as such it leaves some researchers floundering. What they need is a "strong structuration theory" that supplies an ontology-in-situ, an ontology that connects universal abstractions to the "ontic," to "particular social processes and events in particular times and places," by employing "meso-level ontological concepts" that incorporate "variations and relative degrees in abstract concepts" (8). Insofar as Stones suggests that Giddens neglects these connections altogether he exaggerates – look, for example, at the discussion of systems in chapter 4 of *The Constitution of Society*, the discussion of empirical research in chapter 6, and much of *The Nation-State and Violence* (1985) published a year later – but Giddens could usefully have done more. It is helpful that, in the course of elaborating his strong structuration theory, Stones has necessarily to return to the deficiencies in Giddens's "weak" structuration theory identified above: the relative inattention to the formation and distribution of the unacknowledged and acknowledged conditions of action, and to the differential knowledgeability and capabilities of actors.

At the heart of Stones's theory are the meso-level of ontology (77–78) and the quadripartite nature of structuration (84–85). "The meso-level of ontology concerns the way in which it is possible to talk about at least some abstract ontological concepts in terms of scales or relative degrees." He lists eight ways in which this is possible. In abbreviated form they are: more or less knowledgeability, more or less critical reflection by agents on their internal structures, the greater or lesser intensity of desires, the fewer or greater number of choices available to agents, the more or less durability or modifiability of external structures, the varying number of unintended consequences of particular actions, the varying importance of unintended consequences to specified agents, and the more or less time modifiable external structures take to change. In order to ensure sensitivity to in-situ variation, "any adequate attempt to investigate the processes of structuration at the substantive level will have to engage, at least at a minimal level, with a combination of hermeneutics and structural diagnostics" (81). That necessarily limits the time scale and geographical scope of any structurational inquiry, though not, according to Parker (2006), as much as Stones supposes.

The first part of the quadripartite nature of structuration is the "*external structures as conditions of action*, which have an existence that is autonomous from the agent-in-focus"; they present the "structural context of action faced by the agent-in-focus" at the outset and as such they can "facilitate or frustrate agents' purposes" (Stones, 2005: 84, 85). The second and third parts concern the agent. The second part is the "internal structures within the agent" (85), that is "the actor's internal phenomenologically inflected perceptions of the external structures" (Stones, 2008: 336). These can be divided analytically into two components. First, there are "the conjuncturally specific internal structures" (2005: 85) (that is "the perception of external structures in the immediate context" (2008: 336)). Second, there are the general-dispositional structures or, following Bourdieu, "habitus" (2005: 85) (that is "those enduring and transposable dispositions, capacities and discourse that have been acquired from past contexts" (2008: 336)). The third is "active agency/agent's practices" and includes "the ways in which the agent either routinely and pre-reflectively, or strategically and critically, draws upon her internal structures" (2005: 85). Alternatively put, active agency includes "a range of aspects, such as creativity, improvisation and innovation, involved when actors draw upon internal structures in producing practical action" (2008: 336). The fourth is "outcomes (as external and internal structures and as events) ... The effects of agents' practices on extant structures can involve change and elaboration or reproduction and preservation" (2005: 85). Outcomes also include "the success or otherwise of agents' purposes irrespective of their effect on structures" (ibid.).

Stones repeatedly refers to research studies that exemplify strong structurational principles. He also discusses two case studies of structuration at length. The first is Morawska's study of the emigration of East European Jews and their resettlement in Jonestown, Pennsylvania, between 1890 and 1940 – a study theoretically informed by structuration theory. The second is Ibsen's play *A Doll's House*. Stones on Ibsen, like Giddens on Willis before him, thus makes plain that you do not have to adopt structuration *theory* to evidence structurationist *principles*. But it remains his belief that social scientists who do look to structuration theory for guidance on how to conduct substantive inquiries will obtain more help from his strong version than from Giddens's "weak" one. Time will tell. An assessment could begin with Jack and Kholeif's (2007) recourse to strong structuration theory in organizations, management, and accountancy research.

For Stones there is more to "knowledgeability" than Giddens himself makes explicit. In a similar vein, Bryant (1991, 1995: ch. 5) argues that there is potentially more to Giddens's (1987) "dialogical model" of social science application than he was originally able or willing to define. In particular, it overcomes many of the deficiencies of the engineering, enlightenment, and interaction models by aligning a post-empiricist philosophy of social science with the engagement of agents in a reconsideration of their reasons for action. In so doing it capitalizes on the "double hermeneutic," the "two-way relation involved between lay language and the language of social science" whereby social scientific concepts "can in principle be appropriated by lay actors" (1979: 248). The "double hermeneutic" is one of Giddens's key concepts, but of itself it does not provide a rationale for a critical social science. For that one has to turn to the "utopian realism" of *The Consequences of Modernity* (1990a) and subsequent works.

Phase 3: Theorizing modernity: The personal and the global in a runaway world

Giddens has always been interested in modernity, as his early *The Class Structure of the Advanced Societies* (1973) confirms – indeed, he has always believed sociology's defining mission to be the analysis of the *modern* world – but it is only after his work on the principles of structuration theory reach their fullest elaboration in *The Constitution of Society* (1984) that he devotes most of his efforts to the analysis of late modernity.

The critique of historical materialism and the institutional dimensions of modernity

The two volumes of *A Contemporary Critique of Historical Materialism* (1981, 1985) provide a link between the second and third phases of Giddens's work. They address the core issues raised by evolutionism and its alternatives and provide new schemata for mapping the historical and contemporary relations between the state and economy in a "globalizing" world. Giddens concludes that:

1   there exists no necessary overall mechanism of social change, no universal motor of history such as class conflict;
2   there are no universal stages, or periodizations, of social development, these being ruled out by intersocietal systems and "time-space edges" (the ever-presence of exogenous variables), as well as by human agency and the inherent "historicity" of societies;
3   societies do not have needs other than those of individuals, so notions such as adaptation cannot properly be applied to them;
4   pre-capitalist societies are "class-divided," but only with capitalism are there "class societies" in which there is endemic class conflict, the separation of the political and economic spheres, property freely alienable as capital, and "free" labor and labor markets;
5   whilst class conflict is integral to capitalist society, there is no teleology that guarantees the emergence of the working class as the universal class, and no ontology that justifies denial of the multiple bases of modern society represented by capitalism, industrialism, surveillance, and the industrialization of warfare;
6   sociology, as a subject concerned pre-eminently with modernity, addresses a reflexive reality influenced by the conceptions both actors and sociologists have of it.

The analysis of premodern, modern, and late modern societies along four partly independent, partly interdependent, dimensions – economic, political, military, and symbolic – none of which has primacy, is, at a minimum, distinctive (though compare Mann, 1986) and instructive. In particular, it attends to features of modernity which sociology has too often ignored: the growth of the administrative power of the state and the industrialization of warfare. It also explores the complex ways in which power figures in time-space distantiation (the stretching of social systems across time-space), including the ways not just nation-states and capitalism but also different types of "locale" – such as cities as "power containers" – exercise domination over both nature and persons. Giddens's critique of historical materialism is one most commentators, Marxist and non-Marxist, respect, even when they differ in their evaluation (see Wright, 1983; Callinicos, 1985; Dandeker, 1990; Jary, 1991).

A projected third volume which was to have dealt with state socialism and its alternatives never appeared. The defeats suffered by the left in Western Europe from 1979 onwards and the collapse of state socialism in Eastern Europe in 1989 revised

Giddens's thinking about possible developments within late modernity and the value of any book focusing on traditional socialist agendas. Instead, *The Consequences of Modernity* (1990a), *Modernity and Self-Identity* (1991a), and *The Transformation of Intimacy* (1992b) offer striking and perceptive comment on the contemporary human condition, without providing a comprehensive and systematic examination of the economics and politics of late modernity. What they do provide is an expanded treatment of reflexivity, a concept that is henceforth always central to Giddens's thinking, not least to his treatment of globalization.[6]

Reflexive modernity

"The reflexivity of modern social life consists in the fact that social practices are constantly examined and reformed in the light of incoming information about those very practices, thus constitutively altering their character" (Giddens, 1990a: 38). But, contrary to Enlightenment expectations, knowledge has not led to certitude; instead, reason has lost its foundation, history its direction, and progress its allure. Even so, modernity has not given way to postmodernity but rather has assumed a new form, that of high or "radicalized modernity." For both Giddens and Beck (Beck, 1986; Beck *et al.*, 1994) radicalized modernity refers to the new patterns of security and danger, trust and risk, which typify late modern societies; and trust and risk involve expectations of what both other people and abstract systems will do. Modernity is radicalized because the intensification of individual and institutional reflexivity in the absence of sure foundations for knowledge has a chronic propensity to "manufacture uncertainty" and generate reordering. It is also radicalized because processes of continuous rationalization transform the familiar contours of industrial society.

High modernity involves the disembedding, or lifting out, of social relations, practices, mechanisms, and competencies from their specific, usually local, circumstances of time and space ("locales"), and their extension, thanks to developments in communications, over much wider spans of time and space. The development of expert systems provides one example of the latter; "symbolic tokens" (media which circulate without regard to the characteristics of those who handle them – such as money) provide another. Both expert systems and symbolic tokens depend on trust, not in individuals, but in abstract capacities. "Trust is related to absence in time and space" (Giddens, 1990a: 33), and it "operates in environments of risk" (ibid.: 54). This last is a reminder that living in late modernity is often unsettling and disorienting; it is disturbingly "like being aboard a careering juggernaut" (ibid.: 53).

One of the features of the contemporary world acknowledged by both postmodernists and Giddens is the plurality of intellectual formations and cultural spaces, but, contrary to postmodern theories, this need not preclude potential convergences, fusions of horizons, larger truths, or agreements on new beginnings. Giddens emphasizes the possibilities of universal truth claims and systematic knowledge, but he is reluctant to enter further epistemological debate and explain precisely how, given his general acceptance of anti-foundationalist and post-empiricist arguments, these are realizable (Bryant, 1992).

Disoriented or not, men and women in an age of high modernity are not subject to the fate and fortune of their premodern forebears; instead institutional and personal reflexivity, including the calculation of risk, inform social practice and continue to have a bearing on the course of events. There is now, according to Giddens, a possibility that "life politics" (the politics of self-actualization) may become more salient than "emancipatory politics" (the politics of class, inequality and exclusion); that new social movements – indeed all variants of Beck's sub-politics – may have more social impact than political parties (especially so where a culture of "post-scarcity" and a humanized technology have begun to challenge work-centered agendas); and that the reflexive project of the self, and changes in gender and sexual relations, may lead the way, via the "democratization of democracy," to a new era of "dialogic democracy" in which differences are settled, and practices ordered, through discourse rather than violence, the commands of duly constituted authority or the separation of the parties.

When modernity is conceived as radicalized "the universal features of truth claims force themselves upon us in an irresistible way given the primacy of problems of a global kind," and "coordinated political engagement [are] both possible and necessary, on a global level as well as locally" (Giddens 1990: 150). But Giddens's account of the opportunities presented by radicalized modernity is highly generalized. It lacks both justified identification of mediate political groupings – despite an obvious interest in feminism and new social movements – and careful attention to the principles of structuration theory. Unfortunately, *Beyond Left and Right: the Future of Radical Politics* (1994a), does not repair these deficiencies. What it does do is explore the paradox of a political left, for long on the defensive, which had, in many respects, fewer radical inclinations than a market-oriented radical right intent on overthrowing tradition and custom at, it sometimes seemed, any cost. Dismissing without much argument any middle-way "market socialism," Giddens responds to the radicalism of the right by drawing on earlier forms of "philosophic conservatism," in combination with elements of socialist thought to construct a six-point framework for a reconstituted radical politics: (a) repair damaged solidarities; (b) recognize the centrality of life politics; (c) accept that active trust implies generative politics; (d) embrace dialogic democracy; (e) rethink the welfare state; and (f) confront violence.

A runaway world

This is hardly a framework, more an agenda – and arguably an agenda more principled than practical at that. Giddens's "brave new world" (1994b) may be worthy, but is it realistic? It may not all be the "argument-by-mantra" of which Judt (1994: 7) complains, but its connections with contemporary political agents and processes in both the state *and* civil society are, to say the least, underspecified. "There is no single agent, group or movement that, as Marx's proletariat was supposed to do, can carry the hopes of humanity," Giddens (1994a: 21) reminds us, "but there are many points of political engagement which offer good cause for optimism." Stop hankering after some new comprehensive, all-connecting, ideologically driven program, Giddens seems to say, and, in this age of high modernity, do what you can where you can – for there is plenty that you can do in the home, workplace, community, and polity. Tony Blair, for one, was listening. Giddens was a guest at the British Prime Minister's weekend residence, Chequers, on November 1, 1997.

Giddens continued to be fascinated by the notion of "a runaway world," and he chose it for the title of a conference in January 1997, which marked his assumption of the directorship of the LSE and the publication of four volumes of commentary on his work (Bryant and Jary, 1997). The conference asked, in effect, what could be done about, or in, a runaway world when there was great hope but less expectation that the imminent defeat of the Conservative government by new Labour at the ballot box would make a difference.

Giddens often links the image of a runaway world to that of riding a juggernaut (as in *The Consequences of Modernity*, chapter 5, and *Modernity and Self-identity*, chapter 1). We think the juggernaut metaphor has the wrong associations and should be abandoned. Juggernaut, in Hindu mythology, is the name of an idol carried in procession on a huge cart; in the past devotees are said to have thrown themselves in front of it. This ultimate in cultural dopism is plainly incompatible with Giddens's approach to human agency. "Runaway world" is more serviceable, but still presents problems. It suggests a world wholly out-of-control which had formerly been under control – both of which are exaggerations – but it also correctly implies that science, social science, and technology no longer offer the promise of any overall control. Indeed, some technologies – such as industrial processes that generate pollutants, nuclear technology, and genetic engineering – are now as much constituents of a world out-of-control as means of controlling it. Double edged, they are as much part of the problem, adding to manufactured uncertainty, as part of any solution.

The specter of a runaway world would seem to prompt three alternative responses. First, try to recover, or secure, control; fix the big picture. Second, resign oneself to loss, or absence, of control and retreat to the private and personal. In the circumstances of late modernity, this is more likely to focus on the self than on the soul. Third, go for limited and local control; accept that there is no one big picture, but fix bits of pictures as and when you can for the purposes in hand. In the last of these, positivism gives way to post-positivism, empiricism to post-empiricism, and ideological conviction to pragmatism; we are left as more or less chastened, or more or less emancipated, mourners at what Gray (1995), a contributor to the London conference, called Enlightenment's wake.

Giddens was cheered, not chastened, by Enlightenment's wake. An age of endings, not just of the millennium but also of modernity and the politics of left and right, also suggested fresh beginnings. The burden of totalizing ambition had been lifted and a world of multiple possibilities beckoned. It is interesting to compare his view of these possibilities with Edmund Leach's, because it is Leach's 1968 Reith Lectures for the BBC, *A Runaway World?*, which first planted the idea. Leach argued that developments such as the population explosion and the technological revolution had seemingly led to a runaway world, and "The runaway world is terrifying because we are gradually becoming aware that simple faith in the limitless powers of human rationality is an illusion" (Leach, 1968: 78–79). In its place, Leach advocated an evolutionary humanism. Some of its features we would question, but three of Leach's injunctions are still worth noting four decades later. First, rethink science along, we would now say, post-empiricist lines. Second, engage with the world to make things happen; men and women can make a difference even if they cannot know all the differences they will make, and even if some of them turn out to be unwelcome. Third, do not be deterred by disorder; the times are always changing, and changing times are always out-of-joint; order is an illusion which affords a sense of security at odds with the inevitability of change. Those who participate in history,

Table 18.2 Reflexivity and risk society – and a possible new order beyond modernity

1. INSTITUTIONAL COMPLEXES OF MODERNITY	→	2. REFLEXIVE/RADICALIZED MODERNITY; THE CHALLENGES OF A RISK SOCIETY	→	3. NEW SOCIAL MOVEMENTS/NEW POLITICS	→	4. UTOPIAN REALIST EXTRAPOLATION OF POSSIBLE BASIS OF A NEW GLOBAL SOCIAL ORDER "BEYOND MODERNITY"
Globalisation – a dialectic of the global and the local		New environments of risk & trust – disembedding and reembedding in a "runaway world" of "manufactured risk"		Increasing importance of life politics alongside emancipatory politics – a politics beyond left & right: the Third Way		Critical Sociology
RULES: (S) *Communication* Abstract and expert systems; Industrialization/technology	⟺	Post-empiricist epistemology; ontological insecurity/loss of tradition; new reflexive bases of self-identity; ecological threats		New forms of active trust, e.g. transformations of intimacy (pure relationships); ecological and counter-cultural movements; women's movement		Dialogical resolutions of issues and a new dialogic politics; repair of damaged solidarities; humanization of technology; global system of planetary care
RESOURCES: (D) *Allocative power* Global capitalism	⟺	Unregulated global capital flows; weightless economy; intensification of work; new global inequalities		Labor movement		More socialized economic organization post-scarcity/less work-centered society; end of poverty, reform of the welfare state – post dependency; the social investment state
RESOURCES: (D) *Authoritative power* Administrative/political power	⟺	Changes in the sovereignty and autonomy of states		Constitutional and civil rights movements		Multi-layered democracy – EU as model; a more coordinated world political order
RULES (L) *Legitimation Sanctions* Military power; values		Threat of nuclear annihilation; internal violence/genocide; fundamentalist reworking of tradition		Peace movement; human rights movements		Reduced risk of global war – demilitarization; democracies without enemies; cosmopolitan democracy

instead of looking on, can at least enjoy the present. That way, Leach continues, you can avoid becoming

> a lonely, impotent and terrified observer of a runaway world. A more positive attitude to change will not mean that you will always feel secure, it will just give you a sense of purpose. You should read your Homer. Gods who manipulate the course of destiny are no more likely to achieve their private ambitions than men who suffer the slings and arrows of outrageous fortune; but gods have much more fun. (Leach, 1968: 9)

There is a conceit, or perhaps a bravura, in Leach's claim that men and women are, or could be, god-like – except that Leach's ancient Greek gods do not determine the course of history, they just make things happen. What Giddens offers is more a version of men and women condemned to take risks but saved by their potential for dialogue. To put it in Weberian terms, gods might favor an ethic of ultimate conviction, but men and women are better served by an ethic of responsibility.

In Giddens's terms, this is the difference between utopianism and utopian realism, where the latter refers to the combination of realism and idealism in the envisaging of "alternative futures whose very propagation might help them be realised" (Giddens, 1990a: 154). Giddens's own utopian realism has at its heart his vision of the possibilities of the more socialized, demilitarized and planetary-caring global order variously articulated within the labor, green, civil rights, women's, and peace movements, and within the wider democratic movement. Our runaway world could even end up as an agreeable postmodernity, a new global social order beyond modernity, characterized by dialogical politics, more socialized economics, and cosmopolitan societies (see Table 18.2). Whether, two decades on from the anticipated post-1989 "new world order," Giddens would now be as sanguine about the attainability of such an outcome must be in some doubt. His more recent writings are narrower in focus and ambition.

From the third way to the politics of climate change

Public intellectuals set agendas, inform debate, influence public opinion and thereby make a difference to political and policy outcomes. To be a successful public intellectual is a major challenge for any social scientist because, as Max Weber ruefully acknowledged, the demands made on, and the skills needed by, someone in public life are different from those required of academics. Giddens was always well aware of this and he says it was only after psychotherapy in the early 1990s that he had the confidence to seek a public role for the first time. Other commentators seem not to know about Giddens's experience of psychotherapy or pass over it in silence. It seems to us a key to understanding the otherwise startling reorientation of his career in the 1990s. Grappling with the ontology of the social and networking in the White House belong to different worlds and are normally the pursuits of different people.

Giddens "the public intellectual" has won widespread public attention in Britain and access to politicians and their advisers in many countries all over the world. In the autumn of 1998 he published *The Third Way*, an attempt to define a politics beyond left and right for new Labour. Much of the force of Giddens's argument, and much of its appeal to Tony Blair and to politicians abroad, lay in the claim that socialism and the Old Left had died of exhaustion and maladjustment to a changed world, and their successors, neoliberalism and the New Right, unable to sustain the contradictions between market fundamentalism and conservatism, were now dying too. But what of the successor third way? According to Giddens (1998b: 64), "the overall aim of third way politics should be to help citizens pilot their way through the major revolutions of our time: *globalization, transformations in personal life* and our *relationship to nature*." In all three cases, Giddens argues (with echoes of Saint-Simon) that wise action on our part can make a difference to how these revolutions work themselves out.

Giddens's third-way program has as its components the radical center, the new democratic state (the state without external enemies – a pre-9/11 formulation), an active civil society, the democratic family, the new mixed economy, equality as inclusion, positive (enabling) welfare, the social investment state, the cosmopolitan nation (which balances cultural pluralism and solidarity), and cosmopolitan (outward-looking) democracy. It is notable that Giddens's state still has a lot to do in making social investments, in regulating capitalism at home, and in reforming and devising the international institutions with which to combat market fundamentalism globally. Giddens discussed the latter with the financial speculator, George Soros, and edited a book on it with the economic commentator, Will Hutton (Hutton and Giddens, 2000a).

Not all the concepts and ideas in Giddens's version of the third way figure in Tony Blair's similarly titled Fabian society pamphlet, published shortly afterwards (Blair, 1998). In particular, Blair refers disparagingly to the "fundamentalist Left," but it is market fundamentalism and especially the minimal regulation of international capital markets that disturbs Giddens more. Giddens's ecological concerns also do not make it into Blair's pamphlet, and nor does his critique of the self-exclusion of the privileged from the social mainstream. Blair's use of Giddens is selective, and his vision is less radical. Be this as it may, third-way thinking (recast as the "new center" by Chancellor Schröder in Germany) influenced governments in most of the European Union and beyond, and secured plaudits from, *inter alia*, Romano Prodi, President of the European Commission, and Fernando Henrique Cardoso, President of Brazil. Such developments enabled Giddens to edit a volume entitled *The Global Third Way Debate* (2001a: cf. Jary, 2002).

Giddens also delivered the 1999 Reith Lectures on BBC radio. He took as his title *Runaway World* but omitted any reference to juggernauts. The lectures are prestigious and may have served to make some of his ideas more widely known, especially as three of the five were delivered outside Britain (in Delhi, Hong Kong, and Washington). Each lecture was followed by discussion, and among the questioners were Hillary Clinton and Tony Blair. Audio and video versions of the series were accessible on the World Wide Web, along with an interactive web site. Given that the lectures contained nothing new, the global multimedia were the message.

In May 2001, new Labour was re-elected in Britain with another huge majority but without the popular enthusiasm evident in 1997; the turn-out of only 59 percent was the lowest since 1918. Giddens had already responded to critics in *The Third Way and its Critics* (2000b); he now came up with *Where Now for New Labour?* (2002). His answers largely amounted to more of the same; they were worthy, often complex, and far from populist. They represent as has so much of new Labour – and here again there are echoes of Saint-Simon – a politics without great passion.

In countries other than Britain a failure to stir the voters had contributed to electoral reverses of the center-left. Acknowledging this, Giddens was prepared to call for a more ideological debate about the good society but what he had to say about balancing the state, civil society, and the market, and about differences between government, the state, and the public interest, was still decidedly cerebral and unlikely to excite voters.[7]

Giddens took part in a succession of private conferences with the leading politicians of the center-left on both sides of the Atlantic, including gatherings in the Clinton White House and at Chequers, the country house of the British prime minister. Out of these there developed the Progressive Governance Network of international policy makers and academics which held conferences in New York, Florence, and Berlin. This was then institutionalized in 2002 as the Policy Network, based in London. Policy Network declares itself "an international think-tank dedicated to promoting progressive policies and the renewal of social democracy" (Giddens, 2007: vi; also see www.policy-network.net). It has an international program of research, publications, and events. The events have included seven progressive governance summits, the first in Washington and the latest in London in 2008. Bill and Hillary Clinton, Tony Blair, Al Gore, Gerhard Schröder (formerly Chancellor of Germany), Romano Prodi, and José Manuel Barroso (former and current presidents of the European Commission) are just some of those brought together by these means. Tony Giddens has been one of the key academics involved throughout.

All seven of Giddens's books since 2002 have Policy Network associations. Only *Over to You, Mr Brown* (2007) is directed specifically at a British readership. It was published just before Gordon Brown took over from Tony Blair as prime minister in 2007, is subtitled *How Labour Can Win Again*, and is about how to rebuild a progressive consensus. Giddens was always much closer to Blair than Brown and there is scant evidence that the new prime minister has heeded it. At the time of writing (November 2009), Britain is only a few months away from a general election which commentators and polls suggest Labour will lose heavily. This is therefore an appropriate moment to point out that neither Blair nor Brown have come close to implementing the full range of Giddens's third-way thinking, nor have they taken on board his revisions and critiques. Giddens's claim remains valid that no alternative to the third way has emerged offering a better accommodation between market and state. After the world banking crisis it also bears repeating that Giddens has argued from the start that market fundamentalism could be the ruin of us all, that new international regulatory financial structures are urgently needed, that the self-isolation of the rich damages the rest of society and has to be countered, and that environmental issues have to have a much higher priority or we will all suffer the consequences. The similarities between the third way and the campaigning Obama are striking, although President Obama, perhaps anxious to achieve clear water between himself and Clinton, has never acknowledged them.[8]

Two other books also deserve a mention. Consistent with his long-standing view of the declining independent political and economic power of the nation-state, Giddens's *Europe in the Global Age* (2007) advances a view of "the struggle for Europe" that is "Eurorealist" in that it is "sober but ambitious" (xii). The struggle for Europe has an internal dimension "in the sense of a clash between different versions of what the Union represents, and what form it should assume in the future" (ix).

Giddens regards the EU "as an experiment in government without a state" (212), and defines it "as a democratic association (or community) of semi-sovereign nations" (217), "drawing upon collective capabilities" (211). He does not engage with the complexities of what others have called multi-level governance or the difficulties of securing endorsement for such a union from its citizens (cf. Bryant 2008). What he does do is address at the European level themes familiar from his third-way writing such as the supersession of the traditional welfare state by the post-industrial welfare society, and the pursuit of a new egalitarianism which optimizes the balance, or the trade-offs, between social justice and economic dynamism. These necessitate reform of the European social model. Controversially, Giddens thinks that Britain has done more in recent times to stimulate enterprise and reform labor markets than the "blocked societies" of Germany and France and has consequently suffered less unemployment. The external dimension refers to the struggle "that Europe has to engage in to assert itself in a world of far-reaching transformation" (ix). Europe has to respond positively to the challenges of globalization, economic, ecological, political, and ideological. Key concepts he introduces – "assertive multilateralism," "blocked societies," "the ensuring state" "everyday democratisation," "preventative welfare," etc. – convey the tenor of the work.

The Politics of Climate Change (2009) also has its continuities with previous work in that it extends the theme of new dimensions of risk in a globally interconnected and to some extent runaway world. It is centered on "Giddens's paradox": that "the dangers posed by global warming aren't tangible, immediate or visible in the course of day-today life," but "waiting until they become visible and acute before being stirred to serious action will, by definition, be too late" (2). The paradox is hardly novel and it will be unfortunate if the eponymous conceit diverts attention from the message. Giddens makes the "startling assertion that, at present, we have no politics of climate change … we do not have a developed analysis of the political innovations that have to be made if our aspirations to limit global warming are to become real" (4); and it is this omission he sets out to remedy. It is not possible to summarize the extensive ground he covers in a few sentences but three points are worth noting. First, the Stern Report (2007) is right that global warming "is the greatest market failure the world has seen" (49), but this must not prompt a retreat from capitalism. Growth will and must continue; capitalist enterprise and new technology are crucial to solutions. Second, the issue of global warming has to be addressed in tandem with that of energy security. Here in particular, states have an interest in action leading to greater energy efficiency. Third, global warning constitutes risks, but, as ever, risks also afford opportunities.

Social scientists familiar with Giddens's work before his public-intellectual turn can reflect on the third way, Europe and climate change books and, mindful of *The Consequences of Modernity* (1990) and *Beyond Left and Right* (1994), tease out continuities – but they are quite thin. It is tempting to speak of Giddens-lite, but this is also to miss the point. Without the making of structuration theory Giddens would not have come to look beyond left and right to articulate the politics of the third way, reform of the European social model and climate change, but how Giddens arrived at his current thinking is irrelevant to its appeal. He is now writing for a readership way beyond the academy with a view to influencing opinion, policy, and practice. To this end, he is pitching what he has to say somewhere between rigorous and referenced academic analysis and the desperately brief, superficial and slanted pieces that are the staple of journalism in Britain certainly and no doubt in many other countries too.

A CONCLUDING EVALUATION OF GIDDENS'S OEUVRE

Giddens's commentary on leading figures, schools, and traditions is unsurpassed in volume, range, and consistent quality. It would be a commendable achievement even if he had done nothing else. But, of course, he has. It is arguable that of all the approaches to the agency–structure and macro–micro debates on offer, and they now run into double figures, Giddens's is the most persuasive – not least because of the long list of theorists and theoretical approaches he has critically appropriated.[9] The principles of structuration theory have also proved useful to an impressive number of researchers in a dauntingly wide range of disciplines even if Stones is right that without further elaboration their application represents a tougher challenge than it needs to. In addition, Giddens has done as much as anyone to make concern for time-space an essential of social theory and empirical research design.

Beginning with *The Consequences of Modernity* (1990a), Giddens has played a leading role in establishing globalization and its concomitants as one of the biggest topics in contemporary social science. Giddens has also provided some of the ingredients for a theory of *late* modernity, such as the focus on the dialogic resolution of issues and the acknowledgment of the continuing importance of traditions (see especially his contribution to Beck *et al.*, 1994). He has come close to reconsideration of "evolutionary" issues (see Jary, 1991; Craib, 1992), including the role of the aesthetic, the ludic, and perhaps also the religious dimensions of culture (see Tucker, 1993). It would, however, sometimes have been more helpful to point up the similarities with Habermas than the differences. The similarities on the dialogic conception of knowledge and the justification of values, and on new social movements, are evident; despite his protestations, there is also the potential for an approach to evolution with some resemblance to Habermas's.

And, whatever the limitations of his more recent work, Giddens has coined, appropriated, and given currency to a host of concepts which can be expected to continue to figure in discourse about late or postmodernity for a long time yet: reflexive and radicalized modernity, institutional reflexivity, detraditionalization, manufactured uncertainty, and global risk environments, emancipatory politics and life politics or the politics of self-actualization, narratives and projects of the self, the sequestration of experience and ontological security, the democratization of democracy and dialogic democracy, cosmopolitan democracy, the pure relationship, the transformation of intimacy and confluent love, utopian realism, active and passive trust, the ensuring state, positive and preventative welfare, and many more.

To pay attention to the phases of Giddens's writing career and to aspects of his works is all very proper, but it misses the most important feature of all his work up until the mid-1990s – grand synthesis. Craib (1992), a perceptive but not always sympathetic critic, argues that Giddens's oeuvre, whatever its flaws, is probably the best there has been at integrating (a) commentary, (b) theorization of the constitution of society and the self, and (c) analysis of premodern, modern, and late modern societies. Craib had his doubts about the feasibility of such grand synthetic ventures, but he also acknowledged that without them sociology could so easily have fragmented into a host of self-contained and self-absorbed specialities of ever-declining consequence for our understanding of the world at large. Giddens, perhaps more than any other single figure in sociology, held the whole discipline together and connected it to other social sciences. With Giddens's attentions now elsewhere, who else is there to carry the torch?

Having made what we believe to be a formidable case for Giddens, we now want to return to criticisms of our own. There has long been a need for Giddens to develop further the principles of structuration theory in order to deal more convincingly with the objections raised by critics. It is highly improbable that Giddens will now ever face up to the task and he has shown no interest in encouraging anyone else to do so – which makes Stones's efforts all the more admirable. The non-appearance of a major systematic treatment of economic and political relations in late modern societies, to fill the gap left by the abandonment of the projected third volume of the contemporary critique of historical materialism, is also a serious omission. It is a pity, too, that Giddens has shown negligible interest in developing further the connections between the core of structuration theory and an analysis of radicalized modernity in which more justified instances of utopian realism inform a thorough examination of its economics and politics. There are also unresolved tensions in Giddens's description of continuities and contingencies in modernity and his depiction of knowledgeable and capable agents in a runaway world.

The early Giddens who eschewed judgments in *Capitalism and Modern Social Theory* (1971a) contrasts greatly with the pundit of the 1990s and the associate of world leaders in the 2000s. The close referencing of the early and middle Giddens differs markedly from the light referencing of *The Consequences of Modernity* (1990a) and subsequent books. The books of the 1990s offer brilliant sketches, countless *aperçus*, engaging prompts, and much else, but fall short of a comprehensive and systematic account of the global age, as do the books of the 2000s. Rigorous scholarship and analysis had increasingly given way to invention and communication relatively unencumbered by literatures and *systematic* evidence until the return to evidence trawling in *Europe in the Global Age* (2006) and *The Politics of Climate Change* (2009).

Enough of criticism, Giddens's achievements in social theory and the analysis of high modernity has been immense. He has, of course, also had other commitments. He wanted to secure a brilliant future for the LSE in the difficult circumstances of the chronic underfunding of British universities, and a movement from elite to mass higher education in which greater institutional diversification was inevitable. This was no mean task and, although not all saw it this way, he largely succeeded. And he wanted to contribute prominently and publicly to the fashioning of a politics beyond left and right in which the values of the center-left remain, but the strategies and the policies are rethought. This was no mean ambition and, although not all have seen it this way, he has had his successes at home and abroad. Giddens the utopian realist has the audacity to hope. He believes a combination of technological innovation, economic dynamism, and individual and collective self-interest, reflexivity, imagination, and capability will ensure that the runaway world never entirely runs away from us. In the end it is not so much a threat as a challenge that humankind can and will go on meeting. In sum, Giddens is not just one of the most significant of all contemporary social theorists, he is also one of the most influential public intellectuals of our time and probably the most successful international political networker sociology has ever produced. One can recognize and forgive the occasional trade-offs between intellectual scruple and public impact that this has made necessary.

Reader's Guide to Anthony Giddens

The Constitution of Society (1984) is relatively accessible and the best place to begin engagement with structuration theory in Giddens's own words. Chapter 1, "The elements of structuration theory," presents the core theory. *The New Rules of Sociological Method* (1976a) indicates most clearly why Giddens was moved to formulate what immediately thereafter became structuration theory. Giddens's Introduction to the second edition (1993) offers a reply to Mouzelis (1991) and other critics.

None of Giddens's books on the contemporary world is hard to read. Anyone starting with *A Contemporary Critique of Historical Materialism* (1981) and *The Nation-State and Violence* (1985) and then working through the short, but highly influential, *The Consequences of Modernity* (1990), the path-pointing *Beyond Left and Right* (1994), and the politically significant *The Third Way* (1995), will see how Giddens reached the particular social democratic position he still occupies.

Modernity and Self-Identity (1991) and *The Transformation of Intimacy* (1992b) explore the interrelation of the self and modernity in new ways. *Europe in the Global Age* (2007) promotes a particular version of the "European social model," whilst *The Politics of Climate Change* (2009) bids for political attention on a matter of worldwide concern.

The two best book-length commentaries on Giddens, each entitled *Structuration Theory*, are by Ira Cohen (1989), and Rob Stones (2005). The latter also offers the most important development of the theory since Giddens. Kenneth Tucker's *Anthony Giddens and Modern Social Theory* (1998) is also commendable. Lars Bo Kaspersen's *Anthony Giddens* (2000) provides simple reliable exposition but more contestable evaluation. Stjepan Meštrović's *Anthony Giddens* (1998) offers acerbic criticism of Giddens's synthesis from a postmodern perspective, and Steven Loyal's *The Sociology of Anthony Giddens* (2003) finds Giddens's progressive liberal world-view ultimately incoherent.

The most comprehensive collection of critical assessments of Giddens is Bryant and Jary's *Anthony Giddens* (1996, 4 vols) which also covers uses and applications as does their 2001 collection. Earlier collections by Held and Thompson (*Anthony Giddens and His Critics*, 1989), Clark, Modgil and Modgil (*Anthony Giddens: Consensus and Controversy* 1990) and Bryant and Jary (*Giddens' Theory of Structuration* 1991) remain useful. Held and Thompson's include an important reply from Giddens to his critics. Later ones by O'Brien, Penna, and Hay (*Theorising Modernity* 1999) and Bryant and Jary (*The Contemporary Giddens* 2001) concentrate on identity, modernity, and politics. The latter also contains the most complete bibliography of works by, on and using Giddens from 1960 to 2000.

Notes

1   Three of these from 1995 have been republished as chapter 13, "Brave New World: the New Context of Politics," of Giddens (1996). The best early piece by a journalist on Giddens and his new political role is Boynton's in *The New Yorker* (1997).

2   We have, *inter alia*, drawn on our interviews with Giddens on April 26, 1989 in Cambridge and November 27, 1997 in London.

3   This is not to say that Elias's influence was necessarily evident to students at the time, as one of us, Chris Bryant, a Leicester graduate, can testify.

4   For another view of Elias at Leicester, see Brown (1987).

5   This is, of course, the opposite of C. Wright Mills's (1959) exercise of the sociological imagination, which moves from an examination of "the public issues of social structure" to an enlightening re-view of "the personal troubles of milieu."

6   For an extended discussion of Giddens on reflexivity, see Bryant and Jary (2001: 20–24).

7   On Giddens and the first new Labour government, see Bryant and Jary (2001), especially point IV, "The Public Intellectual," and chapter 12, "The Reflexive Giddens."

8   Newman and de Zoysa (2001) include interesting comment on the American input to the third way. In their major overview of third-way initiatives in many countries, Hale, Leggett and Martell's (2004) contributors discuss criticisms, futures and alternatives. Part I of Leggett (2005) discusses "When Sociology Met Politics: New Labour and the Third Way"; the other parts consider "The Left Critics" and "After the Third Way."

9   But like others we have sometimes wondered whether Giddens's synthesis sufficiently respects the nuances of the approaches it incorporates – a reservation only reinforced by his admission that he hardly ever reads books from cover to cover, he just uses lists of contents and indexes to fillet out the main bits (in *The Guardian*, Higher Education, January 14, 1997).

Bibliography

Writings of Anthony Giddens

1971a. *Capitalism and Modern Social Theory*. Cambridge: Cambridge University Press.

1971b. *The Sociology of Suicide* (editor). London: Frank Cass.

1972a. *Emile Durkheim: Selected Writings* (editor). Cambridge: Cambridge University Press.

1972b. *Politics and Sociology in the Thought of Max Weber*. London: Macmillan.

1973. *The Class Structure of the Advanced Societies*. London: Hutchinson.

1974. *Positivism and Sociology* (editor). London: Heinemann.

1976a. *New Rules of Sociological Method*. London: Hutchinson (2nd edn, 1993).

1976b. Functionalism: *après la lutte*. Social Research, 43: 325–366.

1977a. *Studies in Social and Political Theory*. London: Hutchinson.

1977b. A Theory of suicide. In *Studies in Social and Political Theory*, chapter 9.

1977c. Notes on the Theory of Structuration. In *Studies in Social and Political Theory*, appendix to chapter 2.

1978. *Durkheim*. London: Fontana.

1979. *Central Problems in Social Theory: Action, Structure and Contradiction in Social Analysis*. London: Macmillan.

1981. *A Contemporary Critique of Historical Materialism. Volume 1, Power, Property and the State*. London: Macmillan (2nd edn, 1995).

1982a (editor with G. Mackenzie). *Classes and the Division of Labour: Essays in Honour of Ilya Neustadt*. Cambridge: Cambridge University Press.

1982b (editor with D. Held). *Classes, Conflict and Power: Classical and Contemporary Debates*. London: Macmillan.

1982c. *Profiles and Critiques in Social Theory*. London: Macmillan.

1982d. *Sociology: a Brief but Critical Introduction*. London: Macmillan (2nd edn, 1986).

1984. *The Constitution of Society: Outline of the Theory of Structuration*. Cambridge: Polity.

1985. *A Contemporary Critique of Historical Materialism. Volume 2, The Nation-State and Violence*. Cambridge: Polity Press.

1986. *Durkheim on Politics and the State* (ed.). Cambridge: Polity Press.

1987. *Social Theory and Modern Sociology*. Cambridge: Polity Press.

1987 (editor with J. H. Turner). *Social Theory Today*. Cambridge: Polity Press.

1989. *Sociology*. Cambridge: Polity Press (6th edn, 2009; US edn, *An Introduction to Sociology*. New York: Norton, 1991).

1990a. *The Consequences of Modernity*. Cambridge: Polity Press.

1990b. Structuration theory and sociological analysis. In J. Clark, C. Modgil, and S. Modgil (eds) *Anthony Giddens: Consensus and Controversy*. Lewis: Falmer Press, chapter 22.

1991a. *Modernity and Self-identity: Self and Society in the Late Modern Age*. Cambridge: Polity Press.

1991b. Structuration theory: Past, present and future. In C. G. A. Bryant and D. W. Jary (eds) *Giddens' Theory of Structuration: a Critical Appreciation*. London: Routledge, chapter 8.

1992a. *Human Societies: A Reader*. Cambridge: Polity Press (2nd edn, *Sociology: Introductory Readings*, 1997).

1992b. *The Transformation of Intimacy: Sexuality, Love and Eroticism in Modern Societies*. Cambridge: Polity Press.

1993. Introduction to the Second Edition. *New Rules of Sociological Method*. Cambridge: Polity Press.

1994a. *Beyond Left and Right: the Future of Radical Politics*. Cambridge: Polity Press.

1994b. Brave New World: the New Context of Politics. In D. Miliband (ed.) *Reinventing the Left*. Cambridge: Polity Press, chapter 1.

1995. *Politics, Sociology and Social Theory: Encounters with Classical and Contemporary Social Thought*. Cambridge: Polity Press.

1996. *In Defence of Sociology: Essays, Interpretations and Rejoinders*. Cambridge: Polity Press.

1998. *Conversations with Anthony Giddens: Making Sense of Modernity* (co-author C. Pierson). Cambridge: Polity Press.

1998b. *The Third Way: the Renewal of Social Democracy*. Cambridge: Polity Press.

1999. *Runaway World: How Globalisation is Reshaping Our Lives*. London: Profile.

2000a (editor with W. Hutton). *On the Edge: Living with Global Capitalism*. London: Cape.

2000b. *The Third Way and Its Critics*. Cambridge: Polity Press.

2001a. *The Global Third Way Debate* (editor). Cambridge: Polity Press.

2001b. The Reflexive Giddens: Christopher G. A. Bryant and David Jary in Dialogue with Anthony Giddens. In C. G. A. Bryant and D. W. Jary (eds) *The Contemporary Giddens: Social Theory in a Globalising Age*. Basingstoke and New York: Palgrave.

2002. *Where Now for New Labour?* Cambridge: Polity Press.

2003. *The Progressive Manifesto* (ed.). Cambridge: Polity Press.

2005 (editor with P. Diamond). *The New Egalitarianism*. Basingstoke: Palgrave.

2006 (editor with P. Diamond and R. Liddle). *Global Europe, Social Europe*. Cambridge: Polity Press.

2007. *Europe in the Global Age*. Cambridge: Polity Press.

2007. *Over to You, Mr Brown: How Labour Can Win Again*. Cambridge: Polity Press.

2009. *The Politics of Climate Change*. Cambridge: Polity Press.

Further Reading

Archer, M. S. (1982) Morphogenesis versus structuration: on combining structure and action. *British Journal of Sociology*, 33: 455–488.

Archer, M. S. (1988) *Culture and Agency: The Place of Culture in Social Theory*. Cambridge: Cambridge University Press.

Barrett, J. C. (1988) Fields of discourse: Reconstituting a social archaeology. *Critique of Anthropology*, 7(3): 5–16.

Bastien, D. T., McPhee, R. D., and Bolton, K. A. (1995) a study and extended theory of the structuration of climate. *Communication Monographs*, 87–109.

Beck, U. (1986) *Risk Society: Towards a New Modernity*. London: Sage.

Beck, U., Giddens, A., and Lash, S. (1994) *Reflexive Modernization: Politics, Tradition and Aesthetics in the Modern Order*. Cambridge: Polity Press.

Blair, T. (1998) *The Third Way: New Politics for the New Century*. London: The Fabian Society.

Boland, R. J. (1993) Accounting and the interpretative act. *Accounting, Organizations and Society*, 18: 125–140.

Boynton, R. S. (1997) The two Tonys: Why Is the Prime Minister so interested in what Anthony Giddens thinks? *The New Yorker*, October 6: 2–7.

Brown, R. K. (1987) Norbert Elias in Leicester: Some recollections. *Theory, Culture and Society*, 4: 533–539.

Bryant, C. G. A. (1991) The dialogical model of applied sociology. In C. G. A. Bryant and D. W. Jary (eds) *Giddens' Theory of Structuration: a Critical Appreciation*. London: Routledge, chapter 7.

Bryant, C. G. A. (1992) Sociology without Philosophy? The case of Giddens' structuration theory. *Sociological Theory*, 10: 137–149.

Bryant, C. G. A. (1995) *Practical Sociology: Postempiricism and the Reconstruction of Theory and Application*. Cambridge: Polity Press.

Bryant, C. G. A. (2008) Complexity and citizen disaffection in an enlarged European Union. In S. Eliaeson (ed.) *Building Civil Society and Democracy in New Europe*. Cambridge: Cambridge Scholars Publishing, pp. 88–106.

Bryant, C. G. A. and Jary, D. W. (eds) (1991) *Giddens' Theory of Structuration: a Critical Appreciation*. London: Routledge.

Bryant, C. G. A. and Jary, D. W. (eds) (1997) *Anthony Giddens: Critical Assessments*, 4 vols. London: Routledge.

Bryant, C. G. A. and Jary, D. W. (eds) (2001) *The Contemporary Giddens: Social Theory in a Globalising Age*. Basingstoke and New York: Palgrave.

Burman, P. (1988) *Killing Time, Losing Ground*. Toronto: Wall and Thompson.

Callinicos, A. (1985) Anthony Giddens – a contemporary critique. *Theory and Society*, 14: 133–166.

Carlstein, T. (1981) The sociology of structuration in time and space: A timegeographic assessment of Giddens' theory. *Svensk Geografisk Arsbok*, 57: 41–57.

Cash, J. D. (1996) *Identity, Ideology and Conflict: The Structuration of Politics in Northern Ireland*. Cambridge: Cambridge University Press.

Clark, J., Modgil, C., and Modgil, S. (eds) (1990) *Anthony Giddens: Consensus and Controversy*. London: Falmer Press.

Cohen, I. J. (1989) *Structuration Theory: Anthony Giddens and the Constitution of Social Life*. London: Macmillan.

Cohen, P. S. (1968) *Modern Social Theory*. London: Heinemann.

Connell, R. W. (1987) *Gender and Power*. Cambridge: Polity Press.

Craib, I. (1992) *Anthony Giddens*. London: Routledge.

Dandeker, C. (1989) *Surveillance, Power and Modernity*. Cambridge: Polity Press.

Dandeker, C. (1990) The Nation-state and the modern world system. In J. Clark, C. Modgil, and F. Modgil (eds) *Anthony Giddens: Consensus and Controversy*. Lewis: Falmer Press.

Dunning, E. (1994) Towards a configurational critique of the theory of structuration. Paper presented at the 13th World Congress of Sociology, Bielefeld, Germany.

Elchardus, M. (1988) The rediscovery of Chronos: The new role of time in sociological theory. *International Sociology*, 3(1): 35–59.

Eldridge, J. (1990) Sociology in Britain: A going concern. In C. G. A. Bryant and H. A. Becker (eds) *What Has Sociology Achieved?* London: Macmillan, chapter 9.

Elias, N. (1939) *The Civilizing Process. Volume I, The History of Manners*. Oxford: Blackwell (1978).

Graves, C. P. (1989) Social space in the English medieval parish church. *Economy and Society*, 18: 297–322.

Gray, J. (1995) *Enlightenment's Wake: Politics and Culture at the Close of the Modern Age*. London: Routledge.

Gregson, N. (1989) On the (ir)relevance of structuration theory to empirical research. In D. Held and J. B. Thompson (eds) *Social Theory of Modern Societies: Anthony Giddens and his critics*. Cambridge: Cambridge University Press, 235–248.

Hale, S, Leggett, W., and Martell, L. (eds) (2004) *The Third Way and Beyond: Criticisms, Futures and Alternatives*. Manchester: Manchester University Press.

Held, D. and Thompson, J. B. (eds) *Social Theory of Modern Societies*. Cambridge: Cambridge University Press.

Jack, L. and Kholeif, A. (2007) Introducing strong structuration theory for informing qualitative case studies in organizations, management and accounting research. *Qualitative Research in Organisations and Management: An International Journal*, 2: 208–225.

Jary, D. W. (1991) Society as time traveller: Giddens on historical change, historical materialism and the nation-state in world society. In C. G. A. Bryant and D. W. Jary (eds) *Giddens' Theory of Structuration: a Critical Appreciation*. London: Routledge, chapter 5.

Jary, D. W. (2002) The global Third Way debate. *Sociological Review*, 50: 437–449.

Jary, D. W. and Jary, J. (1995) The transformations of Anthony Giddens. *Theory, Culture and Society*, 12(2): 141–160.

Judt, T. (1994) How much is really left of the Left? *The Times Literary Supplement*, 4773(7), September 23.

Kaspersen, Lars Bo (2000) *Anthony Giddens: An Introduction to a Social Theorist*. Oxford: Blackwell.

Kilminster, R. (1991) Structuration theory as a world-view. In C. G. A. Bryant and D. W. Jary (eds) *Giddens' Theory of Structuration: a Critical Appreciation*. London: Routledge, chapter 4.

Layder, D. (1994) *Understanding Social Theory*. London: Sage.

Leach, E. (1968) *A Runaway World?* London: BBC.

Lee, R. L. M. (1992) The structuration of disenchantment: Secular agency and the reproduction of religion. *Journal for the Theory of Social Behaviour*, 22: 381–402.

Leggett, W. (2005) *After New Labour: Social Theory and Centre-Left Politics*. Basingstoke and New York: Palgrave.

Loyal, S. (2003) *The Sociology of Anthony Giddens*. London: Pluto.

MacIntosh, N. B. and Scapens, R. W. (1990) Structuration theory in management and accounting. *Accounting, Organizations and Society*, 15: 455–477.

Mann, M. (1986) *The Sources of Social Power. Volume 1, A History of Power from the Beginning to* AD *1760*. Cambridge: Cambridge University Press.

Marshall, T. H. (1982) Introduction to A. Giddens and G. Mackenzie (eds) *Social Class and the Division of Labour: Essays in Honour of Ilya Neustadt*. Cambridge: Cambridge University Press.

Mellor, P. A. (1993) Reflexive traditions: Anthony Giddens, high modernity, and the contours of contemporary religiosity. *Religious Studies*, 29: 111–127.

Meštrović, S. G. (1998) *Anthony Giddens: The Last Modernist*. London: Routledge.

Mills, C. Wright (1959) *The Sociological Imagination*. New York: Oxford University Press.

Morawska, E. (1996) *Insecure Prosperity: Small Town Jews in Industrial America 1890–1940*. New York: Cambridge University Press.

Mouzelis, N. (1991) *Back to Sociological Theory: The Construction of Social Orders*. London: Macmillan.

Newman, O. and de Zoysa, R. (2001) *The Promise of the Third Way: Globalization and Social Justice*. Basingstoke and New York: Palgrave.

O'Brien, M., Penna, S., and Hay, C. (eds) (1999) *Theorising Modernity: Reflexivity, Environment and Identity in Giddens' Social Theory*. London: Longman.

Orlikowski, W. J. (1992) The duality of technology; Rethinking the concept of technology in organization. *Organization Science*, 3: 398–427.

Parker, J. (2006) Structurations' future? From "all and every" to who did what, where and why, Review of Stones (2005). *Journal of Critical Realism*, 5: 122–138.

Parsons, T. (1937) *The Structure of Social Action*. New York: McGraw-Hill.

Roberts, J. and Scapens, R. W. (1985) Accounting systems and systems of accounting: Understanding accounting practices in their organisational contexts. *Accounting, Organizations and Society*, 10: 443–456.

Scapens, R. W. and MacIntosh, N. B. (1996) Structure and agency in management accounting research: A response to Boland's interpretive act. *Accounting, Organizations and Society*, 21: 675–690.

Sewell, W. (1992) A theory of structure: Duality, agency and transformations. *American Journal of Sociology*, 98: 1–29.

Shilling, C. (1992) Reconceptualising structure and agency in the sociology of education: Structuration theory and schooling. *British Journal of Sociology of Education*, 13: 69–87.

Shotter, J. (1983) "Duality of structure" and "intentionality" in an ecological psychology. *Journal for the Theory of Social Behaviour*, 13: 19–43.

Sica, A. (1991) The California–Massachusetts strain in structuration theory. In C. G. A. Bryant and D. W. Jary (eds) *Giddens' Theory of Structuration: a Critical Appreciation*, London: Routledge, chapter 2.

Spybey, T. (1984) Traditional and professional frames of meaning in management. *Sociology*, 18: 550–562.

Stern, N. (2007) *The Economics of Climate Change*. Cambridge: Cambridge University Press.

Stinchcombe, A. (1986) Milieu and structure updated: A critique of the theory of structuration theory. *Theory and Society*, 15: 901–914.

Stones, R. (1991) Strategic context analysis: A new research strategy for structuration theory. *Sociology*, 25: 673–695.

Stones, R. (1996) *Sociological Reasoning: Towards a Post-modern Sociology*. London: Macmillan.

Stones, R. (2005) *Structuration Theory*. Basingstoke and New York: Palgrave.

Stones, R. (ed.) (2008) *Key Sociological Thinkers*, 2nd edn. Basingstoke and New York: Palgrave.

Sydow, J. and Windeler, A. (1996) Managing inter-firm networks: A structurationist perspective. In C. G. A. Bryant and D. W. Jary (eds) *Anthony Giddens: Critical Assessments, vol. 4*. London: Routledge, chapter 93.

Thompson, J. B. (1989) The theory of structuration. In D. Held and J. B. Thompson (eds) *Social Theory of Modern Societies: Anthony Giddens and His Critics*. Cambridge: Cambridge University Press, chapter 3.

Tucker, K. H. (1993) Aesthetics, play and cultural memory: Giddens and Habermas on the postmodern challenge. *Sociological Theory*, 11: 194–211.

Tucker, K. H. (1998) *Anthony Giddens and Modern Social Theory*. London: Sage.

Whittington, R. (1992) Putting Giddens into action: Social systems and managerial agency. *Journal of Management Studies*, 29: 693–712.

Willis, Paul (1977) *Learning to Labour: How Working-class Kids get Working-class Jobs*. Farnborough: Saxon House.

Wright, E. Olin (1983) Giddens' critique of Marxism. *New Left Review*, 138: 11–35.

Yates, J. and Orlikowski, W. J. (1992) Genres of organizational communication: A structurational approach to studying communication and media. *Academy of Management Review*, 17: 299–326.

19

Giorgio Agamben

CATHERINE MILLS

Born in Rome in 1942, Giorgio Agamben completed studies in Law and Philosophy with a doctoral thesis on the political thought of Simone Weil at the University of Rome. He was close to Italian intellectuals and literary figures such as Giorgio Caproni and Elsa Morante, and has collaborated with Pier Paolo Pasolini (including playing a role in the film *The Gospel According to St Matthew*) and Italo Calvini. Much of his work can be read as ongoing conversations with other contemporary European scholars such as Jacques Derrida, Jean-François Lyotard, Jean-Luc Nancy, and Antonio Negri. His work is also steeped in the concerns of French thinkers such as Georges Bataille, Pierre Klossowski, and Guy Debord, one of the key figures of the Situationist movement. In 1974–1975, he was a fellow at the Warburg Institute in London, a position that led to his influential book, *Stanzas* (S). Throughout his career, Agamben has taught at a number of universities, including the Universities of Macerata and Verona, as well as a number of American institutions such as the University of California.

Perhaps most important for Agamben's philosophical development, though, was his participation in Martin Heidegger's seminars in the late 1960s on Hegel and Heraclitus as a postdoctoral scholar, which shaped his interest in language and poetics, as well as his sense of philosophy as vocation. Additionally, he served as editor of the Italian edition of Walter Benjamin's collected works. The influence of these figures is palpable throughout Agamben's work. Heidegger's influence is especially evident in the earlier work and in the specific style of philosophical analysis that Agamben adopts. Walter Benjamin provides Agamben with the conceptual tools for the resolution or *euporic* overcoming of the *aporias* that he claims give rise to the violence of modern democracy and consumer capital.

Even so, the problematic introduced to philosophy by Aristotle's dictum that man is an animal that has language, and hence politics, is most central to Agamben's

The Wiley-Blackwell Companion to Major Social Theorists, First Edition.
Edited by George Ritzer and Jeffrey Stepnisky.
© 2011 Blackwell Publishing Ltd. Published 2011 by Blackwell Publishing Ltd.

thought, and especially his later political thought. For Aristotle, the having of language or logos permits humanity to distinguish between the just and the unjust, and it is this that sets humans apart from other animals. That this thought provides a touchstone for Agamben does not, however, mean that he endorses or finds it unproblematic. Rather, in a manner of thinking that borrows from Heidegger, he sees it as both covering over the true ethos of the human and disclosing the direction of thought for recovering a more originary understanding of it. This is particularly evident in his focus on what it means that human beings *have* language, where the key question is, what is the nature of this having? In addressing this question, Agamben's work does not follow a straightforward path of development either conceptually or thematically. Instead, his work over the past three decades constitutes an elaborate and multifaceted engagement with several key problems, which reappear in one guise or another in almost every text that he has written.

While Agamben is not obviously a theoretician of the social, his work has nevertheless been influential in disciplines such as Sociology, primarily because of his construal of the camp as the "nomos of the modern," an idea developed in his discussions of biopolitics. This characterization of modernity draws upon, but also contrasts with, figures within classical social theory (most notably Marx and Weber) as well as within contemporary social theory (especially Foucault). In order to grasp the full significance of this notion, though, it is important to place it within the broader philosophical project that Agamben is undertaking. In order to assess Agamben's work, then, as well as its impact within social theory, I will first provide a background introduction to this philosophical context, with particular focus on his discussions of the concepts of "experience," "infancy" and his approach to a philosophy of language.

Philosophical Context – Language, Experience, and Infancy

Some of the most difficult problems that Agamben addresses derive from the history of metaphysics in Western philosophy, particularly the tendency that he diagnoses in metaphysical thought to presuppose and posit a negative foundation for being and language. This position is elaborated most explicitly in *Language and Death* (LD), where Agamben's project is primarily to diagnose and elaborate this metaphysical tendency towards negative foundation. This text takes as its starting point Heidegger's suggestion of an essential relation between language and death. From this, Agamben argues that Western metaphysics have been fundamentally tied to a negativity that is increasingly evident at the heart of the *ethos* of humanity. In his analysis of Heidegger and Hegel, Agamben isolates their reliance upon and indeed radicalization of negativity, by casting *Da* ["here/there"] and *Diese* ["this"] as grammatical shifters that refer to the pure taking place of language. Agamben draws upon the linguistic notion of *deixis* [indication or pointing out] to isolate the self-referentiality of language in pronouns or grammatical shifters, which he argues do not refer to anything beyond themselves but only to their own utterance (LD: 16–26).

The key problem that this approach makes apparent is that both Hegel and Heidegger ultimately maintain a split within language – which he sees as a consistent element of Western thought from Aristotle to Wittgenstein – in their identification of an ineffability or unspeakability that cannot be brought into human discourse but which is nevertheless its condition. Agamben calls this mute condition of language "Voice," and concludes that a philosophy that thinks only from the foundation of Voice cannot deliver the resolution of metaphysics that contemporary nihilism demands. Instead, he suggests, this is only possible in an experience of infancy that has never yet been: it is only in existing "in language without being called there by any Voice" and dying "without being called by death" (LD: 96) that humanity can return to its proper dwelling place or *ethos*, to which it has never been and from which it has never left. This points toward the necessity of an *"experimentum linguae"* in which what is experienced is language itself, and the limits of language become apparent not in the relation of language to a referent outside of it, but in the experience of language as pure self-reference.

Published in Italian in 1978, *Infancy and History* constitutes one of Agamben's earliest attempts to grasp the implications of such an experience of language. Consisting of a series on interconnected essays on concepts such as history, temporality, play, and gesture, *Infancy and History* provides an important entrance to Agamben's later work on politics and ethics, and provides the necessary background for understanding his importance within social theory. Of particular importance in this text is the eponymous essay on the concept of infancy, in which Agamben proposes a new understanding of the concept of experience. In this, Agamben argues that the contemporary age is marked by the destruction or loss of experience, in which the banality of everyday life cannot be experienced per se but only undergone, a condition which is in part brought about by the rise of modern science and the split between the subject of experience and of knowledge that it entails. Against this destruction of experience, which is also extended in modern philosophies of the subject such as Kant and Husserl, Agamben argues that the recuperation of experience entails a radical rethinking of it as a question of language rather than of consciousness, since it is only in language that the subject has its site and origin. Infancy, then, conceptualizes an experience of being without language, not in a temporal or developmental sense of preceding the acquisition of language in childhood, but as a condition of experience that ontologically precedes and makes possible *any* appropriation of language.

In addition to these reflections on the having of language, one of the most consistent threads throughout Agamben's work is the problem of potentiality. In this regard, Agamben focuses on Aristotle's proposal in Book Theta of *Metaphysics*, that "a thing is said to be potential if, when the act of which it is said to be potential is realized, there will be nothing im-potential, that is, there will be nothing able not to be" (HS: 45). He argues that this ought not be taken to mean simply that "what is not impossible is possible," since this would condemn Aristotle's claim to being completely trite. Instead, this idea highlights the suspension or setting aside of im-potentiality in the passage to actuality, where this suspension does not entail the destruction of im-potentiality, but rather to its fulfillment. That is, through the turning back of potentiality upon itself – its "giving of itself to itself" – impotentiality, or the potentiality to not be, is fully realized in its own suspension such that actuality appears as *not not-being*. This formulation is central to the passage of voice to speech or signification and to attaining toward the experience of language as such that Agamben attempts to elaborate. But he also claims that in this formulation

Aristotle bequeaths to Western philosophy the paradigm of sovereignty, since it reveals the undetermined or sovereign founding of being. As he concludes, "an act is sovereign when it realizes itself by simply taking away its own potentiality not to be, letting itself be, giving itself to itself" (HS: 46). In this way then, the relation of potentiality to actuality described by Aristotle accords perfectly with the logic of the ban that Agamben argues is characteristic of sovereign power, thereby revealing the fundamental integration of metaphysics and politics.

Before considering these ideas of the ban and sovereignty in more detail though, it is also worth outlining the key ideas of Agamben's first major contribution to contemporary philosophy of aesthetics in his acclaimed book *Stanzas*. In this text, he develops a dense and multifaceted analysis of language and phantasm, entailing engagement with modern linguistics and philosophy, as well as psychoanalysis and philology. While dedicated to the memory of Martin Heidegger, this book also evidently bears the influence of Aby Warburg. Agamben argues in *Stanzas* that to the extent that Western culture accepts the distinction between philosophy and poetry, knowledge founders on a division in which "philosophy has failed to elaborate a proper language…and poetry has developed neither a method nor self-consciousness" (S: xvii). The urgent task of thought, and particularly that which Agamben names "criticism," is to rediscover "the unity of our own fragmented word." Criticism is situated at the point at which language is split from itself – in for instance, the distinction of signified and signifier – and its task is to point toward a "unitary status for the utterance," in which criticism "neither represents nor knows, but knows the representation" (S: xvii). Thus, against both philosophy and poetry, criticism "opposes the enjoyment of what cannot be possessed and the possession of what cannot be enjoyed" (S: xvii).

In order to pursue this task, Agamben develops a model of knowledge evident in the relations of desire and appropriation of an object that Freud identifies as melancholia and fetishism. In this, he also questions the "primordial situation" of the distinction between the signifier and the signified, to which Western reflections on the sign are beholden. He concludes this study – which encompasses discussion of fetishism and commodity fetishism, dandyism, the psychoanalysis of toys, and the myths of Narcissus, Eros, and Oedipus amongst other things – with a brief discussion of Saussurian linguistics, claiming that Saussure's triumph lay in recognizing the impossibility of a science of language based on the distinction of signified and signifier. However, to isolate the sign as a positive unity from Saussure's problematic position is to "push the science of the sign back into metaphysics" (S: 155). This idea of a link between the notion of the unity of the sign and Western metaphysics is, in Agamben's view, confirmed by Jacques Derrida's formulation of grammatology as an attempt to overcome the metaphysics of presence that Derrida diagnoses as predominant within Western philosophy from Plato onwards.

Yet, Agamben argues that Derrida does not achieve the overcoming he hopes for, since he has in fact misdiagnosed the problem: metaphysics is not simply the interpretation of presence in the fractures of essence and appearance, sensibility and intelligibility and so on, and it is to see either the sign or the signified as originary. Rather, the origin of Western metaphysics lies in the conception that "original experience be always already caught in a fold…that presence be always already caught in a signification" (S: 156). Hence, *logos* is the fold that "gathers and divides all things in the 'putting together' of presence. And the human [*zoon logon echon*] is precisely this fracture of presence, which opens a world and over which language holds itself " (S: 156). Ultimately then, an attempt to truly overcome metaphysics requires that the semiological algorithm S/s must reduce to solely the barrier (/) itself rather than one side or the other of the distinction, where that barrier is understood as the "topological game of putting things together and articulating" (S: 156).

AGAMBEN'S CONTRIBUTION TO SOCIAL THEORY

Biopolitics and the camps

At this point, we are in a better position to turn directly to Agamben's contribution to social theory, which primarily rests on his theorization of biopolitics, which springs directly from his engagements in metaphysics and the philosophy of language. Undoubtedly, *Homo Sacer* (HS) is Agamben's best-known work, and probably also the most controversial. In this book, Agamben develops his analysis of the condition of biopolitics, specifically in response to Michel Foucault's claims in the first volume of his *History of Sexuality* series. Foucault argues here that the "threshold of modernity" was reached with the transition from sovereign power to biopower, in which the "new political subject" of the population became the target of a regime of power that operates through governance of biological life itself. But while engaged with this thesis, it would be erroneous to suppose that Agamben is at all faithful to it. He explicitly rejects the historical typography that Foucault suggests (though Foucault is himself more measured in other essays) and proposes a more integral link between sovereignty and biopower, such that Western politics have always been biopolitical. Agamben goes so far as to suggest that "the production of a biopolitical body is the original activity of sovereign power" (HS: 6). What distinguishes modern democracy from the Ancient polis, then, is not the integration of biological life into the sphere of politics, but that the nexus between sovereignty and the biopolitical body is revealed in an unprecedented way in modernity.

The extent to which biopolitics can be read back into the Greek polis is of course highly contestable – and the apparent sweeping historical breadth of Agamben's thesis is probably its weakest aspect. In order to assess the plausibility of Agamben's claim, though, it is essential to keep in mind the methodological commitments that underpin the (only) apparently historical claim. Agamben has characterized his methodology as aiming at the identification and clarification of "paradigms." By "paradigm" he does not mean to align himself with Thomas Kuhn; rather, a paradigm is "an example which defines the intelligibility of the set to which it belongs and at the same time which it constitutes" (WIP). The paradigm allows for the intelligibility of a generality by virtue of the knowability of a singularity, where the generality is not inductively derived from "the exhaustive enumeration of the individual cases." Instead, it entails only the comparison of a singular example "with the object or class that the paradigm will make intelligible" (ibid.). Thus, in this view, the singular example illuminates the general by virtue of its singularity. Rather than building up empirical evidence through exhaustive historical detail, Agamben picks out a singular example and uses this to excavate the conceptual heart of the paradigm at issue – in this case, of the paradigm of biopolitics. Whether this methodology is compelling is a question in its own right. But, even if it is granted, it does not guarantee the veracity of the claims about Western politics that Agamben makes (if, indeed, that is the criteria against which they should be judged).

Setting these methodological concerns aside, it might be argued that *Homo Sacer* is not so much an attempt to correct or complete Foucault's account of biopolitics, as an attempt to complete Walter Benjamin's critique of Carl Schmitt, the German jurist who was to become one of the strongest intellectual supporters of the German Nazi Party. In *Political Theology*, Carl Schmitt summarizes his strongly decisionistic account of sovereignty by claiming that the sovereign is the one that decides on the exception. For Schmitt, it is in the capacity to decide on whether a situation is normal or exceptional, and thus whether the law applies or not (since the law can only apply in a normal situation) that sovereignty is manifest. This casts sovereignty as the "border-line concept" of order and the exception, where the sovereign decides whether the situation that confronts it is truly an exception or the normal order. This also gives the sovereign the prerogative to suspend the law in any situation understood as exceptional. Contemporary "states of emergency," in which normal civil liberties and rights are usually suspended, could be seen as an example of this condition. Contrary to this formulation, in his "Theses on the Philosophy of History" Benjamin posits that the state of emergency is not simply an irruption within the normal order, but has in fact become the rule. His concern here is specifically with the rise of Fascism in Germany during the 1930s, and he argues that in order to combat the rise of Fascism, the inauguration of a real state of exception (rather than the false, nihilistic exception that suspends the law while leaving it in force) is required.

In addressing this conflict between Schmitt and Benjamin, Agamben argues that in contemporary politics, the state of exception identified by Schmitt in which the law is suspended by the sovereign, has in fact become the rule. This is a condition that he identifies as one of *abandonment*, in which the law is in force but has no content or substantive meaning – it is "in force without significance." The structure of the exception, he suggests, is directly analogous to the structure of the ban identified by Jean-Luc Nancy, who claims that in the ban the law only applies in no longer applying. The subject of the law is simultaneously turned over to the law and left bereft by it, simultaneously exposed and abandoned. Agamben uses the figure of *homo sacer* – who "can be killed but not sacrificed" – in Roman law to elaborate this condition. According to Agamben, the sacredness of *homo sacer* does not so much indicate a conceptual ambiguity internal to the sacred, as many have argued, as the abandoned status of sacred man in relation to the law. The sacred man is "taken outside" both divine and profane law as the exception and is thus abandoned by them. Importantly, that the exception has become the norm or rule of contemporary politics means that it is not the case that only some subjects are abandoned by the law; rather, Agamben states that in our age, "we are all virtually *homines sacri*" (HS: 115).

For Agamben, the key figure of biopolitics understood as an exceptional situation in which law operates through its suspension is "bare life." This notion emerges from the distinction made between natural life (*zoe*) and a particular form of life (*bios*) in Aristotle's account of the origins of the polis. The distinction relegates natural life to the domain of the household or *oikos* and at the same time identifies a specifically political form of life. For Aristotle, politics is not simply about *living*, but *living well;* what is at stake in politics is not *life* per se, but the *good life.* In Agamben's interpretation of Aristotle, this division indicates that Western politics is founded upon that which it excludes – the natural life that is simultaneously excluded from the polis and implicated in it (by virtue of its exclusion). *It is this exclusion and implication of natural life that gives rise to the idea of "bare life," understood as the politicized form of natural life.* The question to ask here is how natural life is politicized. Agamben's response to this question is through its exposure or abandonment to death, that is, to the power of sovereignty. Hence, bare life is not conceptually equivalent to natural life though it often confused with it, not least because of Agamben's own inconsistency. At its most specific though, bare life can be defined as "life exposed to death" (HS: 88), that is, life exposed and abandoned to its own negativity.

Perhaps one of the most controversial aspects of Agamben's thesis in *Homo Sacer* is the identification of the concentration camp as the characteristic space of contemporary politics. He argues that the camps, such as those of the Boer War, of the Second World War, and of refugee camps the world over, are the "nomos of the modern," by which he means they materialize the organizing principles of modern politics. The camps do not entail a fundamental break with the political rationality of modernity, but reveal its hidden logic and in doing so, reveal the increasing convergence of democracy and totalitarianism. The camp is the space opened when the exception becomes the rule or the normal situation, as was the case in Germany in the period immediately before and throughout the Second World War. Further, what is characteristic of the camp is the indistinguishability of law and life, in which bare life becomes the "threshold in which law constantly passes over into fact and fact into law" (HS: 171). This indiscernibility of life and law effectively contributes to a normative crisis, for here it is no longer the case that the rule of law bears upon or applies to the living body, but rather, the living body has become "the rule and criterion of its own application" (HS: 173) thereby undercutting recourse to the transcendence or independence of the law as a source of legitimate authority. Provocatively, if the camps are the "nomos" or "hidden matrix" of modern politics, then the normative crisis evident in them is not specifically limited to them, but is actually characteristic of our present condition, a condition described as one of "imperfect nihilism."

Importantly, in addition to this, Agamben argues that the logic of the "inclusive exclusion" that structures the relation of natural life to the polis, the implications of which are made most evident in the camps, is perfectly analogous to the relation of the transition from voice to speech that constitutes the political nature of "man" in Aristotle's account. For Aristotle, the transition from voice to language is a founding condition of political community, since speech makes possible a distinction between the just and the unjust. Agamben writes that the question of how natural bare life dwells in the polis corresponds exactly with the question of how a living being has language, since in the latter question "the living being has logos by taking away and conserving its own voice in it, even as it dwells in the polis by letting its own bare life be excluded, as an exception, within it" (HS: 8). Hence, for Agamben, the caesura introduced into the human by the definition of man as the living animal who has language and therefore politics is foundational for biopolitics, for this disjuncture allows the human being to be reduced to bare life. In this way, metaphysics and politics are fundamentally entwined, and it is only by overcoming the central dogmas of Western metaphysics that a new form of politics will be possible.

Rather than leading to political despair, though, this allows Agamben to point toward a way out or beyond the crisis of contemporary politics. Agamben's theorization of the "coming politics" relies upon a logic of *euporic* resolution to the *aporias* that characterize modern democracy, including the *aporia* of bare life (P: 217). In *Means without End* (ME), he argues for a politics of pure means, wherein "politics is the sphere neither of an end in itself nor of means subordinated to an end; rather, it is the sphere of a pure mediality without end intended as the field of human action and of human thought" (ME: 117). In developing this claim, Agamben claims that the coming politics must reckon with the dual problem of the post-Hegelian theme of the end of history and with the Heideggerian theme of *Ereignis* [roughly, "event"; "appropriation"], in order to formulate a new life and politics in which both history and the state come to an end simultaneously. This experiment of a new politics without reference to sovereignty and associated concepts such as nation, the people and democracy, requires the formulation of a new "happy life," in which bare life is never separable as a political subject.

The politics of pure means that Agamben envisages here is given more content in the formulations of "play" and "profanation" that he develops in other texts. In *Infancy and History* (IH), and specifically the chapter "In Playland," he analyzes the function of rituals and play in relation to time, and claims that the revelatory characteristic of toys is to make present and tangible human temporality in itself. Agamben begins this essay by citing Collodi's description of Playland in *Pinocchio*, in which a population entirely composed of boys partakes in all manner of games, creating a noisy and unconstrained pandemonium of play, the effect of which is to change and accelerate time and halt the repetition and alteration of the calendar. Drawing on Benveniste's study of play and the sacred, Agamben posits that "Playland is a country whose inhabitants are busy celebrating rituals, and manipulating objects and sacred words, whose sense and purpose they have, however, forgotten…In play, man frees himself from sacred time and 'forgets' it in human time" (IH: 70). Additionally, play preserves profane objects and behaviors that otherwise no longer exist, evident in the use that children make of objects that have outlasted their functional use-value but are still taken up as toys. The philosophical importance of the toy is that it reveals the fundamental historicity of the object and of the human: "[it] makes present and renders tangible human temporality in itself, the pure differential margin between the 'once' and the 'no longer'" (ibid.: 71–72).

Agamben returns to the thematic of play in his more recent work, *Profanations* (P). Rather than tying play to the question of time and history as in the earlier discussion, here he discusses it within the context of the necessity of resistance to the current "extreme phase" of spectacular capitalism, in which representation and the commodity form have colonized all social relations. Agamben isolates profanation as a process of extracting things from the realm of the sacred and returning them to a "free use of men" (P: 73), such that the thing so returned is "pure, profane, free of sacred names" (ibid.). One of the ways that such profanation can be effectuated is in play, since "play frees and distracts humanity from the sphere of the sacred, without simply abolishing it" (ibid.: 76). But the impact of play is not felt solely in relation to the sacred strictly understood, for as with children "who play with whatever old things fall into their hands," play can also be used to free humanity in relation to economics, law and so on. Importantly, the reference to freeing humanity does not mean setting these spheres aside and overcoming their oppressive effects through destruction. Nor does it entail restoring a more natural or uncontaminated use to the things that are rendered as toys in the children's play kit. Instead, play gives onto a new use: play releases objects and ideas from the inscribed use within a given sphere and severs their instrumental attachment to an end or goal. As Agamben writes, "[t]he freed behaviour still reproduces and mimics the forms of the activity from which it has been emancipated, but, in emptying them of their sense and of any obligatory relationship to an end, it opens them and makes them available for a new use" (ibid.: 85–86). Given that Agamben commends play as a political task, the question to ask is what value an activity that repeats and mimics while severing the connection to an end has as a means of political liberation or resistance. Responses to this question are divided: some commentators see Agamben as rightly pointing to the political power of a kind of extreme passivity, most clearly embodied in Herman Melville's figure of Bartleby. Others see his absolutist rejection of the contemporary terms of politics as dangerous and misguided.

Ethics

Given his view that camps provide the clearest manifestation of the condition of contemporary nihilism, it is no surprise that Agamben takes them as a starting point for an elaboration of a new ethics. In *Remnants of Auschwitz* (RA), the third installment of the *Homo Sacer* series, Agamben develops an account of an ethics that is cleansed of juridical reference, where the term "law" is taken to encompass normative discourse in its entirety. The key idea he pursues is that ethics take the form of testimony, and entails bearing witness to that to which one cannot bear witness. The starting point for this book is the problem of skepticism in relation to the Nazi concentration camps of the Second World War, since for revisionists the very condition of having survived the camps contradicts the claims that their *telos* was extermination. The central figure that Agamben uses is the *Muselmänner*, those in the camps who had reached such a state of physical decrepitude and existential disregard that "one hesitates to call them living: one hesitates to call their death death" (Levi cited in RA: 44). For Agamben, the *Muselmann* indicates a fundamental indistinction between the human and the inhuman, such that it impossible to definitively separate one from the other. The key question that arises for Agamben is whether there is in fact a "humanity to the human" over and above biologically belonging to the species, and it is in reflection upon this that Agamben develops his account of ethics. In this, he rejects recourse to standard moral concepts such as dignity and respect, claiming that "Auschwitz marks the end and the ruin of every ethics of dignity and conformity to a norm … The *Muselmann* … is the guard on the threshold of a new ethics, an ethics of a form of life that begins where dignity ends" (RA: 69).

In order to provide "signposts" for this new ethical terrain, Agamben returns to the definition of the human as the being who has language, along with his earlier analyses of deixis, to bring out a double movement in the human being's appropriation of language. In an analysis of pronouns such as "I" that allow a speaker to put language to use, he argues that the subjectification effected in this appropriation is conditioned by a simultaneous and inevitable de-subjectification. Because pronouns are nothing other than grammatical shifters or "indicators of enunciation," such that they refer to nothing other than the taking place of language itself, the appropriation of language in the identification of oneself as a speaking subject requires that the psychosomatic individual simultaneously erase or desubjectify itself. Consequently, it is not strictly the "I" that speaks, and nor is it the living individual: rather, as Agamben writes, "in the absolute present of the event of discourse, subjectification and desubjectification coincide at every point and both the flesh and blood individual and the subject of enunciation are perfectly silent" (RA: 117).

Importantly, Agamben argues that it is precisely this non-coincidence of the speaking being and living being and the impossibility of speech revealed in it that provides the condition of possibility of testimony. Testimony, he claims, is possible only "if there is no articulation between the living being and language, if the 'I' stands suspended in this disjunction" (RA: 130). What is at stake in testimony is bearing witness to this disjuncture, that is, bearing witness to the impossibility of speech and making it appear within speech. In this way, he suggests, the human is able to endure the inhuman. Further, testimony is not simply a practice of speaking, but as an ethos, understood as the only proper "dwelling place" of the subject. The additional twist that Agamben adds here to avoid a notion of returning to authenticity in testimony is that while testimony is the proper dwelling place or "only possible consistency" of the subject, it is not something that the subject can simply assume as its own. As his account of subjectification and desubjectification indicates, there can be no simple appropriation of language that would allow the subject to posit itself as the ground of testimony, and nor can it simply realize itself in speaking. Instead, testimony remains forever unassumable.

This also gives rise to Agamben's account of ethical responsibility. Against juridical accounts of responsibility that would understand it in terms of sponsorship, debt, and culpability, Agamben argues that responsibility must be thought as fundamentally unassumable, as something which the subject is consigned to, but which it can never fully appropriate as its own. Responsibility, he suggests, must be thought without reference to the law, as a domain of "irresponsibility" or "non-responsibility" that necessarily precedes the designations of good and evil and entails a "confrontation with a responsibility that is infinitely greater than any we could ever assume." While it may seem as if Agamben is leaning toward a conception of ethical responsibility akin to Emmanuel Levinas's conception of infinite responsibility toward the absolute Other, this is not the case. In fact, Agamben sees Levinas as simply radicalizing the juridical relation of sponsorship in unexpiatable guilt. In distinction from this, Agamben argues that "ethics is the sphere that recognizes neither guilt nor responsibility; it is…the doctrine of happy life" (RA: 24). But it is difficult to see how such a notion of ethics as happy life might be developed, especially since resources for further explicating a concept of non-responsibility cannot be sought in Levinas. Agamben has not taken his account of ethics any further than in *Remnants*, and it is not hard to imagine that it is ultimately a philosophical dead-end. A non-responsibility derived from the idea of bearing witness to the desubjectivation in every subjectivation is flimsy ground for approaching the multifaceted ethical question of living well.

Messianism

The conceptions of politics and ethics that Agamben develops converge in the notion of "happy life," or what he calls "form-of-life" at other points. What Agamben means by this is particularly unclear, not least because he sees the attainment of this condition as requiring a fundamental overturning of the metaphysical grounds of Western philosophy, but also because they gesture toward a new politics and ethics that remain largely to be thought. What is clear within this though is that Agamben draws upon Benjamin's formulation of the necessity of a politics of pure means and, correlative to that, his conception of temporality and history, which taps a deep vein of messianism that runs through Judeo-Christian thought. This vein of messianism emerges in Agamben's thought in a number of formulations, particularly those of "infancy," "happy life" and "form-of-life," and the notion of "whatever singulari-ties." What is also common to all these concepts is a concern with the figuration of humanity at the end of history, a concern that Agamben develops in discussion of the debates between Bataille and Kojeve over the Hegelian thesis of the end of history.

The importance of the notion of "happy life" or "form of life" is that they ought to provide the foundation of a new politics, in which it is no longer possible to iso-late bare life as political object. He seeks a politico-philosophical redefinition of politics no longer founded upon the Aristotelian separation of natural life and polit-ical life. Instead, happy life will be such that no separation between *bios* and *zoe* is possible, and life will find its unity in a pure immanence to itself, in "the perfection of its own power." As he states,

> The "happy life" on which political philosophy should be founded thus cannot be either the naked life that sovereignty posits as a presupposition so as to turn it into its own subject or the impenetrable extraneity of science and of modern biopolitics that everybody tries in vain to sacralize. This "happy life" should be rather, an absolutely profane "sufficient life" that has reached the perfection of its own power and its own communicability – a life over which sovereignty and right no longer have any hold. (ME: 114–115)

This conception of a "form of life" or happy life that exceeds the biopolitical caesurae that divide the human from itself is developed in reference to Benjamin's conception of happiness in "Theologico-Political Fragment" (TPF) Here he paints a picture of two arrows pointing in different directions but nevertheless reinforcing each other, one of which indicates the force of historical time and the other that of Messianic time. For Benjamin, while happiness is not and cannot bring about the redemption of Messianic time on its own, it is nevertheless the profane path to its realization – happiness allows for the fulfillment of historical time, since the Messianic kingdom is "not the goal of history but the end" (TPF: 312). This debt also brings into focus Agamben's reliance on the Benjaminian formulation of communicability as such, or communicability without communication, a thematic which is central to his construal of the necessity of an *experimentum linguae* discussed earlier.

Agamben probably goes furthest toward sketching the outlines of a new political condition founded on happy life in *The Coming Community* (CC), though it is also the case that many of the ideas that he presents here, such as "whatever singularity," remain suggestive. In taking up the problem of community, Agamben enters into a broader engagement with this concept by others such as Maurice Blanchot and Jean-Luc Nancy, and in the Anglo-American scene, Alphonso Lingis. The broad aim of the engagement is to develop a conception of community that does not presuppose commonality or identity as a condition of belonging. Within this, Agamben's conception of "whatever singularity" indicates a form of being that rejects any manifestation of identity or belonging and wholly appropriates being to itself, that is, in its own "being-in-language." Whatever singularity allows for the formation of community without the affirmation of identity or "representable condition of belonging," in nothing other than the "co-belonging" of singularities itself. Importantly though, this entails neither a mystical communion nor a nostalgic return to a *Gemeinschaft* that has been lost; instead, the coming community has never yet been. Interestingly, Agamben argues in this elliptical text that the community and politics of whatever singularity are heralded in the event of Tiananmen Square, which he takes to indicate that the coming politics will not be a struggle between states, but instead, a struggle between the state and humanity as such, insofar as it exists in itself without expropriation in identity. Correlatively, the coming politics do not entail a sacralization of humanity, for the existence of whatever singularity is always irreparably abandoned to itself; as Agamben writes, "The Irreparable is that things are just as they are, in this or that mode, consigned without remedy to their way of being. States of things are irreparable, whatever they may be: sad or happy, atrocious or blessed. How you are, how the world is – this is the irreparable" (CC: 90).

Agamben returns to the provocative thread of the irreparable within a critical analysis of the definition of man as the being that has language in *The Open* (TO). Agamben begins this text with reflection on an image of the messianic banquet of the righteous on the last day, preserved in a thirteenth-century Hebrew Bible, in which the righteous are presented not with human heads, but with those of animals. In taking up the rabbinic tradition of interpreting this image, Agamben suggests that the righteous or "concluded humanity" are effectively the "remnant" or remainder of Israel, who are still alive at the coming of the Messiah. The enigma presented by the image of the righteous with animal heads appears to be that of the transformation of the relation of animal and human and the ultimate reconciliation of man with his own animal nature on the last day. But for Agamben, reflection on the enigma of the posthistorical condition of man thus presented necessitates a fundamental overturning of the metaphysico-political operations by which something like man is produced as distinct from the animal in order for its significance to be fully grasped. Agamben concludes with the warning that tracing the "no longer human or animal contours of a new creation" will not be sufficient to stop the "anthropological machine" of modern biopolitics. Instead, this requires risking ourselves in the hiatus and central emptiness that separates the human and animal within man. Thus, for Agamben, "the righteous with animal heads … do not represent a new declension of the man-animal relation," but instead indicates a zone of non-knowledge that allows them to be outside of being, "saved precisely in their being unsavable" (TO: 92).

While attention to the messianic is a consistent feature of much of Agamben's work, his approach to messianism is most thoroughly outlined in *The Time That Remains* (TR). In this text, he proposes an interpretation of Pauline theology that emphasizes its messianic dimension, and argues that Paul's "Letter to the Romans" actually aligns conceptually with the messianic threads that run through the thought of Walter Benjamin. In the course of showing that Benjamin appropriates Pauline messianism, Agamben develops an intriguing understanding of messianic time that draws together a number of aspects of previous work on time, history, metaphysics, and politics. He argues that messianic time is distinct from both the time of prophecy, which is always future referential and announces the coming of the Messiah, and from the eschaton, or the eschatological concern with the Last Day and End of Time. Taking up Paul's term for the messianic event – *ho nyn kairos*, or "the time of the now" – Agamben argues that messianic time is a "time that contracts itself and begins to end…time that remains between time and its end" (TR: 62). Messianic time, then, is not end time nor futural time; rather, it is "the time that time takes to come to an end" (TR: 67).

But as such, messianic time is not external to or opposed to chronological time – it is internal to it, in that it contracts chronological time and begins to bring it to an end. This contraction of time, Agamben suggests, is like the muscular contraction of an animal before it leaps. While not the leap itself, messianic time is akin to that contraction that makes the leap possible; it is the time "left to us" before the end and which brings about the end. As *kairos*, the time of the now is neither identifiable with nor opposed to chronological time, but is instead internal to it as a seized and contracted *chronos* – as "the pearl embedded in the ring of chance" *kairos* is "a small portion of *chronos*, a time remaining" (TR: 69). Thus, according to Agamben, Pauline messianism identifies two heterogeneous times – "one *kairos* and one *chronos*," the relation of which is identified in the term "para-ousia," which literally means next to, and more specifically, being beside being, being beside itself. In this way, messianic time "lies beside itself, since, without ever coinciding with a chronological instant, and without ever adding itself onto it, it seizes hold of the instant and brings it forth to fulfilment" (ibid.: 71). Agamben avers that the result of this, as Benjamin writes in "On the Concept of History," is that every moment is "the small gateway in time through which the Messiah might enter."

IMPACT AND ASSESSMENT

By far the most influential text of Agamben's in relation to social theory has been his *Homo Sacer*, and, to a lesser extent, related texts such as *State of Exception* and *Means without End*. In the context of post-9/11 global geopolitics and institutions and events such as Guantanamo Bay, the Abu Ghraib revelations, extraordinary renditions and the massive movements of refugees around the world, Agamben's diagnoses of the camps and of bare life have struck a chord. Consequently, his understanding of contemporary political exceptionalism has provided many scholars of politics and society with a theoretical vocabulary and a certain critical leverage in their own projects. Despite the contemporary popularity of Agamben's political theory, though, it is worth considering some of the implications of his theorizations further in order to assess their actual value for understanding and critiquing contemporary conditions of existence.

As we can see from the summary of Agamben's work above, notions such as that of "bare life" arise from a deep engagement with the history of philosophy, particularly Aristotle and Heidegger. Further, these formulations are built upon prior ontological and political theorems, and also provide the basis for further reflections on political concepts such as rights, subjectivity and identity, community and so on. In short, as simple as the idea of "bare life" might initially appear, it really only makes sense within the context of a complex web of philosophical ideas about language, the "nature" of humanity, sovereignty, time, and messianism. This means that anyone wishing to use the notion of "bare life" to analyze a socio-political phenomenon has to ask the question of what other theoretical commitments are entailed in doing so; for instance, the idea of bare life is closely related to the positive formulation of "form-of-life," and through that, with Agamben's concern with beatitude and messianism. Unless it can be shown that the idea of bare life can be extracted from this framework – that it does not conceptually entail a positive turn to form-of-life – then the analyst of bare life is also committed to a theory of political and social change based on messianism.

That, of course, may not necessarily be a problem in itself, and the difficulties entailed in extracting a catchy idea or formulation from a broader theoretical framework are hardly unique to Agamben's work. However, they may be a little more pointed in his case than in some others when we consider the methodology that informs his analysis of Western politics. In extrapolating from Benjamin's claim that the exception has become the rule, Agamben takes the concentration camp as paradigmatic of the logic of the sovereign ban that he diagnoses as the originary relation of Western politics. Thus, he argues that the Nazi genocide was indicative of a hidden logic intrinsic to Western politics, and the paroxysms of the Second World War merely brought this logic to light in an unprecedented way. Underpinning this view is a methodological commitment to the notion of the "paradigm," which, according to Agamben, allows for the intelligibility of a general condition or logic on the basis of a singular example. This means that Agamben's characterizations of the logics of Western politics are not based on empirical evidence per se, and in this, they are certainly short on historical detail. It also presupposes that there *is* a hidden logic to Western politics as a whole – stretching, in this account, from Aristotle to Adolf Hitler – which, for some reason, is now coming to light. For many political theorists, this might appear more as an article of faith than a thesis that could be defended in a reasoned way.

Indeed, Agamben has been criticized for his "conceptual absolutism" from several quarters. This broad critique has several aspects. First, it rejects the sense of historico-philosophical continuity that Agamben relies upon in favor of an approach that is sensitive to historical specificity, to transformations and shifts in the ways of thinking and acting that inform systems of governance. Second, it rejects the totalizing analysis of contemporary politics and the reduction of the complexity of current global and local socio-political conditions to one systematic logic that supposedly underlies and corrupts all contemporary ways of understanding and doing politics. Third, it rejects Agamben's outright dismissal of standard contemporary political concepts such as that of human rights on the basis that these are merely part of the biopolitical machine and thus cannot have an instrumental value in local political struggles.

These critiques may seem damning, but so far they seem to have done little to dampen enthusiasm for Agamben's work. And to be sure, there is a very compelling quality to his writings in their apparent pellucidity. His readings of major philosophers are insightful and often profound, while his reflections on contemporary conditions of existence are often searching and provocative. Ultimately, then, we are not yet in a position to know whether or not the impact of his work will endure beyond a passing fascination that probably occludes at least as much as it reveals the real value of a thing.

Reader's Guide to Giorgio Agamben

Because the popularity of Agamben's work is a relatively recent phenomenon, there are limited resources available at this stage for readers seeking an overview of his work. Catherine Mills's critical introduction, *The Philosophy of Agamben* (2008) and Alex Murray's *Giorgio Agamben* (2010) are the two main thematic introductions. Leland de la Durantaye's *Giorgo Agamben: A Critical Introduction* (2009) is also a useful source for a discussion of each of Agamben's books up until *State of Exception*. Excellent collections of critical essays are Andrew Norris's *Politics, Metaphysics and Death: Essays on Giorgio Agamben's Homo Sacer* (2005), Matthew Calarco and Steven DeCaroli's *Giorgio Agamben: Sovereignty and Life* (2007) and Alison Ross's *The Agamben Effect (South Atlantic Quarterly)* (2008). For particularly interesting political and sociological analyses using Agamben's work, see Sergei Prozorov, *The Ethics of Postcommunism: History and Social Praxis in Russia* (2009) and Bulent Diken and Carsten Bagge Laustsen, *The Culture of Exception – Sociology Facing the Camp* (2005).

Bibliography

Writings of Giorgio Agamben

1991. *Language and Death: The Place of Negativity*, trans. K. E. Pinkus and M. Hardt. Minneapolis, MN: University of Minnesota Press.

1993. *Infancy and History: Essays on the Destruction of Experience*, trans. L. Heron. London: Verso.

1993. *Stanzas: Word and Phantasm in Western Culture*, trans. R. L. Martinez. Minneapolis, MN: University of Minnesota Press.

1993. *The Coming Community*, trans. M. Hardt. Minneapolis, MN: University of Minnesota Press.

1995. *Idea of Prose*, trans. M. Sullivan and S. Whitsitt. Albany, NY: SUNY Press.

1998. *Homo Sacer: Sovereign Power and Bare Life*, trans. D. Heller-Roazen. Stanford, CA: Stanford University Press.

1999. *Potentialities: Collected Essays in Philosophy*, ed. and trans. D. Heller-Roazen. Stanford, CA: Stanford University Press.

1999. *Remnants of Auschwitz: The Witness and the Archive*, trans. D. Heller-Roazen. New York: Zone Books.

1999. *The End of the Poem: Studies in Poetics*, trans. D. Heller-Roazen. Stanford, CA: Stanford University Press.

1999. *The Man Without Content*, trans. G. Albert. Stanford: CA: Stanford University Press.

2000. *Means without End: Notes on Politics*, trans. Casarino and Binetti. Minneapolis, MN: University of Minnesota Press.

2002. What Is a Paradigm? Available online at www.egs.edu/faculty/agamben/agamben-what-is-a-paradigm-2002.html (accessed November 25, 2010).

2004. *The Open: Man and Animal*, trans. K. Attell. Stanford, CA: Stanford University Press.

2005. *State of Exception*, trans. K. Attell. Chicago, IL: University of Chicago Press.

2005. *The Time That Remains: A Commentary on the Letter to the Romans*, trans. Patricia Daley. Stanford, CA: Stanford University Press.

2007. *Profanations*, trans. J. Fort. New York: Zone Books.

Further Reading

Benjamin, W. (1996) Critique of violence. In M. Bullock and M. W. Jennings (eds) *Selected Writings, Volume 1, 1913–1926*, E. Jephcott (trans.). Cambridge, MA: Harvard University Press, pp. 236–252.

Benjamin, W. (2002) Theological-political fragment. In H. Eiland and M. W. Jennings (eds) *Selected Writings, Volume 3, 1935–1938*, E. Jephcott (trans.). Cambridge, MA: Harvard University Press, pp. 305–306.

Benjamin, W. (2003) On the concept of history. In H. Eiland and M. W. Jennings (eds) *Selected Writings, Volume 4, 1938– 1940*. Cambridge, MA: Harvard University Press, pp. 389–400.

Calarco, M. and DeCaroli, Steven D. (eds) (2007) *Giorgio Agamben: Sovereignty and Life*. Stanford, CA: Stanford University Press.

Debord, G. (1995) *The Society of the Spectacle*. D. Nicholson-Smith (trans). New York: Zone Books.

DeCaroli, S. D. (2001) Visibility and history: Giorgio Agamben and the exemplary. *Philosophy Today*, 45: 9–17.

de la Durantaye, L. (2009) *Giorgio Agamben: A Critical Introduction*. Stanford, CA: Stanford University Press.

Diken, B. and Laustsen, C. (2005) *The Culture of Exception – Sociology Facing the Camp*. New York: Routledge.

Foucault, M. (1981) *The History of Sexuality, Volume 1: An Introduction*. R. Hurley. (trans.). London: Penguin.

Mills, C. (2008) *The Philosophy of Agamben*. Durham UK: Acumen Press.

Murray, A. (2010) *Giorgio Agamben*. London: Routledge.

Nancy, J.-L. (1993) Abandoned being. In Holmes *et al.* (eds and trans.)*The Birth to Presence*. Stanford, CA: Stanford University Press, pp.36–47.

Norris, A. (ed.) (2005) *Politics, Metaphysics and Death: Essays on Giorgio Agamben's* Homo Sacer. Durham: Duke University Press.

Prozorov, S. 2009. *The Ethics of Postcommunism: History and Social Praxis in Russia*. New York: Palgrave.

Ross, A. (ed.) (2008) *The Agamben Effect (South Atlantic Quarterly)*. Durham: Duke University Press.

Wall, T. C. (1999) *Radical Passivity: Levinas, Blanchot and Agamben*. Albany: SUNY Press.

20

Ulrich Beck

IAIN WILKINSON

The Person

Ulrich Beck was born on May 15, 1944, in the Pomeranian town of Stolp (now Słupsk), (then a part of the Greater German Reich and now part of Poland). His father, Wilhelm Beck, was a naval officer, and when not looking after young Ulrich and her other four children, his mother, Magarete von Schulz-Hausmann, worked as a nurse. From an early age he had a questioning mind and soon acquired an appetite for intellectual debate. By his teenage years, Beck had refined moral and political arguments in opposition to his father's National Socialism; and as an exchange student he had wearied of the intellectual shortcomings of the culture of evangelical Christianity that he experienced in his host-family in the USA. As a young man he sought the company of friends who shared his passion to question the pre-siding values of his times; particularly insofar as this served as a means to identify opportunities for progressive personal and social change. This passion has sustained his career to this day.

As a student at the Ludwig-Maximilian University of Munich (1967–1972), he first enrolled to take courses in philosophy and for a while was preoccupied with studying traditions of German idealism. Beck's decision to shift the direction of his studies towards sociology was in part motivated by a rejection of the intellectual sectarianism that he encountered among the professors of philosophy at Munich. At the same time, he was very attracted to the open culture of debate that he encoun-tered when attending Karl Martin Bolte's sociology seminars. Here Beck found a spirit of inquiry that matched his own. Under Bolte's encouragement and supervision, Beck became a committed sociologist. In 1972 he submitted a thesis for his doctoral degree that critically compared contrasting positions in the so-called "Value Dispute" in German and American sociology (Beck [1972]1974). After "habilitation" in 1979

The Wiley-Blackwell Companion to Major Social Theorists, First Edition.
Edited by George Ritzer and Jeffrey Stepnisky.
© 2011 Blackwell Publishing Ltd. Published 2011 by Blackwell Publishing Ltd.

he started his career as a university professor at the universities of Münster (1979–1981) and Bamberg (1981–1992), Beck's early research (1972–1979) largely revolved around developments in the sociology of industry and labor relations, particularly in connection with German post-war welfare reforms. Bolte's interest in charting the bearing of processes of welfare reform upon the subjective meaning of work was taken up by Beck in some of his early publications on the experience of individualization and has remained a core consideration in the development of his theoretical project through to this day (Beck, 1983). Individualization is also one of the headline topics of interest featured in various publications he has co-authored with his wife, Elizabeth Beck-Gernsheim, who has a longstanding interest in the bearing of this phenomenon upon women's experience of work and family life (Ostner, 2003). She also studied at Munich under the supervision of Bolte.

Beck shot to fame with the publication of his book *Risikogesellschaft: Auf dem Weg in eine Andere Moderne* (1986), which was later translated into English as *Risk Society: Towards a New Modernity* (1992). The inspiration for this project was rooted in his involvement as a student with Germany's nascent environmental social movements. From its earliest years, in contrast to the American and British experience, German environmentalism was characterized by a particularly pronounced debate about doomsday scenarios relating to the scarcity of the world's natural resources and the hazardous properties of pollutants associated with the nuclear and chemical industries (Rucht and Roose, 1999). For many, the Chernobyl disaster that took place on April 26, 1986 confirmed the truth of these fearful depictions of our future, and in the aftermath of this crisis, Beck's *Risk Society* was read as a highly prescient account of the social and political ramifications that follow in the wake of people waking up to the fact that they are living on the brink of ecological catastrophe.

In 1992 Beck returned to the Ludwig-Maximilian University of Munich to take up a position as Professor of Sociology and Director of the Institute of Sociology. From this time onwards, his works were widely translated and the influence of his thought spread throughout Europe and the English-speaking world. This was in part due to the extent to which his arguments were taken up as key matters for analysis and debate by theorists such as Zygmunt Bauman and Anthony Giddens. Indeed, in some quarters, along with these and the French sociologist, Pierre Bourdieu, Beck is now fêted as one of the new "canonical" figures in contemporary sociology (Outhwaite, 2009).

Whilst marking out the distinctiveness of his theoretical concerns in relation to the characterizations of modernity outlined by Giddens and others, the full scope and ambition of Beck's sociology has been brought into view. His interest in processes of individualization and emergent forms of environmental risk consciousness is part of a larger project that aims to chart the institutional transformations and types of experience that are driving industrialized nations along a course of social development that he refers to as *reflexive modernization*. He holds that this amounts to a more radical "second phase of modernity," that in many respects breaks with both the experience and traditions of understanding of an earlier phase that has been diminishing in force and receding from view since the 1960s. Accordingly, whilst working to make known the parameters and traits of reflexive modernization, Beck aims to be particularly attentive to social processes and cultural formations that are setting the stage for new ways of living in society.

Whilst a large number of his publications through the 1990s and 2000s are designed to refine and/or amend his original thesis on risk society, he has also produced a large body of work that details how the dynamics of globalization are inclined to produce the *cosmopolitanization* of societies. In the context of these debates, Beck demonstrates a vision for sociology that is in many ways akin to theorists in the so-called "classical" tradition; for above all else, he appears to be concerned with the potential for sociological inquiry to both make known major social transitions and to broaden the horizon of human possibility. Whilst acutely attuned to the risks inherent within our modernization, as well as the many unintended consequences of this process, he is also deeply committed to nurturing forms of critical thinking that serve to open up world politics and society to reform. In this respect, he holds that he is searching for a "second enlightenment" and is working to fashion forms of sociological thinking to fit this purpose (Beck and Willms, 2004: 200–201).

Following the appointment of Anthony Giddens as Director of the London School of Economics in 1997, Beck was invited to take up a position as British Journal of Sociology and LSE Centennial Professor of Sociology. At present, he spends his time working at both the London School of Economics and the Ludwig-Maximilian University of Munich. At the latter, he directs the "Reflexive Modernization" research center which is funded by the *Deutsche Forschungsgemeinschaft* (DFG). He remains a prolific author and is still working to develop new avenues for sociological inquiry.

THE SOCIAL CONTEXT

Eric Hobsbawm (1994) depicts the key junctures in the history of the twentieth century as "a sort of triptych" in which a middle period of economic advancement and progressive social change is flanked on either side by eras of social crisis, economic decline, and great violence. On this account, Beck grew up in an era of unprecedented economic growth, social transformation, and democratic reform; a time that, in retrospect, appears to have been the century's "Golden Age." This was also the experience under which he forged the early part of his academic career.

During this time West Germany was celebrated as both an "economic miracle" (*Wirtschaftswunder*) and a model example of a society governed by corporatist principle. A new political culture of social democracy was set in place along with an expansion of state welfare provision. These developments were also accompanied by the rise of a mass consumer society. This was a period of unprecedented political stability sustained on the one hand by a general commitment to an ethic of civic individualism, and on the other, by a resolute faith in the proficiency of managerialism. On many accounts, a general mood of optimism was inspired by dramatic improvements in people's living standards and social opportunities. Under these conditions, it was widely understood that capitalism could be disciplined to deliver "a less deferential, more egalitarian and forward-looking society" (Mazower, 1998: 290–330).

Few anticipated the prolonged experience of "crisis" that the majority of social commentators now tend to feature as the presiding concern of the closing decades of the twentieth century. On many accounts, the 1973 oil crisis introduced instabilities into the world economy that have had lasting consequences for the organization of state and capital. This moment in time is understood to mark the beginning of a more intensive phase of economic globalization that through the 1980s and 1990s saw the creation of a new international division of labor and a concerted drive to apply new information and communication technologies to the reorganization of capitalist modes of production. This is also a period in which many Western nation states moved to abandon earlier corporatist and welfarist principles so as to allow the "free market" more control and influence over the role of government and the workplace. For many, particularly those born into the poorer sections of society, these changes have resulted in a radical reversal of fortune and social opportunity; and in this respect, most social commentators are inclined to agree that, in their political systems and economic arrangements, modern capitalist societies are experiencing a pronounced crisis of legitimacy.

Looking back to the 1960s, the possibility that these critical conditions were set to be further aggravated by social conflicts over the development and implementation of industrial technologies scarcely figured as a political concern. Indeed, it is striking to note that on September 3, 1966, Jerome D. Frank saw fit to use his presidential address to the Society for the Psychological Study of Social Issues to ask why environmental risks appeared to weigh so little upon the minds of the American public (Frank, 1966). At this point "risk consciousness" was debatable more in terms of its absence than in terms of its presence within anxieties relating to the hazardous side effects of industrialization.

Whilst the environmental critique of industrial modernity was already well developed before the fallout from the Chernobyl disaster, it is widely held that this event served to raise the profile of ecological issues on the political agenda. Since the 1980s, the burgeoning science of climate change, coupled to increased expressions of alarm over the depletion of natural resources and destruction of the natural environment, have made the politics of global ecology a critical matter for any movement to secure a future for modernity. In this respect, it is now largely accepted that the endemic crises of capitalism are inextricably bound to a "crisis of nature"; both in relation to limitations in the natural resources available for industrialization and in the toxic results of the ways they are put to use in the production and consumption of capitalist goods and services.

In order to appreciate the character and scale of the problems that drive Beck to theorize society, it is important to situate his work as the product of an experience of unmitigated crisis within prevailing conditions of modernity. It is equally important to appreciate that he is alert to the progressive potential of industrial modernization and holds an abiding interest in the possible ways in which governments might act to reform societies for the better. The experience of his formative years has made a lasting impression on the overall character of his sociological ambition. Whilst his sociological theory is dedicated to diagnosing the critical state of modernity in an age of mounting ecological catastrophe, it also demonstrates a deep commitment to the task of understanding how modern societies might be reformed so as to further the bounds of progress and social opportunity. At the same time as he seeks to warn his readers about the destructive potential of modernity, he also aims to inspire them in the task of building a better social world.

The Intellectual Context

During the period in which Beck has devised his sociological theory, debates have congregated around the contention that we are living amidst multiple endings; everything is "post" and "after." It is argued that we are witnessing a series of fundamental and unprecedented changes in the social structure, political organization, and cultural experience and of modern societies. Many work from the understanding that, whilst we may not have arrived at a point where it is possible to announce the full-blown arrival of a distinctly new kind of society, nevertheless, we should certainly recognize ourselves to be living through the end of what has gone before. There is no consensus as to the ways in which new information technologies and new transnational economic arrangements are combining to reconfigure the experience of work and employment, yet on many accounts, there is something "post-industrial" about what is now taking place here. Similarly, whilst the character and meaning of "postmodernism" is subject to a great conflict of interpretations, most commentators are inclined to treat this as an axial matter for debate when charting key developments in contemporary processes of cultural reproduction and exchange. Further, many hold that events such as the 1989 revolutions in Eastern Europe and the collapse of the Soviet Union mark a definitive break in post-war history that finally brought an end to Marxism as a credible political philosophy. In these terminal contexts, the work of social theory is characterized by a pronounced struggle to forge concepts that are adequate to grasp the dynamics of contemporary social change; and on many accounts, this is also likely to buckle under the weight of the challenge to set new parameters for social critique and political reform.

When explaining the character of his approach to social theory, Ulrich Beck expresses a great deal of frustration with theoretical perspectives that do no more than diagnose some "post" condition or "end" state of society. He holds that, more often than not, these amount to a lazy accommodation to the fact of change; particularly insofar as they fail to take on the creative challenge of imagining the world anew (Beck, 1990). By contrast, he holds that social theory should aspire to be a highly innovative enterprise. It should provide us with orientating scripts that serve both as a resource for negotiating the dilemmas of the present and as a means to re-shape the horizon of possibility. On Beck's account, social theory should concern far more than an announcement of endings; rather, it should articulate a vision of the world that serves as a roadmap for life.

Whilst Beck's work might be identified as a type of critical theory, it is only on rare occasions that he ventures to elaborate on matters of philosophical principle. In this regard, he should not be approached as a critical theorist in the vein of the Frankfurt School. He is not so much concerned with fashioning a contribution to the philosophical discourse of modernity as he is with advancing the narrative traditions of sociology so that these are better suited to make known the presiding social character and emergent properties of our times (Beck and Gane, 2004: 152–156). Whilst his work has inter-disciplinary appeal, his key point of reference is sociology and the forms of inquiry that operate within this field. More directly, he is concerned to devise a narrative script for sociology that casts nascent forms of cultural consciousness and social behavior in conceptual relief, so that the contours of new types of society are brought into view.

He holds that a great deal of sociology falls short of meeting with this task, and that this is largely a consequence of the extent to which the discipline is theoretically hamstrung by an antiquated conceptual vocabulary that is ill-suited to grasp the dynamics of contemporary processes of social change. On this account, it is no longer possible to demarcate the boundaries of the social world via concepts such as "household," "nation state," and "class"; for these terms of analysis are unable to make adequate sense of the force and scale of the transnational dynamics of culture economy and society in our times. Whilst the sociological imagination was once celebrated for its capacity to make clear the interplay between history, self and social circumstance, Beck contends that it is now possessed by a quality of mind that labors under the dead weight of its intellectual history to a point where it is unable to make known its object of study and cannot hope to live up to its promise. In this respect, he is inclined to present his work as a grand attempt to reinvigorate critical traditions of sociological inquiry under social circumstances in which conditions of modernity are being further radicalized in their dimensions and (unintended) consequences.

THE THEORY

When reading Beck's social theory students should understand that they are presented with "work in progress." He is constantly revising and updating his ideas, and in order to fashion a sociological narrative that is adequate to meet the demands of our day, he is prepared to court the possibility that critics will accuse him of self-contradiction and self-obfuscation. Beck often writes with the aim of provoking his readers into further sociological thought and debate. In this regard, he makes explicit ongoing conceptual and analytical difficulties. Generally speaking, he does not set out to guide us towards a fully digested and settled point of view on the world; rather, he is more concerned with opening up fields of inquiry and with issuing invitations to us to join him in the ongoing task of making sociological sense of the novelty in our times.

Beck is known above all else for his sociological thesis on "risk society" and this remains a core component of his thinking, but it is important to understand that his analysis of society in relation to the problematics of risk is just one element of an elaborate programme of research dedicated to documenting the social transformations that take place under the spur of *reflexive modernization*. Beck's thinking about such matters as the dynamics of *risk consciousness*, the intensification of processes of *individualization* or the *cosmopolitanization* of social attitudes and behaviors is part of broad-ranging project of sociological inquiry that aims to attend to a series of radical changes that are currently taking place within the institutional foundations and cultural experience of modern societies. Above all else, Beck is working to provide us with a vanguard account of the cumulative unintended side effects of modernization; one that also points to new possibilities for political reform and social progress.

The key to making sense of his work lies in an appreciation of the social problems raised by reflexive modernization. In this context, the sociological inspiration behind

Beck's analysis of risk and the political ambition of his heralding of processes of cosmopolitanization are brought into view. It is also from here that one might grasp what is sociologically and politically at stake in his concern to set the intellectual foundations in place for a "second enlightenment."

Reflexive modernization

There are three principle areas of debate that tend to feature in Beck's account of reflexive modernization: the first concerns the dimensions and character of a series of institutional and cultural changes that are setting the foundations in place for a new kind of society ; the second involves an effort to account for the political potential of the social consciousness that emerges under the spur of these changes; the third demarcates a project of research that aims to forge frameworks of understanding that places these issues in sociological relief. At the same time as Beck's writings on reflexive modernization attempt to develop a sociologically informed overview of the possible futures that lie before us, they are also designed to draw analytical attention towards the kinds of political values and initiatives that promote the development of more egalitarian and democratic forms of society.

When used as a label for a process of social change, reflexive modernization refers to conditions that result from the cumulative unintended consequences of the ways people are made to live in modern industrial societies. Beck writes:

> [B]y virtue of its inherent dynamism, modern society is undercutting its formations of class, stratum, occupation, sex roles, nuclear family, plant, business sectors and of course, also the prerequisites of natural techno-economic progress. This new age, in which progress can turn into self-destruction, in which one kind of modernization undercuts and changes another, is what I call the stage of reflexive modernization. (Beck, 1994: 2)

Beck tends to assume that his readers are acquainted with Marx's account of the dynamics of capitalism and these are frequently mentioned in passing as a part of the conditions that are working to radically transform society. The need for capitalism constantly to revolutionize the conditions and relations of production is one of the motor forces of reflexive modernization. In this respect, Beck depicts reflexive modernization in a Marxian vein as a process of "creative destruction." At the same time, however, he emphasizes that he does not believe this to be leading us ineluctably towards a state of crisis that ends in the rupture of revolution.

Beck holds that we are witness to a large-scale process of social change; but there is nothing particularly "dramatic" or "explosive" about the ways in which this is set in motion. He holds that reflexive modernization takes place as a consequence of the ways in which ordinary conditions of social life surreptitiously transform the institutional formations and cultural experience of society. Reflexive modernization takes place through the acquisition of common-sense attitudes that are rooted in everyday conditions of work and family life. It results from an incremental transformation of moral values and social aspirations that are conditioned by an increasingly pronounced experience of individualization. It occurs through the reconfiguration of cultural dispositions and moral solidarities that take place as people grow accustomed to working under conditions of flexible employment. It grows out of the experience of managing a "work-family balance" that demands an ongoing negotiation with gender roles and familial responsibilities. It also incorporates a cultural process in which populations are made increasingly alert to the fact that industrialization has side effects that create hazardous conditions for *both* the natural and social world; and that these place the survival of society and nature in jeopardy.

At the same time as reflexive modernization refers to institutional changes that result from transformations in the organization of Western capitalism, Beck also places a great deal of emphasis on the extent to which it takes place through shifts in social understanding and self-awareness. In this respect, reflexive modernization takes place both within the structure of social institutions and in the cultural attitudes people acquire as these shape their lives. It involves the acquisition of new ways of living in society and new approaches to thinking about the social demands, moral obligations, uncertainties, and risks of modern life.

Within this frame of analysis, the "first" modernity of the classical period of sociology is portrayed as a period where societies were organized within the boundaries of nation states that ran economies with the aim of securing full employment. Beck holds that under these conditions it was widely assumed that people's social roles were given by class, and that class position was the major co-ordinate of self-identity. He also notes that here it would have been hardly possible to imagine a world in which modern technologies deliver unforeseen consequences that risk global environmental disaster.

When describing the social transformations that take place under the spur of reflexive modernization, Beck is referring to the experience of Western and Northern European societies since the Second World War. The 1960s tends to be identified as a key decade in which this transition took root; and fifty years later it is understood to have developed to a point where it is possible to demarcate a clear set of processes as setting the stage for a new "second modernity" (Beck and Lau, 2005). He points to the intensifying force of globalization in the world economy, enhanced levels of welfare provision in advanced industrialized nations, the transformation of gender roles and identities, the increasing use of flexible employment practices and the burgeoning global ecological crisis as all combining to create conditions for a new kind of society and new problems for sociological understanding (Beck, Bonss, and Lau, 2003).

Beck argues that for now at least the new "second" modernity can only be described "as a process of transformation of the first modernity" (Beck and Willms, 2004: 31). Too much is still caught up in the winds of change. He contends that whilst we are now witness to a marked discontinuity with the recent past, it is not possible to provide a categorical statement on what is likely to result from this. On Beck's terms, we are only just beginning to take stock of the cumulative unintended consequences of modernization; and now, more often than not, this only serves to make us more cognizant of the fact that the future is precariously unknowable and most likely uncontrollable.

Beck always takes care to emphasize that in the context of his theory, the "reflexive" component of "reflexive modernization" does not refer to a heightened state of critical self-reflection. Whilst theorists such as Anthony Giddens and Pierre Bourdieu tend to use this word to refer to a mindset that enables individuals to reflect critically upon past practices and experiences so as to reform how they think and act towards the future, for Beck being "reflexive" is liable to arouse a profound sense of intellectual frustration. He understands reflexive modernization to involve the experience of being *confronted* with the knowledge that a previous way of life is being rendered increasingly unattractive, impractical, and unmanageable. It also involves us awakening to the fact that we require a radically new approach to understanding the world; and that at present we do not possess an adequate means to achieve this.

When detailing what is involved in the sociological study of "reflexive modernization," he tends to represent this as a project of research beset with the task of *re*learning how to theorize the social world. Beck argues that most existing tools of sociological analysis have been shaped under historical and social circumstances that no longer apply to the world in which we find ourselves today. Accordingly, to make sense of what is sociologically at stake in reflexive modernization we require new concepts, new theories, and new research methodologies. He works from the premise that past social attitudes and institutional approaches to problem-solving are no longer suited to meet the sociological and political challenges at hand. On Beck's account, the advent of "reflexive modernization" signals a stage within the development of modern societies where the discipline of sociology must be re-founded on new intellectual grounds and with new projects of research. This is the position from which he turns to reflect upon the parameters of a "risk society" and the development of new "cosmopolitan" attitudes and institutional behaviors.

The risk society

It is when developing his narratives about risk that Ulrich Beck points to some of the most radical consequences of the cumulative unintended consequences of industrialization. Here he is particularly concerned to have us dwell upon the sociological implications of large-scale hazards that are created as "side effects" of the institutional arrangements, economic conditions, and technological achievements of industrial modernity. For the most part, his earliest accounts of the "risk society" tend to focus on hazards associated with the nuclear and chemical industries. The original thesis was developed in the aftermath of events such as the Union Carbide chemical plant disaster at Bhopal on December 3, 1984, the Cubatão (Vila Parisi) oil spill fire disaster of February 25, 1984 (at another Union Carbide chemical plant) and Chernobyl nuclear plant disaster of April 26, 1986. These are all taken as evidence in support of the view that a new "era of disasters" is already upon us; one that is set to radically change the ways people think and act in the world (Beck, 1987, 1992).

With such matters being featured as headline topics of concern, some of the earliest commentaries on his work tended to represent Beck as a sociological ally of "green" social movements and as a writer who demonstrates how the portent of environmental catastrophe might be taken up by Western traditions of sociological theory (Goldblatt, 1996; Strydom, 2002). Whilst problems of environmental risk are featured throughout his work, subsequent publications have included a more elaborate range of issues as evidence for the fact that "risk" is a central concern for societies experiencing intensifying processes of reflexive modernization. For Beck, the arena of risks also includes AIDS, livestock diseases such as foot and mouth disease and avian flu, scientific controversies surrounding genetic technologies (particularly in relation to the manufacture of foods), the uncontrollability of global financial markets and the threat of terrorist attacks (Beck, 2002a; Beck, 2005: 243–244; Beck,

2006: 33–34). Whilst quite different in many of their features and effects, neverthe-less, Beck holds that each of these hazards share some characteristics that demon-strate the novelty of the problems that he is concerned with here. First, they all exist as *unintended side effects* of processes of technological and scientific modernization. Second, there is so much uncertainty surrounding the magnitude of the disasters that they might visit upon society that their final consequences are *incalculable*. Third, they cannot be contained within national borders and have the potential to wreak havoc on a *global scale*. Finally, each *confront* modern societies with demands for mitigation and restitutive action for the sake of planetary survival.

Beck's representation of the reality of the risks we face is open to a great deal of critical debate and he readily admits to this. In more cautious passages of writing, he notes that "hazards are subject to historico-cultural perceptions and assessments which vary from country to country, from group to group, from one period to another" (Beck, 1995a: 91). He confesses that the rationality of risk perception is always open to social definition (Beck, 1992: 59). Due to the extent to which many of these hazards are not made immediately available to sensory experience and only become "socially available" to people via the visual imagery and news reports of mass media, there are occasions where he portrays the risk society as a kind of "shadow kingdom" where the reality of the threats we face shall always be open to speculation (Beck, 1995a: 100). At the same time he consistently brings emphasis to the extent to which public debates about risk are liable to arouse a widespread sense of anxiety and political concern. In later revisions of the risk society thesis, he argues that it is the public "staging of risk" in the mass media that matters here (Beck, 2009). Accordingly, Beck is largely concerned to explore the character and consequences of the "risk consciousness" that develops among populations in con-nection with media representations of what *might* take place under *anticipated* events of catastrophe wrought by modernization. In this respect, it is "the political anticipations, actions and reactions in response to the staging [of risk]" that he takes up as a key problem for sociological analysis (Beck, 2009: 10).

When describing the various dimensions and qualities of "risk consciousness," Beck charts the emergence of a new political awareness of the need for radical social change. He aims to explain how people stand to acquire knowledge of the fact that they inhabit a form of society that has unwittingly created the conditions for its own annihilation. He is also concerned to dwell upon the potential for this knowledge to inspire movements of social critique and political reform. Accordingly, the risk soci-ety thesis can be read as an account of the ways in which the conditions for social revolution are created in response to a burgeoning knowledge of modernity as being instituted upon technological and social processes that create a surfeit of catastrophic side effects.

It is also important to locate this component of his thesis alongside a broader account of transformations in the organization and experience of work, gender rela-tions, and family life. A substantial portion of the risk society thesis is devoted to the contention that people are disposed to become anxiously preoccupied with risk as a consequence of a more pronounced experience of uncertainty in conditions of every-day life. There are three core processes of social change that he tends to highlight here as *combining* to produce a "radicalized" experience of individualization that impresses upon people the understanding that life must be lived as an ongoing negotiation with risk. In the first place, along with many other sociologists, Beck holds that since the 1970s there has been a steady decline in a tradition of employment that offered people a "job for life" and this has been replaced by a more precarious environment of short-term work contracts that demand a great deal of "flexibility" from individuals both in their work practices and organization of time (Beck, 2000a). Second, he points to the radical redefinition of gender roles that has taken place under the spur of "second wave feminism" and the post-war expansion of higher education as a development that has brought large sections of society into a conscious, and often deeply unsettling, debate with their own gender identities, obligations, and aspirations (Beck and Beck-Gernsheim, 1995). Thirdly, he refers us to the proliferation of family forms that follow in the wake of these changes. Indeed, it is via a depiction of the tensions that are likely to be brought into people's relationship when they have children that Beck emphasizes the extent to which risk is now being adopted as a co-ordinate of self-identity and day-to-day experience. He contends:

> The capacity of men and women to work together to raise kids is becoming ever more difficult. It is here that two completely different worlds with opposing imperatives meet and clash. In the labour market, flexibility is preached as if it were the highest virtue. Flexibility means the ability to make ever quicker short-term adjustments to changing economic requirements. But the world of living together is characterized by exactly the opposite imperative … [T]he demands of healthy relationships, the demands of parenting and the needs of children are all in clear contradiction to the ever more insistent demand for labour market flexibility … Each of the various ways in which work can be flexibilized – contractually, spatially, and temporally – intensifies the extent to which both work and everyday life are becoming permeated by risk. (Beck and Willms, 2004: 162–164)

Beck argues that under such circumstances social life is being restructured so that individuals are being "institutionally forced to construct their own lives to a qualitatively new degree, resulting in a more indeterminate co-existence" (Beck and Willms, 2004: 63–68). Indeed, in this respect, he even ventures to depict "second modernity" as a society where "the individual becomes for the first time in history the basic unit of social reproduction" (ibid.). Current transformations in the experience of work, gender roles and family life are held to have produced social situations and political cultures where individuals are cast as having no-one to blame but themselves for the problems that beset their lives. They are made to take personal responsibility for the fates that befall them in a precarious world of risk and chance (Beck and Beck-Gernsheim, 2002).

Beck claims that this ever-intensifying experience of individualization makes people feel more vulnerable towards society and their future. He holds that the anxieties experienced over the conduct of everyday life are liable to bleed into those associated with large-scale risks to the globe. Beck represents the common experience of a "risk society" as one where the majority of individuals are fraught with anxieties of self-identity and social purpose; and as they gather every evening around "the village green of television," he suggests that, more than ever before they are bound to become consciously aware of the fact that problems of global society are entwined with their personal biographies and fate (Beck, 1992: 131–138).

In light of this worrying portrayal of the reality of our social situation, it may seem strange to some that Beck does not conclude his thesis on a pessimistic note. He does not regard the advent of risk society as reason to indulge in "postmodern panic" or to forsake all hopes for a better future; rather, he draws hope from the possibility that these might be the only conditions under which societies can be moved towards "ecological enlightenment" (Beck, 1995b). He argues:

> This all-encompassing and all-permeating insecurity is not just the dark side of free-dom. What is important is to discover it as the bright side. The introduction of insecu-rity into our thoughts and deeds may help to achieve the reduction of objectives, slowness, revisability and ability to learn, the care, consideration, tolerance and irony that are necessary for the change to a new modernity. (Beck, 1997: 168)

This is the hope that animates his thinking about the progressive force of "cosmo-politanism" and wider processes of "cosmopolitanization" in our times.

Cosmopolitanism

Beck frequently moves to make explicit the political motives behind his work. He is convinced that current processes of industrial modernization have brought global society to the brink of environmental catastrophe, and that we are living under con-ditions that are bound to give rise to a great deal of social distress, economic diffi-culty and political unrest. The dramatic tone of his writing is designed as a call for critical thought and political action. He is working to make clear the grounds under which people may not only be moved to save the world, but also, to promote social practices and to set institutions in place for building more humane forms of society.

His thesis on the risk society has been developed alongside a series of publications that outline the forms of politics that might emerge in the wake of people being made alert to the fact that processes of modernization have created hazards on an unprec-edented scale. There are differences in the problems featured as key topics of inquiry in books such as *Ecological Politics in an Age of Risk* (1995a), *Ecological Enlightenment* (1995b), *The Reinvention of Politics* (1997) and *Democracy without Enemies* (1998), but all these works make clear his commitment to the development of a form of envi-ronmental politics that aims to open up arenas of democratic debate over the design and implementation of modern technologies and industrial processes. In these con-texts, Beck explains his desire for a more "ecologically enlightened" form of rational-ity and questions how this might acquire the power to shape the institutional organization and industrial logics of modernization. He also explores the possible ways in which industry and state can be made more democratically and legally accountable to populations intent on moving from a situation of "organized irrespon-sibility" towards "the utopia of a responsible modernity" (Beck, 1999: 133–152).

At this stage in his writing, occasional references are made to the possible contri-bution of "cosmopolitan" values to the refashioning of social solidarities, demo-cratic principles, and political ideologies. Whilst setting out the parameters of a new "ecological politics" Beck occasionally dwells on the potential for political alliances to be forged among non-governmental organizations and global social movements; and at first, this is his principle sphere of reference when assessing the prospects for a new style of "cosmopolitan politics." In this context, he points to "sub-political" organizations and pressure groups who share in the understanding that "the central human worries are 'world' problems" and who work "from below" to present "local" problems as "global" concerns needing "glocal" solutions. Here Beck's interests lie in cosmopolitanism as a broad-based political movement that aims to break with the narrow agendas and institutional confines of national politics so as to promote global human rights along with the social reforms required to make these a living reality. Accordingly, he presents cosmopolitanism as a progressive response to the cumulative crises of a world risk society that aims to "reinvent" politics on behalf of a humanitarian movement for "responsible globalization" (Beck, 1999: 1–47; Beck, 2000b: 64–108).

More recently, he has moved to announce that "the cosmopolitan outlook" is "the key concept and topic of the reflexive second modernity" (Beck, 2006: 21). In a new trilogy of major works, *Power in the Global Age* (2005), *Cosmopolitan Vision* (2006) and *Cosmopolitan Europe* (2007), as well as numerous articles, Beck has outlined a programme of sociological inquiry that, in its thematic range and ambition, is of an order akin to his thesis on risk society. Beck's "cosmopolitan turn" may well come to be recognized as a further disciplinary defining event; and he does not shy away from expressing his hope that this proves to be the case. His declarations of cosmopolitan principle and depictions of the "cosmopolitanization" of social life are accompanied by calls for a new approach to sociological research.

Whilst acknowledging his indebtedness to earlier traditions of cosmopolitan thought and drawing inspiration from Stoic philosophy as well as figures such as Immanuel Kant, Karl Jaspers, and Hannah Arendt, Beck makes clear that, on his account, cosmopolitanism concerns much more than questions of abstract principle. In contrast to the portrayal of cosmopolitanism as an ethical standpoint, legal position, or political choice, he contends that he is seeking to attend to a *really existing* process of social and cultural change. Beck argues that a *banal* form of cosmopolitanism now exists as a contingent product of people's everyday relationships and patterns of consumption; and that in this respect, we can speak of the *cosmopolitanization* of societies. He writes:

> [C]osmopolitanization crosses frontiers like a stowaway, as an unforeseen consequence of market decisions: people develop a taste for a particular kind of pop music or for "Indian" food; or they respond to global risks by sorting out their money in states whose policies conform to the neoliberal ideal of responsiveness to the imperatives of the global market. "Cosmopolitanization" in this sense means latent cosmopolitanism, *unconscious* cosmopolitanism, *passive* cosmopolitanism which shapes reality as side effects of global trade or global threats such as climate change, terrorism or financial crises. My life, my body, my "individual existence" become part of another world, of foreign cultures, religions, histories and global interdependencies, without my realizing or expressly wishing it. (Beck, 2006: 19)

He goes on to claim that a new "cosmopolitan society" is being created out of this process; a society where people are alert to the fact that their lives are "*simultaneously* global and local" and move to interact with one another on this basis (Beck, 2002b: 36). In such a setting, Beck holds that it is possible to detect the emergence of a new kind of civility that is characterized by an active and ongoing recognition of our global interrelatedness and shared responsibility for planetary conditions. Indeed, whilst the "cosmopolitan society" remains a "world risk society," he holds that we are now witnessing the development of social ties and interdependencies that impress upon people that they must cooperate transnationally to survive. For Beck, it is now the case that cosmopolitan ideals are being met by a social reality that sets the stage for the creation of a new political "regime"; a regime that treats global human rights and the health of our natural environment as a paramount concern and moves to reform society so that such values are upheld in every sphere of life (Beck, 2005). He contends:

> Cosmopolitanization ... [is] a multidimensional process that has irrevocably changed the historical "nature" of social worlds and the status of individual countries within those worlds. It involves the formation of multiple loyalties, the spread of transnational lifestyles, the rise of non-state political actors (from Amnesty International to the World Trade Organization), and the development of global protest movements against (neo-liberal) globalism and for a different (cosmopolitan) globalization involving worldwide recognition of human rights, worker's rights, global protection of the environment, an end to poverty and so on. All these tendencies may be seen as the beginning, however deformed, of an institutionalized cosmopolitanism – paradoxically in the shape of anti-globalization movements, an International Criminal Court or the United Nations. (Beck, 2004: 136)

In this context, Beck calls for the development of a sociology that attends to the ways in which people's interrelationships transcend national boundaries so as to make their "transnationality" a focal point of analysis. Whilst this involves an effort to document and chart some of the banal processes of cosmopolitanization that are taking place within richer nations, it challenges social researchers to open up new vistas of inquiry into the multiple conditions and experiences of modernity that exist around the globe. He endorses a "methodological cosmopolitanism" that actively works to include non-Western experiences and frames of understanding within its accounts of the social world. Indeed, in this respect he holds that a cosmopolitan sociology should be particularly attentive to global inequalities in people's material conditions, political freedoms and social opportunities (Beck, 2002b; Beck and Sznaider, 2006).

Whilst Beck's thesis on the risk society aims to equip us with conceptual frameworks for making sense of a new complex of social problems, his analysis of cosmopolitanism is largely devoted to an exploration of the conditions under which we might search for their solutions. Whilst the earlier project is geared to announce the arrival of a new age of catastrophe and social upheaval, the later work raises the hope that our salvation lies in a cosmopolitan future. Throughout his writing there is an ongoing debate over the possibility of reforming the theoretical discourse and research agendas of sociology. His "cosmopolitan vision" for sociology suggests that, in terms of the transnational mapping of multiple experiences of modernity, and in its attempts to understand the stock of our times in terms of the *shared* fate of humanity, its work has hardly begun; yet he holds firm to the conviction that this remains vital for sustaining the hope that we might yet create a new "enlightened" world order for society.

Assessment

There is a considerable conflict of interpretations surrounding Beck's work (Gabe, 2004). In part, this may be due to inconsistencies in his documentation of the expository roles and critical purposes of key terms of analysis. Beyond this, the volume of his output, his willingness to adapt his arguments for a wide variety of audiences and the fact that he often approaches the task of writing more with a mind to provoke debate than with the aim of outlining a systematic approach to thinking, have made it possible to chart a number of interpretive paths through his work. One should not expect to find any consensus when it comes to summarizing the core tenets of his sociological theory; and certainly, there are many ways of evaluating its contribution to the field.

His work has attracted a great deal of comment and criticism. Whilst few are inclined to present themselves as standing in full agreement with his depiction of the social world, it appears to be widely understood that by situating your work in relation to Beck's project, its sociological interests and political commitments are brought into relief. Indeed, at least in the context of British sociology, many work at promoting their favored agendas for sociology, or move to explain the distinctiveness of their approach to study, via a critical commentary on Beck's work. Here there are at least three common criticisms that are leveled towards his social theory.

First, many contend that his portrayal of current social trends lacks the support of evidence drawn from empirical research. For example, it is argued that there is a large amount of empirical research that establishes that the social distribution of employment and health risks is heavily stratified by class; and further, that class remains a core component of self-identity and social consciousness (Bottero, 2005; Devine *et al.*, 2005; *Sociology*, 2005). In this context, Beck is accused of overemphasizing the prevalence and social significance of individualization; or rather, critics complain that, when analyzing this phenomenon, he fails to pay due heed to the continuing relevance of class as a determining force upon people's social opportunities and life chances (Atkinson, 2007; Cebulla, 2007; Mythen, 2005). In a similar vein, he is criticized for his lack of attention to large-scale data sets and cross national surveys that document current employment trends across different sectors of national and transnational economies; and it is argued that much of the available data serves to undermine his claims about the general character and effects of labor market "flexibility" (Doogan, 2009). A range of commentators also make reference to the extent to which empirical studies of risk perceptions serve to cast doubt on his accounts of emergent forms of social subjectivity (Irwin, 2001; Irwin *et al.*, 1999; Tulloch and Lupton, 2003). In this context, it appears that very few people are prone to display the forms of "risk consciousness" that Beck profiles within his narratives on risk society; whilst worrying about everyday problems of work and family life, most have no time or inclination to reflect upon matters of global risk (Wilkinson, 2001).

Second, there are a range of disputes surrounding his depictions of past experience and the history of ideas. In this regard, Beck tends to be criticized for failing to provide a sufficiently elaborate and historically qualified account of the cultures and traditions against which he seeks to depict the novelty of the present. The effort that is put into his documentation of current social trends and new cultural and political formations is not carried over into the judgments that he places on the past. Some complain that in order to cast his arguments in their most strident form, Beck tends to deploy stereotypical reconstructions of the past that either ignore or downplay any evidence that does not suit his purpose (Elliott, 2002). For example, it is argued that when criticizing the "methodological nationalism" of classical sociological theory he ignores some of the antecedents of cosmopolitan social thought (Inglis, 2009). Similarly, it is argued that there is a wealth of evidence to suggest that the experience of "risk consciousness" is considerably older than Beck suggests. For example, Bryan Turner contends that the understanding that individual thoughts and actions are implicated (albeit as an unintended consequence) within the creation of global mega-hazards may be recognized as a longstanding component of many religious worldviews; particularly in the context of attempts to reconcile faith in Divine Providence with the experience of a world in which there appears to be an unjustifiable amount of suffering (Turner, 1994: 180–181).

Finally, Beck is often taken to task for his tendency to exaggerate the extent to which problems and experiences of risk are shared around the globe. It is argued that he fails to attend to the uneven social distribution, geographical spread, and human consequences of different types of risk and hazard (Bromley, 2000; Culpitt, 1999; Draper, 1993; Dryzek, 1995; Mythen, 2004). At no point does Beck moderate his account of the risk society with any documentation of the incidence of harm. In terms of the numbers of fatalities involving hazardous materials, India, Mexico, Russia, Brazil, and China are the countries most deserving of the label "risk society" (de Souza, 2000). These are also the countries where the largest numbers of occupational accidents and fatalities take place. At a conservative estimate, when compared to countries such as the United Kingdom and United States, the rates at which people are injured or killed in the workplace is three times higher in developing countries (Hämäläinen et al., 2006). Accordingly, whilst there are passages where Beck argues that the proliferation of large-scale industrial hazards in the developing world has latent "boomerang effects" that strike back at populations living in rich countries, on almost any scale, these are far less devastating than those visited upon the poor countries of the world (Beck, 1992: 36–44). In this respect, it is argued that he should be more careful to moderate his account of "world risk society" with a detailing of the *multiple* conditions of modernity that exist around the globe and how these frequently involve people in very different dilemmas of risk and experiences of harm (Wilkinson, 2009: 85–96).

Beck is certainly aware of these criticisms and occasionally makes reference to them in his work. In recent publications he appears to be increasingly concerned to take up the task of charting global differences in conditions of modernity and inequalities in the experience of risk (Beck, 2005, 2008, 2009). He also claims that, in collaboration with colleagues working at the Research Center on Reflexive Modernization in Munich, he is working to better illustrate his theory with data drawn from empirical research (Beck and Sznaider, 2006; Beck, 2007). At the same time, however, Beck's priorities seem to be fixed in the direction of bringing critical force and volume to his narratives on "risk society" and the "cosmopolitan vision." The majority of his publications are dedicated to updating and refining terms of sociological debate as set within his own enterprise. In this regard, he does not appear to be too worried by critics who question its sociological value and precision.

Ultimately, the judgment that is brought to Beck's work may well reflect the value that is placed upon the art of writing sociological narratives to fit our times. It is also likely to be the case that enthusiasm for his project is moderated by the importance placed on using sociology as a means to forecast the possible futures that lie before us. Very few have ventured to write with the political conviction, boldness of vision and sociological ambition that Beck demonstrates in his work. Most sociologists build their careers around critical commentaries on the works of the grand theorists; and by setting out their stall out in opposition to a particular element in a theorist's work, effectively acknowledge the relevance and importance of the grander project. Beck's sociology demonstrates a rare cast of imagination. He offers a distinctive vision of modernity and opens up new avenues of inquiry into its institutional design, developmental logics, and latent consequences. In this respect, he offers an authoritative script that provides many with a sociological orientation for their research and a means to express its value; and all the more so where they are moved to join in the task of understanding how national fates may be entwined both for better and worse by the unfurling catastrophe of climate change and the destruction of our natural environment.

Reader's Guide to Ulrich Beck

Readers seeking a good overview of Beck's project of social theory should consult his interviews with Johannes Willms (2004) and Nicholas Gane (2004). Those searching for an introduction to his thesis on the risk society should consult Gabe Mythen's *Ulrich Beck: A Critical Guide to the Risk Society* (2004). Short overviews of this component of his work are also included in general surveys of the sociological literature on risk provided by Lupton (1999), Mythen and Walklate (2006) and Wilkinson (2009). Robert Fine's (2007) introduction to cosmopolitanism provides a concise overview of Beck's contribution to debates on this area. More critical assessments of Beck's "cosmopolitan turn" are provided in recent articles by Inglis (2009) and Martell (2009).

Bibliography

Writings of Ulrich Beck

1974. Objectivität und Normativität. Die Theorie-Praxis-Debatte in der modernen deutschen und amerikanischen Soziologie. Reinbek: Rowohlt. Doctoral thesis, University of Munich, 1972.

1983. Janseits von Stand und Klasse? Soziale Ungleichheiten gesellschaftliche Individualisierungsprozesse und die Entstehung neuer sozialer Formationen und Identitäten. In R. Kreckel (ed.) *Soziale Ungleichheiten Soziale Welt*, Sonderband 2. Gottingen: Schwartz, pp. 37–74.

1987. The anthropological shock: Chernobyl and the contours of the risk society. *Berkeley Journal of Sociology*, 32(1): 153–165.

1990. On the way toward an industrial society of risk? An outline of argument. *International Journal of Political Economy*, 20(1): 51–69.

1992. *Risk Society: Towards a New Modernity*. London: Sage Publications.

1994. The reinvention of politics: towards a theory of reflexive modernization. In U. Beck, A. Giddens, and S. Lash (eds) *Reflexive Modernization: Politics, Tradition and Aesthetics in the Modern Social Order*. Cambridge: Polity Press.

1995a. *Ecological Politics in an Age of Risk*. Cambridge: Polity Press.

1995b. *Ecological Enlightenment: Essays on the Politics of the Risk Society*. New York: Prometheus.

1996. Risk and the provident state. In S. Lash, B. Szerszynski, and B. Wynne (eds) *Risk Environment and Modernity: Towards a New Ecology*. London: Sage Publications, pp. 27–43.

1997. *The Reinvention of Politics*. Cambridge: Polity Press.

1998. *Democracy Without Enemies*. Cambridge: Polity Press.

1999. *World Risk Society*. Cambridge: Polity Press.

2000a. *The Brave New World of Work*. Cambridge: Polity Press.

2000b. *What is Globalization?* Cambridge: Polity Press.

2000c. The cosmopolitan perspective. *British Journal of Sociology*, 51(1): 79–105.

2000d. Risk society revisited: Theory, politics and research programmes. In B. Adam, U. Beck, and J. Van Loon, (eds) *The Risk Society and Beyond: Critical Issues for Social Theory*. London: Sage Publications, pp. 211–229

2002a. The silence of words and political dynamics of the world risk society. *Logos*, 1(4): 1–18.

2002b. The cosmopolitan society and its enemies. *Theory, Culture & Society*, 19(1–2): 17–44.

2004. Cosmopolitan realism: on the distinction between cosmopolitanism in philosophy and social science. *Global Networks*, 4(2): 131–156.

2005. *Power in the Global Age*. Cambridge: Polity Press.

2006. *Cosmopolitan Vision*. Cambridge: Polity Press.

2007. Beyond class and nation: reframing social inequalities in a globalizing world. *British Journal of Sociology*, 58(4): 679–705.

2008. World at risk: The new task of critical theory. *Development and Society*, 37(1): 1–21.

2009. *World at Risk*. Cambridge: Polity Press.

1995 (with E. Beck-Gernsheim). *The Normal Chaos of Love*. Cambridge: Polity Press.

2002 (with E. Beck-Gernsheim). *Individualization: Institutionalized Individualism and its Social and Political Consequences*. London: Sage.

2008 (with E. Beck-Gernsheim). Global generations and the trap of methodological nationalism for a cosmopolitan turn in the sociology of youth and generation. *European Sociological Review*, 25(1): 25–36.

2003 (with W. Bonss and L. Lau). The theory of reflexive modernization: problematic, hypotheses and research programme. *Theory Culture & Society*, 20(2): 1–33.

2004 (with N. Gane). The cosmopolitan turn. In N. Gane, *The Future of Social Theory*. London: Continuum.

2007 (with E. Grande). *Cosmopolitan Europe*. Cambridge: Polity.

2005 (with C. Lau). Second modernity as a research agenda: theoretical and empirical explorations in the "meta-change" of modern society. *British Journal of Sociology*, 56(4): 525–557.

2006 (with N. Sznaider). Unpacking cosmopolitanism for the social sciences a research agenda. *British Journal of Sociology*, 57(1): 1–23.

2004 (with J. Willms). *Conversations with Ulrich Beck*. Cambridge: Polity Press.

Further Reading

Atkinson, W. (2007) Beck, individualization and the death of class: a critique. *British Journal of Sociology*, 59(3): 349–366.

Barry, J. (1999) *Environment and Social Theory*. London: Routledge.

Bottero, W. (2005) *Stratification: Social Division and Inequality*. London: Routledge.

Bromley, S. (2000) Political ideologies and the environment. In D. Goldblatt (ed.) *Knowledge and the Social Sciences: Theory, Method, Practice*. London: Routledge, pp. 74–114.

Cebulla, A. (2007) Class or individual? A test of the nature of risk perception the individualization thesis of risk society theory. *Journal of Risk Research*, 10(2): 129–148.

Cottle, S. (1998) Ulrich Beck, risk society and the media. *European Journal of Communications*, 13(1): 5–32.

Culpitt, I. (1999) *Social Policy and Risk*. London: Sage Publications.

de Souza Jr., A. B. (2000) Emergency planning for hazardous industrial areas: A Brazilian case study. *Risk Analysis*, 20(4): 483–493.

Devine, F., Savage, M., Scott, J., and Crompton, R. (eds) (2005) *Rethinking Class, Identities, Cultures and Lifestyles*. Basingstoke: Palgrave.

Doogan, K. (2009) *New Capitalism? The Transformation of Work*. Cambridge: Polity Press.

Draper, E. (1993) Risk society and social theory. *Contemporary Sociology: A Journal of Reviews*, 22(1): 641–644.

Dryzek, J. S. (1995) Toward an ecological modernity. *Contemporary Sociology: A Journal of Reviews*, 28: 231–242.

Elliott, A. (2002) Beck's sociology of risk: A critical assessment. *Sociology*, 36(2): 293–315.

Fine, R. (2007) *Cosmopolitanism*. London: Routledge.

Frank. J. D. (1966) Galloping technology: A new social disease. *Journal of Social Issues*, 12(1): 1–14.

Gabe, M. (2004) *Ulrich Beck: A Critical Introduction to the Risk Society*. London: Pluto Press.

Goldblatt, D. (1996) *Social Theory and the Environment*. Cambridge: Polity Press.

Hajer M. and Kesselring, S. (1999) Democracy in the risk society? Learning from the new politics of mobility in Munich. *Environmental Politics*, 8(3): 1–23.

Hämäläinen, P., Takala, J., and Saarela, K. J. (2006) Global estimates of occupational accidents. *Safety Science*, 44: 137–156.

Hobsbawm, E. (1994) *The Age of Extremes*. London: Abacus.

Inglis, D. (2009) Cosmopolitan sociology and the classical canon: Ferdinand Tönnies and the emergence of global *Gesellschaft*. *British Journal of Sociology*, 60(4): 813–832.

Irwin, A. (2001) *Sociology and the Environment*. Cambridge: Polity Press.

Irwin, A., Simmons, P., and Walker, G. (1999) Faulty environments and risk reasoning: the local understanding of industrial hazards. *Environment and Planning A*, 31: 1311–1326.

Lash, S., Szerszynski, B., and Wynne, B. (eds) (1996) *Risk Environment and Modernity: Towards a New Ecology*. London: Sage Publications.

Lupton, D. (1999) *Risk*. Routledge: London.

Martell, L. (2009) Global Inequality, human rights and Power: A critique of Ulrich Beck's Cosmopolitanism. *Critical Sociology*, 35(2): 253–272.

Mazower, M. (1998) *Dark Continent: Europe's Twentieth Century*. London: Penguin.

Mythen, G. (2004) *Ulrich Beck: A Critical Introduction to the Risk Society*. London: Pluto Press.

Mythen, G. (2005) Employment, individualization and insecurity: Rethinking the risk society perspective. *Sociological Review*, 53(1): 129–149.

Mythen, G. (2007) Reappraising the risk society thesis: Telescopic sight or myopic vision? *Current Sociology*, 55(6): 793–813.

Mythen, G. and Walklate, S. (eds) (2006) *Beyond the Risk Society: Critical Reflections on Risk and Human Security*. London: McGraw Hill.

Ostner, I. (2003) Individualization – The origins of the concept and its impact on German social policies. *Social Policy & Society*, 3(1): 47–56.

Outhwaite, W. (2009) Canon formation in late 20th-Century British sociology. *Sociology*, 43(6): 1029–1045.

Rucht, D. and Roose, J. (1999) The German environmental movement at a crossroads. *Environmental Politics*, 8 (1): 59–80.

Smith, M. (2006) Environmental risks and ethical responsibilities: Arendt, Beck and the politics of acting into nature. *Environmental Ethics*, 28(3): 227–246.

Sociology (2005) Class, culture and identity. Special Issue. *Sociology*, 39(5): 797–1040

Strydom, P. (2002) *Risk, Environment and Society*. Buckingham: Open University Press.

Tulloch, J. and Lupton, D. (2003) *Risk and Everyday Life*. London: Sage Publications.

Turner, B. S. (1994) *Orientalism, Postmodernism and Globalism*. London: Routledge.

Vedby Rasmussen, M. (2006) *The Risk Society at War: Terror, Technology and Strategy in the Twenty-First Century*. Cambridge: Cambridge University Press.

Wilkinson, I. (2001) *Anxiety in a Risk Society*. London: Routledge.

Wilkinson, I. (2009) *Risk, Vulnerability and Everyday Life*. London: Routledge.

21

Donna Haraway

JANET WIRTH-CAUCHON

THE PERSON

Donna Haraway is a feminist science studies scholar whose work has had wide influence in science studies, cultural studies, and feminist theory. Through her critical studies of technoscience, primatology, and companion species, she has opened new terrain in social theory. Fundamental to her work and her contribution to social theory is a transformed understanding of the categories of nature and culture as well as their interrelationships. Haraway's original and innovative writing provides a new critical language for addressing the complexities of technoscientific knowledge practices, as well as how these can be reimagined for more sustainable and life-affirming worlds.

Donna Haraway is Professor at the History of Consciousness Program at the University of California, Santa Cruz, a position she has held since 1980. She was born in 1944 in Denver, Colorado, and was educated in Catholic schools. She attended Colorado College on a scholarship from the Bettcher Foundation, and graduated in 1966, completing a degree in zoology, with minors in philosophy and literature. Following graduation, she spent a year in France on a Fulbright scholarship, studying evolutionary philosophy and theology at the Faculté des Sciences, Université de Paris. She did graduate studies in biology at Yale University, and also became politically active in the antiwar and civil rights movements. She earned a PhD in biology at Yale University, moving from marine biology to evolutionary ecology, studying with Evelyn Hutchinson, an ecologist who specialized in the study of lake ecology. Haraway credits Hutchinson's encouragement of broad intellectual interests in his graduate students with fostering her love of biology and enabling her to study biology historically and culturally. She completed a dissertation that she describes as "a hybrid between history of science, philosophy, and biology" (2000: 19), on the emergence of the organicist model in developmental biology, that drew on Thomas

The Wiley-Blackwell Companion to Major Social Theorists, First Edition.
Edited by George Ritzer and Jeffrey Stepnisky.
© 2011 Blackwell Publishing Ltd. Published 2011 by Blackwell Publishing Ltd.

Kuhn's *The Structure of Scientific Revolutions* to study scientific change. The dissertation was published in 1976 in revised form as *Crystals, Fabrics, and Fields: Metaphors of Organicism in Twentieth-Century Developmental Biology*. The significance of this early study for Haraway's body of work is that its main themes – the centrality of metaphor and language in scientific knowledge making; the stress on interactive relational processes as constitutive of forms; the favoring of complex process over reductive, causal thinking – are early statements of themes that appear, in different form or scale – in Haraway's later work. This manner in which materiality and meaning intertwine is a theme running through her work on primate studies, technoscience, and animal studies.

In 1970, she moved to the University of Hawaii and taught courses in biology while completing her dissertation, then moved to Johns Hopkins University in 1974, teaching the history of science. While at Johns Hopkins she read and taught women's studies with Nancy Hartsock. In 1980, she took the position in feminist theory in the History of Consciousness program, which she embraced as an innovative interdisciplinary environment that enabled her to work on the several areas she was interested in, including science and technology studies, primate studies and feminist theory. In 2000, she was awarded the J. D. Bernal award for distinguished contributions to the field from the Society for Social Studies of Science, the third woman to have been given the prize.

The Intellectual and Social Context

Haraway was among those in her generation engaged in the social movements of the late 1960s and 1970s, most prominently the women's liberation, civil rights, and antiwar movements. While at Yale in the late 1960s, she was involved in the anti-Vietnam war movement as well as anti-racist and welfare rights activism. The women's health movement and reproductive politics of the 1970s were important catalysts for Haraway's critical studies of technoscience (Haraway, 1997: 193; 2004: 339), as were the environmental and labor movements. One line of development in feminist science studies in the 1970s and 1980s that influenced Haraway's work emerged in the critiques of scientific objectivity and value neutrality, frequently grounded in critiques of biological determinism in sex differences research (Subramaniam, 2009). Feminists studying the masculinist basis of science argued that including women as the subjects of scientific knowledge, and starting inquiry from women's vantage points, would lead to more useful knowledge because it would include perspectives and lived experiences of those historically excluded from science. Sandra Harding (1986) argued for a concept of "strong objectivity," an expanded objectivity that includes recognition of social communities affected by scientific practices. Haraway articulated the issues in her essay "Situated Knowledge: The Science Question in Feminism and the Privilege of Partial Perspective" (1988, reprinted in Haraway, 1991), discussed in more detail below. The problem, as Haraway saw it, was how to acknowledge the constructedness of science and the social character of knowledge claims, while refusing to capitulate to a relativism that would not be able to make a difference in the world. In Haraway's words, it is a problem of "how to have simultaneously an account of radical historical contingency for all knowledge claims ... and a no-nonsense commitment to faithful accounts of a 'real' world, one that can be partially shared and friendly to earth-wide projects of finite freedom, adequate material abundance, modest meaning in suffering, and limited happiness" (1991: 187).

While feminists such as Sandra Harding as well as Evelyn Fox Keller (1985), Anne Fausto-Sterling (1985), and others were pushing forward with feminist critiques of gender and science, related developments in the social studies of science were taking place in the work of scholars such as Bruno Latour (1987, 1988), Andrew Pickering (1992), and Steve Woolgar (1988). Haraway's work has been associated with and frequently in dialogue and debate with this work, and Haraway has cited as an influence Latour's actor-network theory that ascribes agency to nonhuman actants in interactive relationship with human knowers (Haraway, 1997: 284, n. 23; Penley and Ross, 1991: 3). Like Latour, Haraway resists a concept of a "transcendent social" outside of scientific technical practice; she understands scientific encounters inside a laboratory or field site, where humans interact with a range of human and nonhuman objects, as themselves thoroughly social encounters.

Another important force shaping Haraway's work emerges in the debates in feminism regarding differences of race, class, gender, and sexuality. In a 2006 interview, Haraway describes the feminist movement as a "complicated heritage," the source of a critical effort to imagine alternative social worlds, that was also a period of working through racial and class divisions within feminist movements (2006: 136). Critiques of mainstream feminism by women of color and postcolonial writers, such as Trinh T. Minh-ha (1986/7), bell hooks (1981), and Chela Sandoval (1990) challenged the exclusive focus on women's issues or gender outside of the contexts of colonialism, race, class, or sexuality. These writers developed an intersectional approach that focused on multiple and interlocking oppressions. Haraway's work has taken up this critique, opening up the universal category of "woman" that erases differences, and insisting on the "relentless intersectionality" that postcolonial and anti-racist feminist theorists developed in feminist theory (2004: 329). Haraway seeks "new geometries" of oppositional politics beyond the familiar identity categories that, she argues, are not supple enough for complex and changing social relations. Haraway draws on anti-racist and postcolonial theory to rethink the politics of difference in ways that account for this complexity; that constructs "possible postcolonial, nongeneric, and irredeemably specific figures of critical subjectivity, consciousness, and humanity" (2004: 48). This is evident throughout her work, including her discussion of racial exclusions in feminism and the need for new forms of coalition in "A Manifesto for Cyborgs" (1985, reprinted in Haraway, 1991); the intersecting racial, gendered, and colonial narratives in primatology in *Primate Visions* (1989), the study of racial and global disparities in women's experiences of reproductive technology and the racialized hetero-normative logic of genetics in *Modest_Witness* (1997), and the analysis of postcolonial ecological justice struggles in *When Species Meet* (2008).

Another important social and intellectual context was Marxist and socialist feminism. Haraway's early work in the late 1970s and 1980s was identified as socialist feminist, and Haraway drew on Marxist categories for analysis of gender relations and women's position. In her 1988 essay, "Situated Knowledges," she writes that Marxism provided a "promising resource" for a feminist critique of knowledge as embodied and historically contingent. There also she noted the limitations of Marx's "ontological theory of the domination of nature in the self-construction of man" and its exclusive focus on wage labor (1991: 186). In "A Manifesto for Cyborgs," Haraway asserted that the Marxist privileging of labor, and socialist feminists' extension of the category to include women's work, was based on a "Marxian humanism, with its pre-eminently Western self" (1991: 158). The cyborg essay was in part an effort to transform the analytic categories available to socialist feminists in the face of what Haraway termed "the informatics of domination," marked by global capitalist communications systems that imposed new forms of control on women in the "integrated circuit" (1991: 170).

Haraway has continued to draw on Marxian concepts in her later work addressing the material relations of technoscience, as in her adaptation of Marx's analysis of commodity fetishism to analyze the commodification of the gene in *Modest_Witness* (1997). In her most recent work on companion species, Marx's analysis of exchange value is a point of departure for Haraway's development of a concept of "encounter value" with dogs as "lively capital" in capitalist technoculture (2008: 46).

Haraway's discursive study of scientific knowledge and practice is also informed by the work of Michel Foucault (Sofoulis, 2002; Braidotti, 2006; Vint, 2008). As Zoe Sofoulis (2002) has noted, Foucaultian influence is evident in the "A Cyborg Manifesto," in Haraway's view of the always-open possibility of reversal and resistance in the face of power. In her studies of technoscience in *Modest_Witness*, she draws on Foucault's concept of biopower to develop what she terms "technobiopower," designating a regime marked by the "implosion of biologics and informatics," where not "life," but "life, enterprised up" that is, genetically altered, legally patented and commodified forms of life, are the new political objects of management (1997: 12).

Another notable aspect of Haraway's work is her development of a vocabulary outside of the framework of psychoanalysis that was so predominant in feminist and cultural theory in the 1980s and 1990s. Haraway sought to find another language in order to avoid its preoccupation with Oedipal conflicts and a hetero-normative nuclear family. While she views the unconscious as still being a "useful theoretical object" (2000: 125), she seeks ways to explore unconscious commitments that may not be confined to family structures or stories, such as for instance within models of friendship, and of "work and of play – and of connections to nonhumans" (2000: 126).

The Work

Science, meaning, and materiality

A central aspect of Haraway's work is her insistence on the connection of meaning and materiality, their co-presence in scientific knowledge making and other cultural practices. Haraway envisions the braided, intertwining skein of culture and meaning with the material; they are not separable. One may foreground particular aspects as a heuristic strategy, but this is done provisionally and with an awareness of the complexity of biosocial "naturecultures" (2008: 25). Thus, while she is a historian of science, and her work takes up the deconstructive critique of scientific discourses that reproduce hierarchical relations of race, sex-gender, class, and culture, she views these discourses as embedded in material processes and relations that have agency and that "act back" on those discourses. Haraway addresses this most explicitly in her recent work on companion species relationships, yet it is fundamental to her previous studies of the cyborg figure, technoscience, and primatology. While Haraway's reading of science focuses on language, metaphor, discourse, and narrative, she stresses the agency of material processes and nonhuman entities – the objects of knowledge making practices – asserting that "nature is made, but not entirely by humans; it is a co-construction among humans and non-humans" (2004: 66). Haraway foregrounds the inseparability of meaning and materiality with her term "material-semiotic" to describe scientific processes and entities (1997: 218; 1989: 172). She adapts Charles Sanders Peirce's term "semiosis," particularly Teresa de Lauretis's (1984: 167–175) elaboration of the concept that stresses meaning-making as a social, material process (2004: 201; 1997: 127).

Haraway's attention to the agency of material processes is illustrated in her use of biology. Trained as a biologist, Haraway says that she reads biology "in a double way," not only for understanding biological processes, but also for "the way the world works metaphorically" (Haraway, 2000: 24). Haraway has given particular attention in her work to processes of complex interaction and relational co-creation, not only at the level of molecules, cells, and tissues, but also in cultural and social processes and histories. In her work on companion species and cross-species interaction and relation, she draws on her early study of embryology, as well as the work of biologist Scott Gilbert, to define the process of "reciprocal induction," as "morphogenetic interactions through which cells and tissues of a developing embryo reciprocally shape each other through cascades of chemical-tactile communications" (2008: 219). Haraway sees this process of "coshaping" – a dynamic, active process immanent to matter – occurring at many levels of human-animal-technological relations, including that of human-dog co-evolution in her work on companion species. Unlike a biological determinism, which reduces complex social processes to biological causes, Haraway assumes a two-way interaction between the social and the biological. Haraway reads the underlying processes of reciprocal co-shaping at many levels of scale, from cells, to bacteria, to ecological zones, to cross-species interdependence. She strives to capture this dynamism and complexity with her language, forging new metaphors, figures, and stories that evoke this relational process.

Primatology: Science and storytelling

In her 1989 study of primatology, *Primate Visions*, Haraway envisions primatology as a "historically changing craft of narrating the history of nature" (1989: 4). *Primate Visions* is a cultural history of the science of primatology, paying attention to how gender and race figure into the ways primates are imagined, hunted, and studied in the laboratory and in the field, and narrated in science and popular culture. Haraway studies the primate as a figure, a material-semiotic object around which collect cultural myths of nature, the primitive, human civilization, and racial and gendered differences. Grounded in an approach that views the natural sciences as historically specific, Haraway sees primates as especially potent figures to study, as they are situated at the boundaries between animal and human and regularly signify the meanings of human's relationships to nature. Primatology tells stories about human origins, as "the cradle of culture, of human being distinct from animal existence ... the Western imagination of the origin of sociality itself, especially in the densely meaning-laden icon of 'the family'" (11). Moving through the history of primatology, Haraway's comprehensive study includes Carl Akeley's early twentieth-century safari expeditions and construction of the African Hall of apes in the American Museum of Natural History, the mid-twentieth-century laboratory and field studies, including those by Robert Yerkes, Sherwood Washburn, Dian Fossey, and Jane Goodall, and the feminist primatologists of the 1970s and 1980s who transformed the field. She details the initial entrance of women into primate studies, especially Jane Goodall, focusing on the operations of gender and race in the reception of women into the field. In popular accounts of Goodall's work with chimpanzees at the Gombe National Reserve in Tanzania, for example, she was portrayed as a representative of (white European) civilization making connection with primitive wilderness. Haraway shows how Goodall was cast as a savior and healer of nature in these accounts. At the same time, African people were systematically excluded from these popular accounts of Goodall's work, at a time when they were engaged in movements for national independence from colonial power.

Haraway's reading of primatological narratives is not limited to the *ex post facto* narrative of scientific findings, but rather, with "science in the making," how the very constitution of a problem – the questions that are asked, what concepts and categories are seen as central and what is extraneous to the problem – depend upon meaning and tropes. Further, scientific categories and stories – the "tropic as tools to think with" – emerge within particular historical conditions. For example, she studied primatologists' conceptualization of the natural social unit of primate society, a category that organized data collection and was central to accounts of primate evolution. While in the 1930s, Robert Yerkes assumed the monogamous heterosexual pair was the natural unit to study, by the 1960s and 1970s feminist primatologists focused on mother-infant pairs, female-female interactions and larger, fluid social groups. This new focus on females changed the science; its effect was to transform how scientists of both sexes observed and interpreted female primates.

Haraway then examines the work of several women in the field of primatology in the 1970s and 1980s, including Jeanne Altmann, Linda Marie Fedigan, Adrienne Zihlman and Sarah Blaffer Hrdy. Haraway frames how these primatologists negotiate the paradoxical positions of woman, feminist, and scientist. She studies their feminist discursive strategies to "understand again how the politics of being female are part of the stakes in the scientific contest for what may count as human" (1989: 330). Primatologists whose feminism shaped and enabled their thinking, field observations, and interpretations of primate behavior told different stories: downplaying the male dominance themes favored in the existing accounts, and including a focus on the everyday activities and agency of female primates. In building evolutionary accounts, for example, Altmann argued that a longer time frame was needed to show the variability of female reproductive success, a neglected theme in previous work. Feminist primatologists emphasized primates' female agency through their everyday activities, and noted constraints in the demands of their lives.

Yet these feminist narratives were not fully free of the discursive and cultural constraints that Haraway noted in existing primatology. Haraway draws on Foucault's understanding of discourse as both reinforcing and resisting power, and reads feminist primatology as sometimes "pervaded by and reproducing the very logics of domination and appropriation it struggles against" (1989: 287). For example, a theory centered on female primates' active reproductive strategies, such as that articulated by Sarah Blaffer Hrdy, can be seen as resistive in the sense that it is reworking the evolutionary narrative centered only on male competition, but it also reproduces a sociobiological logic of liberal individualism and competition between females. Feminist primatologists told stories about primates to meet their own feminist ends, and in particular ways shaped by the particular discourses of the historical time period.

Nature as witty agent

Haraway notes that all of her work has addressed the question of "what gets to count as nature" (2000: 50). She views nature as a discursive figure, a *topos*, with its condensed spatial and rhetorical meanings: as "place or topic for consideration of common themes" (2004: 126). While focused on the discursive and material practices through which science constructs the boundaries of nature and culture, one of the most significant aspects of Haraway's approach is her conception of nature or the material world and its objects, as having agency, as "lively," active partners in relation with humans, not passive inert objects of knowledge. As she writes, "Actors come in many and wonderful forms" (1991: 198), and Haraway's insistence on the liveliness and agency of the nonhuman world includes biological processes, nonhuman animals, whether these be primates, laboratory mice, or dogs, as well as nonhuman technologies and machines, all of which become players in the interactions of science practice. She conceptualizes science as a relation or conversation with that agentic world, an active process that materializes the boundaries of scientific objects.

Yet an important caveat here is that simply decoding what counts as nature is not a guarantee for certainty about its workings nor that of scientific practice. The lack of guarantee is embodied in a figure that Haraway takes up in her work to view the world as "witty agent," that of the Coyote or Trickster from Native American mythology. Tricksters have a cunning intelligence and sense of humor, and have the ability to change shape and move across different contexts. Haraway's figuration of the world as witty agent signifies that the world-as-trickster may surprise us and disrupt our expectations. Acknowledging the agency of nature counters a view of it as resource for technoscience, and helps avoid distortions or errors in accounts of the worlds studied. It suggests humans are not the authors of nature, but rather are in relationship to it and thus could be more sensitive to and responsible to the forms and dynamics of these nonhuman processes.

Figuration in technoscience

Haraway addresses her critical reading of scientific practice and narrative to *figurations,* defined as "material-semiotic nodes or knots in which diverse bodies and meanings coshape one another … where the biological and literary or artistic come together with all of the force of lived reality" (Haraway, 2008: 4). Figures are condensed points of intersection where multiple cultural meanings and material conditions converge. In *Modest_Witness*, for example, Haraway examines the figures of technoscience such as the gene, OncoMouse™, a genetically altered laboratory mouse, the fetus, and the computer chip. Haraway refers to these as "performative images that can be inhabited ... We inhabit and are inhabited by such figures that map universes of knowledge, practice and power" (1997: 11). Haraway's reading of figures resembles a Foucaultian genealogy, as she traces the threads in the histories out of which figures become possible and emerge. In an interview, Haraway has likened her deconstruction of figures to unwinding a ball of yarn, tracing the threads of discourse and institutional conditions of their emergence, to redescribe figures in their multiple contexts. "They lead out into worlds, you can explode them, you can untangle them, you can somehow loosen them up" (2004: 338). Her reading of figures is not one of *representing* technoscience, but rather, "*articulating* clusters of processes, subjects, objects, meanings, and commitments" (1997: 63).

Yet in another sense, Haraway writes of figurations as productive, performative narratives or cultural technologies specific to Western culture, that have historically operated as "world-making machines" (180), producing what counts as reality. Drawing on Eric Auerbach's study of figuration in *Mimesis* (1953), Haraway reads scientific figures, practices and narratives as embodying a specifically Western and Christian sense of time and history, which she refers to as "salvation history," "a story that tends to fulfillment, to an ending that redeems and restores meaning" (1997: 44). She argues that technoscience is deeply invested in and reproduces salvation narratives, drawing on their tropes and story forms in secular form. These "sacred secular" salvation stories focus on the origins of life, the beginnings of time and civilization, the story of Man as progress, scenarios of apocalypse and disaster, and ultimate redemption and fulfillment.

Salvation history's approach to time is deferral to a promised fulfillment or salvation, so that "ordinary materialization," living within finite limits, is neglected in favor of living in the "time zone of amazing promises" (1997: 41). This sense of time and history infuses the figures of technoscience, which in the promises they hold, are "chronotopes," Mikhail Bakhtin's term for figures that organize a cultural sense of time and space. In the chronotope, which is "a center for concretizing representation" time, in Bakhtin's words, "becomes, in effect, palpable and visible; the chronotope makes narrative events concrete, makes them take on flesh" (Bakhtin, 1981: 250). This is illustrated in Haraway's reading of the gene as figure of technoscience in *Modest Witness* (1997). Haraway argues that the gene is fetishized, conceived as a stand-in or metonym for life. If, as Haraway holds, biology and evolution are comprised of ongoing interactive processes, in mutually sustaining, interdependent relations between multiple processes, then no one unit or aspect can be singled out as a discrete entity-unto itself, independent of these complex interactions. Yet the reductive view of the gene reduces it to information or code, a thing-in-itself and a "master element" that determines the organism's evolution. Haraway points to sociobiologist Richard Dawkins's view that the "body is merely the gene's way to make more copies of itself" (1997: 133). For Haraway, this misrepresents the complexity of both human beings as well as genes themselves, thereby illustrating Alfred North Whitehead's concept of the "fallacy of misplaced concreteness," that as Haraway writes, mistakes "abstractions for concrete entities, which are themselves ongoing events" (Haraway, 1997: 147).

Haraway's aim is not merely to untangle the figures' historical threads, but to inhabit and refigure their potential meanings, a refiguration oriented toward constructing alternative trajectories and other possible futures. Haraway occupies these figures of technoscience to "mutate" them, to reimagine from within the possible new relations engendered by a more responsible, accountable, transparent and democratic science.

The best-known example of this refiguration, though it pre-dates Haraway's use of the term, is the cyborg, from her 1985 essay, "A Manifesto for Cyborgs." Haraway calls the manifesto an ironic political myth, a "blasphemy" that nonetheless aims to remain "faithful to feminism, socialism and materialism" (1991: 149). The cyborg is a figure "in the belly of the monster," militaristic technoscience, that Haraway reoccupies and refigures toward feminist, anti-racist ends. The cyborg is a cybernetic organism, the coupling of organic body and machine that is a familiar staple of science fiction from the 1950s and after, and "also a powerful social and scientific reality in the same historical period" (1989: 17). Read against the grain of salvation history, the cyborg is a being that does not trade in the origin stories of Edenic birth, separation from the fullness of nature, or ultimate redemption. It is neither fully natural nor fully artificial, a boundary creature, that breaks down what Haraway would later term "human exceptionalism" (2008: 11) by blurring the boundaries between the human and animal, between the human and machine, and between the physical and nonphysical.

These blurred boundaries challenge social and feminist theory's assumption of the dualisms of mind and body, human and machine, and nature and technology that no longer apply in a postmodern world of coding and information processing. Haraway's incorporation of the machinic into the organic was also a response to certain strains in the discourses of ecofeminism that held a vision of an originary, pure nature that for Haraway was no longer workable as a basis for a feminist political response to technoscience. The meshing and connection of body and machine, in effect, undermines the distinction between the natural and the artificial, and puts into question the "natural" as a secure ground of knowledge and politics, an "imagined organic body to integrate our resistance" (1991: 154). Identity and being must become consciously crafted rather than naturally assumed. Haraway argues that survival depends upon thinking in new ways in order to avoid reinforcing these category dualisms, and to avoid either technophobia or its corollary, an uncritical celebration of technology.

Haraway's essay also addressed the politics of race and gender in global economic terms. Ultimately, the effect of cybernetic technologies, which Haraway refers to as "C3I" (command, communications, control, intelligence) has been "the translation of the world into a problem of coding" (164). Electronics and communication systems and industries facilitate a new global information economy, in which women, particularly in the developing world, play central roles. She argues that this state of affairs marks "an emerging system of world order ... a polymorphous, information system" which she calls "the informatics of domination" (161). This economic, military and political order must be confronted in socialist feminist politics and action.

The cyborg, then, is also a new political subject addressed to these technological, racial and gendered global relations. For feminist politics, a natural identity or unity of woman can no longer be assumed as an "innocent," history-free zone that feminism would try to liberate. Instead, Haraway holds out the promise of "women of color" as "a cyborg identity, a potent subjectivity synthesized from fusions of outsider identities" (174). She looks to writing by women of color who, in "seizing the tools to mark the world that marked them as other" have the power to transform cultural myth systems. Haraway turns to Chela Sandoval's (1991) concept of "oppositional consciousness" to articulate a feminist position that acts on the basis of conscious coalition and political alliance rather that that of natural identity (156).

Haraway's strategy of refiguration in "A Cyborg Manifesto" also draws on science fiction, which for her is political theory, a means of contesting for alternative possible worlds. She turns to cyborg figures from science fiction in the works of writers such as Octavia Butler (1987), Joanna Russ (1975), and Vonda McIntyre (1983) that challenge the status of human and that demonstrate boundary transgressions between humans and machines. She reads Vonda McIntyre's *Superluminal*, for example, that features characters with bionic implants, all of whom "explore the limits of language … and the necessity of limitation, partiality, and intimacy" in their fusion with technology (1991: 179). Octavia Butler's novel *Dawn*, which Haraway explored in more detail in the final chapter of *Primate Visions*, features Lilith, an African American woman who must negotiate genetic and reproductive exchange with an alien species. For Haraway, this is a tale that evokes the genocidal history of slavery that depends on Lilith's fight for survival and agency as she "mediates the transformation of humanity through genetic exchange" (1991: 179).

Among the figures that Haraway reads in her later work on technoscience in *Modest Witness* (1997) is OncoMouse, the first patented animal genetically altered to carry genes for cancer. Haraway reads OncoMouse as metonym for technoscience; it is a living, breathing animal, yet it is a figure for the imaginary relations of capitalism, a "dense node" of meaning. OncoMouse, as a patented animal, signifies the implosion of the biological with the commodity form. OncoMouse also becomes Haraway's interlocutor, a point of view that Haraway inhabits, as she encourages us to see the technoscientific world through the mouse's eyes. From this point of view, the question she poses to technoscientific practices and culture is "*Cui bono?* For whom does OncoMouse live and die?" (1997: 113). Haraway uses this point of view to invite readers to reflect on this question and to "take up and reconfigure technoscientific tools" in order to articulate the relationships between science and ethics differently.

Situated knowledge, modest witnessing, and diffraction

In Haraway's account of interactive knowledge making, the human partner in the process, whether a molecular biologist or science studies scholar, must acknowledge and practice from an awareness of their locatedness in these relations of knowledge. In her essay, "Situated Knowledge," Haraway reviews feminist critiques of objectivity (including her own past positions) and the alternatives they offer, to argue for knowledge practices as situated. Haraway begins with the critique of the positivist or empiricist conception of objectivity that purports to be able to conduct research from a detached, neutral position, which she refers to as "a conquering gaze from nowhere," a "God-trick" that authorizes "unlocatable, and so irresponsible, knowledge claims" (1991: 188). This claim to be able to observe from a neutral position, which she refers to in her later work as the "modest witness" (1997), is made from the "unmarked category" of universal, generic human that has historically excluded the lives, concerns or vantage points of those in culturally "marked" categories of racial, class, or gendered difference (1991: 188).

In critiquing the claims of objectivity, Haraway describes two "poles of a tempting dichotomy:" strong social constructionism and feminist standpoint theory. The strong social constructionist position argues that all knowledge claims are socially constructed and therefore contestable claims that reflect not truth, but the claims-making activities of the researcher. The risk of this perspective is that it can lead to a form of relativism in which no truth claims are seen as better or more adequate than any others. This can lead to a lack of engagement or accountability that is not unlike the disengagement of the positivist account; as Haraway argues, "Relativism is a way of being nowhere while claiming to be everywhere equally" (1991: 191).

The alternative, feminist critical empiricism, or feminist standpoint theory, draws on Marxist historical materialism to argue that located, embodied knowledge from women's particular vantage points can provide a more accurate perspective for making knowledge. Haraway considers the possibility of this critical standpoint "from below," cautioning against romanticizing it as a ground of authenticity or unity outside the entanglements of history or society. Further, Haraway cautions against a search for an ultimate standpoint, that would be "innocent" (1991: 191), free of the surrounding influences that feminists have argued compromise the claims of the positivist position. As she continues to emphasize in her work, Haraway sees such social locations as themselves immersed in, and complicit with, other contexts, subjects, and objects of knowledge practice – not only of the knowers' socio-historical location, but also in interaction with local and global discourses. Relationality, in all its complexities, takes precedence over fixed location.

Haraway's strategy in striving for both a sensitivity to socially constructed and contingent knowledge claims, and a less relativist, more embodied feminist empiricism that "takes a stand" for a better world, is crafting a new metaphor based on vision. Emphasizing that eyes "are active perceptual systems, building in translations and specific *ways* of seeing" (190), Haraway stresses the embodied specificity and partiality of vision, seeing from a particular vantage point, rather than the illusion of transcendent sight. Because it is partial, it is limited, and this vulnerability means that it must be more actively accountable for its mode of seeing, its "visual system," and the exclusions it might create. This is to be contrasted with both the "gaze from nowhere" of the unmarked category, as well as the vantage point of the subjugated, which, while having a better chance of a more critical vantage point due to its outsider position or "view from below" the dominant realms of power, nonetheless carries the risk of recreating a totalizing view outside history. Drawing on Nancy Hartsock's (1983) historical materialist conceptualization of a feminist standpoint, Haraway argues that a standpoint is not a location, but a fragile achievement, "the always fraught but necessary fruit of the *practice* of oppositional and differential consciousness ... not an abstract philosophical foundation" (1997: 198–199; see also p. 304, n. 32). For Haraway, this constructed, partial, vulnerable practice creates the conditions for connection with others across difference.

Haraway returned to this figure of the unlocatable "view from nowhere" in *Modest_Witness@Second_Millenium: FemaleMan© Meets OncoMouse™* (1997). Haraway derives the "modest witness" from the seventeenth-century chemist Robert Boyle, whose experiments with the air pump established the scientific method. Valid observations required a disinterested, neutral observer, a modest witness that Boyle's method represented. Yet, as Haraway argues, drawing on Steven Shapin and Simon

Schaffer's study *Leviathan and the Air Pump* (1989) this not only works to "stabilize matters of fact as objectively given," but it also established credible knowing, and as well as who could legitimately occupy the position of knower. Only those in the "unmarked" position of racial, gendered, and class privilege, were legitimized as credible witnesses. Haraway's intervention is to "mutate" the modest witness, to "queer the elaborately constructed confidence" of this position (1997: 24), to reimagine witnessing as more visible, accountable, implicated in and responsible to the worlds s/he studies.

Haraway further develops an optic metaphor to propose a situated knowledge practice of *diffraction*. Diffraction is a phenomenon in physics referring to the bending of light waves when encountering interference. A record of these waves yields not a simple copy or reflection of what is registered, but includes the interference patterns produced, and thus in Haraway's words, "shows the history of their passage" (2000: 103). In taking up this metaphor, Haraway refigures the process of knowing as not only embodied and located, but as explicitly opposed to representation, to a mirroring reflection of the "real." Diffraction registers the "difference patterns" and not "reflection of the same displaced elsewhere" (1997: 16; 268). It thereby seeks to avoid the illusions of objectivity, by inserting the knower more visibly into the field of knowledge. For Haraway, it is a kind of multiple literacy, when different discourses are read through one another, to productive effect (Haraway, in Schneider, 2005: 149).

Yet diffraction is not the same gesture as reflexivity, proposed by science studies scholars in the "strong social constructionist" position such as Steve Woolgar, wherein the knower turns the mirror back onto their own knowledge claims and their production. For Haraway, reflexivity does not escape the warp of mirroring, and "seems not to be able to get beyond self-vision as the cure for self-invisibility" (1997: 33). As she had argued in "Situated Knowledge," the aim is to "make a difference in the world" (36), to "take sides" in knowledge making rather than attempting to remain outside of the action.

Companion species

In *The Companion Species Manifesto* (2003) and *When Species Meet* (2008), Haraway studies relationality and cross-species interdependence in human–animal relations, as well as the entanglements of technologies, ecologies, and cultures. In this work, Haraway moves further into the terrain of the challenge to human exceptionalism, not through the blurred boundaries between human and technology, but to that between human and nonhuman animals. Haraway, in seeking to explore the "ontics and antics of significant otherness, in the ongoing making of the partners through the making itself" (2008: 165), studies the interactions of human and animal beings, their comingling and co-dependency across the "Great Divides" – Bruno Latour's term for Western cultural separation between nature and culture (Latour, 1993: 97; Haraway, 2008: 9). Companion species is a category that "insists on the relation as the smallest unit of being and of analysis" (Haraway, 2008: 165).

An animating theme in the companion species work is the co-evolution of dogs and humans in interaction with one another and with cultural technologies including cohabitation, selective breeding, and genetic testing to trace canid evolution. In this account of co-evolution, nature and culture implode, as species diversity and survival itself becomes dependent upon human management and scientific tracking systems. One of Haraway's main sites for the discussion of dog–human interactions is agility sport, drawing on her own experiences with agility sport trials with her Australian shepherd. In describing how she and her dog "co-trained" one another, she adapts Vinciane Despret's term "becoming-with," where humans and the animals they study mutually shape one another. As Haraway writes, humans and animals become "partners-in-the-making through the active relations of coshaping, not ... possessive human or animal individuals whose boundaries and natures are set in advance of the entanglements of becoming together" (2008: 208). Haraway asks how thinking and politics could be transformed by a respect and regard for animals in their difference, an acknowledgment and response that took the "risk of an intersecting gaze" (21). This requires avoiding anthropocentric projections and fantasies, in order to "meet dogs as strangers, as significant others, so that both can learn the corporeal semiosis of cross-species trust and enter the open of risking something new" (2008: 243).

A prominent example of this respect is Haraway's discussion of Barbara Smuts's efforts to study baboons. Smuts departed from her initial efforts to "habituate" to the animals – that is, to try to remain invisible in their presence – when she realized that she had to respond to their behavioral social cues and greeting rituals in order for the animals to feel comfortable with her. "Smuts had to enter into, not shun, a responsive relationship" with the baboons (25). Here Haraway uses this example to show how humans and animals are "together in situated histories, situated nature-cultures, in which all the actors become who they are *in the dance of relating*" (25, emphasis in original).

Haraway's framing of mutual human–animal responsiveness is grounded in an ethics of responsibility to other beings across the "discredited breach of nature and culture" (2004: 10), She argues for the importance of taking up the responsibility of involvement, curiosity, and care of nonhuman beings. Haraway turns to the etymology of her phrase: companion, Latin for *cum panis*, "with bread," connotating "messmates at table," and species, with its Latin root, *specere*, "to look" or regard, as well as its use as "kin and kind," the "the relentlessly 'specific' or particular and to a class of individuals with the same characteristics" (17). Haraway views the making and remaking of species as a process of "ongoing kin-kind work" (2006: 144) that remakes the categories. In this, she argues for a practice of "worldliness," which is curiosity about and responsibility towards others.

Haraway's framing renders difference as productive, to enable greater responsiveness to and knowledge of the other and of self, and in new and unexpected directions. This is created through a commitment to mutual knowing, expressed through the metaphor of a mutual gaze: "The ethical regard that I am trying to speak and write can be experienced across many sorts of species differences. The lovely part is that we can know only by looking and by looking back. *Respecere*" (164).

In addressing the social contexts for this mutual coshaping, she draws on Mary Louise Pratt's study of colonial encounters in her book *Imperial Eyes* (1992). Pratt uses the term "contact zone," to emphasize how cultures coming into contact, even in such asymmetrical relations of power, nonetheless alter one another and develop in particular directions only through their interactions. A parallel concept comes from anthropologist James Clifford's work on borders and contact regions where cultures become entangled. Haraway quotes Clifford to illustrate the relational aspects of cultural development: "Contact approaches presuppose not sociocultural wholes subsequently brought into relationship, but rather systems already constituted relationally, entering new relations through historical processes of displacement" (Clifford, 1997: 7, quoted in Haraway, 2008: 217). Haraway shows contact zones and cross-species interdependence in further examples from developmental biology and ecology, as well as ecological justice struggles, to argue that "most of the transformative things in life happen in contact zones" (219).

Haraway's ethical vision in the challenge to human exceptionalism is respect and regard across differences. It is also to avoid moral absolutes that in effect, allow humans to deny responsibility for their involvement with animals. Engagement with animals creates the conditions for being accountable to them, in working with them in asymmetrical relations, in for example, agriculture or laboratory research. Haraway rejects a humanist assumption of the superiority and rights of humans over animals, but also rejects an absolute prohibition for the use of lab animals, instead arguing for an ethics of "nonmimetic sharing" of suffering as an obligation to the animals one uses in research. A nonhumanist, companion species ethic strives for a recognition of the animals with which one is in relationship, in order to do what one can to lessen suffering, without seeking recourse to a comforting transcendent moral distance from them.

IMPACT

Haraway's work has had a transformational impact on a range of fields in cultural studies, science studies and feminist theory. One of the most influential essays has been "A Manifesto for Cyborgs," which has become, in the words of N. Katherine Hayles, a "legend of late 20th-century scholarship" (Hayles, 2006: 159). Haraway's cyborg figure, that stressed irony, partiality and the fusion of opposed terms, as well as affinity across differences, offered an alternative model – and new ways to think about – political subjectivity. As Zoe Sofoulis notes in her detailed review, the Cyborg Manifesto had a "seismic" effect, "jolting many out of their categorical certainties" and thereby transforming debates about identity in feminist and cultural studies (Sofoulis, 2002: 84).

The essay helped inaugurate "cyberculture" studies that drew on science fiction and developments in technology to explore the implications of body-technology fusions and linkages (Bell, 2007). As Haraway has noted, some of this work is based on a partial reading that focuses only on the technology-human interface, ignoring the feminist and anti-racist critique, leading to a "very blissed-out, techno-sublime position" (Haraway, 2004: 325). Yet as Sofoulis notes, Haraway's work created openings for exchange between social studies of science, feminist theory, and the humanities, in bringing themes and concepts from science studies into feminist and cultural theory. It encouraged feminists to acknowledge their complicity with technology, to "find something other than victim metaphors linking women with an idealized Nature from which technology was excluded" (Sofoulis, 2002: 85). The historical timing of the essay in the midst of the emergence of the Internet and World Wide Web fostered burgeoning exploration of virtual spaces, networks, and gender, race, and sexuality, in effect launching a new field of cyberfeminism (Sofoulis, 2001; Kirkup, et al., 1999).

While one review has argued that the cyborg was limited to its own historical juncture, such that it has outlived its usefulness and is now a "dead metaphor"

(Bartsch *et al.*, 2001: 141), others have found continued relevance in the cyborg figure. Sarah Franklin, in an assessment of the cyborg essay twenty-one years after its publication, argues that further advances in biotechnology since the publication of the cyborg essay and *Modest_Witness* make the cyborg more relevant than ever (Franklin, 2006). Franklin holds that Haraway's analysis of biotechnology as informatics is urgently necessary to address the "cyborg embryo," in developments such as assisted reproductive technologies, gene transfer, and tissue engineering, developments that fundamentally alter the meaning of the biological itself.

Haraway's work has had wide influence in science studies, and is among those scholars who incorporate matter and non-human objects or actants into their accounts of scientific practice, and as such, constitutes a turn toward ontological questions about the "nature of nature" (Barad, 2007: 72). Haraway's work, for example is central to Karen Barad's elaboration of scientific knowledge and practice in *Meeting the Universe Halfway: Quantum Physics and the Entanglement of Matter and Meaning* (2007). Barad's development of a performative conception of scientific practice builds on Haraway's concept of materialized figuration to develop an extensive account of science as a set of material-discursive practices. Barad's concept of "intra-action," in particular, in which the agencies of knowledge "do not precede, but emerge through, their interaction" (Barad, 2007: 33), resembles Haraway's relationality.

In feminist theory, Haraway's work figures prominently in the emergence of a "new materialism," in the assessment of Stacey Alaimo and Susan Hekman, the editors of *Material Feminisms* (2008). As they point out, new materialists do not simply bring in material themes nor critique their absence, but rather formulate new ways of understanding the relationship between matter and discourse. Haraway's work has been fundamental to this development, and she has created new frameworks for conceptualizing nature as enmeshed in human and nonhuman technological relations. Alaimo and Hekman note that one of the significant areas that Haraway's and others' revisioning of nature promises to transform is environmentalism. Rather than a "wilderness" model dedicated to the protection of an untouched nature, and that often pits the welfare of people against that of nature, a relational model such as Haraway's addresses the linked worlds of people, animals, and technologies affected by environmental issues.

Similarly, Haraway's work on companion species, with its critique of human exceptionalism and privileging of cross-species relationality, has contributed to the emerging field of animal studies more broadly (Lundblad, 2004). In addressing the question of cross-species relations, Haraway makes a contribution to related work in posthumanism in the sense articulated by Cary Wolfe as "the embodiment and embeddedness of the human being in not just its biological but also its technological world" (Wolfe, 2009: xv), though Haraway prefers the more expansive terrain captured by the term "companion species" over that of posthumanism (2006: 140).

ASSESSMENT

Haraway's work has helped to bring contemporary developments in technoscience and technoculture into the foreground of social theory. Her accounts of primatology and critical readings of technoscience figurations have given an enriched view of science as social practice, as imbued with and operative through cultural narratives and tropes, as well as a set of practices in action, as "science-in-the-making." In concepts such as the cyborg, figuration, diffraction, and material-semiotic objects, she has provided an original language to comprehend the ways technoscience has altered social relations, for example, the implosion or collapse of the biological and the informational, and the ways that coding and cybernetic systems logic has transformed social and economic relations.

Yet Haraway's language also draws on these biological and technological metaphors to reimagine cultural relations, to think toward possible alternative futures. Her ontology of relationality stresses the entanglement and co-creation of beings *through* these assemblages of human, technical, and animal relations. Haraway inquires into how these entanglements could be reimagined for more hopeful, life-affirming, and sustainable worlds. Haraway calls this reimagination a form of "cosmopolitics," a term she draws from Isabelle Stengers, in which "decisions must take place somehow in the presence of those who will bear their consequences" (2008: 83).

What is notable about this vision of politics is that it foregoes an effort to arrive at or hold out for an ideal world of nature, a kind of purity or self-certainty that Haraway's work has cautioned against. In this sense the political implications of Haraway's social theory are different from those that operate with more idealized conceptions of nature free of the contaminating effects of technology. For Haraway, this is a fantasy that reinforces a dualism between nature and culture, and that impedes the possibility of concrete engagement with others "on the ground," that is nonetheless animated by moral responsibility toward nonhuman nature.

While Haraway has in much of her work foregrounded cultural constructions of "what counts as nature," her emphasis on the agency of nature and of nonhuman actors works to dismantle social theory's prevailing conception of nature as a blank surface upon which culture writes, a passive resource for cultural projects. Haraway's ontology of relationality conceptualizes nature as lively, as a partner interimplicated with culture, an ongoing *enactment* or "corporealization," comprising "the interactions of humans and nonhumans in the distributed, heterogeneous work processes of technoscience" (1997: 141). Relationality, and an enlivened conception of nature, then, provides social theory with a transformed conception of culture as "naturecultures" – including scientific practices and relations with nonhuman animals, as more complex and emergent in material relations.

Haraway's concepts of situated knowledge and diffraction helped move social theory beyond the impasse between the relativism of a pure social constructivist position, and the risk of essentialism in the empiricist and standpoint theories. Haraway's epistemological contribution, particularly in the "Situated Knowledge" essay, is in her account of knowledge as embodied and situated, partial or interested in its vantage point, which helped avoid a "false choice between realism and relativism" in thinking about knowledge (1997: 16). But her metaphors freed embodiment from its fixed sense of location; while stressing the situated character of knowledge, Haraway's conception of vision is not a static conception of a position on a grid of cultural identities or significations, which can work to foreclose on the possibility of movement and change (Massumi, 2002: 9). Instead, she stresses vision as an active perceptual system, and knowledge making as emergent and enacted through changing relations with the worlds one is studying, not all of whom, Haraway stresses, are human. This includes immersing oneself in, and drawing from, the worlds and discourses of technoscience.

Another distinctive aspect of Haraway's work is her mode of writing and criticism that foregrounds her own "literary moves" (2004: 337). Haraway uses stories, figures, and tropes in science and science fiction as a means of redescribing or reimagining social reality. She describes "category work," strategies of "foregrounding and backgrounding," categories, and of using one set of categories to interrupt other categories, all of which she strives to make visible in her writing as "thinking technologies that have materiality and effectivity" (2004, 335). As Nina Lykke stated in an interview with Haraway, in Haraway's writing, "theoretical content, methodology, style and epistemology go hand in hand" (Lykke, 2004: 332). Haraway's use of humor and irony, for example, are a way of holding disparate categories in tension (Bartsch, 2001: 131). In her commitment to keeping categories in play, she writes in such a way as to keep meanings and their construction visible and open to contestation, to expose her own thinking practices.

In summary, Haraway's work has contributed a nuanced account of technoscience and of knowledge making that is attentive to difference and heterogeneity, without reinscribing the dualisms that can obscure the complexities of social life. For Haraway, technoscience is not confined to what scientific specialists are doing, but rather is our shared cultural condition, requiring active engagement and ethical responsibility to all those it affects. With her concepts of situated knowledge, figuration, and diffraction, she has articulated a strategy of knowing based on embodied vision that incorporates the discursive as well as material constructedness of knowledge. At the same time, her focus on nonhuman objects and actors has helped enrich what is meant by nature by enlivening it as a partner in relationship to human natural-cultural practices. Finally, Haraway's enhanced sense of relationality, captured in her use of metaphors, stories, and diffracted writing, provides an ethical vision of hope for possible alternative worlds.

Reader's Guide to Donna Haraway

The Haraway Reader (2004) is a collection of writings spanning the range of Haraway's work, and includes a previously published interview. The chapter "Morphing in the Order," originally published in 2000, is a particularly helpful retrospective reflection on her previous studies of primatology and technoscience. Haraway's 1991 collection, Simians, Cyborgs, and Women, provides a set of early essays, including her important contribution to feminist standpoint theory in "Situated Knowledges: The Science Question in Feminism and the Privilege of Partial Perspective," originally published in 1988 in Feminist Studies. Her extended critique of technoscience, including discussions of genetics, reproductive technologies, and racial taxonomies, is Modest_Witness @Second_Millennium. FemaleMan© Meets OncoMouse™. Feminism and Technoscience (1997). For animal and companion species studies, see The Companion Species Manifesto: Dogs, People, and Significant Otherness (2003) and When Species Meet (2008).

A good starting place for an overview and thematic discussion of Haraway's work is Joseph Schneider's Donna Haraway: Live Theory (2005), which includes an interview conducted for the book, as well as a comprehensive bibliography. For another thematic introduction as well as rich biographical material, see the extended interview in *How Life A Leaf: An Interview with Thyrza Nichols Goodeve* (2000). A helpful review of Haraway's "A Cyborg Manifesto" and its impact on a range of fields is Zoe Sofoulis's "Cyberquake: Haraway's Manifesto," in Darren Tofts *et al.*'s, edited volume *Prefiguring Cybercultures* (2002). For a more recent assessment of "A Cyborg Manifesto," see the series of articles in *Theory, Culture, and Society* edited by Mike Featherstone and Nicholas Gane (23(7, 8)). Haraway's contribution to cyberculture theory is discussed in David Bell's 2007 volume, *Cyberculture Theorists: Manuel Castells and Donna Haraway*.

Acknowledgment

I would like to thank the Five Colleges Women's Studies Research Center, Mount Holyoke College, for support during the writing of this chapter.

Bibliography

Writings of Donna Haraway

1976. *Crystals, Fabrics and Fields: Metaphors of Organicism in Twentieth-Century Developmental Biology*. New Haven: Yale University Press (North Atlantic Books, 2004).

1989. *Primate Visions: Gender, Race, and Nature in the World of Modern Science*. New York and London: Routledge.

1991. *Simians, Cyborgs, and Women: The Reinvention of Nature*. New York and London: Routledge.

1997. *Modest_Witness @Second_Millennium. FemaleMan© Meets OncoMouse™. Feminism and Technoscience*. New York and London: Routledge.

2003. *The Companion Species Manifesto: Dogs, People, and Significant Otherness*. Chicago: Prickly Paradigm Press.

2004. *The Haraway Reader*. New York and London: Routledge.

2008. *When Species Meet*. Minneapolis: University of Minnesota Press.

Interviews with Donna Haraway

1991. Cyborgs at Large. In Constance Penley and Andrew Ross (eds) *Technoculture*, Minneapolis: University of Minnesota.

1994. Possible Worlds: an Interview with Donna Haraway. Avery Gordon, in Michael Ryan and Avery Gordon (eds) *Body Politics: Disease, Desire, and the Family*. Boulder, Colorado: Westview Press.

1995. Writing, Literacy and Technology: Toward a Cyborg Writing. In Gary Olson and Elizabeth Hirsh (eds) *Women Writing Culture*. Albany: State University of New York Press, pp. 45–77.

2000. *How Like A Leaf: An Interview with Thyrza Nichols Goodeve*. New York and London: Routledge.

2004. Cyborgs, coyotes and dogs: A kinship of feminist figurations and there are always more things going on than you thought? Methodologies as thinking technologies. An interview with Donna Haraway conducted in two parts by Nina Lykke, Randi Markussen, and

Finn Olesen. In Donna Haraway, *The Haraway Reader*. New York and London: Routledge, pp. 321–342.

2005. Conversations with Donna Haraway. In Joseph Schneider, *Donna Haraway: Live Theory*. New York: Continuum Press, pp. 114–156.

2006. "When We Have Never Been Human, What Is to Be Done?" Interview with Donna Haraway Nicholas Gane. *Theory, Culture, Society*, 23(7, 8): 135–158.

Further Reading

Alaimo, Stacy and Hekman, Susan (eds) (2008) *Material Feminisms*. Indiana University Press.

Bakhtin, M. M. (1981) *The Dialogic Imagination: Four Essays*. Edited by Michael Holquist, trans. by Caryl Emerson and Michael Holquist. Austin: University of Texas Press.

Balsamo, Anne (1996) *Technologies of the Gendered Body: Reading Cyborg Women*. Durham, NC: Duke University Press.

Barad, Karen (2007) *Meeting the Universe Halfway: Quantum Physics and the Entanglement of Matter and Meaning*. Durham and London: Duke University Press.

Bartsch, Ingrid, DiPalma, Carolyn, and Sells, Laura (2001) Witnessing the postmodern jeremiad: (Mis)understanding Donna Haraway's method of inquiry. *Configurations*, 9(1): 127–164.

Bell, David (2007) *Cyberculture Theorists: Manuel Castells and Donna Haraway*. New York: Routledge.

Braidotti, Rosi (2006) Posthuman, all too human: Toward a new process ontology. *Theory, Culture, Society*, 23 (7, 8): 197–208.

Butler, Octavia (1987) *Dawn*. New York: Warner Books.

Campbell, Kristen (2004) The promise of feminist reflexivities: Developing Donna Haraway's project for feminist science studies. *Hypatia*, 19(1): 162–182.

Clifford, James (1997) *Routes: Travel and Translation in the Twentieth Century*. Cambridge, MA: Harvard University Press.

Clough, Patricia and Schneider, Joseph (2001) Donna J. Haraway. In Anthony Elliott and Bryan Turner (eds) *Profiles in Contemporary Social Theory*. London: Sage, pp. 338–349.

De Lauretis, Teresa (1984) *Alice Doesn't: Feminism, Cemiotics, Cinema*. Bloomington: Indian University Press.

Fausto-Sterling, Anne (1985) *Myths of Gender: Biological Theories About Women and Men*. New York: Basic.

Featherstone, Mike and Gane, Nicholas (2006) Introduction. *Theory, Culture, Society*, 23 (7, 8): 1–4.

Franklin, Sarah (2006) The cyborg embryo: Our path to transbiology. *Theory, Culture, Society*, 23(7, 8): 167–187.

Harding, Sandra (1986) *The Science Question in Feminism*. Ithaca: Cornell University Press.

Hartsock, Nancy (1983) The feminist standpoint: Developing the ground for a specifically feminist historical materialism. In Sandra Harding and Merrill B. Hintikka (eds) *Discovering Reality*. Dordrecht: Kluwer Academic Publishers, 283–310.

Hayles, Katherine (2006) Unfinished work: From cyborg to cognisphere. *Theory, Culture, Society*, 23(7, 8): 159–166.

hooks, bell (1981) *Ain't I A Woman: Black Women and Feminism*. Boston, MA: South End Press.

Ihde, Donald and Selinger, Evan (eds) (2003) *Chasing Technoscience: Matrix for Materiality*. Bloomington: Indiana University Press.

Keller, Evelyn Fox (1985) *Reflections on Gender and Science*. New Haven, CT: Yale University Press.

Kirkup, Gill, Janes, L., Woodward, K., and Hovenden, F. (eds) (1999) *The Gendered Cyborg: A Reader*. New York and London: Routledge.

Latour, Bruno (1987) *Science in Action: How to Follow Scientists and Engineers through Society*. Cambridge, MA: Harvard University Press.

Latour, Bruno (1988) *The Pasteurization of France*. Cambridge, MA: Harvard University Press.

Latour, Bruno (1993) *We Have Never Been Modern*. Trans. Catherine Porter. Cambridge, MA: Harvard University Press.

Lundblad, Michael (2004) The Animal Question. *American Quarterly*, 56(4): 1125–1134.

Massumi, Brian (2002) *Parables for the Virtual: Movement, Affect, Sensation*. Duke University Press.

McIntyre, Vonda (1983) *Superluminal*. Boston: Houghton Mifflin.

Penley, Constance and Ross, Andrew (1991) *Technoculture*. University of Minnesota Press.

Pickering, Andrew (ed.) (1992) *Science as Practice and Culture*. Chicago: University of Chicago Press.

Pratt, Mary Louise (1992) *Imperial Eyes: Travel Writing and Transculturation*. New York: Routledge.

Russ, Joanna (1975) *The Female Man*. Boston: Beacon Press.

Sandoval, Chela (1990) Feminism and racism. In Gloria Anzaldua (ed.) *Making Face, Making Soul: Haciendo Caras*. San Franciso: Aunt Lute, pp. 55–71.

Sandoval, Chela (1991) US third world feminism: The theory and method of oppositional consciousness in the postmodern world. *Genders*, 10: 1–24.

Schneider, Joseph (2005) *Donna Haraway: Live Theory*. New York: Continuum Press.

Sofoulis, Zoe (2002) Cyberquake: Haraway's manifesto. In Darren Tofts, Annemarie Jonson, and Alessio Cavallaro (eds) *Prefiguring Cyberculture: An Intellectual History*, Cambridge: MIT Press, pp. 84–104.

Subramaniam, Banu (2009) Moored metamorphoses: A retrospective essay on feminist science studies. *Signs: Journal of Women in Culture and Society,* 34(4): 951–980.

Trinh T. Minh-ha (1986/7) She, The Inappropriated Other. *Discourse*, 8.

Vint, Sheryl (2008) A family of displaced figures: An overview of Donna Haraway. *Science Fiction Film and Television*, 1(2): 289–301.

Wolfe, Cary (2009) *What Is Posthumanism?* Minneapolis: University of Minnesota Press.

Woolgar, Steve (1988) *Science, the Very Idea!* London: Tavistock Publications.

22

Bruno Latour

SAL RESTIVO

THE ONCE AND FUTURE PHILOSOPHER

Bruno Latour is, with the possible exception of Thomas Kuhn, the most widely influential student of science and society of the last fifty years. Like Kuhn, his most influential writings are more philosophical than scientific. His writing style, focus, and concepts address the interests of a wide audience and have gained him credibility across the intellectual landscape. He has been concerned throughout his career with the nature of "the social," but as a philosophical and ethnomethodological idea rather than a (social) scientific concept. The difference between social theory driven by ethnomethodology and sociological theory may help explain the wide influence of Latour's theories. Briefly, ethnomethodology describes the accounts people give of their own lives and sense-making activities; it does not share the theoretical or methodological toolkits, scientific and causal perspectives on, and assumptions about social life characteristic of sociology as a scientific enterprise. That difference is at the same time a source of tension between Latour's "sociology of associations" and classically driven sociology. Latour views "the social" within sociology as too general, too encompassing, and a "garbage" or residual category.

Latour was born into an elite family of wine growers in Beaune, Burgundy (close to Dijon, France) in 1947. His earliest studies in Dijon focused on theology and philosophy. He did a dissertation on the Catholic writer Charles Péguy. Latour received his doctorate in philosophy from the University of Tours in 1975. The French philosopher Michel Serres was an early influence on Latour. Latour was drawn to Serres's opposition to a privileged metalanguage for science, and his idea of translating between accounts. Serres's (1983) use of Hermes (and more recently *angels*) as a model for the messenger who translates between accounts and domains also appealed to Latour. Latour's mature social theory is greatly indebted to Serres.

The Wiley-Blackwell Companion to Major Social Theorists, First Edition.
Edited by George Ritzer and Jeffrey Stepnisky.
© 2011 Blackwell Publishing Ltd. Published 2011 by Blackwell Publishing Ltd.

Latour was stationed in Africa during his military service. Under the guidance of anthropologist Marc Augé, Latour carried out a study of colonialism, race, and industrial relations in Côte d'Ivoire. In 1975, with the aid of an invitation from his long time neighbor in Dijon, the neuroendocrinologist (and future Nobelist) Roger Guillemin, Latour moved to La Jolla, California to begin his celebrated laboratory ethnography at the Salk Institute. The study was carried out in collaboration with sociologist Steve Woolgar and funded by Fulbright and NATO fellowships. Latour taught at the École des Mines de Paris Centre de Sociologie de l'Innovation from 1982 to 2006. He is currently professor in the Centre de sociologie des organizations and vice president for research at the Institut d'études politiques de Paris.

Latour and Woolgar's pioneering laboratory ethnography *Laboratory Life: The Social Construction of Scientific Facts* (1979) helped launch the field of science and technology studies, already by then a developing research arena still trying to find its way onto the academic stage after a decade of research, publications, and meetings. This book (reissued in 1986) contained an agenda that unfolded into a career that has taken Latour far beyond science studies. That career has followed to some extent at least the path to becoming a dominant French philosopher schematized in sociologist Michelle Lamont's (1987) analysis of the career of Jacques Derrida. Briefly, some of the factors Lamont mentions that apply to Latour are: strong theoretical trademark; diffusion potential based on being ambiguous and adaptable; addressing fundamental questions and transcending classical works; and diffusion by prestigious scholars and journals. Reviewers consistently describe his works as provocative and important, radically original, witty, stylistically dazzling, and bold in their approach to problems everyone has become embroiled in. These problems have been generated in the contexts of structuralism, postmodernism, grammatology, narrative, and social and cultural critiques of history and theory.

In an intellectual world characterized by widespread skepticism about the status of sociology as a science (a skepticism that has a foothold even within the sociological community), Latour's criticism of the scientific claims of traditional sociology has been readily embraced and his status enhanced. His antipathy to sociology and to causal science has driven him away from sociology and anthropology (in spite of his self-definitions) and toward philosophy.

Latour is a founding member of the Society for Social Studies of Science (1975), a former president of the society (2004–2005), and a recipient of the society's J. D. Bernal Prize for distinguished contributions to the field (1992). Latour presented some initial findings from the Salk study at the first meeting of the society (November 1976) in a paper titled "Including Citation Counting in the System of Actions of Scientific Papers." There are already hints in this paper of an actor-network theory (ANT), Latour's major contribution to social theory (e.g. as explicated most recently in Latour, 2005). The development of ANT is also the work of Michel Callon and John Law (e.g. Law and Callon, 1988, 1989).

THE SOCIAL AND INTELLECTUAL CONTEXTS

By the time *Laboratory Life* was published, Karin Knorr-Cetina, Steve Woolgar, Doug McKegney, Sal Restivo (with Michael Zenzen), and a few others were already engaged in field studies of science. Sharon Traweek, who would become one of the most prominent anthropologists of science, was already working outside of this network at the SLAC national accelerator laboratory in Stanford, California. By the early 1980s, the work of the ethnographers had revolutionized our understanding of scientific practice. In combination with the studies undertaken by Harry Collins, Trevor Pinch, David Edge, Michael Mulkay, David Bloor, Donald MacKenzie, Steve Shapin, and others (primarily representing the Edinburgh and Bath schools) on replication, discourse, mathematics, and social histories of science, the ethnographies of science produced a new narrative in answer to the question "What is science?" Latour is one of the most prominent guides to our liminal times. The liminality of our era reaches to most of the fundamental categories and classifications that have guided human cultures for millennia in some cases and for the last few hundred years in the case of industrial societies. This liminality is driving some of the most significant and influential intellectual movements of our era. Nature–society, human–machine, male–female, person–fetus, and life–death are among the powerful dualisms that have become dramatically problematic. The very idea of science (along with those "good" terms rationality, truth, and objectivity) has been embraced by this liminality that threatens to engulf all of our values, goals, and gods. Traditional dichotomies have given way to complexities, non-linearities, and chaotic, fractal, and multi-logical ways of thinking, speaking, and seeing. We have encountered new phenomena across time and space on and off the planet; engaged new ideas, experiences, and values from east to west and north to south (politically, economically, and culturally); and we have endured enormous leaps in our knowledge about how the world around us works. The result is that we have been forced into new epistemological and ontological territories. It is important not to ignore the cultural inertia that sustains classical dichotomies. That inertia is fuel for caution when reading Latour's criticisms and challenges. Nonetheless it is difficult to ignore the signs of worldview and paradigm shifts and essential tensions that are widely visible features of our everyday and professional lives.

Our liminal era is producing hybrid ideas and concepts and monstrous entities on a new scale. One day we are accosted by cyborgs, the next day by *robosapiens*; cloned sheep march with "natural" cows and horses; mice are patented; some women sell their eggs, some men donate their sperm. No one has exploited this situation on the public and professional stages better than Latour. His prominence has tended to obscure the innovative contributions in this arena by feminist social theorists, beginning with Mary Daly in the 1970s and including scholars such as Donna Haraway, Gloria Andalzua, and Susan Leigh Star. Latour, nonetheless, has been a leader in exploring new ways of reworking our systems of categories and classifications. He has been among the leaders documenting the changes in worldview our emerging human ecologies are calling forth. Such efforts, now as in all liminal eras, necessarily strike us as awkward, counterintuitive, and obscure to different degrees. Latour's particular mix of counter-intuitives, even where his critics consider him wrongheaded and misguided, has the virtue of drawing our attention to the limits of our reigning categories and classifications. In a world of hybrids, monsters, and uncertainties it should not surprise us that Latour has produced theories and concepts that are themselves hybrids, monsters, and embodiments of uncertainty.

Latour can appear on the one hand as a charlatan and on the other as a creative strategist in the midst of uncertainties and complexities. Like science in one of his best-known graphics, he is Janus-faced. One face knows, the other face does not know yet.

This image gives us "science and technology" on the one hand and technoscience on the other hand. Perhaps to understand Latour we must look both ways – forward and backward in time. His advice is to recognize that we need to shift our activities and viewpoints just as science, nature, and actors/actants in general shift theirs. Here we have the foundation for a strategy that avoids dichotomies old and new as we move through time and space. Latour is not dogmatically opposed to dichotomies per se, only to those that are uninteresting and obstruct our research (Gane, 2004: 79).

Prior to the emergence of science and technology studies (variously science studies, technology studies, social studies of science and technology, and the new sociology of science) in the late 1960s, the question "What is science?" was primarily addressed by scientists themselves, philosophers and historians of science, and science writers. Sociologists of science also studied science but they were not seen by scientists as encroaching on their jurisdiction because (1) they championed science and viewed themselves as scientists, (2) they studied the sciences scientists themselves viewed as embodying the best of what science could offer the world, especially physics, and (3) they did not claim any analytical purchase on the content of science.

The new sociologists of science associated with science studies included social critics of science (such as Restivo, Ravetz, Rose, and Levidow) but for the most part still adopted an uncritical to worshipful orientation to science (in the works, for example, of Bloor and H. Collins). But it was their claim that they were now prepared to study the actual content of science that would eventually upset some scientists and many philosophers and historians of science. Latour became the whipping boy for these defenders of the faith because he was so outspoken, and so widely and wildly visible through his writings, lectures, and interviews. Underneath the attacks on Latour and science studies was a fervent resistance to sociology as a science, discipline, and profession and a widespread ignorance about the nature and findings of sociology. The so-called "science warriors" who initiated the science wars (see, for example and notably, Gross and Levitt, 1994) read postmodernism in general and the idea that science was socially constructed as meaning that science was arbitrary, not objective, and more fiction than truth. The science wars of the 1990s brought some scientists and philosophers into open conflict with social scientists and humanities scholars over the nature of science. Briefly, the conflict pitted "realists" (who believed in an objective "reality out there") against "social constructionists" whom they assumed (incorrectly) to be making relativist claims and challenging the validity of science (for the details of this controversy, see Restivo and Croissant, 2007: 225ff.). Latour, while trying in different ways to mollify the scientists and philosophers, at the same time has joined them in opposing a certain kind of sociology or perhaps sociology per se. Latour does not want to alienate the scientists who are his "subjects" and an important segment of the audience he wants to cultivate. One of the things he shares with many physical and natural scientists is a skepticism about the value and even the possibility of a scientific sociology.

THE MAJOR WORKS

Laboratory Life, Latour's best-known work (co-authored with Woolgar), was part of a movement that reworked our conventional ideas about how science works. The book is discussed in more detail further on. In *Science in Action* (1987), Latour offered readers a systematic rendering of this reworking, and showed us how to think anew about science and technology. He tied together the major achievements of science studies, namely the emphasis on practice, construction, the central role of inscription, and the institutional context of modern science. Latour turned these achievements into a general theory of science as a network building activity. With this book, we are a few steps closer to articulating the actor-network theory adumbrated in *Laboratory Life*. Latour's next book, *The Pasteurization of France* (1988), contributed to the development of actor-network theory by demonstrating that it takes more than a great man to produce and ground a discovery.

Louis Pasteur (1822–1895) is best known to the general public for inventing pasteurization. He contributed to reducing deaths due to puerperal fever, and developed the first rabies vaccine. Latour demonstrates that Pasteur's success in developing pasteurization was dependent on a network of forces that included public hygiene actors, physicians, and government interests. Pasteur's triumph – substantively and methodologically – was the outcome of competing forces and interests within a specific historical context. Pasteur's success (as an actant in a network of actants) in relation to other microbiologists was dependent on mobilizing various elements of the French public from farmers and industrialists to scientists and politicians.

Latour argues that society and scientific facts co-create each other simultaneously. Two Latourian axioms begin to come into sharper focus in this book. One is that it doesn't make sense to think in terms of "science and society;" the other is that there is no way to "reduce" the case of Pasteur to disciplinary sociology. But where Latour and his acolytes see the triumph of "irreductionism" over sociological reductionism, some critics see just another example of sociological analysis (e.g. see especially Restivo, 2005, but also Star and Griesemer, 1989; Amsterdamska, 1990). The problem here turns once again on the assumptions ethnomethodologists make about the world compared to the assumptions of scientific sociologists. Latour does not admit social facts amenable in the manner of Durkheim to scientific *qua* theoretical analysis. Therefore, Latour views sociology as reducing social life to scientific explanations; thus his alternative notion of "irreductionism." If we think of this sort of strategy in relation to physics instead of sociology, what could be made of an ethnomethodological physics? The very idea is self-destructive. If one assumes the reality of a physical world, the analysis of that world in terms of disciplinary physics is not reductionist. If one assumes the reality of a social world, the analysis of that world in terms of disciplinary sociology is not reductionist. Latour does not admit such a social reality, so in his terms scientific sociology is by definition reductionist (see the discussion on the debate between Latour and Bloor below).

In *We Have Never Been Modern* (1993), Latour continues to confound the taken for granted boundaries that separates humans and things, the physical and the social sciences, and the sciences and the humanities. Where hybrids abound, the myth of modernity totters. This book is a way station on Latour's path to an increasingly systematic and well-articulated actor-network theory. If modernity is a myth so must be one of its defining features, the idea of progress.

Latour's *Aramis* (1996) is a cautionary tale about technology and progress. Reviewers have described the book as "quirky" and filled with "stylistic excrescences" on the one hand, and as "eminently readable" and "strange and deep" on the other. Latour tells the story of a robotic transit system the French government designed for Paris during the 1970s and early 1980s. He tells this story by inventing a new genre, "scientifiction." The book interweaves fictional and real characters into a Rashomonesque tapestry designed to demonstrate once again the limits of sociology and the promise of actor-network theory. This book more than anything else Latour has written demonstrates his impressive capacity to mobilize wit, style, concepts, perspectives, bibliographies, empirical facts, and theoretical resources to create challenging hybrid theories. Even those who do not agree with his understanding of the sociological enterprise must conjure with an approach to reality which adopts sociology as one and only one of the resources to be brought to bear on a question or problem. It is difficult to argue with this approach, one that Nietzsche ([1887]1956: 255) long ago anticipated when he argued that the more eyes one brings to a situation the more objective the viewing will be. The heterogeneity of sociology itself affords us many different sociological eyes with which to view social reality. Symbolic interactionism in particular offers an important approach to the social that is in some ways competitive with ANT and in others a resource for ANT.

Pandora's Hope (1999) is purportedly Latour's reply to a scientist friend's question: "Do you believe in reality?" Latour mobilizes ANT in defense of the reality of science studies and the flawed nature of his friend's question. He begins by rehearsing the contributions of science studies to our understanding of science and reality. This is followed by case studies in which Latour's dictum "follow the scientists" is the research imperative. Latour's account of science studies is designed to answer skeptics and critics of the field. From the very beginning, science studies has been about documenting in ethnographic detail and with Geertzian "thick descriptions" (Geertz, 1973) the details of scientific practice. Latour, more than most of his colleagues, is concerned to bring into sharp relief the ways in which technology and science, the material and the human merge as our pictures of reality emerge, evolve, transform, and stabilize. Where and why given all this complexity did the idea that there is a reality we can fathom that is independent of our humanity come from? Latour wants to be the champion of ordinary people who are submissive to and intimidated by the warring claimants to "the facts" and ultimate truths.

Politics of Nature: How to Bring the Sciences into Democracy (2004) evidences the culmination of Latour's evolution from philosopher to sociologist and anthropologist to *über*-philosopher and naked metaphysician. Even if and where his metaphysics is in some self-contradictory sense "empirical," it is a philosophy more idealistic than realistic. The title and subtitle sizzle with the promise of saving us from ourselves, or more correctly from our categories and classifications, and from political tendencies driven by outmoded worldviews. In spite of his penchant for the empirical, his profound understanding of science and technology as interwoven practices, and his decades of critically dismantling our conventional ideas about science and society, in the end he has divorced himself from real problems, practical solutions, and the guidelines of the ecological-sociological imagination. We nonetheless are forced to engage with the limits of our taken for granted categories and classifications, and this is why the book is worth out attention.

Latour, who has traditionally shown little concern for a normative politics, now turns to a politics rooted in Plato's allegory of the Cave. He argues that that myth has given the West its ideas about science and society and the concept of the philosopher-scientist. Unlike the rest of humanity who only have access to the Cave's shadows, the philosopher-scientist can travel between the world of truth and the world of shadows, the social world. The myth of the Cave becomes a new starting point for an old idea in science studies: we have to distinguish the myth of Science from the actual practices of the sciences. Latour argues further that we have to distinguish on similar grounds the power politics of the Cave from politics in action. These distinctions flow from and reinforce the Latourian project of blurring the distinction between nature and society and between things and humans. The point of his argument is that we should reach our views on reality, the external world, and nature not by way of the travels and tales of scientists moving between the worlds of truth and the social world but rather through a representative "due process." In place of an assembly of things and an assembly of humans, Latour proposes a new constitutional politics in which there are no special envoys and no barrier to go over and come back from. The sciences and one could say "the politics" are no longer concerned respectively with nature and with interests. Scientists and politicians now work together to construct our view of reality. Curiously (but in a way that is consistent with the ethnomethodological program), the due process that gives us reality with representation leads us to all of the old forms – a reality out there, subjects and objects, humans, a cosmos – we constructed under the old constitution.

In *Reassembling the Social* (2007), Latour mobilizes all of his resources to mount a focused challenge to reigning ideas about society and "the social." He reiterates his claim that following Durkheim's imperative to explain social facts with social facts means "explaining" stable things in terms of other stable things. However useful this methodology may have been historically it is now obstructing and obscuring our ability to understand social life. The old theories and methods left out too many "things" or "facts" that enter into the social domain. These other things and facts cannot be taken into account if we think of the social as a kind of thing, a level of reified material reality. To understand scientists, we must follow them and document all the connections they make and engage; to understand society, we must follow it everywhere it goes and document all the connections it makes and engages. The new social science must focus on the process of assembling the social without prejudging what is and what is not social. Here, then, is the introduction to actor-network theory that many of Latour's admirers and critics have been waiting for. Here is Latour assembling actor-network theory.

The Theory

Working out actor-network theory has leveraged Latour's development of an alternative sociology, a sociology of associations opposed to a sociology of the social. Latour views this distinction as parallel to pre-relativistic physics (conventional sociology with its Durkheimian roots) versus relativistic physics (the sociology of associations, grounded in ethnomethodology, material-semiotics, and most recently in the work of Durkheim's contemporary Gabriel Tarde). The main methodological principle emerging out of Latour's studies and made explicit in *Science in Action* (1987) was "follow the scientists and engineers." This was the portal that led to ANT.

Already in the first chapter of *Laboratory Life*, Latour (with Woolgar) begins to dismantle the very idea of the social. Their concern with "the social" is different, they stress, from that of traditional (notably Mertonian) sociologists of science. It has become increasingly clear that Latour's understanding of "the social" is not just different from that of sociologists of science but that of sociologists in general. The focus on "the social" in *Laboratory Life* emphasizes the construction of "sense" in science, rather than the sorts of variables the Mertonians addressed (such as norms, rewards, and competition).

What, then, are the socially available procedures for constructing ordered accounts out of practices, discourses, and environments that appear initially to be chaotic? Some of Latour's colleagues discuss this in terms of constructing facts out of contingencies. Latour has mounted a formidable attack on cultural patterns of practice and discourse, categories and classifications that have concretized over centuries and resist our efforts to learn anew, to adapt to new situations, and to strategize politically in the wake of new political and ecological imperatives. It is important to recognize that while the laboratory scientists are constructing order out of disorder, Latour and Woolgar are constructing an orderly account out of the initial appearance of disorder in the laboratory. Later Latour (1988: 161) would say that one order is being created out of other orders. On the surface, the effort to make this approach seem like something innovative is belied by how closely it imitates classical ethnographies. At least some sociologists of the social appear to operate essentially as Latourian sociologists of associations but without losing the Durkheimian sense of the social.

It is instructive here to review accounts of anthropologists engaging a culture for the first time. Raymond Firth's (1936) introduction to *We, the Tikopia*, for example, clearly describes a process of creating order out of disorder or out of other orders. Such accounts demonstrate that Latour's effort to create a new sociology has continuities with classical ethnography. The Firth example is one of many more one could point to that demonstrate that Latour's sociology has been a part of classical and modern sociology all along. What *is* innovative is the idea that the account given by Latour and Woolgar is not privileged over the accounts given by the scientists themselves in terms of giving us access to a sociology of science. Even here, however, we hear echoes of ethnomethodology and anticipations of the new ethnography and the commitment to making anthropology the science of giving a voice to the Other. *Laboratory Life* plants the seeds of an assault on Durkheimian sociology and of the future science wars.

The marks of ethnomethodology pervade this account, and postmodern French philosophy (notably the works of de Certeau and Serres) underwrites the emphasis Latour and Woolgar place on science as the production of "fictions," connoting here literature and writing accounts and not falsehoods. After all the exegesis and critical evaluation is completed, it will turn out that Latour and Woolgar have made an invaluable contribution to the sociology of science, independent of the distinction between the social and associations. That is, they have neither denied the "out-thereness" of reality, nor the existence of facts; but they have stressed and empirically demonstrated that facts and realities are social accomplishments, the result of the practical, discursive work of scientists. On this point, they are at one with their post-Mertonian colleagues (including Bloor, Knorr-Cetina, R. Collins, Leigh Star, and Restivo), all of whom, however, distance themselves from Latour's claims about the demise of the social.

In 1986, Latour and Woolgar published the second edition of *Laboratory Life*. They added a postscript and eliminated the word "social" from the subtitle. In a section on "The Demise of the Social," Latour and Woolgar carry out the promise of their original study to understand how scientists themselves distinguish between "social" and "technical" factors. The idea of the social was useful to the Mertonians in their development of the concept of science as a social institution. It was equally useful to the Edinburgh School in its development of a sociology of scientific knowledge (SSK), constructed on the foundation of Bloor's "strong programme." Latour and Woolgar now claim that "the social" is no longer useful.

Perhaps the single most important focus for critics of ANT is that it seems to assign agency to nonhumans. ANT has been described by its founders as a material-semiotic method that maps relations between things and between concepts simultaneously. This means that the interactions we can observe in a bank, for example, are not just the interactions between people, but rather the network of interactions involving people, their ideas and concepts, and technologies. It is not clear why, when ANT is described in this way, it is any different from the way anthropologists view culture holistically in terms of the network of relations between socifacts, mentifacts, and artifacts (to use David Bidney's (1967) categories). This is a good place to recall the work of Ludwik Fleck ([1935]1979) who anticipated so much of Latour, not to mention Fleck's contributions to Kuhn's (1962) thinking. The anthropologist Mary Douglas (1986) has succinctly explicated the significance of Fleck and Durkheim for any sociology of knowledge.

Latour identifies more closely with anthropology than to sociology. The foil he makes of sociology from this position is somewhat forced. Opposing sociology from the anthropological perspective is based on a distinction without a difference, a matter of professional, disciplinary, and historical contingencies. His identification with anthropology as an interpretive discipline (as opposed to sociology-as-science) probably allows him to mobilize more humanities scholars, and anti-quantitative STS scholars and social scientists.

Let's look again at the example of the bank. In ANT terms, the bank is a network that under certain conditions can be treated as a unity, as an actor/actant. ANT stresses that networks are transient, constantly engaged in making and re-making themselves. Our relationships and our networks constantly have to be reconstituted, re-produced. Again, it is not clear what this idea achieves that hasn't already been achieved by sociologists like Harold Garfinkel and Erving Goffman. These two exemplars might readily be dismissed because they are idiosyncratic in the context of mainstream sociology. But we could as easily demonstrate the point with Weber and the sociologists who have followed in his wake, Merton no less than R. Collins.

Basic Concepts in Actor-Network Theory

ANT's focus is on actants. The term "actant" appears in the work of Lucien Tesnière as early as 1959. It is also associated with the works of Greimas ([1966]1986) and Kristeva (1967). Latour introduced the term "actant" into science studies to avoid speaking of "actors" acting or systems behaving. It is characteristically difficult to pin Latour down on definitions which seem to flow from him like Zen koans (cf. Zammito, 2004: 189). Giving him the benefit of the doubt, we can argue that this is just what is necessary in order to capture something about a world of great complexity and uncertainty that seems constantly to be outrunning our efforts to stabilize it conceptually. Latour's critics see shallow maneuvering, comic effects, and attention-getting strategies in his work. It doesn't help the matter when Latour himself refers to his work as a joke, and tweaks his readers with ambiguities and contradictions. We, however, have to consider whether he has hit on a strategy that has at least temporary relevance for a period in which worldviews are undergoing stress and change (cf. Restivo, 1985: 129–156). It is important to keep in mind that the heritage of the laboratory studies has been to keep the focus on matters that are not yet settled, not yet closed, and still mired in different degrees of controversy.

The critiques leveled against Latour often mischaracterize his position. Indeed, these are critiques that have been leveled against science studies researchers in general (notably in the science wars). Latour (1999: 299–300) claims explicitly that his critics are attacking someone with his name who defends all the absurdities he disputes: that science is socially constructed, that science is nothing more than discourse, that there is no "reality out there," that "everything goes" in science, that science is conceptually empty, that the more ignorant you are the better; that everything is political; that subjectivity and objectivity are inter-mingled; and "that the mightiest, manliest, and hairiest scientist always wins provided he has enough 'allies' in high places."

How is it that critics could make such a mistake? One answer is that Latour demands with the authority of the ethnographer that we rethink ideas about science that have gone unexamined; another is that science studies has invaded territories long held by more traditional disciplines; and finally, we cannot dismiss the possibility that the very idea of a sociology of science breaches powerful ideologies of science.

Already in his presentation at the first meeting of the Society for Social Studies of Science (1976), Latour is at work redefining things in the world of science so as to extend what it includes; he begins to draw the outlines of what he will later capture in the term "actant." In his 4S paper, he defines "literature" as a continuum which includes drafts, corrected manuscripts, private and public preprints, oral presentations of papers, posters, abstracts, and the finally published papers, reprints and copies. The very process of ethnography forces Latour to focus on the frontiers of science, watching unsettled science where we find chains of conflict, controversy, and modalities. What Latour sees in his Salk laboratory study is not facts plain and simple, but a continuous chain of activities.

In *The Pasteurization of France*, Latour mobilizes ANT in the interest of providing what amounts to a "thick description" (Geertz) of actants, of an actor-network. Society is not formed with the social alone; in this particular case, for example, we have to add the action of microbes. We cannot speak of something – science – done in laboratories and then speak of groups, classes, interests, and laws in a separate narrative. Instead we have to speak of actor-networks, and instead of thinking in terms of "forces" that cause this or that, we must think and speak of "weaknesses," "entelechies," "monads," or more generally "actants." Latour uses "actor," "agent," or "actant" without assuming actions or properties. They are "autonomous figures," and they can be individuals or crowds, figurative or nonfigurative.

These ideas can be very confusing, but the main thing is to avoid using the term "actor" which is often limited to humans; the virtue of the term "actant" is that it can refer to humans and nonhumans. People and things have "spokespersons" in the assemblage of an ANT and Latour borrows the term "actant" from semiotics to describe what the spokesperson represents. He now can describe the power of the scientific laboratory in terms of the number of actants it can mobilize around its findings and interests. In general, then, power is a function of the number of allies "the laboratory" or anyone, or any network can shape and enroll – mobilize – to support its findings and interests in an agonistic arena. If Pasteur speaks for microbes, the Curies can be said to speak for plutonium, Cantor for transfinite numbers, Einstein for photons, and so on. Perhaps the simplest definition of actant is the one Latour offers in the glossary for *Politics of Nature*; but he once again confuses his readers by pairing actor and actant as one entry. Actant applies to humans and non-humans, he writes. This is followed by "an actor is any activity that modifies another activity in a trial." Presumably, this is what he means by "actant," the non-anthropomorphic sibling of "actor." It helps to reflect on the use of the concept of actant in semiotics to reveal more clearly what Latour is trying to accomplish.

Originally, the concept of actant was invented to help readers of stories identify characters as one sort of actant or another: helper or opponent (the conflict axis); subject or object (the project axis); and sender or receiver (the communication axis). Characters could also be combinations of two or more actants. This framework offers a primitive narrative organization for a fairy tale. Something or someone is missing as the result of a villainous act. The subject lacks this object. The sender and the receiver contract to retrieve the missing object. The sender is high on the hierarchies of status, power, and privilege, which means the receiver incurs an obligation in this contract. The subject, with or without a helper, retrieves the object in combat with an anti-subject (opponent). This is known as "the test" (Hawkes, 1977; Tesnière, 1959). Latour (1987: 89–90) has translated this framework and imported it into science studies. The "things" that stand behind the texts of science are like the heroes of our epics. In some stories, heroes defeat dragons and save maidens. In some stories, hero scientists "resist precipitation" or "triumph over bismuth." The essence of the hero does not appear to us all at once but over time and retrospectively. What at one point is a list of actions eventually becomes clear as an essence.

Actants are characters, and they require spokespersons to turn them into actors (Akrich and Latour, 1992). By pairing humans and nonhumans, Latour makes it possible to assemble the greatest number of actants in a single world, an assembling carried out by the collective. The result is that there is no longer any need "to defend the subject against reification, or to defend the object against social construction. Things no longer threaten subjects. Social construction no longer weakens objects" (Latour, 2004: 80–81). The creation of an actor-network is known as "translation." Notice that Latour considers it useful to focus on a single actor (read "actant") and to see translation from that actor's perspective. The process of translation occurs in four stages. First a focal actor identifies and aligns itself with other actors who share its identities and interests. The focal actor sets itself as an "obligatory passage point" (OPP), and in this way renders itself "indispensable" (Callon, 1986). This is known as the problematizing stage. At the *interessement* stage, the focal actor is engaged in convincing others to accept its definition(s) of identities and interests. The stage in which the others accept the focal actor's definition(s) is known as enrollment. The fourth stage, mobilization, solidifies the shape, form, and scope of the network.

Six additional concepts help to flesh out the basic conceptual skeleton of ANT: inscription, irreversibility, punctualization, depunctualization, token, and techno-science. Inscription creates technologies designed to protect the interests of actors and networks (cryptography technologies are a transparent exemplar). Keeping in mind that *interessement* involves interrupting and ultimately triumphing over com-peting definitions, the idea of irreversibility refers to how likely it is to return to a situation in which alternative possibilities exist (Walsham, 1997). As Hardy, Phillips, and Clegg (2001: 538) note: "These strategies help to create convergence by locking actors into the network. The more fixed or stable it appears, the more 'real' and durable it becomes, and the less controversy and ambiguity are evident ... The aim, then, is to put relations between actors into 'black boxes' where they become a mat-ter of indifference – scientific 'facts,' technical artifacts, modes of thought, habits, forces, objects." The laboratory studies, viewed from this perspective, describe the process of translation from macrocosm (larger "outside" world) to microcosm (the laboratory), from laboratory activity to laboratory inscriptions, and from the labo-ratory back to the outside world (Callon, Lascoumes, and Barthe, 2009).

Punctualization refers to the fact that the components of complex systems, such as those of an automobile, are hidden from the view of the user. If a car breaks down, this can provoke the driver to recognize that the car is a collection of parts rather than just a vehicle that s/he can drive from place to place. This kind of aware-ness can also be kindled when parts of a network begin working in conflict with the network as a whole. This is referred to as "depunctualization." Social order in gen-eral and the working automobile in the example above are achievements of the act-ants interacting within actor-networks. Such creations are known as "tokens" or "quasi-objects" and they get passed from actants/actors to actants/actors across actor-networks. The more tokens circulate through a network the more they get punctualized and reified; a decrease in the circulation of a token results in depunctu-alization and a decrease in reification.

Early on in *Science in Action*, Latour (1987: 29, 174–175) "forges" the word "technoscience" in order to avoid endlessly writing "science and technology." Technoscience refers to "all the elements tied to the scientific contents no matter how dirty, unexpected or foreign they seem." This leaves "science and technology" (in quotes) "to designate *what is kept of technoscience* once all the trials of respon-sibility have been settled." We can see Latour's ANT strategy at work here. The term "technoscience" appears to have been introduced into philosophy by the Belgian philosopher Gilbert Hottois (1984) in the late 1970s. Hottois's concept of techno-science was not tied to a social theory of science but rather to Percy Bridgeman's notion of operationalization. In both cases, the term technoscience is designed to broaden our notions of science and technology. Notice that for Latour, technoscience implies a stage as well as a new stability. It is a stage within which science and tech-nology are composed of many different kinds of elements (or actants). Once the tri-als of responsibility are settled, we can once more distinguish science and technology (or in Latour's more exact terms, "science and technology").

Latour's translations within science studies revolve around mobilizing the concept of the actant and ANT and result in a clear separation between ANT and the strong programme (hereafter SP) in the sociology of scientific knowledge. Latour's principle antagonist is the author of SP, David Bloor. Latour's theory and critique of "the social" achieves a dramatic focus in his "vehement" (Bloor, 1999: 81) criticism of the sociology of knowledge and of SP. Bloor (1999: 82) claims that Latour's criticism of SP systematically misrepresents the programme and his alternative, "in so far as it is different, is unworkable." Latour and Bloor differ on what to do about the "subject-object schema." Latourian sociology simply rejects the schema. Bloor points out that there are many levels and interpretations of the schema, and that at least one is sociologically viable.

Latour versus Bloor

Latour criticizes sociology and SP for relying on "Society" to explain things. He is opposed to a Durkheimian sociology that explains social facts with social facts, and a SP that uses Society to explain Nature (Latour, 1992: 278). The issue for Latour is that sociology and SP do not take into account the ways in which non-social things and processes contribute to "Society," that is, to the social organization of our lives. Latour adopts the term "anthropology" for a project that is non-sociological, non-reductionist, non-naturalistic, and non-causal and not anything like the anthropological tradition that runs from Durkheim to Mary Douglas. That tradition is central to SP. Latour mistakenly assumes that the goal of SP is to use society to explain nature. The goal of SP is in fact to explain not nature but "shared beliefs about nature" (Bloor, 1999: 87). The debate between Bloor and Latour is not easily resolved. The reason in part is that differences in metaphysics (as Latour recognizes) and more broadly differences in worldview are at issue. We must in the end compare and contrast entire worldviews rather than little bits and pieces of epistemology, methodology, and ontology, a general strategy elegantly outlined by the philosopher of science Clifford Hooker (1975).

Latour wants to interrogate everything: science, nature, society, causality, and so on. Bloor wants to carry out interrogations on the grounds of the successful sciences. Parenthetically, notice that this could easily degenerate into a conflict between a Latourian antagonism to causal science and a Bloorian scientism. In his reply to Bloor, Latour raises the banner of anti-absolutism, the very banner Bloor waves in the face of those SP critics who understand relativism as the opposite of realism. Bloor has consistently stressed that relativism in SP is opposed to absolutism and even defined relativism as "disinterested research" (a classic philosophical and sociological definition of science; see Barnes and Bloor, 1982: n. 47).

Could it be that the result of this debate is to demonstrate that Bloor and Latour are at one on the nature of science and society? This would not be an unusual outcome. After all of his efforts to distance himself from Lakatos in *Against Method* (1975), Feyerabend joins him. And all radical appearances to the contrary, the more Kuhn explains Kuhn the clearer he makes it that he is more a traditional internalist historian of science than a sociologist of knowledge. The outcome of all of Latour's interrogations is that he lands on Bloor's territory. When we have interrogated all of the old forms – the subject/object schema, external reality, society, and nature using Latour's (2004) proposed new constitution and parliament, in the wake of the due process he demands, all of the old forms will be back. Latour's slogan is "No reality without representation." If all the forms are the same before and after representation, before and after due process, what has Latour added to our discourse except the Strong Programme and SSK? Bloor, indeed, claims just this, that Latour (1999: 113) has given us SSK "couched in a fancy vocabulary."

CRITIQUE AND OPPOSITION

Four main questions have occupied Latour's acolytes and critics – is he a constructionist (social or otherwise); is he a relativist; does he grant machines and material objects agency; and what discipline can he be assigned to? Latour himself claims that he is not a *social* constructionist; he is a relativist only in the same way, he says, that Einstein is a relativist; he is frustratingly ambivalent about the agency of objects; and if not a dominant French philosopher he is at least an *über-denker*. Forced to discipline him, I would choose philosophy over sociology or anthropology. Let's look more closely at Latour and social constructionism.

Latour's early education and training in philosophy and theology and his continuing exercise of philosophical analytical and discursive strategies in his research and writing underpin his defense of metaphysical narratives. His view of how the world works and what it "is" bears some resemblance to the views of the late physicist David Bohm. Bohm was at least as sensitive as Latour to the volatility and dynamics of the material world as well as the world of humans, their languages, and their cultures. Bohm's science is strikingly consistent with Latour's metaphysics (Restivo, 1985: 121–125).

As we approached the second millennium, the flux of categories and classifications and the proliferation of hybrids and monsters, increasingly came to dominate our everyday lives and the horizons of humanity. These are times that require great courage and imagination to engage, so it is not surprising that only a few thinkers like Latour come to the fore. But his work and his ideas are strengthened by the fact that a thinker like Bohm, stressing science as opposed to metaphysics, has seen contemporary liminal dynamics through the very lenses that Latour is seeking to change. Bohm (1976) even championed a verb-based language as one way of coordinating language and reality.

Does Latour consider himself a relativist? Yes and no. Is his sociology more metaphysics than science? Yes and no. Do machines have agency? Yes and no. It is easy to view Latour as a sort of Zen master, prying open black boxes, challenging the taken-for-granted, shaking us out of our complacency about everyday language – by drowning us in language games designed to enlighten us. There is method behind what sometimes can appear to be Zen sociology or less charitably, just a little joking. When the philosopher Graham Harman described Latour as an empirical metaphysician, Latour countered by stressing that while philosophy and metaphysics are significant aspects of his research program the main thrust of his approach is to engage in empirical research. He accepted with good humor someone's description of him as a "serial re-describer." Latour's approach has roots in ethnomethodology, arguably a methodology of translation (translating phenomena into the language of ethnomethodology) but certainly not a scientific methodology. Nonetheless, Latour's book *Politics of Nature* is nothing if not an exercise in unadulterated metaphysics.

He addresses issues ranging from science and philosophy to world politics, ecology, and the body. He is always "trespassing" onto the territories of other scholars and specialties. This is, on the one hand, characteristic of the general theorist, and especially of the philosopher. On the other, this opens Latour up to attacks on many different fronts.

The difference between the sociologists of the social and the sociologists of association is a red herring. Latour claims that the former can be called on to study stable social orders, but that the latter are needed to study and understand social orders in process. But there is no reason to make such a distinction unless one is ready to defend the claim that in any field of study you need two different sciences to study statics and dynamics. For the Durkheimian "sociologists of the social," the other issue is that if we make "everything" social, we lose sight of the unique qualities that obtain in the social interactions of humans – the ties that bind: belongingness, community, solidarity, emotional coupling. Indeed, when he chooses Tarde over Durkheim as his starting point, he reveals why his social theory does not rise to the level of a scientific sociology. At the same time, he ignores the influence of Tarde on pragmatism and Chicago school sociology. Tarde is a more subtle sociologist than I can demonstrate here, but see Tarde ([1899]2009).

Tarde locates the origin of social changes in the "individual" and the "single mind" (cited in Latour, 2005: 15). For Durkheim, society precedes the individual; the individual is a social unit, a social fact. Humans come onto the evolutionary scene not as individuals who then at some Hobbesian point choose to come together socially by way, for example, of a social contract. Rather, humans emerge everywhere, always, and already social. Latour's preference for Gabriel Tarde over Emile Durkheim amounts to an attack on the sociological imagination (C. Wright Mills), the sociological cogito (Randall Collins), social constructionism (Sal Restivo, Karin Knorr-Cetina), and the form of symbolic interactionism inspired by Anselm Strauss. In Latour's defense, it is important to note that the sociology of associations stresses the in-betweenness of things classically held to be inside individuals. Emotions, for example, are in-between, relational; so is consciousness. When humans and objects interact, relational phenomena emerge. There are forms of emotion that characterizes our relations with the shells we pick up as we stroll along a beach, and with the computers and robots we interact with. The more interactive and the more humanoid the object the more salient the emotional relationship will be. In this sense, then, the concept of actants and networks of actants can be enlightening. The problem is not to lose sight of the unique nature of the relationships between human beings, and the roots of a certain privileged form of being human in those relationships. We are different kinds of humans interacting with each other and interacting with objects.

Latour is a formidable social theorist, but this does not automatically make his work sociological. His criticism of the sociologists of the social ignores the fact that sociologists as different as George Lundberg, Nicolai Bukharin, Howard Becker, and Randall Collins have addressed the very issues and problems Latour claims require ANT. Like many philosophers, he is prepared to claim jurisdiction over a discipline (sociology in this case) and to define idiosyncratically the nature and subject matter of the field. If sociology has to be reconfigured, so be it. Latour has tried to do this without understanding first what it is that sociologists do. He has abandoned social constructivism/ionism without persuading many of his science studies colleagues that he has discovered an alternative to the constituting activities of social relations. And that, after all, is what social construction means: we have no recourse outside of our interactions – our social humanity – for constituting the world (Restivo, 2005). Latour has underestimated the diversity of contemporary "sociology." This has trapped him in a caricature of a universe he doesn't inhabit and sees only from afar. It is important to keep in mind continuously that the issues here turn on whether we accept ethnomethodology as a mode or school of sociology or rather as an opponent of or alternative to sociology.

David Berreby (1994) conjured the image of a boxing match when he titled an essay, "And now [one can almost hear the implied 'in this corner'], overcoming all binary oppositions … that damned elusive Bruno Latour." Latour's elusiveness is due in great part to the increasingly philosophical voice he has adopted combined with the wider and wider scope of the issues he has taken on. His philosophy, once empirically grounded, has moved onto a metaphysical plane divorced from the social and political realities of everyday life. If he started his career with the promise of helping to fashion a Copernican revolution in the sociology of science, he has evolved into a thinker who reminds us more of Rousseau or Hobbes. This helps explain his ready dismissal of the perspectives and findings of the social sciences. His plan for bringing the sciences into "democracy" is more Platonic and transcendental than empirical. He writes more and more in a tradition that pays serious attention to bats, armadillos, aliens, and idealized humans in trying to achieve insights about real humans and the human condition. His ideas about democracy, for example, owe more to the Platonic philosophical imagination than to empirical political economy.

His elusiveness is as much a function of his unquestionably elegant literacy and logic as it is to his cleverness, wit, and playfulness. He is without question an engineer of brilliant insights on science and society. Yet he seems to put some of his readers into an adoring trance with his neologisms, doodles, and wit. On the other hand, his critics describe him as obscure and self-indulgent. He wants a reasoned dialogue with his reader but he wonders whether he is raising questions for himself and himself alone (Latour, 2004: 6). It is always worth navigating Latour's counterintuitives but the dangers are everywhere – solipsistic meanderings, clichés, pithy Confucianisms (e.g. "today's enemy is tomorrow's ally"). It is the game of plurals that is his forte. Where once it was obvious that we had science and nature, he leads us toward sciences and natures – and politics. He is a piper leading us out of Plato's cave where the West's view of "science and society" was born.

Science studies have given us the sciences as social practices and discourses. This empirically grounded view of the sciences is indisputable. The further lesson that Latour draws from science studies, that sociology's conventional toolkit must be eliminated, is far less convincing. The disagreements on this point and on the social construction conjecture with Bloor, Restivo, Knorr-Cetina, and others do not trouble Latour. He advocates something akin to Richard Rorty's (1981) imperative to keep the conversation going. For Latour, there is nothing sinister or dangerous about these disagreements; they are merely differences to be played out on the field of "politics." The pluralism in Latour's theory, to the extent that it is salient, does not rise to the level of the pluralist theories developed by the feminists, black and queer social theorists, and women and minority voices in Brazil, Africa, India, and elsewhere outside the Euro-American sphere.

This then continues the conversation of the Western philosophers, and does so politely under the rules of a gentlemen's club. It is, however, hard to ignore the vocabulary of warfare that marks Latour's rhetoric. If this rhetoric was derived from sociological theory, from conflict theory for example, it might be more persuasive. In Latour's hands, this rhetoric is just another strategy for mobilizing adherents and a philosophical undertaking rather than an empirically grounded political economy.

His most recent philosophy *cum* metaphysics – empirical or not, science-like or not – is more like the story-telling he advised as an alternative to explanation early in his career. At the end of the day, it will fall to Latour's readers to balance the applause of his most adoring acolytes against the damnations of his most volatile critics. This won't be easy because Latour transforms ANT as he goes. In Latour (1999: 1), four things do not work with ANT: actor, network, theory, and the hyphen; in Latour (2005: 9), ANT fits Latour's project "very well." Are networks, indexed in Latour (2005), the key idea, or is circulation, not indexed in that same volume, more to the point (Latour, 1999: 19)? If, however, the balance is true, and readers weigh the pros and cons fairly, they might readily and reasonably conclude that Latour is a social theorist to conjure with, a social theorist to think with, and one of the most learned and eloquent guides to our time and place as the twenty-first century unfolds.

Reader's Guide to Bruno Latour

One of the best ways to engage Latour's ideas is to follow him through one of his many interviews. Gane's (2004) interview allows Latour to articulate his views on sociology. See also Crawford's (1993) interview with Latour on the eve of the outbreak of the science wars; and his review of *We Have Never Been Modern* (Crawford, 1994). For an in depth reading of Latour as a social theorist, see Zammito (2004). Zammito contextualizes Latourian social theory at the near end of the post-positivism study of science that has Willard Quine at the far end. Zammito characterizes Latour in relation to some of his more prominent colleagues in science studies including Haraway, Longino, and Pickering. Zammito tends to side with Latour in the Latour-Bloor debate. Perhaps the best introduction to Latour as a philosopher can be found in Harman (2009). Latour himself can be as good a guide to his ideas as his champions and translators. For one example, see his essay in WIRED (Latour, 2003). For those readers coming to Latour for the first time, Dave Harris (2005) of University College Plymouth has written an accessible guide to Latour's Science in Action and the basic ideas of Actor-Network Theory. One of the earliest critiques of ANT arose in the context of the development of the concept of boundary objects in the works of Susan Leigh Star and her colleagues (Star and Griesemer, 1989; Star, 1989; Bowker and Star, 1999). For a Marxist perspective on ANT, see Rudy and Gareau (2005). The symposium they introduce highlights the most persistent criticism of Latour and ANT, the failure to address issues of social justice, inequality, and power. Among Latour's colleagues in STS, Restivo (2005) and Amsterdamska (1990) have written essays that criticize him on the same grounds, even in the wake of his increasing focus on democracy and world peace. In her review of *Science in Action*, Olga Amsterdamska criticizes Latour for what she claims is a "might makes right" approach to understanding science, a constant rhetoric of warfare, and a confused understanding of reality; Restivo's review of

Politics of Nature focuses on Latour's turn to philosophy and the poverty of his sociology. For a recent defense of a "post-ANT" ANT, see Gad and Jensen (2010). Gad and Jensen come close to arguing that ANT is little more than a distillation of how to do science based on what we have learned from the ethnographers of science about scientific practice but without causality and with a deification of complexity and uncertainty.

Acknowledgments

I would like to thank the following readers for their kudos and cautions, criticisms and suggestions on this chapter during various stages of its preparation: Randall Collins (Pennsylvania), Jennifer Croissant (Arizona), Abby Kinchy (RPI), Michelle Lamont (Harvard), Julia Loughlin (Syracuse), Jerry Ravetz (Oxford), and Leigh Star (Pittsburgh).

Bibliography

The writings of Bruno Latour

1979 (with S. Woolgar). *Laboratory Life: The Social Construction of Scientific Facts.* Thousand Oaks, CA: Sage Publications.

1986 (with S. Woolgar). *Laboratory Life: The Construction of Scientific Facts: With a New Postscript by the Authors.* Princeton NJ: Princeton University Press.

1987. *Science in Action.* Cambridge, MA: Harvard University Press.

1988. *The Pasteurization of France.* Cambridge, MA: Harvard University Press.

1988. A relativist account of Einstein's relativity. *Social Studies of Science,* 18: 3–44.

1992. Where are the missing masses? The sociology of a few mundane artifacts. In W. E. Bijker and J. Law (eds) *Shaping Technology/Building Society: Studies in Sociotechnical Change.* Cambridge: MIT Press, pp. 225–258.

1992 (with M. Akrich). A summary of a convenient vocabulary for the semiotics of human and non-human assemblies. In W. E. Bijker and J. Law (eds) *Shaping Technology/Building Society: Studies in Sociotechnical Change.* Cambridge, MA: The MIT Press, pp. 259–264.

1993. *We Have Never Been Modern.* Cambridge, MA: Harvard University Press.

1996. *Aramis, or The Love of Technology.* Cambridge, MA: Harvard University Press.

1996. Social theory and the study of computerized work sites. In W. J. Orlikowski, G. Walsham, M. R. Jones, and J. I. DeGross (eds) *Information Technology and Changes in Organizational Work.* London: Chapman & Hall, pp. 295–307.

1999. For Bloor and beyond: A response to David Bloor's "Anti-Latour." *Studies in History and Philosophy of Science,* 30(1): 113–129.

1999. Factures/fractures: From the concept of network to the concept of attachment. *Research,* 36: 20–31.

1999. On recalling ANT. In J. Law and J. Hassard (eds) *Actor-Network and After.* Oxford: Blackwell, pp. 15–25.

1999. *Pandora's Hope: Essays on the Reality of Science Studies.* Cambridge, MA: Harvard University Press.

2002. Gabriel Tarde and the end of the social, In P. Joyce (ed.) *The Social in Question: New Bearings in History and the Social Sciences.* London: Routledge, pp. 117–132.

2002. *La Frabrique du droit. Une ethnographie du Conseil d'Etat.* Paris: La Découverte.

2002. *War of the Worlds: What About a Peace*. Chicago: Prickly Paradigm Press.

2002 (with M. Akrich, M. Callon, *et al.*). The key to success in innovation; Part I: The art of interessement and the key to success in innovation; Part II: The art of choosing good spokespersons. *International Journal of Innovation*, 6(2): 187–225.

2003. The promise of constructivism. In D. Ihde and E. Selinger (eds) *Chasing Technoscience: Matrix for Materiality*. Bloomington: Indiana University Press, pp. 27–46.

2003. The World Wide Lab; Research Space: Experimentation without representation is tyranny. *WIRED*, November 6: 147.

2003. What if we were talking politics a little? *Contemporary Political Theory*, 2(2): 143–164.

2004. How to talk about the body? The normative dimension of science studies. In M. Akrich and M. Berg (eds) Bodies on trial. *Body and Society*, 10(2, 3): 205–229.

2004. *Politics of Nature: How to Bring the Sciences into Democracy*. Cambridge, MA: Harvard University Press.

2004. Why has critique run out of steam? From matters of fact to matters of concern. *Critical Inquiry*, 30(2): 225–248.

2005 (with P. Weibel (eds)). *Making Things Public: Atmospheres of Democracy*. Cambridge, MA: MIT Press.

2007. *Reassembling the Social: An Introduction to Actor-Network Theory*. Oxford: Oxford University Press.

2008. The Netz-works of Greek deductions: A review of Reviel Netz's *The Shaping of Deductions in Greek Mathematics*. *Social Studies of Science*, 38(3): 441–459.

2008. Will non-humans be saved. *Journal of the Royal Anthropological Institute*, 15: 459–475 (publication of the annual Henry Myers Lecture, Royal Institute of Anthropology, London, September).

2008 (with Albena Yaneva). Give me a gun and I will make all buildings move: An ANT's view of architecture. In Reto Geizer (ed.) *Explorations in Architecture: Teaching, Design, Research*. Basel: Birkhäuser, pp. 80–89.

2009. Perspectivism: Type or bomb? *Anthropology Today*, 25(2), April: 21–22.

2009. Spheres and networks. Two ways to reinterpret globalization. *Harvard Design Magazine*, 30, Spring/Summer: 138–144.

Forthcoming. Tarde's idea of quantification. In Mattei Candea (ed.) *The Social After Gabriel Tarde: Debates and Assessment*.

Further Reading

Amsterdamska, Olga (1990) Surely you are joking, Monsieur Latour! *Science, Technology, and Human Values*, 15(4), Autumn: 495–504.

Barnes, B. and Bloor, D. (1982) Relativism, rationalism and the sociology of knowledge. In Martin Hollis and Steven Lukes (eds) *Rationality and Relativism*. Oxford: Basil Blackwell, pp. 21–47.

Berreby, D. (1994) And now, overcoming all binary oppositions, it's ... that damned Elusive Bruno Latour. *Lingua Franca*, 4(6), October: 26.

Bidney, D. (1967) *Theoretical Anthropology*. New York: Schocken Books (2nd edn, Edison NJ: Transaction Publishers, 1995).

Bloor, D. (1999) Anti-Latour. *Studies in History and Philosophy of Science*, 30(1): 81–112.

Bohm, D. (1971) *Chance and Causality in Modern Physics*. Philadelphia: University of Pennsylvania Press.

Bohm, D. (1976) *Fragmentation and Wholeness*. Jerusalem: Van Lee Jerusalem Foundation.

Bowker, G. C. and Star, S. L. (1999) *Sorting Things Out: Classification and its Consequences.* Cambridge, MA: MIT Press.

Callon, M. (1986) Some elements of a sociology of translation: Domestication of the scallops and the fishermen of St Brieuc Bayin. In John Law (ed.) *Power, Action and Belief: A New Sociology of Knowledge.* London: Routledge & Kegan Paul, pp. 196–233.

Callon, M., Lascoumes, P., and Barthe, Y. (2009) *Acting In An Uncertain World: An Essay On Technical Democracy.* Cambridge, MA: MIT Press.

Crawford, T. Hugh (1993) Interview with Bruno Latour. *Configurations,* 1(2), Spring: 247–268.

Crawford, T. Hugh (1994) Book review: B. Latour, *We Have Never Been Modern. Configurations,* 2(3), Fall: 578–580.

Douglas, M. (1986) *How Institutions Think.* Syracuse: Syracuse University Press.

The Eighth Social Study of ICT workshop, SSIT8 (2008): The Habitat of Information: Social and Organizational Consequences of Information Growth, April 25.

Feyerabend, P. (1975) *Against Method.* London: Verso.

Firth, R. (1936) *We, the Tikopia.* New York: American Book Company.

Fleck, L. ([1935]1979) *Genesis and Development of a Scientific Fact.* Chicago: University of Chicago Press (orig. publ. in German).

Gad, C. and Jensen, C. B. (2010) On the consequences of post-ANT. *Science, Technology, and Human Values,* 35(1), January: 55–80.

Gane, N. (2004) Bruno Latour: The social as association. In Nicholas Gane, *The Future of Social Theory.* New York: Continuum, pp. 77–90.

Geertz, C. (1973) Thick description: Toward an interpretive theory of culture. In C. Geertz, *The Interpretation of Cultures: Selected Essays.* New York: Basic Books, pp. 3–30.

Greimas, A. J. ([1966]1986) *Sémantique structurale.* Paris: Presses universitaires de France.

Gross, P. R. and Levitt, N. (1994) *The Higher Superstition.* Baltimore: The Johns Hopkins Press.

Hardy, C., Phillips, N., and Clegg, S. (2001) Reflexivity in organization and management studies: A study of the production of the research "subject." *Human Relations,* 54(5): 3–32.

Harman, G. (2009) *Prince of Networks: Bruno Latour and Metaphysics.* Melbourne AU: re.press.

Harris, David (2005) Reading guide to Latour, B (1987) *Science in Action.* Available online at www.arasite.org/latour.html (accessed November 25, 2010).

Hawkes, T. (1977) *Structuralism and Semiotics.* Berkeley: University of California Press.

Hooker, C. (1975) Philosophy and metaphilosophy of science: Empiricism, popperianism, and realism. *Synthèse,* 32: 177–231.

Hottois, Gilbert (1984) *Le signe et la technique. La philosophie à l'épreuve de la technique,* Paris: Aubier Montaigne.

Kornfeld, W. and Hewitt, C. (1981) "The scientific community metaphor" IEEE transactions on systems, man and cybernetics. SMC-11.

Kristeva, Julia (1967) L'Expansion de la sémiotique. *Information sur les sciences sociales,* 6(5), October: 169–181.

Kuhn, T. (1962) *The Structure of Scientific Revolutions.* Chicago: University of Chicago Press.

Lamont, M. (1987) How to become a dominant French philosopher: The case of Jacques Derrida. *American Journal of Sociology,* 93(3), November: 584–622.

Law, J. (1987) Technology and heterogeneous engineering: The case of Portuguese expansion. In W. E. Bijker, T. P. Hughes, and T. J. Pinch (eds) *The Social Construction of Technological Systems: New Directions in the Sociology and History of Technology.* Cambridge, MA: MIT Press, pp. 111–134.

Law, J. and Callon, M. (1988) Engineering and sociology in a military aircraft project: A network analysis of technical change. *Social Problems*, 35: 284–297.

Law, J. and Callon, M. (1989) On the construction of sociotechnical networks: Content and context revisited. *Knowledge and Society*, 9: 57–83.

Martin, M. and McIntyre, L. C. (eds) (1994) *Readings in the Philosophy of the Social Sciences*. Cambridge, MA: MIT Press.

Nietzsche, F. ([1887]1956) *The Geneology of Morals* (bound with *The Birth of Tragedy, 1872)*. New York: Doubleday Anchor.

Prades, J. (1992) *La Technoscience: Les fractures des discours*. Paris: Editions L'Harmattan.

Restivo, S. (1985) *The Social Relations of Physics, Mysticism, and Mathematics*. Dordrecht: D. Reidel.

Restivo, S. (2005) Politics of Latour, review essay. *Organization and Environment*, 8(1), March: 111–115.

Restivo, S. and Croissant, Jennifer (2007) Social constructionism in science and technology studies. In Jim Holstein and Jaber Gubrium (eds) *Handbook of Constructionist Research*. New York: Guilford, pp. 213–229.

Rorty, R. (1981) *Philosophy and the Mirror of Nature*. Princeton: Princeton University Press.

Rudy, A. P. and Gareau, B. J. (eds.) (2005) Actor-Network Theory, Marxist economics, and Marxist political ecology, a symposium. *Capitalism Nature Socialism*, 16(4), December: 85–90.

Serres, M. (1983) *Hermes: Literature, Science, Philosophy*. Baltimore: Johns Hopkins University Press.

Star, S. L. (1989) The structure of ill-structured solutions: Boundary objects and heterogeneous distributed problem solving. In Les Gasser and M. N. Huhns (eds) *Distributed Artificial Intelligence, Vol. 2, Research Notes in Artificial Intelligence*. London: Pitman, pp. 37–53.

Star, S. L and Griesemer J. R. (1989) Institutional ecology, "Translations" and boundary objects: Amateurs and professionals in Berkeley's Museum of Vertebrate Zoology, 1907–39. *Social Studies of Science*, 19(4): 387–420.

Tarde, G. ([1899]2009) *Social Laws: An Outline of Sociology*. Bibliolife, Open Source (orig. publ. by Macmillan in London).

Tesnière, L. (1959) *Eléments de syntaxe structurale*. Paris: C. Klinsieck.

Toews, David (2003) The new Tarde: Sociology after the end of the social. *Theory, Culture and Society*, 20: 81–98.

Walsham, G. (1997) Actor-Network Theory and IS research: Current status and future prospects. In A. S. Lee, J. Liebenau, and J. I. DeGross (eds) *Information Systems and Qualitative Research*. London: Chapman and Hall, pp. 466–480.

Zammito, John (2004) Women, ANTs, and (other) dangerous things. In John Zamnito, *A Nice Derangement of Epistemes: Post-Positivism in the Study of Science from Quine to Latour*. Chicago: University of Chicago Press, pp. 183–231.

23

Judith Butler

MOYA LLOYD

THE PERSON

Currently, the Maxine Elliott Professor in the Departments of Rhetoric, Comparative Literature and Gender and Women's Studies at the University of California, Berkeley, Judith Butler, was born in 1956 in Cleveland, Ohio to an Ashkenazi Jewish family of Hungarian, Polish, and Russian extraction. She trained initially as a philosopher. As she notes in a rare autobiographical essay, her first introduction to philosophy was a "radically deinstitutionalized one" (Butler, 2004a: 235). Closeted in the basement of her family home, smoking, the "sullen and despondent" teenage Butler read her parents' philosophy books (2004a: 236): amongst them, Søren Kierkegaard's *Either/Or*, Arthur Schopenhauer's *The World as Will and Representation* and, of particular note, Baruch Spinoza's *Ethics*, whose idea of the *conatus* (the desire to be that endures even in desolation) made a significant and long-lasting impression on her (see Butler, 2006a).

By contrast, Butler's "institutionalized philosophical career" (2004a: 238) began at the synagogue she attended in her hometown. As punishment for persistently missing Hebrew class, the fourteen-year-old Butler was required to take classes with her rabbi. Tutorials followed: on Spinoza, existential theology and the relation of German idealism to Nazism, all topics selected by Butler. This philosophical education continued at Bennington College, Vermont, and then at Yale University, where she received her BA in philosophy 1978. She remained at Yale as a graduate student, gaining her MA in 1982 and then her PhD in philosophy in 1984. Prior to her graduate studies, Butler won a Fulbright scholarship enabling her to attend the lectures and seminars of Hans Georg Gadamer at the University of Heidelberg.

After Yale, Butler spent three years at Wesleyan University, first as a visiting faculty member and then postdoctoral fellow at the Center for the Humanities, during

The Wiley-Blackwell Companion to Major Social Theorists, First Edition.
Edited by George Ritzer and Jeffrey Stepnisky.
© 2011 Blackwell Publishing Ltd. Published 2011 by Blackwell Publishing Ltd.

which time she revised her thesis for publication as *Subjects of Desire: Hegelian Reflections in Twentieth-Century France*. Following a year (1987–1988) spent at Princeton at the Institute for Advanced Study Butler became Assistant Professor of Philosophy at George Washington University. It was while at Princeton and George Washington that Butler wrote *Gender Trouble*. By the time the book was published in 1990, however, Butler had moved to Johns Hopkins University where she stayed until 1993 when she joined the faculty of the University of California, Berkeley, where she has remained since.

Since *Gender Trouble*, Butler has written eight further monographs. In 1993 *Bodies That Matter* appeared. In 1997 she published two books: *The Psychic Life of Power* and *Excitable Speech*. This was followed in 2000 by *Antigone's Claim* and in 2004 by both *Precarious Life* and *Undoing Gender*. 2005 saw the publication of *Giving an Account of Oneself* and 2009 *Frames of War*. A tenth anniversary edition of *Gender Trouble* was issued in 1999, complete with a new preface. That same year, *Subjects of Desire* was also reissued, it too with a new preface. Butler has also collaborated on a number of books, including *Feminist Contentions* with Seyla Benhabib, Drucilla Cornell and Nancy Fraser and in 2000, *Contingency, Hegemony, Universality* with Ernesto Laclau and Slavoj Žižek.

Judith Butler is very much an activist academic. Since the mid-to-late 1970s, she has been actively involved in both gay and lesbian and in feminist politics. In 1982 she participated in the Barnard Sexuality Conference, often reckoned to mark the start of the "sex wars" in feminism, reporting on the conference for *Gay Community News*, a radical gay and lesbian periodical of the time. Between 1994 and 1997 she chaired the International Gay and Lesbian Human Rights Commission. In addition, Butler has lent her support to a variety of causes to do with sex, gender, and sexuality, including petitioning for the recognition of kinship relations not based on marriage (same-sex or otherwise) and supporting the work of the Intersex Society of America. She has engaged in political debates about hate-speech and affirmative action. Drawing on her theoretical interests in ethical responsibility, mourning, and violence, she has spoken out against the wars in Afghanistan and Iraq; prisoner detention at Abu Ghraib and Guantanamo Bay; and intervened publically in debates about the Palestine–Israel conflict, supporting the cultural boycott of organizations and institutions that are not explicitly opposed to the occupation.

Amongst her many honors, which include the Brudner Prize for Lifetime Achievement at Yale in 2004 and an Andrew W. Mellon Foundation Distinguished Achievement Award for her contribution to scholarship in the humanities in 2008, in 2007 the scholar who was determined to maintain some distance from the "institutionalized life" of philosophy was elected a member of the American Philosophical Society.

THE SOCIAL CONTEXT

A significant factor influencing the development of Butler's thought was the rise of identity politics; specifically within the women's movement and the gay and lesbian movement. For all their differences, these two movements shared a number of important characteristics: each sought to overcome the specific forms of oppression and marginalization members of their particular group (women or gays and lesbians) experienced; each challenged conventional understandings of politics and political action; and each based its politics around the affirmation of a shared identity. Very soon each also found itself dividing internally over that latter idea.

Within the women's movement, the initial catalyst was the criticism of Black women and women of color that not all women experienced oppression in the way imagined by those at the heart of the movement. Soon other dissenting voices were added to these. Within the academy, the challenge to the idea of a unified female/feminine identity came from feminists influenced by psychoanalytic and/or post-structuralist ideas. The gay and lesbian movement underwent a parallel series of developments. Immanent criticisms were leveled by lesbians and gays of color about its ethnocentrism. Increasingly, tensions surfaced between gays and lesbians about the values and direction of the movement, with some lesbians becoming more and more critical of the masculinism of gay culture. During the so-called "sex wars" of the late 1970s and early 1980s, lesbians were further divided between the "sex radicals" ("pro-sex" lesbians who affirmed the value of practices such as sado-masochism and pornography), and those lesbians, often radical feminists, who conceived of women as essentially life affirming and (often) of "sex" as a social construct designed to oppress women. Together these developments not only brought to the fore questions about how sex and sexuality ought to be theorized, paving the way for the emergence of queer theory. They also placed the question of how to understand identity – women's or gay and lesbian identity – center-stage.

Another vital element in understanding the development of Butler's thought is the impact that the Holocaust and its aftermath had on it. Like many other Jews, Butler's family had direct experience of the camps: her mother lost most of her family in them. Moreover, her Jewish education was framed by these events; they provided the context for ethical debate, raising in particular questions about acknowledging mourning and loss. They shaped her choice of reading material; her refusal to engage with Nietzsche initially was because of his purported anti-Semitism (Butler, 2000d). This confrontation with the past, together with her Judaism more broadly – the values and interpretive practices she has embraced, its philosophical heritage – has influenced and indeed continues to influence much of her work. She has become increasingly open about it over time in both interviews and writing (see, for instance, Butler, 2000d, 2004a, 2006b, 2010) and one of her current projects is a book on Jewish philosophy, examining pre- and post-Zionist criticisms of state violence.

The final event of importance in shaping Butler's thinking is September 11, 2001, when almost three thousand people were killed in a series of terrorist attacks in the US. Like other Left intellectuals Butler found herself in fundamental opposition with the policies adopted by the Bush Administration in the aftermath of 9/11, particularly what appeared to be a rush to unwarranted violence. In a series of publications, therefore, Butler spoke out against these policies by showing how they reinforce a series of politically and ethically problematic distinctions between human lives that are valued, grievable and in need of protection, and those that are none of those things (2002a, 2003a, 2004a, 2009).

THE INTELLECTUAL CONTEXT

Endeavoring to assess the intellectual influences on Butler is not easy because she draws on such a wide range of traditions in philosophy, psychoanalysis, gay and lesbian criticism, and feminism. Nevertheless, it is possible to isolate a few of the most salient. The first, after her Jewish education, is undoubtedly the work of German Idealist philosopher, Georg Wilhelm Friedrich Hegel, the theorist *par excellence* of alterity and recognition. Butler's doctoral thesis, "Recovery and Invention: The Projects of Desire in Hegel, Kojève, Hyppolite, and Sartre," supervised by Maurice Natanson, a phenomenologist and scholar of Husserl, is an examination of the influence on conceptions of desire of Hegelian ideas in France during the 1930s and 1940s. Hegelian themes (particularly desire, Otherness, and recognition) have continued to shape her work since then both directly and indirectly; indeed, she has suggested herself that "[i]n a sense, all of my work remains within the orbit of a certain set of Hegelian questions" ([1987]1999a: xiv). And so it seems: *The Psychic Life of Power* contains an essay on Hegel and "the unhappy consciousness" (1997a: 31–62). Hegel's ideas of recognition are explored in both *Giving an Account of Oneself* and in *Undoing Gender*. Butler's understanding of "universality" is heavily indebted to Hegel (see, for instance, 1996a; Butler in Butler, Laclau and Žižek, 2000).

Most readers of Butler tend to pigeonhole her, however, as a "poststructuralist"; someone steeped in particular French traditions of thought associated with Jacques Derrida, Michel Foucault, Jacques Lacan, and Julia Kristeva, amongst others, centering on ideas such as anti-essentialism, anti-foundationalism, suspicion of grand narratives, an opposition to teleological accounts of history, and a distrust of metaphysics. This is certainly true but it was not always thus. Butler was initially resistant to and skeptical of such approaches. Instead, she concentrated her attentions on phenomenology (the influence of which can be seen in the essays leading up to the publication of *Gender Trouble*), existentialism, the Frankfurt School, as well as hermeneutics and German Idealism, as already mentioned. Matters changed, however, when she left Yale for Wesleyan.

The first signs of this are the revisions made to her doctoral thesis for publication. *Subjects of Desire* contains new material on Kristeva, Foucault, Derrida, and Gilles Deleuze. Around the same time, Butler also began publishing a series of articles on sex, gender, and sexuality (1986a, 1986b, 1988, 1989a, 1989b, 1989c). Most of them center on the feminist phenomenologist Simone de Beauvoir, whose ideas were to prove particularly influential in the development of Butler's account of gender performativity. Increasingly, however, in these articles, Butler begins to blend insights taken from the work of Michel Foucault with those of Beauvoir. Foucault's ideas had been particularly important in debates on identity in the gay and lesbian movement, because of his anti-essentialist view, advanced in *The History of Sexuality: volume one*, that homosexuality is a discursive construct. For Butler, though this approach to identity is important, it is his idea on sex and on norms that prove to be most significant. By contrast, Derrida's inspiration appears most explicitly when Butler sets out to address the concerns about agency that followed the publication of *Gender Trouble* and in her treatment of hate-speech in *Excitable Speech*. As we will see, it is the idea of iterability or citationality that Derrida develops in his critical reading of J. L. Austin that Butler evokes.

Her work is also shaped by feminist debates. The first, alluded to above, is one that preoccupied feminism throughout the late 1970s and much of the 1980s concerning the "subject" of feminism. It centered round the question "What is a woman?" and whether a universal shared experience of oppression was the necessary ground of feminist politics (see Lloyd, 2005). The other body of feminist ideas influencing Butler as will become clear is that associated with thinkers as diverse as Monique Wittig, Adrienne Rich, and Gayle Rubin, which centered on the idea that the naturalization of heterosexuality, based on the assumption of binary sex, was political, serving to secure male privilege – patriarchy – and to marginalize homosexuality. *Gender Trouble*, in particular, addresses both.

Butler is also influenced by psychoanalysis, particularly by Freud, though to a lesser degree by Jacques Lacan too. Although commentators often gloss over it, Butler's theorization of subjectivity is, as *The Psychic Life of Power* makes particularly clear, a psychoanalytically informed one. For all that, however, Butler is nevertheless deeply critical of the investment of both forms of psychoanalysis in presumptive heterosexuality (see Lloyd, 2007).

THE THEORY

Performativity – rethinking sex, gender, and sexuality

Butler's principal contribution to feminist theory is her discussion of gender performativity; an approach that in its attempt to denaturalize heterosexuality is also regarded as foundational to queer theory. Her concern in *Gender Trouble*, in particular, is with the way sex and gender are produced in terms of "the heterosexual matrix" (an expression that evokes Wittig's idea of the "heterosexual contract" (1980, 1981)). The argument Butler advances is important for a number of reasons: first, because it calls into question the way that the relation between sex and gender had been conventionally conceived within feminism. Second, because the account of gender performativity she develops, in fact, encompasses far more than just simply gender; it extends to matters of sex, sexuality and the body as well. Finally, it has significant implications for how identity is conceived; not as the expression of an inner truth of the self or a natural property of the subject but rather as an effect of power/discourse.

A basic feature of Anglo-speaking feminism throughout the 1970s and 1980s was its attempt to distinguish sex from gender. Sex connoted the innate biological traits distinguishing men from women while gender was explained as the social, psychological, and cultural features ascribed to men and women (that is, masculinity and femininity). Feminists stressed the distinction in order to demonstrate that since gender was constructed it could be challenged or even eliminated. In so doing, however, they *assumed* rather than questioned the naturalness of sex (and, indeed, the body). When, therefore, in *Gender Trouble*, Butler begins her interrogation of the relation between sex and gender and, in particular, contends that sex is constructed, she is responding to this over-sight in much prior feminist work. Instead of assuming that sexual difference is the natural (biological) substratum on which gender is built, she contends radically and controversially that gender is, in fact, the "apparatus" producing it as such (Butler, 1990a: 7). She thus not only disputes those logics that assume sex causes gender (or, putting it differently, that gender identity is an expression of sex); she also contests the feminist assumption that sex and gender must necessarily share the same binary structure, with femininity mapping onto female bodies and masculinity onto male ones.

Butler bases her argument that sex is the product of the gender apparatus, in part, on Foucault's claims, in *The History of Sexuality*, that sex is not an idea "*in itself*" but one "that was formed inside the deployment of sexuality" (1978: 152). He denaturalizes sex by suggesting that within this deployment it is a means to unify a range of "anatomical elements, biological functions, conducts, sensations, and pleasures" (Foucault, 1978: 154). Butler denaturalizes it by demonstrating how it operates in the service of presumptive heterosexuality where it is a component element of the "heterosexual matrix": the "hegemonic discursive/epistemic model of gender intelligibility through which bodies, genders, and desires are naturalized" as heterosexual (1990a: 151 n.6). Here biological sex is seen naturally to give rise both to the pertinent gender identity (masculine for men; feminine for women) and to desire for a person of the opposite sex (and gender). It is precisely the normative – or, rather, hetero-normative – dimensions of these relations (between sex, gender, and desire) that Butler sets out to trouble, first, as we have just seen, by showing that sex is a construct that is presented as pre-discursive or natural and, second, by producing an account of gender that is able both to demonstrate how the subject acquires a gender identity and how hetero-normative idealizations of gender can be challenged. She does the latter by arguing that gender is performative.

The concept of performativity initially originates in speech act theory; specifically, in the work of English philosopher, J. L. Austin where it is used to denote a specific kind of linguistic utterance: words that "do" things (1962). The idea of *gender* performativity, by contrast, grows out of Butler's engagement with Beauvoir's idea that "One is not born, but rather becomes, a woman" (1983 [1949]: 295; see Butler, 1986a, 1986b, 1988, 1989a). It thus begins life as part of Butler's attempt to develop a phenomenological account of gender centered on a "politics of performative gender acts" (1988: 530). In these early articles, Butler is interested in three aspects of Beauvoir's work: the implied distinction between sex and gender suggested by being born versus becoming a woman; Beauvoir's understanding of the body as an "historical idea" (Butler, 1989a: 254); and what the verb "to become" signifies in respect of gender. The first two are central to the arguments discussed above: that there is no necessary connection between sex and gender and that "lived or experienced 'sex,'" as Butler puts it, "is always gendered" (1986a: 39). The last aspect – the concern with becoming – is the key to understanding gender as performative.

Butler speculates that, according to Beauvoir, what it means to "become" a woman is not just that gender is constructed; it implies that it is also "a process of constructing ourselves ... a purposive and appropriative set of acts" (1986a: 36). These are not freely chosen acts; at least, not entirely. They are acts that are constrained by established gender norms. Understood thus, gender is to be conceived of as "an incessant project, a daily act of reconstitution and interpretation" of these norms (Butler, 1986a: 40); or, as Butler writes of Beauvoir elsewhere, it is "an identity instituted through a *stylized repetition of acts*" (1988: 519).

For all her sympathy for Beauvoir's position there is, nevertheless, one facet that troubled Butler: its apparent individualism. To redress this deficiency therefore, in

"Performative Acts and Gender Constitution" (Butler, 1988), she supplements Beauvoir's phenomenological account of acts with a so-called "theatrical" account, deriving from the work of social anthropologist Victor Turner. She draws on Turner's contention that human life as ritual social drama depends on the repetition of social performances to highlight how compulsory heterosexuality secures its hegemonic status. The repetition of a performance, for Turner, is the means by which its accrued meanings are re-enacted and the social laws it embodies routinely legitimated. The same is true for gender performances, Butler suggests: they are the means by which the binary, hetero-normative, structure of sex and gender is maintained and the illusion of an essential sex or true gender identity produced. As such gender reality is *performative*: "real only to the extent that it is performed" (Butler, 1988: 527).

By the time *Gender Trouble* is published, however, Butler's argument has shifted in notable ways: the reading of Beauvoir outlined above has been abandoned; all *explicit* references to a phenomenological theory of constituting acts have disappeared from the text; and Butler's debt to Turner is hidden in a footnote. Yet the basic substance of and much of the language used in this earlier account remains – that the illusion of a gendered self is a result of the "*stylized repetition of acts*" (Butler, 1990a: 140); that such acts are fundamentally corporeal – though they are now presented as parts of Butler's *own* account of gender performativity. This time, too, the idea that distinguishes Butler's work from earlier dramaturgical accounts of social performance, such as that of Erving Goffman, that "there is no gender identity behind the expressions of gender" (Butler, 1990a: 25), is iterated not via Turner and Beauvoir but by way of Nietzsche's claim in *On the Genealogy of Morals* that "there is no 'being' behind doing, effecting, becoming" (cited in Butler, 1990a: 25). Gender, it is now said, exists *only* in the "doing" – the repetition – of a specific (normalizing and historically sedimented) corporal repertoire or "style of the flesh"; a doing that constitutes the gendered subject not one performed *by* them.

Significantly, for Butler, the repetition that produces the illusion of a gender identity is also the practice that has the capacity to denaturalize heterosexuality. In an argument indebted to Esther Newton, Butler suggests in *Gender Trouble* that the same imitative structure that underpins drag, the focus of Newton's anthropological study *Mother Camp*, underpins gender. *Both* are forms of impersonation; however, although drag is often assumed to parody an original identity, it is Butler declares, in fact, a parody "*of* the very notion of an original" (1990a: 138; see also Butler, 1991). *All* gender is a form of imitation. Even though heterosexual genders (those where sex, gender, and desire converge) may *appear* to be natural, they are not. Their *naturalization* rests on their miming what idealized heterosexual gender is supposed to be like. The only difference when the drag queen apes femininity is that his performance potentially exposes this derivativeness by *de*-naturalizing the relations between sex, gender and desire, since his sex does not accord with his gender performance, which raises further questions about his sexuality.

The purpose of Butler's argument here is to demonstrate that heterosexuality, though compulsory can be (momentarily) destabilized. While there are often costs attached to violating heterosexual norms, those norms can be subverted. In the original preface to *Gender Trouble* she proposes parody as a strategy with the potential to resignify and to proliferate the categories of sex, gender, body and sexuality "beyond the binary frame" (Butler, 1990a: x). She makes it clear, however, that parody is subversive *only* when it divulges the constituted character of gender and thus discloses its performativity, a clarification several of her readers missed. Butler's next book, *Bodies That Matter* is, in part, a response to the criticisms directed at *Gender Trouble* and, in particular, to the charges that drag was necessarily subversive and that one's gender could be redesigned at will (Butler, 1993a). Her aim here is to demonstrate how, when there is no " 'doer' behind the deed," political action to destabilize gender norms is nevertheless possible (Butler, 1990a: 25). Her answer involves a reorientation of the notion of performativity via Derrida's account of iterability.

Derrida sketches this idea in his discussion of the distinction Austin sets out in *How to Do Things with Words* between serious and non-serious uses of language (1988). Derrida takes issue with Austin's description of the latter, found in poems and plays, as "parasitic upon" ordinary language use (Austin, 1962: 22), suggesting instead that it reveals a feature common to all language: namely, its citationality. Language in general succeeds, Derrida comments, precisely because it "repeat[s] a 'coded' or iterable utterance" (1988: 18). Gender, Butler proposes, shares a similar citational structure. Performativity is a temporal process of "regularized and constrained repetition of [gender] norms" (Butler, 1993a: 95). Their reiteration, however, is not performed by a subject; the subject is its effect. This has implications for agency. Agency, for Butler, is not an innate property of the individual. It is a possibility that inheres within the practice of citation that secures and sustains the regulatory force of gender norms. What operates as a mechanism of constraint is thus also the locus of subversion. Every performance of gender can also be a way to "*work ... the weakness in the norm*" (Butler, 1993a: 237).

Butler also modifies her earlier position in another way. Where previously she had viewed the proliferation of genders as a means to subvert the heterosexual matrix, she now explicitly refutes that suggestion. Discussing drag once more, she proposes, instead, that its "critical promise" rests exclusively on its capacity to denaturalize heterosexuality (Butler, 1993a: 237) by exposing it as a regulatory fiction.

The body

Once the full implications of Butler's critique of sex/gender were grasped, it quickly became apparent that her critique posed a radical challenge to feminism's prevailing understanding of the body – or more specifically, the sexed body. Although feminists challenge the dualisms associating women with the body and irrationality and men with the mind and reason, this has not usually equated with contesting the "reality" of women's biology and, in particular, its reproductive capacity. When Butler declared that sex is "always already gender" (1990a: 7) she did precisely that. She questioned not only the actuality of sex as a thing in itself; she also challenged the idea that sex difference is an ontological truth of the flesh that shapes women's lives on a daily basis (see, for instance, Bigwood, 1991; Segal, 1994; and Nussbaum, 1999).

The basic difficulty her theory presents is that by arguing, as she had in *Gender Trouble*, that there is no such thing as the "body" existing outside of or prior to culture Butler *appears* to treat the body purely as a text shaped exclusively by discourse. *Gender Trouble*, recall, centers on the performative production of *both* gender *and* the sexed body. Her strategy (drawing on Foucault and Wittig) is precisely to show how "sex" is constructed as a "reality-effect" that, in turn, structures our perception of the body as naturally "sexed." What's more, she owns here that it is impossible to determine whether a "physical" corpus exists prior to its construction as such (Butler, 1990a: 114). The question this raised is what about the materiality of the body.

In *Bodies That Matter*, she responds to this question, not by acknowledging that there is a body that precedes discourse, though at times she appears to concede that some such exists (Butler, 1993a: 67). Maintaining her position that the sexed body cannot be apprehended directly, Butler sets about interrogating the concept of materiality per se. She does so by focusing on the discourse of construction. Her aims: to differentiate her position from that of linguistic idealism – that is, the claim that language, *tout court*, constitutes the body – and to confront directly the problem of apparently doing away with "sex" by defining it as fictive. Instead, therefore, of simply upholding the argument she advances in *Gender Trouble*, where "sex" – and the body – were classified as products of the gender apparatus, an apparatus that is itself also a construction, in *Bodies That Matter* she modifies it by way of the concept of materialization.

Matter is now conceptualized "not as a site or surface, but as a *process of materialization that stabilizes over time to produce the effect of a boundary, fixity, and surface we call matter."* Consequently, matter is never just brute matter; it is "always materialized" (Butler, 1993a: 9). Although "sex" is a fiction, it is a fiction with real material effects. It is one of the principal ways in which the body is lived. Sex, for Butler, is still conceived of as gendered, in the sense that it is apprehensible only through gender norms *but* – and the "but" is crucial – it is no longer assumed to be identical with gender. "Sex" has its own material effects because it functions specifically as a regulatory norm of *embodiment*, the necessary reiteration of which (for example, at every birth) sustains its force.

Notably, however, Butler's discussion does not end here. Materialization is inextricably entwined with signification. The "bodies that matter" of her title are those bodies whose materialization renders them intelligible. The bodies that make sense according to the scheme of sexed materiality wrought and supported by presumptive heterosexuality. There is, however, a realm of abject bodies that do not make sense within this scheme, because of which they do not matter; indeed, their exclusion from the realm of intelligibility is precisely what guarantees the force of the norms defining the bodies that do matter. To matter (or to materialize), for Butler, is thus also to be meaningful, to have value. In terms of sex, it is to fit within the dualist morphology established by hetero-normativity. Having an anatomically anomalous body – being intersexed, for example – is to be "outside" that frame, an exclusion that has a profound impact on how gender and sexuality are then actually lived.

There is one final reorientation of Butler's account of the body to note. Beginning in *The Psychic Life of Power*, Butler's most emphatically psychoanalytic book, and developing through *Undoing Gender* and *Precarious Life*, she begins to conceptualize the body as innately vulnerable. Right from birth, she surmises, the subject's existence – literal and psychic – depends on its "primary vulnerability to the Other" (Butler, 1997a: 21). The body is mortal, susceptible to violence, open to the loving/passionate/angry touch of the Other. Far from being autonomous, through our bodies, from the start we are "given over" to others (Butler, 2004b: 26). The main implications of this are two-fold. First, although we might struggle for rights to control our own bodies, those bodies are never simply *"our own"* (Butler, 2004b: 25). They are not just co-dependent on other bodies; as the earlier discussion demonstrated they also depend for their intelligibility – their very viability – on the operation of particular norms. Struggles for corporeal rights are, thus, also fundamentally struggles with these norms.

The body is also "invariably in community" (Butler, 2004b: 27) in a second sense. Connections with others constitute a sense of identity defining who we are. This is made clear by experiences such as grief and mourning, when "I think I have lost 'you' only to discover that 'I' have gone missing as well" (Butler, 2004b: 22). The "dispossession" that follows loss – though Butler implies a parallel dispossession may be at work in love and desire, for instance – brings about a change in the self, as it reveals existence to be always a being-with-others. Vitally, these moments of dispossession are also moments when ethical relations are illuminated and questions about how to respond to the Other posed; whether, in particular, to respond in ways that make life possible or to respond in ways which intensify life's ineradicable precariousness. I will return to the question of ethics and how it is tied to the livable life below. First, however, I want to return to performativity, this time in relation to hate-speech.

Hate-speech and resignification

Although Butler certainly breaks new ground with the contention that gender is performative, it does not constitute her only contribution to contemporary interrogations and reformulations of the concept of performativity. In *Excitable Speech*, she engages more explicitly than previously with speech act theory in order to produce a highly original response to the problem of hate-speech.

The issue of hate-speech or "words that wound" came to the fore in various discussions in the US throughout the 1980s and 1990s. The first centered on the concerns of critical race theorists that racially assaultive speech should be removed from First Amendment protection (the First Amendment safeguards freedom of speech) to become prosecutable as a form of "fighting words." The second focused on feminist worries about pornography, particularly the impact of its graphic sexual imagery on women. They too sought state censorship as the solution and on the same grounds. As Catherine MacKinnon, one of the foremost advocates of this position puts it: "Protecting pornography means protecting sexual abuse *as* speech" (1994: 7). Both rest their arguments on the claim that words wound immediately and directly. To say that they wound, however, is not to capture the whole story, for their utterance also subordinates those to whom they are addressed. Hate-speech is, as Mari Matsuda comments, "a mechanism of subordination" (in Matsuda *et al.*, 1993: 36). Another way to parse this all is, of course, to propose that such words are performative; they do what they say.

At first glance, the parallels with Butler's argument seem striking: both stress the performativity of language, its construction of reality in inegalitarian and exclusionary ways, and its constitution of subjectivity. One might expect Butler, therefore, to be sympathetic to their case. Yet she is not. It is not just that she dislikes the strategy being proposed for dealing with assaultive speech – its regulation by the state. It is rather that her objection is a linguistic one. She contends that speech and conduct (words and what they do) are always dissociable because they are always in some fundamental way temporally distinct, and because of this, paradoxically, hate-speech itself always constitutes an opportunity for its own reversal; its utterance is also the site to defuse its power.

The defense given by the advocates of censorship rests on the assumption that hate-speech is, what Austin called, "illocutionary speech" – the "performance of an act *in* saying something" (1962: 99). Butler's rests on another of Austin's distinctions, namely "perlocutions": utterances that "produce certain consequential effects" on others (Austin, 1962: 101). In other words, where *by* saying something certain effects follow. Butler, however, does not deny that illocutionary speech-acts enact their effects as they are uttered – harming as they are spoken – rather she contends that their *force* (their ability to succeed in harming) rests, like perlocutionary utterances, on their prior usage. Reading Austin through Derrida's conceptualization of performativity-as-citationality, Butler argues that wounding words wound (directly or indirectly) not because their speaker expects them to work like this – she rejects the idea of the sovereign subject able to control entirely the meaning of their utterances – but because they have been "coded" as wounding words. Hateful language contains what Butler describes as a "condensed historicity" (1997b: 3), resulting from its repetition over time. Hate-speech is only identifiable as hate-speech, in other words, because it is "*a citation of itself*" (Butler, 1997b: 80); and it is its re-citation that engenders its force. Consequently, egregious speech can only to continue to harm *if* it is repeated. Paradoxically, however, this requirement for its repetition is also where its potential to be contested and *re*-signified resides.

Butler returns once more to Derrida's critical engagement with Austin to develop her case. One of the areas where Derrida dissented from Austin was over what Austin called "infelicitous" utterances; speech acts that fail to attain their ends. Austin explained this failure by way of the social conventions that underpin them; where, for instance, saying "I do" fails because one of the parties to a marriage is already married or the person before whom marriage vows are sworn is not authorized to conduct a marriage ceremony. Derrida, however, prefers to see language as having an intrinsic capacity to fail because of its iterable structure. *Différance* is Derrida's term for the idea that each time a term is used a difference (or differentiation) is introduced, with the result that its meaning is perpetually deferred. The very condition that makes for a successful performative – its citationality or "excitability," as Butler sometimes characterizes it – is also what puts it in jeopardy.

Butler thus draws from Derrida's approach the idea that all terms have the innate potential to break with their existing contexts and be re-signified in new, unpredictable ways; including hate-speech. Such "redoubling of injurious speech" is already evident in rap music, political satire, and parody (Butler, 1997b: 14). Ironically too, she surmises, it is also present in arguments in support of its censorship. Given its capacity for de-contextualization Butler proposes the most effective way to counter hate-speech is not with its legal suppression but with more speech.

The essence of hate-speech is name-calling. To allow that name-calling has injurious force, that it subordinates those to whom it is directed (at least some of the time), requires Butler to demonstrate the connection between language and subjectivity – or, more precisely, subjectification. In both *Excitable Speech* and in *The Psychic Life of Power*, Butler turns in response to the idea of interpellation developed by Louis Althusser. According to Althusser a subject is formed when it is interpellated or "hailed" by an authority figure, such as a police officer calling "Hey, you there." Recognizing itself in the call, the individual turns, and in that instant is transformed into a subject. Where in *Psychic Life*, Butler is interested in the question of why the subject turns in the first place, why it responds to the voice of the law, in *Excitable Speech* her concern is somewhat different. It is the fact that *all* interpellations – whether by an authority figure or not, whether by an actual speaker or by an institution (by way of forms, documents, employment applications) – call the subject into being, giving it existence.

All such interpellations, for Butler, are injurious insofar as they foreclose other interpellative possibilities but not all are conventionally harmful in the way hate-speech is. Its success in harming depends on its being received in a particular way; as a demeaning address that the addressee accepts as demeaning. If, however, the addressee instead of receiving such speech as hate-speech, appropriates the term and resignifies it in a positive or affirmative way then not only does s/he defuse it of its pernicious potential but s/he refuses to be constituted linguistically by it as an object of hate/a hateful object (see also Butler, 1993a: 226–230, 1993b, 2000b: 352–353). The problem with seeking to prosecute those who utter noxious language is that although they are certainly responsible for its recitation, their prosecution reduces the scene of utterance to a face-to-face encounter between addressor and addressee when the problem, as Butler conceives it, is the reiteration that leads to its sedimentation as noxious language. Because this process of sedimentation, this history, is not prosecutable (Butler, 1997b: 50) then as words are the vehicle of injury, so too should they be the locus of resistance.

Ethics and "becoming human"

In a conversation with political philosopher, William Connolly, in 2000, Butler declared:

> I confess to worrying about the turn to ethics, and have recently written a small essay that voices my ambivalence. [This is "Ethical Ambivalence" (2000d).] I tend to think that ethics displaces from politics, and I suppose for me the use of power as a point of departure for a critical analysis is substantially different from an ethical framework. (2000c)

In 2005, Butler published *Giving an Account of Oneself*, described on its dust jacket as "her first extended study of moral philosophy" where she "offers a provocative outline for a new ethical practice." What then is to be made of these twin claims? Has she abandoned her own earlier stance on ethics or is what is "provocative" about the ethical practice she sketches precisely that it adopts the same starting point as the critical political practice that she values – that it begins from power?

If there is a consistent normative aspiration in Butler's work it focuses on the idea of a "livable life," a concept which, although latent in her work from *Subjects of Desire* onwards, gains increasing prominence with the publication of *Undoing Gender*. Drawing inspiration from Spinoza's concept of the *conatus*, Butler contends that although everyone has this desire "to persist in one's own being" this is only possible, as Hegel realized, "on the condition that we are engaged in receiving and offering recognition" (2004a: 31). Livability, described as "the ability to live and breathe and move" (Butler, 2004a: 31; see also Butler, 2000d: 27), is not, however, an ability readily available to all. To give and gain recognition depends on being already normatively recognizable as human. "[I]f there are no norms of recognition by which we are recognizable," she writes, "then it is not possible to persist in one's being, and we are not possible beings; we have been foreclosed from possibility." Which is why, she determines that "possibility is a necessity" for those so-excluded (Butler, 2004a: 31).

There are two inter-twining factors that condition this distribution of possibility. The first is our constitutive relations with others; the second is what Butler refers to in *Frames of War* as the "schemas of intelligibility" that "condition and produce [the] norms of recognizability," which prepare the ground for recognition (2009: 7).

From as early as *Gender Trouble*, Butler had drawn attention to the role that dependence on the Other has in the constitution of subjectivity. I am referring here to her discussion of gender melancholia, which Butler regards as central to the formation of gendered subjectivity. Drawing on the work of Freud, Butler proposes that at the heart of normative heterosexuality there is a disavowed loss – denial – of homosexual desire. It occurs as part and parcel of the resolution of Oedipal situation. In melancholia, the individual, unable to get over loss in the usual way, incorporates the lost object into its ego, identifying with it and adopting certain of its characteristics. In gender melancholia, the fact that the boy identifies with his father and the girl with her mother suggests to Butler that the lost desire for the parent of the same sex is installed melancholically in the child's ego: hence the identification. The initial desire is present but foreclosed; that is, heterosexual desire is bought at the cost of denying prior homosexual desire.

The point is that the subject comes to exist, to "be," in other words, through its primary dependency on the Other; indeed through its absorption of the Other into the self as part of the production of that self. What is important in relation to psychic subjectivity is that because primary attachments of these kinds are foreclosed – "rigorously barred" from consciousness (Butler, 1997a: 23) – the subject is always, to some extent, opaque to itself. However, although it may not readily know that it is dependent on the Other for its psychic survival, this dependence is revealed in the moments of "dispossession" noted earlier. Moments of loss, grief, passion, and so forth that expose "the ties we have to others, that shows us that these ties constituted what we are, ties or bonds that compose us" (Butler, 2004b: 22).

Life is precarious by virtue of this fundamental dependency. Calling on Emmanuel Levinas, Butler surmises that this fundamental dependency is also the source of our ethical responsibilities towards others (2005a: 88); responsibilities that arise, according to Levinas, *prior* to our "being" because of the unwilled demand the Other makes on us. For him, therefore, the demand is pre-ontological. Calling on Foucault, Butler, however, notes that once the ethical question: "How ought I to treat you?" is posed, "I am caught up not only in the sphere of normativity but in the problematic of power" (2005a: 25); caught up, that is, in politics. Because norms establish who is ontologically recognizable as human they also delimit the ethical scene by determining who is capable of offering and accepting recognition. For Butler, importantly therefore, ethical encounters, like so much in her work, are also essentially struggles with norms. And, to return to where this section began, as such they are deeply implicated in the distribution of possibility and entwined with power. What then to do to cultivate an ethical responsive to the Other that is also capable of transforming these limiting norms?

One suggestion is made in the context of her discussion of the violence that followed 9/11; it is the nurturing of "a point of identification with suffering itself" (Butler, 2004b: 30). It rests, in this particular case, on the development of what might be called "an ethics of grief" (Gutterman and Rushing, 2008: 129). Threaded through Butler's work from almost the beginning has been an interest in mourning and, specifically, in the conditions that produce some lives as publicly unmournable. A legacy of her Judaism, for sure, the concern was revived for Butler during the AIDS crisis in the US, when she notes those who lost their partners were often unable to acknowledge these losses publicly (Butler, 2010). It is behind her interest in Sophocles's *Antigone* developed in *Antigone's Claim* (Butler, 2000a). It is central to her critique of 9/11 and the wars that followed, where public grief has been far from evenly distributed (2004b). Her underlying point in these discussions is that identifying who is worthy of public grief is also a means to identify who is recognizable as "human."

Grief, for Butler, though is also an ethical and political resource. Ethics, she writes at the end of *Giving an Account*, "requires us to risk ourselves." It is the occasion when "our willingness to become undone in relation to others constitutes our chance of becoming human" (Butler, 2005a: 136). As noted earlier, grief is a disorienting experience exactly because it reveals our dependency on another; their loss is our undoing. As such, it opens us up to the "ways in which we are, from the start ... already given over, beyond ourselves, implicated in lives that are not our own" (Butler, 2004b: 28). The problem after 9/11, Butler proposes, was that instead of "tarrying with grief" (2004b: 30) the desire for revenge won out and an ethical and political opportunity was subsequently missed; an opportunity to envisage a world not of sovereign mastery where violence is met with retaliatory violence but a world in which violence might actually be diminished. For it is only by abiding with the pain and anguish of loss, she surmises, that we can become better attuned to the *shared* fragility of human life. Without this we cannot develop a politics or an ethics that enhances the livability of life or the possibility of "becoming human" for those – ourselves or others – who are outside the current frame of recognition and, who as such, do not figure as recognizably human in its terms.

IMPACT AND ASSESSMENT

A central difficulty assessing the impact of Butler's work is that it has been so wide-ranging. *Gender Trouble*, alone, has been translated into over twenty languages and has shaped debates in fields as diverse as geography, philosophy, design, politics, and performance studies. Indeed, this one book has been credited with defining the relation between feminism and postmodernism, setting the terms of the debate over identity in the US and elsewhere, inspiring – even founding – queer theory and politics and rendering its author one of the most cited feminist theorists of the last twenty years. To this can be added, amongst many other developments, the impact her ideas on life's precariousness have had on international relations theory, how her ideas on the human and recognition have been taken up in explorations of asylum and immigration, and the critical reception her ethical work is receiving.

A second problem arises because Butler is a "living" author; not only in the sense that she continues to write but rather because of how she does so. As she puts it, "part of what being a 'living' author means, as I understand it, is to be always underway"; that is, "always in the process of restaging and finding new experimental possibilities for prior positions"; taking a stand in one text only to forget it in another; "approaching the same thematic from another angle with a different set of questions"; and failing to reconcile competing claims (Butler, 2006b: 281). A living author, for Butler, is one who resists systematicity and totalization; it is one whose writing is, we might say, performative: it perpetually resignifies what went before.

This process of resignification extends not only to Butler's own compositional practice where she does, indeed, restage ideas she has previously advanced: witness her rethinking in *Bodies that Matter* of aspects of *Gender Trouble* or her turn to Austin and Althusser in *Excitable Speech* to remedy some of the shortcomings of her earlier Foucauldian account of constitution. What is more controversial from the perspective of her critics is that this practice extends also to her sources. Butler is routinely charged with reading into them concepts that are not present there (as with the whole idea of sex and gender in Beauvoir's work) or with bypassing the key concerns of a thinker to make a different point (as, for instance, when she neglects Wittig's materialism); in short, with misinterpreting them. (For further discussion see Lloyd, 2007.) Certainly her evaluations and engagements often chart a different course to those commonly plotted. The explanation for this may be found in Butler's conception of texts as "living" entities, which are not merely open to interpretation but rather are "extended and augmented with every interpretation" (2006b: 278); a conception at once indebted to Talmudic scholarship, hermeneutics and deconstruction. Those who construe interpretation in a different vein will, no doubt, continue to worry nonetheless about the purported "eccentricity" of some of Butler's readings.

Perhaps the area that has troubled her critics most, however, has to do with politics. From the debates with Nancy Fraser and Seyla Benhabib over norms, agency, and subjectivity in *Feminist Contentions* (Benhabib *et al.*, 1995; see also Stone, 2005) through to Nussbaum's accusation of political quietism in "The Professor of Parody" (1999), questions have arisen about the adequacy of Butler's account of politics. Certainly, she is not a political theorist in the received sense: she contests both the wisdom and the possibility of prescribing a specific political programme (of the kind often found in feminist works) on the grounds that politics is contingent and unpredictable, "an incalculable effect" (1994b: 38; see also 1999d). She refuses the idea that political action needs to be grounded, whether in a truth, a shared collective experience, or a foundational concept such as "Woman." Instead, what is far more subversive are "moments of degrounding" (Butler, 1994b: 38) when what is natural or taken-for-granted is exposed as a normalizing constraint and thus denaturalized.

Although Butler acknowledges that her work has a normative orientation (to do with extending the field of possibilities for livable life), she questions the need to stipulate an abstract set of norms to guide political action, to measure political success or to ground critique (2004a: 219–221; see also 1994b: 39). In so doing, she specifically differentiates herself from the likes of Jürgen Habermas and feminists, such as Nancy Fraser. Norms, for Butler, are always social, embedded in practices, productive of intelligible social orders and action. They "confer reality" (2004a: 52) and, as such, are forever normalizing and exclusionary. Because of which they can never be neutral or abstract in the sense Habermas and others assume. The point of politics, as a consequence, for Butler is thus not to recommend other, more ideal norms but rather to contest and refashion those that already exist.

Where her critics espy an inadequate conception of politics, her sympathizers, however, discern something else. They spot in her work an alternative, even incommensurable, approach to politics, one centered on political insurrection *within* the terms of power rather than its overcoming; one that in denaturalizing sites of power, in effect, politicizes them, opening them up to "democratising resistance" (Chambers and Carver, 2008: 162); one that questions the sufficiency of traditional approaches to politics and allied conceptualizations of the political (Lloyd, 2005; Jagger, 2008); and, finally, one centered on struggles with the norm.

While the jury is almost certainly still out on whether she has a tenable conception of politics, the status of Butler's recent foray into ethics presents equally, if not tougher, questions for her readers. First, because of the difficulties, noted earlier, of squaring her previous view of ethics as "an escape from politics" (Butler, 2000d: 15; see Rushing, forthcoming) with the fact that she has begun to develop an ethical argument of her own centered on responsibility. Second, because of concerns about the emphasis Butler places in this ethics not just on grief and mourning but on the ineradicable vulnerability of human life and whether, or not, it betokens what Bonnie Honig (forthcoming) calls a "resurgent *mortalist* humanism." This is a humanism predicated not on a common conception of the human but on the idea of a "common human vulnerability" (Butler, 2004b: 31) to the other. And, finally, because the ethical responsiveness that (potentially) emerges from an acknowledgement of shared vulnerability is one with the apparent capacity to circumvent entrenched political divisions between people. Understanding the *relationship* between ethics and politics, including which term has priority, is thus central to understanding precisely what it is ethics adds to Butler's earlier account of political engagement.

Reader's Guide to Judith Butler

The only current anthology of Butler's writings is *The Judith Butler Reader* edited by Sarah Salih (2004). Salih's 2002 book, *Judith Butler*, provides a basic, accessible introduction to Butler's writing up to *The Psychic Life of Power* and *Excitable Speech*. A more challenging read is Vicki Kirby's *Judith Butler: Live Theory* (2006), which is notable for its exploration of the psychoanalytic dimensions of Butler's thought. Readers interested specifically in Butler's discussions of sex, gender, sexuality and the body, might profitably begin with either Gill Jagger's lucid introduction, *Judith Butler: Sexual Politics, Social Change and the Power of the Performative* (2008) or with Moya Lloyd's 2007 study, *Judith Butler: from Norms to Politics*, which focuses, in particular, on feminism and politics and provides a comprehensive and critical exploration of all of Butler's principal texts from *Subjects of Desire* to *Giving an Account of Oneself*. Samuel Chambers and Terrell Carver's *Judith Butler and Political Theory* (2008) offers a significant critical assessment of the key political concepts in Butler's writing and will be of especial interest to those already familiar with Butler's work. Recent important texts exploring Butler's work in relation to ethics include Elena Loizidou's *Judith Butler:*

Ethics, Law, Politics (2007), written from a critical legal studies perspective, and Annika Thiem's *Unbecoming Subjects* (2008), which seeks to assess Butler's thinking from the perspective of moral philosophy. There are also a number of useful edited collections examining Butler's work, including Carver and Chambers (2008), with essays on topics such as Butler's phenomenology, the significance of her work for ethics, sovereignty, law and rights; Armour and St. Ville (2006), which utilizes Butler's work to address questions of religion (Christian, Islamic, and Buddhist); and Davies (2008), which assesses the contribution of Butler's thought to work in the Social Sciences and Humanities.

Bibliography

Writings of Judith Butler

1986a. Sex and gender in Simone de Beauvoir's *Second Sex*. *Yale French Studies*, 72: 35–49.

1986b. Variations on sex and gender: Beauvoir, Wittig and Foucault. *Praxis International*, 5(4): 505–516.

1987. *Subjects of Desire: Hegelian Reflections in Twentieth-Century France*. New York: Columbia University Press.

1988. Performative acts and gender constitution: An essay in phenomenology and feminist theory. *Theatre Journal*, 40(4): 128–142.

1989a. Gendering the body: Beauvoir's philosophical contribution. In A. Garry and M. Pearsall (eds) *Women, Knowledge, and Reality: Explorations in Feminist Philosophy*. Boston, Unwin and Hyman, pp. 252–162.

1989b. Sexual ideology and phenomenological description: A feminist critique of Merleau-Ponty's *Phenomenology of Perception*. In J. Allen and M. Young (eds) *The Thinking Muse: Feminism and Modern French Philosophy*. Bloomington: Indiana University Press, pp. 83–100.

1989c. The body politics of Julia Kristeva. *Hypatia*, 3(3): 104–118.

1989d. Foucault and the Paradox of Bodily Inscriptions. *The Journal of Philosophy*, LXXXVI: 601–607.

1990a. *Gender Trouble: Feminism and the Subversion of Identity*. London: Routledge.

1990b. The force of fantasy: Feminism, Mapplethorpe, and discursive excess. *differences: A Journal of Feminist Cultural Studies*, 2(2): 105–125.

1990c. Gender trouble, feminist theory and psychoanalytic discourse. In L. Nicholson (ed.) *Feminism and Postmodernism*. London: Routledge, pp. 324–340.

1991. Imitation and gender insubordination. In D. Fuss (ed.) *Inside/Out: Lesbian Theories, Gay Theories*. London: Routledge, pp. 13–31.

1992. Contingent foundations: Feminism and the question of "postmodernism." In J. Butler and J. Scott (eds) *Feminists Theorize the Political*. London: Routledge, pp. 35–57.

1992 (with J. Scott (eds)). *Feminists Theorize the Political*. London: Routledge.

1993a. *Bodies That Matter: On the Discursive Limits of "Sex."* London: Routledge.

1993b. Critically queer. *GLQ: A Journal of Gay and Lesbian Studies*, 1: 17–32.

1993c. Poststructuralism and postMarxism. *Diacritics*, 23(4): 2–11.

1994a. Against proper objects. *differences: A Journal of Feminist Cultural Studies*, 6(2–3): 1–26.

1994b. Gender as performance: An interview with Judith Butler. *Radical Philosophy*, 67: 32–39.

1995 (with S. Benhabib, D. Cornell, and N. Fraser). *Feminist Contentions: A Philosophical Exchange*, with an introduction by L. Nicholson. London: Routledge.

1996a. Universality in culture. In J. Cohen (ed.) *For Love of Country? Debating the Limits of Patriotism*. Boston: Beacon Press, pp. 45–52.

1996b. An affirmative view. *Representations*, 55: 74–83.

1997a. *The Psychic Life of Power: Theories in Subjection*. Stanford, CA: Stanford University Press.

1997b. *Excitable Speech: The Politics of the Performative*. London: Routledge.

1998a. Merely cultural. *New Left Review*, 227: 33–44.

1998b. How bodies come to matter: An interview with Judith Butler. *Signs: Journal of Women in Culture and Society*, 23(2): 275–286.

1999a. *Subjects of Desire: Hegelian Reflections in Twentieth-Century France*, with new preface. New York: Columbia University Press.

1999b. *Gender Trouble: Feminism and the Subversion of Identity*. Tenth Anniversary Edition. London: Routledge.

1999c. Revisiting bodies and pleasures. *Theory, Culture, Society*, 16(2): 11–20.

1999d. On speech, race and melancholia: An interview with Judith Butler. *Theory, Culture and Society*, 16(2): 163–174.

2000a. *Antigone's Claim: Kinship between Life and Death*. New York: Columbia University Press.

2000b. Changing the subject: Judith Butler's politics of radical resignification. *jac*, 20(4): 731–765.

2000c. Politics, power and ethics: A discussion between Judith Butler and William Connolly. *Theory and Event*, 4(2). Available online at http://muse.jhu.edu/journals/theory_and_event/v004/4.2butler.html (accessed June 13, 2005).

2000d. Ethical ambivalence. In M. Garber, B. Hansen, and R. L. Walkowitz (eds) *The Turn to Ethics*. London: Routledge, pp. 15–28.

2000 (with E. Laclau and S. Žižek). *Contingency, Hegemony, Universality: Contemporary Dialogues on the Left*. London: Verso.

2000 (with J. Guillory and K. Thomas (eds)). *What's Left of Theory? New Work on the politics of Literary Theory*. London: Routledge.

2001. The end of sexual difference? In E. Bronfen and M. Kavka (eds) *Feminist Consequences: Theory for the New Century*. New York: Columbia University Press, pp. 174–203.

2002a. Guantanamo limbo. *The Nation*. Available online at www.thenation.com/doc/20020401/butler (accessed February 26, 2010).

2002b. Is kinship always already heterosexual? *differences: A Journal of Feminist Cultural Studies*, 13(1): 14–44.

2002c. What is critique? An essay on Foucault's virtue. In D. Ingram (ed.) *The Political*. Oxford: Blackwell, pp. 212–226.

2002 (with R. Post and K. A. Appiah, T. C. Grey, and R. B. Siegel). *Prejudicial Appearances: The Logic of American Antidiscrimination Law*. Durham, NC: Duke University Press.

2003a. Peace is a resistance to the terrible satisfactions of war. Interview with Jill Stauffer. Available online at http://believermag.com/issues/200305/?read+interview_butler (accessed April 8, 2010).

2003b. No, it's not anti-Semitic. Judith Butler defends the right to criticize Israel. *London Review of Books*. August, 21: 19–21.

2004a. *Undoing Gender*. London: Routledge.

2004b. *Precarious Life: The Powers of Mourning and Violence*. London: Verso.

2004c. Jews and the bi-national state. *Logos*, 3(1).

2005a. *Giving an Account of Oneself*. New York: Fordham University Press.

2005b. Merleau-Ponty and the Touch of Malebranche. In T. Carman and M. B. N. Hansen (eds) *The Cambridge Companion to Merleau-Ponty*. Cambridge: Cambridge University Press, pp. 181–205.

2005c. Photography, war, outrage. *PMLA*: 822–827.

2006a. The desire to live: Spinoza's *Ethics* under pressure. In V. Kahn, N. Saccamano, and D. Coli (eds) *Politics and the Passions, 1500–1850*. Princeton, NJ: Princeton University Press, pp. 111–130.

2006b. Afterword. In E. T. Armour and S. M. St. Ville (eds) *Bodily Citations: Religion and Judith Butler*. New York: Columbia University Press, pp. 276–291.

2007 (with G. C. Spivak). *Who Sings the Nation-State? Language, Politics, Belonging*. London: Seagull Books.

2008. Sexual politics, torture, secular time. *The British Journal of Sociology*, 59(1): 1–23.

2009. *Frames of War: When is Life Grievable?* London: Verso.

2010. As a Jew, I was taught it was ethically imperative to speak up. Interview with Udi Aloni. *Haaretz*. Available online at www.haaretz.com/hasen/spages/1152017.html (accessed February 26, 2010).

Further Reading

Armour, E. T. and St. Ville, S. M. (eds) (2006) *Bodily Citations: Religion and Judith Butler*. New York: Columbia University Press.

Austin, J. L. (1962) *How to Do Things with Words*, 2nd edn. Oxford: Oxford University Press.

Beauvoir, S. de (1983[1949]) *The Second Sex*. Trans. H. M. Parshley. Harmondsworth: Penguin.

Bigwood, C. (1991) Renaturalizing the body (with the Help of Merleau-Ponty). In Welton, D. (ed.) *Body and Flesh: A Philosophical Reader*. Oxford: Blackwell, pp. 99–114.

Carver T. and Chambers, S. A. (eds) (2008) *Judith Butler's Precarious Politics: Critical Encounters*. London: Routledge.

Chambers, S. A. and Carver, T. (2008) *Judith Butler and Political Theory: Troubling Politics*. London: Routledge.

Davies, B. (ed.) (2008) *Judith Butler in Conversation. Analyzing the Texts and Talk of Everyday Life*. London: Routledge.

Derrida, J. (1988) *Limited Inc*. Evanston, IL: Northwestern University Press.

Foucault, M. (1978[1976]) *The History of Sexuality, Volume 1: An Introduction*. Trans. R. Hurley. Harmondsworth: Penguin.

Gutterman, D. S. and Rushing, S. L. (2008) Sovereignty and suffering: towards an ethics of grief in a post-9/11 world. In S. A. Chambers and T. Carver (eds) *Judith Butler and Political Theory: Troubling Politics*. London: Routledge, pp. 127–141.

Honig, B. (forthcoming) Antigone's two laws: Greek tragedy and the politics of humanism, *New Literary History*.

Jagger, G. (2008) *Judith Butler: Sexual Politics, Social Change and the Power of the Performative*. London: Routledge.

Kirby, V. (2006) *Judith Butler: Live Theory*. London: Continuum.

Lloyd, M. (2005) *Beyond Identity Politics: Feminism, Power, Politics*. London: Sage.

Lloyd, M. (2007) *Judith Butler: From Norms to Politics*. Cambridge: Polity.

Loizidou, E. (2007) *Judith Butler: Ethics, Law, Politics*. London: Routledge.

MacKinnon, C. A. (1994) *Only Words*. London: Harper Collins.

Matsuda, M. J., Lawrence III, C. R., Delgado, R., and Crenshaw, K. W. (1993) *Words that Wound: Critical Race Theory, Assaultive Speech and the First Amendment*. Boulder, CO: Westview Press.

Nussbaum, M. (1999) Professor of Parody. Available online at www.akad.se/Nussbaum.pdf (accessed April 19, 2010).

Rushing, S. L. (forthcoming) Preparing for politics: Butler's ethical dispositions. *Contemporary Political Theory*, 9(3).

Salih, S. (2002) *Judith Butler*. London: Routledge.

Salih, S. (ed.) (2004) *The Judith Butler Reader*. Oxford: Blackwell.

Segal, L. (1994) *Straight Sex: The Politics of Pleasure*. London: Virago.

Stone, A. (2005) Towards a genealogical feminism: A reading of Judith Butler's political thought. *Contemporary Political Theory*, 4(1): 4–24.

Thiem, A. (2008) *Unbecoming Subjects: Judith Butler, Moral Philosophy, and Critical Responsibility*. New York: Fordham University Press.

Wittig, M. (1980) The straight mind. *Feminist Issues*, 1(1): 103–111.

Wittig, M. (1981) One is not born a woman. *Feminist Issues*, 1(2): 47–54.

Index

abandonment 469
accountability 95, 102, 104, 120
accounting practices 104, 106, 114, 120
accumulated (dis)advantage ("Matthew
  Effect") 78
actants 528, 529–30
action
  affirmative 542
  and capital 380
  and communication 296–8, 362
  and dialectical materialism 50
  and experience 296, 378
  and global warming 454
  and institutional rules 119–20
  and reflexivity 375
  and structure 115, 364, 365, 385, 438
  and texts 272, 276–8
  Bourdieu on 362–5, 371–2, 375, 376,
    378–81, 385, 386, 387, 389n.3
  collective 380
  communicative 296, 340, 343–51
  Elias on 33
  expressive 233
  frame of reference 295, 301
  Garfinkel on 89–101, 105–9, 111–116,
    118, 120

Giddens on 438, 439, 441, 443, 444,
  445, 452
Goffman on 145, 146
Habermas on 343–51
institutional ethnography and 274
instructed 90
local 145, 401
Luhmann on 295–9, 301
Mead on 362
Merton on 69, 76, 77, 80, 84
political 184, 491, 508, 526, 543,
  548, 555
practical 100, 374, 445
purposive 77, 231–4
rational 220, 231, 346
scientific 96
Smith (Dorothy E.) on 271–4,
  276–80, 282
subaltern 426
systems 295, 348
theory 19, 70, 84, 292, 438
  see also behavior; social action
actor-network theory (ANT) 3–4, 521, 522,
  525–32, 536
actors 528–30
actual, the 181, 184

The Wiley-Blackwell Companion to Major Social Theorists, First Edition.
Edited by George Ritzer and Jeffrey Stepnisky.
© 2011 Blackwell Publishing Ltd. Published 2011 by Blackwell Publishing Ltd.

Adorno, Theodor 17, 162, 325, 342
aesthetics
    materialization of 327
    modernist 160
    of the self 251, 253–4
    see also transaesthetics
affirmative action 542
Africa 396, 399
Agamben, Giorgio 6, 464–79
    and Aristotle 464–7, 469–70
    and Deleuze 189–90
    and Derrida 467
    and Foucault 468
    and Heidegger 464, 465
    as a person 464–5
    impact/assessment of 476–8
    on ethics 11, 466, 472–4
    philosophical context 465–8
agency 3, 145, 279–80, 368, 401, 548
    active 445
    of nonhuman world 504, 506, 533
    see also structure-agency distinction
aggregation 234
"Agnes" study 94–5
Ahmad, Aijaz 427
Alaimo, Stacey 514
Alexander, Jeffrey C. 386–7
Algeria 365, 366–7, 371–2
alienation 46, 49, 51–2, 55, 314, 315
Althusser, Louis 242, 316, 551
ambivalence 80, 164, 170
animals, *see* companion species
anomie 67, 76, 77
ANT, *see* actor-network theory (ANT)
anthropoemia 164
anthropology 316–17, 531–2
anthropophagia 164
Apel, Karl Otto 343
Appadurai, Arjun 10
archeology 246
Archer, Margaret 440–2
architecture 160
Arendt, Hannah 258, 263
"aristocratic critique" of capitalism 317
Aristotle 464–70
Aron, Raymond 368
Arrighi, Giovanni 406, 407
art 46–7, 51, 54, 254, 327, 385
Ashby, Ross 294

assemblage 4, 187, 190
assimilation 164
Austen, Jane 422
Austin, J.L. 551
autogestion 58–9
autopoiesis 293, 300

Bachelard, Gaston 245, 246
Bacon, Francis 187
Badiou, Alain 44, 181
Bakhtin, Mikhail 277, 507
balancing operations 201, 203, 208, 211
Baltasound 127
ban 467, 469
Barad, Karen 514
Baran, Paul A. 397
Barber, Elinor 68
"bare life" 469–70
Bataille, Georges 316–18
Baudrillard, Jean 8, 10, 11, 90, 310–38
    and neo-Marxism 314–18
    and postmodernism 318–23
    and "the object" 323–5
    as a person 310–11
    early writings 311–14
    in the 1990s 325–9
    reader's guide to 335
    theory fictions 329–33
Bauman, Janina 162–3, 172
Bauman, Zygmunt xvi, 6, 8, 10, 36,
        155–74, 481
    as a person 155–6
    context 156–7
    interpretations of 170–2
    reader's guide to 172
    work 157–70
Béarn 372–3
Beauvoir, Simone de 544, 546–7
Beck, Ulrich 9, 480–99
Becker, Gary 259–60
Becker, Howard 112, 534
Beck-Gernsheim, Elizabeth 481
becoming 187
behavior
    and civilizing processes 23, 25, 26–9
    choice 73–4
    codes of 27, 32
    deviant 76
    interaction order 135–8

responsive versus purposive 230–3
see also action
behaviorism 197–8, 201–2
Beilharz, Peter 170
Bell, Jeffrey 181
Benjamin, Walter 464, 469, 474, 476
Berger, Joseph 224
Bergson, Henri 177, 182–3
Berlin Wall 1, 329
Berreby, David 535
Bienenstock, Elisa Jane 213
biology 504
biopolitics 256–7, 468–72
biopower 255–6
Blackshaw, Tony 171
Blair, Tony 448, 451, 452, 453
Blau, Peter 198, 199, 200, 214
Bloor, David 531–2
Blumer, Herbert 132
body 5, 7, 546–50
  "without organs" 187
  see also cyborg
Bohm, David 533
Bonacich, Philip 213
Bourdieu, Pierre 3, 8, 90, 91, 361–94
Brenner, Robert 401
Breton, André 47
Brown, George Spencer 301
Brown, Gordon 453
Burgess, Robert 197, 198
Burke, Kenneth 103, 105, 134, 148
Burt, Ronald S. 208
business networks 209–10
Butler, Judith 5, 6, 7, 11, 541–60
  as a person 451–2
  impact and assessment 554–6
  intellectual context 542–5
  reader's guide to 556–7
  social context 543–3
  theory 545–54

Campbell, Donald T. 303, 304
camps 470, 472
Canguilhem, Georges 245, 246
capital 379–80, 381, 383
capitalism
  "aristocratic critique" of 317
  as "zero sum game" 261–3
  ceiling effects 406

core/periphery hierarchy 399–401
crises 345, 483
crisis of legitimacy 483
critique of 315, 317, 345, 355
emergence of 399–1,
    405, 406
finance 186
global 403–5
liberal 256, 258, 260, 262
persistence of 185
replacement by new system 407
Carroll, Lewis 177
Cartwright, Dorwin 196
Castoriadis, Cornelius 169
categorization 374–5
Cave allegory 525–6
censorship 550–1
Chase-Dunn, Christopher 404–5
Chicago School 110, 120,
    261, 534
  second 132–2
choice behavior
  and information 74, 79
  and institutional patterns 73–5
chronotope 507
cinema 8, 187–8
civil inattention 136
civilization 26–7
civilizing processes 23, 26–9
Clark, Kenneth 82
class relations 29, 399–402
Clifford, James 512
climate change 454, 483
cloning 331
Cobb-Douglas utility function 221
codes of behavior 27, 32
coevolution 300
Cohen, Bernard P. 224
cohesion 203, 212
Cohn-Bendit, Daniel 52, 53, 312
Cold War 329
Coleman, James S. 3, 219–39, 384
collectivities 76
colonialism 58, 256, 264,
    366–7, 399
  see also imperialism
Columbia School 83
commitment 212
commodities 313, 315, 320

communication
  and action 296–8, 362
  Baudrillard on 321
  components of 297
  Garfinkel on 96–8
  Habermas on 344–5
  Luhmann on 296–9, 302–3
  see also communicative action; language;
    symbols
communicative action 296, 340,
    343–51
communism 159, 331
communitarianism 169
community 168–9, 475
companion species 511–13
conceptual frames 271
conformism 160, 163
consequences 77–8
constellations 182
constitutive orders 118, 119, 120
constraint 27–8, 76, 102, 119,
    441, 442
consumer culture 7–9, 166, 259,
    312–15, 320–1, 327,
contingency 298, 303
contrapuntal reading 422
conversational analysis 108, 115
conversational interaction 127, 128,
    129, 140
convexity condition 224
Cook, Karen 195, 197, 198, 204, 208
Cooley, C.H. 134, 146
coordination, of activities 273
co-presence 135
core/periphery relations 397–405
corporations 374
correspondence analysis 376
coshaping 504
cosmopolitanism 169, 491–3
cosmopolitanization 492–3
cosmopolitics 515
court ritual 25–6
Craib, I. 45–6
critical theory 112–13, 156, 256, 334–5,
    342–4, 348, 353, 355
criticism
  Agamben on 467
  Said on 418–19
critique 249–50, 254, 255

cultural capital 380, 383, 384
cultural goals 77
cultural structure 74, 75
culture
  aestheticization of 327
  Alfred Weber on 16
  and imperialism 421–3
  Bauman on 159–60
  of critique 159
  see also consumer culture
cyberculture studies 513
cybernetic systems theory 299–300
cyborg 508–9, 513–14

Dada 47
Davis, Mark 171, 172
Dawkins, Richard 507
Debord, Guy 8, 55
decivilization 32
dedifferentiation 320
deductive theories 221–2
deference 138
deixis 465, 472
Deleuze, Gilles 4, 8, 175–92
  and Agamben 189–90
  and Bacon 187
  and Bergson 177, 182–3
  and Foucault 175, 188, 189
  and Hegel 180
  and Hume 177, 180–1
  and Kant 182–3
  and Nietzsche 177, 181, 182, 183
  and Sartre 176
  and Spinoza 177
  as a person 175–9
  impact 190
  reader's guide to 191
  work 179–90
dependency theory 397, 399
depunctualization 531
Derrida, Jacques
  and Agamben 467
  and Butler 544, 548, 551
  Said's critique of 417
Descartes, René 26, 325
desire 185–7
desiring machines 186
deviance 71–2
Dewey, John 109

dialectical materialism 47–8, 52
 and action 50
 see also Marxism
dialectics 50, 56–8
différance 551
difference, processes of 184
differentiation
 distinguished from differenciation 184
 in consumer society 314
 segmentary 304
 theory 304–5
 see also dedifferentiation
diffraction 511
discipline 252, 265
discourse
 ethics 343, 347, 349–51
 Foucault on 244, 245
 of race war 256, 261
 principle 350
 Smith on 276–7
documentary method 93, 102
double contingency theories 298
doxa 373–4
drag 547–8
drama metaphor 137
dualistic ontology 181
Dunning, Eric 18, 434–5
Durkheim, Emile 102, 111, 118, 119, 137
 and Garfinkel 120–1
 and Goffman 133–4
 and Latour 534
 and Merton 70

ecofeminism 508
economic capital 380, 383
economic liberalism 161
economic restructuring 280–2
economy 7, 10, 167, 209, 303, 316–17,
  327, 334, 347
 general 316–18
 of practices 381
 world 401, 402, 483, 487
 see also political economy
ego identity 143
elementary theory 213
Elias, Norbert 5, 6, 13–43
 and Giddens 434–5
 and Mannheim's programme 24
 as a person 14–21

influence 19–21, 35–6
 on ethics 23, 24
 on evolutionary theory 31
 on German social development 32
 on philosophy 14, 22
 on social science 30–1
 on sociology 23
 reader's guide to 37
 reception of work 34–6
 writings 21–2
Elliot, Anthony 171–2
Emerson, Richard M. 193–218
 as a person 193–6
 assessment of 213–14
 impact 207–13
 reader's guide to 214
 social/intellectual context 196–9
 theory 197–207
emotions 534
Engels, Friedrich 270
Enlightenment, The 161, 253–4,
  325, 449
 Habermas on 342, 353–4
enterprise society 8, 259–60
episteme 189, 246
epistemological breaks 245
equidependence 213
established–outsiders relations 23,
  29–30
 see also outsiders
ethics
 Agamben on 11, 466, 472–4
 and power 7
 and technoscience 509
 Butler on 11, 552–4, 556
 Elias on 23, 24
 discourse 343, 347, 349–51
 of being 253
 of consumer culture 7
 of nonmimetic sharing 513
 of the self 251
 see also morality
ethnomethodology 89–96, 100–3, 114–15,
  117, 119, 520
 the term 107
Europe
 and emergence of capitalism 399,
  405, 406
 Bauman on 170

European Union
  Giddens on 453–4
  Habermas on 351–3
everyday life 51–5, 93
evolutionary humanism 449–51
evolutionary theory 31, 303, 304
exchange networks 202–7
  and economy 209
  and marketing 209
  and microeconomic theory 213
  and organizational studies 208–9
  balanced/unbalanced 204
  cross-category 202
  definition 202
  experiments 204–6, 211–13
  intra-category 202, 203, 206
  positive/negative connections 202, 206
  power distribution in 212–13
exchange relations 201–7
  and values 206–7
  as ongoing exchange 212
  between states 211
  in personal relations 210
  position of actor in 202
  reciprocal exchange 211–12
  theory of commitment 212
  use of power in 204, 211
exclusion 140, 164, 290, 549–50
  inclusive 470
  of women 272, 275
  racial 502
existentialism 48, 368
expected value model 213
experience
  Agamben on 466
  distinguished from action 296
  status of 276
expressions, Goffman on 135

fabrications 139
face 138
fairy-tale framework 530
false consciousness 185
family
  Deleuze on 176
  dynamics of relationships 210
  proliferation of forms 490
Fanon, Frantz 423
fascism 161, 185

FDA (Food and Drug Administration) 208
feedback loops 74, 77–8, 81
feminism
  and Butler 542, 544, 545, 548, 554, 556
  and Haraway 502, 508–10, 513–14
  and historical materialism 510
  and knowledge 509–10
  and primatology 505–6
  Smith 272, 274–6, 278–9, 283
  socialist 502
  subject of 545
fields 379–84
figurational sociology 14, 19
figurations 506–8
film 187–8
fire 36
Flaubert, Gustave 382
Fleck, Ludwik 528
Fleming, James 105
focused interaction 136
focused interview 67
focus group methodology 67
Foerster, Heinz von 300
Food and Drug Administration (FDA) 208
footing 140, 146
Fordism 167, 168, 259
formalism 113
form-of-life 474, *see also* happy life
Foucault, Michel 8, 240–67
  and Agamben 468
  and Butler 544, 546, 553
  and Deleuze 175, 188, 189
  and Haraway 503, 507
  and Nietzsche 242, 243, 247–8
  and Smith 276–7, 281–2
  archeological approach 246
  as a person 241–3
  critiques of work 264, 417
  influences on 241–4
  key concepts 250–5
  methodology 244–50
  on discourse 244, 245, 276–7
  on Enlightenment 253–4
  on enterprise society 8, 259–60
  on governmentality 246–7, 281
  on juridical-economic order 260–1
  on knowledge 249–51
  on neoliberalism 7, 257–64
  on political economy 247, 255–64

on power 6–7, 248, 250–2, 255–6, 261
on sex 546
on the nation-state 255, 256, 261
reader's guide to 264–5
understanding of origin 248
frames 139
Frank, Andre Gunder 405
Frankfurt School 315, 339, 342
Franklin, Sarah 514
Freiburg School 257, 258, 261
French Communist Party (PCF) 45, 47–8
Freud, Anna 29
Freud, Sigmund
and Marx 184–5
and the Oedipal complex 182, 187
Friedkin, Noah 213
Friedmann, Georges 47
functional analysis 73, 84
functionalism 73, 293
functional-structural theory 293–4

game metaphor 137, 362–3
game theory 213
Gandillac, Maurice de 176
Garfinkel, Harold 89–124
and Durkheim 120–1
and ethnomethodology 89–96, 100–3,
107, 114–15, 117, 119
and Habermas 93
and Marx 116
and Parsons 100–1, 105–7
as a person 103–8
assessment of 117–21
documentary method 93, 102
influence of 113–17
intellectual context 110–13
jury study 94
on gender 94–5
on social structure 3
reader's guide to 121
social context 108–10
theory of communication 96–8
theory of information 98–100
gay and lesbian movement 543
gender
Butler on 545–9
displays 137, 143, 144
Garfinkel on 94–5
Goffman on 143–4

identity 2, 546–7
melancholia 553
performativity 545–9
relation to sex 545–6
roles 115, 165, 487, 490
gene 507
genealogy 247–50, 264
general economy 316–17
Generation X 168
genetic engineering 351, 449
Germany 341–2
Berlin wall 329
development of habitus in 32
unification 352
Weimar period 19–20
Giddens, Anthony 3, 9, 432–63
and Elias 434–5
and Habermas 455
as a person 433–6
evaluation of work 455–7
paradox 454
reader's guide to 457
theory 433, 436–55
gift-giving 212, 316, 372
Gillmore, Mary 195, 198, 204
Gills, Barry 405
Gini coefficient 227, 229–30, 235
global capitalism 403–5
global class system 403–4
global financial crisis 186, 404
Global South 397, 399
global warming, see climate change
globalization 10–12
and nation states 166
Baudrillard on 11, 328, 332–3
Bauman on 10, 165, 166, 168–9
dark side of 331
Habermas on 11, 350–1
of neoliberalism 263, 280–1
"responsible" 11, 492
Wallerstein on 11, 398, 403–4
see also world-system perspective
goals 77, 207
Goffman, Erving 112, 125–54
and Bourdieu 367
and Durkheim 133–4
and Mead 134
and Simmel 133–4, 147
as a person 126–30

Goffman, Erving (*cont'd*)
  frame analysis 138–40
  influence of 144–9
  intellectual context 132–4
  interaction studies 135–8
  popular works 140–4
  reader's guide to 149
  social context 130–2
Goldfrank, Walter 395
Goldhagen, Daniel 340
Goodall, Jane 505
Goode, William J. 224
Goudsblom, Johan 19, 20, 33, 35, 36
Gouldner, Alvin 131–2
governmentality 246–7, 281
Greek philosophy 254–3
grief 7, 550, 553, 554, 556
Griffith, Alison 279
Group Analytic 18
groups 76
  established–outsider relations 29–30
  influence on behavior 78
growth, economic 262–3
Guattari, Félix 176, 177, 178,
    179, 182, 184–9
Gulf War 326, 329–30
Guterman, Norbert 47

Habermas, Jürgen, 339–60
  and Garfinkel 93
  and Gidddens 455
  and Luhmann 306
  and Marxism 342–3, 345, 347,
    348, 353
  and Weber 340, 345, 346, 348
  as a person 339–41
  assessment of 354–5
  influence of 353–4
  intellectual context 342–4
  reader's guide to 356
  social context 341–2
  theory 344–53
habitus 26, 28, 32, 362–3,
    377–9
Haecceities 102, 122n.1
Halbwachs, Pierre 175
Hall, Thomas D. 404–5
happiness 474
happy life 471, 473–4

Haraway, Donna 500–19
  and Foucault 503, 507
  and Marxism 502–3
  as a person 500–1
  assessment of 514–16
  influence of 513–14
  intellectual/social context 501–3
  reader's guide to 516–17
  work 503–13
Hardt, Michael 179–80
Harvey, David 404
hate-speech 550–2
Hayek, F. 261
health care 210–11
Hegel, Georg
  and Butler 544, 552
  and Deleuze 180
  and Lefebvre 48–50
Heidegger, Martin 464, 465
Hekman, Susan 514
heterosexuality 544, 546–7, 553
higher education 369
  see also universities
high schools 227–8, 232–3
Historians' Dispute 340
historical materialism 322, 345
  and feminism 510
  critique of 446–7, 456
Hochfeld, Julian 156, 162
Holocaust, The
  and Butler 543
  and recognition 6
  Bauman on 162–4
  Habermas on 340
  see also camps
Homans, George 198, 200, 203, 214
homines aperti 16
homo clausus 16, 26
homo oeconomicus 259–60
homo sacer 469
homosexuality 553
Hönigswald, Richard 15–16
Horkheimer, Max 17, 162, 325, 342
Hottois, Gilbert 531
Hughes, Everett C. 112, 127, 132–3, 134
human capital 259, 384
human rights 261, 425
humanism 161
  and Lefebvre 46, 48, 51, 55

evolutionary 449–51
Said on 423–6
Sartre on 423
see also posthumanism
Hume, David 177, 180–1
Hurricane Katrina 168
Husserl, Edmund 291, 295, 345
Hyman, Herbert 67
hyperreality 319, 320–1
hypothetico-deductive theory 221
Hyppolite, Jean 176, 242

identity 5–6
Bauman on 169–70
concepts of 142–3
Smith on 5
stigmatized 142–3
see also self, the
ideology 270–1, 373–4
immanence 177, 180, 189–90
"immanent reversal" 325
imperialism 421–3
see also colonialism
implosion 320, 321
income distribution 226
incongruity 91, 134, 148, 292
indexicality 92
individualization 489–90, 494
individualism 145, 146
inequality 261, 290
infancy 466
information 297
and choice behavior 74, 79
and social structures 78–9
Garfinkel's theory of 98–100
inscription 531
institutional constraint 102
institutional ethnography 273–4, 277–82
institutional practices 119–20
institutional reflexivity 144
institutional rules 119–20
institutional technologies 280
institutions
access to 77
and seduction 323
and social order 118, 119
and technology 275, 280
and the world systems perspective
398, 401

Beck on 491
Bourdieu on 369, 370, 375–6, 378, 379,
380, 384
coercive 142
disciplinary 2, 244, 247, 249, 252
economic 440, 441
formal 113, 118, 119, 120
Foucault on 244, 247, 249, 252,
256, 257
Garfinkel on 93, 94, 95, 102, 113, 114,
116, 119, 120
Giddens on 440, 441, 443, 452
Goffman on 141, 142
legal 440
Merton on 3, 76, 77, 81
of work 115
political 440
public 256, 380
reflexive modernization within 487
ruling 283
science and 9, 81
social support for 78
total 141, 142
intellectuals 161, 424, 451
intelligibility 120–1
interaction
analysis of 129, 213
and consciousness 281
and individualism 111
and social structure 145, 146
and work 97
as exchange 201
behaviorism and 198
between social and biological 504
Bourdieu on 363
communicative 96, 97
computer-mediated 98
conversational 127, 128, 129, 140
cross-species 504, 511, 512
Emerson on 201
female-female 505
Garfinkel on 89, 92, 93, 96, 98, 107,
111, 113, 118
Giddens on 439, 440
Goffman on 5, 112, 113, 126–42, 145,
146, 147, 149, 292
Habermas on 348
Hughes on 112
in nonhuman world 506, 515

interaction (*cont'd*)
   in world-systems perspective 398, 405
   Luhmann on 301–2
   Merton on 75, 76, 80, 82
   models 445
   networks 398
   order 5, 118, 126, 129, 131, 132, 134,
      138, 140, 145, 147, 292, 301
   self-other relations in 348
   social organization of 111
   studies of 112, 114, 135–8
   see also communication; exchange
     relations; power-dependence theory
interaction contexts 76
interactionism 112, 133, 525, 534
interaction systems 301–2
Internet 209
interpellation 551–2
interpreters 161
invisible hand 258, 263
irreductionism 524
irreversibility 531
Irwin, Robert 428
Islam 419

Jackson, Nancy 278
Jacobinism 162
Jacobsen, Michael Hviid 171
Jameson, Fredric 186
Jarry, Alfred 316, 324–5
Jaspers, Karl 16, 341
Jefferson, Gail 108
Jenkins, Richard 385–6
Jews 163, 164
Johnson, Guy 104–5
juggernaut metaphor 449
juridical-economic order 260–1
jury 94, 107

Kabylia 366–7, 371–2, 389n.8
Kant, Immanuel 92, 164, 182–3, 253,
   346, 349
Kaufmann, Felix 107
kernel 213
Kilminster, Richard 170
Klein, Melanie 187
knowledge
   and feminism 509–10
   differentiation of disciplines 376

   Foucault on 249–51
   Haraway on 509–11, 515
   ideological forms of 271
   Smith on 281–2
   truth of 421
Kohl, Helmut 341
Kohlberg, Lawrence 348
Koyré, Alexandre 389n.1
Kuhn, Alfred 197
Kuhn, Thomas 500–1

labeling theory 120, 375
laboratory ethnography 521
Labour Party 157, 158
Lacan, Jacques 178, 187
laissez-faire 257–8, 260
Lamont, Michelle 521
language
   Agamben on 465–8, 472, 473, 475, 477
   and communication 92–3, 98, 99,
     298, 302
   and information theory 98, 99
   and science 501, 504
   and structures 115
   and subjectivity 551
   and the body 549
   Aristotle on 464–5, 470
   as a game 362, 364, 533
   Deleuze on 177
   Derrida on 548, 551
   Habermas on 344, 345, 351, 354
   Haraway on 501
   hateful 551, 552
   Lefebvre's theory of 57
   of mathematics 222
   performativity of 550
   religious 351
   Smith on 271, 276, 277–8
   turn towards 99, 276–8
   verb-based 533
   Wittgenstein on 362
Lassalle, Ferdinand 59
Latour, Bruno 520–40
   actor-network theory (ANT) 3–4, 521,
     522, 525, 526–32, 536
   and Durkheim 534
   as a person 520–1
   critiques of 533–6
   debate with Bloor 532–3

major works 523–6
reader's guide to 536–7
social/intellectual context 521–3
theory 526–8
law
  Agamben on 469–70, 472, 474
  and morality 350
  Foucault on 260–1
  Roman 469
Lawler, Edward 212
Layder, Derek 440
Lazarsfeld, Paul 66, 70, 104, 105, 111
Leach, Edmund 449–51
leakage effects 78
Lefebvre, Henri 8, 44–64
  and everyday life 51–5
  and French Communist Party 47–8
  and Hegel 48–50
  and humanism 48
  and Marxism 45–6
  and praxis 49, 50–2
  and radical art 46–7, 51, 54
  and revolution 51–2, 58–60
  and space 6, 45, 55, 56–8
  and totality 49–50, 59–60
  influence of 60
  on the state 58–9
  reader's guide to 61
legislators 161
Leibniz 188
Levinas, Emmanuel 473, 553
Lévi-Strauss, Claude 164, 368
liberal capitalism 256, 258, 260, 262
liberalism
  economic 161
  Foucault on 257
  transformations in 257
  see also neoliberalism; ordo-liberalism
life 469–70
lifeworld 345–6
liminal era 522
linguistic turn 276–8
liquid modernity 164–5, 167–8
liquidity metaphor 167
livability 552–3
Livingston, Eric 100
local orders 91, 92, 101, 102, 116, 118–20
  see also local social orders
local social orders 91, 119

see also local orders
logic 49
love 168, 303
Luhmann, Niklas 287–309
  and Habermas 306
  and Husserl 291, 295
  and Parsons 289, 290, 291, 292, 295
  as a person 287–8
  assessment of 305–6
  differentiation theory 304–5
  double contingency theory 298
  impact of 305–5
  intellectual context 291–3
  reader's guide to 307
  social context 288–91
  systems theory 4, 293–301
  theory of communication 296–9
  theory of society 301–5
  theory of sociocultural evolution 303–4
  theory of symbolically generalized media
    of communication 302–3
Lukács, George 47, 48, 49, 315, 342, 348
Lynch, Michael 100

machines 186–7
macro–micro distinction 3, 118, 149,
    233–5, 455
Malinowski, Bronislaw 212
Malowist, Marian 399
manners 26–7
Mannheim, Karl 17, 20–1, 24, 34–5
mapping 279, 280, 283
Marcuse, Herbert 48
market 262, 258–9
marketing 209
Marx, Karl
  and Bauman 165
  and Freud 184–5
  and Garfinkel 116
  on finance capital 186
  on ideology 270
  Paris manuscripts 48
Marxism
  and Baudrillard 314–18, 324, 326
  and Bourdieu 8, 381, 386, 387
  and critical theory 343
  and Habermas 353, 355
  and Lefebvre 44, 45–8, 51, 59, 60
  and Luhmann 289

Marxism (*cont'd*)
  and schizoanalysis 185
  Deleuze and Guattari on 185, 186
  dissident (Renaissance) 156
  false consciousness in 185
  growth in 1970s 415
  Haraway on 502
  structuralist/humanist camps in 51
  Western 48, 342, 348,
    354, 397
mass media 290, 489
  see also media
materiality 503–4
mathematical functions 222–4
"Matthew Effect" 78
Maturana, Humberto 292, 293, 300
Mauss, Marcel 316, 318
McChrystal, Stanley A. 233
McClosky, Herbert 104
Mead, George Herbert 134, 146, 362
meaning
  and language 98–9
  and materiality 503–4
  and social systems 294–5
  disappearance of 321–2, 329
media 81, 320–2, 324
  see also mass media
mediation 57, 59
mental hospitals 140–2
Merleau-Ponty, Maurice 176, 242
Merton, Robert K. 65–88
  and Durkheim 70
  and Weber 70
  as a person 65–6
  assessment of 84–5
  impact of 82–3
  intellectual career 66–9
  reader's guide to 85
  social/intellectual context 69–71
  theory 71–82
messianic time 476
messianism 474–6
microeconomic theory 213
microenvironments 76
micro–macro distinction 3, 118, 149,
    233–5, 455
middle-range theories 72
Milgram and Zimbardo experiments
    163–4

Mills, C. Wright 119–20
  and Bauman 156, 167, 171
  and Wallerstein 396
misrecognition 373–5
modernity 160–4
  and the Holocaust 162–4
  and waste 168
  Baudrillard on 321, 322, 330–1
  Bauman on 160–8
  consumers' 166
  Giddens on 445–55
  high 447–8
  Latour on 524
  liquid 164–5, 167–8
  producers' 167
  solid 167, 168
modern societies 319, 320
modes
  of adaptation 77
  of being 23
  of connectivity 182
"modest witnessing" 509–12
Molm, Linda 198, 203, 211
moments 52–3, 57
mondialization 58
money 303
Moore, Wilbert 106, 107
morality
  Garfinkel on 92
  Habermas on 348–50
  in post-war society 111
  see also ethics
Morhange, Pierre 47
Mouzelis, Nicos 442
mutual intelligibility 89, 92, 99, 100, 101,
    102, 120
mutual reflexivity 93

Nancy, Jean-Luc 469
narratives 422–3
nation-state, the
  and globalization 10
  and social theory 11
  and world-system theory 405
  declining power of 453
  Foucault on 255, 256, 261
  Habermas on 341, 346
  irrelevance of 403
natural life 469–70

nature 506, 514, 515
Nazism 163, 164, 340
needs 313–14
neo-Darwinism 303, 304
neoliberalism
  and communitarianism 169
  and growth 262
  and individualization of failure 262
  and state intervention 258
  Foucault on 7, 8, 257, 261, 262, 264
  German 341
  rise of 1
  uncertainty of 165
  see also liberalism
neo-Marxism 314–18
  see also Marxism
network identity 209–10
networks 4, 209
  business 209–10
  see also actor-network theory; exchange
    networks
Neustadt, Ilya 18, 434
New Deal 108, 109, 261, 262
newism 167–70
new Labour 432, 436, 449, 451–3
New World Order 330, 451
Newton, Esther 547
Nietzsche
  and Baudrillard 317
  and Deleuze 177, 181, 182, 183
  and Foucault 242, 243, 247–8
Nizan, Paul 47
nowism 167–70
Nussbaum, Martha 263

Obama, Barack 453
objectification 48
objectivity 270, 296, 442, 509–11
  Manheim on 24
  strong 501
objects 99–100
  boundary 99
  system of 312–14
  triumph over subjects 323–5
observation 300–1
Odum, Howard W. 104, 105
Oedipal complex 182, 187
Offe, Claus 167
old age 189

OncoMouse 509
ontology
  and structuration theory 443, 444
  critical 254, 255, 259
  Deleuze on 183
  dualistic 181
  Foucault on 254, 255, 257
  Giddens on 433, 438, 443, 444
  of governmentality 282
  of institutional ethnography 279, 280
  of relationality 515
  of the self 433
  of the social 433
  practical 4, 187
open positions 136
operations 298–301
operative coupling 300
opportunity-structure 78
ordo-liberalism 257–9
organizations
  Luhmann on 301–2
  network perspective 208–9
  normal 302
  resource dependence perspective 207–8
Orient, the 5
Orientalism 5–6, 419–21, 427–8
orthodoxy 373
Osborne, Peter 54
Ossowski, Stanislaw 156, 162
outsiders 159, 166
  perspectives 374, 424
  see also established–outsiders relations

Palestine 413–15, 425–7
panopticon 248–9
paradigms 71, 468–9
para-ousia 476
Paris Commune 52
Parnet, Claire 188
parrhesia 254–5
Parsons, Talcott 109, 111
  and Garfinkel 101, 105, 106–7
  and Luhmann 289, 290, 291, 292, 295
  and Merton 70
  double contingency theory 298
  on social and psychic systems 295
  on universities 290
  "Parsons's Plenum" 100–1
Pasteur, Louis 524

pataphysics 324–5
PCF (French Communist Party) 45, 47–8
Pen, Jan 226
Pence, Ellen 279
performativity 546, 550, 551
personal identity 143
personality 76
philosophies group 47
philosophy
  Deleuze on 188–9
  Elias critique of 14, 22
physiocrats 258, 262
Plato 525
play 471–2
Poder, Paul 171
Poisson distributions 224–5
Poland 397, 399
Policy Network 459
political economy
  Baudrillard on 319–20
  Foucault on 247, 255–64
  see also economy
Politzer, Georges 47
poor, the 166
positivism 99, 113, 197, 343, 449
postcolonial studies 426
posthumanism 514
  see also humanism
postmodernism 60, 160, 484
postmodernity 160–5, 318–23
postmodern societies 319, 320
post-secular society 9, 351–2
poststructuralism 5, 115–16, 180,
    276, 277
  and Baudrillard 310, 315, 321, 326
post-war world 160–1, 165, 167
potentiality 466–7
power 6–7
  Agamben on 7
  as measurable concept 200
  balance of 29–30
  Butler on 7, 553–4
  distribution in exchange
    networks 212–13
  Elias on 6
  Emerson on 6, 200
  field of 383
  Foucault on 6–7, 248, 250–2,
    255–6, 261
  Giddens on 7, 439–40
  Lefebvre on 6, 58
  Merton on 79
  social 199–201, 207
  total 203
  use of in exchange relations 204
  see also power-dependence theory
power-dependence theory 195, 200–7
  and economy 209
  and family studies 210
  and health care 210–11
  and organizational studies 207–8
  and relations between states 211
  and theory of structural holes 208–9
  and values 206–7
  equation 200
  of cohesion 212
power/knowledge 251
practical actions 100
practice 364–5
practice theory 3
pragmatism 101, 112, 115–16
Pratt, Mary Louise 512
praxis 49, 50–2
premodern societies 318–19
primary frameworks 139
primatology 504–6
prisons 112, 141, 142, 246, 247
probability distributions 224–7
process sociology 14, 32–4
profanation 471–2
Proust, Marcel 182
psychic systems 295
psychoanalysis 182, 185–6
  see also schizoanalysis
psychosis 186
public places 136
public sphere 341, 347, 349, 350, 352, 353,
    355
punctualization 531
purposive behavior 230–3
Putnam, Robert 384

quasi-objects 531
queer theory 543

race 105, 106, 109, 114
  Coleman on 228–9
race war discourse 256, 261

racism 163, 256
rank 224, 234
rational action paradigm 231
rationalities 95–6
reading, contrapuntal 422
reality
    disappearance of 327–8, 329
    Latour on 525–6
    virtual 327–8
    see also hyperreality
reciprocal induction 504
reciprocity 203
recognition 5–6, 553–4
record keeping 95
reentry 301
reference groups 67, 74, 75–6, 78
reflexive modernization 481, 486–8
reflexivity 375–7, 447–8
Régulier, Catherine 45
Reich, Wilhelm 185
reification 315, 348
Reisman, David 111
relationships 168, 210
relativism 510
religious ritual 137
resource dependence perspective
    207–8, 209
responsibility 473
responsive behavior 230–3
revolution
    and everyday life 51–2
    and Lefebvre 51–2, 59–60
    urban 55–6
    world 397, 406, 408n.6
reward-structures 79
risk consciousness 489, 494, 495
risk society 10, 488–91, 495
ritual 137–8
Robinson, William I. 403–4, 405
role-set 67, 75
Ross, Kristin 52, 53
Rossi, Peter H. 219
rules 90, 93
ruling relations 272–3, 279, 280, 283
"runaway world" 448–51
Ryazanov, David 48

SAB (Scientific Advisory Board) 208
Sacher-Masoch, Leopold von 182

Sacks, Harvey 100, 108
Said, Edward E. 412–29
    and Derrida 417
    and Foucault 264, 417
    and humanism 423–6
    and Orientalism 5–6, 419–21, 427–8
    as a person 412–31
    assessment of 427–9
    criticism of 418–19
    influence of 426–7
    intellectual context 415–16
    on Palestine 413–15, 425–7
    on culture and imperialism 421–3
    reader's guide to 429
    social context 414–15
    theory 416–26
salvation history 507
Sanderson, Stephen K. 400–1
Sarason, Seymour 104
Sartre, Jean-Paul 176, 423
Schachter, Stanley 194, 197
Schegloff, Emmanuel 108
schizoanalysis 184–7
schizophrenia 186
Schmidt, Christian 56–7
Schmitt, Carl 469
science 9–10
    as game 363–3
    Latour on 9, 523–8
    Merton on 9, 68, 79, 81
    nature of 522–3
    see also technoscience
science fiction 509
science wars 9, 523
Scientific Advisory Board (SAB) 208
scientific sociology 105, 112–14
scientification 525
Scotson, John L. 18, 29
Scott, Joan 276
Scott, W. Richard 208
secondary adjustments 142
second nature 160
Second World War 196
    see also post-war world
secularization 345, 348, 351–2
seduction 323
self, the 5–6
    aesthetics of 251, 253–4
    Elias on 5

self, the (*cont'd*)
  ethics of 251
  Goffman on 5, 137, 146
  presentation of 137, 138
  see also identity
self-control 17, 26
self-defeating prophecy 77
self-fulfilling prophecy 77
self-reference 299–300
self-substitutive orders 305
self-talk 139–40
Selznick, Peter 104
semiosis 504
Sen, Amartya 263
sense making 139
sensory motor scheme 188
serendipity 71
Serres, Michel 520
sex
  Butler on 5, 545–9, 555
  Foucault on 546
  relation to gender 545–6, 549
  see also gender
sexism 269–70
sexual favors 210
"sex wars" 542, 543
"shoulders of giants" metaphor 68
signs 312–14, 322
sign value 312–13, 322
Simmel, G. 133–4, 147, 148
Simpson, George 65, 66, 70
simulations 319–22
situational proprieties 135–6, 137
Situationists, the 8, 51, 52
Skinner, B.F. 197
Smith, Adam 258, 262
Smith, Dennis 170
Smith, Dorothy 10–11, 268–86
  and feminism 272, 274–6, 278–80, 283
  and Foucault 276–7, 281–2
  and Goffman 149
  and Marx 270–2, 283
  as a person 268–70
  impact of work 278–80, 282–3
  linguistic turn 276–8
  on economic restructuring and
    governance 280–2
  reader's guide to 284
  scholarly work 270–4

Smith, George 279
Smith, Kate 81
Smuts, Barbara 512
sobriety 189
social action 145, 228, 229, 230
  and interaction 111
  classical concerns with 118
  Coleman on 228
  conditions for 33
  description of 112
  factors shaping 376
  freedom of 228–9
  Garfinkel on 89–92, 96, 97, 98, 101,
    113, 115
  Goffman on 145
  Luhmann on 296
  Merton on 77, 80
  Parsons on 109
  purposive 77
  study of 230
  Znaniecki on 105–6
  see also action
social capital 365, 380, 384
social categories 76
social change 77, 80, 81
social character 76
social choices 76–7, 80
social constructionism 510, 533–5
social development 31
social dilemmas 212
social energy 80
social engineering 158, 161, 163
social exchange theory 194–5, 199–13
  and values 206–7
  impact of 207–13
social facts 102
social identity 142–3
social inquiry 271–2
social interdependencies 27, 33
social learning 77
social mechanisms 78–9
social occasion 135
social order 101–2, 118
social policy 258
social power 199–201, 207
social practices 77
social relations, Smith 271
social science, Elias on 30–1
social situation 135

social structure 2–4
  and information 78–9
  and interaction 145, 146
  and social actions 364–5
  Garfinkel on 3
  Goffman on 145–6
  Merton on 3, 74–6, 79–81
  see also structure-agency distinction
social systems 4
  and environment 294
  and meaning 294–5, 302
  and psychic systems 295
  complexity of 294, 299
  concept of autopoiesis 293, 300
  distinction of action and experience 296
  elements of 299–301
  Luhmann's system theory 293–301
  operationally closed 300
social-gathering 135
socialism 157–9
socialist feminism 502–3
socialization 92–3
socially expected durations (SED) 69, 79
society
  concept of 301, 302
  immortal 102
  Luhmann's theory of 301–5
  Merton on 81
  post-secular 9, 351–2
  sociocultural evolution of 303–4
sociology of scientific knowledge (SSK) 528, 533
Sofoulis, Zoe 513
Sørensen, Aage B. 220, 224, 226
sovereignty
  Agamben on 467, 470, 474, 477
  and Aristotle 467
  as form of power 255
  Bataille on 316
  Baudrillard on 316, 328
  challenges to 350
  Foucault on 255, 325, 468
  of states 450
  Schmitt on 469
  significance of Butler's work for 557
space 6, 45, 52–8
  see also time-space
spatial turn 45
specialization 34–5

Spilerman, Seymour 220
Spinoza, Baruch 177, 183, 184, 185
SSK (sociology of scientific knowledge) 528, 533
Stalin, Josef 47–8
states
  Elias theory of formation 26, 28
  exchange relations between 211
  gardening 163, 168
  Habermas on 350
  Lefebvre on 58–9
  Max Weber definition of 28
  see also nation-state
statistics 111, 112, 114
status
  and relative rank 224, 232
  average 226, 234–5
  distribution 226–7, 234
  inequality 226–7, 236n.3
  in high school environment 232–3
  model for production 224, 226–7, 232, 234
status-set 75
stigma 142–3
Stinchcombe, Arthur 72–4, 219
Stones, Rob 443–5
structural coupling 300
structural holes 208–9
structural principles 440
structuralism 253, 368
structuration 365, 444–5
  theory 440–5
structure-agency distinction 3, 8, 77, 145, 253, 279–80
  see also actor-network theory; habitus; structuration
subjectivity 252–5
suicidal prophecy 77
Surrealism 47
symbolic exchange 316, 318, 319
symbolic violence 373, 375
symbols 31–2, 134
symptoms 182
Szasz, Thomas 112, 120

"taming of warriors" 25, 38n.5
Tarde, Gabriel 534
taste 327, 383–4
taxation 28

technocracy 341, 347
technology 9–10
technoscience 10, 506–9
    the term 531
Terror War 331, 332
terrorism 332
Tester, Keith 171, 172
testimony 473
Thatcherism 167
theory fiction 329–33
third-way politics 451–3
Thompson, James D. 208
Thompson, John 441
Tiananmen Square 475
time
    Bergson theory of 183
    chronotope 507
    Elias on 31
    messianic 476
    sequential 97
time-image 188
time-space 440
tokens 531
total institutions 140–2
totality 49–50, 59–60
total man 50–1
total power 203
Tournier, Michel 176
toys 471–2
transaesthetics 327
transcendental empiricism 180
transnational relations 403
transversality 178
"travelling theory" 417–18
tribalism 169
"Trust" requirement 90, 93, 111
truth 303, 421
truth-telling 254–5
Tumin, Melvin 104
Turner, Bryan 428, 495
Turner, Jonathan 199, 211, 214
Turner, Susan 279
Turner, Victor 547
tutorial exercises 91
Tzara, Tristan 47

uncertainty 168
understanding 297
unfocused interaction 136

unique adequacy 91, 114
United States 403, 404, 407
universalization 333
universities 290
    see also higher education
urban, the 55–6
urbanization 55
urban revolution 55–6
urban space 52–3
utility functions 221, 223
utopianism 451
utopias 158–9
utterance 297, 298

values 23, 206–7, 260
Varcoe, Ian 170
Vietnam war 271, 329
violence 27, 28, 373
virtual, the 181, 184
visual sociology 143
vitalism 182

Waite, Geoffrey 60
Wallerstein, Immanuel 395–411
    and class analysis 401–2
    and Mills 396
    and world-system perspective 397–408
    as a person 395–400
    critique of 400–8
    on globalization 11, 398, 403–4
    reader's guide to 408
Warner, W. Lloyd 127, 133, 134
Warraq, Ibn 428
warrior code 32
Warsaw Ghetto 163
Washington consensus 263
waste 168
Weber, Alfred 16–17, 25
Weber, Max
    and Habermas 340, 345, 346, 348
    and Merton 70
    and Simmel 148
    on fields 381
    on the Russian Revolution 159
    on the state 28
Weider, Larry 100
Weimar Germany 19–20
welfare state 167, 261, 262, 345, 346, 405, 454

West, the 27, 419–21
"whatever singularity" 474–5
Willer, David 213
Wittgenstein, Ludwig 89, 99, 362, 389n.3
Wolfe, Cary 514
Wolff, Kurt 107
women movement 543
women's standpoint 274–6
Woolgar, Steve 521, 527, 528
wordliness 512
world empires 405
world-system perspective 397–408
  and class relations 401–2
  and global capitalism 403–5
  and politics-economics relation 402

core/periphery hierarchy 399
endogenous/exogenous processes
  400–1
evolution in modern system 406–8
premodern system 405–6
see also globalization
Wouters, Cas 35

Yamagishi, Toshio 195, 198, 204
Yegenoglu, Meyda 427
Yugoslavian wars 370

zero-sum games 261–3
Zelditch Jr., Morris 224
Znaniecki, Florian 105–6, 110